CW01018750

The Statutes at Large
by Great Britain

THE

Statutes at Large,

FROM THE

$_0^{th}$ to the 33^d Year of King GEORGE II.

To which is prefixed,

A TABLE containing the TITLES of all the STATUTES during that Period.

VOL. XXII.

By DANBY PICKERING, of Gray's-Inn, Efq;
Reader of the Law Lecture to that Honourable Society.

CAMBRIDGE,
rinted by JOSEPH BENTHAM, Printer to the UNIVERSITY; for CHARLES BATHURST, at the Crofs-Keys, oppofite St. Dunftan's Church in Fleet-Street, London. 1766.

CUM PRIVILEGIO.

A

TABLE of the STATUTES,

Containing the Titles of all fuch Acts as are extant in print, from the Thirtieth to the Thirty Second Year of King GEORGE II. inclufive.

A TABLE of the STATUTES.

a 2   mited

mited for executing and performing several provisions, powers and directions in certain acts of this session of parliament.

Cap. 38. For amending, widening, and keeping in repair several roads in and near to the town of *Tenbury* in the counties of *Salop*, *Worcester* and *Hereford*.

Cap. 39. For repairing and widening several roads leading to, thro' and from the town of *Frome* in the county of *Somerset*; and for giving further powers to the trustees in an act passed in the twenty fifth year of his present Majesty's reign, for repairing the roads from the town of *Warminster* in the county of *Wilts*, to the city of *Bath* in the county of *Somerset*, and other roads therein mentioned.

Cap. 40. For enlarging the terms and powers granted by two acts of parliament, one passed in the third, and the other in the seventeenth year of the reign of his present Majesty, for repairing the road leading from a gate called *Shipston Toll-gate* at *Bridgetown* in the parish of *Old Stratford* in the county of *Warwick*, through *Alderminster* and *Shipston* upon *Stower*, to the top of *Long Compton Hill* in the said county of *Warwick*; and also for repairing the road leading from the first milestone standing on the said *Shipston* road, through a lane called *Clifford Lane*, and through *Mickleton* and *Chipping Campden*, to a place called *Andover's Ford*, in the county of *Gloucester*.

Cap. 41. For amending, widening, and keeping in repair, the road from the turnpike road at the bottom of *Shaw Hill*, in the parish of *Melksham*, through *Googes Lane*, *Corsham*, *Biddestone*, and *West Yatton*, to the turnpike road at *Upper Combe*, in the parish of *Castlecombe*, in the county of *Wilts*.

Cap. 42. For the ascertaining and

collecting the poor's rates; and for the better ordering and regulating the poor in the parish of Saint *Luke*, in the county of *Middlesex*.

Cap. 43. For amending, widening, and keeping in repair, the road from the town of *Hitchin* in the county of *Hertford*, through the town of *Shefford* and *Carrington Cotton End*, to a lane opposite a farm house called *Saint Leonard's*, leading into the turnpike road from *Saint Alban's*, to the town of *Bedford*; and also the road from the turning-out of the aforesaid road into *Henlow Field*, to *Gerford Bridge*; and also the road from the town of *Henlow*, over *Henlow Bridge*, to *Arlesey* in the county of *Bedford*.

Cap. 44. For amending, widening, and keeping in repair, the road leading from *Burleigh Bridge* in the the town of *Loughborough*, to *Ashby de la Zouch*, in the county of *Leicester*.

Cap. 45. For amending, widening, and keeping in repair, the roads from the east end of the town of *Hertford*, in the county of *Hertford*, through *Watton*, to *Broadwater*; and from the town of *Ware*, through *Watton*, to the north end of the town of *Walkern* in the said county.

Cap. 46. For amending, widening, making commodious, and keeping in repair, the road from the *Cross Keys*, otherwise *Bricker's Barn*, in the parish of *Corsham*, in the county of *Wilts*, to Bath-*Easton Bridge*, in the county of *Somerset*.

Cap. 47. For making the river *Blyth* navigable from *Halesworth Bridge*, in the county of *Suffolk*, into the haven of *Southwould*.

Cap. 48. For repairing and widening the road from *Towcester*, through *Silverston* and *Brackley*, in the county of *Northampton*, and *Ardley* and *Middleton Stoney*, to *Weston Gate*, in the

of

A TABLE of the STATUTES.

enlarging the highways between the top of *Kingfdown Hill* and the city of *Bath*, and for amending feveral other highways therein mentioned, leading to the faid city; and alfo for repairing feveral other roads therein mentioned.

Cap. 68. For repairing and widening the roads leading from *Spalding High Bridge*, through *Littleworth*, and by *Frognall*, and over *James Deeping Stone Bridge*, in the county of *Lincoln*, to *Maxey Outgang*, in the county of *Northampton*, adjoining the high road there.

Cap. 69. For amending, widening, and keeping in repair, the roads from the town of *Wrexham*, in the county of *Denbigh*, to *Pentre Bridge*, in the county of *Flint*; and from the town of *Mold*, to *Northop*, *Holywell*, and *Rhuddlan*, in the same county; and from thence to the *Ferry Houfe* oppofite to the town of *Conway*, in the county of *Carnarvon*; and from *Ruthin* to the faid town of *Mold*.

Private Acts.

Anno 30 Georgii II.

1. An act to enable *Oliver Cramer* efquire, and the heirs of his body, to take and ufe the furname of *Coghill*, purfuant to the will of *Marmaduke Coghill* efquire, deceafed, and to bear the family arms of *Coghill*.

2. An act to enable the reverend *Thomas Collier* clerk, and his iffue, to take and ufe the furname of *Barnard*.

3. An act for naturalizing *John Baptift Durand*, and *Bartholomew Rilliet*.

4. An act for naturalizing *John Frederick Falwaffer*.

5. An act for dividing an! enclofing the common fields, common paftures, common meadows, common grounds, and greens, in the manor and parifh of *Prior's Hardwick*, in the county of *Warwick.*

6. An act for confirming and eftablifhing certain articles of agreement, and an award, for dividing and inclofing the common fields, common downs, meadows, and paftures, within the manor of *Barton Stacy*, in the parifh of *Barton Stacy*, in the county of *Southampton*.

7. An act for dividing and inclofing the common field, common meadows, common pafture, common grounds, and commonable lands, in the townfhip of *Burchefter*, otherwife *Burcefter*, otherwife *Biffiter Market End*, in the county of *Oxford*; and for extinguifhing all right of common in certain common meadows, common paftures, and inclofed grounds, in the faid townfhip.

8. An act for confirming and eftablifhing two feveral articles of agreement, for inclofing and dividing *Northwood Hanchurch Heath*, and *Toft Green*, in the manor and parifh of *Trentham*, in the county of *Stafford*.

9. An act for dividing and inclofing a certain piece of pafture ground, called *Whitgift Pafture*, in the county of *York*; and for giving a compenfation, in lieu of tythes, to the impropriator of the rectory of *Whitgift* aforefaid.

10. An act for varying and poftponing certain limitations in a grant made by King *Charles* the Second, of a duty on coals fhipped in the river *Tyne*, to *Charles* late duke of *Richmond* and *Lenox*; and for enabling the prefent duke of *Richmond*, *Lenox*, and *Aubigny*, to make a jointure on his intended marriage with lady *Mary Bruce*.

11. An act for fettling a certain yearly fum upon the right honourable *Ann Fitzroy*, commonly called countefs of *Eufton*, wife of the right honourable *Auguftus Fitzroy* efquire, commonly called earl of *Eufton*, out of certain yearly penfions iffuing

ing

ing out of the hereditary revenue of the excise, and comprised in certain letters patent bearing date the two and twentieth day of *October* in the twenty-sixth year of the reign of King *Charles* the Second, in part of the jointure agreed to be secured to her upon her intermarriage with the said right honourable *Augustus Fitzroy* esquire, commonly called earl of *Euston*.

12. An act for vesting the estate and interest late of *Robert Cheatham* esquire, deceased, in the duties granted by certain acts of parliament, for maintaining a lighthouse on the *Edystone* rock, in trustees, in trust to raise money to be applied towards rebuilding the said lighthouse.

13. An act to impower the warden and society of *The King's-Town*, of *Sutton Coldfield*, in the county of *Warwick*, to grant part of a common called *Sutton Coldfield Park*, unto *Simon Luttrell* esquire, and his heirs.

14. An act to enable *Mary Jeffreys*, the wife of *Jeffrey Jeffreys* esquire, a lunatick, and the committee or committees of his estate for the time being, to make leases of the parts and shares of the said *Mary Jeffreys*, of divers lands, tenements and hereditaments, in the county of *Devon*, devised by the will of Sir *William Maurice*, deceased, during the continuance of the said lunatick's interest therein.

15. An act for establishing and rendering effectual certain articles of agreement for inclosing the common fields and grounds in the manor of *Stragglethorpe*, within the parish of *Beckingham*, in the county of *Lincoln*; and for making a compensation to the rector of the said parish, for the glebe lands and tythes in *Stragglethorpe* aforesaid.

16. An act for dividing, allotting, and inclosing, the common, open

and arable fields, and waste grounds in *Earlstone*, in the parish of *Burghcleare*, in the county of *Hants*.

17. An act for dividing and inclosing the common fields, common meadows, common pastures, common grounds, and commonable lands within the township of *Piddington*, in the county of *Oxford*.

18. An act for dividing and inclosing certain common pastures and common grounds, in the manor and parish of *Wingerworth*, and in the hamlet of *Tupton*, in the parish of *North Wingfield* respectively, in the county of *Derby*.

19. An act to enable *Thomas Turner* esquire, and his issue, to take and use the surname and arms of *Payler*.

20. An act for naturalizing *John Jacob Thompsons*.

21. An act for vesting the settled estate of *George William* earl of *Coventry*, in the county of *Cambridge*, in trustees, in trust to sell the same; and to lay out the money arising by such sale, in the purchase of other lands and hereditaments lying nearer to his estate in the counties of *Worcester*, *Gloucester*, and *Warwick*, to be settled to the uses therein mentioned.

22. An act for discharging *John* lord *Trevor*, executor of *Thomas* lord *Trevor*, deceased, from the sum of eight thousand and eight hundred pounds, agreed by the said *Thomas* lord *Trevor*, to be laid out in the purchase of lands, and for confirming the application made by the said *John* lord *Trevor*, of the said eight thousand and eight hundred pounds towards the discharge of the sum of ten thousand pounds, charged on the manor of *Bromham*, and other the estates late of the said *Thomas* lord *Trevor*, in the county of *Bedford*.

23. An act for impowering the guardians of *Henry* lord *Arundell* of *Wardour*,

or unto such other person or persons as the court of *Chancery* shall direct.

52. An act for dividing and inclosing certain open and common fields, lying within the parish or township of *Morten*, otherwise *Morten Morrel*, in the county of *Warwick*.

53. An act for dividing and inclosing several commons or wastes, and also several common fields, meadows, pastures, and waste grounds lying within the manor of *Wimeswould*, in the county of *Leicester*.

54. An act for confirming a partition between *William* earl of *Dartmouth*, and *Frances Katherine* countess of *Dartmouth*, his wife, and Sir *William Maynard* baronet, of several estates in the counties of *Bucks*, *Middlesex*, *Surrey*, *Suffolk*, and *Hertford*, and in the city of *London*, and for vesting and settling the entire premisses to the several uses therein mentioned.

55. An act to impower *Elizabeth*, the wife of *Henry Thomas Carr* esquire, a lunatick, to make an appointment of a sum of three thousand pounds, towards the payment of the said lunatick's debts; and for other purposes therein mentioned.

56. An act for sale of part of the settled estate of *William Thomson* esquire, in the county of *Berks*, to raise money towards discharging several mortgage debts and incumbrances affecting other parts of his settled estates, in the same county.

57. An act for impowering the receiver general of his Majesty's customs, to release and discharge the estate and effects of *George Buchanan* and *William Hamilton*, from a debt due to his Majesty, upon payment, by the assignees under the commission of bankruptcy against them, of a sum of money therein mentioned.

58. An act to enable *Samuel Jackson* esquire, now called *Samuel Dodington*, and his heirs male, to take and use, in exchange for his and their own surname and arms, the surname and arms of *Dodington*, pursuant to the will of *George Dodington* esquire, deceased.

59. An act to enable *James Newsam* esquire, and his issue, to take and use the surname of *Craggs*.

Anno 31 *Georgii* II.

Cap. 1. For continuing certain laws made in the last session of parliament, for prohibiting the exportation of corn, malt, meal, flour, bread, biscuit, and starch; and for prohibiting the making of low wines and spirits, from wheat, barley, malt, or any other sort of grain, or from meal or flour; and to allow the transportation of wheat, barley, oats, meal, and flour, to the *Isle of Man*, for the use of the inhabitants there; and for reviving and continuing an act made in the same session, for discontinuing the duties upon corn and flour imported, and upon corn, grain, meal, bread, biscuit, and flour, taken from the enemy; and to permit the importation of corn and flour into *Great Britain* and *Ireland*, in neutral ships; and to authorize his Majesty, with the advice of his privy council, to order and permit the exportation of such quantities of the commodities aforesaid, as may be necessary for the sustentation of any forces in the pay of *Great Britain*, or of those of his Majesty's allies acting in support of the common cause; and to prohibit the payment of any bounty upon the exportation of any of the said commodities to be made during the continuance of this act.

Cap. 2. For continuing and granting to his Majesty certain duties upon malt, mum, cyder, and perry, for the service of the year one thousand seven hundred and fifty-eight.

Cap.

A TABLE of the STATUTES.

year one thousand seven hundred and fifty eight; and for empowering the proper officers to make forth duplicates of exchequer bills, tickets, certificates, receipts, annuity orders, and other orders, in lieu of such as shall be lost, burnt, or otherwise destroyed; and for obliging the retailers of wines, commonly called *Sweets*, or *Made Wines*, to take out a wine licence.

Cap. 32. For repealing the duty granted by an act made in the sixth year of the reign of his late Majesty, on silver plate, made, wrought, touched, assayed, or marked in *Great Britain*; and for granting a duty on licences, to be taken out by all persons dealing in gold or silver plate; and for discontinuing all drawbacks upon silver plate exported; and for more effectually preventing frauds and abuses in the marking or stamping of gold or silver plate.

Cap. 33. For enabling his Majesty to raise the sum of eight hundred thousand pounds, for the uses and purposes therein mentioned; and for further appropriating the supplies granted in this session of parliament.

Cap. 34. For enlarging the times for the first meetings of commissioners or trustees, for putting in execution certain acts of this session of parliament; and for other purposes therein mentioned.

Cap. 35. To continue several laws therein mentioned, for granting a liberty to carry sugars of the growth, produce, or manufacture, of any of his Majesty's sugar colonies in *America*, from the said colonies directly into foreign parts, in ships built in *Great Britain*, and navigated according to law; for the preventing the committing of frauds by bankrupts; for giving further encouragement for the importation of naval stores from the *British* co-

lonies in *America*; and for preventing frauds and abuses in the admeasurement of coals in the city and liberty of *Westminster*; and for preventing the stealing or destroying of madder roots.

Cap. 36. For continuing certain laws therein mentioned relating to *British* sail cloth, and to the duties payable on foreign sail cloth; and to the allowance upon the exportation of *British* made gunpowder; and to the encouragement of the trade of the sugar colonies in *America*; and to the landing of rum or spirits of the *British* sugar plantations, before the duties of excise are paid thereon; and for regulating the payment of the duties on foreign exciseable liquors; and for the relief of *Thomas Watson*, with regard to the drawback on certain *East Indian* callicoes; and for rendering more commodious the new passage leading from *Charing Cross*.

Cap. 37. To permit the exportation of certain quantities of malt now lying in his Majesty's storehouses; and to allow the bounty upon such corn and malt as was shipped and cleared for *Ireland*, on or before a limited time; and to authorize the transportation of flour, meal, bread, and biscuit, to the islands of *Guernsey* and *Jersey*, for the use of the inhabitants there, in lieu of the wheat, malt or barley, which may now, by law, be transported to those islands.

Cap. 38. For applying a sum of money granted in this session of parliament towards carrying on the works for fortifying and securing the harbour of *Milford* in the county of *Pembroke*.

Cap. 39. For vesting certain messuages, lands, tenements, and hereditaments, for the better securing his Majesty's docks, ships, and stores, at *Portsmouth*, *Chatham*, and *Plymouth*, and for the better fortifying

fying the town of *Portfmouth*, and citadel of *Plymouth*, in truftees, for certain ufes; and for other purpofes therein mentioned.

Cap. 40. To afcertain the weight of truffes of ftraw, and to punifh deceits in the fale of hay and ftraw in truffes in *London*, and within the weekly bills of mortality, and within the diftance of thirty miles thereof; and to prevent common falfemen of hay and ftraw from buying the fame on their own account, to fell again; and alfo to reftrain falefmen, brokers, or factors, in cattle, from buying on their own account, to fell again, any live cattle in *London*, or within the weekly bills of mortality, or which are driving up thereto.

Cap. 41. To amend and render more effectual an act paffed in the twenty ninth year of his prefent Majefty's reign, intituled, *An act for inclofing, by the mutual confent of the lords and tenants, part of any common, for the purpofe of planting and preferving trees fit for timber or underwood; and for more effectually preventing the unlawful deftruction of trees.*

Cap. 42. For making perpetual feveral acts therein mentioned, for preventing theft and rapine on the northern borders of *England*; for the more effectual punifhing wicked and evil difpofed perfons going armed in difguife, and doing injuries and violences to the perfons and properties of his Majefty's fubjects, and for the more fpeedy bringing the offenders to juftice; and alfo two claufes to prevent the cutting or breaking down the bank of any river, or fea bank; and to prevent the malicious cutting of hop binds; for the more effectual punifhment of perfons malicioufly fetting on fire any mine, pit, or delph of coal, or canal coal; and of perfons unlawfully hunting or

taking any red or fallow deer in forefts or chafes; or beating or wounding the keepers or other officers in forefts, chafes, or parks; and alfo fo much of an act as relates to the power of appealing to the circuit courts in civil cafes, in *Scotland*.

Cap. 43. For repairing and widening feveral roads in the counties of *Dorfet* and *Devon*, leading to and through the borough of *Lyme Regis*.

Cap. 44. For repairing the road from the village of *Magor*, to the bridgefoot, in the town of *Chepftow*, in the county of *Monmouth*; and other roads in the counties of *Monmouth* and *Gloucefter*.

Cap. 45. For afcertaining and collecting the poors rates, and for better regulating the poor in the parifh of Saint *Mary Magdalen Bermondfey* in the county of *Surry*.

Cap. 46. To amend an act paffed in the laft feffion of parliament, intituled, *An act for building a bridge or bridges crofs the river of* Thames, *from a certain place in* Old Brentford, *in the parifh of* Ealing, *in the county of* Middlefex, *known by the name of* Smith, *or* Smith's Hill, *to the oppofite fhore in the county of* Surrey.

Cap. 47. For the more eafy and fpeedy repairing of publick bridges within the county of *Devon*.

Cap. 48. For enlarging the term and powers granted by an act of parliament paffed in the twenty fourth year of his prefent Majefty's reign, for enlarging the term and powers granted by an act paffed in the third year of the reign of his prefent Majefty, for repairing and amending the feveral roads leading from *Woodftock*, through *Kiddington* and *Enftone*, to *Rollright Lane*, and *Enftow Bridge* to *Kiddington* aforefaid; and for making the faid act more effectual.

Cap. 49. For amending feveral roads leading

A TABLE of the STATUTES.

leading from the town of *Tiverton*, in the county of *Devon*.

Cap. 50. For repairing and widening the roads from *Donington High Bridge* to *Hale Drove*, and to the *Eighth Mile Stone*, in the parish of *Wigtoft*, and to *Langret Ferry*, in the county of *Lincoln*.

Cap. 51. For repairing the high road leading from *Brent Bridge* in the county of *Devon*, to *Gasking Gate*, in or near the borough of *Plymouth*, in the said county.

Cap. 52. For enlarging the term granted by an act made in the twenty sixth year of his present Majesty's reign, intituled, *An act for laying a duty of two pennies Scots, or a sixth part of a penny sterling, upon every Scots pint of ale and beer which shall be brewed for sale, brought into, tapped, or sold, within the town and parish of* Preston Pans, *in the shire of* East Lothian, *otherwise* Haddingtoun, *for repairing the harbour of the said town, and for other purposes therein mentioned.*

Cap. 53. To explain, amend, and render more effectual an act passed in the ninth and tenth years of the reign of his late majesty King *William* the Third, intituled, *An act for erecting hospitals and workhouses within the city and county of the city of* Exon, *for the better employing and maintaining the poor there.*

Cap. 54. For repealing so much of the act of the fifteenth year of his present Majesty, for enlarging the term and powers granted by an act of the thirteenth year of his late majesty King *George* the First, for repairing the roads from *Cirencester Town's End* to *Saint John's Bridge* in the county of *Gloucester*, as directs that the inhabitants of the several parishes and hamlets therein named, shall pass toll free; and for repairing the street from the *High Cross* in *Cirencester* to the *Town's End* there; and for other purposes

therein mentioned; and for enlarging the terms and powers granted by the said two former acts.

Cap. 55. For enlarging the term and powers granted by an act of the twenty fifth year of his present Majesty's reign, intituled, *An act for repairing the post road from the city of* Edinburgh, *through the counties of* Linlithgow *and* Sterling, *from the* Boat-house Ford, *on* Almond Water, *and from thence to the town of* Linlithgow, *and from the said town of* Falkirk, *and from thence to* Stirling; *and also from* Falkirk *to* Kilsyth, *and to* Inch Bellie Bridge, *on the post road to the city of* Glasgow; *and for building a bridge cross* Almond Water.

Cap. 56. For enlarging the powers granted by an act passed in the eighteenth year of the reign of his present Majesty, intituled, *An act for rendering more effectual the several acts passed for the erecting of hospitals and workhouses within the city of* Bristol, *for the better employing and maintaining of the poor thereof*; and for making the said act more effectual.

Cap. 57. For making more effectual four several acts of parliament, made in the sixth year of the reign of her late majesty Queen *Ann*; the eleventh year of the reign of his late majesty King *George* the First; and in the tenth and thirteenth years of the reign of his present Majesty respectively, for repairing the highways from *Old Stratford* in the county of *Northampton* to *Dunchurch*, in the county of *Warwick*.

Cap. 58. To continue and render more effectual two acts of parliament made in the twelfth year of the reign of his late Majesty, and in the eighteenth year of the reign of his present Majesty, for repairing the roads leading from *Birmingham* to *Edghill*, in the county of *Warwick*.

Cap. 59. For building a bridge cross
the

Studley Lane End; and also the road leading from *Yarnbrook*, to the turnpike road at *Melksham*, in the said county of *Wilts*.

Cap. 69. To continue and render more effectual an act made in the fifteenth year of his present Majesty's reign, intituled, *An act for laying a duty of two pennies scots, or one sixth part of a penny sterling, upon every* Scots *pint of ale and beer which shall be brewed for sale, brought into, tapped, or sold, within the town of* Kirkcaldy, *and liberties thereof.*

Cap. 70. To enable the trustees appointed for putting in execution an act passed in this session of parliament, intituled, *An act for repealing so much of an act of the fifteenth year of, his present Majesty, for enlarging the term and powers granted by an act of the thirteenth year of his late majesty King* George *the First, for repairing the roads from* Cirencester Town's *end to* Saint John's Bridge, *in the county of* Gloucester, *as directs that the inhabitants of the several parishes and hamlets therein named, shall pass toll free; and for repairing the street from the* High Cross *in* Cirencester, *to the town's end there, and for other purposes therein mentioned; and for enlarging the terms and powers granted by the said two former acts;* to reduce all or any of the tolls granted by the said act; and for appointing additional trustees for putting the said acts in execution.

Cap. 71. For regulating, governing, preserving, and improving, the oyster fishery in the river *Colne*, and waters thereto belonging.

Cap. 72. For extending the navigation of the river *Calder*, to or near to *Sowerby Bridge* in the parish of *Halifax*; and for making navigable the river *Heble, Halig* or *Halifax Brook*, from *Brooksmouth* to *Salter Hebble Bridge*, in the county of *York*.

Cap. 73. For repairing and widening the roads from *Chawton Pond*, in the parish of *Chawton*, in the county of *Southampton*, through *Rumsdean Bottom, Westmeon, Warnford, Exton, Bishop's Waltham,* and over *Sherrill Heath*, and through *Wickham* and *Fareham*, to the town of *Gosport*; and from *Exton* aforesaid, through *Droxford*, to the east end of *Sherrill Heath*, in the said county.

Cap. 74. For repairing and widening the roads from the town of *Bishop's Waltham*, in the county of *Southampton*, over the top of the down called *Stephen's Castle Down*, and through *Salt Lane* and *Tichborne*, to the town of *New Alresford*; and from the *Market House* in the said town of *New Alresford*, through *Old Alresford, Bradley Lane,* and over *Herriard Common*, to the town of *Odiham* in the said county.

Cap. 75. For repairing and widening the roads from the town of *Stockbridge*, in the county of *Southampton*, to the city of *Winchester*; and from the said city, through *Bellmour Lane*, to the top of *Steven's Castle Down*, near the town of *Bishop's Waltham*, in the said county; and from the said city of *Winchester*, through *Otterborne*, to *Bargate*, in the town and county of the town of *Southampton*.

Cap. 76. For relief of the coalheavers working upon the river *Thames*; and for enabling them to make a provision for such of themselves as shall be sick, lame, or past their labour, and for their widows and orphans.

Cap. 77. For repairing and widening the road from the *Swan Inn* at *Leatherhead*, to the *Maypole* at the upper end of *Spital* or *Somerset Street*, in the parish of *Stoake*, near the town of *Guldeford*, in the county of *Surry*.

Cap. 78. For repairing and widening the

the road from the town of *Gulde-ford*, to the *Directing Post* near the town of *Farnham*, in the county of *Surrey*.

Private Acts.

Anno 31 Georgii II.

1. An act to enable *John* earl of *Sandwich*, *Wellbore Ellis* esquire, and *Thomas Potter* esquire, to take in *Great Britain*, the oath of office as vice treasurer and receiver general and paymaster general of all his Majesty's revenues in the kingdom of *Ireland*; and to qualify themselves for the enjoyment of the said offices.

2. An act for transferring certain *South Sea* annuities, standing in the name of the late treasurer to the commissioners for building fifty new churches, unto the respective rectors of eight of those churches, and for vesting certain sites for churches purchased by the said commissioners, in trustees, in order to sell the same for the purposes therein mentioned.

3. An act to enable *George Amyand* and *John Anthony Rucker* of *London*, merchants, agents for the *Embden East India* company, to sell and dispose of the cargo of the ship the *Prince Ferdinand of Prussia*, to the united company of merchants of *England* trading to the *East Indies*, and to enable the said united company to purchase land, sell, and dispose of, the same or any part thereof; and to impower the said *George Amyand* and *John Anthony Rucker*, to make insurances upon the said ship and cargo.

4. An act to enable *Mary Woollett* spinster (notwithstanding her infancy) upon her marriage with *Robert Mead Wilmot* esquire, to settle and convey her estate and interest in certain messuages, lands, and hereditaments, in the county

of *Kent*, and in two several sums of two thousand pounds, and three hundred pounds, to the uses in certain articles of agreement mentioned.

5. An act to dissolve the marriage of *Godfrey Wentworth* esquire, with *Dorothea Pilkington* his now wife, and to enable him to marry again, and for other purposes therein mentioned.

6. An act for dividing and inclosing certain wastes or commons called *Brancepeth*, and *Stockley* moors or commons, within the manor and parish of *Brancepeth*, in the county of *Durham*.

7. An act for dividing and inclosing certain open and common fields, in *Great Glen*, in the county of *Leicester*, called the *Upper* or *North End Fields*, and all the common pastures, common meadows, and common and waste grounds, within the said fields.

8. An act for naturalizing *George Clifford*.

9. An act for vesting the forests and manors of *Singleton* and *Charlton*, and other manors, lands, tenements, and hereditaments, in the counties of *Sussex* and *Wilts*, in trustees, and their heirs, upon the trusts therein mentioned, freed and discharged from the estates, uses, and trusts, to which the same are at present subject; and for other purposes therein mentioned.

10. An act for inclosing and dividing the moors and commons within the chapelry of *Hamsterly*, in the manor of *Wolsingham*, in the county of *Durham*.

11. An act for confirming a contract of lease of mines between *Charles* duke of *Queensborough* and *Dover*, of the one part; and *Ronald Crawfurd*, *James Crawfurd*, and *Daniel Telfer*, of the other part; and for enabling the said duke, and his heirs of entail, to grant leases in

terms

A TABLE of the STATUTES.

A TABLE of the STATUTES.

for

exchequer for the service of the year one thousand seven hundred and fifty nine; and for relief of *Samuel Taylor*, with respect to a bond entered into by him for securing the duties on tobacco imported.

Cap. 32. For the more effectual preventing the fraudulent importation of cambricks and *French* lawns.

Cap. 33. To explain and amend an act made in the last session of parliament, intituled, *An act for granting to his Majesty several rates and duties upon offices and pensions; and upon houses; and upon windows or lights; and for raising the sum of five millions by annuities and a lottery, to be charged on the said rates and duties;* so far as the same relates to the rates and duties on offices and pensions.

Cap. 34. For the better preventing the importation of the woollen manufactures of *France* into any of the ports in the *Levant* sea, by or on the behalf of any of his Majesty's subjects; and for the more effectual preventing the illegal importation of raw silk and mohair yarn into this kingdom.

Cap. 35. For augmenting the salaries of the puisne judges in the court of *King's Bench*, the judges in the court of *Common Pleas*, the barons of the coif in the court of *Exchequer* at *Westminster*, the judges in the courts of *Session* and *Exchequer* in *Scotland*, and justices of *Chester*, and the great sessions for the counties in *Wales*.

Cap. 36. For enabling his Majesty to raise the sum of one million for the uses and purposes therein mentioned; and for further appropriating the supplies granted in this session of parliament.

Cap. 37. For repairing and widening the high road leading from the town of *Mansfield* in the county of *Nottingham*, through the towns of

Pleasley, *Glapwell*, *Heath*, and *Normenton*, and the liberty of *Hasland*, to the turnpike road leading from the town of *Derby*, to the town of *Chesterfield* in the county of *Derby*.

Cap. 38. For repairing and widening the roads from *Chappel Bar*, near the west end of the town of *Nottingham*, to *Newhaven*; and from *The Four-Lane-Ends* near *Oakerthorpe*, to *Ashborne*; and from the *Cross Post* on *Wirksworth Moor*, to join the road leading from *Chesterfield*, to *Chappel-en-le-Frith*, at or near *Longston* in the county of *Derby*; and from *Selston*, to *Annesley Woodhouse* in the county of *Nottingham*.

Cap. 39. For repairing and widening the roads from the east end of the town of *Chard*, to the south end of *West Moor*; and from the west end of the *Yeovil* turnpike road, through *Ilminster*, to *Kenny Gate*; and from the west end of *Pease Marsh Lane*, to *Horton Elm*; and from Saint *Raine Hill*, to *Ilminster*; and from *White Cross*, to *Chillington Down*; and from a place called *Three Oaks*, over *Ilford Bridges*, to *Bridge Cross* in the county of *Somerset*.

Cap. 40. For repairing several roads leading to the town of *Bridgewater*, in the county of *Somerset*; and for amending and rendering more effectual several acts for amending several roads from the cities of *Gloucester* and *Bristol*, and several other roads in the said acts mentioned, in the counties of *Somerset* and *Gloucester*.

Cap. 41. For repairing and widening the road from the cross at *Broken Cross* in *Macclesfield*, in the county of *Chester*, through *Macclesfield Forest*, to the present turnpike road at the south end of the township of *Buxton*, in the county of *Derby*.

Cap. 42. For making the river *Stort* navigable, in the counties of *Hertford* and *Essex*, from the *New Bridge*

in

6

Wear, *and port and haven of* Sunderland, *in the county of* Durham; as relates to making the said river navigable between the said two places called *South Biddock,* or *Biddock Ford,* and *New Bridge,* in the county of *Durham.*

Cap. 65. For continuing, amending, and rendering more effectual, so much of an act made in the twentieth year of his present Majesty's reign, intituled, *An act for the better preservation and improvement of the river* Wear, *and port and haven of* Sunderland, *in the county of* Durham; as relates to the port and haven of *Sunderland,* and the river *Wear,* between *South Biddock,* or *Biddock Ford,* and the said port and haven.

Cap. 66. For amending and widening the roads leading from *Stretford's Bridge* in the county of *Hereford,* to the new inn in the parish of *Winstanstow* in the county of *Salop;* and also the road from *Blue Mantle Hall,* near *Mortimer's Cross,* to *Aymstrey* in the said county of *Hereford;* and for repealing so much of an act made in the twenty second year of the reign of his present Majesty, as relates to the road from *Mortimer's Cross* to *Aymstrey Bridge.*

Cap. 67. For repairing the road from the south end of the south street, in the parish of *South Malling,* near the town of *Lewes,* to *Glyndbridge;* and from thence through *Firle Street under the Hill,* to *Longbridge* in the parish of *Alfriston,* in the county of *Sussex.*

Cap. 68. For repairing and widening the road from *Modbury,* through the town of *Plympton,* to the north end of *Lincotta Lane,* in the county of *Devon.*

Cap. 69. For repairing, amending, and widening the roads from the south west end of *Nether Bridge,* in the county of *Westmorland,* by *Sizerghfellside,* to *Levens Bridge,* and from thence through the town of *Millthrop,* to *Dixies;* and from the town of *Millthrop* aforesaid to *Hangbridge,* and from thence to join the *Heron Syke* turnpike road, at the guide post near *Clawthrop Hall,* in the county aforesaid.

Cap. 70. For repairing and widening the road leading from the east side of *Barnesley Common,* in the county of *York,* to the middle of *Grange Moor,* and from thence to *White Cross;* and also the road from the guide post, in *Barugh,* to a rivulet called *Barugh Brook,* and from thence for two hundred yards over and beyond the same rivulet or brook into the township of *Cawthorne,* in the said county.

Cap. 71. For repairing and widening the high road from *Wetherby* to *Grassington,* in the county of *York.*

Private Acts.

Anne 32 Georgii II.

1. An act for dividing and inclosing the common fields, common pastures, common meadows, common grounds, and waste grounds, in the parish of *Ecton,* in the county of *Northampton.*

2. An act to enable the most noble *Francis* duke of *Bridgewater,* to make a navigable cut or canal from a certain place in the township of *Salford,* to or near *Worsley Mill,* and *Middlewood,* in the manor of *Worsley,* and to or near a place called *Hollin Ferry,* in the county palatine of *Lancaster.*

3. An act for dividing and inclosing the open, arable, meadow, pasture, and waste grounds, in the parish of *Honington,* in the county of *Warwick.*

4. An act for establishing and rendering effectual, certain articles of agreement for inclosing and dividing the commons and waste grounds,

A TABLE of the STATUTES.

A TABLE of the STATUTES.

made between the most noble *John* duke of *Bedford*, and *Ambrose Reddall* gentleman, *Judy* his wife, and *Elizabeth* their only child.

23. An act for vesting part of the estates intailed by the will of the most noble *Charles Noel* duke of *Beaufort*, deceased, in trustees to be sold; and for purchasing other estates to be settled to the like uses; and for impowering the guardian and trustees named in the said will, to make leases of the said duke's estates, in the counties of *Gloucester*, *Wilts*, *Hants*, *Devon*, *Dorset*, *Glamorgan*, and *Brecon*, during the minority of his children.

24. An act for settling the real and leasehold estates of the most honourable *Margaret Brydges*, commonly called marchioness of *Carnarvon*, wife of the most honourable *James Brydges* esquire, commonly called marquis of *Carnarvon*, and late *Magaret Nicoll*, spinster, an infant, for the benefit of the said marquis and marchioness, and their issue; and for applying part of the personal estate of the said marchioness for the purposes therein mentioned.

25. An act for empowering *Henry Arthur* earl of *Powis*, and *Barbara* countess of *Powis*, to make leases of the estate late of *William* marquis of *Powis*, deceased, in the county of *Montgomery*, for twenty one years, or three lives, at the improved rent.

26. An act for making a partition and division of certain lands and hereditaments, in the county of *Surrey*, agreed to be purchased by *Thomas* late lord *Onslow*, and for settling and limiting the same, for the benefit of the several persons claiming, under his marriage settlement and will, respectively; and also for selling and disposing of timber growing on the estate devised, by his will, for the purposes therein mentioned.

27. An act for raising money out of the personal estate of the late duchess of *Buckinghamshire* and *Normanby*, deceased, to renew a lease of certain manors and estates in the county of *York*, in the manner, and for the purposes therein mentioned.

28. An act to enable *William Walley* and others to sell and convey three undivided fourth parts of a messuage or farm, and several pieces or parcels of land and hereditaments, lying in or near the parish of *Hayes*, in the county of *Kent*, unto the right honourable *William Pitt*, in fee simple, and for investing the purchase-money in other lands and hereditaments, to be settled to the same uses and estates, as the said three undivided fourth parts are now subject to; and to enable the trustees named in the will of *William Cleaver* the elder, deceased, to convey certain pieces or parcels of land, in the parish of *Hayes* aforesaid, part of the estate devised by the will and codicil of the said *William Cleaver*, unto the said *William Pitt*, in fee simple, in exchange for part of the said first mentioned lands.

29. An act to repeal an act made in the last session of parliament, intituled, *An act to enable* Charles Bagot, *now called* Charles Chester, *and his sons, to take the surname of* Chester, *and for carrying an agreement therein mentioned, into execution*; and for explaining and altering that agreement, and giving better directions for the carrying the same, so explained and altered, into execution.

30. An act for carrying into execution the articles made on the marriage of Sir *Edward Blackett* baronet, with dame *Anne* his wife, by a settlement to be made with, and under, certain variations and provisions, more beneficial for the issue of the said marriage.

31. An act to impower the honourable *Edward Bouverie* and *William Bou*

Bouverie, respectively, to make leases of *Chester's Key* and *Brewer's Key*, and other tenements and buildings, in the city of *London*, devised by the wills of *Bartholomew Clarke* and *Hitch Younge*, esquires, deceased.

32. An act to impower certain persons to enfranchise several customary lands and hereditaments, parcel of the several manors of *Nicol Forest, Solport* and *Bewcastle*, in the county of *Cumberland*, late the estates of the honourable *Catherine Widrington* widow, deceased, directed to be settled to certain uses, by the will and codicil of the said *Catherine Widrington*; and for other purposes therein mentioned.

33. An act for transferring to the guardians of *Charles William Molyneux*, an infant, a certain power of leasing, contained in the marriage settlement of *Richard* late lord viscount *Molyneux* deceased, during the minority, and for the benefit, of the said infant.

34. An act to exchange lands between *Samuel Wegg* esquire, and the dean and chapter of the cathedral church of *Saint Paul*, in the city of *London*.

35. An act for vesting divers lands and hereditaments in the counties of *Cornwall* and *Devon*, settled and entailed on *Denys Rolle* esquire, and his issue, in him, in fee simple, and for settling other lands and hereditaments in the said county of *Devon*, of greater value, to the same uses.

36. An act for vesting the manor of *Duxford*, and divers lands and hereditaments in the county of *Cambridge*, part of the settled estate of *James Barry* esquire, and *Elizabeth* his wife, in trustees, to be conveyed to *Richard Crop* esquire, pursuant to articles, and for settling other estates in the county of *York*, of greater value, in lieu thereof, to the uses of their marriage articles.

37. An act for sale of the inheritance of part of the settled estate of *John Caryll* esquire, in the county of *Sussex*, to discharge incumbrances affecting the same.

38. An act to impower *William Warburton* esquire, to make leases of part of his settled estate in *Malvern Chace*, for ninety nine years, in order for the cultivating and improving of the same.

39. An act for sale of part of the settled estates of *Thomas Buckley* esquire, in the county of *Lancaster*, for discharging an incumbrance affecting the same, prior to his marriage settlement.

40. An act for giving further time to trustees, therein named, to execute certain trusts vested in them, in and by an act of parliament made in the sixteenth year of the reign of his present Majesty, intituled, *An act for vesting the remainder in fee of several lands in* Ireland, *in trustees, in order to sell the same to protestant purchasers.*

41. An act for dividing and inclosing several open fields, meadows, and commons, within the lordship and liberty of *Loughborough*, in the county of *Leicester*.

42. An act for dividing and inclosing certain open and common fields, called *Little Barrington* common fields, and a common or waste called *The Downs*, within the manor of *Little Barrington*, in the county of *Gloucester*.

43. An act for dividing and inclosing the open and common fields of *Hoton*, in the county of *Leicester*, and all the lands and grounds within the same fields.

44. An act for dividing and inclosing the open arable fields, open meadows, and common pasture grounds, in the parish of *Sileby*, in the county of *Leicester*.

45. An act for inclosing and dividing the common fields and common grounds

grounds of, and in, the manor and parish of *Harmston*, in the county of *Lincoln*.

46. An act for dividing and inclosing several fields, meadows, pastures, common and waste grounds in the parish of *Everton*, in the county of *Nottingham*.

47. An act for dividing and inclosing the open and common fields of *Breedon*, *Tonge*, and *Wilson*, in the manor of *Breedon*, and county of *Leicester*, and certain commonable and waste grounds, within the respective liberties thereof.

48. An act for inclosing and dividing the common fields, in the manor of *East Cotham*, in the county of *York*, and extinguishing the right of warren of the lord of the said manor in part of a tract of ground called the *Sea Batts*, or *Coney Warren*, in *East Cotham* aforesaid.

49. An act for dividing and inclosing the open fields and meadows, common pasture, and waste grounds, in the manor of *Thistleton*, in the county of *Rutland*.

50. An act for dividing and inclosing the common fields, common pastures, common meadows, common grounds, and waste grounds, in the manor and parish of *Slapton*, in the county of *Northampton*.

51. An act for dividing and inclosing the open and common fields of *Oadby*, in the county of *Leicester*, and all the lands and grounds within the same fields.

52. An act for dividing and inclosing certain open, common, and arable fields, meadows, pastures, and waste grounds, within the manor of *Burstall*, in the parish of *Belgrave*, in the county of *Leicester*.

53. An act for dividing and inclosing several open fields, and commonable lands, within the manor and parish of *Coleby*, in the county of *Lincoln*.

54. An act for dividing and inclosing the open and common fields of *Desford*, in the county of *Leicester*, and the lands and grounds therein, and also such lands, in the lordship of *Peckleton*, in the said county, as lie open to the said fields.

55. An act for dividing and inclosing several open and common fields, common meadows, common pastures, and common grounds, in the manor or lordship of *Bartin*, otherwise *Barton in Fabis*, in the several parishes of *Barton* and *Clifton*, in the county of *Nottingham*.

56. An act for dividing and inclosing certain open and common fields, meadows, common pastures, and waste grounds, in the parish or township of *Bolton upon Dearne*, in the county of *York*.

57. An act for dividing and inclosing certain open, arable fields, in the manor of *Bishops Waltham*, in the county of *Southampton*.

58. An act to enable *Arthur Hill* esquire, and *Arthur* his son, and their issue male, to take the name and arms of *Trevor*.

59. An act to enable *Robert Dobyns* esquire, now called *Robert Yate*, and his first and other sons, and their heirs male, to take and use the surname of *Yate*, in pursuance of the will of *Walter Yate* esquire, deceased.

60. An act for naturalizing *John Christian Suhring*, and *John Henry Subring*.

The END *of the* TABLE.

THE
STATUTES at Large, &c.

Anno Regni GEORGII II. *Regis Magnæ Britanniæ, Franciæ, & Hiberniæ, tricesimo.*

AT the parliament begun and holden at West-minster, the thirty first day of May, Anno Domini *one thousand seven hundred and fifty four, in the twenty seventh year of the reign of our sovereign Lord* GEORGE *the Second, by the grace of* GOD, *of* Great Britain, France, *and* Ireland, King, *defender of the faith,* &c. *And from thence continued by several prorogations to the second day of* December, *one thousand seven hundred and fifty six, Being the fourth session of this present parliament.*

CAP. I.

An act to prohibit, for a time to be limited, the exportation of corn, malt, meal, flour, bread, biscuit and starch.

WHEREAS the exportation of any sort of corn, meal, malt, flour, bread, biscuit and starch, out of the kingdoms of Great Britain or Ireland, may, at this time be greatly prejudicial to his Majesty's subjects; be it therefore enacted by the King's most excellent majesty, by and with the advice and consent of the lords spiritual and temporal, and commons, in this present parliament assembled, and by the authority of the same, That no person or persons whatsoever, at any time or times before the twenty fifth day of *December* in the year of our Lord one thousand seven hundred and fifty seven, shall, directly or indirectly, export, transport, carry or convey, or cause or procure to be exported, transported, carried or conveyed out of or from the said kingdoms of *Great Britain* or *Ireland*; or load or lay on board, or cause or procure to be laden or laid on board in any ship or other vessel, or boat, in order to be exported or carried out of the said kingdoms of *Great Britain* or *Ireland*, any

No corn, &c. to be exported from Great Britain or Ireland, before 25 Dec. 1757.

B

sort

fort of corn, meal, malt, flour, bread, bifcuit or ftarch, under the penalties and forfeitures herein after mentioned; that is to fay, That all the faid commodities that fhall be fo exported, fhipped or laid on board, or loaded to be exported, fhipped or carried out, contrary to this act, fhall be forfeited; and that every offender or offenders therein fhall forfeit the fum of twenty fhillings for every bufhel of corn, malt, meal or flour; and twelve pence of lawful money of *Great Britain*, for every pound weight of bread, bifcuit or ftarch, and fo in proportion for any greater or lefs quantity, which fhall be fo exported, fhipped or put on board to be exported; and alfo the fhip, boat or veffel, upon which any of the faid commodities fhall be exported, fhipped or laden to be exported, and all her guns, tackle, apparel and furniture, fhall be forfeited; and one moiety of all the

One moiety of the forfeiture to go to the King, the other to the profecutor.

faid penalties and forfeitures fhall be to the King's majefty, his heirs and fucceffors, and the other moiety to him or them that will fue for the fame; and for offences which fhall be committed in that part of *Great Britain* called *England*, fuch penalties and for-

Method of recovery thereof if in England, Wales,

feitures fhall be recovered by action of debt, bill, plaint or information, in any of his Majefty's courts of record at *Weftminfter*, or before the juftices of affize, or at the great feffions in *Wales*, or by information at any general quarter feffions of the peace for the county, city, riding, divifion or place, where the offence fhall be committed; and in fuch fuit, no effoin, protection, privilege or wager of law, fhall be allowed; and for offences which fhall be committed in that part of *Great Britain* called *Scotland*, by action, or fummary bill or information in the

Scotland,

courts of feffions or exchequer in *Scotland*; and for offences which fhall be committed in *Ireland*, in his Majefty's courts of record

or Ireland.

in *Dublin*, or at the general quarter feffions of the peace for the county, city or place, where the offence fhall be committed; and

Mafter and mariners if convicted, to be committed.

that the mafter and mariners of any fuch fhip, boat or veffel, wherein any fuch offence fhall be committed, knowing fuch offence, and wittingly and willingly aiding and affifting thereunto, and being thereof duly convicted in any fuch courts as aforefaid, fhall be imprifoned for the fpace of three months without bail or mainprize

II. And be it further enacted by the authority aforefaid,

Officers impowered to feize the veffels, and commodities;

That it fhall and may be lawful to and for any perfon or perfons, being an officer or officers of the cuftoms, or being lawfully authorized in this behalf by the lord high treafurer of *Great Britain*, or the commiffioners of the treafury for the time being, or any three or more of them, to take or feize all fuch of the faid commodities, not allowed to be exported by this act, or by his Majefty's royal proclamation, or fuch order of council, in purfuance of this act, as he or they fhall happen to find, know, or difcover to be laid on board any fhip or other veffel or boat, at fea, or in any port, or in any navigable river or water, to the intent or purpofe to be exported, tranfported or conveyed, out of *Great Britain* or *Ireland*; contrary to the true intent of this act; and alfo the fhip, veffel or boat, in which the fame

fhall

shall be found, and to bring the said goods to the king's ware-house or warehouses belonging to the custom-house, next to the place where such seizures shall be made, or to some other safe place (where there are no such warehouses) in order to be proceeded against according to law; and in case of recovery, to be divided according to the directions of this act. *and to lodge the goods in the King's warhouses.*

III. Provided always that this act, or any thing herein contained, shall not extend to prohibit the exportation or carrying out of such, or so much of the said commodities, as shall be necessary to be carried in any ship or ships, or other vessel or vessels, in their respective voyages, for the sustenance, diet and support of the commanders, masters, mariners, passengers or others, in the same ships or vessels only; or for the victualling or providing any of his Majesty's ships of war, or other ships or vessels in his Majesty's service; or for his Majesty's forces, forts or garrisons; any thing herein contained to the contrary notwithstanding. *Necessary provision for ships on their voyage; and for the King's ships, forces, forts, or garrisons, are excepted.*

IV. Provided also, That this act, or any thing herein contained, shall not extend to prohibit any person or persons to ship or put on board any of the commodities aforesaid, to be carried coastwise; that is to say, from any port, creek, or member of the kingdoms of *Great-Britain* or *Ireland*, to any other port, creek, or member of the same respectively, having such or the like coast-cocquet or sufferance for that purpose, and such or the like sufficient security being first given for the landing and discharging the same in some other port, member or creek of the said kingdoms, and returning a certificate in six months, as is required by law in cases where goods which are liable to pay duties on exportation, or carried coast-wise from one port of *Great-Britain* to another, and not otherwise. *The said commodities may be carried coastwise, if a cocquet be granted for the same, and selike curity given.*

V. Provided also, That this act, or any thing herein contained, shall not extend to any of the said commodities which shall be exported, or shipped to be exported, out of or from *Great-Britain* to *Ireland*, or from *Ireland* to *Great-Britain*, or from *Great-Britain* or *Ireland* to *Gibraltar*, or unto any of his Majesty's islands or colonies in *America*, that have usually been supplied with any of the said commodities from *Great-Britain* or *Ireland*, for the sustentation of the inhabitants of the said islands, colonies or dominions, or for the benefit of the *British* fishery in those parts only; so as the exporter do, before the shipping or laying on board the same, declare the island, colony or dominion, islands, colonies or dominions, for which the said commodities are respectively designed, and do become bound with other sufficient security, in treble the value thereof, to the commissioners or chief officer or officers of his Majesty's customs, belonging to the port or place where the same shall be shipped or put on board (who hath or have hereby power to take such security in his Majesty's name, and to his Majesty's use) that such commodities shall not be landed or sold in any parts whatsoever, other than the kingdoms, dominions, islands or colonies for which the same shall be so declared; and *The said commodities may be exported to Gibraltar, or the British islands or colonies in America, the exporter declaring where the same are designed for, and giving security.*

that

that a certificate under the hand and seal of the collector, comptroller or other chief officer of the customs; or if no such, or the naval officer, or some other principal officer of the port where the same shall be landed, shall within the respective times herein after for that purpose mentioned (the dangers of the seas excepted) be returned to the officers who took the said bonds, that the said commodities have been landed at the port or place for which the same shall be so declared; and for the taking of

such security, and giving such certificates (which the respective officers aforesaid are hereby on demand required to give) no fee or reward shall be demanded or received; and if any officer shall make any false certificate of any such commodities being so landed, such officer shall forfeit the sum of two hundred pounds, and lose his employment, and be incapable of serving his Majesty, his heirs or successors, in any office relating to the customs; and if any person shall counterfeit, rase or falsify any such certi-

ficate, or knowingly publish any such counterfeit, rased or false certificate, he shall forfeit the sum of two hundred pounds, and such certificate shall be void and of none effect; which said penalties for offences committed in Great Britain or Ireland, shall be recovered in the same courts, and in the same manner, as the other penalties inflicted by this act are recoverable; and for offences committed in the colonies or plantations in America, or other the dominions belonging to the crown of Great Britain in Europe, shall be recovered in the high court of admiralty, or in any other chief court of civil or criminal jurisdiction in such respective colonies, plantations or dominions; and shall be divided

into equal moieties between his Majesty and the informer; and the said bond or bonds, if not prosecuted within three years, shall be void.

VI. Provided also, That nothing herein contained shall extend to prohibit the exportation of beans to the British forts, castles and factories in Africa, or for the use of the ships trading upon that coast, that usually have been supplied with the same from Great Britain or Ireland, so as the like security be given for the exporting thereof, as is required by this act to be given by persons carrying any of the said commodities to the British colonies in America.

VII. Provided also, That nothing herein contained shall extend to prohibit the united company of merchants of England, trading to the East-Indies, from exporting any of the said commodities to any of their forts, factories or settlements, for the support of the persons residing there, so as the like security be given for the exporting thereof, as is required by this act to be given by persons carrying any of the said commodities to the British colonies in America.

VIII. Provided also, That this act, or any thing herein contained, shall not extend to any wheat, malt or barley, to be transported out of or from the port of Southampton only, unto the islands of Jersey and Guernsey, or either of them, for the only use of the inhabitants of those islands, so as the exporter
before

before the lading of the wheat, malt or barley, or laying the exporter giv-
same on board, do become bound with other sufficient security ing security.
(which the customer or comptroller of the same port hath hereby
power to take, in his Majesty's name, and to his Majesty's use;
and for which security no fee or reward shall be given or taken), .
that such wheat, malt or barley, shall be landed in the said islands Certificate of
of *Jersey* and *Guernsey*, or one of them (the danger of the seas the landing to
only excepted) for the use of the inhabitants there, and shall be returned
not be landed or sold in any other parts whatsoever, and to re- within a limit-
turn the like certificates of the landing the same there, as are ed time.
herein before required on the exportation of the said commodities to the *British* colonies in *America*, and within the time for
that purpose herein after mentioned; and so as the quantity of Quantity to be
wheat, malt and barley, which, at any time or times after the exported not
passing of this act, and before the twenty-fifth day of *December* to exceed 5000
one thousand seven hundred and fifty-seven, shall be shipped at quarters.
the said port for *Jersey* and *Guernsey*, or either of them as aforesaid, doth not exceed in the whole five thousand quarters any
thing herein contained to the contrary notwithstanding.

IX. And be it further enacted by the authority aforesaid, Commissioners
That the commissioners of the customs for the time being shall, of the customs
and they are hereby required to give a full and true account in to lay before
writing to both houses of parliament, at the beginning of the both houses of
next session thereof, of all corn, meal, malt, flour, bread, biscuit parliament an
and starch, that shall before that time be exported to any place account of the
whatsoever, by virtue or in pursuance of any of the liberties or corn, &c. ex-
powers hereby given or granted for that purpose. ported.

X. Provided, That nothing in this act contained shall extend Malt made for
to any malt declared or made for exportation on or before the exportation
fourth day of *December* one thousand seven hundred and fifty-six, before 4 Dec.
which shall be exported; provided the proprietor or proprietors 1756, may be
thereof shall produce to the collector or chief officer of the port exported, the
where such malt shall be exported, a certificate or certificates proprietor
from the officer or officers with whom the entry of the corn in- certificate
tended to be made into such malt for exportation shall have been thereof from
made, that the said malt was actually declared or made for ex- the proper of-
portation on or before the said fourth day of *December* one thou- ficer.
sand seven hundred and fifty-six; nor to any other of the commodities aforesaid which shall be cleared out of any custom- Vessels cleared
house within *Great Britain*, before the twenty-fifth day of *De*- out before 25
cember one thousand seven hundred and fifty-six; or out of any permitted to
custom-house in *Ireland* before the twenty-fifth day of *December* proceed on
one thousand seven hundred and fifty-six; but that such ships their voyages.
and vessels shall be permitted to proceed on their voyages; any
thing herein contained to the contrary in any wise notwithstanding.

XI. Provided always, and be it enacted by the authority His Majesty
aforesaid, That in case his Majesty at any time or times before by proclama-
the twenty-fifth day of *December* one thousand seven hundred and tion, or order
fifty-seven, shall (in his royal discretion) judge it to be most for in council,
the benefit and advantage of this kingdom, to permit the expor- may at any
ta- time before 2

tation of corn and other the commodities aforesaid, or any of them, that then it shall and may be lawful to and for his Majesty, by his royal proclamation or proclamations to be issued, by and with the advice of his privy council, or by his Majesty's order in council, to be published in the *London Gazette*, from time to time to permit and suffer all and every person or persons, natives and foreigners (but not any particular person or persons) at any time or times before the twenty-fifth day of *December* one thousand seven hundred fifty-seven, to export or carry out of the kingdoms of *Great Britain* or *Ireland*, or out of both or either of them, all or any of the commodities aforesaid, to all or any other place or places, and upon or without giving security for the landing thereof in such place or places, and returning certificates of such landing, as to his Majesty shall seem meet, and as in such proclamation or proclamations, or such orders of council, to be published in the *London Gazette*, shall be expressed and declared; any thing herein contained to the contrary notwithstanding.

XII. And be it further enacted by the authority aforesaid, That all certificates of the landing and discharging of the said commodities to be exported, other than coastwise, shall be returned within the respective times following; that is to say, Where the bonds are taken in respect of any of the said commodities to be exported from *Great Britain* or *Ireland*, to any of the said colonies or plantations in *America*, within eighteen calendar months after the date of the said bonds; and where to *Gibraltar*, with twelve calendar months after the date of such bonds; and where to the islands of *Guernsey* or *Jersey*, within six calendar months after the date of such bonds; and where from *Great Britain* to *Ireland*, or from *Ireland* to *Great Britain*, within six calendar months after the date of such bonds respectively.

CAP. II.

An act to make provision for the quartering of the foreign troops in his Majesty's service, now in this kingdom.

WHEREAS difficulties have lately arisen in providing quarters for the foreign troops in his Majesty's service, which have been brought over for the defence of Great Britain; be it enacted by the King's most excellent Majesty, by and with the advice and consent of the lords spiritual and temporal and commons in this present parliament assembled, and by the authority of the same,

That the said foreign troops brought over as aforesaid, shall and may, during their continuance here, be quartered, and be received and provided for in quarters, in the same manner to all intents and purposes as the *British* troops now are; and that the billeting, quartering, receiving and providing for such foreign troops, in the manner aforesaid, shall be deemed and taken to have been, and to be legal, valid and effectual, to all intents and purposes whatsoever.

CAP.

CAP. III.

An act for granting an aid to his Majesty by a land-tax, to be raised in Great-Britain, *for the service of the year one thousand seven hundred and fifty seven; and for discharging certain arrears of land taxes incurred before the time therein mentioned; and for the more effectual collecting of arrears for the future.* 4s. in the pound.

CXV. AND whereas several arrears of land taxes, granted by former acts of parliament, do still remain unsatisfied, which ought to have been levied, assessed, or re-assessed by the respective commissioners in such acts named or appointed, some of which being since dead, or removed to distant places; it is hereby declared and enacted by the authority aforesaid, That the commissioners by this act named or appointed, or so many of them as are hereby impowered to cause the monies by this act granted to be assessed or raised, shall, and they are hereby impowered to cause the monies so in arrear upon the said land taxes, to be assessed, re-assessed, levied and answered, as fully and effectually as any commissioners appointed by former acts might have done in that behalf; and the said assessors, collectors, and receivers, shall respectively assess, re-assess, levy, receive, and answer the several arrears, in such manner, and under such penalties, and by such means, and as fully and effectually as in this act they are impowered and required, with respect to the several sums by this act charged.

Arrears of former land taxes to be levied by the present commissioners.

CLXXVI. Provided always, and it is hereby likewise enacted by the authority aforesaid, That all the monies arisen or to arise into the exchequer, of or for the said surplusses, excesses or over-plus monies, and other revenues, composing the sinking fund (except such monies thereof, as are by this, or any other act or acts of this or any former session or sessions of parliament, especially charged upon the said sinking fund, or to be paid out of the same, or out of any revenues or branches composing the said sinking fund) shall be appropriated, reserved, and employed to and for the discharging the principal and interest of such national debts and incumbrances, as were incurred before the twenty fifth day of *December* one thousand seven hundred and sixteen, and are declared to be such national debts as may be redeemed, and are provided for by act of parliament, in such manner and form, as shall be directed and appointed by any future act or acts of parliament to be discharged therewith, or out of the same, and to none other use, intent or purpose whatsoever; any thing in this act contained to the contrary notwithstanding.

Sinking fund appropriated to discharge national debt incurred before 25 Dec. 1716.

CLXXVII. And whereas several orders of loan or exchequer bills made upon and in pursuance of an act of parliament of the twenty-eighth year of his Majesty's reign, (*Intituled, An act for granting an aid to his Majesty by a land tax, to be raised in* Great Britain, *for the service of the year one thousand seven hundred and fifty five*) still remain unpaid, for want of sufficient money arising by the said act being come into the exchequer to answer and pay

Deficiency of the land tax 28 Geo. II. how to be supplied.

the

the fame ; and it is uncertain how much thereof the monies a-
rising by the said act will be able to answer and discharge ; be
it enacted by the authority aforesaid, That if the money arisen
or to arise into the exchequer, for or on account of the said aids,
on or before the twenty-ninth day of *September* which shall be
in the year of our Lord one thousand seven hundred and fifty
seven, shall not be sufficient to discharge the whole principal and
interest due, or to grow due, on the several orders of loan or
exchequer bills made upon and in pursuance of the said act, that
then so much money as shall then appear to be deficient or wanting for answering the purposes aforesaid, shall and may be supplied and made good out of any the monies arising into the exchequer by or from the loans or exchequer bills on this act, or
any other monies or loans that are or shall be appropriated for
the service of the year one thousand seven hundred and fifty seven ; and the commissioners of the treasury, or any three or
more of them, or the high treasurer for the time being, shall direct and apply the same accordingly ; any thing herein before
contained to the contrary notwithstanding.

CAP. IV.

An act for continuing and granting to his Majesty certain duties upon
malt, mum, cyder, and perry, for the service of the year one thousand
seven hundred and fifty seven; and concerning the interest to be paid
for monies to be borrowed as well on the credit of this act, as on the credit of an act of this session of parliament, for granting an aid to his majesty by a land tax.

CAP. V.

An act for granting to his Majesty a sum not exceeding one million fifty
thousand and five pounds, and five shillings, to be raised by way of
lottery.

Natives and foreigners may contribute to the sum of 1,050,605l. 5 s. for
the purchase of tickets in the present lottery, at 1 l. 1 s. each ticket. Purchase money to be paid to the chief cashier of the bank. Subscribers for
100 tickets, depositing the one moiety of the purchase money, allowed to 1
June next to make good the second payment. Subscribers for any less
number, to pay the whole of the purchase money at the time of subscribing. Receipts to be given for the sums paid, &c. and the bearers intitled
to tickets in respect thereof. Cashier to attend at the bank from 9 to 3
o'clock, to receive subscriptions. Cashier to give security ; and to pay the
monies into the exchequer. Treasury to apply the monies to the services
voted by the commons. Managers and directors of the lottery to be appointed by the treasury. Books to be prepared with three colums, in each
of which 66,667 tickets to be printed. Tickets to be of an oblong form,
and joined with oblique lines, &c. Tickets in the 3d column to have the
words following printed on them : this ticket entitles the bearer to such
prize as may belong thereunto. Tickets to be signed. Books to be prepared for 14 classes, with 2 columns, on each of which 66,667 tickets to be
printed. Chances of the tickets in the 14 classes to be determined by
drawing the tickets in the books with three columns. Managers
to examine the books with the tickets, and deliver them to the cashier, and take a receipt for the same. Cashier to give a ticket for every
sum of 1l. 1s. paid in, and permit the adventurer to write his name on the
corresponding ticket. Cashier to redeliver the books to the managers, by 1
August, and account for the sums received. Tickets undisposed of to be
returned into the exchequer. Tickets of the middle column to be rolled up,
and tied; and cut off indenturewise into a box marked with the letter
(A) box to be locked up and sealed. Books to be prepared with 2 columns,

hmns, on each of which 66,667 tickets to be printed. The number and value of the fortunate tickets. 756 prizes. Fortunate tickets: 1 of 10,000l. 1 of 5,000l. 1 of 3,000l. 1 of 1,000l. 2 of 500l. 10 of 100l. 100 of 50l. 200 of 20l. 440 of 10l. with 300l. to the firft drawn ticket, and 300l. 3s. 6d. to the laft drawn. Tickets of the outermoft columns to be rolled up and tied, and cut out indentwife into a box marked with the letter (B). Box to be locked up and fealed. Publick notice to be given of times of cutting the tickets into boxes. The lottery to begin drawing 5 September. Method to be obferved in drawing, &c. After each day's drawing the boxes to be locked up and fealed. Numbers of the fortunate tickets, and the fums to be printed. Difputes relating thereto, to be adjufted by the managers. Penalty of forging tickets or certificates, felony. Managers to be fworn. The oath. Adventurer not paying his whole confideration-money by the times limited, fhall lofe the advance money. Tickets not difpofed of fhall be delivered into the exchequer. Managers, &c. to be paid by the commiffioners of the treafury out of the lottery money. Penalty of felling chances or fhares of tickets, for a lefs time than the drawing of the lottery; or of laying wagers relating to the chance of tickets; where to be fued for. Application thereof. Perfons felling fhares in tickets of which they are not poffeffed, &c. to forfeit 500l. Application thereof. Offences committed in Ireland againft acts made here, for preventing unlawful lotteries, declared to be punifhable, and may be fued for in Dublin. After the drawing of the lottery, the tickets to be exchanged for certificates. Managers to give notice of the time for taking in the tickets, and delivering out the certificates, &c. Book to be kept for entering perfons names, and the numbers of their tickets, &c. Certificates to be figned, &c. 525,002l. 12s. 6d. to be paid out of the fupplies into the bank before 20 Jan. next, for payment of the prizes. Cafhier to make payment thereof accordingly. Treafury to pay the incident charges attending the execution of this act; and to make allowance to the bank, &c. for their trouble and pains. 20l. penalty on officer taking any fee, &c. for receiving or paying monies on this act. Perfons fued on this act may plead the general iffue. Treble cofts.

C A P. VI.

An act for punifhing mutiny and defertion; and for the better payment of the army and their quarters.

C A P. VII.

An act to difcontinue for a limited time the duties upon corn and flour imported; and alfo upon fuch corn, grain, meal, bread, bifcuit and flour, as have been or fhall be taken from the enemy, and brought into this kingdom.

WHEREAS *the difcontinuing of the duties for a limited time upon corn and flour imported into this kingdom, and alfo upon fuch corn, grain, meal, bread, bifcuit, and flour, as have been or fhall be taken from the enemy, and brought into this kingdom, may be of advantage to his Majefty's fubjects;* be it therefore enacted by the King's moft excellent majefty, by and with the advice and confent of the lords fpiritual and temporal and commons in this prefent parliament affembled, and by the authority of the fame, That no fubfidy, cuftom, rate, duty, or other impofition whatfoever, fhall be demanded, collected, received or taken, upon any corn or flour which fhall be imported into this kingdom, at any time or times before the twenty fourth day of *Auguft* next; nor fhall any fubfidy, cuftom, rate, duty, or other impofition whatfoever, be demanded, collected, received or taken, upon

The enumerated commodities for a time limited may be landed duty free, and carried coaftwife.

any

any corn, grain, meal, bread, biscuit or flour, which have been or shall be taken from the enemy, and brought into this kingdom, at any time or times before the said twenty fourth day of *August*; but that all such corn and flour, and also all such corn, grain, meal, bread, biscuit and flour, shall and may be imported, brought in, and landed, duty free, and may also be carried coastwise, under such regulations as corn of the growth of this kingdom is now allowed to be carried coastwise, at all times before the said twenty fourth day of *August*; any former law, statute, act or acts of parliament to the contrary in any wise notwithstanding.

Entry to be made thereof;   II. Provided always, and be it further enacted by the authority aforesaid, That a due entry shall be made in such manner and form as were used and practised before the making of this act, of all corn, grain, meal, bread, biscuit and flour, which shall be imported or brought into this kingdom, before the said twenty fourth day of *August*, at the custom-house belonging to the port into which the same shall be imported or brought in, or other-

otherwise to be subject to duty.   wise in default of making such entry, such corn, grain, meal, bread, biscuit and flour, shall be liable and subject to such and the same duties, as were payable upon the importation thereof before the making of this act; any thing in this act contained to the contrary notwithstanding.

III. And be it further enacted by the authority aforesaid, That if any action or suit shall be commenced against any person or persons, for any thing done in pursuance of this act, in that part of *Great Britain* called *England*, the defendant or defen-

General issue.   dants in any such action or suit may plead the general issue, and give this act and the special matter in evidence, at any trial to be had thereupon; and that the same was done in pursuance and by the authority of this act; and if it shall appear so to have been done, the jury shall find for the defendant or defendants; and if the plaintiff shall be nonsuited, or discontinue his action; after the defendant or defendants shall have appeared; or if judgment shall be given upon any verdict or demurrer against the plaintiff, the defendant or defendants shall and may recover

Treble costs.   treble costs, and have the like remedy for the same, as any defendant or defendants hath or have in other cases by law; and

Suits in Scotland.   if such action or suit be commenced or prosecuted in that part of *Great Britain* called *Scotland*, the court before whom such action or suit shall be brought, shall allow the defender to plead this act on his defence; and if the pursuer shall not insist on his action, or if judgment shall be given against such pursuer, the defender shall and may recover the full and real expences he may have been put to by any such action or suit.

CAP. VIII.

An act for the speedy and effectual recruiting of his Majesty's land forces and marines.

WHEREAS for recruiting his Majesty's land forces and marines, it is necessary that a new supply of men be forthwith raised *raifed within the kingdom of* Great Britain, *by common confent and grant in parliament ;* be it therefore enacted by the King's moft excellent majefty, by and with the advice and confent of the lords fpiritual and temporal and commons in this prefent parliament affembled, and by the authority of the fame, That within and throughout the feveral and refpective counties, fhires, ftewartries, ridings, cities, boroughs, cinque ports, parifhes, towns and places of *Great Britain,* a fpeedy and effectual levy of able-bodied men to ferve his Majefty as foldiers, fhall be forthwith had, made, practifed and put in execution, according to the rules and directions of this prefent act.

A levy of able bodied men to be madethroughout Great Britain.

II. And it is hereby further enacted, That the juftices of the peace of every county, fhire, ftewartry, riding, liberty or place, within *Great Britain,* and all and every the perfons who were named, or otherwife appointed to be commiffioners for putting in execution an act of parliament made and paffed at *Weftminfter* in the twenty eighth year of the reign of his prefent Majefty, intituled, *An act for granting an aid to his Majefty by a land-tax, to be raifed in* Great Britain, *for the fervice of the year one thoufand feven hundred and fifty five ;* and *for the relief of the inhabitants of certain places in the county of* Lincoln, *in refpect of arrears of the land-tax,* or any fubfequent act or acts of parliament for that purpofe, within the feveral and refpective counties, fhires, ftewartries, ridings, cities, boroughs, cinque ports, towns and places, therein particularly expreffed, who are ftill living, and have duly qualified themfelves according to the faid acts, or fhall duly qualify themfelves according to this prefent act in that behalf, fhall be commiffioners for putting in execution this prefent act, and the powers therein contained, within and for the fame counties, fhires, ftewartries, ridings, cities, boroughs, cinque ports, towns and places of *Great Britain,* for which they were fo named or appointed refpectively ; and that all and every the other perfons who are named or otherwife appointed to be commiffioners for putting in execution an act paffed in the prefent feffion of parliament, intituled, *An act for granting an aid to his Majefty by a land tax to be raifed in* Great Britain, *for the fervice of the year one thoufand feven hundred and fifty feven ;* and *for difcharging certain arrears of land taxes incurred before the time therein mentioned ;* and *for the more effectual collecting of arrears for the future,* within or for the faid counties, fhires, ftewartries, ridings, cities, boroughs, cinque ports, towns and places, or any of them refpectively, or fuch of the perfons laft mentioned, as fhall alfo duly qualify themfelves according to this act in that behalf, fhall alfo be commiffioners for putting in execution this prefent act, and the powers therein contained, within and for the fame refpective counties, fhires, ftewartries, ridings, cities, boroughs, cinque ports, towns and places of *Great Britain,* for which they are fo named or appointed refpectively ; and that all and every the juftices of the peace, and magiftrates of corporations and burghs in any part of *Great Britain,* who are or fhall be in any of his Majefty's commiffions of the peace, or in the magiftracy

Juftices of the peace, commiffioners of the land tax, and magiftrates of corporations to put this act in execution.

of

of fuch corporation or burgh, at any time during the execution of this act, who shall duly qualify themfelves according to this prefent act in that behalf (although not fpecially named or appointed commiffioners by the faid act) shall be likewife commiffioners for putting in execution this prefent act, and all the powers therein contained, within the limits of their commiffions and jurifdictions refpectively: all which commiffioners by this act intrusted with the execution of the fame, are hereby strictly enjoined and required to ufe their utmost care and diligence that his Majefty's fervice, in making fuch levies as aforefaid, be not difappointed or neglected.

and to take care, that his Majefty's fervice be not neglected.

III. And be it further enacted by the authority aforefaid, That the high sheriff of every county, or his deputy, immediately upon receiving notice for that purpofe from the fecretary at war, shall fend precepts to the refpective bailiffs, or others who are ufually employed to fummon juries, although in liberties out of the ordinary jurifdiction of the faid high sheriff, directing them to fummon the feveral juftices of the peace, and commiffioners of the land tax, within their refpective divifions and liberties, to attend at the ufual place of meeting in every divifion, upon a certain day in the faid precepts named, within the time limited by the fecretary at war (notice of which day shall be fent to the war office and admiralty, upon the iffuing of the precepts by the sheriff) to qualify themfelves for the execution of this act; and the faid commiffioners shall then and there appoint the feveral times and places for the fucceeding meetings in each of their refpective fub-divifions during the continuance of this act; and the faid juftices of the peace, and commiffioners of the land tax, at fuch their first meeting, or at fome other meeting to be held as foon as it can be conveniently, shall iffue their precepts to the high constables, headboroughs, or other proper officers for the refpective hundreds, lathes, rapes, wapentakes or other fub-divifions, within the faid counties, shires, stewartries, ridings or divifions, as aforefaid; which precept shall contain an account of the times and places appointed for the fucceeding meetings, and shall be returnable on a day therein to be named, within twenty days, and not lefs than fourteen days, from the time of iffuing thereof; and fuch high constables, headboroughs or other proper officers, are hereby required forthwith to fignify the times and places appointed for fuch meetings, to the feveral commiffioners refiding within their refpective districts; and the faid commiffioners affembled at fuch first meeting to qualify themfelves as aforefaid, shall alfo give notice of the time and place of all and every fucceeding meeting to be appointed as aforefaid, to the military officer whom they shall have learned, by notice from the fecretary at war, to be directed to attend this fervice.

High sheriffs, &c. upon notice from the fecretary at war, to iffue precepts for the commiffioners to meet, and qualify themfelves.

Notice of the day of meeting to be fent to the war office. Commiffioners to appoint the times and places of their fucceeding meetings, and iffue precepts for that purpofe to the high constables, &c.

and to give notice thereof alfo to fuch military officers as shall attend this fervice.

IV. Provided always, and it is hereby enacted, That all reafonable charges or expences incurred by any sheriff or deputy sheriff in the execution of this act, shall be allowed in the accounts of fuch sheriff at the receipt of his Majefty's exchequer.

Sheriffs to be allowed by the exchequer their expences in the execution of this act.

V. And

V. And, for the encouragement of fit and able persons vo- Every person
luntarily to enter into his Majesty's service, be it enacted, That voluntarily in-
every such person who shall, on or before the first day of *May* listing himself,
one thousand seven hundred and fifty seven, voluntarily enter intitled to ſL.
himself into his Majesty's service, before the said commissioners, ney.
at their first or any subsequent meeting, shall, by warrant of any
three or more of the said commissioners, receive the sum of three
pounds out of the money of the land tax, arisen or to arise in
the years one thousand seven hundred and fifty six, and one
thousand seven hundred and fifty seven, or either of them, then
being in the hands of any receiver general, or of any collector
thereof, within the county or place for which the said commissioners are appointed; and thereupon the commissioners then Volunteers to
present, or any three of them, shall forthwith cause such volun- be delivered
teers to be delivered to the officers appointed to receive them; to the military
and shall cause an entry to be made in some book to be kept by officers, and
the said commissioners, or such clerk as they shall appoint, of an entry to be
the names of such volunteers, and of the parishes or places of made of their
their last abode (if they can be known) and of the time and names, places
place when and where they did so enter themselves, and of the of abode, sums
sums paid to them, and by whom such payments were made, paid them,
and of the names of the officers or persons who received such cers receiving
volunteers, and for what regiment or company they were re- them.
ceived; and shall cause true copies or duplicates of such entries, Duplicates
attested by three or more of the said commissioners then present, thereof to be
within forty days after the delivery of such volunteers, to be transmitted
transmitted into the office of his Majesty's secretary at war for the to the war
time being, to be compared with the muster-rolls. office.

VI. And it is hereby declared, That the pay of every such Volunteers to
volunteer shall commence from the time that he shall so enter receive pay
himself into his Majesty's service, and that every such volun- from the time
teer, after he shall have continued in the military service of his of their enter-
Majesty, his heirs and successors, during the space of three ing; and to be
years, if the war shall then be ended, or otherwise at the end discharged at
of the war, shall be at liberty (if he think fit) to demand his the end of
discharge from the colonel or commanding officer of the regi- three years, or
ment or company to which he shall belong; and such discharge of the war, if
shall be granted to him *gratis* in writing under the hand of such it.
colonel or commanding officer, who is hereby impowered and
required to give the same accordingly, on pain of suffering the
penalties usually inflicted for disobedience to orders; any thing
herein contained to the contrary notwithstanding.

VII. And it is hereby further enacted, That the warrants by Warrants for
this act directed to be issued by the said commissioners for the bounty-mo-
encouragement of volunteers as aforesaid, shall be satisfied by ney to be paid
such receivers or collectors as aforesaid, to whom such warrants without any
shall be directed, without any abatement for fees, gratuities, deduction.
charges, poundage, or any other pretence whatsoever, and shall
be allowed upon their accounts; any law or statute to the contrary notwithstanding; and the said receivers general, and their Receivers ge-
respective deputies, and the said collectors of the land tax mo- neral, and collectors, to at-
ney,

tend meeting of commissioners, to pay the bounty.

40 s. of every pound paid out of the land tax, to be repaid into exchequer by the paymasters of the forces.

Amended by a subsequent act of this session.

Three commissioners impowered to levy such men as are herein described;

and to call in the assistance of parish and town officers;

and to meet in their sub-divisions,

and issue general search warrants, &c. for bringing persons within the description of this act before them at their second meeting.

ney, or any of them, upon the summons of the said commissioners, or any three or more of them, shall attend at the said meetings for receiving volunteers as aforesaid, and duly pay to the said volunteers the rewards prescribed by this act, as they will answer at their peril any delay or obstruction to his Majesty's service which may happen by their defaults.

VIII. Provided always, and it is hereby enacted, That it shall be lawful for the lord high treasurer, or commissioners of the treasury for the time being, to cause forty shillings of every pound of the money which shall be supplied out of the land tax money for the year one thousand seven hundred and fifty six, and one thousand seven hundred and fifty seven, or either of them, for payment of the encouragements aforesaid, to be repaid into his Majesty's exchequer by the respective paymasters of his Majesty's forces, out of such money as they shall receive for the said forces, to make good the respective credits on the said land taxes, and to be applied to the satisfaction of such principal and interest (if any) as shall be remaining thereupon.

IX. And it is hereby further enacted by the authority aforesaid, That the said commissioners, or any three or more of them, in their respective places or stations, shall be, and are hereby authorized and impowered to raise and levy, and to cause to be raised and levied, at any time or times during the continuance of this act, within their several limits and jurisdictions, all able-bodied idle and disorderly persons, who cannot, upon examination, prove themselves to exercise and industriously follow some lawful trade or employment, or to have some substance sufficient for their support and maintenance, to serve his Majesty as soldiers; and to require and command all and every the high constables, churchwardens, overseers of the poor, petty constables, headboroughs and tythingmen, and other parish and town officers, or any of them, within their respective limits and jurisdictions, to be aiding and assisting to them the said commissioners, or any three or more of them, in the performance of this his Majesty's service; and for that purpose the said commissioners, or any three of them, are to meet in their respective sub-divisions, according to the appointment of the justices and commissioners as aforesaid, and to issue out their warrants, under their hands and seals, thereby requiring and commanding such churchwardens, overseers of the poor, petty constables, headboroughs, tythingmen, or other parish or town officers, or else requiring and commanding the said high constables to issue their precepts to such churchwardens, overseers, petty constables, headboroughs, tythingmen, and other parish and town officers as aforesaid, every or any of them, to make or cause to be made a general search within their respective parishes, townships, constablewicks, or other places, for all such persons as they can find, who are or shall appear to them to be within the description of this act, and to bring all such persons before the commissioners, who have power to execute this act, in and for such county, shire, stewartry, riding or division, at such time and place as shall have been

been appointed by the justices and commissioners as aforesaid, for the second meeting of the said commissioners, in their respective sub-divisions, which time and place shall be prefixed in the said warrants and precepts respectively; and afterwards the said commissioners, within their respective limits and divisions, shall meet at such convenient time or times as they shall think fit, in order to issue their like warrants or precepts, for making general searches for persons within the said description, and for bringing them before the commissioners at any future times and places appointed by the justices and commissioners as aforesaid, during the continuance of this act.

X. Provided always, That in case the second meeting appointed to be held in any sub-division, shall be at so great a distance of time, as may render it inconvenient to issue warrants for bringing persons before such commissioners at the second meeting, then the commissioners of such sub-division respectively may adjourn themselves to some convenient day, previous to such second meeting, in order to issue their warrants as aforesaid.

If the second meeting be too distant, commissioners in their sub-divisions may adjourn to a previous day.

XI. Provided always, and it is hereby enacted, That it shall and may be lawful to and for the churchwardens, overseers of the poor, constables, headboroughs, tythingmen, and other officers of any parish or township, or any of them, at any time after the said second meeting of the said commissioners, without tarrying for any such warrant or precept as aforesaid, to search for, and apprehend all, or any such persons as they, or any of them shall find, or shall appear to them, or any of them, to be within the description of this act, and to secure such persons (in case they shall think it necessary) in the gaol or house of correction, or publick prison where debtors are not usually confined, of the county, town or place, where such persons shall be apprehended, and the keeper of such gaol, house of correction or prison, shall receive such persons without fee or reward, and the parish officers shall allow such keeper six pence by the day for each person, during the time that they shall remain there, and shall convey them before the commissioners, at their next meeting for listing of soldiers, to be examined, and (if judged within the description of this act) to be listed and delivered into his Majesty's service, according to the true intent and meaning hereof.

After such second meeting, the parish and town officers may search for and secure such persons as come within the description of this act, and convey them before commissioners to be listed.

XII. And be it further enacted by the authority aforesaid, That the commissioners for executing this act, who shall attend this service at the place or places for listing soldiers as aforesaid, shall strictly examine the persons who shall be brought before them, by the said churchwardens, overseers, constables, headboroughs, tythingmen, or other parish or town officers, as aforesaid; and in case the said commissioners, or the major part of them then present, upon examination of the persons so brought before them, shall find that such persons shall come within the descriptions herein mentioned, and the said commissioners, and the officer or officers who shall be appointed to receive the impressed men, shall judge them to be such as are hereby intended

Commissioners to examine the said persons,

and if found proper for the service,

to

to be entertained as foldiers in his Majefty's fervice, then and in fuch cafe the faid commiffioners fhall caufe fuch perfons to be delivered over by the faid churchwardens, overfeers, conftables, headboroughs, tythingmen or other parifh or town officers, to fuch officers or perfons as fhall be appointed to receive fuch recruits as aforefaid, fuch officers or perfons giving a receipt under their hands, acknowledging what men are fo delivered to him or them, which receipt they are hereby required to give.

XIII. And be it further enacted, That the refpective officers who fhall receive fuch new raifed men, fhall pay to the clerk appointed by the commiffioners, for the ufe of the officers of the parifh or town fo employed in the raifing fuch men, for their pains and fervices therein, twenty fhillings of lawful money of Great Britain, for every man fo raifed; and fhall alfo pay for every fuch new raifed man, who fhall have a wife or family, any fum not exceeding forty fhillings, nor lefs than ten fhillings of lawful money of Great Britain, to the faid clerk, to be by him paid over as is herein after directed, into the hands of the churchwardens or overfeers of the poor, for the benefit of fuch parifh or townfhip, in which fuch new raifed man fhall have gained a fettlement, and whofe wife and family may become chargeable to fuch parifh or townfhip refpectively; which fum fhall be fettled by the commiffioners prefent at the meeting when fuch perfon fhall be inlifted, or any three or more of them, regard being had to the number of children, or other particular circumftances of fuch perfon fo inlifted, for both which payments the clerk fhall give a receipt, and the fum of fix pence per diem, for keeping every fuch new raifed man who fhall be delivered as aforefaid, according to the number of days that the officers of the faid parifh or town fhall have kept him in cuftody, purfuant to the powers granted by this act, until fuch delivery; the faid allowances of twenty fhillings, and of fix pence per diem, in cafe of difpute, to be afcertained and diftributed to or amongft the faid churchwardens, overfeers, conftables, headboroughs, tythingmen, and fuch other parifh and town officers, or any of them, according to the judgment and direction of the faid commiffioners, or the major part of them then prefent.

XIV. Provided always, and be it further enacted by the authority aforefaid, That the faid commiffioners, or any three or more of them, in their refpective divifions, are hereby authorized and impowered, by and out of the faid fum of twenty fhillings, herein before directed to be paid for the ufe of the officers of the parifh or town fo employed in the raifing of fuch men, to allot and order fuch fum as they fhall think fit, to the refpective high conftables within their refpective limits and jurifdictions, for their pains and fervice in the execution of this act, not exceeding the fum of two fhillings.

XV. Provided always, That no perfon fhall be inlifted by the faid commiffioners by virtue of this act, who is not fuch an able-bodied man as is fit to ferve his Majefty, and is free from ruptures and every other diftemper, or bodily weaknefs or infirmity,

mity, which may render him unfit to perform the duty of a foldier; and that no man be inlifted for his Majefty's fervice by
virtue of this act, who fhall appear in the opinion of the commiffioners, or officer or officers appointed to receive the impreff-
ed men, to be under the age of feventeen years, or above the age
of forty five years, or a known papift, or who fhall be under the
fize of five feet four inches without fhoes.

XVI. *And for the better preventing any difputes which may arife
about paying for the fubfiftence of thofe perfons, who, having been
apprehended and detained by virtue of this act, may afterwards be
difcharged upon examination before the commiffioners and military officers;* be it further enacted by the authority aforefaid, That if
any perfon being judged by the commiffioners not to be within
the defcription of this act, fhall be by them difcharged, the officers of the parifh or town fhall be intitled to no confideration, for
their expences in keeping fuch perfon; and if any perfon being
judged by the commiffioners to be within the defcription of this
act, fhall be rejected by the military officer, fuch officer fhall pay
to the officers of the parifh or town fix pence *per diem*, for the
whole time that they fhall have kept every fuch perfon, to be
charged to the account of his refpective regiment or company;
and every officer who fhall object to any perfon delivered to him
by the commiffioners, fhall fpecify his objection to fuch perfon,
whether it fhall be to his age or fize, or bodily difability, and the
grounds of fuch objection fhall be forthwith (as far as may be)
enquired into by the faid commiffioners, and they fhall proceed
accordingly; and every officer who fhall refufe or difcharge any
perfon delivered to him by the commiffioners as fit to ferve his
Majefty within the defcription of this act, fhall without delay
tranfmit to his Majefty's fecretary at war, his reafon for fuch refufal or difcharge, in writing, attefted by himfelf.

XVII. And it is hereby enacted and ftrictly enjoined by the
authority aforefaid, That the inhabitants of every parifh and
townfhip, where any perfons defcribed as aforefaid, do abide,
or are to be found, at the inftance of any one or more of the
commiffioners appointed for the execution of this act, or of any
churchwarden, overfeer of the poor, or conftable of the fame
parifh or townfhip, fhall (not having a lawful or reafonable excufe to the contrary) be aiding and affifting in the furtherance of
his Majefty's fervice by this act defcribed.

XVIII. *And to encourage fuch inhabitants and others to affift in
difcovering and apprehending fuch perfons defcribed as aforefaid;* it
is hereby further enacted by the authority aforefaid, That if any
perfon fhall difcover and give information of any able bodied
man fit to ferve his Majefty within the defcription of this act,
fo that he fhall be apprehended and inlifted before the commiffioners as aforefaid, fuch perfon, for every man fo difcovered
and inlifted, fhall receive from the officer to whom fuch man
fhall be delivered, the fum of ten fhillings out of the twenty fhillings, which he is elfewhere directed to pay to the officers of
the parifh or town, for every man inlifted by virtue of this act,

and the remainder only of the faid twenty fhillings fhall in that cafe be paid to fuch officers.

Clerks to be
appointed by
the commiff-
oners at their
firft general
meeting.
Clerks to be
appointed for
attending the
meeting of
commiffioners
in their fub-
divifions.
Clerks to be
paid by the
officer 2s. for
every man in-
lifted.

XIX. And be it further enacted by the authority aforefaid, That it fhall and may be lawful to and for the faid commiffioners, at their firft general meeting affembled, to appoint a clerk to attend them, then and at each of their fubfequent meetings, and for the commiffioners of the feveral fub-divifions, to appoint a clerk to attend them at their refpective meetings in each fub-difion wherein foldiers are to be lifted as aforefaid ; and fuch refpective clerks, as a reward for their labour and pains in the execution of this act, fhall be intitled to and fhall receive for every man who fhall be lifted in purfuance of this act, at the meetings whereon they fhall refpectively attend, the fum of two fhillings of lawful money of *Great Britain*, to be paid by the refpective officer who fhall receive fuch new raifed men refpectively.

The fecond
and fixth fec-
tions of the
articles of war
to be read
before com-
miffioners to
new raifed
men.
Names of the
men, parifh,
time of inlift-
ing, &c. to be
entered in a
book.

XX. And be it further enacted by the authority aforefaid, That the faid commiffioners, or fuch of them as fhall be prefent at fuch meeting for lifting of foldiers as aforefaid, fhall caufe the fecond and fixth fections of the articles of war againft mutiny and defertion, to be read to fuch new raifed men, in the prefence of the faid commiffioners then there ; and the faid commiffioners, or the major part of them prefent, fhall forthwith caufe an entry or memorial to be made, in a book or books to be kept by them or their clerks for that purpofe, of the names of fuch new raifed men, and of the parifhes or places of their laft abode (if they can be known) and of the time and place when and where fuch men were delivered to the faid officers or perfons appointed to receive them, and the names of the officers or perfons who received them, and for what regiment or company they were fo received, and the fums paid, and fhall caufe true copies or

Attefted copy
thereof to be
tranfmitted
within 40
days, to the
admiralty, or
office of fecre-
tary at war,
on penalty of
10l.
Application of
the penalty.

duplicates of fuch entries, attefted by the faid commiffioners, or any three or more of them then prefent, within forty days after the delivering fuch men as aforefaid, to be tranfmitted into the admiralty or office of his Majefty's fecretary at war for the time being, to be compared with the mufter-roll ; and every clerk for every neglect or default, in not tranfmitting the faid copies or duplicates of fuch entries, to the admiralty or office of the fecretary at war as aforefaid, fhall forfeit the fum of ten pounds, one moiety thereof to the ufe of his Majefty, his heirs and fucceffors, and the other moiety to fuch perfon or perfons who fhall inform or fue for the fame, in fome of the courts of record at *Weftminfter*, or the court of feffions in *Scotland* ; and it is hereby declared, that the pay of every fuch new raifed man, fo

Commence-
ment of fol-
dier's pay.
After articles
of war read,
foldiers deem-
ed to be lifted,
and fubject to
martial law.
No lifted per-
fon to be taken
out of the fer-
vice, but for

delivered to the officers or perfons appointed to receive them as aforefaid, fhall commence from the time of his being taken and fecured as aforefaid ; and from and after fuch delivery as aforefaid, and reading the faid articles of war, every perfon fo raifed fhall be deemed a lifted foldier to all intents and purpofes, and fhall be fubject to the difcipline of war, and in cafe of defertion, fhall be proceeded againft as a deferter by any law now in force, or by any law to be made for punifhment of deferters ;
and

and no person so listed, shall be liable to be taken out of his Majesty's service, by any process other than for some criminal matter.

some criminal matter.

XXI. Provided nevertheless, and be it enacted by the authority aforesaid, That it shall be lawful for the commissioners, who shall have been present at any such meeting where any new raised man shall have been delivered over as aforesaid, or for the major part of them, upon the demand of such man, or of any other person on his behalf, signified to their clerk within four days after such meeting, and by him notified to each of the said commissioners, to appoint a further meeting of the same commissioners, to be holden within six days after the making of such demand; and if upon further and more certain information, the said commissioners, or the major part of them at such further meeting, shall find that such new raised man was not, at the time of his being delivered over as aforesaid, within the description of this act, they are hereby required to certify the same under their hands and seals to his Majesty's secretary at war, who on the receipt of such certificate shall cause the man to be forthwith discharged, upon his paying to the officer to whom he was delivered over, the sum of six pence for his maintenance for each day that he shall have been detained, under the authority of this act; and the clerk appointed by the commissioners shall repay to such officer (without fee or other deduction) the several sums before paid to him by the said officer, and shall give back the receipts taken as above directed, in exchange for a copy of the man's discharge; and in case no such discharge shall have been obtained as aforesaid, then the said clerk shall, after the expiration of fourteen days, from the time that such new raised man was delivered over as aforesaid, pay over, without fee or deduction, to the persons respectively intitled thereto, under the directions of this act, the several sums deposited in his hands for that purpose.

Commissioners present at the delivering over any recruit, may appoint a further meeting; and finding him not to be within the description of the act, are to certify the same to the secretary at war, and the man to be discharged, upon payment of his subsistence-money. Officer to be repaid, and receipts to be returned. If no discharge be obtained, clerk to pay over the sums deposited to the proper persons.

XXII. Provided always, That nothing in this act contained shall be construed to extend to impower the said commissioners to inlist any person as a soldier until the several sums herein directed to be paid by the respective officers appointed to receive such new raised men, shall be first paid to the person or persons respectively authorized to receive the same.

None to be inlisted 'till the sums payable by the officers are first paid.

XXIII. And be it further enacted by the authority aforesaid, That the officer or officers, and other person or persons appointed to attend the said commissioners, and to receive such impressed men, shall, in case he or they shall find it necessary, secure such impressed men in some secure house or place to be provided by the justices of the peace in their petty or special sessions for that purpose; but in case no such house or place shall be so provided, then in the gaol of the county, town or place where such man shall be received into his Majesty's service, or in the house of correction, or other publick prison of such county, town or place where debtors are not usually confined: and the keeper of such gaol, house of correction or prison shall receive such im-

Officers may secure impressed men.

pressed

preſſed men until they can be removed, without fee or reward;

Keeper to be allowed their ſubſiſtence-money.
Civil officers, if required, to be aiding in ſecuring them.

and ſuch keeper ſhall be allowed the uſual ſubſiſtence for ſuch men during the time they ſhall remain there, from the officer by whom they ſhall be delivered as aforeſaid; and the conſtables, headboroughs, and other civil officers, ſhall (if required) be aſſiſting to ſuch officer in conveying ſuch man or men, to ſuch ſecure place, gaol or houſe of correction; and ſhall be allowed ſuch reaſonable ſum or ſums, as the major part of the commiſſioners then preſent ſhall appoint to be paid by the officer or officers who ſhall require ſuch aſſiſtance.

Commiſſioners may levy a fine not exceeding 10l. on gaoler for eſcape of men, and on pariſh officers for neglect of duty.

XXIV. And it is hereby further enacted by the authority aforeſaid, That it ſhall and may be lawful to and for the ſaid commiſſioners, or any three or more of them, to impoſe upon any gaoler or keeper of a houſe of correction or priſon, who ſhall ſuffer any perſon committed to his cuſtody in purſuance of this act to eſcape; or upon any high conſtable, churchwarden, overſeer, petty conſtable, headborough, tythingman, or other pariſh or town officer, for every wilful neglect or default in the execution of any warrant, order or precept, to them or any of them directed in purſuance of this act, a fine not exceeding ten pounds; and to cauſe every ſuch fine to be levied by diſtreſs and ſale of the offenders goods, rendering the overplus (if any be) to the owners, and to pay the ſaid fine to the informer or informers.

Perſons obſtructing the execution of this act to forfeit 10l.

XXV. And be it further enacted by the authority aforeſaid, That if any perſon or perſons whatſoever ſhall wilfully do any act or thing whereby the execution of this act, in the ſearching for, taking and ſecuring ſuch able-bodied men as aforeſaid, ſhall be hindered or fruſtrated, every ſuch perſon ſhall, for every ſuch offence, forfeit any ſum not exceeding ten pounds, to the uſe of the informer or informers; and all and every ſuch offences may be enquired of, heard and finally determined by any two or more of his Majeſty's juſtices of the peace, dwelling in or near the place where ſuch offence ſhall be committed, who have hereby power to cauſe the ſaid penalty to be levied by diſtreſs and ſale of the offenders goods and chattels, rendering the overplus (if any be) to the owners;

For want of diſtreſs, offender to be committed.

and if the offenders have no goods and chattels ſufficient to anſwer the ſaid penalty, then to commit him or her to the county gaol or houſe of correction, there to remain for the ſpace of three months, without bail or mainprize.

Perſons who have a vote in the election of members of parliament, not liable to be liſted.

XXVI. Provided always, and it is hereby declared, That this act ſhall not extend to the taking or levying any perſon to ſerve as a ſoldier, who ſhall make it appear to the ſatisfaction of the commiſſioners then preſent, that he hath any vote in the election of any member or members to ſerve in parliament, in any county, city, borough, town, port or place within the kingdom of *Great Britain*.

No military officer may be a commiſſioner.

XXVII. And it is hereby enacted, That no perſon who at the time of the execution of this act, ſhall have any military office or employment in *Great Britain* (other than in the militia) ſhall

shall execute any power or authority by this act given to commissioners as aforesaid.

XXVIII. And be it further enacted by the authority aforesaid, That if any action, plaint, suit or information, shall be commenced or prosecuted against any person or persons, for what he or they shall do in pursuance or execution of this act, the same shall be commenced within six months after the offence committed, and such person or persons so sued in any court whatsoever, shall and may plead the general issue Not guilty, and upon any issue joined, may give this act and the special matter in evidence; and if the plaintiff or prosecutor shall become nonsuit, or forbear further prosecution, or suffer a discontinuance, or if a verdict pass against him, the defendant shall recover treble costs; for which they shall have the like remedy, as in any case where costs by the law are given to defendants. *Limitation of actions. General issue. Treble costs.*

XXIX. And for the better obviating such frauds and abuses as may be practised in discharging of soldiers; it is hereby further enacted by the authority aforesaid, That no private soldier who shall be duly listed into his Majesty's service by virtue of this act (during the time such soldier shall remain in *Great Britain*) shall be discharged from his Majesty's service, without the consent of the colonel, or in his absence, the field officer commanding in chief the regiment, first had and obtained in writing under their hands and seals for that purpose, in which writing the cause of his discharge shall be expressed, and a duplicate or copy of every such discharge, forthwith transmitted to the secretary at war, to be by him kept and entered in a book; or if a marine, without the consent of the lord high admiral, or the commissioners of the admiralty for the time being first had and obtained; and any officer that shall presume to discharge any soldier inlisted pursuant to this act, in any other manner contrary to this act, shall for such offence be cashiered. *No soldier or marine to be discharged without a certificate from his colonel, &c. of which a duplicate to be transmitted to the secretary at war. Officer breaking this order, to be cashiered.*

XXX. Provided always, and it is hereby enacted, That every person who shall be impressed upon this act, after he shall have continued in the military service of his Majesty, his heirs and successors during the space of five years, if the war shall then be ended, or otherwise at the end of the war, shall be at liberty if he think fit to demand his discharge from the colonel, or in his absence, the officer commanding the regiment or company to which he shall belong, and such discharge shall be granted to him *gratis* in writing under the hand of such colonel or officer, who is hereby impowered and required to give the same accordingly; any thing herein contained to the contrary notwithstanding. *Impressed men after five years service, to be discharged, if they demand it.*

XXXI. And be it further enacted, That the said several clerks to the said commissioners, provided the said copies or duplicates be duly transmitted into the office of the admiralty, or secretary at war, as aforesaid, shall have and receive by the hands of the paymasters of his Majesty's land forces and marines, or one of them, such rewards as the lord high treasurer or commissioners of the treasury for the time being, upon consideration of *Clerks to be rewarded for their trouble, in transmitting the duplicates.*

the

the numbers of men lifted in the feveral counties, cities, boroughs, or other places, and the pains and charges of the feveral clerks in this fervice, fhall judge the faid clerks feverally and refpectively to deferve.

His Majefty, may fufpend by proclamation, &c. the execution of this act;

XXXII. Provided always, That his Majefty, when he fhall be fatisfied by the faid returns of the commiffioners, or otherwife, that a fufficient number of recruits in the whole fhall be raifed for his prefent fervice, may be gracioufly pleafed to fufpend or ftop the further execution of this act by proclamation, or order in council, or other publick notice in the *London Gazette*; any thing herein contained to the contrary notwithftanding.

or may fufpend or inforce the act, in any county or place.

XXXIII. Provided alfo, That his Majefty, when he fhall judge it expedient for his fervice, may at any time fufpend or enforce the execution of this act, in any county or place of *Great Britain*, by notice from his Majefty's fecretary at war; any thing herein contained to the contrary notwithftanding.

Perfons employed in the execution of this act, exempted from the penalties of act 25 Car. 2. c. 2.

r W. & M. feff. 1. c. 8.

and 13 & 14 W. 3. c. 6.

XXXIV. Provided always, and be it further enacted by the authority aforefaid, That no commiffioner, churchwarden, overfeer, conftable, headborough, tythingman, or other parifh or town officer, who fhall be employed in the execution of this act, fhall be liable for or by reafon of fuch execution, to any of the penalties mentioned in an act made in the twenty fifth year of the reign of King *Charles* the Second, *For preventing dangers which may happen from popifh recufants*; or in one other act made in the firft year of the reign of King *William* and Queen *Mary*, intituled, *An act for abrogating the oaths of allegiance and fupremacy, and appointing other oaths*; or in one other act made in the parliament holden in the thirteenth and fourteenth years of the reign of the late King *William* the Third, intituled, *An act for the further fecurity of his Majefty's perfon, and the fucceffion of the crown in the proteftant line; and for the extinguifhing the hopes of the pretended prince of* Wales, *and all other pretenders, and their open and fecret abettors.*

Commiffioners in England, not to act till they have taken the oaths appointed

XXXV. Provided always, and be it enacted, That no perfon or perfons hereby appointed to be a commiffioner or commiffioners for any county, riding, city, borough, cinque port or place, of *England*, *Wales*, or *Berwick upon Tweed* (except fuch as duly qualified themfelves to be juftices of the peace, or commiffioners for executing the faid act for the land tax made and paffed in the twenty eighth year of his prefent Majefty's reign, or any fubfequent act or acts of parliament for that purpofe) fhall be capable, in *England*, *Wales*, or *Berwick upon Tweed*, of acting as a commiffioner or commiffioners in the execution of this act, or executing any the powers of the commiffioners therein mentioned (unlefs it be the power hereby given of adminiftering oaths) until fuch time as he or they refpectively fhall have taken the oaths appointed by an act of parliament made in

by 1 W. & M. feff. 1 c. 8. and 13 W. 3. c. 6.

the firft year of the reign of King *William* and Queen *Mary*, intituled, *An act for the abrogating the oaths of fupremacy and allegiance, and appointing other oaths*; and alfo in the faid act, intituled,

led, *An act for the further fecurity of his Majefty's perfon, and the fucceffion of the crown in the proteftant line ; and for extinguifhing the hopes of the pretended prince of* Wales, *and all other pretenders, and their open and fecret abettors* ; which oaths it fhall and may be lawful to and for any two or more of the faid commiffioners to adminifter, and they are hereby required to adminifter the fame to any other of the faid commiffioners ; and that no perfon or perfons hereby appointed to be a commiffioner or commiffioners for any part of *Scotland* (except fuch as duly qualified themfelves, according to the laws of *Scotland*, to be commiffioners there for executing the faid act for the land tax made and paffed in the twenty eighth year of his prefent Majefty's reign, or any fubfequent act or acts of parliament for that purpofe) fhall be capable of acting as a commiffioner or commiffioners in the execution of this prefent act in any part of *Scotland*, until fuch time as he or they refpectively fhall have duly qualified themfelves according to the laws of *Scotland* for that purpofe.

nor commiffioners in Scotland, till they have qualified themfelves as the laws there direct.

XXXVI. Provided always, and be it enacted, That if any perfon hereby appointed a commiffioner for any county, city, town or place, in *England, Wales,* or *Berwick upon Tweed* (except as before excepted) fhall prefume to act as a commiffioner in the execution of this act, before he fhall have taken the faid oaths which by this act he is required to take, and in the manner hereby prefcribed, he fhall forfeit to his Majefty the fum of two hundred pounds, to be recovered by action of debt, or on the cafe, bill, fuit or information, in any of his Majefty's courts of record at *Weftminfter*, wherein no effoin, protection, wager of law, or more than one imparlance fhall be allowed ; and that if any perfon hereby appointed a commiffioner for any fhire, ftewartry, burgh or place in *Scotland* (except as before excepted) fhall prefume to act as a commiffioner in the execution of this act, before that he fhall have qualified himfelf according to the laws in *Scotland*, he fhall forfeit to his Majefty the fum of fifty pounds, to be recovered in the court of exchequer in *Scotland*, in the fame manner as any other penalties are there recoverable.

Commiffioners in England acting before they have taken the oaths,

forfeit 200 l.

and commiffioners in Scotland, 50 l.

XXXVII. Provided alfo, That in cafe there fhall not be a fufficient number of commiffioners for any city, borough, town, port or place of *Great Britain* (for which by this act commiffioners are fpecially appointed) capable of acting according to the refpective qualifications required by this act, then and in every fuch cafe, any the commiffioners appointed for the county, fhire or ftewartry at large, within which fuch city, borough, town or place doth ftand, or which is next adjoining thereto, may act as commiffioners in the execution of this act, within fuch city, borough, town, port or place ; any thing herein contained to the contrary notwithftanding.

Commiffioners for the county, at large, &c. may act for any city, &c.

XXXVIII. Provided always, and be it enacted by the authority aforefaid, That no commiffioner of the land tax, not being a juftice of the peace, or a magiftrate of a corporation or a borough, fhall be capable of acting as a commiffioner in the execution of this act, or of any of the powers therein contained,

Qualification of commiffioners for counties at large within England.

C 4

ed,

ed, in or for any county at large within *England*, the dominion of *Wales*, (the counties of *Anglesey*, *Merioneth*, *Cardigan*, *Caermarthen*, *Glamorgan*, *Montgomery*, *Pembroke*, *Caernarvon* and *Monmouth* excepted) or in or for any of the ridings in the county of *York*, unless such person by himself, or his tenants or trustees was taxed, or did pay in the same county or riding, for the value of one hundred pounds *per annum* or more of his own estate, by virtue of the said act, for the land tax made and passed in *England* in the twenty eighth year of his Majesty's reign, or any subsequent act or acts of parliament for that purpose, or unless such person so appointed to be a commissioner, shall at the time of the execution of this act, by himself, his tenants or trustees, enjoy an estate of lands, tenements or hereditaments, of the said yearly value of one hundred pounds or more within the said county or riding respectively; any thing herein contained to the contrary notwithstanding.

Persons disabled presuming to act, forfeit 50 l.
XXXIX. And it is hereby further enacted, That if any person intended by this act to be disabled for the cause last-mentioned, shall nevertheless presume to act as a commissioner in the execution of this act, or any of the powers therein contained, every such person for such offence, shall forfeit the sum of fifty pounds, to any person or persons who will inform or sue for the same, to be recovered in any of his Majesty's courts of record at *Westminster*, or in the *Exchequer* of *Scotland* as aforesaid.

Commissioners may act for any city, being inhabitants, or inns of court.
XL. Provided nevertheless, and it is hereby enacted, That no person who is appointed to be a commissioner for executing this act in any part of *Great Britain*, shall be disabled for the cause last-mentioned from acting as a commissioner, within and for any city, borough, cinque port, or corporate town only, whereof he shall be an inhabitant at the time of the execution of this act, or from acting as a commissioner within any of the inns of court or inns of *Chancery*.

XLI. *And whereas some doubts may arise whether mayors, bailiffs, and other chief magistrates of cities, boroughs, towns corporate and cinque ports, for which commissioners are specially appointed by virtue of this act, can act as commissioners for executing this act in the said cities, boroughs, towns corporate and cinque ports;* be it further enacted by the authority aforesaid, That all mayors, bailiffs, and
Mayors, bailiffs, &c. to act as commissioners specially appointed.
other chief magistrates who are appointed commissioners for executing this act, shall be, and have power to act as commissioners for executing this act, within and for any city, borough, town corporate or cinque port, wherein they inhabit at the time of executing this act, as well where commissioners are specially appointed by this act, as where they are not.

XLII. *And whereas it may often be expedient for his Majesty's service, that the commissioners hereby appointed, shall execute this act in cities, towns, or other places, when it may not be convenient to enforce the execution thereof through the county in which such city, town or place shall be respectively situate;* be it therefore enacted by the authority aforesaid, That the mayor or other chief magistrate giftrate of every city, town or place, shall (upon receiving notice for that purpose from the secretary at war) immediately proceed to put this act in execution within their respective jurisdictions, in the same manner to all intents and purposes, as if such mayor, or other chief magistrate, had received such notice from the sheriff of the county in which such city, town or place shall be respectively situate; any thing in this act contained to the contrary notwithstanding.

Civil magistrate, upon notice from the secretary at war, to enforce this act within his jurisdiction.

XLIII. And it is hereby provided and enacted, That no bailiff's follower or assistant, employed or belonging to any sheriff, bailiff of liberties, marshalsea court, or any other person or persons that shall be so employed, by any one that shall have the power of executing any warrant or process whatsoever, shall be deemed thereby to follow or exercise any calling or employment, or to have a sufficient support and maintenance within the intent and meaning of this act.

Bailiffs followers and assistants, &c. not exempted by this act.

XLIV. And forasmuch as great inconveniencies may happen by impressing men, during the time of harvest; be it therefore enacted by the authority aforesaid, That from and after the twenty fifth day of *May* one thousand seven hundred and fifty seven, until the twenty fifth day of *October* following, no harvest labourer, or person working at hay harvest or corn harvest work within the time aforesaid, within the kingdom of *Great Britain*, shall be impressed by virtue of this act, but shall be free and exempted from the same during the time aforesaid, provided they have a certificate under the hands of the minister, and of one churchwarden or overseer of the poor, or elders of the parish or place where they live, allowed under the hand and seal of one justice of the peace of the same county, shire, stewartry, riding, city or place, which certificate shall be given *gratis*.

Labourers, having proper certificates, not liable to be impressed in harvest time.

XLV. And for the more easy and better putting this act in execution; be it enacted by the authority aforesaid, That any three or more commissioners for putting this act in execution, in the several ridings of the county of *York* (being justices of the peace) though not all of the same riding, may, within the castle of *York*, or limits thereof, execute the powers of this act.

Commissioners for executing this act within the castle of York.

XLVI. And whereas divers soldiers who have deserted his Majesty's service, have been harboured in a certain place called Threapwood, lying within or near the counties of Chester and Flint, or one of them, and adjoining to the town of Cuddington in the said county of Chester; be it further enacted by the authority aforesaid, That the commissioners hereby appointed for the county of Chester, and the officers of the said town of Cuddington, shall execute this act in the said place called Threapwood, according to the true intent and meaning thereof.

Commissioners for executing this act in Threapwood.

XLVII. And be it further enacted by the authority aforesaid, That if at any of the meetings of the commissioners by this act appointed, in any of their sub-divisions, they shall not be attended by some proper officer appointed for the receiving of recruits, either through negligence or any unavoidable accident; then and in that case, it shall and may be lawful to and for the said

Officer not attending to receive recruits. Commissioners may adjourn, and order the detention of the

imprelled men.

said commissioners to adjourn themselves to some other convenient day, and they are hereby authorized to give directions for detaining in custody, all such persons as shall have been then brought before them by the parish officers to be inlisted, or such of them as they shall think duly qualified for his Majesty's service; and the said commissioners shall give notice to any of the

Notice of adjournment to be given to any officers attending this service, &c.

officers attending on this service, in the county or place where such sub-divisions shall lie, of the day of such adjournment; and the said officer is hereby required, either to attend himself, or to appoint some other officer to attend such commissioners, and to receive such persons as the said commissioners shall inlist into his Majesty's service; and the officer so receiving the re-

Officer to pay subsistence money for every recruit;

cruits, shall pay to such person as the commissioners shall appoint, six pence *per diem*, for the subsistence of every recruit then inlisted, from the day of the last meeting of the commissioners, to the said day of adjournment, the same to be charged to the account of the several regiments or companies into which the

and incidental charges.

said recruits shall be inlisted, together with such charges and expences as shall appear to the said commissioners to have been incurred on account of the detaining the said persons from the day of the former meeting of the said commissioners, to the day of such second meeting, not exceeding three pounds.

Continuance of this act.

XLVIII. And be it further enacted by the authority aforesaid, That this act, and every thing herein contained, shall be and continue in force until the end of the next session of parliament.

Form for making entries pursuant to the act.

XLIX. And be it further enacted by the authority aforesaid, That the several entries which the commissioners of the land tax are by this act required to make, of the names and descriptions of all volunteers, and also of all impressed men, together with the other particulars herein before directed, be made according to the form hereunto annexed.

Recruit's Name.	Parish.	Height.		Age.	Description of the Recruits.	For what corps pressed.	For what corps entered voluntarily.	Bounty paid.	Bounty due.	Officer who received or refused the recruit, and on what day.	On what grounds refused.
		Feet.	Inches.								

CAP. IX.

An act to prohibit for a limited time the exportation of corn, grain, meal, malt, flour, bread, bifcuit, ftarch, beef, pork, bacon, and other victual (except fifh and roots and rice, to be exported to any port of Europe foutbward of Cape Finifterre) from his Majefty's colonies and plantations in America, unlefs to Great Britain or Ireland, or to fome of the faid colonies and plantations; and to permit the importation of corn and flour into Great Britain and Ireland in neutral fhips; and to allow the exportation of wheat, barley, oats, meal and flour, from Great Britain to the ifle of Man, for the ufe of the inhabitants there.

WHEREAS *the exportation of any fort of corn, grain, meal, malt, flour, bread, bifcuit, ftarch, beef, pork, bacon, or any other fort of victual, from any of his Majefty's colonies or plantations in* America, *may, at this time, be greatly prejudicial to his Majefty's fubjects;* be it therefore enacted by the King's moft excellent majefty, by and with the advice and confent of the lords fpiritual and temporal, and commons, in this prefent parliament affembled, and by the authority of the fame, That no perfon or perfons whatfoever, at any time or times during the continuance of the prefent war with *France,* fhall, directly or indirectly, export, tranfport, carry, convey, or caufe or procure to be exported, tranfported, carried or conveyed out of or from any of the *Britifh* colonies or plantations in *America,* or load or lay on board, or caufe or procure to be laden or laid on board, any fhip or other veffel or boat, in order to be exported or carried out of the faid colonies or plantations, any fort of corn, grain, meal, malt, flour, bread, bifcuit, ftarch, beef, pork, bacon, or other fort of victual, whether the faid commodities fhall, or fhall not be, the produce or manufacture of, or made in the refpective colonies or plantations from whence the fame fhall be defigned to be exported, under the penalties and forfeitures herein after mentioned; that is to fay, That all the faid commodities that fhall be fo exported, fhipped or laid on board, or loaded to be exported, fhipped or carried out contrary to this act, fhall be forfeited, and that every offender or offenders therein, fhall forfeit the fum of twenty fhillings of lawful money of *Great Britain,* for every bufhel of corn, grain, meal, malt or flour, and twelve pence of the like money, for every pound weight of bread, bifcuit, ftarch, beef, pork, bacon, or other victual, and fo in proportion for any greater or lefs quantity, which fhall be fo exported, fhipped or put on board to be exported, and alfo the fhip, boat or veffel, upon which any of the faid commodities fhall be exported, fhipped or laden to be exported, and all her guns, tackle, apparel and furniture fhall be forfeited; and one moiety of all fuch penalties and forfeitures fhall be to the

Enumerated commodities prohibited to be exported from the Britifh plantations, &c. during the war with France.

King's

King's majefty, his heirs and fucceffors, and the other moiety to him or them that will fue for the fame ; which faid penalties and forfeitures fhall be recovered in the high court of admiralty, or any other chief court of civil or criminal jurifdiction, in fuch refpective colonies or plantations ; and that the mafter and mariners of any fuch fhip, boat, or veffel, wherein any fuch offence fhall be committed, knowing fuch offence and wittingly and willingly aiding and affifting thereunto, and being thereof duly convicted in any fuch courts as aforefaid, fhall be imprifoned for the fpace of three months without bail or mainprize.

Officers impowered to feize the veffels and commodities ;

II. And be it further enacted by the authority aforefaid, That it fhall and may be lawful to and for any perfon or perfons, being an officer or officers of the cuftoms, or being lawfully authorized in this behalf by the lord high treafurer of *Great Britain*, or the commiffioners of the treafury for the time being, or any three or more of them, to take or feize all fuch of the faid commodities not allowed to be exported by this act, or by his Majefty's royal proclamation, or fuch order of council in purfuance of this act, as he or they fhall happen to find, know or difcover, to be laid on board any fhip or other veffel or boat at fea, or in any port, or in any navigable river or water, to the intent or purpofe to be exported, tranfported or conveyed out of any of the faid colonies or plantations, contrary to the true intent of this act ; and

and lodge the fame in the King's warehoufes.

alfo the fhip, veffel or boat in which the fame fhall be found, and to bring the faid goods to the King's warehoufe or warehoufes, belonging to the cuftom-houfe next to the place where fuch feizures fhall be made, or to fome other fafe place (where there are no fuch warehoufes) in order to be proceeded againft according to law, and in cafe of recovery, to be divided according to the directions of this act.

Neceffary provifions for fhips on their voyage ;

III. Provided always, and be it further enacted by the authority aforefaid, That this act, or any thing herein contained, fhall not extend to prohibit the exportation or carrying out of fuch or fo much of the faid commodities as fhall be neceffary to be carried in any fhip or fhips, or other veffel or veffels in their refpective voyages, for the fuftenance, diet and fupport of the commanders, mafters, mariners, paffengers or others, in the fame fhips or veffels only, or for the victualling or providing any of his Majefty's fhips of war, or other fhips or veffels in his Majefty's fervice, or for his Majefty's forces, forts or garrifons ; any thing herein contained to the contrary notwithftanding.

and for the King's fhips ; forces, forts, or garrifons excepted. The faid commodities may be carried from the faid colonies or plantations to Great Britain or Ireland, &c.

IV. Provided alfo, and be it further enacted by the authority aforefaid, That this act, or any thing herein contained, fhall not extend to prohibit the exportation of any of the faid commodities from the faid colonies or plantations to *Great Britain* or *Ireland*, or from any of the faid colonies or plantations, to any other of the faid colonies or plantations, or from any other port or place in any one of the faid colonies or plantations, to any port or place in fuch colony or plantation refpectively, fo as the exporter do before the fhipping or laying on board the fame, declare the

king-

kingdom, ifland, plantation or colony, and the port or place fo*taking out a* which the faid commodities are refpectively defigned, and take *cocquet for* out a cocquet or cocquets, expreffing the particulars of fuch com-*the fame, and* modities, and do likewife become bound with two fureties of *giving fecurity.* known refidence in the faid colonies or plantations, and of abi-lity to anfwer the penalty mentioned in the bonds, in treble the value of fuch commodities, to the chief officer or officers of his Majefty's cuftoms, or the naval officer, or fome other principal officer belonging to the port or place where the fame fhall be fhipped or put on board, or to fuch perfon or perfons as fhall be appointed for that purpofe, by the lord high treafurer of *Great Britain*, or the commiffioners of the treafury for the time being, or any three or more of them (who are hereby impowered to take fuch fecurity in his Majefty's name, and to his Majefty's ufe) that fuch commodities fhall not be landed or fold in any parts whatfoever, other than the kingdom, ifland, plantation, colony, port or place refpectively, for which the fame fhall be fo declared, and that a certificate under the hand and feal, or hands and feals of the collector, comptroller, or other chief officer of the cuftoms, or if no fuch, of the naval officer or fome other principal officer of the port or place where the fame fhall be landed, or fuch perfon or perfons as fhall be appointed for that purpofe by the lord high treafurer of *Great Britain*, or the com-miffioners of the treafury for the time being, or any three or more of them, fhall, within the refpective times herein after mentioned (the danger of the feas excepted) be returned to the officer or officers, or perfon or perfons, to whom fuch fecurity fhall have been given as aforefaid, that the faid commodities, ex-preffing the particulars thereof, have been landed at the port or place for which the fame fhall have been fo declared; and for the taking of fuch fecurity, and giving fuch cocquets and certifi-cates (which the refpective officers and perfons aforefaid are hereby on demand required to give) no fee or reward fhall be demanded or received; and if any fuch officer or perfon fhall *Penalty on of-* make any falfe certificate of any fuch commodities being fo *ficer making a* landed, fuch officer or perfon fhall forfeit the fum of two hun-*falfe certifi-* dred pounds, and lofe his employment, and be incapable of ferv-*cate;* ing his Majefty, his heirs or fucceffors, in any office relating to the cuftoms; and if any perfon fhall counterfeit, rafe or falfify *and on perfons* any cocquet or certificate, or knowingly publifh any fuch coun-*counterfeiting* terfeit, rafed or falfe cocquet or certificate, he fhall forfeit the *&c. certifi-* fum of two hundred pounds, and fuch cocquet or certificate fhall *cates.* be void and of none effect; which faid penalties for offences committed in *America*, fhall be recovered in the fame courts, *Penalties* and in the fame manner, as the other penalties inflicted by this *where to be* act are recoverable; and for offences which fhall be committed *recovered.* in that part of *Great Britain* called *England*, fuch penalties fhall be recovered by action of debt, bill, plaint or information, in any of his Majefty's courts of record at *Weftminfter*, or before the juftices of affize, or at the great feffions in *Wales*, or by in-formation at any general quarter feffions of the peace for the
county

county, city, riding, divifion or place, where the offence fhall be committed; and in fuch fuit no effoin, protection, privilege, or wager of law fhall be allowed; and for offences which fhall be committed in that part of *Great-Britain* called *Scotland*, by action or fummary bill or information in the courts of feffions or exchequer in *Scotland*; and for offences which fhall be committed in *Ireland*, in his Majefty's courts of record in *Dublin*, or at the general quarter-feffions of the peace for the county, city or place, where the offence fhall be committed; and for offences which fhall be committed in any other of the dominions belonging to the crown of *Great Britain* in *Europe*, in the high court of admiralty, or any other chief court of civil or criminal jurifdiction in fuch dominions refpectively; and fuch penalties when recovered, fhall be divided in equal moieties between his Majefty and the informer; and upon all actions, fuits and informations, that fhall be brought, commenced, or entered in the faid colonies and plantations upon this act, the offences may be laid or alledged to have been committed in any colony, province, county or precinct, within the faid plantations, at the pleafure of the profecutor or informer.

Officer fufpecting certificate to be falfe, not to vacate the bonds.   V. Provided alfo, That in cafe the officer or officers, or perfon or perfons, to whom any certificate fhall be returned, fhall not have caufe to fufpect that fuch certificate is falfe and counterfeit, the bonds fhall not be cancelled or the fecurity vacated, until fuch officer or officers, or perfon or perfons, fhall have been informed from the perfon or perfons in whofe name fuch certificate fhall appear to have been granted, that the matter and contents of fuch certificate are juft and true.

Commodities may be carried by land, or acrofs rivers, &c. from one plantation to another.   VI. Provided alfo, That nothing in this act contained fhall extend or be conftrued to extend to prohibit the tranfporting, carrying, or conveying any of the commodities herein before mentioned, by land, or acrofs rivers, by common ferries, or up or down the faid rivers, or acrofs harbours where clearances have not ufually been taken, from any one of the faid plantations or colonies to any other plantations or colonies, or to any part of the fame plantation or colony, or to fubject the perfons tranfporting, carrying or conveying, or caufing to be tranfported, carried or conveyed, any of the faid commodities in manner aforefaid, to any of the reftrictions or regulations herein before prefcribed, with refpect to fuch commodities exported by fea, from one colony to another.

Bonds to be fued within 3 years.   VII. Provided neverthelefs, That the faid bond or bonds (if not profecuted within three years) fhall be void.

Commodities, cleared before 25 March 1757, may be exported.   VIII. Provided always, and it is hereby declared, That nothing in this act contained fhall extend to any of the commodities aforefaid, which fhall be cleared out of any cuftom-houfe in any of the colonies or plantations before the twenty fifth day of *March* one thoufand feven hundred and fifty feven; any thing herein contained to the contrary notwithftanding.

His Majefty by proclamation,   IX. Provided always, and be it enacted by the authority aforefaid, That in cafe his Majefty at any time or times during the

con-

continuance of this act, shall in his royal discretion judge it to be expedient to permit the exportation of corn, and other the commodities aforesaid, or any of them, from the said colonies and plantations, that then it shall and may be lawful to and for his Majesty by his royal proclamation or proclamations to be issued, by and with the advice of his privy council, or by his Majesty's order in council, from time to time, to permit and suffer all and singular his Majesty's subjects (but not any particular person or persons) to export or carry out of all of the said colonies or plantations in any ship or ships, vessel or vessels, duly navigated, owned, and qualified according to law to trade there, all or any of the commodities aforesaid to all or any other place or places, and upon or without giving security for the landing thereof in such place or places, and returning certificates of such landing, as to his Majesty shall seem meet, and as in such proclamation or proclamations, or such orders of council, shall be expressed and declared; any thing to the contrary notwithstanding.

or order in council, may at any time permit the exportation of corn, &c from the colonies or plantations, &c.

X. And be it further enacted by the authority aforesaid, That all certificates of the landing and discharging of the said commodities to be exported, shall be returned within the respective times following; that is to say, Where the bonds are taken in respect of any of the said commodities to be exported to *Great Britain* or *Ireland* within eighteen calendar months after the date of the said bonds; and in respect of any of the said commodities to be exported from any of the said colonies or plantations to any other of the said colonies or plantations, or from any port or place in any one of the said colonies or plantations, to any other port or place in such colony or plantation respectively, within twelve calendar months after the date of such bonds respectively.

Times limited of returning the certificates from the ports where the corn, &c. has been landed.

XI. Provided always, and be it further enacted by the authority aforesaid, That this act shall not extend to prohibit the exportation of any rice from the said colonies or plantations directly to any part of *Europe* southward of *Cape Finisterre*, but that rice shall and may be shipped and exported directly to any part of *Europe* southward of the said cape, in such manner as the same might have been exported if this act had not been made; any thing herein contained to the contrary notwithstanding.

Prohibition not to extend to exporting of rice.

XII. Provided also, and be it further enacted by the authority aforesaid, That this act shall not extend to any fish or roots which shall be exported or carried coastwise, but that fish and roots of all sorts shall and may be exported and carried coastwise, in such manner as the same might have been exported or carried coastwise, if this act had not been made; any thing herein contained to the contrary notwithstanding.

Fish or roots may be exported, or carried coastwise.

XIII. *And whereas by an act passed this present session of parliament, intituled,* An act to prohibit, for a time to be limited, the exportation of corn, malt, meal, flour, bread, biscuit and starch, *it was enacted, That no person, at any time before the twenty fifth day of* December *one thousand seven hundred and fifty seven, should export,*

Act of this session.

port,

port, or carry out of or from the kingdoms of Great Britain or Ireland, any sort of corn, meal, malt, flour, bread, biscuit or starch, under the penalties and forfeitures therein mentioned; but with several provisions and savings in the said act contained: And whereas the inhabitants of the isle of Man have, for several years last past, been supplied with considerable quantities of corn, meal and flour, from Great Britain and Ireland; and they are now in great want thereof, no provision or saving having been made in the said act for supplying **Wheat, &c. may be exported from Southampton and Exeter unto the isle of Man,** them therewith; be it therefore enacted by the authority aforesaid, That the said recited act, or any thing therein contained, shall not extend to any wheat, barley, oats, meal or flour, to be transported out of or from the ports of *Southampton* or *Exeter* only, unto the said isle of *Man*, for the only use of the inhabitants of that island, so as the exporter, before the lading of such wheat, barley, oats, meal or flour, or laying the same on board, do become bound, with other sufficient security (which the customer or comptroller of either of the said ports respectively hath hereby power to take in his Majesty's name, and to his Majesty's use, and for which security no fee or reward shall be given or taken) that such wheat, barley, oats, meal or flour, shall be landed in the said isle of *Man* (the danger of the seas only excepted) for the use of the inhabitants there, and shall not be landed or sold in any other parts whatsoever, and to return the like certificates of the landing the same there, as are by the said act required on the exportation of the said commodities to the *British* **not more than 2,500 quarters.** colonies in *America*, and within the time for that purpose therein mentioned; and so as the whole quantity of wheat, barley, oats, meal or flour, which, at any time or times after the passing this act, and before the said twenty fifth day of *December* one thousand seven hundred and fifty seven, shall be shipped at both the said ports **One moiety to be shipped at each of the said ports.** for the said isle of *Man* as aforesaid, shall not exceed in the whole two thousand five hundred quarters; one moiety whereof to be exported at the said port of *Southampton*, and the other moiety thereof to be exported at the said port of *Exeter*; any thing in **Act of this session.** the said recited act to the contrary notwithstanding.

XIV. *And whereas by an act made in this present session of parliament (intituled,* An act to discontinue, for a limited time, the duties upon corn and flour imported, and also upon such corn, grain, meal, bread, biscuit and flour, as have been, or shall be, taken from the enemy, and brought into this kingdom) *corn and flour is allowed to be imported into this kingdom, duty free, for and during such time as in the said act is mentioned: And whereas it is necessary that such importation shou'd be allowed to be made in ships belonging to* **Corn and flour may be imported duty free, from any kingdom, &c. in amity, into Great Britain,** *any state in amity with his Majesty, as well as in ships belonging to Great Britain, and from any port or place whatsoever;* be it therefore enacted by the authority aforesaid, That it shall be lawful, during the time, and under the regulations, mentioned in the said act, for any person or persons whatsoever to import and bring into this kingdom, in any ship or vessel belonging to *Great Britain*, or to any kingdom or state in amity with his Majesty, his heirs and successors, from any port or place whatsoever corn and

and flour duty free ; any act or acts of parliament to the contrary notwithstanding.

XV. *And whereas, if the importation of corn and flour into* Ireland *was permitted, for a limited time to be made in ships belonging to any state in amity with his Majesty, the same may be of advantage to his Majesty's subjects*; be it therefore enacted by the authority aforesaid, That it shall be lawful, at any time or times before the twenty-fourth day of *August* next, for any person or persons whatsoever to import and bring into the kingdom of *Ireland*, in any ship or vessel belonging to any kingdom or state in amity with his Majesty, his heirs or successors, corn and flour from any port or place whatsoever; any act or acts of parliament to the contrary notwithstanding.

or Ireland.

XVI. And be it further enacted by the authority aforesaid, That if any action or suit shall be commenced against any person or persons for any thing done in pursuance of this act, the defendant or defendants in any such action or suit may plead the general issue, and give this act, and the special matter, in evidence, at any trial to be had thereupon, and that the same was done in pursuance, and by the authority, of this act; and if it shall appear so to have been done, the jury shall find for the defendant or defendants; and if the plaintiff shall be nonsuited, or discontinue his action, after the defendant or defendants shall have appeared; or if judgment shall be given, upon any verdict or demurrer, against the plaintiff, the defendant or defendants shall and may recover treble costs, and have the like remedy for the same as any defendant or defendants hath or have in other cases by law.

General issue.

Treble costs.

CAP. X.

An act to prohibit for a limited time the making of low wines and spirits, from wheat, barley, malt, or any other sort of grain, or from any meal or flour.

WHEREAS *it is expedient that the distillation or extraction of low wines or spirits, from wheat, barley, malt, and all other sorts of grain, should be prohibited for a limited time*; be it therefore enacted by the King's most excellent majesty, by and with the advice and consent of the lords spiritual and temporal and commons in this present parliament assembled, and by the authority of the same, That from and after the eleventh day of *March* one thousand seven hundred and fifty seven, no low wines or spirits whatsoever shall be made, extracted, or distilled, within this kingdom, from any wheat, barley, malt, or any other sort of grain, or from any meal or flour, for and during the space of two calendar months.

Wheat and all sorts of grain, meal and flour, prohibited to be made use of in distillation for 2 months; continued by cap. 15. till 24 Dec. 1757. on penalty of 100l. and forfeiture of such grain, with the wines and spirits; &c.

II. And be it further enacted by the authority aforesaid, That if, during the time before limited, any distiller, or maker of low wines or spirits, or any other person or persons whatsoever, shall make, extract or distil, or cause or procure to be made, extracted, or distilled, any low wines or spirits, from any wheat, barley, malt, or other grain, or from any meal or flour; or shall use or mix, or cause or procure to be used or mixed, any wheat, barley, malt, or other grain, or any meal or flour, in any worts or wash, in order for the making, extracting or distilling, low wines or spirits; or shall put or lay, or cause or procure to be put or laid, in any tun, wash-batch, cask, copper, still, or other vessel or utensil, any wheat, barley, malt or other grain, or any meal or flour, for the purpose of preparing any worts or wash, or for making, extracting or distilling, low wines or spirits, whether such tun, wash-batch, cask, copper, still, or other vessel or utensil, hath or hath not been duly entered at the excise office; that then, and in each and every of the said cases, such distiller or maker of low wines or spirits, or other person or persons acting contrary to the directions of this act, or the person or persons in whose custody or possession any such tun, washbatch, cask, copper, still, or other vessel or utensil, which shall be made use of, contrary to the intention of this act, shall be found, shall respectively, for every such offence, forfeit and pay the sum of two hundred pounds; and all such wheat, barley, malt, and other grain, and such meal and flour, and such worts and wash, low wines and spirits, shall be also forfeited.

All wheat, &c. found within the time limited, in any work-house, &c. belonging to a distiller forfeited, and 100l.

III. And be it further enacted by the authority aforesaid, That if any wheat, wheat meal, or wheat flour, shall, within the time herein before limited, be found in any workhouse, stillhouse, storehouse, warehouse, or any other place, wherein low wines or spirits, or worts or wash, shall be made, extracted, distilled or prepared, or where any low wines or spirits, or worts or wash, shall have been made, extracted, distilled or prepared, since the first day of *January* one thousand seven hundred and fifty seven, all such wheat, meal and flour shall be forfeited, and the person or persons in whose possession such workhouse, stillhouse, storehouse, warehouse, or place shall be, shall, for every such offence respectively, also forfeit and pay the sum of one hundred pounds.

Officer, &c. may enter suspected houses,

IV. And be it further enacted by the authority aforesaid, That during the time herein before limited, it shall be lawful for any person or persons, who shall be authorized for that purpose by the commissioners of excise for the time being, or any two or more of them, within the limits of the chief office of excise in *London*, or by one or more justice or justices of the peace in any other part of *Great Britain*, at any time or times, with any officer of excise, to enter into any workhouse, stillhouse, storehouse, warehouse, or any other place wherein any low wines or spirits, or worts or wash shall be, or are suspected to be made, extracted, distilled or prepared, or wherein low wines or spirits, or worts or wash shall have been made, extracted, distilled or prepared, since the first day of *January* one thousand seven hundred and fifty seven, and shall have free admittance into the same, and may inspect all the materials, vessels and utensils, therein contained (giving thereby as little interruption as may be to the business which shall be carrying on);

and inspect the materials and utensils therein;

and

and in case any such officer of excise, shall have reason to suspect that any wheat, barley, malt or other grain, meal or flour, is mixed in any worts or wash, or in any other material or preparation, for making, extracting or distilling low wines or spirits, it shall be lawful for such officer, at any time or times, during the said term, upon payment of two shillings and six pence, to take a sample not exceeding two quarts, of any such worts or wash, material or preparation, which shall be found in any such house or other place as aforesaid ; and in case any distiller or maker of low wines or spirits, or the owner or occupier of any such house or place, or any workman or servant to any such distiller, owner or occupier belonging, shall refuse to admit such person or persons, as shall be so authorized, or any officer of excise, into any such house or place, or shall obstruct or hinder any such officer or person or persons, in making such inspection as aforesaid, or shall not allow any such officer to take such sample, after the said sum of two shillings and six pence shall be paid or tendered for the same, such distiller, owner or occupier, shall, for every such offence respectively, forfeit and pay the sum of one hundred pounds ; and it shall be lawful for any such officer of excise, or other person or persons authorized as aforesaid, having a warrant for that purpose from any two or more of the commissioners of excise, or any justice or justices respectively as aforesaid, to seize, take and carry away, all such wheat, wheat meal, and wheat flour, as shall be found in any such house or other place, together with all the sacks, bags, and other things, in which the said commodities shall be contained.

and take samples, paying for the same. Distiller refusing admittance, or obstructing officer forfeits 100l.

and the officer may seize, and carry away the wheat, &c. found.

V. And be it further enacted by the authority aforesaid, That if any distiller or maker of low wines or spirits for sale or exportation, shall, after the eleventh day of *March* one thousand seven hundred and fifty seven, and before the eleventh day of *May* one thousand seven hundred and fifty seven, be possessed of, or have in his, her or their custody or possession, or in the custody or possession of any person or persons in trust, or for the use or benefit of such distiller or maker of low wines or spirits, more than five quarters of wheat, wheat meal, or wheat flour, at any one time, in any one or more place or places (not being a place or places for preparing, making, extracting, distilling, or keeping worts or wash, low wines or spirits) every such distiller or maker of low wines and spirits, shall, for every such offence respectively, forfeit all such wheat, meal and flour, exceeding the said quantity of five quarters, and also the sum of five pounds for every quarter so forfeited.

Distiller, or other person for him having more than 5 quarters of wheat, &c. in his custody,

forfeits the same, and 5l. for every quarter.

VI. Provided always, That this act shall not extend to inflict the said last mentioned penalty and forfeiture upon any distiller or maker of low wines or spirits, who shall be the actual grower of wheat, and shall be possessed of any quantity of such wheat grown by him or her in the straw, or after the same is threshed out or separated from the straw ; provided such wheat shall not be kept in his or her possession, or in the possession of any other person or persons in trust for him or her, for a greater space of time

Distillers not to forfeit for wheat of their own growth,

if sold within 10 days after being threshed ; and not kept in workhouse, &c.

time than twenty days after the fame fhall be threfhed or fepa-
rated from the ftraw; and fo as fuch wheat be not kept in any
place ufed for making, extracting or diftilling low wines or fpirits,
or for preparing or keeping worts or wafh.

VII. Provided alfo, That this act fhall not extend to inflict
the faid laft mentioned penalty and forfeiture upon any diftiller
or maker of low wines or fpirits, who practifes the trade of a
miller, and who was poffeffed of, and worked any mill or mills
for the grinding of wheat, on or before the firft day of *January*,
one thoufand feven hundred and fifty feven, for or upon account
of any quantity of wheat, wheat meal, or wheat flour, which
fhall, during the time herein before limited, be found in any
fuch mill or mills; any thing herein contained to the contrary
notwithftanding.

VIII. And be it further enacted by the authority aforefaid,
That in cafe any officer or officers of the excife, or any other
perfon or perfons, fhall, at any time or times, have caufe to fufpect that any wheat, wheat meal, or wheat flour, exceeding the
quantity of five quarters, fhall be laid or kept in any fuch ftorehoufe, warehoufe, grainary, or other place or places, as aforefaid, belonging to any diftiller or maker of low wines or fpirits,
contrary to the true intent and meaning of this act, then, and in
every fuch cafe, upon oath made by fuch officer or officers, or
other perfon or perfons, before the commiffioners of excife for
the time being refpectively, or any two or more of them, or before one or more juftice or juftices of the peace refiding near the
place where fuch officer or officers, or other perfon or perfons,
fhall fufpect the fame to be laid and kept, fetting forth the ground
of his or their fufpicion, it fhall and may be lawful to and for the
faid commiffioners, or juftice or juftices of the peace refpectively, before whom fuch officer or officers, or other perfon or perfons, fhall make oath as aforefaid, (if he or they fhall judge it
reafonable) by fpecial warrant under his or their refpective hands
and feals, to authorize and impower fuch officer or officers, or
other perfon or perfons, authorized as aforefaid, by day or by
night (but if in the night, then in the prefence of a conftable,
or other lawful officer, of the peace) to enter into all and every
ftorehoufe, warehoufe, grainary, or other place or places, where
he or they fhall fo fufpect that any wheat, wheat meal, or wheat
flour, exceeding the quantity of five quarters, as aforefaid, fhall
be laid or kept, belonging to any fuch diftiller, or maker of low

wines or fpirits; and to feize, take and carry away, all fuch
wheat, meal and flour, as he or they fhall fo find (over and above
the faid quantity of five quarters, together with all the facks,
bags, or other things, wherein the fame fhall be contained);

and fuch diftiller or maker of low wines or fpirits, or the perfon
or perfons in whofe cuftody or poffeffion fuch wheat, meal or
flour, belonging to fuch diftiller fhall be found, fhall, for every
fuch offence refpectively, forfeit and pay the faid penalty of five
pounds for every quarter, exceeding the faid quantity of five
quarters; and the faid officer or officers, and other perfon or
persons,

persons, is or are hereby impowered by such warrant, together with such other person or persons as he or they shall take to his or their assistance, to enter such storehouses, warehouses, grainaries, and other place or places, and break open the doors thereof, in case they be not forthwith opened on demand.

IX. And be it further enacted by the authority aforesaid, That all penalties and forfeitures by this act imposed, shall be sued for and recovered by action of debt, bill, plaint or information, in any of his Majesty's courts of record at *Westminster*; or in the court of *exchequer* in *Scotland*; and that the court before whom the same shall be recovered, may, and are hereby authorized (if they shall think fit) to mitigate all or any of the pecuniary penalties herein before inflicted, to any sum not less than one fourth part of the sum herein respectively mentioned; and that one moiety of all the penalties and forfeitures, when recovered, shall be to the use of his Majesty, his heirs and successors; and the other moiety to him or them who shall sue for the same, or give information of, or discover the offence. *[Penalties how to be recovered; Court may mitigate the same; Application thereof.]*

X. Provided always, That all suits, prosecutions or informations, for offences committed against this act, shall be commenced and made within the space of two calendar months after the fact is committed, and not otherways; any thing herein contained to the contrary notwithstanding. *[Suits to be commenced within two months after the offence.]*

XI. *And whereas there have been contracts made by the distillers with several persons for yest, to be delivered and received at future times after the twenty ninth day of* September *one thousand seven hundred and fifty six*; be it therefore further enacted by the authority aforesaid, That all contracts or bargains made by any distiller or distillers with any person or persons whatsoever, for any yest to be delivered at any time during the continuance of this act, shall be, and are hereby declared to be suspended. *[Contracts for delivery of yest suspended.]*

XII. And be it further enacted by the authority aforesaid, That if any action or suit shall be commenced against any person or persons, for any thing done in pursuance of this act, such action or suit shall be commenced within the space of four calendar months next after the offence shall be committed, and if such action or suit shall be commenced or prosecuted in that part of *Great Britain* called *England*, the defendant or defendants in any such action or suit may plead the general issue, and give this act and the special matter in evidence, at any trial to be had thereupon; and that the same was done in pursuance and by the authority of this act; and if it shall appear so to have been done, the jury shall find for the defendant or defendants; and if the plaintiff shall be nonsuited, or discontinue his action, after the defendant or defendants shall have appeared, or if judgment shall be given upon any verdict or demurrer against the plaintiff, the defendant or defendants shall and may recover treble costs, and have the like remedy for the same, as any defendant or defendants hath or have in other cases by law; and if such action or suit be commenced or prosecuted in that part of *Great Britain* called *Scotland*, the court before whom such action or suit *[Limitation of actions. General issue. Treble costs.]*

fhall be brought, fhall allow the defender to plead this act on
his defence ; and if the purfuer fhall not infift on his action, or
if judgment fhall be given againft fuch purfuer, the defender
fhall and may recover the full and real expences he may have
been put to by any fuch action or fuit.

CAP. XI.

An act for the regulation of his Majefty's marine forces while on fhore.

CAP. XII.

*An act to amend an act made in the twenty ninth year of the
reign of his prefent Majefty, intituled,* An act to render
more effectual an act paffed in the twelfth year of the
reign of his late majefty King *George,* to prevent unlawful combinations of workmen employed in the
woollen manufactures, and for better payment of their
wages ; and alfo an act paffed in the thirteenth year of
the reign of his faid late Majefty, for the better regulation of the woollen manufacture ; and for preventing
difputes among the perfons concerned therein ; and for
limiting a time for profecuting for the forfeiture appointed by the aforefaid act, in cafe of payment of the
workmens wages in any other manner than in money.

29 G. 2. c. 33.
12 G. 1. c. 34.
13 G. 1. c. 23.
W HEREAS *by an act made and paffed in the twenty ninth
year of the reign of his prefent Majefty, intituled,* An act
to render more effectual an act paffed in the twelfth year of the
reign of his late majefty King *George,* to prevent unlawful combinations of workmen employed in the woollen manufactures,
and for better payment of their wages ; and alfo an act paffed
in the thirteenth year of the reign of his faid late Majefty, for
the better regulation of the woollen manufacture, and for preventing difputes among the perfons concerned therein ; and for
limiting a time for profecuting for the forfeiture appointed by
the aforefaid act, in cafe of the payment of the workmens wages
in any other manner than in money ; *it was, amongft other things,
enacted, That from and after the twenty fourth day of* June, *one
thoufand feven hundred and fifty fix, it fhould be lawful for the juftices of the peace affembled at any of their general or quarter feffions
held next after* Michaelmas *yearly, to make rates for the payment of
wages to weavers, and others employed in the woollen manufactures,
according to the number of yards that the chains are laid upon the
warping bars, and not otherwife: which rates by the faid act were
to continue for one year from the making thereof: and whereas, from
the great variety of the faid manufacture of broad cloth, as well in
refpect to breadth and colour, as to the quantity and quality of the
material of which the fame is compofed, it is found impracticable to
form any general rate of wages that would be juft, adequate, and
fuitable to the feveral branches and circumftances of the faid manufacture: and whereas great mifchiefs and inconveniencies have arifen,*
and

and may arise, from the exercise of the aforesaid power and authority given by the above recited act to the justices of the peace, to make rates for the payment of wages, as therein mentioned: for remedy whereof, may it please your Majesty, that it may be enacted; and be it enacted by the King's most excellent majesty, by and with the advice and consent of the lords spiritual and temporal and commons in this present parliament assembled, and by the authority of the same, That so much of the said recited act as enacts, That it shall and may be lawful for the justices of the peace assembled at any of their general or quarter sessions held next after *Michaelmas* yearly, to make rates for the payment of wages to weavers, and others employed in the woollen manufactures, according to the number of yards that the chains are laid upon the warping bars, and not otherwise, shall be, and the same is hereby repealed. *Clause in the recited act repealed.*

II. And be it further enacted by the authority aforesaid, That all or any contracts or agreements made, or hereafter to be made and entered into, between any clothier or maker of mixed, medley or white broad cloth, and the weaver or weavers employed by such maker, in respect to any wages to be paid to such weaver or weavers, shall, from and immediately after the first day of *May* one thousand seven hundred and fifty seven, be, and are hereby declared to be good, valid and effectual, to all intents and purposes; any rate made or to be made in pursuance of any law, statute or usage, to the contrary thereof in any wise notwithstanding. *Agreements entered into between clothier and weaver, to be binding;*

III. And be it further enacted by the authority aforesaid, That the aforesaid contracts or agreements shall extend only to the actual prices or rates of workmanship or wages to be paid, and not to the payment thereof in any other manner than in money, contrary to the intent and meaning of the said recited act of the twenty ninth year of his present Majesty's reign. *but to extend only to the wages, which are to be paid in money.*

IV. And be it further enacted by the authority aforesaid, That if any clothier or maker of any mixed, medley or white broad cloth, shall refuse or neglect to pay to the weaver or weavers employed by him or them his or their wages or price agreed on in money, within two days next after the work shall be performed and delivered to such employer, or some person on his behalf (the same being demanded of such employer or person employed on his behalf); then and in every such case, every such clothier or person so offending, shall for every such offence forfeit and pay the sum of forty shillings; to be recovered in such manner and form, and by such ways and means, and to be paid, applied, and disposed of, as the several penalties and forfeitures incurred and made payable by the said recited act made in the twenty ninth year of his present Majesty's reign, are thereby directed and appointed to be recovered and applied. *Clothier not paying the same within 2 days after delivery of the work,* *to forfeit 40 s.*

CAP. XIII.

An act to rectify a mistake in an act passed this session of parliament, intituled, An act for the speedy and effectual recruiting of his Majesty's land forces and marines.

Cap. 8.

WHEREAS *by an act made this present session of parliament, intituled,* An act for the speedy and effectual recruiting his Majesty's land forces and marines; *it is enacted, That for the encouragement of fit and able persons voluntarily to enter into his Majesty's service, every person who should voluntarily enter himself into his Majesty's service, in the manner therein mentioned, should receive the sum of three pounds out of the money of the land tax arisen, or to arise, in the years one thousand seven hundred and fifty six, and one thousand seven hundred and fifty seven: and whereas in the provision made by the said act for the repayment of part of the sums so to be supplied out of such land taxes, for such encouragement as aforesaid, the word* Pound *is by mistake inserted, instead of the words* three pounds; be it enacted by the King's most excellent majesty, by and with the advice and consent of the lords spiritual and temporal, and commons, in this present parliament assembled, and by the authority of the same, That it shall be lawful for the lord high treasurer, or commissioners of the treasury for the time being, to cause forty shillings of every three pounds which shall be so supplied out of the said land tax money for payment of the encouragements aforesaid, to be repaid into his Majesty's exchequer by the respective paymasters of his Majesty's forces, out of such money as they shall receive for the said forces, to make good the respective credits on the said land taxes, and to be applied to the satisfaction of such principal and interest (if any) as shall be remaining thereupon; any thing in the said act contained to the contrary notwithstanding.

Forty shillings of every three pounds paid out of the land tax, to be repaid into the exchequer by the paymasters of the forces.

CAP. XIV.

An act for continuing an act of this present session of parliament, intituled, An act to discontinue, for a limited time, the duties upon corn and flour imported; and also upon such corn, grain, meal, bread, biscuit and flour, as have been, or shall be taken from the enemy, and brought into this kingdom.

Cap. 7.

WHEREAS *an act made in this present session of parliament, intituled,* An act to discontinue, for a limited time, the duties upon corn and flour imported; and also upon such corn, grain, meal, bread, biscuit and flour, as have been, or shall be taken from the enemy, and brought into this kingdom, *which will expire upon the twenty fourth day of* August *one thousand seven hundred and fifty seven, hath been found useful and beneficial: and whereas it is found necessary that the said act should be continued for a longer time; be* it therefore enacted by the King's most excellent majesty, by and

and with the advice and confent of the lords fpiritual and temporal and commons in this prefent parliament affembled, and by
the authority of the fame, That the faid act fhall be, and the *Recited act*
fame is hereby further continued from the expiration thereof, *continued to*
until the fifteenth day of *November* next. *15 November next.*

CAP. XV.

*An act for continuing an act of this prefent feffion of par-
liament, intituled,* An act to prohibit, for a limited time,
the making of low wines and fpirits from wheat, barley, malt, or any other fort of grain; or from any meal
or flour.

WHEREAS *an act made in this prefent feffion of parliament,* *Cap. 10.*
intituled, An act to prohibit, for a limited time, the making of low wines and fpirits from wheat, barley, malt, or any
other fort of grain; or from any meal or flour; *which will expire
upon the eleventh day of* May, *one thousand seven hundred and fifty
seven, hath been found useful and beneficial: and whereas it is found
necessary that the said act should be continued for a longer time;* be
it therefore enacted by the King's moft excellent majefty, by and
with the advice and confent of the lords fpiritual and temporal,
and commons, in this prefent parliament affembled, and by the *The recited*
authority of the fame, That the faid act fhall be, and the fame *act continued*
is hereby continued from the expiration thereof, until the ele- *to 11 Decem-*
venth day of *December* next. *ber next.*

II. Provided always, and be it enacted by the authority afore- *His Majesty*
faid, That in cafe his Majefty, at any time or times after the *impowered by*
eleventh day of *May* one thoufand feven hundred and fifty feven, *proclamation*
and before the eleventh day of *December* one thoufand feven *or order of*
hundred and fifty feven, fhall, in his royal difcretion, judge it *council, to fu-*
to be moft for the benefit and advantage of this kingdom, to *spend the act*
permit the making of low wines and fpirits from wheat, bar- *and permit di-*
ley, malt or any other fort of grain, or from any meal or flour, *stillation from*
that then it fhall and may be lawful to and for his Majefty, by *wheat, &c.*
his royal proclamation or proclamations to be iffued, by and
with the advice of his privy council, or by his Majefty's order
in council, to be publifhed in the *London Gazette*, from time to
time, to permit and fuffer all and every perfon and perfons, natives and foreigners (but not any particular perfon or perfons)
at any time or times after the faid eleventh day of *May* one thoufand feven hundred and fifty feven, and before the faid eleventh
day of *December*, one thoufand feven hundred and fifty feven, to
make low wines and fpirits from wheat, barley, malt, or any
other fort of grain, or from any meal or flour; any thing
herein contained to the contrary notwithftanding.

CAP.

CAP. XVI.

An act to extend the liberty granted by an act of the twenty third year of the reign of his present Majesty, of importing bar iron from his Majesty's colonies in America, *into the port of* London, *to the rest of the ports of* Great Britain; *and for repealing certain clauses in the said act.*

23 G. 2. c. 29. WHEREAS *by an act made in the twenty third year of the reign of his present Majesty, intituled,* An act to encourage the importation of pig and bar iron from his Majesty's colonies in *America*; and to prevent the erection of any mill or other engine for slitting or rolling of iron; or any plating forge to work with a tilt hammer; or any furnace for making steel in any of the said colonies, *it is enacted, That from and after the twenty fourth day of* June *one thousand seven hundred and fifty, no subsidy, custom, imposition, rate or duty whatsoever, should be payable upon bar iron made in, and imported from, his Majesty's colonies in* America, *into the port of* London: *and whereas the admission of such bar iron into the rest of the ports of* Great Britain, *duty-free, will be advantageous to the iron manufacture, as well as to the general trade and commerce of these kingdoms*; be it therefore enacted by the King's most excellent majesty, by and with the advice and consent of the lords spiritual and temporal, and commons, in this present parliament assembled, and by the authority of the same, That from and after the twenty fourth day of *June* one thousand seven hundred and fifty seven, the several and respective subsidies, customs, impositions, rates and duties, now payable on bar iron made in, and imported from, his Majesty's colonies in *America*, into any port of *Great Britain*, shall cease, determine, and be no longer paid; and that the said act, and every clause, matter and thing, therein contained, so far as relates to the importation of bar iron from *America* (except that is altered or repealed by this act) shall, and is hereby declared to extend to all the ports in *Great Britain*, as fully as if the same were repeated and re-enacted in this present act; any law, statute, or usage to the contrary notwithstanding.

Bar iron to be imported from America, duty free.

Clauses in the recited act relating to the importation thereof, extended to all the ports of Great Britain.

II. *And whereas by the said act of the twenty third year of his present Majesty, it is enacted, That no bar iron whatsoever shall be permitted to be carried coastwise, unless mention be made in the certificate to be granted for that purpose, of the day on which the subsidies, customs, impositions, rates and duties, payable upon the importation thereof, were paid, and of the name of the person or persons by whom the same were paid*; be it enacted by the authority aforesaid, That from after the said twenty fourth day of *June* one thousand seven hundred and fifty seven, the said clause shall be, and is hereby declared to be repealed.

Clause relating to certificates for duties paid, on being carried coastwise repealed.

III. *And whereas by the said act of the twenty third year of his present Majesty, it is enacted, That no bar iron imported into the port of* London *by virtue of the said act, shall be carried or conveyed by land, beyond ten miles from any part of the port of* London;

be

be it enacted by the authority aforesaid, That from and after the twenty fourth day of *June* one thousand seven hundred and fifty seven, the said clause shall be, and is hereby declared to be repealed.

Clause prohibiting the carrying thereof by land 10 miles from London, repealed.

IV. *And whereas by the said act of the twenty third year of his present Majesty, it is enacted, That all bar iron imported from any of his Majesty's colonies in* America *into the port of* London, *shall be stamped with such mark or stamp as the commissioners of the customs shall direct, in three different parts of each bar, which provision will be for the future unnecessary*; be it enacted by the authority aforesaid, That the said act, so far as relates to the stamping or marking of *American* bar iron, in the port of *London*, shall, from and after the twenty fourth day of *June* one thousand seven hundred and fifty seven, be, and is hereby declared to be repealed.

Clause requiring the bars to be stamped, repealed.

CAP. XVII.

An act for the importation of fine organzined Italian *thrown silk.*

WHEREAS *by an act made in the second year of the reign of their late majesties King* William *and Queen* Mary, *intituled*, An act for the discouraging the importation of thrown silk; *amongst other things in the said act contained, the bringing in of thrown silk of the growth or production of* Italy *is prohibited, unless imported in such ships or vessels, and navigated in such manner, as in and by an act made in the twelfth year of the reign of King* Charles *the Second, intituled*, An act for the encouraging and encreasing of shipping and navigation, *is directed and allowed, and brought from same of the ports of those countries or places, whereof the same is the growth or production, and which shall come directly by sea, and not otherwise: and whereas there is at present very great and immediate want of organzined thrown silk from* Italy, *for the use and purpose of warp in the silk manufacture, without which the manufacture cannot be carried on, and many thousands of manufacturers must be unemployed*; be it therefore enacted by the King's most excellent majesty, by and with the advice and consent of the lords spiritual and temporal, and commons, in this present parliament assembled, and by the authority of the same, That it shall and may be lawful to and for any person or persons to import or bring into this kingdom, from any port or place, or in any ship or vessel whatsoever, until the first day of *December* one thousand seven hundred and fifty seven, organzined thrown silk, of the growth or production of *Italy*; any thing contained in the said recited acts, or any other act, to the contrary thereof notwithstanding.

2 W. & M. sess. 1. c. 9.

and 12 Car. 2. c. 18.

Liberty given to import organzined thrown silk from Italy for a limited time.

II. Provided always, That this act, nor any thing herein contained, shall extend to give liberty to import any *Italian* thrown silk, that shall be coarser than a sort thereof, known and distinguished by the name of *Third Bolonia*, nor any sorts of silks commonly called *Tram*, of the growth of *Italy*, nor any other thrown

Silks of a particular sort prohibited to be imported under this act, under penalty of forfeiture.

thrown silk of the growth or production of *Turkey, Persia, East India*, or *China*, under the penalty of forfeiting all such thrown silks, as shall be brought over and imported contrary to the purport, true intent, and meaning of this act; one moiety whereof to the use of his Majesty, his heirs and successors, and the other moiety to such person or persons who shall seize, inform, or sue for the same; to be recovered by bill, plaint or information, in any of his Majesty's courts of record at *Westminster*; wherein no essoin, protection, or wager of law shall be allowed.

All organzined thrown silk wheresoever landed, to be brought up to the custom-house at London, under penalty of forfeiture.

III. *And for the better and more effectual execution of this act, and to prevent the importation of any sort of thrown silk not organzined*; be it further enacted and declared, That all such organzined thrown silk, as is allowed to be imported by this act, wheresoever landed, shall be brought to his Majesty's custom house at *London*; to the intent that no other sort of thrown silk may be imported, than that allowed by this act, under the penalty of forfeiting all such thrown silk as shall be imported contrary to the purport, true intent and meaning of this act; one moiety whereof shall be to the use of his Majesty, his heirs and successors, and the other moiety to such person or persons who shall seize, inform or sue for the same; to be recovered by bill, plaint or information, in any of his Majesty's courts of record, wherein no essoin, protection or wager of law shall be allowed; any thing to the contrary hereof in any wise notwithstanding.

CAP. XVIII.

An act for the relief and encouragement of the captors of prizes, with respect to the bringing and landing prize goods in this kingdom.

7 & 8 W. 3. c. 20.

WHEREAS the duties granted by an act passed in the seventh and eighth years of the reign of the late King William the Third, upon French wines and other goods of the growth, product or manufacture of France, as well as several other duties upon various goods imported into this kingdom, are by law not to be drawn back upon the re-exportation thereof into foreign parts: and whereas such duties have been found in several instances to be equal to the value of the goods which have been taken as prize from the French, and thereby the captors have so far lost the benefit of their prizes; which discouragement hath often induced captors to carry their prizes directly to foreign parts, to the prejudice of this kingdom: therefore be it enacted by the King's most excellent majesty, by and with the advice and consent of the lords spiritual and temporal and commons in this present parliament assembled, and by the authority of the same, That any goods of the growth, product or manufacture of *France*, or of any of the dominions belonging to the crown of *France*, that have been or shall hereafter be taken during the continuance of the present war, and brought hither by any of his Majesty's ships of war or privateers, shall and may, upon condemnation thereof as lawful prize, be land-

Prize goods, after condemnation, may be lodged in private warehouses, under the King's locks;

ed

ed in any port within this kingdom, and secured under the King's locks in warehouses provided at the sole expence of the captors, with the privity and approbation, and under the care and inspection of the commissioners, or other principal officers for collecting and managing the respective duties of customs and excise, to which such goods are liable; and upon admission of *Duties are to* any such goods taken since his Majesty's declaration of war a- *be paid there-* gainst *France*, into such warehouses, there shall be paid by the *on, but no* captors, or their agents, the following duties only; which shall *drawback on* not be afterwards drawn back or repaid upon the exportation of *exportation.* the same goods; that is to say, For all such goods (except wines *What duties* and vinegar, and such goods as are herein after enumerated) of *are payable on* the growth, product or manufacture of *France*, or any of the *goods, if taken* dominions belonging to the crown of *France*, taken as afore- *by the King's* said by any of his Majesty's ships of war, the half of the old *ships;* subsidy granted by the act of tonnage and poundage passed in the twelfth year of the reign of King *Charles* the Second; and *12 C. 2. c. 4.* the whole of the further subsidy of poundage granted by an act passed in the twenty first year of the reign of his present Ma- *21 G. 2. c. 2.* jesty, being what is commonly called *The subsidy one thousand* *what if taken* *seven hundred and forty seven*; and for the like goods if taken by *by privateers.* any private ship of war, the half of the said old subsidy, and no more; which duties shall be collected, paid and applied in the *Customary al-* same manner, and to the same purposes, whereunto they are *lowances and* by law appropriated, subject nevertheless to the customary and *discounts to be* legal discounts and abatements, and allowances for damage; *made.* and for every ton of *French* wine and *French* vinegar taken as *Duties on* aforesaid, either by his Majesty's ships of war or privateers, the *French wine* sum of three pounds; and so after the same rate for any greater *and vinegar.* or lesser quantity; to be paid into the receipt of his Majesty's exchequer, as part of the duties arising by an act passed in the eighteenth year of the reign of his present Majesty, intituled, *18 G. 2. c. 9.* *An act for granting to his Majesty several additional duties upon all* *wines imported into* Great Britain; *and for raising a certain sum of* *money by annuities and a lottery, in manner therein mentioned, to be* *charged on the said additional duties.*

II. And be it further enacted by the authority aforesaid, That *Duty to be paid* the half of the old subsidy granted by the said act of the twelfth *ad valorem,* of *Charles* the Second, and the whole of the further subsidy of *upon the* poundage, granted by the said act of the twenty first year of the *goods here e-* reign of his present Majesty, which is directed by this act to be *numerated.* paid for such prize goods taken by his Majesty's ships of war; and the half of the old subsidy granted by the said act of the twelfth of *Charles* the Second, which is directed by this act to be paid for such prize goods taken by private ships of war, shall be payable *ad valorem*, and no otherwise, upon the oath of the captors or their agents, upon the following goods; that is to say, upon all sorts of woollen and silk manufactures, and hats, handkerchiefs, checks, knives and nails, notwithstanding the same may have been rated in the book of rates of the twelfth year of the reign of *Charles* the Second, or the additional book

of

How the fame of rates of the eleventh year of the reign of his late majesty King
are to be levi- *George* the First; and that the said duties *ad valorem* respectively
ed, &c. on the goods before enumerated, shall be levied and collected
by the same rules and regulations, and under the same penalties
11 G. 1. c. 7. and forfeitures, as are directed and prescribed in and by an act of
the eleventh year of the reign of his late majesty King *George* the
First, intituled, *An act for rating such unrated goods and merchan-*
dizes as are usually imported into this kingdom, and pay duty ad valorem,
upon the oath of the importer; and for ascertaining the value of all
goods and merchandizes not inserted in the former or present book of
rates; and for repealing certain duties upon drugs and rags; and for
continuing the duty upon apples; and for ascertaining the method of ad-
measuring pictures imported.

Military or   III. Provided always, That no duties or customs whatsoever
ship stores ex- shall be demanded or taken for any prize goods consisting of any
empted from military or ship stores; any thing in this or any other act con-
duty. tained to the contrary notwithstanding.

Prize goods   IV. And it is hereby further enacted by the authority afore-
taken since the said, That any prize goods of the growth, product or manufac-
declaration of ture of *France*, or any of the dominions belonging to the crown
war, may be of *France*, which shall be received into any warehouse in pursu-
exported, ance of this act, or which are now remaining in any warehouse
in this kingdom, where they have been secured, under the King's
locks, by the permission of the commissioners of the customs, shall
upon payment and may, upon payment of the respective duties before directed
of the duties by this act (if the same have been taken since the declaration of
of this act; war) be exported at any time directly from thence, either by the
captors or their agents, or by any other person or persons, without paying any further duty of customs or excise for the same;
and if such goods shall have been taken before the said declara-
and such as tion of war, the same shall and may be exported in like manner,
were taken be- without payment of any duty of customs or excise whatsoever;
fore, may be the person or persons exporting the same, giving sufficient secu-
exported with- rity in double the value of the goods, before the delivery thereof
out paying out of the warehouse, that the same shall be really and truly ex-
any duty; the ported, and not brought back again or relanded in any part of
exporter giv- *Great Britain*, or the islands of *Guernsey, Jersey, Alderney, Sark*
ing security. or *Man*; which security the customer or collector of the port
from whence the same are intended to be exported, is hereby
required and authorized to take in his Majesty's name, and to
his Majesty's use.

Goods taken   V. Provided always, and it is hereby further enacted by the
out of the authority aforesaid, That if any goods shall be taken out of any
warehouse for warehouse, wherein they are secured as aforesaid, to be consumed
home con- in this kingdom, the person or persons so taking out the same,
sumption, to shall first pay up the remainder of the duties which would have
pay the duties been due and payable to his Majesty thereon, if the same had
payable on im- been regularly imported by way of merchandize into this king-
portation. dom; and such goods shall, in all other respects, be liable to the
same restrictions and regulations to which they would have been
subject, if this act had not been made.

VI. P ro

VI. Provided neverthelefs, That nothing in this act shall extend, or be conftrued to extend, to charge any wine with the before-mentioned duty of three pounds *per* ton, which shall at the time of landing the fame be damaged, corrupt or unmerchantable, and which shall be given up by the captors or their agents, to the officers of the cuftoms, to be publickly fold, in order to be diftilled into brandy, or to be made into vinegar, in the manner directed by an act paffed in the twelfth year of the reign of his late majefty King *George* the Firft, intituled, *An act for the improvement of his Majefty's revenues of cuftoms, excife and inland duties.* *{right margin: Damaged wines, if given up to the King's officers, not liable to the duty of 3l. per ton. 12 G. 1. c. 28.}*

VII. Provided alfo, That nothing in this act contained shall extend, or be conftrued to extend, to leffen or any ways alter the duties which by law are due and payable upon goods that are the growth, product or manufacture of any other country or place, except *France* and the dominions belonging to the crown of *France*, which may be taken as prize and condemned in this Kingdom. *{right margin: The duties payable on goods of the growth of other countries, not altered by this act.}*

CAP. XIX.

An act for granting to his Majefty feveral rates and duties upon indentures, leafes, bonds and other deeds; and upon news papers, advertifements and almanacks; and upon licences for retailing wine; and upon coals exported to foreign parts; and for applying, from a certain time, the fums of money arifing from the furplus of the duties on licences for retailing fpirituous liquors; and for raifing the fum of three millions, by annuities, to be charged on the faid rates, duties and fums of money; and for making perpetual an act made in the fecond year of the reign of his prefent Majefty, intituled, An act for the better regulation of attornies and folicitors; *and for enlarging the time for filing affidavits of the execution of contracts of clerks to attornies and folicitors; and alfo the time for payment of the duties omitted to be paid for the indentures and contracts of clerks and apprentices.*

Moft gracious Sovereign,

WE, your Majefty's *moft dutiful and loyal fubjects, the commons of* Great Britain *in parliament affembled, towards raifing by the moft eafy means the neceffary fupplies to defray your Majefty's publick expences, have freely and voluntarily refolved to give and grant unto your Majefty the feveral rates and duties, and fums of money berein after mentioned; and do moft humbly befeech your Majefty that it may be enacted;* and be it enacted by the King's moft excellent majefty, by and with the advice and confent of the lords fpiritual and temporal and commons in this prefent parliament affembled, and by the authority of the fame, That from and after *{right margin: Additional duties}* after the fifth day of July one thousand seven hundred and fifty seven, there shall be raised, levied, collected and paid throughout the kingdom of *Great Britain*, onto and for the use of his Majesty, his heirs and successors,

on indentures, leases, bonds and other deeds.
32 Ann. c. 9.

For every skin or piece of vellum or parchment, or sheet or piece of paper, upon which shall be ingrossed, written or printed in *Great Britain*, any indenture, lease, bond or other deed, for which a stamp duty of six pence is payable, by virtue of an act made in the twelfth year of the reign of her late majesty Queen *Anne*, over and above all other rates and duties by the said act, or by any other act of parliament imposed, an additional stamp duty of one shilling.

Upon news papers.
10 Ann. c. 19.

For and upon every news paper or paper containing publick news, intelligence or occurrences printed in *Great Britain*, to be dispersed and made publick, whether the same be contained in half a sheet, or any less piece of paper, or in any paper larger than half a sheet, and not exceeding one whole sheet, over and above all other rates and duties by an act made in the tenth year of the reign of her late majesty Queen *Anne*, or by any other act of parliament imposed, an additional duty of one half penny.

Upon advertisements in news papers.

For every advertisement to be contained in the *London Gazette*, or any other printed paper in *Great Britain*, to be dispersed or made publick weekly, or oftener, over and above all other rates and duties by an act made in the tenth year of the reign of her late majesty Queen *Anne*, or by any other act of parliament imposed, an additional duty of one shilling; and,

Upon advertisements in pamphlets, or periodical works, &c.
Upon sheet almanacks.
9 Ann. c. 23.

For every advertisement contained in or published with any paper or pamphlet whatsoever, printed in *Great Britain*, to be dispersed or made publick yearly, monthly, or at any other interval of time exceeding one week, a duty of two shillings.

For every almanack or calendar for one particular year, or for any time less than a year, printed on one side only of any one sheet or piece of paper, over and above the duty charged thereon by an act made in the ninth year of the reign of her late majesty Queen *Anne*, an additional duty of one penny.

Upon other almanacks.

For every other printed almanack or calendar for any one particular year, over and above the duty charged thereon by the said act, an additional duty of two pence; and,

Upon almanacks to serve for several years.
Upon licences for retailing wine, where no other licence is taken out.

For every almanack or calendar made to serve for several years, the said several additional duties for every such year; and,

For every piece of vellum or parchment, or sheet or piece of paper, on which shall be ingrossed, written or printed any licence for retailing of wine, to be granted to any person who shall not take out, either a licence for retailing of spirituous liquors, or a licence for retailing of beer, ale or other exciseable liquors, over and above all other rates and duties payable by virtue of any former act or acts of parliament, imposing any duties on stampt vellum, parchment and paper, an additional duty of five pounds.

Upon licences for retailing

For every piece of vellum or parchment, or sheet or piece of paper, on which shall be ingrossed, written or printed any licence

cence

cence for retailing of wine, to be granted to any person who shall take out a licence for retailing beer, ale and other exciseable liquors, but shall not take out a licence for retailing of spirituous liquors, over and above all other rates and duties payable by virtue of any former act or acts of parliament, imposing any duties on stampt vellum, parchment and paper, an additional duty of four pounds; and,

wine, where a licence for beer only is taken out.

For every piece of vellum or parchment, or sheet or piece of paper, on which shall be ingrossed, written or printed any licence for retailing of wine, to be granted to any person who shall also take out a licence for retailing of spirituous liquors, over and above all other rates and duties payable by virtue of any former act or acts of parliament, imposing any duties on stamp vellum, parchment and paper, an additional duty of forty shillings.

Upon licences for retailing wine, where licence for spirituous liquors is taken out.

II. And be it further enacted by the authority aforesaid, That from and after the fifth day of *July* one thousand seven hundred and fifty seven, no person whatsoever, unless he be authorized and enabled in the manner herein after prescribed, shall sell or utter by retail, that is, by the pint, quart, pottle or gallon, or by any other greater or less retail measure, or in bottles in any less quantity than shall be equal to the measure of the cask or vessel in which the same shall have been or may lawfully be imported, any kind of wine or wines, or any liquor called or reputed wine, upon pain to forfeit, for every such offence, the sum of one hundred pounds; the one moiety of every such penalty to be to the use of the King, his heirs and successors, and the other moiety to him or them who will inform for the same; the said penalty to be recovered in such manner as the penalties for offences committed against any laws imposing any duties on stampt vellum, parchment or paper are directed to be recovered.

100l. penalty on retailing wine unlicensed.

III. And be it further enacted by the authority aforesaid, That from and after the said fifth day of *July* one thousand seven hundred and fifty seven, any two or more of his Majesty's commissioners appointed for managing the duties arising by stamps on vellum, parchment or paper, and no other person whatsoever, shall grant licences under their hands and seals, to such persons as they shall think fit, to sell and utter by retail in manner aforesaid, any kind of wine or wines, or liquor called or reputed wine whatsoever, in any city, town or other place within *Great Britain* for the space of one year from the date of such licences.

Commissioners for stamps to grant wine licences.

IV. Provided nevertheless, That if before the fifth day of *July* one thousand seven hundred and fifty seven, the agents or commissioners authorized by virtue of the said act made in the twelfth year of the reign of King *Charles* the Second, shall have granted a licence to any person to sell wine by retail for the space of one year, or for any term not then expired, the person so licenced shall be enabled to sell wine by retail for the space of one year from the date of such licence, or until the expiration of the term for which the licence shall be so granted; any thing in this act before contained to the contrary notwithstanding.

Licences granted by former commissioners to be good for the term they were granted for. 12 Car. 2. c. 25.

New licences
to be taken
every year,
and the duty
paid at the
same time.

V. And be it further enacted by the authority aforesaid, That every person who shall take out such licence for retailing wine as aforesaid, to endure for the space of one year, shall take out a fresh licence ten days at the least before the expiration of that year for which he shall be so licensed, if he or she shall continue to sell wine by retail, and in the same manner shall renew such licence from year to year, paying down the respective sums due for such licences; and so yearly and every year, as long as he or she shall continue to sell or utter wine by retail, in manner aforesaid.

Licences to be
granted to per-
sons at a di-
stance, upon
application in
their behalf,
and payment
of duty.
12 Car. 2. c.
25. in part re-
pealed.

VI. And be it further enacted by the authority aforesaid, That upon application made by, or in behalf of, any person not residing in the weekly bills of mortality, for a licence to retail wine, the said commissioners for the time being shall deliver or cause to be delivered such licence, upon payment of the duty payable thereupon.

VII. *And whereas, by virtue of an act made in the twelfth year of the reign of King Charles the Second, intituled, An act for the better ordering the selling of wines by retail; and for preventing abuses in the mingling, corrupting and viciating of wines; and for settling and limiting the prices of the same; his Majesty's agents for granting licences to sell and utter wine by retail, are enabled to grant such licences to persons retailing wines, on the terms and for the yearly rents in the said act mentioned: And whereas it was provided by the said act, that the rents, revenues and sums of money thence arising, except what should be allowed for the salaries or wages of his Majesty's said agents, and the officers and ministers to be appointed for the better carrying on of the said service, which was not to exceed six pence out of every pound thereof, should be duly and constantly paid and answered into the receipt of his Majesty's exchequer, which revenue is now vested in his Majesty, his heirs and successors, and is part of the revenue established for the better support of his Majesty's houshold, and of the honour and dignity of the crown of Great Britain: And whereas his Majesty, for the benefit of the publick, has been graciously pleased to consent to an abolition of the said revenue, and to accept in lieu thereof a yearly income, equal to the net produce of the said revenue arising from licences to retail wine;* be it further enacted by the authority aforesaid, That the said act made in the twelfth year of the reign of King *Charles* the Second, except so much thereof as relates to the preventing abuses in the mingling, corrupting and viciating of wines, and to settling and limiting the prices of the same, shall from and after the said fifth day of *July* one thousand seven hundred and fifty seven be repealed, and the yearly rents and sums of money thereby payable by virtue of the said act on licences to retail wine, shall cease and determine.

and the com-
mission for
granting licen-
ces by virtue
thereof to
cease.

VIII. Provided also, and be it further enacted by the authority aforesaid, That from and after the said fifth day of *July* one thousand seven hundred and fifty seven, the commission whereby agents and commissioners are appointed by virtue of the said act for granting licences to retail wine, shall cease and determine.

IX. Pro-

IX. Provided always, That this act, or any thing herein contained, shall not in any wise be prejudicial to the privileges of the two univerfities in that part of *Great Britain* called *England*, or either of them, nor to the chancellors or scholars of the fame, or their fucceffors, but that they may ufe and enjoy fuch privileges as they have heretofore lawfully ufed and enjoyed; any thing herein contained to the contrary notwithftanding.

Privileges of the univerfities referved to them.

X. Provided alfo, That this act, or any thing therein contained, shall not extend to be prejudicial to the mafter, wardens, freemen and commonalty of the *vintners* of the city of *London*, or to any other city or town corporate, but that they may ufe and enjoy fuch liberties and privileges, as they have heretofore lawfully ufed and enjoyed.

Privileges of the vintners company of London, referved to them.

XI. Provided neverthelefs, That no perfon, who, from and after the faid fifth day of *July* one thoufand feven hundred and fifty feven, shall be admitted to the freedom of the faid company of *vintners* of the city of *London*, by redemption only, shall be exempted from the obligation of taking out a licence for felling or uttering wine by retale, or from the payment of the duties hereby granted on licences to retail wine; but that the freemen only of the faid company, who have been already admitted to their freedom, or who from and after the faid fifth day of *July* one thoufand feven hundred and fifty feven, shall be admitted to their freedom in right of patrimony or apprenticefhip, shall be entitled to fuch exemption.

Exemption from the duty not to extend to perfons purchafing their freedom in the faid company.

XII. Provided alfo, and be it enacted by the authority aforefaid, That this act, or any thing herein contained, shall not in any wife extend to debar or hinder the mayor and burgeffes of the borough of Saint *Albans* in the county of *Hertford*, or their fucceffors, from enjoying, ufing and exercifing, all fuch liberties, powers and authorities, to them heretofore granted by feveral letters patents, under the great feal of *England*, by Queen *Elizabeth* and King *James* the Firft, for the erecting, appointing and licenfing of three feveral wine taverns, within the borough aforefaid, for and towards the maintenance of the free fchool there; but that the fame liberties, powers and authorities, shall be and are hereby eftablifhed and confirmed, and shall remain and continue in and to the faid mayor and burgeffes, and their fucceffors, to and for the charitable ufe aforefaid, and according to the tenor of the letters patents aforefaid, as though this act had never been made; any thing in this act contained to the contrary in any wife notwithftanding.

Power of the corporation of St. Albans to grant licences, referved to them.

XIII. Provided always, and be it enacted by the authority aforefaid, That from and after the faid fifth day of *July* one thoufand feven hundred and fifty feven, there shall be paid to his Majefty, his heirs and fucceffors, out of the monies which shall arife from the new duties on licences to retail wine, by four quarterly payments, on the tenth day of *October*, the fifth day of *January*, the fifth day of *April*, and the fifth day of *July* yearly, in every year, the fum of feven thoufand and two pounds fourteen fhillings and three pence, which appears to have been the neat annual

700:l. 14s. 3d to be paid annually, as an equivalent to his Majefty, out of the duties on licences for wine.

nual produce of the former duties on licences for retailing wine, at a medium of six years, ending the fifth day of *January* one thousand seven hundred and fifty seven.

His Majesty impowered to grant pensions to the late commissioners, out of the duties on wine licences.

XIV. Provided nevertheless, and be it enacted by the authority aforesaid, That out of the several duties before-mentioned, payable by virtue of this act for licences to retail wine, his Majesty, his heirs and successors, be, and he or they is and are hereby impowered to grant, by warrant or warrants under his or their sign manual, during pleasure, to the several agents or commissioners for managing the duties on wine licences granted by the said act made in the twelfth year of the reign of King *Charles* the Second, and their officers, or to such of the said agents or officers as his Majesty, his heirs and successors, shall think proper objects of his or their royal bounty, such yearly allowances as his Majesty, his heirs and successors, shall judge fit, so as no allowance to any such agent or commissioner shall exceed five hundred pounds by the year, and so as no such allowance to be made to

Pensions not to exceed a certain sum.

any other such officer, shall exceed the present annual amount of the salaries and wages due and payable to such officers respectively.

XV. *And whereas the duties on licences for retailing wine, granted by this act, are subjected to the payment of the yearly sum of seven thousand and two pounds fourteen shillings and three pence, as an equivalent for a revenue vested in his Majesty, his heirs and successors, by virtue of an act of the parliament of England, made before the union of the two kingdoms of England and Scotland: And whereas his Majesty is by this act impowered to grant, during pleasure, out of the produce of the duties for retailing wine hereby granted, to the agents and officers employed in the collection of the revenue hereby repealed, certain yearly allowances, which may amount to the sum of three thousand three hundred and ten pounds: And whereas that part of Great Britain called Scotland was not subject to the payment of any part of the revenue arising from wine licences so vested in his Majesty, his heirs and successors, as aforesaid, it having been agreed by the fourteenth article of the treaty of union, that the kingdom of Scotland should not be charged with any other duties laid on by the parliament of England before the union, except those consented to by the said treaty, and ought not to be subject to any part of the duties granted by this present act, applicable as an equivalent to the said former revenue, or in consequence thereof, but to such a proportion only of the duties granted by this present act as is applicable to the publick service;* be it provided and enacted by the authority aforesaid, That in all cases

Proportional duties payable in Scotland, for licences to retail wine.

where a duty of five pounds is herein before directed to be paid on a licence for retailing wine, a duty of three pounds six shillings and eight pence, and no more, shall be paid for a licence to retail wine in that part of *Great Britain* called *Scotland;* and that in all cases where a duty of four pounds is herein before directed to be paid for such licence, a duty of two pounds thirteen shillings and four-pence, and no more, shall be paid for a licence to retail wine in that part of *Great Britain* called *Scotland;* and that in all cases where a duty of two pounds is herein be-

before directed to be paid for every such licence, a duty of one pound six shillings and eight pence, and no more, shall be paid for a licence to retail wine in that part of *Great Britain* called *Scotland*; any thing in this act contained to the contrary thereof in any wise notwithstanding.

XVI. Provided also, and be it further enacted by the authority aforesaid, That it shall and may be lawful for the said commissioners for managing the duties on stamped vellum, parchment and paper, to collect and recover, or cause to be collected or recovered, for the use of his Majesty, his heirs and successors, all such arrears of rent for licences to retail wine, or of forfeitures for retailing wine without licence, which shall have been incurred at any time before the said fifth day of *July* one thousand seven hundred and fifty seven; for which purpose, as well as for the better enabling them to execute the trusts hereby in them reposed, all the books, registers, papers, instruments, or other writings belonging to the said agents appointed by virtue of the said act made in the twelfth year of the reign of King *Charles* the Second, for granting licences to retail wine, shall, as soon as conveniently may be, be transferred to the custody of the said commissioners for managing the duties on stamped vellum, parchment and paper.

Commissioners for the stamps impowered to levy the duties, due on wine licences before 5 July, 1757.

XVII. And be it further enacted by the authority aforesaid, That for the better and more effectual levying, collecting, and paying all the said additional and new duties herein before granted, the same shall be under the government, care and management, of the commissioners for the time being appointed to manage the duties charged on stamped vellum, parchment and paper; who, or the major part of them, are hereby required and empowered to employ the necessary officers under them for that purpose; and to cause such new stamps to be provided to denote the said several duties, as shall be requisite in that behalf, and to do all other things necessary to be done for putting this act in execution with relation to the said several rates and duties herein before granted, in the like, and in as full and ample manner, as they, or the major part of them, are authorized to put in execution any former law concerning stamped vellum, parchment or paper.

The new duties put also under their management.

XVIII. Provided always, and be it further enacted by the authority aforesaid, That to prevent the multiplication of stamps upon such pieces of vellum or parchment, or sheets or pieces of paper, on which several duties are by several acts of parliament imposed, it shall and may be lawful for the said commissioners, instead of the distinct stamps directed to be provided to denote the several duties on the vellum, parchment or paper, charged therewith, to cause one new stamp to be provided, to denote the said several duties on every piece of vellum or parchment, or sheet or piece of paper, charged with the said several duties.

One new stamp to be provided to denote the several duties on vellum, paper, &c.

XIX. And be it further enacted by the authority aforesaid, That all vellum, parchment and paper, upon which any indenture, lease, bond or other deed, by this act charged with a duty

Indentures, leases, bonds, &c. charged

E 3 of

with a duty of
1s. to be
brought to the
office to be
stampt.
of one shilling, shall, from and after the said fifty day of *July* one thousand seven hundred and fifty seven, be ingrossed, written or printed, shall be brought to the head office for stamping or marking vellum, parchment and paper; and the said commissioners by themselves, or by their officers employed under them, shall forthwith, upon demand to them made by any person or persons, from time to time, stamp or mark any quantities or parcels of vellum, parchment or paper, to be used for the purpose of ingrossing, writing, or printing such indentures, leases, bonds and other deeds, he or they paying to the receiver general of the stamp duties for the time being, or his deputy or clerk, the several duties payable for the same by virtue of this act; which stamp or mark to be put thereupon in pursuance of this act, shall be a sufficient discharge for the duty hereby payable for the vellum, parchment or paper so stamped or marked.

Commissioners to take
care that all
parts be sufficiently furnished with
stamps.
XX. And be it further enacted by the authority aforesaid, That the said commissioners for the time being, shall take care that the several parts of the kingdom of *Great Britain*, shall, from time to time be sufficiently furnished with vellum, parchment and paper, stamped and marked as by this act is directed, to the end that the subjects of his Majesty, his heirs and successors, may have it in their election, either to buy the same of the officers and persons to be employed by the said commissioners at the usual and most common rates above the said duties, or to bring their own vellum, parchment or paper, to be stamped and marked as aforesaid.

Prices of
stamps to be
set yearly,
and marked ;
and the usual
allowance
made for
prompt payment.
XXI. And be it further enacted by the authority aforesaid, That the price of such stamped vellum, parchment or paper, shall be yearly set, and such price marked, and such allowance made on present payment of the said duties, for any quantity of the said vellum, parchment or paper, so to be sold, in such manner as by any former law relating to stamped vellum, parchment or paper, is directed.

Stamps may
be altered and
renewed.
XXII. And be it further enacted by the authority aforesaid, That such stamps as the said commissioners are hereby directed and authorized to provide and use, shall and may be altered and renewed, in such manner, as any other stamps on vellum, parchment or paper, are, by any former law relating to stamped vellum, parchment or paper, directed to be altered and renewed; and that all persons who shall have in their custody or possession, any vellum, parchment or paper, marked with the stamp or mark which shall be so altered or renewed, or on which, being already stamped with a stamp denoting any former duty, a new stamp is hereby directed to be impressed, shall have the like remedy and allowance as by any former law relating to stamped vellum, parchment or paper, is in like cases directed.

Duties to be
paid to the
receiver general of the
stamps ;
XXIII. And be it further enacted by the authority aforesaid, That the several duties herein before granted, shall be paid from time to time into the hands of the receiver general, for the time being, of the duties on stamped vellum, parchment and paper; who shall keep a separate and distinct account

of

of the several rates and duties, and pay the same (the necessary and paid by charges of raising, paying and accounting for the same, being him into the deducted) into the receipt of the exchequer, for the purposes exchequer. herein after expressed, at such time, and in such manner, as any former duties on stamped vellum, parchment or paper, are directed to be paid; and that in the office of the auditor of the said receipt shall be provided and kept a book or books, in which all the monies arising from the said several rates and duties, and paid into the said receipt as aforesaid, shall be entered separate and apart from all other monies paid and payable to his Majesty, his heirs or successors, upon any account whatsoever; and the These duties said money so paid into the said receipt of exchequer as afore- to be part of said, subject to the payment herein before directed to be made a fund. thereon, shall be part of the fund established by this act, for the several purposes in this act mentioned.

XXIV. And be it further enacted by the authority aforesaid, Commission- That the said commissioners, and all other officers who shall be ers and other employed in the collection or management of the said several officers to o- duties herein before granted, shall in the execution of their offi- ders of the ces, observe and perform such rules and orders, as they respec- treasury. tively shall from time to time receive from the commissioners of the treasury, or the treasurer of the exchequer for the time be- No fee to be ing; and that no fee or reward shall be taken or demanded taken by them. by any such commissioners or officers from any of his Majesty's subjects, for any matter or thing to be done in pursuance of this act; and in case any officer employed in the execution of this act, Officers to an- in relation to the said duties, shall refuse or neglect to do or per- swer all da- form any matter or thing by this act required to be done or per- mages occa- formed by him, whereby any of his Majesty's subjects shall or may sioned by ne- sustain any damage whatsoever, such officer so offending shall glect of duty. be liable by any action to be founded on this statute, to answer to the party grieved all such damage, with treble costs of suit.

XXV. And be it further enacted by the authority aforesaid, Commission- That the said commissioners, and their officers, shall be subject ers and officers to such penalties and forfeitures for any breach of the trust in liable to pe- them reposed, or for diverting or misapplying the money re- nalties, &c. ceived in pursuance of this act, as by any former law relating to for breach of stamped vellum, parchment or paper are inflicted; and that all trust, or mis- powers, provisions, articles, clauses, distribution of penalties application of and forfeitures, and all other matters and things prescribed or Powers, &c. appointed by any former act or acts of parliament relating to the of former acts duties on vellum, parchment and paper, on which any inden- relating to ture, lease, bond, or other deed, shall be ingrossed, written or stamps ex- printed, or to the rates and duties on news papers and adver- act. tisements, and almanacks, and not hereby altered, shall be in full force and effect, with relation to the additional duties here- by imposed, and shall be applied and put in execution for the raising, levying, collecting and securing the said additional and new rates and duties hereby imposed, according to the true in- tent and meaning of this act, as fully, to all intents and pur- poses, as if the same had severally and respectively been hereby enacted, with relation to the faid additional and new rates and duties hereby impofed.

XXVI. *And for preventing a diminution of the revenue arifing from the duties payable on almanacks, by fubjecting the venders of un-ftamped almanacks to the fame penalties as by an act made in the fix-teenth year of his prefent Majefty's reign, are inflicted on the venders of unftamped news papers;* be it enacted by the authority afore-said, That every perfon who, from and after the faid fifth day of *July* one thoufand feven hundred and fifty feven, fhall fell, utter or expofe to fale any almanack, liable to any duty by this or any former act impofed, fuch almanack not being ftamped or marked as by this or any former act is directed, every perfon fo offending fhall, for every fuch offence, be liable to the fame punifhment as is inflicted on any hawker of unftamped news papers by the faid act made in the fixteenth year of the reign of his prefent Majefty; and every juftice of the peace fhall have the like power to convict fuch offender, as by the faid act is granted, with relation to the conviction of offenders againft the faid act; and every perfon who fhall apprehend fuch of-fender, fhall be intitled to the like reward, as by the faid act is granted for the apprehenfion of offenders againft the faid act.

XXVII. And be it further enacted by the authority aforefaid, That if any perfon, from and after the faid fifth day of *July* one thoufand feven hundred and fifty feven, fhall counterfeit or forge, or procure to be counterfeited or forged, any feal, ftamp or mark, to refemble any feal, ftamp or mark, directed or al-lowed to be ufed by this or any other act of parliament for the purpofe of denoting the duties by this or any other act of par-liament granted, or fhall counterfeit or refemble the impreffion of the fame, with an intent to defraud his Majefty, his heirs and fucceffors, of any of the faid duties; or fhall utter, vend or fell, any vellum, parchment or paper liable to any ftamp-duty, with fuch counterfeit ftamp or mark, knowing the fame to be counterfeit; or fhall privately and fraudulently ufe any feal, ftamp or mark, directed or allowed to be ufed by this or any other act of parliament relating to the ftamp-duties, with intent to defraud his Majefty, his heirs and fucceffors, of any of the faid duties; every perfon fo offending, and being there-of lawfully convicted, fhall be adjudged a felon, and fhall fuffer death as in cafes of felony, without benefit of clergy.

XXVIII. *And whereas the duties upon coals exported to foreign parts in* Britifh *veffels, are lefs than the duties payable on coals car-ried coaftwife, to be ufed in this kingdom, whereby foreigners may be fupplied therewith at a lefs expence than the fubjects of this realm, to the great prejudice of the trade and manufactures of this kingdom; and an additional duty on coals fo exported, will be a proper aid to be granted to his Majefty, for the purpofes of this act;* be it enacted by the authority aforefaid, That from and after the faid fifth day of *July* one thoufand feven hundred and fifty feven, there fhall be raifed, levied, collected and paid to his Majefty, his heirs and fucceffors, for every chaldron of coals, *Newcaftle* meafure, which

fhall

16 G. 2. c. 26.
Hawkers of unftamped al-manacks, their punifhment.

Penalty of counterfeiting or forging the feals or ftamps, &c. death.

Additional duty on coals fhipped for foreign parts, not belonging to the Britifh dominions.

shall be shipt for exportation to any part beyond the seas, except to *Ireland*, the *Isle of Man*, or his Majesty's plantations, an additional duty of four shillings, and after the same rate for any greater or less quantity, over and above the present duties now payable for the same; which said additional duty hereby granted, shall be raised, levied, collected and paid, in the same manner, and under such penalties and forfeitures, and by such rules, ways and methods, as the former duties payable to his Majesty upon the exportation of coals, are raised, levied, collected and paid, as fully, and to all intents and purposes, as if the several clauses, powers, directions, penalties and forfeitures relating thereto, were particularly repeated, and again enacted in the body of this present act.

XXIX. And be it further enacted by the authority aforesaid, That in the office of the auditor of the receipt of the exchequer, a book or books shall be provided and kept, in which all the monies arising from the said additional duty, and paid into the said receipt, shall be entered separate and apart from all other monies paid or payable to his Majesty, his heirs and successors, upon any account whatsoever; and the said money so arising from the said additional duty, and paid into the said receipt of exchequer, shall be part of the fund established for the several purposes herein after mentioned. *Book to be kept by the auditor for entering the said duties separately. The said duties to be part of a fund.*

XXX. *And whereas by an act made in the sixteenth year of the reign of his present Majesty, intituled,* An act for repealing certain duties on spirituous liquors, and on licences for retailing the same; and for laying other duties on spirituous liquors, and on licences to retail the said liquors; *the sum of twenty shillings yearly is directed to be paid by every person retailing such liquors (except as is therein excepted) to be granted in the manner mentioned in the said act: and whereas by an act made in the same session of parliament, intituled,* An act for repealing the several rates and duties upon victuallers and retailers of beer and ale, within the cities of *London* and *Westminster*, and the weekly bills of mortality; and for transferring the exchequer bills unsatisfied thereupon, to the duties for licences to sell spirituous liquors and strong waters by retail; and also for enabling his Majesty to raise a sum of money, for the service of the year one thousand seven hundred and forty three, to be further charged on the said duties for licences; *it was amongst other things enacted, That from and after the twenty fourth day of* June *one thousand seven hundred and forty three, the several rates and duties imposed by an act made in the twelfth year of the reign of his late majesty King* George *the First, upon all victuallers and retailers of beer and ale, within the cities of* London *and* Westminster, *and the weekly bills of mortality, should cease and determine, and be no longer paid; and it was thereby also enacted, That from and after the said twenty fourth day of* June *the principal sum of four hundred and eighty one thousand four hundred pounds, in exchequer bills, part of the sum of five hundred thousand pounds, advanced by the governor and company of the bank of* England, *at an interest after the rate of three pounds* **Recital of clauses in two acts of 16 Geo. 2. c. 8. and c. 12.**

per

per centum per annum, which exchequer bills had been made forth inpursuance of the said act made in the twelfth year of the reign of his said late Majesty, and then remained unsatisfied and undischarged, together with the interest thereupon, and the charges of circulating the same, should be transferred from the said rates and duties then charged with the same, and be charged, together with the sum of five hundred eighteen thousand six hundred pounds directed to be raised by the afore recited act made in the sixteenth year of his present Majesty's reign, upon the duties granted by the said other act of parliament made in the sixteenth year of his present Majesty's reign: and whereas by an act made in the nineteenth year of the reign of his

19 Geo. 2. c. 6.

present Majesty, intituled, An act for establishing an agreement with the governor and company of the bank of *England*, for cancelling certain exchequer bills upon the terms therein mentioned; and for obliging them to advance the sum of one million upon the credit of the land tax and malt duties, granted to his Majesty for the service of the year one thousand seven hundred and forty six; *reciting, that in pursuance of the said recited act made in the sixteenth year of his present Majesty's reign, the said sum of four hundred eighty one thousand four hundred pounds, in exchequer bills, as also the said further sum of five hundred eighteen thousand six hundred pounds, amounting together to the principal sum of one million were charged upon the said duties arising from licences as aforesaid, at an interest after the rate of three pounds per centum per annum; and that the said exchequer bills, by paying off part of the said principal sums, did then amount to no more than the principal sum of nine hundred eighty six thousand eight hundred pounds; and also reciting, that the said governor and company of the bank of* England *were willing and contented that the said sum of nine hundred eighty six thousand eight hundred pounds, in exchequer bills, remaining unsatisfied on the said duties payable for licences to sell spirituous liquors by retail, might be cancelled and discharged, and in lieu thereof to accept of an annuity of thirty nine thousand four hundred and seventy two pounds, being the interest on the said sum, at the rate of four pounds per centum per annum, to be charged on the same securities: and further reciting, that the said governor and company were also willing, upon the terms by them proposed, to advance and pay into the receipt of his Majesty's exchequer, for the service of the year one thousand seven hundred and forty six, the sum of one million, upon the credit of the rates and duties and assessments arising by the malt and land tax, granted for the service of the said year, at four pounds per centum per annum, for exchequer bills to be issued for that purpose, it was thereby enacted, That all the said exchequer bills charged upon the said duties, should be discharged, cancelled and made void, and the interest thereof, together with the charges of circulating the same, should be fully cleared and paid off; and that in lieu of the said principal sum of nine hundred eighty six thousand eight hundred pounds, in exchequer bills, the said governor and company should be intitled to have and receive at his Majesty's exchequer, one annuity or yearly sum of thirty nine thousand four hundred and seventy two pounds, being after the rate of four pounds* per centum per annum,

and

and upon the said principal sum to be paid in the manner mentioned in the said act, till the redemption thereof by parliament, with such provisions for making good the deficiencies of the said rates and duties as are in the said act contained: and whereas by another act made in the twentieth year of the reign of his present Majesty, intituled, An act 20 Geo. 2. c. 39. *for granting a duty to his Majesty to be paid by distillers, upon licences taken out by them for retailing spirituous liquors; the several distillers within the cities of* London *and* Westminster, *borough of* Southwark, *or weekly bills of mortality, are permitted to take out yearly licences for retailing spirituous liquors, upon payment of five pounds for every such licence: and whereas by an act made* and 24 Geo. 2. *in the twenty fourth year of the reign of his present Majesty, intituled,* c. 40. An act for granting to his present Majesty an additional duty upon spirituous liquors, and upon licences for retailing of the same; and for repealing the act made in the twentieth year of his present Majesty's reign, *intituled,* An act for granting a duty to his Majesty to be paid by distillers, upon licences to be taken out by them for retailing spirituous liquors; and for the more effectual restraining the retailing of distilled spirituous liquors; and for allowing a drawback upon the exportation of *British* made spirits; and that the parish of Saint *Mary le Bon* in the county of *Middlesex* shall be under the inspection of the head office of excise; *it is enacted, That from and after the twenty fourth day of* June *one thousand seven hundred and fifty one, the said duty of five pounds payable by every distiller for a licence to sell spirituous liquors by retail, shall cease, determine, and be no longer paid; and that in lieu of the said duty, an additional duty of twenty shillings per annum, should be paid for every licence to be taken out for retailing spirituous liquors: and whereas the said last mentioned duty, not being by the last mentioned act appropriated, is subject to the disposition of parliament: and whereas the said several duties of twenty shillings, and twenty shillings, for yearly licences, to retail spirituous, have not been paid into the receipt of his Majesty's exchequer, distinctly and apart from each other, but on account thereof hath been kept as if the same were consolidated, and the surplus of the said duties so united, after reserving sufficient to pay the annuity due to the bank of* England *on the credit of the first of the said duties, which is now, in consequence of an act made in the twenty third year of the reign of his present Majesty for reducing the rates of interest of the several annuities therein mentioned, reduced to the yearly sum of thirty four thousand five hundred and thirty eighty pounds, and will in consequence of the said act be from and after the fifth day of* January *one thousand seven hundred and fifty eight, reduced to twenty nine thousand six hundred and four pounds, hath from time to time, been disposed of by parliament for the publick service: and whereas the revenue arising from the said several duties so united, will be more than sufficient to pay the said annuity, and the security of the governor and company of the bank of* England, *for the payment thereof will be enlarged by charging the said annuity, as well on the said duty granted by the act made in the twenty fourth year of his present Majesty's reign, as on the said former duty granted by an act* made

*made in the sixteenth year of his prefent Majefty's reign, and it will
be for the publick fervice to grant the furplus of the faid duties fo
united, for the purpofes of this act, in addition to the feveral rates
and duties hereby impofed*; be it further enacted by the authority

Surplus of the former duties on licences for retailing fpirituous liquors, to be kept apart,

aforefaid, That from and after the tenth day of *October* one
thoufand feven hundred and fifty fix, the furplus or remainder
of the monies arifen, or which fhall from time to time arife,
by the faid feveral rates and duties on licences for retailing fpirituous liquors, after paying and referving, from time to time,
at the receipt of his Majefty's exchequer, money fufficient to
fatisfy and pay the faid annuity due and payable to the governor
and company of the bank of *England* as aforefaid, fhall at the faid
receipt of exchequer, be kept diftinctly and apart from all other

and to go towards paying the annuities granted by this act.

branches of the publick revenue ; and the fame fhall be and is
hereby declared to be, an additional fund and fecurity for payment of the feveral annuities granted by this act, in the manner herein after mentioned, and for no other ufe or purpofe
whatfoever.

The additional duties, and furplus aforefaid, appropriated to the payment of the annuities granted by this act.

XXXI. And be it further enacted by the authority aforefaid,
That the feveral annuities which by this act fhall be granted and
made payable, with refpect of the principal fum of three millions, to be raifed in manner and form as is hereafter directed,
fhall be charged and chargeable upon and payable out of the feveral additional and new rates and duties by this act impofed on
ftampt vellum, parchment and paper, whereon the faid indentures, leafes, bonds, or other deeds, fhall be ingroffed, written
or printed; and alfo upon and out of the faid additional and
new duties on news papers, advertifements, almanacks; and
alfo upon and out of the faid duty on licences for retailing
wine; and alfo upon and out of the furplus of the duties upon
licences for retailing fpirituous liquors; and alfo upon and out
of the faid additional duty on coals exported to foreign parts;
and the faid feveral additional and new rates and duties, and
the faid furplus, are hereby appropriated for that purpofe accordingly.

XXXII. *And whereas feveral perfons have fubfcribed towards
the faid fum of three millions for the purchafe of annuities, after the
rate of three pounds* per centum per annum, *transferrable at the
bank of* England, *and redeemable by parliament; and alfo of annuities for lives, payable for every one hundred pounds contributed, after
the rate of one pound two fhillings and fix pence* per centum per
annum; *and the faid fubfcribers or contributors have, in purfuance
of the refolutions of the commons of* Great Britain *in parliament affembled, depofited with and paid to, the firft or chief cafhier or cafhiers of the governor and company of the bank of* England, *fifteen pounds
for every one hundred pounds by them refpectively fubfcribed, and are
defirous to pay the remaining principal fums by them fubfcribed as
aforefaid, at the times and in the manner herein after appointed in
that behalf*; be it therefore enacted by the authority aforefaid,

Contributors who have paid into the bank 15l. per cent.

That it fhall and may be lawful to and for all fuch refpective contributors who have already depofited with or paid to, the faid
                                                        cafhier

cashier or cashiers of the said governor and company of the bank of England, the sum of fifteen pounds for every one hundred pounds by them subscribed respectively, to advance and pay unto the said cashier or cashiers of the governor and company of the bank of *England*, the remaining sums by them subscribed respectively towards the said sum of three millions, on or before the respective days or times, and in the proportions in this act hereafter limited in that behalf; that is to say, the sum of ten pounds *per centum*, being part of the sum so remaining, on or before the fourth day of *June* one thousand seven hundred and fifty seven; the sum of fifteen pounds *per centum*, other part thereof, on or before the seventh day of *July* then next following; the sum of fifteen pounds *per centum*, other part thereof, on or before the eighteenth day of *August* then next following; the sum of fifteen pounds *per centum*, other part thereof, on or before the twenty first day of *September* then next following; the sum of fifteen pounds *per centum*, other part thereof, on or before the tenth day of *November* then next following; and the remaining sum of fifteen pounds *per centum*, on or before the twenty second day of *December* then next following.

towards purchasing annuities under this act, are to pay the remainder of their subscriptions, viz. 10l per cent. by 4 June, 15l. per cent. by 7 July, 15l. per cent. by 18 August, 15l. per cent. by 21 Sept. 15 per cent. by 10 Nov. and 15l. per cent. by 22 December.

XXXIII. And be it further enacted by the authority aforesaid, That every such contributor, for and in respect of every one hundred pounds by him subscribed, shall be intituled to an annuity after the rate of three pounds *per centum per annum* transferrable at the bank of *England*, and redeemable by parliament; and shall also be intitled for every one hundred pounds so subscribed, to an annuity for life, after the rate of one pound two shillings and six pence *per centum per annum*.

Contributor intitled to 3l. per cent. transferrable annuities, and an annuity for life of 1l. 2s. 6d. per cent.

XXXIV. And be it further enacted by the authority aforesaid, That the annuities which shall become due and payable to the several contributors, their executors, administrators and assigns, after the rate of three pounds *per centum per annum*, shall commence and be computed from the said fifth day of *July* one thousand seven hundred and fifty seven, and shall be paid by half-yearly payments, by even and equal portions, on the fifth day of *January* and the fifth day of *July* in every year; and that the annuities for lives which shall be due and payable, after the rate of one pound two shillings and six pence *per centum per annum*, shall be paid in like manner, by half-yearly payments, by even and equal portions, on the fifth day of *January* and the fifth day of *July* in every year; the first half-yearly payment to be made on the fifth day of *January* one thousand seven hundred and fifty eight, if such contributors respectively shall, on or before that time, have appointed their nominees; or upon such of the said half-yearly days of payment, as shall be next after the respective appointments of their nominees.

3l. per cent. annuities to commence from 5 July 1757. and to be paid half-yearly. Life annuities to be paid half-yearly also.

XXXV. And be it further enacted by the authority aforesaid, That the said cashier or cashiers of the governor and company of the bank of *England* who shall have received, or shall receive any part of the said contributions towards the said sum of three millions, shall give receipts in writing to every such contributor.

Receipts to be given to contributors for money paid in by them; which may be assigned.

tributor for all such sums; and that the receipts to be so given shall be assignable by indorsement thereupon made, at any time before the fifth day of *January* one thousand seven hundred and fifty eight, and no longer.

Cashier of the bank to give security;

XXXVI. Provided always, That such cashier or cashiers shall give security to the good liking of any three or more of the commissioners of the treasury for the time being, or the high treasurer for the time being, for duly answering and paying into the receipt of his Majesty's exchequer for the publick use, all the monies which they have already received, and shall here-after receive, from time to time, of and for the said sum of three millions, and for accounting duly for the same, and for per-

and pay the monies into the exchequer.

formance of the trust hereby in them reposed; and shall from time to time pay all such monies so received, and account for the same in the exchequer, according to the due course thereof.

Treasury to apply the money to the services voted by the commons.

XXXVII. And be it further enacted by the authority afore-said, That it shall and may be lawful for three or more of the commissioners of the treasury, or the high treasurer for the time being, to issue and apply, from time to time, all such sums of money as shall be so paid into the receipt of his Majesty's exche-quer by the said cashier or cashiers, to such services as shall then have been voted by the commons of *Great Britain* in this pre-sent session of parliament.

Contributors names to be entered in books at the bank.

XXXVIII. And be it further enacted by the authority afore-said, That in the office of the accomptant general of the governor and company of the bank of *England* for the time being, a book or books shall be provided and kept, in which the names of the said contributors shall be fairly entered, which book or books the said respective contributors, their respective executors, ad-ministrators and assigns, shall and may, from time to time, and at all seasonable times, resort to and inspect, without any fee or charge; and that the said accomptant general shall, on or before

Duplicate thereof to be transmitted to the exche-quer.

the fifth day of *July* one thousand seven hundred and fifty eight, transmit an attested duplicate fairly written on paper, of the said book or books, into the office of the auditor of the receipt of his Majesty's exchequer, there to remain for ever.

Contributors duly paying their subscrip-tions,

XXXIX. And be it further enacted by the authority afore-said, That such contributors duly paying the whole sum sub-scribed, at or before the respective times in this act limited in that behalf, and their respective executors, administrators and assigns, shall have, receive and enjoy, and be intitled by virtue of this act, to have, receive and enjoy, the said several annui-ties by this act granted in respect of the sum so subscribed, out of the monies by this act appropriated for payment thereof, and

to have sure estates in the annuities,

shall have good and sure interests and estates therein, according to the several provisions in this act contained, as well in respect of the said transferrable annuities, after the rate of three pounds *per centum per annum*, as of the said annuities for lives, after the rate of one pound two shillings and six pence *per centum per an-*

and the same to be tax-free.

num, and that the said several annuities shall be free from all taxes, charges and impositions whatsoever.

XL. And be it further enacted by the authority aforesaid,
That

That as soon as such respective contributors, their respective executors, administrators and assigns, shall have completed the payment of the monies by them respectively subscribed towards the said sum of three millions, for the purchase of the said several annuities, such sums, for and in respect of such transferrable annuities, after the rate of three pounds *per centum per annum*, in which they shall become interested, shall, from and after the fifth day of *July* one thousand seven hundred and fifty seven, be placed to their credit, and made transferrable in the books of the bank of *England* to be kept for that purpose.

On completing their payments, contributors to have their annuities placed to their credit, and the same to be transferrable.

XLI. Provided always, That in case any such contributors who have already deposited with, or shall hereafter pay to the said cashiers, any sum or sums of money at the times and in the manner before mentioned, in part of the sums so by them respectively subscribed, or their respective executors, administrators and assigns, shall not advance or pay to the said cashier or cashiers the residue of the sums so subscribed, at the times and in the manner before mentioned; then and in every such case, so much of the respective sums so subscribed as shall have been actually paid in part thereof to the said cashier or cashiers, shall be forfeited for the benefit of the publick; any thing in this act contained to the contrary thereof in any wise notwithstanding.

Contributors not duly paying the whole of their subscriptions, forfeit what they shall have paid.

XLII. And be it further enacted by the authority aforesaid, That the several annuities which by this act are granted and made payable in respect of the said sum of three millions, shall be charged and chargeable upon, and payable out of the several rates, duties, and sums of money, composing the fund hereby established for the payment thereof, and the said several rates, duties and sums of money are hereby appropriated for that purpose accordingly.

The duties and sums granted by this act to be a fund for payment of the annuities.

XLIII. And be it further enacted by the authority aforesaid, That the said accomptant general for the bank of *England* for the time being, shall, in a book or books to be provided and kept for that purpose, give credit to the said respective contributors, and their respective executors, administrators and assigns, for the principal sums by them respectively subscribed and paid; and the persons to whose credit such principal sums shall be so placed, their respective executors, administrators and assigns, shall and may have power to assign and transfer the same, or any part, share, or proportion thereof, to any other person or persons, or body or bodies politick or corporate whatsoever, in other books to be provided and kept by the said accomptant general for that purpose; and every principal sum so assigned and transferred, shall carry an annuity after the rate of three pounds *per centum per annum*, and shall be taken and deemed to be stock transferrable according to the true intent and meaning of this act, until redemption thereof by parliament, according to a proviso herein after contained for that purpose.

Contributors to have credit in proper books, for the sums paid in by them;

the same to be transferred in other books.

Annuities deemed transferrable stock.

XLIV. And, for the more easy and sure payment of the said transferrable annuities after the rate of three pounds per centum per annum; be it further enacted by the authority aforesaid, That the said governor and company of the bank of *England*,

A chief cashier and accomptant general, to be employed at the bank.

and their successors, shall, from time to time, until the said annuities, after the rate of three pounds *per centum per annum*, shall be redeemed as aforesaid, appoint and employ one or more sufficient person or persons within their office in the city of *London*, to be their chief or first cashier or cashiers, and one other sufficient person within the same office, to be their accomptant general; and that so much of the monies from time to time arising into the said receipt of the exchequer, from the said rates and duties, and sums of money by this act granted and appropriated, as shall be sufficient, from time to time, for payment of the said annuities, after the rate of three pounds *per centum per annum*, shall, by order of the commissioners of the treasury, or any three or more of them, or the treasurer of the exchequer for the time being, without any further or other warrant to be sued for, had and obtained, in that behalf, from time to time, at the respective half-yearly days of payment in this act appointed for payment thereof, be issued and paid at the said receipt of exchequer, to the said first or chief cashier or cashiers of the said governor and company of the bank of *England*, and their successors for the time being, by way of imprest, and upon account for payment of the said annuities, after the rate of three pounds *per centum per annum*, at such times, and in such manner and form, as are by the said act prescribed in that behalf; and that such cashier or cashiers, to whom the said money shall from time to time, be issued, shall from time to time, without delay, apply and pay the same accordingly, and render his or their account thereof, according to the due course of the exchequer.

Treasury to issue money from time to time, to the said cashier, for payment of the annuities.

XLV. And be it further enacted by the authority aforesaid, That the said accomptant general for the time being shall from time to time inspect and examine all receipts and payments of the said cashier or cashiers, and the vouchers relating thereto, in order to prevent any fraud, negligence or delay; and that all persons who shall be intitled to any of the said annuities after the rate of three pounds *per centum per annum*, and all persons lawfully claiming under them, shall be possessed thereof as of a personal estate, which shall not be descendible to heirs, nor liable to any foreign attachment by the custom of *London* or otherwise; any law, statute or custom, to the contrary notwithstanding.

Accomptant general to inspect the receipts and payments.

Annuities to be deemed a personal estate.

XLVI. And be it further enacted by the authority aforesaid, That all the monies to be advanced or contributed by virtue of this act, towards the said sum of three millions, on which the said annuities, after the rate of three pounds *per centum per annum*, shall be attending, shall be deemed one capital and joint stock; and that all persons and corporations whatsoever, in proportion to the monies by them severally advanced, for the purchase of the said annuities, after the rate of three pounds *per centum per annum*, or to which they shall become intitled by virtue of this act, shall have and be deemed to have a proportional interest and share in the said stock, and in the said annuities attending the same, at the rate aforesaid; and that the said whole capital

Sums contributed to be deemed a joint stock;

capital or joint stock, or any share or interest therein, shall be *and may be assigned or transferred.* assignable and transferrable as this act directs, and not otherwise.

XLVII. Provided also, and it is hereby enacted by the authority aforesaid, That at any time upon one year's notice to be *Annuities declared to be redeemable by parliament.* printed in the *London Gazette*, and affixed upon the *Royal Exchange in London*, and upon repayment by parliament of the said sum of three millions, or any part thereof, by payments not less than five hundred thousand pounds at one time, in such manner as shall be directed by any future act or acts of parliament in that behalf, and also upon full payment of all arrearages of the said annuities after the rate of three pounds *per centum per annum*, then, and not till then, such or so much of the said annuities as shall be attending on the principal sums so paid off, shall cease and determine, and be understood to be redeemed; and that any vote or resolution of the house of commons, signified by the speaker in writing, to be inserted in the *London Gazette*, and affixed on the *Royal Exchange* in *London* as aforesaid, shall be deemed and adjudged to be sufficient notice within the words and meaning of this act.

XLVIII. And be it further enacted by the authority aforesaid, *Books to be kept for entering assignments or transfers of annuities.* That books shall be constantly kept by the said accomptant general for the time being, wherein all assignments or transfers of the said annuities, after the rate of three pounds *per centum per annum*, shall at all seasonable times be entered and registered; which entry shall be conceived in proper words for that purpose, and shall be signed by the parties making such assignments or transfers; or if such parties be absent, by their respective attornies, thereunto lawfully authorized in writing under their hands and seals, to be attested by two or more credible witnesses; and that the several persons to whom such transfers shall be made, shall respectively under-write their acceptance thereof; and that no other method of assigning and transferring the said annuities, or any part thereof, or any interest therein, shall be good or available in law. *Method of assigning and transferring the same.*

XLIX. Provided always, That all persons possessed of any *Annuities may be devised by will.* share in the said joint stock of annuities, or estate and interest therein, may devise the same by will in writing, attested by two or more credible witnesses; but that no payment shall be made *Entry to be made thereof.* on any such devise, till so much of the said will as relates to any share, estate, or interest in the said joint stock of annuities, be entered in the said office; and that in default of such transfer or devise, such share, estate, or interest in the said joint stock of annuities, shall go to the executors or administrators; and *Stamp duties not chargeable on transfers.* that no stamp duties whatsoever, shall be charged on any of the said transfers; any law or statute to the contrary notwithstanding.

L. Provided always, and be it enacted by the authority aforesaid, That out of the monies arising from the contributions to- *Treasury to defray all incidental charges.* wards raising the said sum of three millions, any three or more of the commissioners of the treasury, or the high treasurer for the time being, shall have power to discharge all such incident charges

charges as shall necessarily attend the execution of this act, in

and to settle the allowances to be made to the cashiers and accomptant general, such manner as to them shall seem just and reasonable; and also to settle and appoint such allowances as shall be thought proper for the service, pains and labour, of the said cashier or cashiers, for receiving, paying and accounting for the said contributions; and also shall have power to make out of the fund hereby established, or out of the sinking fund, such further allowances as shall be judged reasonable for the service, pains and labour of the said cashier or cashiers, for receiving, paying and accounting for the said annuities, after the rate of three pounds *per*

to be at the disposal of the governor and company of the bank. *centum per annum*, payable by virtue of this act; and also for the service, pains and labour of the said accomptant general, for performing the trust reposed in him by this act; all which allowances to be made as aforesaid, in respect to the service, pains and labour of any officer or officers of the said governor and company, shall be for the use and benefit of the said governor and company, and at their disposal only.

Bank to continue a corporation till the annuities are are redeemed. LI. Provided always, and be it enacted by the authority aforesaid, That the said governor and company of the bank of *England*, and their successors, notwithstanding the redemption of all or any their own funds, in pursuance of the acts for establishing the same, or any of them, shall continue a corporation till all the said annuities, after the rate of three pounds *per centum per annum*, by this act granted, shall be redeemed by parliament, according to the proviso herein before contained in that behalf; and that the said governor and company of the bank of *England*, or any member thereof, shall not incur any disability for or by reason of their doing any matter or thing in pursuance of this act.

LII. *And whereas in pursuance of a resolution of the commons of* Great Britain *in parliament assembled, divers persons did subscribe the sum of three hundred thirteen thousand one hundred pounds, and no more, towards the sum of two millions five hundred thousand pounds, by the said resolution directed to be raised in manner therein mentioned, by annuities for lives, with the benefit of survivorship, or for terms of years certain: and whereas by a subsequent resolution of the commons of* Great Britain *in parliament assembled, all subscribers towards the said sum of two millions five hundred thousand pounds, pursuant to the said former resolution, who, instead of the annuities therein mentioned, should choose to accept the annuities proposed by the said subsequent resolution, and who, on or before the fourth day of* May *one thousand seven hundred and fifty seven, should, in books to be opened at the bank of* England *for that purpose, express their consent, or not express their dissent thereunto, were, upon their compliance with the terms in the subsequent resolution last-mentioned, for every one hundred pounds so by them subscribed, intitled to the several annuities by the said subsequent resolution proposed; in which case the sums so by them before advanced, were to be deemed part of their contribution, for the purchase of the annuities, by the subsequent resolution proposed: and whereas several of the persons so subscribing the sum of three hundred thirteen thousand one hundred*

pounds,

pounds, towards the sum of two millions five hundred thousand pounds, directed to be raised on the terms of the said first mentioned resolution, induced by the allowance of three pounds per centum, stipulated by the said resolution to be made to them for all previous payments, may have advanced more than the sum of fifteen pounds per centum, by the said last-mentioned resolution directed to be paid by way of deposit for every one hundred pounds subscribed; be it enacted by the authority aforesaid, That the first or chief cashier or cashiers of the governor and company of the bank of England, shall restore to every such subscriber who, before the fourth day of June one thousand seven hundred and fifty seven, shall have demanded restitution thereof, so much money as shall exceed the amount of such deposit, together with interest for the same, after the rate of three pounds per centum per annum, from the time of such previous payments to the time of such demand; the said interest to be paid by the said cashier or cashiers out of the monies contributed by virtue of this act.

Subscribers to the sum of 2,500,000l. pursuant to a former resolution of the commons accepting of the present terms, to be repaid with interest so much of their deposit money as exceeds 15l. per cent. of the sums subscribed.

LIII. *And whereas several of the persons who subscribed towards the said sum of two millions five hundred thousand pounds, on the terms of the said first-mentioned resolution, may have been prevented, either by absence or ignorance of the said last-mentioned resolution, from complying with the terms thereof*; be it enacted by the authority aforesaid, That all such persons shall be at liberty, if they think fit, at any time before the fourth day of June one thousand seven hundred and fifty seven, either to demand restitution of the deposit of ten pounds per centum, made by them on the terms of the said first-mentioned resolution, which the said cashier or cashiers is and are hereby required to return accordingly, or to subscribe the like sums on the terms of the resolution last-mentioned; and that in the stead of any person or persons so demanding and obtaining restitution of the sums by him, her or them subscribed, towards the said sum of two millions five hundred thousand pounds, directed to be raised in pursuance of the said first-mentioned resolution, any other person or persons shall, on or before the fourth day of June one thousand seven hundred and fifty seven, be admitted to subscribe towards completing the sum directed to be raised in pursuance of the resolution last-mentioned, he, she or they, paying at the time of such subscription the several sums then payable according to the terms of the said resolution.

Time allowed to subscribers to the former scheme to withdraw or subscribe into this.

Others may subscribe in their room.

LIV. *And whereas for the greater encouragement of persons to become contributors to the said sum of three millions, directed by this act to be raised, it is intended that each contributor shall for every one hundred pounds contributed be also intitled to an annuity for life, after the rate of one pound two shillings and six pence per centum per annum*; be it further enacted by the authority aforesaid, That every person who shall advance and pay unto the said cashier or cashiers of the governor and company of the bank of England, at or before the respective days and times, and in the respective proportions herein before directed, the principal sum of one hundred pounds, or divers entire sums of one hundred pounds,

Contributors to have an annuity for life of 1l. 2s. 6d. for every 100l. paid in, for the purchase of the annuities granted by this act, shall, for or in respect of every principal sum of one hundred pounds so to be advanced and paid, be intitled to have and receive at the receipt of his Majesty's exchequer during his or her life, or the life of some other person, to be nominated by him or her, or by his or her assigns, an annuity of one pound two shillings and six pence *per centum per annum*, over and above the annuity of three pounds *per centum per annum*, before by this act made payable at the bank of *England* to each contributor of one hundred pounds; which annuity so payable at the exchequer as aforesaid, shall be paid by half-yearly payments, on the fifth day of *January* and the fifth day of *July* in every year; the first payment thereof to be made on the fifth day of *January* one thousand seven hundred and fifty eight, if such contributors respectively shall on or before that time have appointed their nominees in manner herein after-mentioned, or upon such of the said half-yearly days of payment as shall be next after the respective appointments of their nominees; and that the said cashier or cashiers of the governor and company of the bank of *England*, shall, as soon as he or they shall have received from any such contributor forty pounds *per centum*, of the several sums by them respectively subscribed, forthwith give to such contributor or his or her assigns, a certificate by him or them signed, directed to the auditor of the receipt of his Majesty's exchequer, to be printed or written upon cheque paper, and cut out indentwise, through some flourish or device, to be contrived by the said cashiers, containing the names and additions of such contributors, or his or her assigns, together with the annuity payable to him, her or them, in respect of the sum so contributed; which certificate shall be assignable by indorsement thereon to be made and witnessed by two persons at any time or times before the fifth day of *January* one thousand seven hundred and fifty eight; and that in order to prevent the auditor of the said receipt from being imposed upon by any counterfeit or forged certificate, the said cashiers shall transmit to the said auditor the counterpart of the cheques of all the certificates given by them to such contributors as aforesaid; upon which counterparts shall be expressed the number of such certificate, the contributors name, and the annuity contained therein.

over and above the annuity of 3l. per cent. per annum, to be paid half-yearly.

Cashier to give to contributors, on payment of 40l. per cent. certificates,

which may be assigned.

Counterpart of the cheques of certificates to be transmitted to the auditor of the exchequer.

LV. And be it further enacted by the authority aforesaid, That the same cashier or cashiers shall, within seven days after the said twenty second day of *December* one thousand seven hundred and fifty seven, transmit to the auditor of the said receipt of the exchequer a book fairly written on paper, signed by him or them, containing the names of the several contributors towards raising the said sum of three millions, the principal sums by them respectively paid, and the annuities payable in respect thereof, at the rate aforesaid, to the end that the said auditor may be thereby satisfied that the full and entire sum payable by each contributor, hath been paid to such cashier or cashiers; which books shall remain in the office of the auditor of the said receipt for ever.

Cashier to transmit to the auditor, a book of the contributors names, and sums paid.

LVI. And

LVI. And be it further enacted by the authority aforefaid, That every fuch contributor, or fuch other perfon as fhall be poffeffed of any fuch certificate by this act directed to be given by any fuch cafhier, fhall, before the fifth day of *January* one thoufand feven hundred and fifty eight, deliver, or caufe to be delivered, every certificate fo to him or her given, to be exchanged for orders to be made out in the manner herein after mentioned ; and fhall alfo at the fame time name to the faid auditor, his or her own, or fome other life, during which he or fhe, or his or her affigns, fhall be intitled to receive a dividend or fhare of the yearly fund by this act directed to be fet apart, out of the faid feveral rates, duties and fums of money, by this act granted to his Majefty, upon pain of forfeiting not only the half-year's annuity which fhall become due and payable to him or her, or his or her affigns, on the fifth day of *January* one thoufand feven hundred and fifty eight, in refpect of every principal fum of one hundred pounds, to be advanced as aforefaid, but alfo all fubfequent half-yearly payments, until he or fhe, or his or her affigns, fhall have produced to the auditor of the receipt fuch certificate or certificates, and fhall have appointed a nominee or nominees as aforefaid.

Contributors to bring their certificates to be exchanged for orders, and to name nominees for the life annuities.

LVII. And be it further enacted by the authority aforefaid, That the auditor of the faid receipt of exchequer fhall, as foon as conveniently may be after fuch certificate or certificates fhall be delivered to him, caufe fuch and fo many order or orders for payment of fuch annuities, to be made out in the exchequer for fuch certificate or certificates, as fhall be defired by the faid feveral and refpective contributors, or their affigns ; taking care that the annuity or annuities made payable by fuch order or orders, do not exceed in the whole the annuity or annuities fpecified and expreffed in fuch certificate or certificates, in exchange for which fuch order or orders fhall be fo made out as aforefaid ; which order or orders fhall be made out upon vellum or parchment, and fhall contain the names, firnames, additions and places of abode, of the refpective contributors or their affigns, and of their nominees, and the reputed ages and parents of their nominees, with other defcriptions, which fhall beft afcertain the perfon of fuch nominees ; and alfo the annuities payable during the lives of fuch refpective nominees out of the yearly fund herein after directed to be fet apart for that purpofe ; and all fuch orders fhall be figned by the commiffioners of the treafury, or any three or more of them, or the high treafurer for the time being ; and after figning thereof, the fame fhall be firm, good, valid and effectual in law, according to the purpofe and true meaning thereof, and of this act, and fhall not be determinable by or upon the deaths or removals of any commiffioner or commiffioners of the treafury, or high treafurer ; nor fhall they, or any of them, have power to revoke, countermand, or make void, fuch orders fo figned as aforefaid.

Such a number of orders for certificates to be made out as the contributors fhall defire ;

the fame to be figned by 3 commiffioners of the treafury.

LVIII. And it is hereby enacted, That in the offices of the auditor of the faid receipt of the exchequer, and clerk of the

Books to be provided at the exchequer

for entering the names of contributors, assigns and nominees.

pells severally, there shall be provided and kept one or more book or books, in which shall be fairly entered the names of all such contributors, or their assigns, and their nominees, during whose lives respectively the several dividends of the said yearly fund hereafter directed to be set apart shall be payable, at the time when the same shall be nominated as aforesaid; which books it shall be lawful for the respective contributors, their executors, administrators or assigns, from time to time, to have resort to, and to inspect without fee or reward.

The yearly sum of 33,750l. appropriated for payment of life annuities.

LIX. And it is hereby further enacted by the authority aforesaid, That out of the monies arising by virtue of this act, there shall yearly and every year be separated and kept apart at the said receipt of exchequer, the sum of thirty three thousand seven hundred and fifty pounds; which said sum of thirty three thousand seven hundred and fifty pounds shall be, and is hereby declared to be a yearly fund, for answering and paying the annuities as aforesaid, and shall yearly and every year be equally divided among the said contributors, their executors, administrators or assigns, during the lives of their respective nominees, in proportion to the principal sums by them advanced, by two equal half

Payment to be made half-yearly.

yearly payments; that is to say, on the fifth day of *January* and fifth day of *July* in every year; the first payment thereupon to be made on the fifth day of *January* one thousand seven hundred and fifty eight, if such contributors respectively shall, on or before that time, have appointed their nominees, or upon such of the said half yearly days of payment, as shall be next after the respective appointments of their nominees.

Annuity to cease upon the death of the nominee.

LX. And be it further enacted by the authority aforesaid, That upon the death of every such nominee, the share of the said fund which was payable during his or her life, shall cease and determine.

Orders may be assigned toties quoties during the life of the respective nominees.

LXI. And be it further enacted by the authority aforesaid, That it shall and may be lawful to any such contributor, or his or her executors, administrators or assigns, at any time during the life of his or her nominee or nominees, by proper words of assignment to be indorsed on his or her, or their order, to be witnessed by two persons, to assign or transfer his, her or their right, title, interest, and benefit of such order or orders, to any other person or persons; which being notified in the office of the auditor of the said receipt of the exchequer, the officers there shall cause an entry or memorial thereof to be made in the book of registry for such orders, without fee or charge; and after such entry made, such assignments shall intitle such assignee or assignees, his, her or their executors, administrators or assigns, to the benefit thereof, and payment thereon; and such assignee or assignees may, in like manner, assign again, and so *toties quoties*; and afterwards it shall not be in the power of such person or persons who shall make such assignment, to make void, release, or discharge the same, or any monies thereby due, or any part thereof.

LXII. And, for preventing all frauds in receiving any share of the yearly fund hereby appointed to be set apart as aforesaid; be be it further enacted by the authority aforefaid, That every contributor, his or her executors, adminiftrators, affigns or agents, upon demand of any half yearly payment of his or her refpective fhares of the faid yearly fund (unlefs the nominee appears in perfon at the faid receipt) fhall produce a certificate of the life of his, her or their refpective nominee, figned by the minifter and churchwardens of the parifh where fuch nominee fhall be then living, upon the day when the faid half yearly payments fhall become due (if fuch nominee fhall be then refiding in that part of *Great Britain* called *England*, dominion of *Wales*, or town of *Berwick* upon *Tweed*) or otherwife, it fhall and may be lawful to and for every fuch contributor, or his or her executors, adminiftrators or affigns, at his or her election, to make oath of the truth of his, her or their refpective nominee's life upon the day when the faid half yearly payment fhall become due, before one or more juftices of the peace of the refpective county, riding, city, town or place, wherein fuch perfon, at the time of making fuch oath, fhall refide; and in like manner every fuch contributor, his or their executors, adminiftrators, affigns or agents, whofe nominee fhall refide in any town or place, being extraparochial, upon the day where any of the faid half yearly payments fhall become due, fhall make a like oath before any fuch juftice or juftices aforefaid, of the life of fuch nominee on that day (which oath the faid juftice or juftices of the peace are hereby impowered to adminifter) and fuch juftice or juftices fhall make a certificate thereof; for which oath and certificate no fee or reward fhall be demanded or paid; and the faid certificate fhall be filed in the office of the auditor of the faid receipt of the exchequer.

At demanding the annuity, certificate from the minifter and churchwardens to be produced of the life of the nominee, if refident in England

or the fame to be certified, on oath, before a juftice;

and in places extraparochial

The certificates to be filed in the auditor's office.

LXIII. And be it further enacted by the authority aforefaid, That if any perfon fhall be guilty of a falfe oath, or fhall forge any certificate touching the premiffes, and be thereof lawfully convicted, fuch perfon fhall incur the pains and penalties inflicted upon perfons committing wilful perjury and forgery.

Penalty of making a falfe oath, or forging a certificate;

LXIV. And be it further enacted by the authority aforefaid, That in cafe any nominee fhall, at the time of fuch demand, be refident in that part of *Great Britain* called *Scotland*, or in the kingdom of *Ireland*, and any one or more of the barons of the *exchequer* there for the time being fhall certify, that upon proof to him or them made (which proof he and they is and are hereby authorized and required to take in a fummary way) it doth feem probable to him or them that the faid nominee is living (which certificate is to be given on examination made without fee or charge) the faid certificate being filed as aforefaid, fhall be a fufficient warrant for making the faid half yearly payment to the refpective contributors, their executors, adminiftrators or affigns; and in cafe any fuch nominee fhall, at the time of fuch demand, be refident in any parts beyond the feas, the proprietors of all fuch orders, or their agents, fhall produce certificates of the life of his, her or their refpective nominees, under the hand of the *Britifh* minifter refiding at the place where any fuch nominee fhall be

Nominee being refident in Scotland, or Ireland, barons of the exchequer there to grant certificates;

if refident in foreign parts, the Britifh minifter, if any,

liying upon the day when such half yearly payment shall become due; which certificates shall be given without fee or reward; and in case no *British* minister shall reside at the place where any such nominee shall live, then the said proprietors of such orders, or such agents, shall produce a certificate of the life of his, her or their respective nominees, under the hand and seal of the chief magistrate of any city, town or place, where any such nominee shall be then living upon the day when the said half yearly payment shall become due as aforesaid; and every such agent or agents shall also annex to every such certificate or affidavit to be made by him or them, before one or more of the barons of the *exchequer*, that he or they do believe that such certificate is true; which certificate being filed as aforesaid, shall be a sufficient warrant for making the said half yearly payment to the respective contributors, their executors, administrators or assigns; and if any person or persons shall receive one or more half yearly payments upon his, her or their annuity or annuities, for any time beyond the death of his, her or their nominee or nominees, when the same ought to cease, such person or persons knowing such nominee or nominees to be dead, shall forfeit treble the value of the monies so by him, her or them, received, and also the sum of five hundred pounds; the moiety whereof shall go to his Majesty, his heirs and successors, and the other moiety to him or them who will sue for the same, by action of debt, bill, suit or information, in which no essoin, protection, privilege, wager of law, injunction, or more than one imparlance shall be allowed.

LXV. And be it further enacted by the authority aforesaid, That every contributor, his or her executors, administrators or assigns, within one month next after notice of the death of his, her or their respective nominee or nominees, shall certify such death to the auditor of the said receipt of exchequer for the time being, and shall also within three months after such notice, deliver or cause to be delivered up to the said auditor, his, her, or their order or orders, by which he, she or they, was and were intitled during the life of such nominee to any share of the said yearly fund, in case such order and orders be in his, her or their hands or power; and in default thereof, such contributor, his or her executors, administrators and assigns, shall forfeit the sum of ten pounds; to be recovered by action of debt, as aforesaid, and to be had and received for the use of any person who shall sue for the same.

LXVI. And be it further enacted by the authority aforesaid, That all the annuities payable to such contributors out of the said yearly fund, shall be free from all taxes, charges and impositions whatsoever.

LXVII. *And whereas it may so happen that in process of time, several of the standing orders may be lost, burnt or destroyed, or may become defaced, obliterated, or incumbered with many assignments thereon, and it may be necessary that new orders should be made forth in lieu thereof;* be it therefore enacted by the authority aforesaid, That in all or any the said cases, any three or more of the

the commiffioners of the treafury now being, or the high trea- Orders loft,
furer, or any three or more of the commiffioners of the treafury burnt or de-
ftroyed, &c.
for the time being, fhall, and they are hereby impowered, from may be renew-
time to time (upon certificate under the hand of the lord chief ed;
baron, or any other of the barons of the coif of his Majefty's
court of exchequer, that he or they are fatisfied, by proof upon
oath before him or them made, that any fuch order or orders
have been loft, burnt or otherwife deftroyed) to caufe new orders to be made forth at the exchequer, to be made by him or
them, in lieu of fuch orders fo certified to be loft, burnt or deftroyed; and the refpective officers in the faid exchequer are
hereby directed to pay the intereft which fhall from time to time
become due on fuch new orders, as if the original order or orders had been produced; and all fuch payments fhall be allowed
in their refpective accounts; provided that the perfon or perfons Proprietor
intitled to receive the intereft due upon any fuch order or orders giving fecurity
do give fecurity to the King, to the good liking of the perfon appointed to pay the fame into the exchequer for the ufe of the publick, fo much money as fhall be paid thereupon, if the order or
orders fo certified to be loft, burnt or otherwife deftroyed, be
hereafter produced; and the faid commiffioners of the treafury,
or the high treafurer for the time being, fhall alfo have power to New orders
caufe new ftanding orders to be made forth, for and in lieu of may be iffued
fuch orders as fhall become defaced, obliterated or otherwife in- in lieu of fuch
cumbered as aforefaid; which faid order or orders fhall be, at as become de-
faced, &c.
the fame time delivered up and cancelled, and the new order or or-
ders to be made out in lieu thereof, fhall be made payable, and
delivered to the perfon or perfons who fhall appear to be the
proprietor or proprietors of the faid order or orders fo to be delivered up and cancelled, at the time of fuch delivery as aforefaid; and the auditor of the receipt as aforefaid, fhall always take Entry thereof
care that fuch entries or memorandums be made upon the faid to be made on
new orders, as may denote their being made in lieu of fuch de- the new or-
ders.
faced, obliterated, incumbered or otherwife defective orders cancelled, and as may fecure the publick againft any double payments, for or by reafon of the making out or iffuing fuch new
orders in manner aforefaid.

LXVIII. *And for preventing all frauds and abufes in or about
the faid ftanding orders, or any affignments thereof, or the receiving
the annuities due or to grow due thereon;* be it enacted by the au- Penalty of for-
thority aforefaid, That if any perfon or perfons whatfoever fhall ging or coun-
forge or counterfeit, or procure to be forged or counterfeited, or terfeiting cer-
knowingly or wilfully act and affift in the forging or counter- tificates, &c.
feiting any certificate or certificates to be given by fuch cafhier or of fraudu-
or cafhiers, or any order or orders to be made forth in lieu there- lently receiv-
of, in purfuance of this prefent act, or any affignment or affign- ing annuities.
ments of fuch order or orders, or of the annuities payable
thereon, or of any receipt or difcharge to the exchequer, for the
annuities due or to grow due on any fuch order or orders, or of
any letter of attorney, or other authority or inftrument, to tranf-
fer,

fer, affign, alien or convey any fuch order or orders, or to receive
the annuities due or to grow due thereon, or any part thereof;
or fhall forge or counterfeit, or procure to be forged or counterfeited, or knowingly or wilfully act or affift in the forging or counterfeiting any the name or names of any of the proprietors of any
fuch order or orders, in or to any fuch pretended affignment or
affignments, receipt, letter of attorney, certificate, inftrument or
authority; or fhall falfely and deceitfully perfonate any true and
real proprietor or proprietors of any of the faid orders, and thereby affign, or endeavour to affign, any of the faid orders, or receive or endeavour to receive the money of fuch true and lawful
proprietor, as if fuch offender were the true and lawful owner
thereof; then, and in every fuch cafe, all and every fuch perfon and perfons being thereof lawfully convicted in due form of
law, fhall be adjudged guilty of felony, and fhall fuffer death as
in cafes of felony, without benefit of clergy.

No fee to be taken for receiving or paying the contributions or annuities,

LXIX. And be it further enacted, That no fee, reward or
gratuity whatfoever fhall be demanded or taken of any of his
Majefty's fubjects for receiving or paying the faid contribution
monies, or any of them, or for paying the faid feveral annuities, or any of them, or for any transfer of any fum great or
fmall, to be made in purfuance of this act, upon pain that any
offender or perfon offending by taking or demanding any fuch
fee, reward or gratuity, fhall forfeit the fum of twenty pounds
to the party aggrieved, with full cofts of fuit; and that all re-

or iffuing receipts, &c.

ceipts and iffues, and all other things directed by this act to be
performed in the exchequer, fhall be done and performed by the
officer there, without demanding or receiving, directly or indirectly, any fee, reward or gratuity for the fame; and in cafe

Penalty on officer taking fees, mifapplying the public money, or otherwife neglecting his duty.

the officers of the exchequer fhall take or demand any fuch fee
or reward, or fhall mifapply or divert any of the monies to be
paid into the exchequer upon this act, or fhall pay or iffue out
of the fame, otherwife than according to the intent of this act,
or fhall not keep fuch books, regifters, or make entries, and do
and perform all other things which by this act they are directed
and required to do and perform; every fuch offender fhall forfeit his place, and be for ever after incapable of any office or
place of truft whatfoever, and fhall anfwer and pay treble cofts
of fuit, to any contributor, or perfon claiming under him, that
will fue for the fame, to be recovered by action of debt, bill,
plaint or information, in any of his Majefty's courts of record
at *Weftminfter*, wherein no effoin, protection, privilege or wager
of law, injunction or order of reftraint, or any more than one
imparlance fhall be granted or allowed; and in the faid action,
the plaintiff upon recovery fhall have full cofts of fuit, one third
of which fum fhall be paid into the faid receipt of exchequer for
the benefit of his Majefty, his heirs and fucceffors, and the
other two thirds fhall be to and for the ufe of the profecutor.

LXX. Provided always, and be it enacted, That in cafe
any officer of the exchequer fhall make payment of any fhare or
fhares of the faid yearly fund of thirty three thoufand feven hundred

dred and fifty pounds, by this act directed to be set apart for the purposes aforesaid, upon any such certificate or certificates as aforesaid, such officer shall not incur any penalty, forfeiture or disability, though the said certificate be forged or false, or the said nominee be dead, unless the said officer did know, at the time of such payment, that the said nominee was dead, or that the said certificate was forged or false.

Officer unwittingly paying money on false certificates, not to incur any penalty thereby.

LXXI. And it is hereby enacted by the authority aforesaid, That if at any time or times it shall happen that the produce of the said several rates and duties and sums of money hereby granted for payment of the said several annuities, shall not be sufficient to pay and discharge the several and respective annuities, and other charges directed to be paid thereout, at the end of any or either of the respective half-yearly days of payment, at which the same are hereby directed to be paid, then, and so often, and in every such case, such deficiency or deficiencies shall and may be supplied out of any of the monies which at any time or times shall be or remain in the receipt of the exchequer, of the surplusses, excesses, overplus monies, and other revenues composing the fund commonly called *The sinking fund*, (except such monies of the said sinking fund as are appropriated to any particular use or uses, by any former act or acts of parliament in that behalf) and such monies of the said *sinking fund*, shall and may be, from time to time, issued and applied accordingly; and if at any time or times before any monies of the several rates and duties and sums of money hereby granted, shall be brought into the exchequer as aforesaid, there shall happen to be a want of money for paying the several annuities as aforesaid, which shall be actually incurred and grown due at any of the half-yearly days of payment before mentioned, that then and in every such case the money so wanted shall and may be supplied out of the monies of the *sinking fund*, (except as before excepted) and be issued accordingly.

Deficiencies of the duties to be made good out of the sinking fund.

Occasional want of money for payment of annuities, to be supplied out of the sinking fund.

LXXII. Provided always, and be it enacted by the authority aforesaid, That whatever monies shall be issued out of the *sinking fund* shall, from time to time, be replaced by and out of the first supplies to be then after granted in parliament.

Monies issued out of the sinking fund, to be replaced.

LXXIII. Provided always, and be it enacted by the authority aforesaid, That in case there shall be any surplus or remainder of the monies arising by the said several rates and duties, after the said several and respective annuities, and all arrears thereof, are satisfied, or money sufficient shall be reserved for that purpose, such surplus or remainder shall, from time to time, be reserved for the disposition of parliament, and shall not be issued but by the authority of parliament, and as shall be directed by future act or acts of parliament; any thing in any former or other act or acts of parliament to the contrary notwithstanding.

Surplus of the duties to be reserved for disposition of parliament.

LXXIV. And it is hereby enacted by the authority aforesaid, That if any person or persons shall at any time or times be sued or prosecuted for any thing by him or them done or executed in pursuance of this act, or of any matter or thing in this act contain-

Persons sued on this act, may plead the general issue.

tained, fuch perfon or perfons fhall and may plead the general
iffue, and give the fpecial matter in evidence for his or their defence; and if upon the trial a verdict fhall pafs for the defendant or defendants, or the plaintiff or plaintiffs fhall become

Treble cofts.

nonfuited, then fuch defendant or defendants fhall have treble
cofts to him or them awarded againft fuch plaintiff or plaintiffs.

**2 Geo. 2. c. 23.
made perpetu-
al.**

LXXV. And be it further enacted by the authority aforefaid,
That an act made in the fecond year of the reign of his prefent
Majefty, intituled, *An act for the better regulation of attornies and
follicitors*, which was to be in force from the firft day of *June* one
thoufand feven hundred and twenty nine for the term of nine
years, and from thence to the end of the next feffion of parliament; and which by an act made in the twelfth year of his prefent Majefty's reign, was explained and amended, and further
continued until the twenty fourth day of *June* one thoufand feven hundred and forty eight, and from thence to the end of the
next feffion of parliament; and which by an act made in the
twenty third year of his prefent Majefty's reign, was explained
and amended, and further continued until the twenty fourth day
of *June* one thoufand feven hundred and fifty feven, and from
thence to the end of the next feffion of parliament; by which
the payment of feveral ftamp duties on the admiffion of attornies and follicitors is enforced and regulated, fhall, from and after the expiration thereof, be further continued and made perpetual.

LXXVI. *And whereas divers perfons through miftake, abfence, or
fome un-voidable accident, to the prejudice of infants and others, have
omitted to caufe affidavits to be made and filed in the proper offices, of
the actual execution of feveral contracts in writing, to ferve as clerks
to attornies and follicitors, within the times limited by law for that
purpofe, and many perfons may be in danger of incurring certain difabi-*

**Time allowed
to make and
file affidavits
of execution
of indentures,
&c. omitted to
be done within
the time limit-
ed by law.**

lities by fuch omiffions; be it therefore enacted by the authority
aforefaid, That all and every perfon and perfons who have
omitted to caufe fuch affidavit or affidavits to be made and filed
as aforefaid, and who fhall, on or before the firft day of *Michaelmas* term one thoufand feven hundred and fifty feven, caufe one or
more affidavit or affidavits to be made and filed in fuch manner
as is directed by the laws in being, fhall be, and are hereby indemnified, freed and difcharged from and againft all penalties,
forfeitures, incapacities and difabilities, in or by any act or acts
of parliament mentioned, incurred or to be incurred for or by
reafon of any neglect or omiffion, in caufing fuch affidavit or affidavits to be made out and filed in fuch manner as is required
by the laws in being; and fuch affidavit or affidavits fo to be
made and filed as aforefaid, fhall be as effectual to all intents
and purpofes, as if the fame had been made and filed within
the refpective times limited by the laws in being for that purpofe.

LXXVII. *And for the relief of any perfon or perfons, who,
through neglect or inadvertency, hath or have omitted to pay the feveral rates and duties, or any part thereof, upon monies given, paid, contracted or agreed for, with or in relation to any clerk, apprentice or
fervant who hath been put or placed to or with any mafter or miftrefs*

10

to learn any profession, trade or employment, and to have such inden-
tures or other writings which contain the covenants, articles, contracts
or agreements, relating to the service of such clerk, apprentice or ser-
vant stampt within the times by the several acts of parliament for
those purposes respectively limited; or who have also, in like manner,
omitted to insert and write in words at length, in such indentures or
other writings as aforesaid, the full sum or sums of money, or any Time allowed
part thereof, received, or in any wise directly or indirectly given, for payment
paid, or agreed or contracted for, with or in relation to every such of duties omit-
clerk, apprentice or servant as aforesaid; be it enacted, That upon ted to have
payment of the rates and duties upon monies, or such part of paid on ap-
such monies so neglected or omitted to be paid as aforesaid, on prentices fees;
or before the first day of *September* one thousand seven hundred and for ten-
and fifty seven, to such person or persons to whom the same dentures to be
ought to be paid, and tendering the said indentures, or other stampt, &c.
writings, to be stampt at the same time, or at any time on or
before the twenty ninth day of *September* one thousand seven
hundred and fifty seven, (of which timely notice is to be given
in the *London Gazette*) the same indentures, or other writings,
shall be good and available in law or equity, and may be given
in evidence in any court whatsoever; and the clerks, apprentices or servants therein named shall be capable of following and
exercising their respective intended trade or employment, as fully as if the said rates and duties so omitted had been duly paid,
and the full sum or sums received or agreed for as aforesaid,
had been inserted; and the persons who have incurred any penalties by the omissions aforesaid, shall be acquitted and discharged of and from the said penalties; any thing in the said
former acts to the contrary notwithstanding.

CAP. XX.

An act more effectually to prevent the spreading of the dis-
temper now raging amongst the horned cattle in this
kingdom.

WHEREAS *the contagious distemper now rages amongst the*
horned cattle in this kingdom; for the preventing the spread-
ing thereof; be it enacted by the King's most excellent majesty, His Majesty
by and with the advice and consent of the lords spiritual and impowered to
temporal and commons in this present parliament assembled, make orders
and by the authority of the same, That it shall and may be to prohibit
lawful to and for the King's most excellent majesty, his heirs the removing
and successors, by and with the advice of his or their privy horned cattle
council, from time to time, to make such rules, orders and re- from one
gulations, or to vary or repeal the same, as his Majesty in his county or
great wisdom shall judge most expedient and effectual, in *Great* place to ano-
Britain, *Ireland*, and all other his Majesty's dominions there- ther,
unto belonging, or any part or parts thereof, for prohibiting or
preventing the driving or removing of any oxen, bulls, cows,
calves, steers or heifers infected or not infected with the said
distemper, from or out of any such county, riding, division,
hundred,

hundred, parish or place to any fair or market, or to any other such county, hundred, parish or place as shall for that purpose

and the sale or use of cattle infected, or of their hides, &c.

and for burial of such as shall die of the said infection, &c.

be, specified in such rules, orders or regulations; and for prohibiting the sale, disposition or other use of any such cattle as shall be infected with the said distemper, or of any hides or skins, or other parts of such infected cattle; and also for the burial of any such beasts as shall die of such infectious distemper, or be killed whilst the same is so infected, and every part thereof, within such time and in such manner as shall be specified in such rules, orders and regulations as aforesaid; and also for the cutting and gashing of the hide or skin of every such infected beast, before the burial thereof, in such manner as to render the same intirely useless; any law, statute, custom or usage to the contrary notwithstanding; and also for such further purposes as his Majesty in his great wisdom shall judge most expedient and effectual to put a stop to or prevent the spreading of the said distemper.

19 G. 2. c. 5.
20 G. 2. c. 4.

His Majesty's order in council of 22 March 1747, confirmed and enforced;

II. *And whereas his Majesty hath, in pursuance of two acts of parliament of the nineteenth and twentieth years of his Majesty's reign, by his order in council bearing date the twenty second day of March one thousand seven hundred and forty seven, made and established certain rules, orders and regulations, for the better preventing the spreading of the said infection, and putting a stop to the distemper, which rules, orders and regulations have been found beneficial*; be it therefore enacted by the authority aforesaid, That the said order in council, and all the rules, orders and regulations therein contained and inserted (except such and so much of them, or any of them respectively, as his Majesty, his heirs and successors, at any time or times, during the continuance of this present act, shall with the advice of his and their privy council judge proper and expedient to repeal, alter or vary) shall be in force; and

Obedience to such other order as shall be made, enforced under penalty of 10l.

the same, and also such other rules, orders and regulations, variations and additions as shall be made by virtue of and in pursuance and under the power and authority of this present act, shall be observed and obeyed by all his Majesty's subjects, during the continuance of this act, under the penalty of ten pounds, inflicted and directed to be levied by this act, for every offence committed against the same.

Powers given by order of council to justices, magistrates and officers, confirmed.

III. And it is hereby further enacted and declared, That all the powers and authorities given by the said order of council, or which shall be given by any subsequent order of council, by virtue of the authority aforesaid, to justices of the peace and other magistrates, and to commissioners of the land tax, inspectors and other officers appointed in that behalf, shall be duly executed, and are hereby established and enacted, and declared to be as good and valid in the law, to all intents and purposes, during the continuance of the said order or orders, as if the same were herein repeated and expresly enacted.

50l. penalty on persons obstructing, &c.

IV. And be it further enacted, That from and after the first day of *June* one thousand seven hundred and fifty seven, all and every person and persons who shall by force or threats intimidate,

date,

date, hinder or prevent the said justices, magistrates, commissioners, inspectors or other officers from executing the said rules, orders and regulations, or from performing their respective duties in relation thereto; or who shall enter into any combination, confederacy or subscription to disobey the said order or orders in council, or to defeat, hinder or prevent the execution thereof, shall forfeit and pay the sum of fifty pounds, to be recovered by bill, plaint, suit or information in any of his Majesty's courts of record at *Westminster*, by any person or persons who shall inform and sue for the same, to go and be paid to and for the sole use and benefit of such person or persons respectively, with full costs of suit.

the execution of orders, or entering into a combination to disobey, or defeat the same.

V. *And, to the end that all persons may know how to demean themselves in the premisses*; be it further enacted by the authority aforesaid, That this act, and his Majesty's order in council, dated the twenty second day of *March* one thousand seven hundred and forty seven, on such *Sunday* in every calendar month as the minister shall think proper, shall be publickly read immediately after prayers, in all parish churches, chapels and other places set apart for divine worship; and that when and as often as his Majesty, his heirs or successors, shall make any rules, orders and regulations, or shall vary or repeal the same, by virtue or in pursuance of this act, every such rule, order, regulation, variation and repeal, shall be notified and published in such manner as his Majesty shall think proper, and shall be publickly read upon the next *Sunday* after the receipt of the same, and on such *Sunday* in every calendar month as the minister shall think proper, during the time such rules, orders, regulations and variations shall continue in force in such manner as aforesaid, within such counties, ridings, divisions, hundreds, parishes and places as shall be specified in such rules, orders, regulations, variations and repeals for that purpose; and every such order, rule, regulation, variation and repeal, together with this act, shall be kept by the minister of every such parish church, chapel or place, who shall permit any person residing within his parish, chapelry or place to read the same, during the time such rule, order or regulation shall continue in force; and the churchwardens or chapelwardens of every parish or place shall provide a printed copy of this act, for the purpose aforesaid, at the expence of the parish or chapelry.

This act, and his Majesty's order in council of 22 March 1747, to be read publickly in church on Sundays; and such new orders, &c. as shall hereafter be made, to be read in like manner.

Printed copy of all such orders, together with this act, to be kept by the minister, for the use of the parishioners; and to be provided at the parish expence.

VI. And be it enacted by the authority aforesaid, That it shall and may be lawful to and for the King's most excellent Majesty, by one or more proclamation or proclamations, to be issued at any time or times during the continuance of this act, under the great seal of *Great Britain*, to prohibit and forbid all and every person and persons, bodies politick and corporate whatsoever, to import or bring, or cause or procure to be imported or brought, directly or indirectly, or export, carry or send, or cause to procure to be exported, carried or sent, directly or indirectly, into or from or out of *Great Britain*, *Ireland*, and the dominions thereunto belonging, or any part thereof, any

His Majesty impowered to prohibit by proclamation, occasionally, the importation or exportation of horned cattle, raw hides, or other part of such beasts.

ox,

ox, bull, cow, calf, steer or heifer, or any raw hides or skins, or any other part of such beast, for such time or times, under such rules, orders and regulations, as his Majesty, his heirs and successors, by the advice aforesaid, shall judge most expedient and effectual to prevent or stop the spreading of the said distemper.

Where justices prohibit the holding fairs or markets for sale of horned cattle,

VII. *And, to prevent the distemper amongst the horned cattle being spread and increased by tanners and others buying the hides and skins of infected beasts,* it is hereby further enacted, That when the justices of the peace at their general quarter sessions, or at any adjournment thereof within their respective counties, ridings and divisions, shall prohibit the holding of any fair or fairs, market or markets, for buying and selling of such horned cattle,

no tanner is to bring any raw hide into his tan-yard, before he gives notice to the officer of excise of the district,

every tanner, tawer or dresser of hides and skins shall, before he brings any raw hide or skin of any bull, ox, cow, calf, steer or heifer, into his tan-yard, workhouse, warehouse or place used for dressing or manufacturing of hides or skins, give notice to the officer of excise of the district in which such tan-yard or dressing place is situated, and whose survey the said tanner, tawer or dresser of hides shall be under, and subject to, for the time being, and produce to the said officer a certificate under

and produces a certificate concerning the health of the beast,

the hand and seal, or hands and seals, of one or more justice or justices of the peace, or commissioner or commissioners of the land tax, rector or vicar, qualified as herein after mentioned, specifying the colour of such hide or skin, the name and place of abode of the owner of such hide or skin, and that, upon examination on oath of one or more credible person or persons, it appeared to the person or persons signing and sealing such certificate, that the beast, from which such hide or skin was taken,

which the officer is to enter in a book. Tanner guilty of a breach of orders, forfeits 10 l.

was found, and free from infection; which certificate shall, by the said officer, be entered into a book to be kept for that purpose: and if any tanner, tawer or dresser of hides or skins, shall bring, or suffer to be brought, into his tan-yard or tan-pits, or other place used for dressing or manufacturing hides or skins, any such raw hide or skin, or shall tan or dress, or manufacture any such raw hide or skin, without giving such notice, and producing such certificate, as aforesaid, every person so offending shall, for every such offence, forfeit the sum of ten pounds; to be recovered, levied and applied, as the several forfeitures are by this act directed to be recovered, levied and applied.

Officer to have liberty to enter and search for hides suspected to be clandestinely brought in.

VIII. And it is hereby further enacted, That all and every or any of the officers of excise acting and employed in any district wherein any tan-yard, workhouse or warehouse, or place for dressing or manufacturing of hides or skins is situate and being, shall and may at all times by day or by night (and if in the night, then in the presence of a constable or other officer of the peace) be permitted, upon his or their request, to enter into any such tan-yard, workhouse, warehouse or place, in order to search for hides and skins suspected to be brought and conveyed into the same respectively, contrary to and against the tenor and true meaning

meaning of this act, and then and there to search and examine; or cause to be searched or examined, any tan-pit, fat or other place, where any such hide or skin is suspected to be laid, hid, put or concealed; and if any tanner, tawer, or other person or persons whatsoever, shall obstruct or hinder any such officer or officers in the execution of his or their duty, power or authority, given to, vested in, and required of, him and them respectively by this act, every person so offending, and being thereof lawfully convicted as aforesaid, shall, for every such offence, forfeit and pay the sum of ten pounds, to be recovered, applied and disposed of, in manner herein after mentioned.

Person obstructing him forfeits 10 l.

IX. *And whereas it is necessary to encourage and promote the breeding of cattle, the number being greatly decreased by the said mortality*; be it therefore enacted by the authority aforesaid, That it shall and may be lawful for his Majesty, by advice of his privy council, to prohibit and forbid the killing or slaughtering of cow-calves in such counties and places, and in such manner, and at such times, as his Majesty, during the continuance of this act, shall judge proper; and all and every person offending against such order and prohibition, shall forfeit and pay the sum of ten pounds, to be recovered, levied and applied, as other forfeitures by this act are to be recovered, levied and applied.

His Majesty, by advice of his privy council, may prohibit, occasionally, the killing of cow calves.

X. *And, to prevent any doubts which may arise in the construction of this act*, be it further enacted by the authority aforesaid, That the removal, driving or sale of every ox, bull, cow, calf, steer or heifer, contrary to any such rule, order or regulation, shall be deemed a distinct and separate offence, within the intent and meaning of this act; any thing herein contained to the contrary notwithstanding.

Offender against such prohibition, forfeits 10 l.

What shall be deemed a distinct and separate offence.

XI. And be it further enacted by the authority aforesaid, That all and every the rules, orders, regulations and variations, to be made by virtue, and in pursuance, of this act, are hereby required to be punctually observed and obeyed by all his Majesty's subjects; and all and every person and persons who shall offend against any such rule, order, regulation or variation, and shall be thereof convicted in *Great Britain* or *Ireland*, by his, her, or their own confession, or by the oath or oaths of one or more credible witness or witnesses before any justice or justices of the peace for any county, riding, division, city, liberty or town corporate, where such offence or offences shall be committed (which justice or justices is and are hereby impowered and required to hear and determine the same, and to examine any witness or witnesses upon oath concerning the same) shall forfeit and lose the sum of ten pounds; one moiety thereof to the informer, and the other moiety to the poor of the parish where such offence shall be committed; to be levied by the churchwardens, overseers of the poor, constables, high constables of the hundred, rape or wapentake, or one or more of them, by warrant or warrants under the hand and seal, or under the hands and seals, of the justice or justices of the peace who shall convict such offender, by distress and sale of the goods

Observation of orders made under authority of this act, enjoined, under penalty of 10 l. on conviction of the offender before a justice;

one moiety to go to the informer, the other to the poor, and to be levied by distress and sale;

and chattels of such offender, rendering the overplus (if any be) to the owner thereof; and for want of such distress, such offender shall be committed by such justice or justices to the common gaol or house of correction of such county, riding, division, city, liberty or town corporate, there to remain for the space of three months, to be reckoned from the day of such commitment; and all and every person and persons who shall offend against any such rule, order or regulation, in any other of his Majesty's said dominions, shall be deemed, adjudged, and taken to be guilty of a great misdemeanor, and be prosecuted and punished by fine and imprisonment, according to the laws and usage of the same dominions respectively.

where no distress, the offender to be committed for 3 months. Offenders out of Great Britain or Ireland, to be punished according to the laws and usage of the country.

XII. And be it further enacted by the authority aforesaid, That it shall and may be lawful for any person or persons, who shall be convicted before such justice or justices of the peace as aforesaid, of any of the offences against this act, to appeal from such conviction to the justices of the peace at their next general or quarter sessions to be holden for the county, riding, division, city, liberty or town corporate, in which such offences shall be committed, he, she or they, giving immediate notice to such justice or justices of such intended appeal, and likewise giving security to the satisfaction of such justice or justices, to pay all and every the penalties and forfeitures, to which he, she or they, shall be liable by such conviction; and the costs, charges and expences, of trying such appeal, in case such conviction shall be affirmed; and the said justices in their next general or quarter sessions, are hereby authorized and required to hear, try, and finally determine the same, upon the merits of the cause, and examination of witness on oath, and to order costs to be paid as shall be just, if they shall think it reasonable so to do.

Appeal may be made from any justice to the next quarter-sessions, upon giving notice and security.

XIII. Provided nevertheless, That if it shall appear to the said justices, that there was not sufficient time between such conviction and such quarter-sessions, to give notice to all parties to attend such appeal, that then it shall and may be lawful for such justices to adjourn the hearing thereof to their next subsequent general or quarter sessions, at which they are hereby required to hear, try, and finally determine the same; and in case there shall be no determination on the said appeal at such next or subsequent general or quarter sessions, the judgment and conviction of the justice or justices shall stand and be in full force; and no writ of *Certiorari* shall be allowed to remove the conviction or order of sessions, or any other proceedings thereupon, into any of his Majesty's courts of record at *Westminster*, or of his Majesty's courts of great session in the principality of *Wales*, or the counties palatine.

The justices may adjourn the hearing the appeal to the next quarter-sessions, and if not then determined, the former judgment to stand good; conviction not removeable by certiorari.

XIV. And be it further enacted by the authority aforesaid, That it shall and may be lawful for any justice or justices of the peace, if he or they shall be informed, that any person or persons can give any evidence relating to any of the offences aforesaid, to summon such person or persons to appear before him or them, and to examine such person or persons on oath in relation

Justices may summon and examine witnesses on oath, touching any of these offences,

2   lation

lation thereunto; and in case such person or persons shall refuse or neglect to appear pursuant to such summons, then such
justice or justices shall issue out his or their warrant or warrants,
for apprehending and bringing such person or persons before
him or them; and in case such person or persons shall refuse to
be examined upon oath, to commit such persons to the common
gaol or house of correction for such county, riding, division,
city, liberty or town corporate, there to remain until he, she
or they shall submit to be examined as aforesaid; and in case of
any appeal to the general or quarter sessions, to compel such
person or persons to enter into a recognizance, with condition
to appear at the said general or quarter sessions, and to give evidence upon trial of such appeal.

and commit such as refuse to give evidence; and in case of an appeal compel them to enter into a recognizance to appear, &c.

XV. And be it further enacted by the authority aforesaid,
That for the more easy and speedy convicting of any person or
persons who shall offend against this act, it shall be sufficient for
any justice or justices of the peace, who shall convict any person
or persons of any or either of the said offences, to draw such
conviction in the following form of words, as the case shall happen, or in any other form of words to the same effect (that is
to say)

Form of conviction to be observed by justices;

Middlesex. A B. *is convicted on his, her or their own confession*
(or on the oath of   ) *of having in this
kingdom* (specifying the offence, and the time and place,
when and where the same was committed)

        Given under my (or our) *hand and seal* (or hands
            and seals) *this
            day of*

Which said conviction in the same or like form of words, shall
be good and effectual in the law, to all intents and purposes,
and shall not be quashed, set aside, or adjudged void or insufficient for want of any other form of words whatsoever; and in
case of appeal as aforesaid, the justice or justices who shall convict such offender or offenders, is and are hereby required to
deliver, or cause to be delivered, the conviction in the form a-
foresaid, to the next general or quarter sessions to which the
appeal is made, there to be filed on record.

the same declared to be valid; and in case of appeal, is to be delivered to the next sessions, to be filed.

XVI. Be it further enacted, That the justices of the peace
within their respective limits of their commissions, at their general or quarter sessions, or the major part of them then and
there assembled, within that part of *Great Britain* called *England,* shall have full power and authority, and they are hereby required to order such reasonable salaries and charges as they
shall think proper, to be paid to any inspector or inspectors, or
other person or persons already employed or appointed by the
justices of the peace, or hereafter to be employed or appointed
by the justices of the peace, or the commissioners of the land
tax, to prevent the spreading of the distemper amongst the cat-

Justices to order salaries and charges to be paid to the inspectors of cattle, &c. out of the county rates.

tle,

tle, out of the monies arifen or hereafter to arife, by virtue of an act of parliament paffed in the twelfth year of his Majefty's reign, intituled, *An act for the more eafy affeffing, collecting and levying county rates.*

Commiffioners of the land tax are to put in execution the powers given by this act, or by any order of council.

XVII. And be it further enacted, That the commiffioners of the land tax for the time being in and for every county, riding or divifion, and who have or fhall qualify themfelves to act as fuch refpectively, are hereby impowered and required to put in execution all and every the powers and authorities given to commiffioners of the land tax by this act, or by any order or orders in council purfuant to the fame (except the commiffioners of the land tax within the county of *Middlefex*, and all cities and towns which are counties of themfelves) in as full and ample manner as the juftices of the peace may do within the fame.

Commiffioners in all the fucceeding land tax acts from 1746, authorized to carry into execution the powers vefted in them by the faid orders, and acts continuing them.

XVIII. *And whereas a doubt hath arifen whether commiffioners authorized to put in execution the feveral fucceeding land tax acts, fince the year one thoufand feven hundred and forty fix, were properly impowered to carry into execution the rules, orders and regulations made by his Majefty in council, and the powers and authorities given by the feveral acts of parliament, continuing the fame in force from time to time;* be it therefore declared and enacted, That the commiffioners named in the feveral fucceeding land tax acts, fince the year one thoufand feven hundred and forty fix, to carry the faid refpective land tax acts into execution (having duly qualified themfelves to act therein, according to the directions in the faid acts) are and were authorized to carry into execution the powers and authorities given by fuch rules, orders and regulations, to commiffioners of the land tax, as alfo the powers and authorities given by the feveral acts of parliament continuing the fame in force from time to time.

No horned cattle is to be fold until the fame fhall have been the feller's property 40 days.

XIX. *And to prevent the fpreading of the faid infectious diftemper, by perfons who frequently buy up cattle in infected places, and foon after difpofe of the fame in places free from the infection, contrary to the true intent and meaning of this act, and the orders and regulations made, or which fhall hereafter be made by his Majefty in council;* be it enacted by the authority aforefaid, That from and after the faid firft day of *June* one thoufand feven hundred and fifty feven, no perfon whatfoever by himfelf, his fervant or agent, fhall fell or difpofe of any living ox, bull, cow, calf, fteer or heifer, until the fame fhall have been the property of fuch perfon for the term of forty days at leaft ; and in proof of fuch property, the feller fhall produce a certificate under the hand of the perfon of whom fuch ox, bull, cow, calf, fteer or heifer, was laft bought or purchafed, fignifying the time when he purchafed the fame ; and every perfon who fhall fell or difpofe of any ox, bull, cow, calf, fteer or heifer, without producing fuch certificate, and fhall be thereof convicted by his, her or their own confeffion, or by the oath of one or more credible witnefs or witneffes, before any juftice or juftices of the peace for the county, riding, divifion, city, liberty or town corporate, where the offence fhall be committed, fhall for every ox, bull, cow, calf,

calf, fteer or heifer, fo fold or difpofed of, forfeit and pay the on forfeiture fum of ten pounds; unlefs fuch perfon fhall by himfelf, his a-of 10l. gent or fervant, make oath before the faid juftice or juftices (which oath the faid juftice or juftices is and are hereby im-powered to adminifter) that the faid ox, bull, cow, calf, fteer or heifer, has been his property for more than forty days; the Recovery and faid forfeiture to be adjudged, levied and recovered, in fuch application of manner as is herein after directed to be levied and recovered; the forfeiture. one moiety of the faid forfeiture to be given to the informer, and the other moiety to the poor of the parifh where the offence fhall be committed.

XX. And be it further enacted by the authority aforefaid, The feller That every perfon who fhall, from and after the faid firft day of giving a falfe *June* one thoufand feven hundred and fifty feven, fell or difpofe certificate, and of any ox, bull, cow, calf, fteer or heifer, and fhall give a falfe the perfon ac-or untrue certificate of the time of the fale of fuch cattle, and cepting it for-every perfon who fhall accept of fuch falfe or untrue certificate, feit 10 l. knowing the fame to be fuch, fhall forfeit and pay the fum of ten pounds, to be adjudged, levied, recovered and difpofed of in the manner herein after directed.

XXI. And be it enacted by the authority aforefaid, That if If a drover any drover, or perfon or perfons driving and conducting horned finds any cat-cattle from one place to another, fhall find any beaft or beafts tle ficken in in his drift ficken upon the road fo as to be unable to proceed his drift, he is forward in their journey, fuch drover, or perfon or perfons to give imme-driving fuch horned cattle, fhall forthwith give notice thereof a parifh offi-to the conftable, headborough or churchwarden of the parifh cer, or place wherein fuch beaft or beafts fhall ficken, in order that the fame may be flain and buried, the fkin being firft flafhed, if deemed to be ill of the diftemper now raging amongft the horned cattle, in the opinion of the officer of fuch parifh or place fo fummoned, and of two other fubftantial inhabitants of the faid parifh or place, whom the faid officer is hereby impow-ered, by a note in writing under his hand, to fummon to his affiftance; and in cafe any drover or perfon or perfons driving upon penalty horned cattle, fhall fail herein, or fhall conceal or drive out of of 10l. the way, without giving fuch notice, any fuch fick beaft or beafts, he or they fo offending fhall forfeit and pay ten pounds to the ufe of the poor of fuch parifh or place wherein fuch beaft or beafts fhall be found fick or dead; to be levied on his or their goods and chattels, by warrant under the hand and feal of any juftice of the peace of the county, riding, divifion, liberty, city or town corporate, wherein fuch drover or perfon or perfons driving fuch horned cattle fhall be taken; and in cafe of non-or fix months payment, fuch drover or perfon or perfons fhall be committed imprifon-to the common gaol of fuch county, fhire, ftewartry, riding, ment. divifion, liberty, city or town corporate, there to remain with-out bail or mainprize for the fpace of fix calendar months, or until he or they fhall have paid the faid penalty.

XXII. *And for preventing perfons felling any horned cattle before* No cattle may *they have been in their poffeffion forty days;* it is hereby enacted, be fold unlefs That a certificate be obtained of the number, colour, place of fale, and owner's name; and proof made of their being the feller's property 40 days before; an attefted copy to be given to the buyer, upon penalty of 10 l.

That no perfon or perfons fhall fell or difpofe of any five ox, bull, cow, calf, fteer or heifer, unlefs he, fhe or they fhall, befides his, her or their compliance with the directions of the faid act, firft obtain a certificate under the hand and feal of fome juftice of the peace, or commiffioner of the land tax, fpecifying the colours and number of beafts fo intended to be fold; and the parifh, townfhip or place from whence the fame are brought, or intended to be carried, in order for fale; and the name or names, place or places of abode, of the owner or owners thereof; and that it appears to fuch juftice or commiffioner, upon examination on the oath of one or more credible witnefs or witneffes, that the beafts contained in fuch certificate have been the property and in the poffeffion of fuch perfon or perfons, for at leaft forty days before the date of the faid certificate; and every perfon felling any ox, bull, cow, calf, fteer or heifer, by virtue of fuch certificate, fhall produce the fame and give a true copy thereof, attefted by two or more credible witneffes, to the perfon or perfons buying fuch beafts; and every perfon felling any ox, bull, cow, calf, fteer or heifer, without obtaining fuch certificate, and every perfon buying the fame without receiving a true copy thereof, attefted as aforefaid, fhall forfeit and pay the fum of ten pounds for every ox, bull, cow, calf, fteer and heifer, bought or fold contrary to the true intent and meaning hereof, to be levied, adjudged, recovered, applied and difpofed of, as is herein after directed to be levied, adjudged, recovered, applied and difpofed of.

Juftice may fummon any perfon fufpected of a breach of any of thefe regulations;

and the party is to purge himfelf.

One moiety of the penalty to go to the poor, and the other

XXIII. And be it further enacted by the authority aforefaid, That if one or more juftice or juftices of the peace, during the continuance of this act, fhall fufpect any perfon of buying, felling or driving any ox, bull, cow, calf, fteer or heifer, or of taking off the hide from any infected ox, bull, cow, calf, fteer or heifer, which fhall die of the faid diftemper, contrary to the true intent and meaning of this act, and the rules, orders and regulations made by his Majefty in council, in purfuance thereof, or of not burying any ox, bull, cow, calf, fteer or heifer, contrary to this act and orders, it fhall and may be lawful for fuch juftice or juftices to fummon fuch perfon to appear before him or them, at a reafonable time to be prefixed in fuch fummons; and the proof of complying with the directions of this act and orders, fhall lie on the party fo fummoned; and if fuch perfon fhall neglect or refufe to appear before fuch juftice or juftices (proof being made upon oath of his or her being duly fummoned) or fhall not make it out to the fatisfaction of him or them that he or fhe has fully conformed himfelf or herfelf to this act, rules and orders, fuch perfon fhall be deemed and taken to be duly convicted of the offence or offences for which he fhall be fo fummoned, and incur the feveral penalties and forfeitures inflicted by this act, to be levied, recovered and adjudged, in manner as is herein after mentioned; one moiety of the faid forfeiture to be paid to the overfeer of the poor, and be applied to the ufe of the poor of the parifh where fuch perfon dwells; and
, the

the other moiety to the treasurer of the county, riding or division, to be made part of the county stock; or in that part of *Great Britain*, called *Scotland*, to such person and for such purposes, as the justices in their general quarter-sessions shall direct and appoint.

XXIV. *And for the more effectual preventing the spreading of the said infectious distemper by persons commonly called* Jobbers, *who occupying little or no grazing land, buy up cattle in infected places, and soon after dispose of the same*; be it enacted by the authority aforesaid, That from and after the said first day of *June* one thousand seven hundred and fifty seven, no person whatsoever (butchers and others excepted) buying fat cattle for immediate slaughter) shall purchase any living ox, bull, cow, calf, steer or heifer, without having first obtained a certificate under the hand and seal of some justice of the peace or commissioner of the land tax, acting for the county, riding, division, city, liberty, town or place where such person resides, specifying his or her name, and place of abode, and the number of beasts he or she intends to purchase, and whether such beasts are intended to be purchased by him or herself, or by an agent or servant, and if by an agent or servant, then the name and place of abode of such agent or servant, and that it appears to such justice or commissioner upon examination on the oath of one or more credible witness or witnesses, that such person really occupies land sufficient to graze and keep the number of beasts contained in such certificate, over and above the stock such person is at present possessed of, for the space of three months; and that it may appear no more beasts were bought than were contained in such certificate, every such person shall, upon bringing any cattle into any parish or place, bought in pursuance of such certificate, produce and shew the said certificate to an inspector, churchwarden or overseer of the poor, if any there be, of such parish or place, and shall at the same time acquaint such inspector, churchwarden or overseer, with the place where, and the name of the person of whom such beasts were purchased; and the said inspector, churchwarden or overseer, is hereby required to mark on the back of the said certificate, the number of beasts so brought into any parish or place, and the place where, and the name of the person of whom such beasts were purchased, and the day when such certificate was so produced; and if any person or persons (butchers or others buying fat cattle for immediate slaughter excepted as aforesaid) shall, from and after the said first day of *June* one thousand seven hundred and fifty seven, buy any ox, bull, cow, calf, steer or heifer, without previously obtaining such certificate, or shall buy more than the number contained in the same, or shall not produce the said certificate to an inspector, churchwarden or overseer of the poor, every such person shall, for every beast bought contrary to the true intent and meaning hereof, forfeit and pay the sum of five pounds; the said penalty to be levied, adjudged, recovered, applied and disposed of as is herein after directed.

XV. Pro-

XXV. Provided always, That no cattle shall be deemed to be bought by virtue of such certificate, unless the same are purchased within one month from the date thereof.

XXVI. And be it further enacted by the authority aforesaid, That when and as often as any cattle shall be stopped for want of a proper certificate, the constable or other proper officer of the township or parish where the said cattle shall be so stopped, shall cause such cattle, with all convenient expedition, to be driven back to the next constablewick from whence they last came, and shall give notice thereof to the constable or other proper officer of such next constablewick, who shall, and he is hereby required to receive the said cattle, and to cause the same to be driven through his constablewick, to the next constablewick from whence such cattle were driven, the constable or other parish officer whereof shall receive the same as aforesaid; and so from constablewick to constablewick, until such cattle shall arrive at the first township or place in the said county, riding, division or liberty, through which they were suffered to pass, without a proper certificate, they shall be treated in such and the like manner as cattle which have been within one mile of an infected place are by this act, or by any of his Majesty's orders of council deemed to be treated.

XXVII. *And whereas there are no such officers as overseers of the poor and churchwardens, in that part of* Great Britain *called* Scotland; therefore in order to carry this act in that part of the united kingdom into execution, be it enacted by the authority aforesaid, That all matters and things appointed to be done and executed by the overseers of the poor and churchwardens, in that part of *Great Britain* called *England*, shall, in *Scotland*, be done and executed by the constables, or other officers, to be appointed by the justices of the peace for that purpose, at their respective quarter-sessions or adjournment thereof.

XXVIII. *And in order to make provision in that part of the united kingdom called* Scotland, *for any expence that may attend the execution of this service;* be it enacted by the authority aforesaid, That it may be lawful for the commissioners of the land tax, and they are hereby impowered to assess their respective counties, in a sum not exceeding fifty pounds for each county, to be levied and collected in the same proportions, and according to the same rules, with the land tax; and which sum the respective collectors of the land tax for each county are hereby required to collect and issue, by order of the respective justices of the peace, or the major part of them, assembled at the quarter-sessions or adjournment thereof.

XXIX. And it is hereby further enacted, That wheresoever any person shall, for any offence to be hereafter committed against any law now in being relating to the preventing the spreading of the distemper which now rages amongst the horned cattle in this kingdom, be liable or subject to pay any pecuniary penalty or sum of money upon conviction, before any justice or justices of the peace, it shall and may be lawful for any other

perfon

Marginal notes:

Certificate not good, unless the cattle be purchased within a month after the date. Where cattle are stopt for want of a certificate, they are to be driven back to the place from whence they set out;

and are to be treated as cattle which have been within a mile of an infected place.

In Scotland constables are to execute the powers, &c. vested in the churchwardens;

and the commissioners of the land tax are to assess their counties to defray the expence of such service.

Method of recovery of pecuniary penalties.

person whatsoever, either to proceed to recover the said penalty, by information and conviction, before any justice or justices of the peace, in such manner as is directed by this act; or to sue for the same by action of debt or on the case, bill, plaint or information, in any of his Majesty's courts of record, wherein no essoin, protection or wager of law, or more than one imparlance shall be allowed, and wherein the plaintiff, if he recovers, shall likewise have his double costs.

Plaintiff recovering intitled to double costs.

XXX. Provided, That all suits and actions to be brought by virtue of this act, shall be brought before the end of the next term after the offence committed; and that no offender against any of the laws now in being for the preventing the spreading of the distemper which now rages amongst the horned cattle, shall be prosecuted twice for the same offence.

Limitation of actions.

XXXI. And be it further enacted by the authority aforesaid, That all the commissioners of the land tax, and rectors or vicars who are rated to the land tax for one hundred pounds *per annum*, shall, in their respective parishes, and they are hereby impowered to grant certificates of health for cattle, in as full and ample manner, as any justice or justices of the peace are impowered in any manner whatsoever to do, for which said certificates no fee or reward whatsoever shall be taken.

Commissioners of the land tax, and rectors, and vicars, rated for 100l. per ann. are to grant certificates of health for cattle.

XXXII. And be it further enacted by the authority aforesaid, That from and after the first day of *June* one thousand seven hundred and fifty seven, all persons whatsoever taking upon them to grant certificates in pursuance of this act, or his Majesty's orders relating thereto, shall set forth in every such certificate by virtue of what office he grants such certificate, whether as justice of the peace for any county, city or borough, commissioner of the land tax, or otherwise; and in case any person shall neglect so to do, such person shall, for every such offence respectively, forfeit and pay the sum of ten pounds of lawful money of *Great Britain*, for every such neglect, to be recovered by action of debt, bill, plaint or information, in any of his Majesty's courts of record at *Westminster*, with full costs of suit, wherein no essoin, privilege, protection or wager of law, or more than one imparlance shall be allowed.

Persons granting certificates, are to set forth therein their office,

on penalty of 10l.

XXXIII. And be it further enacted by the authority aforesaid, That the justices of the peace within their respective divisions, at their petty sessions, or the major part of them then and there assembled, within that part of *Great Britain* called *England*, shall have full power and authority to appoint any person or persons to be inspector or inspectors of any houses, buildings, grounds, fields and cattle within their said divisions, to be assistant to the constables, churchwardens and overseers of the poor, in such manner as the justices of the peace at their general quarter sessions are by his Majesty's said order in council, dated the second of *March* one thousand seven hundred and forty seven, impowered to do.

Justices at their petty sessions to appoint inspectors.

XXXIV. Provided, That no seller or buyer of any such cattle shall be obliged to take out either of the said certificates, where

Certificates are not necessary where the buyer and

where both the seller and buyer live in the same parish, or in the next adjacent parish or place, or within five miles distance of each other.

XXXV. Provided, That the seller of such cattle has been in the possession of the cattle so to be sold forty days at the least before such sale, and so as the buyer keeps the said cattle three months at the least, from the time he purchases the same, and so as the distemper that now rages amongst the horned cattle in this kingdom, be not within the space of ten miles of the seller's abode, and that the seller and buyer live in the same county; any thing in this act to the contrary notwithstanding.

XXXVI. *And whereas the magistrates of some corporations situated within counties at large, have in some places presumed to hold fairs and markets for the sale of horned cattle, when the justices of the peace for the county at large have prohibited fairs and markets to be holden in the said county, which in a great measure frustrates the said prohibition, and occasions many disputes;* be it therefore further

enacted by the authority aforesaid, That from and after the said first day of *June* in the year of our Lord one thousand seven hundred and fifty seven, where the justices of the peace for any county at large have already, or shall hereafter think proper, to prohibit fairs and markets to be holden for the sale of horned cattle within such county, such prohibition shall be deemed and taken to extend to all corporations within such county, or surrounded by or lying contiguous to such county, any charter, privilege or exemption to the contrary notwithstanding; and in case any such magistrate shall proclaim or give notice, or cause to be proclaimed or notice to be given, of any fair or market for horned beasts, or shall wilfully and knowingly permit any horned beasts to be brought into or sold at any fair or market within his jurisdiction, during such prohibition as aforesaid, such magistrate shall forfeit and pay the sum of one hundred pounds of lawful money of *Great Britain*, to any person who shall sue for the same in any of his Majesty's courts of record at *Westminster*, wherein no essoin, privilege, protection, wager of law, or more than one imparlance shall be allowed.

XXXVII. And be it further enacted, That from and after the first day of *June* one thousand seven hundred and fifty seven, no justice of the peace, or other magistrate of any corporation, or commissioner of the land tax for such corporation, or rector or vicar within any corporation, shall certify for any horned beast but such as have been kept within his jurisdiction for the time required by law, nor for the hide of any beast but such as have been slaughtered within his jurisdiction; any thing in any former act to the contrary notwithstanding: and in case any such magistrate shall take upon him to grant certificates, otherwise than as aforesaid, such magistrate shall forfeit and pay the sum of twenty pounds of lawful money of *Great Britain*, for every certificate so granted, to any person or persons that shall sue for the same, to be recovered by action of debt, bill, plaint or information, in any of his Majesty's courts of record at *Westminster*,

minster, with full costs of suit, wherein no essoin, privilege, protection, wager of law, or more than one imparlance shall be allowed.

XXXVIII. Be it further enacted by this act, That it shall and may be lawful for any four or more of the justices of the peace, of any county within this realm, at their general quarter-sessions, or any adjournment thereof, upon information given to them that the said distemper is in any neighbouring county, to prohibit for a certain time, or until the distemper shall cease in such county, any ox, bull, cow, calf, steer or heifer, from being driven or removed, or any hides, skins, or flesh carried from such county, or from any hundred, lathe, wapentake, rape, ward, or other division of such county so infected, into the county so making such order ; and in case any person shall act contrary to such order, such person shall incur the penalties and forfeitures enacted against persons driving cattle without certificates.

Upon information that the distemper is in a neighbouring county, the justices may prohibit the removal of cattle or hides from thence.

XXXIX. And be it further enacted by the authority aforesaid, That if action or suit shall be commenced against any person or persons, for any thing done in pursuance of this act, the defendant or defendants in such action or suit may plead the general issue, and give this act and the special matter in evidence, at any trial to be had thereupon ; and that the same was done in pursuance and by authority of this act, or of some rule, order or regulation made or to be made in pursuance of this act ; and if it shall appear so to have been done, then the jury shall find for the defendant or defendants ; and if the plaintiff shall be nonsuited, or discontinue his action after the defendant or defendants shall have appeared ; or if judgment shall be given upon any verdict or demurrer against the plaintiff, the defendant or defendants shall and may recover treble costs, and have the like remedy for the same, as the defendant or defendants hath or have in other cases by law.

Persons sued on this act, may plead the general issue.

Treble costs.

XL. And be it further enacted by the authority aforesaid, That this act shall continue and be in force until the twenty ninth day of *September* one thousand seven hundred and fifty seven, and from thence to the end of the then next session of parliament.

Continuance of the act.

C A P. XXI.

An act for the more effectual preservation and improvement of the spawn and fry of fish in the river of Thames, *and waters of* Medway ; *and for the better regulating the fishery thereof.*

WHEREAS *by an act of parliament made and passed in the ninth year of the reign of her late majesty Queen* Anne, *intituled,* An act for the better preservation and improvement of the fishery within the river of *Thames; and for regulating and governing the company of fishermen of the said river ; it was enacted, That from and after the tenth day of* June one thousand seven

9 Annæ, c. 26.

seven hundred and eleven, it should and might be lawful to and for the court of assistants of the said company, for the time being, or the major part of them present, to make such by-laws and ordinances for the good rule and government of the said company, as they should think fit, so as the same should be always first approved of, or from time to time altered and amended by the court of the mayor and aldermen of the city of London, *and likewise allowed and confirmed according to the form of the statute in that behalf made and provided; and that from and after the said tenth day of* June *there should be yearly elected and chosen by the next court of mayor and aldermen to be held after the tenth day of* June, *out of the six wardens of the said company for the time being, to be nominated by the said court of assistants, one fit person to be a master of the art or mystery of fishermen; and also out of twelve assistants to be nominated as aforesaid, six fit persons to be wardens of the said art or mystery (whereof the water bailiff of the city of* London *for the time being, to be one) and in like manner, out of sixty of the commonalty, to be nominated as aforesaid, thirty fit persons to be assistants of the said company; which said master, wardens and assistants, or any sixteen of them, together with three of the said wardens, should be, and were thereby constituted the court of assistants of the said company, for the time being; and were required to meet and assemble together, from time to time, on the first* Tuesday *in every calendar month in the year, in the hall of the said company, in order to form the said court of assistants, and keep the same for regulating and reforming abuses committed in the said fishery; and for the due ordering and governance of the said company: and whereas in pursuance of the said act of parliament, certain by-laws and ordinances were made for regulating the said fishery, and reforming abuses committed therein, but the said company having ceased to act from about the year one thousand seven hundred and twenty seven, and most of the members thereof being dead, the regulations in the said fishery intended by the said act have not taken place, and the several laws now in force for the preservation of the said fishery, have hitherto proved ineffectual, and by the unwarrantable practices used by fishermen and others, the brood and fry of fish in the said river and waters of* Medway *have been greatly hurt and destroyed: for remedy whereof and for the better preserving the spawn, fry and young brood of fish in the said river of* Thames, *and also in the waters of* Medway, *so far as the same are within the jurisdiction of the mayor of the city of* London, *as conservator of the river of* Thames, *and waters of* Medway, *and for preventing the fishing therein with unlawful and unsizeable nets, engines or other devices; and for the ascertaining the times, seasons, and manner of fishing in the said river and waters, and the size and kind of nets and engines to be used in fishing in the said river and waters; and for regulating the said fishery, and reforming abuses therein; and for the more speedy and effectual apprehending and punishing the offenders;* be it enacted by the King's most excellent majesty, by and with the advice and consent of the lords spiritual and temporal and commons in this present parliament assembled, and by the authority of the same, That the court of the mayor and aldermen of the said city of

London

London for the time being, shall have full power and authority, and they are hereby required on or before the twenty ninth day of *September* in the year of our Lord one thousand seven hundred and fifty seven, to make, frame and set down in writing, such reasonable rules, orders or ordinances, for the governing and regulating all persons who shall fish or drudge in the said river of *Thames*, and also in the said waters of *Medway* (within the said jurisdiction of the said mayor, as conservator as aforesaid) as common fishermen or drudgermen, or otherwise; and for declaration in what manner they shall demean themselves in fishing, and with what manner of nets and engines, and at what times and seasons they shall use fishing in the said river and waters of *Medway*, within the jurisdiction aforesaid, and for ascertaining the assize of the several fish to be there taken; and for the preservation from time to time of the spawn and fry of fish in the said river and waters, within the jurisdiction aforesaid; and for obliging every common fisherman or drudgerman, or other such person who shall fish with a boat, vessel or craft, from and after the said twenty ninth day of *September* one thousand seven hundred and fifty seven, in the said river of *Thames*, and in the said waters of *Medway*, within the jurisdiction aforesaid, to have in his boat, vessel or craft, both his christian and surname, and also the name of the parish or place in which he dwelleth, painted in legible and large characters, in some convenient place where any one may see and read the same; and for preventing such name or mark of distinction from being changed, altered or defaced; and to annex reasonable penalties and forfeitures for the breach of such rules, orders or ordinances, not exceeding the sum of five pounds for any one offence; and such rules, orders and ordinances, or any of them, from time to time, to alter and amend, and such new and other rules, orders and ordinances, touching the matters aforesaid, with such reasonable penalties and forfeitures (not exceeding five pounds for any one offence) from time to time to make, as to the said court in their discretion shall seem meet, for the better putting this act in execution; so as after the making thereof the same be allowed and approved of, from time to time, by the lord chancellor of *Great Britain*, the lord keeper or lords commissioners of the great seal, for the time being, the lord chief justice of the court of *King's Bench*, the lord chief justice of the court of *Common Pleas*, the lord chief baron of the court of *Exchequer*, or any two of them, who are hereby required, on request from time to time to them, or any two or more of them, made by or on the behalf of the said court of mayor and aldermen, to peruse and examine all such rules, orders or ordinances, as shall, from time to time, be made by the said court of mayor and aldermen, in pursuance of this act, and laid before the said lord high chancellor, lord keeper, or lords commissioners of the great seal, for the time being, the said lord chief justice of the court of *King's Bench*, the said lord chief justice of the court of *Common Pleas*, the said lord chief baron, or any two of them, for their allow-

The court of mayor and aldermen of London, impowered to make rules for regulating the fishermen and drudgermen in the Thames and Medway; the rules to be approved of by two of the judges.

allowance and approbation; and they, or any two of them, are
to allow thereof, or alter the fame, before they allow thereof,
as they or any two of them, fhall from time to time think fit; and
for the doing thereof, no fee or reward fhall be paid or taken.

The penalties annexed to the faid rules, confirmed.

II. And be it further enacted by the authority aforefaid,
That no perfon or perfons whatfoever fhall, within the faid jurifdiction of the faid mayor, from and after the firft day of *November* one thoufand feven hundred and fifty feven, wilfully
take, deftroy, fpoil, kill or expofe to fale, or exchange for any
goods, matter or thing, whatfoever, any fpawn, fry or brood of
fifh, or fpatt of oyfters, or any unfizeable or unwholfome fifh,
or fifh out of feafon, or bring fuch fifh on fhore for fale, or ufe
or keep any net, engine or other device whatfoever, which fhall
be prohibited or declared unlawful in and by fuch rules, orders,
and ordinances of the faid court of mayor and aldermen of the
faid city allowed and approved of as aforefaid, upon pain of forfeiting and paying, for every offence, fuch fum and fums of
money as in and by fuch rules, orders or ordinances, fhall be
refpectively appointed, and to be recovered in fuch manner as is
herein after mentioned.

The rules to be printed and publifhed.

III. Provided neverthelefs, and be it enacted by the authority
aforefaid, That fuch rules, orders and ordinances, fo to be from
time to time made by the faid court of the mayor and aldermen,
fhall, within thirty days after the fame fhall be allowed and approved of as aforefaid, be printed and made publick in fuch
manner as the faid court fhall think proper, and from time to
time order.

*Court to fum-
mon occafion-
ally, 12 fifher-
men, and ex-
amine them
touching the
fifhery of the
Thames and
Medway;*

IV. *And to the intent the faid court of the mayor and aldermen of
the faid city may be the better informed what rules, orders and ordinances may be proper to be made from time to time, for the better
regulation and prefervation of the faid fifhery*; be it further enacted by the authority aforefaid, That the faid court fhall at fome
time or times between the twenty fifth day of *June* and twenty
ninth day of *September* next, and fo yearly for ever thereafter,
(if occafion fhall fo require) between the twenty fifth day of
June and twenty ninth day of *September* in every year, order to
be fummoned before them fuch and fo many perfons who fhall
fifh in the faid river of *Thames*, or waters of *Medway*, within
the jurifdiction aforefaid, as common fifhermen or drudgermen
(not exceeding twelve in number) as to the faid court fhall
feem meet to be examined upon oath (if the faid court fhall fo
think fit) touching the fifh and fifhery of the faid river and wa-

*Fifhermen re-
fufing to at-
tend or to be
examined for-
feit 40s.*

ters; and if any fuch common fifherman or drudgerman being
perfonally fummoned by writing to attend the faid court of
mayor and aldermen for the purpofes aforefaid, by the fpace of
fourteen days at the leaft, fhall neglect or refufe fo to do, or in
cafe of attendance fhall refufe to be examined upon oath as a-
forefaid, not having or making appear before the faid court fome
juft or lawful excufe for fuch neglect or refufal; then, and in
every fuch cafe, he or they fo offending fhall, on due proof
made by oath in fuch court of the due fervice of the fummons

in

in manner aforesaid, forfeit and lose the sum of forty shillings, to be levied by distress and sale of his or their goods and chattels, by warrant under the hand and seal of the said mayor, or the recorder of the said city, or any one alderman of the said city, directed to any assistant of the said water bailiff, or any constable, headborough or peace officer, impowering him, them or any of them, to make the said distress for the said forty shillings, and cause the same to be appraised and sold after the expiration of five days from the making such distress, rendering the overplus, if any, to the said offender; which said penal sum shall, as soon as received, be paid to the treasurer of Greenwich hospital for the benefit of the same hospital. *to be levied by distress and sale,* . / *and paid to Greenwich hospital.*

V. And be it further enacted by the authority aforesaid, That for the better preservation of the said fishery of the said river of *Thames*, and waters of *Medway*, within the jurisdiction aforesaid, and for preventing, as much as may be, any abuses from being committed therein, it shall and may be lawful to and for the deputy of the said mayor for the time being, as conservator as aforesaid, commonly called *The water bailiff*, and his assistant and assistants, such assistant and assistants having been named and appointed to be his assistant and assistants, by warrant under the hand and seal of the mayor of the said city for the time being, and likewise for all and every other person or persons who shall for that purpose be specially authorized by any warrant or warrants under the hand and seal of the said mayor, from time to time, and at all times, to enter into any boat, vessel or craft of any fisherman or drudgerman, or other person or persons fishing or taking fish, or endeavouring to take fish, upon the said river of *Thames*, or upon the said waters of *Medway*, within the jurisdiction aforesaid, and there search for, take and seize all spawn, fry, brood of fish, spatt of oysters, and unsizeable, unwholesome or unseasonable fish, and also all unlawful nets, engines and instruments, for taking or destroying fish, as shall then be in any such boat or boats, vessel or craft, in or upon the said river or waters; and to take and seize on the shore or shores adjoining to the said river, or waters of *Medway*, within the jurisdiction aforesaid, all such spawn, fry, brood of fish, spatt of oysters, unsizeable, unwholesome, or unseasonable fish, as shall be there found; and such deputy and assistants, or other persons, who shall be so authorized as aforesaid, shall from time to time, with all convenient speed, after the seizing or taking of any such unlawful nets, engines or instruments, or any spawn, fry, brood of fish, or spatt of oysters, or unsizeable, unwholesome or unseasonable fish, bring or cause the same to be brought, before the mayor of the said city for the time being, or the recorder of the said city, or one of the aldermen of the said city, if seised within the limits of the said city of *London*, and liberties thereof, either upon the said river or on shore, or before the mayor of the said city for the time being, or the recorder of the said city, or one of the aldermen of the said city, or one of his Majesty's justices of the peace of the county in which such seizure

Water bailiff, his assistants, and others authorized by the mayor, / *may enter into fishermens boats, and seize all prohibited fish, nets, &c. on board,* / *and such as shall be found on the shore;* / *and bring them before a proper magistrate;*

zure shall be made, if made upon the said river or waters, out of the limits of the said city, or the liberties thereof, but within the jurisdiction of the said mayor as conservator as aforesaid, or before one of his Majesty's justices of the peace of the county in which the same shall be seised on shore, who shall respectively cause such nets, engines or instruments, or spawn, fry, brood of fish, spatt of oysters, unsizable, unwholesome or unseasonable

and the same being found, to be contrary to the rules, fish, so seised, to be examined; and if the same shall, upon view and examination thereof, or on proof on oath before him or them made (which oath he and they is and are hereby impowered to administer) appear to be unsizeable, unwholesome or unseasonable fish, or unlawful nets, engines or instruments for taking unsizeable fish, or destroying of fish or spawn of fish, contrary to such rules, orders or ordinances, as shall be made by the said court of the said mayor and aldermen, and allowed and approved of as aforesaid, and the intent and meaning of this act, and that the same were so seised as aforesaid, the said mayor, recorder, or any alderman of the said city, or justice respectively, within their respective jurisdictions, shall cause to be forthwith

are to be burnt. burnt or destroyed, as well all such unlawful nets, engines or instruments, as also all such spawn, fry or unsizeable, unwholesome or unseasonable fish, as shall be seised as aforesaid.

Penalty of 10 l. for obstructing an officer in his duty, or rescuing an offender. VI. And be it further enacted by the authority aforesaid, That if any person or persons shall obstruct or hinder the said water bailiff, his assistants, or any of the said officers, or any constable, headborough or other peace officer, in the execution of any of the powers vested in them by this act, or of any warrant or warrants to be issued by the said mayor, recorder, or any alderman of the said city, or justice respectively, in pursuance of this act; or if any person or persons whatsoever shall rescue any person or persons who shall be apprehended or taken by virtue or in pursuance of any of the powers given by this act, the person or persons so offending therein shall, for every such offence, forfeit the sum of ten pounds, on conviction thereof by the oath of one or more credible witness or witnesses, before the said mayor, recorder, or one of the aldermen of the said city, within the said city and liberties, or the jurisdiction aforesaid, or before a justice of the county where the said offence shall be committed, or where the offender shall be apprehended.

Magistrates to determine complaints touching offences against the rules, in a summary way; VII. And be it further enacted by the authority aforesaid, That the mayor, recorder, or any one alderman of the said city, within the said city and jurisdiction aforesaid, and his Majesty's justices of the peace of the respective counties within the jurisdiction aforesaid, or any one of them, shall have full power to hear and determine in a summary way, complaints touching any unlawful or undue fishing, or taking or destroying fish, or any other offences to be committed contrary to any of the rules, orders or ordinances, at any time hereafter to be made by the said court of the mayor and aldermen in pursuance of this act, and which shall be allowed and approved of as aforesaid; and the said mayor, recorder, aldermen and justices, and each of

them

them respectively, within their respective jurisdictions, are and is hereby authorized and required upon view, or upon complaint made on oath to them respectively, of any such offence committed within their respective jurisdictions, contrary to such rules, orders or ordinances, within ten days after the commission of any such offence, to issue his or their warrant or warrants under his hand and seal, or their hands and seals, directed to the water bailiff of the said city, or such his assistant or assistants as aforesaid, or to such constables, headboroughs or other peace officers, as the said mayor, recorder, aldermen or justices, or any one of them shall, from time to time think fit, thereby requiring him or them to apprehend such offender or offenders, and to bring him, her or them, before the said mayor, recorder, aldermen or justices, or any one of them, within their respective jurisdictions, to answer the matters of complaint to be contained in such warrant or warrants; and which warrant or warrants the person and persons to whom the same shall be directed, and their assistants, are hereby authorized, impowered and required, to execute on the said river of *Thames*, or on the waters of *Medway*, or on any part thereof, within the jurisdiction aforesaid, or on any shore adjoining to the said river, or waters of *Medway*; and for that purpose, they, and every of them, are hereby authorized, impowered and required, at all times, to go on board any boat, vessel or craft, in the said river or waters; or in the day time, with a peace officer, to enter any house wherein any such offender or offenders shall be, for the apprehending him, her or them; and when apprehended, to carry him, her or them, as soon as conveniently may be, before the said mayor, recorder, or one of the aldermen of the said city, if apprehended in the said city of *London*, or the liberties thereof; and if apprehended out of the said city of *London*, or the liberties thereof, then before one of the justices of the county where the said offender or offenders shall be taken; and the said mayor, recorder, aldermen and justices, within their respective jurisdictions, or any one of them, are and is hereby authorized and required to summon witnesses, on either side, before them, and to examine them on oath (which oath the said mayor, recorder, aldermen and justices respectively, or any one of them, is and are hereby authorized, impowered and required, to administer) touching the premisses, and thereupon to hear and determine the same; and in case any offender or offenders shall thereupon, by the said mayor, recorder or aldermen, or the said justices, or one of them, be convicted, and adjudged guilty of any such offence, then such offender or offenders shall thereby incur and forfeit such penalty as shall be by such rules and ordinances set and imposed for the same; and that such warrant or warrants, or other act or acts of the said mayor, recorder, aldermen or justices, and the act and acts of the water bailiff, and his assistants, and of all constables, headboroughs and other persons, in obedience to such warrant or warrants, shall be as valid, good and effectual in law, to all intents whatsoever, as if the same were exe-

Margin notes: and upon view or complaint on oath of any offence, to issue their warrants for apprehending offenders, / and to summon witnesses, and examine them on oath. / Upon conviction, offender to forfeit as the rules direct.

cuted within the proper limits of their own city, county or jurifdiction.

VIII. And be it further enacted by the authority aforefaid,
That if any witnefs or witneffes who fhall be fummoned in
purfuance of this act to appear before the faid mayor, recorder,
aldermen, or juftices of the peace, or any one of them, within
their refpective jurifdictions aforefaid, fhall neglect or refufe to
appear according to the direction of the fummons, or appearing
fhall refufe to be examined on oath touching the premiffes, and
no juft excufe fhall be offered for fuch neglect or refufal, every
perfon fo offending, on proof on oath being made of fuch fummons having been ferved on him, her or them, fhall for every
fuch offence, forfeit and lofe fuch fum of money, not exceeding
five pounds, nor lefs than twenty fhillings, as the faid mayor,
recorder, aldermen or juftices, or any one of them, within their
refpective jurifdictions, fhall by warrant under his hand or their
hands order or direct.

IX. And be it further enacted by the authority aforefaid,
That if any affiftant or affiftants of the water bailiff of the faid
city, or any peace officer, fhall wittingly or willingly neglect or
refufe to ferve or execute any warrant or warrants to him or
them directed in purfuance of this act, or fhall otherwife wilfully or wittingly omit the performance of his or their duty in the
execution of this act, and fhall be thereof convicted by the oath
of one or more credible witnefs or witneffes, before the faid
mayor, recorder, or any fuch alderman, or juftice as aforefaid,
within their refpective jurifdictions, every fuch affiftant or peace
officer fo offending fhall forfeit and lofe any fum of money not
exceeding five pounds, as the faid mayor, recorder, alderman,
or juftice, or any one of them, within their refpective jurifdictions fhall think reafonable and direct.

X. And be it further enacted by the authority aforefaid,
That if the faid water bailiff, or any of his affiftants, fhall at any
time hereafter receive any fum of money, gratuity or reward
whatfoever, from any perfon or perfons to prevent, delay or
hinder any profecution ; or compound for, or wilfully conceal
any offence to be committed contrary to this act, and fhall be
thereof convicted by the oath of one or more credible witnefs or
witneffes, before the faid mayor, recorder or aldermen, of the
faid city, or any one of them (and which oath the faid mayor,
recorder and aldermen or any one of them, is and are hereby
authorized to adminifter) fuch water bailiff and his affiftants refpectively, for every fuch offence fhall forfeit and lofe the fum of
five pounds.

XI. *And for the better and more eafy recovery of the feveral penalties and forfeitures to be incurred by difobedience to this act, and
the powers therein contained, and difpofing of the faid forfeitures,
where no particular provifion is already made herein* ; be it further
enacted by the authority aforefaid, That it fhall and may be
lawful to and for the mayor of the faid city of *London* for the
time being, recorder and aldermen of the faid city, or any one
of

Side notes (left margin):

Witnefs re-
fufing to ap-
pear, or to
give evidence,

without juft
caufe, forfeits
not exceeding
5l. nor lefs
than 20s.

Officer neg-
lecting his
duty, forfeits
any fum not
exceeding 5l.

Penalty 5l. on
water bailiff,
or affiftant,
taking any
gratuity to
fcreen, &c. an
offender.

Method of
recovery, and
application of
the forfeiture.

of them, within the said city, or liberties thereof, or within the jurisdiction aforesaid, and to and for any other of his Majesty's justices of the peace, or any one of them, within their respective counties, on the conviction of any person or persons for any offence or offences committed contrary to the true meaning of this act, the forfeiture not being paid, to issue a warrant or warrants under his hand and seal, or their hands and seals respectively, directed to the assistant or assistants of the said water bailiff, or any peace officer, within their respective jurisdictions, impowering him or them to make distress of the goods and chattels of the said offender or offenders, for the sum to be levied by any such warrants; and to cause such goods and chattels, after five days from the distress taken, to be appraised and sold, rendering the overplus, if any, after deducting the forfeiture and the costs and charges of the distress and sale, to the owners; which charges shall be ascertained by the magistrate before whom such offender or offenders shall have been so convicted; and for want of such distress and non-payment, then it shall be lawful for the said mayor, recorder, aldermen and justices, or any one of them, within their respective jurisdictions, by warrant under his hand and seal, to commit such offender or offenders to the common gaol or house of correction of the city or county, where such offender or offenders shall be convicted, there to remain for the space of three months from the time of such commitment, unless payment shall be made of the said penalty, costs and charges, before the expiration of the said three months; and one moiety of all such penalties and forfeitures, when recovered, shall be paid to the informer, and the other moiety thereof shall be paid to the treasurer of *Greenwich hospital* aforesaid, for the use of the said hospital; but in case any such offender or offenders shall think him or themselves aggrieved by such conviction, and shall within the said five days enter into a recognizance with two good and sufficient sureties, in the penal sum of twenty pounds, before such magistrate or magistrates, before whom he, she or they, shall be so convicted, (which said recognizance shall be returned, within the space of fourteen days, to the said court of the mayor and aldermen) conditioned for his personal appearance at some court of the said mayor and aldermen of the said city, to be holden within six weeks after the acknowledging such recognizance, or at the next court of conservacy to be held for the county in which such offence shall be committed, and to stand to and abide such order as shall be made in the premisses by such court, then the goods so distrained shall be returned to the party or parties from whom the same were taken; and the said court of mayor and aldermen, or court of conservacy, is hereby impowered and directed upon a petition of appeal presented to them, by the party or parties so convicted, complaining of such conviction, to appoint a time for the hearing and determining the matter of such appeal, and thereupon to cause notice to be given to the parties, and to summon witnesses to attend at the time so appointed, and then to examine

For want of distress, offender to be committed for 3 months.

One moiety of the penalty to go to the informer, the other to Greenwich hospital. If the offender, aggrieved by such conviction, shall enter into a recognizance, with sureties, to abide the order of the court,

the distress is to be returned; and the court to hear and determine such appeal,

H 2   such

such witneffes upon oath, and finally to hear and determine the matter of such appeal or complaint, and make such order therein, as to such court shall seem meet; and the said courts respectively shall, and they are hereby impowered to order all or any of the penalties laid on or incurred by any of the parties complaining, to be mitigated, or to vacate or set aside such conviction or convictions, or otherwise to ratify and confirm the same, and at their discretion to award such reasonable costs to be paid by the appellant, as to them shall seem meet; and the said court of mayor and aldermen, or court of conservacy, may, on forfeiture of any such recognizance, estreat the same into his Majesty's court of *exchequer*, there to be proceeded upon and executed in the same manner, as estreats returned to the said court of *exchequer*, from any court of conservacy held by the said mayor of the said city.

and to mitigate the penalties, or vacate the conviction, or confirm the same with costs; and on forfeiture of recognizance, to estreat the same into the exchequer.

XII. And be it further enacted by the authority aforesaid, That the mayor, recorder, or any alderman or justice before whom any person shall be convicted in manner prescribed by this act, shall cause such respective conviction to be drawn up in the form, or to the effect following; that is to say,

Form of conviction.

To wit.   BE it remembered, That on this day of   in the   year of his Majesty's reign, A. B. is convicted before me, one of his Majesty's justices of the peace for the city or county of   (as the case shall happen to be) for   (here set forth the offence) and I do adjudge him to pay and forfeit for the same the sum of

Given under my hand and seal, the day and year aforesaid.

to be written on parchment, and transmitted to the court to be filed;

And the said mayor, recorder, alderman or justice before whom such conviction shall be had, shall cause the same so drawn up in the form aforesaid, to be fairly written upon parchment, and transmitted to the court of mayor and aldermen, or court of conservacy, to be filed and kept amongst the records of the said court, to which the same shall be transmitted; and in case any person or persons so convicted shall appeal from the judgment of the said mayor, recorder, or any alderman or justice as aforesaid, to the said court of mayor and aldermen, or court of conservacy, the said court of mayor and aldermen, or court of conservacy, is hereby required upon receiving the said conviction, drawn up in the form aforesaid, to proceed to the hearing and determination of the matter of the said appeal, according to the directions of this act; any law or usage to the contrary notwithstanding.

Conviction, or other proceedings of

XIII. And be it further enacted by the authority aforesaid, That no writ of *certiorari*, or other writ or process for removal of any such conviction, or any proceedings thereon, into any of his Majesty's courts of record at *Westminster*, shall be allowed [the court, not removeable by certiorari,] or granted.

XIV. And it is hereby further enacted, That in case any person, against whom a warrant shall be issued by the said mayor, recorder, or any alderman, or justice of the peace, either before or after conviction as aforesaid, for any offence against this act, shall escape, go into, reside, or be in any other county, riding, division, city, liberty, town or place out of the jurisdiction of such person granting such warrant or warrants as aforesaid ; or if the goods and chattels of any offender convicted of any offence in pursuance of this act, shall be in a different county, riding, division, city, liberty, town or place, than where the said party was convicted, or the warrant of distress granted ; it shall and may be lawful for the said mayor, recorder, or any alderman as aforesaid, or any justice of the peace of the county, riding, division, city, liberty, town or place into which such person shall escape either before or after conviction, or where his goods and chattels shall be, after such conviction ; and they and every of them are hereby required, upon proof made upon oath of the hand writing of the said mayor, recorder, alderman or justice granting such warrant or warrants, to indorse his or their name or names on such warrant ; and the same, when so indorsed, shall be a sufficient authority to all peace officers to execute such warrant in such other county, riding, division, city, town or place out of the jurisdiction of the person granting the said warrant ; and the said mayor, recorder, aldermen and justices respectively, or any one of them, as the case shall happen, after indorsing the said warrant, may, on the offender or offenders being apprehended and brought before the said mayor, recorder, aldermen or justices, or any one of them, within their respective jurisdictions, proceed to hear and determine the complaint, in the same manner as if it had originally arose within their respective jurisdictions, or may direct the offender to be carried to the person who granted the said warrant, to be dealt with according to law.

> If the offender escape out of the jurisdiction of the person granting a warrant against him, or if his goods be in a different county, &c.
>
> any justice of the peace, &c. may indorse the warrant,
>
> and peace officer execute the same ;
>
> and the offender may be tried by such justice,
>
> or remanded back to be tried by the person granting the warrant.

XV. Provided always, and it is hereby enacted and declared, That nothing in this act contained shall extend or enure to prejudice or derogate from the rights, privileges, franchises or authority of the city of *London*, or any rights, privileges or authority exercised by the mayor of the said city for the time being, as conservator as aforesaid ; or to prohibit, defeat, alter or diminish any power, authority or jurisdiction, which at the time of making this act, the mayor commonalty and citizens of *London*, or the mayor of the city of *London*, as conservator of the said river of *Thames* and waters of *Medway*, did or might lawfully claim, use or exercise ; and further, That it shall and may be lawful to and for the said mayor of the said city for the time being, in like manner as he hath used to do in other cases, to inquire of, hear and determine, by presentment or indictment taken before him as conservator of the said river and waters, all unlawful and undue fishing, and taking and destroying fish, and all other offences contrary to such rules, orders and ordinances as shall be made

> Rights and privileges of the city of London, and of the mayor and corporation, reserved.
>
> The mayor, as conservator, may try by presentment or indictment, all unlawful and undue fishing, and o-

ther offences contrary to the rules, and impose suitable fines,

to be applied as penalties inflicted by the court of conservacy.

by the said court of mayor and aldermen, and allowed and approved of as aforesaid; and upon conviction of any such offender or offenders, to impose a fine on him, her or them for the said offence, not exceeding the penalties which shall be inflicted in and by the said rules, orders or ordinances; and which fine or fines, when levied and recovered, shall be applied and distributed in like manner as the penalties inflicted by the said court of conservacy have been usually applied and distributed; but no person shall be punished twice for one and the same offence.

Limitation of actions.

General issue.

Double costs.

Publick act.

XVI. And be it further enacted by the authority aforesaid, That all actions, suits and informations, which shall be commenced and prosecuted against any person or persons for any thing which he, she or they shall do, or cause to be done in pursuance of this act, shall be commenced, sued or prosecuted within six months next after the cause of action shall accrue; and all such persons against whom any such actions, suits or informations shall be commenced, sued or prosecuted, shall and may plead the general issue, and give this act and the special matter in evidence; and if in any such suit, the plaintiff or prosecutor shall become nonsuit, or shall forbear prosecution, or discontinue his suit; or if a verdict shall pass, or judgment shall be given against him upon a demurrer, then, and in any such case, the defendant or defendants shall recover double costs, for which he or they shall have like remedy, as when costs by law are awarded; and this act shall be taken and allowed in all courts within this kingdom as a publick act; and all judges and justices are hereby required to take notice thereof as such, without the same being specially pleaded.

Act 24 G. 2, c. 44, extended to magistrates acting under this act;

and no action is issuable against an officer. till, notice be given him thereof;

XVII. And be it further enacted by the authority aforesaid, That the statute made in the twenty fourth year of his present Majesty's reign, intituled, *An act for the rendering justices of the peace more safe in the execution of their office; and for indemnifying constables and others, acting in obedience to their warrant,* so far as the said act relates to the rendering justices of the peace more safe in the execution of their office, shall extend, and be construed to extend, to the mayor, recorder and every alderman of the said city of *London,* and to every justice and justices of the peace, acting under the authority or in the execution of this act; and no action or suit shall be had or commenced against, nor any writ sued out, or copy of writ served upon the said water bailiff, his assistant or assistants, or any other officer or officers, for any thing done in the execution of this act, until notice in writing shall have been given to him or them, or left at his or their usual place of abode, by the attorney for the party commencing such action, or suing out such writ, one month before the commencing such action, or suing out or serving the copy of the said writ; which said notice in writing shall contain the name and place of abode of the person who is to bring such action, together with the cause of action or complaint; and the name and place of abode of the said attorney, shall be under wrote or indorsed thereon; and the said water bailiff, his assistant or assistants, and

the

the faid other officer or officers fhall be at liberty, and may, by virtue of this act, at any time within one calendar month after fuch notice, tender or caufe to be tendered any fum or fums of money, as amends for the injury complained of to the party complaining, or to the faid attorney; and if the fame is not accepted, the defendant or defendants in fuch action or actions may plead fuch tender in bar of fuch action or actions, together with the general iffue, or any other plea, with leave of the court; and if upon iffue joined upon fuch tender, the jury fhall find the amends tendered to have been fufficient, the faid jury fhall find a verdict for the defendant or defendants; and in fuch cafe, or if the plaintiff fhall become nonfuit, or difcontinue his action; or if judgment fhall be given for the defendant or defendants upon demurrer, the defendant or defendants fhall be intitled to double cofts; and if the jury fhall find that no fuch tender was made, or that the amends tendered were not fufficient; and alfo fhall find againft the defendant or defendants, on fuch other plea or pleas by them pleaded, the faid jury fhall find a verdict for the plaintiff, and fuch damages as they fhall think proper; for which the faid plaintiff fhall have judgment, together with his cofts of fuit.

and he may tender amends for the injury complained of,

and plead the fame, &c. or any other plea, in bar of the action;

and upon a verdict have double cofts.

Plaintiff recovering, intitled to damages and cofts of fuit.

XVIII. Saving always to the King's moft excellent majefty, his heirs and fucceffors, and all bodies politick and corporate, and to the high court of admiralty, and all other courts and perfons, all fines, forfeitures, penalties, amerciaments, and wreck of fea, which of right have been referved and become due and payable to the faid courts and perfons refpectively, for and in refpect of the faid fifhery or drudging; or otherwife, and all rights, titles, eftates, jurifdictions, privileges or franchifes whatfoever, in as full and ample a manner as the fame were or have been, before the making of this act; and alfo all fuch right, title, intereft, claim, privilege and confervation, and inquiry and punifhment of and for the offences aforefaid, as they or any of them lawfully have and enjoy, or of right ought to have and enjoy, by any manner of means; any thing in this act to the contrary notwithftanding.

Refervation of accuftomable rights and privileges, to the crown, and to all bodies politick and corporate, and other perfons,

XIX. Provided always, and be it enacted by the authority aforefaid, That this act, or any thing herein contained, fhall not extend, or be conftrued to extend to prejudice or derogate from any of the rights of the admiralties or vice-admiralties of *Kent* or *Effex*, or any pifcaries or fifhings belonging to or appertaining to the faid city of *London*, or any other city or town corporate, or any lords of manors, proprietors, owners or occupiers of any rivers, creeks, ftreams or fifheries adjacent to or within any part of the faid limits, or to the rights of any other perfon or perfons within the limits aforefaid.

Refervation of rights to the admiralties of Kent and Effex, Pifcaries, &c.

XX. Provided alfo, That nothing in this act contained fhall extend, or be conftrued to extend, to any fifherman or drudgerman who now do or fhall hereafter inhabit or dwell in any of the cinque ports or their members, or in the city of *Rochefter*, or towns or places of *Strood, Chatham, Frindfbury, Gillingham, Milton,*

Places and perfons exempted from the jurifdiction of this act.

tan, Queenborough, Feversham, Whistaple or the places adjacent; but that such fishermen and drudgermen shall and may use and exercise their trades of fishing and drudging, and selling, in as full and ample manner as they have heretofore lawfully done, to all intents and purposes as if this act had never been made.

Fishermen not liable to take out licences, or pay any gratuity for liberty of fishing,

XXI. Provided always, and it is hereby further enacted, That nothing herein contained shall extend or be construed to extend to impower or authorize the said mayor, court of mayor and aldermen, the water bailiff, or any other person whatsoever, to grant any licence or licences, or to make any rules, orders or ordinances whereby any licence or licences shall be required to be taken by any fisherman, drudgerman or other person, for going out to fish, fishing, drudging, or taking fish in any manner of way, or whereby any gratuities, rewards or compensations, under any pretence or denomination whatsoever, shall be paid or payable by any fisherman, drudgerman or other such person, to the water bailiff, or his successors, or to any other person or persons;

or to appear and enter their names,

or whereby any such fisherman, drudgerman or other such person shall be obliged to appear before the said mayor, water bailiff or other person, to enter his or their several name or names, in any register or other book, or whereby any such fisherman, drudger-

or to be restrained from keeping any number of boys.

man or other person as aforesaid, shall be limited or restrained from keeping any number of boys in any one boat, as such fisherman, drudgerman, or other person shall judge proper; any thing in the said act of the ninth year of her late majesty Queen *Anne,* or any other statute, law, custom or usage to the contrary in any wise notwithstanding.

C A P. XXII.

An act to explain and amend an act made in the eighteenth year of his present Majesty's reign, to prevent the misbehaviour of the drivers of carts in the streets in London, Westminster, *and the limits of the weekly bills of mortality; and for other purposes in this act mentioned.*

18 G. 2. c. 32.

WHEREAS *by an act made and passed in the eighteenth year of his present Majesty's reign, intituled,* An act to repeal a clause in an act made in the third year of the reign of King *William* and Queen *Mary,* relating to carts used by persons inhabiting within the limits of the weekly bills of mortality; and to allow such carts to be drawn with three horses; and to prevent the misbehaviour of the drivers of carts in streets within the said limits; *therein reciting (amongst other things) that great inconveniencies had arisen from the irregular behaviour of carmen, draymen and other persons driving carts, drays and other carriages within the cities of* London *and* Westminster, *and suburbs thereof, the borough of* Southwark, *and other streets within the bills of mortality, by their misusing and hindering the passage of his Majesty's subjects through the said streets and highways, and committing other disorders of the like kind; for remedy whereof it was thereby enacted, That from and after the twenty ninth day of* September *one thousand seven hundred*

and

and forty fin, no person or persons whatsoever should drive any cart, car or dray of any kind whatsoever, within the limits aforesaid, unless the master or owner of such cart, car or dray, should place upon some conspicuous part of such cart, car or dray the name of the owner of such cart, car or dray, and the number of such cart, car or dray so belonging unto him, in order that the driver of such cart, car or dray might the more easily be convicted for any disorder or misbehaviour committed by him as aforesaid; and it was thereby further enacted, That every owner of such cart, car or dray residing within the limits aforesaid, should enter his name and place of abode with the commissioners for licensing hackney coaches, for which entry he should pay the sum of one shilling and no more; and the said commissioners were thereby required to receive and register such entry as aforesaid; and it was thereby also enacted, That in case any person or persons should drive any such cart, car, or dray, within the limits aforesaid, not marked, numbered and entered as before directed, every such person so offending should forfeit the sum of forty shillings, and it should be lawful for any person or persons to seize and detain the cart, car or dray, or any of the horses drawing the same, and them to detain until such penalty should be paid: And whereas no provision is made by the said act, to whom the money forfeited shall go and be paid, or to sell the cart, car, dray or horse as shall be seized in pursuance of the said act, to raise the forty shillings forfeited; be it therefore enacted by the King's most excellent majesty, by and with the advice and consent of the lords spiritual and temporal and commons in this present parliament assembled, and by the authority of the same, That one moiety of the money which shall be forfeited by the driver of any cart, car or dray, under the said act, shall go and be paid to the person or persons who shall apprehend and prosecute to conviction any offender or offenders against the said act; and that the other moiety thereof shall go and be paid to the overseers of the poor, if there shall be any, of the parish or place in which the offence shall be committed; and if there shall be no overseers in such parish or place, then to some other officer of such parish or place, for the use of the poor of such parish or place; and if the offender or offenders, on being convicted of any offence against the said act, before any justice of the peace within his jurisdiction, shall not, within the space of twenty four hours after any such conviction, pay the forty shillings forfeited, then the same shall be raised by sale of the cart, car, dray or horse which shall be seized; and every justice of the peace within his jurisdiction, is hereby authorized and required to issue his warrant under his hand and seal, directed to the constable, or some other peace officer of the parish or place in which the cart, car, dray or horse seized shall be, to cause sale to be made thereof with all convenient speed, for raising the money which shall be forfeited for any such offence or offences as aforesaid; rendering to the offender or offenders the overplus, (if any there shall be) after deducting the charges of the sale of any such cart, car, dray or horse, and also the expences the party or parties who shall have made the seizure shall be at by detaining or housing thereof, or keeping any horse seized,

Application of the forfeiture.

On non-payment within 24 hours, distress may be sold.

Overplus to be returned, after deducting all charges.

un-

until sale shall be made thereof in pursuance of this act, or the money forfeited shall be paid.

On changing the property, new owner's name to be affixed on the cart,

II. And be it further enacted by the authority aforesaid, That every time the property of any cart, car or dray, which is or shall be entered with the said commissioners for licensing hackney coaches in pursuance of the said recited or this present act, shall be altered, the new owner or owners thereof shall, from time to time, within seven days next after he, she or they shall become owner or owners thereof, cause the name or names of the former owner or owners thereof to be taken off from every such cart, car or dray, and the name or names of the new and real owner or owners thereof to be put or painted in large and legible characters upon some conspicuous part thereof, and also to be entered with the said commissioners for licensing hackney coaches;

and to be entered; and in default thereof;

and if any omission shall be made in doing thereof, and any person shall drive any such cart, car or dray within the limits aforesaid, not having the name or names of the real owner or owners thereof painted or put thereon, in some conspicuous part thereof, and also entered with the said commissioners for licensing hackney coaches as herein before is directed, every such person so offending in the premisses, shall forfeit for every such offence the sum

Offender to forfeit 40s.

of forty shillings on being thereof convicted, either by his own confession, or by the oath of one or more credible witness or witnesses, before any justice of the peace of the county, city, division or place where any such offence shall be committed; and the said moiety so forfeited, shall go and be applied in like manner as the forty shillings forfeited for any offence committed against the said herein before recited act is hereby directed to go and be applied;

and the cart and horse may be seized and sold.

and every such cart, car and dray, and any horse drawing the same, is and are hereby subjected and made liable to be seized by any person or persons, and also to be sold, to raise and answer the money which shall be forfeited in pursuance of this act, together with the reasonable charges of every such sale, and of housing the cart, car or dray which shall be seized under this act, and keeping the horse which shall be also seized under this act, until sale shall be made thereof, or the money forfeited shall be paid.

III. *And whereas some doubt hath been made whether the justices of the peace of the city of London are authorized to ascertain at their general or quarter sessions of the peace in London, the rates or prices of goods taken up in London, and carried for hire out of London into the city of Westminster, and other places contiguous to London, by the carts, cars or carrooms licensed to work in London, and to compel persons who shall work any such carts, cars or carrooms licensed to work in London, to carry goods from any parts of the said city of London into the said city of Westminster, and other parts adjacent to London; and to enforce payment to the carmen for their labour and carriage of goods, according to the rates or prices which shall be set or ascertained at the said general or quarter sessions of the peace in London, and by reason thereof many inconveniencies have happened to merchants and others; be it therefore further enacted by the authority aforesaid, That the*
ju-

justices of the peace for the said city of *London*, for the time be- *Justices of the*
ing, shall have power and authority, and they are hereby enjoined *city to assess*
and required at the next general sessions of the peace which shall *annually the*
rates of car-
be holden for the said city of *London* after the twenty fourth day *riage of goods,*
of *June* one thousand seven hundred and fifty seven, and so afterwards at the general sessions of the peace which shall be holden
for the said city of *London* next after the twenty fourth day of
June in every year, as occasion shall require, to assess and rate
reasonable rates and prices for the carriage of all goods taken
up in the said city of *London*, and carried by any such licensed
carts, cars or carrooms, as well in the said city of *London* as from
the said city of *London* into the said city of *Westminster*, or any
other place or places not exceeding the distance of three miles
from the said city of *London*; and to make, frame and set down *and to make*
in writing such reasonable rules, orders and ordinances for go- *rules for regu-*
verning and regulating such carts, cars and carrooms, and the *lating carts*
and drivers,
drivers thereof, and to compel payment for carriage of goods *and for pay-*
by such licensed carts, cars or carrooms, according to the rates *ment of their*
or prices which shall be rated, assessed or set at any such sessions *fare,*
of the peace in *London* as aforesaid; and to annex reasonable pe- *and to annex*
nalties for breach of any such rules, orders or ordinances, not *penalties for*
breach of or-
exceeding five pounds for any one offence, as to the major part *ders;*
of the justices at any such sessions of the peace in *London* assembled shall seem meet; and such rules, orders and ordinances, *they may also*
or any of them, from time to time, at any other such sessions of *alter and a-*
the peace as aforesaid in *London*, to alter and amend; and such *mend the*
same, or make
new or other rules, orders and ordinances, touching the matters *new orders.*
aforesaid, with such reasonable penalties and forfeitures (not exceeding five pounds for any one offence) to make, as to the
major part of the justices at any such sessions of the peace assembled shall, from time to time, seem meet, for the better putting
this act in execution.

IV. Provided nevertheless, and be it enacted by the authority *The said rules*
aforesaid, That all such rules, orders and ordinances, so to be *to be printed*
from time to time made at any such sessions of the peace in *and published.*
London shall, within thirty days after the making the same, be
printed and affixed up in some publick places of the said city of
London, and be otherwise made publick, in such manner as the
said justices at their general or quarter sessions of the peace shall
think proper, and from time to time order.

V. *And whereas his Majesty's subjects are frequently interrupted*
and hindered passing on their lawful occasions in the publick streets,
lanes and open passages in the cities of London *and* Westminster,
and within the weekly bills of mortality, by empty pipes, butts, barrels,
casks and other vessels, and also by empty carts, cars, drays or other
carriages, standing or being placed there, and by other obstructions; *Persons wil-*
for remedy whereof, be it further enacted by the authority afore- *fully obstruct-*
said, That no persons, after the said twenty fourth day of *June*, shall *ing the passage*
wilfully obstruct the passing and repassing of his Majesty's sub- *of the streets,*
jects in any such publick streets, lanes or open passages within *&c. with emp-*
ty casks, carts,
the limits herein before mentioned, or put or set any empty *&c.*
pipes,

pipes, butts, barrels, casks or any other vessels in any such publick streets, lanes or open passages within the limits aforesaid, (except for such reasonable time only as shall be necessary for the carrying or removing thereof to or from any house, warehouse, cellar, vault or other place, or for the trimming thereof) or set or place any empty cart, car, dray or other carriage in any such publick street, lane or open passage within the limits aforesaid, except only dur-

except while plying for hire on their proper stands, ing such reasonable time as any such cart, car or other carriage shall be plying for hire, in the place or places appointed or to be appointed for the standing thereof so to ply for hire, by the persons authorized to appoint such the standings thereof, and except during such reasonable time as any such cart, car, dray or other

or taking up, or setting down, a fare, carriage shall be waiting in any such publick street, lane or open passage to load or unload goods or commodities, or to take up or set down a fare; and that every person offending in any of the cases aforesaid, and being convicted of any such offence, either by his own confession, or by the oath of one or more credible witness or witnesses, before any justice of the peace of the county, city, division or place where any such offence shall be committed, shall for every such offence forfeit any sum not ex-

liable to forfeit, not exceeding 20s. nor less than 5s. or to be committed. ceeding twenty shillings, and not less than the sum of five shillings; or shall be committed to the house of correction, or some other prison of the county, city, liberty, division or place in which the offence shall be committed, or the offender shall have been apprehended, there to remain and be kept to hard labour for any time not exceeding one calendar month, as any such justice shall think fit and order.

VI. *And whereas the passage from* Westminster *bridge into the city of* Westminster *is greatly obstructed, and rendered unsafe, by the constant stand of hackney coaches and other carriages, plying for hire near the said bridge;* be it therefore further enacted by the authority aforesaid, That no hackney coachman, carman, or

No coaches or carts to ply for hire in the streets here mentioned. other person or persons, shall, from and after the said twenty fourth day of *June,* ply for hire with any hackney coach, cart, or other wheel carriage, in *Bridge Street, Parliament Street, Great George Street, St. Margaret's Street,* or *Abingdon Street,* in the city of *Westminster,* or any of the said streets; or stop or stay

nor to stop there longer than to take up or set down a fare, in any of the said streets with any such coach, cart, or other wheel carriage, any longer time than shall be reasonable for such coachman, carman, or other person, having the care of any wheel carriage, to wait to take up or set down his fare, or to load and unload goods or other commodities; and that every coachman, carman, or other person, having the care of any such wheel carriage, offending in any of the cases aforesaid, and being convicted of any such offence, either by his own confession, or by the oath of one or more credible witness or witnesses before any justice of the peace for the city and liberty of *Westminster,* which oath such justice is hereby impowered and re-

on forfeiture of a sum not exceeding 20s. quired to administer, shall, for every such offence, forfeit any sum not exceeding twenty shillings, and not less than five shillings; or shall be committed to the house of correction in *Westmin-*

min-

minster, there to remain and be kept to hard labour for any time not exceeding one calendar month, as any such juftice fhall think fit and order.

nor lefs than 5 s. or being committed.

VII. And be it further enacted by the authority aforefaid, That if the driver of any carriage whatfoever in the faid cities of London or Weftminfter, or in any publick ftreet or common highways within the faid weekly bills of mortality, fhall by negligence or wilful mifbehaviour prevent, hinder or interrupt the free paffage of his Majefty's fubjects, in any of the publick ftreets in London or Weftminfter, or in any publick ftreets or common highways within the faid weekly bills of mortality, every fuch driver being convicted thereof, either by his own confeffion, or by the oath of one or more credible witnefs or witneffes before any juftice of the county, city, divifion, liberty or place wherein any fuch offence fhall be committed, and which oath every fuch juftice is hereby impowered to adminifter, fhall for every fuch offence forfeit any fum not exceeding twenty fhillings ; or fhall be committed to the houfe of correction, or fome other prifon of the county, city, liberty, divifion or place in which the offence fhall have been committed, or the offender fhall have been apprehended, there to be kept to hard labour, for any time not exceeding one calendar month, as any fuch juftice fhall think fit and order.

Driver of any carriage, obftructing the paffage in any of the ftreets within the bills of mortality,

forfeits any fum not exceeding 10 s. or may be committed.

VIII. *And for preventing obftructions in all the publick highways of this kingdom* ; be it enacted by the authority aforefaid, That if any perfon, after the twenty fourth day of *June* one thoufand feven hundred and fifty feven, fhall fet, place or leave, any empty waggon, cart, or any other carriage, in any publick highway within this kingdom, fo as in any manner to interrupt or hinder the free paffage of any other carriage, or of his Majefty's fubjects, except only during fuch reafonable time as fuch waggon, cart or carriage fhall be loading or unloading, every perfon fo offending, and being convicted of fuch offence, either by his own confeffion, or by the oath of one or more credible witnefs or witneffes, before any juftice of the peace for the county, riding, divifion, city or place where fuch offence fhall be committed, which oath fuch juftice is hereby impowered and required to adminifter ; fhall, for every fuch offence forfeit and pay any fum not exceeding twenty fhillings, to be levied by diftrefs and fale of the offender's goods and chattels, by warrant under the hand and feal of any juftice of the peace ; and for want of fufficient diftrefs, fuch juftice is hereby impowered and required to commit fuch offender to the houfe of correction, or fome other prifon of the county, riding, divifion, city or place in which the offence fhall be commited, or the offender fhall have been apprehended, there to remain and be kept to hard labour for any time not exceeding one calendar month.

20 s. penalty of obftructing the paffage of any of the highways by empty waggons, &c. except while they are loading or unloading,

to be levied by diftrefs and fale ;

and for want of diftrefs, offender to be committed;

IX. And be it further enacted by the authority aforefaid, That if after the faid twenty fourth day of *June*, the driver of any waggon, cart, car, dray or other carriage, on any publick highway, fhall ride upon any fuch carriage, not having fome

20 s. penalty on driver riding on his waggon or cart, &c. without

other

other perfon on foot or on horfeback to guide the fame (fuch carriages as are refpectively drawn by one horfe only, or by two horfes abreaft, and are conducted by fome perfon holding the reins of fuch horfe or horfes, excepted) or if the driver of any carriage whatfoever on any of the faid highways, fhall by negligence or mifbehaviour caufe any hurt or damage to any perfon paffing or being upon fuch highway; or fhall by negligence or wilful mifbehaviour, prevent, hinder or interrupt the free paffage of any other carriage, or of his Majefty's fubjects on the faid highways; or if the driver of any empty or unloaded waggon, cart or other carriage, fhall refufe or neglect to turn afide and make way for any coach, chariot, chaife, loaded waggon, cart, or other loaded carriage; every fuch driver offending in any of the cafes aforefaid, and being convicted of fuch offence, either by his own confeffion, or by the oath of one or more credible witnefs or witneffes, before any juftice of the peace of the county, riding, divifion or place where fuch offence fhall be committed (which oath fuch juftice is hereby impowered and required to adminifter) fhall for every fuch offence, forfeit any fum not exceeding twenty fhillings, to be levied by diftrefs and fale of the offender's goods and chattels, by warrant under the hand and feal of any juftice of the peace; and for want of fufficient diftrefs, fuch juftice is hereby impowered and required to commit fuch offender to the houfe of correction, or fome other prifon of the county, riding, divifion or place in which the offence fhall be committed, or the offender fhall have been apprehended, there to remain and be kept to hard labour, for any time not exceeding one month.

X. And be it further enacted by the authority aforefaid, That all penalties and forfeitures for offences againft this act on the publick highways, fhall be applied, one moiety to the informer, and the other moiety to the furveyor or furveyors of the highways in the parifh wherein fuch offence fhall be committed, to be by fuch furveyor or furveyors applied in the repair of the highways within fuch refpective parifh.

XI. And be it further enacted by the authority aforefaid, That if any perfon who fhall be apprehended for having committed any offence againft this act, fhall refufe to difcover his name and place of abode, to the juftice or juftices before whom he fhall be brought, fuch perfon fo refufing fhall be immediately delivered over to a conftable or other peace officer, and fhall by him be conveyed to the common gaol, or houfe of correction, of the county or place where the offence fhall be committed, there to remain until he fhall declare his name and place of abode to the faid juftice, or to fome other juftice of the faid county or place.

XII. And be it further enacted by the authority aforefaid, That the pecuniary forfeitures by this act incurred, and for levying whereof no provifion is herein before made, fhall and may be levied by diftrefs and fale of the goods and chattels of every fuch offender (rendring to him the overplus, after the charges
of

of the distress and sale shall be deducted) by warrant under the of the offend-
hand and seal of the justice before whom the offender was con- er's goods.
victed; and one moiety of all which pecuniary forfeitures, Application
whereof the application is not herein before directed, shall be thereof.
paid to the person or persons who shall prosecute to conviction
any offender or offenders against this act; and the other moiety thereof shall be paid to the overseers of the poor, if there
shall be any, of the parish or place in which the offence shall be
committed, or the offender shall have been apprehended; and
if there shall be no overseers in such parish or place, then to
some other officer of such parish or place, for the use of the poor
of such parish or place.

XIII. And be it further enacted by the authority aforesaid, Offenders may
That any person or persons who shall see any of the offences herein be apprehend-
before mentioned, and intended by this act to be redressed, com- ed by any permitted, shall and may by the authority of this act, and without offence com-
any other warrant, apprehend the offender or offenders, and mitted.
shall with all convenient speed then afterwards convey or deliver
every such offender and offenders to a constable, or some other
peace officer of the county, city or place in which the offence
shall be committed, or the offender shall be apprehended, in
order to be conveyed before some justice of the peace of such
county, city or place, there to be dealt with according to law.

XIV. And be it further enacted by the authority aforesaid, Inhabitants of
That in all actions, suits, trials, and other proceedings in pursu- the place
ance of this act, or in relation to any matter or thing herein where any of-
contained, any inhabitant of the parish, town or place in which fence shall be
any offence or offences shall be committed, contrary to the true committed,
intent and meaning of this act, or the said herein before recited witnesses.
act, shall be admitted to give evidence, and shall be deemed a
competent witness, notwithstanding his, her or their being an
inhabitant of the parish or place in which any such offence or
offences shall have been committed.

XV. And be it further enacted by the authority aforesaid, Offenders pu-
That no person, who by virtue of this act shall be punished for nished under
any offence or offences by him, her or them committed, shall this act, not
be punished for the same offence or offences under any other law punishable for
or statute; and that if any action or suit shall be commenced the same of-
against any person or persons for any thing done in pursuance of other.
this act, the defendant or defendants in any such action or suit,
may plead the general issue, and give this act and the special
matter in evidence, at any trial to be had thereupon, and that General issue.
the same was done in pursuance and by the authority of this
act; and if it shall appear so to have been done, a verdict shall
be recorded for the defendant or defendants; and if the plaintiff shall be nonsuited, or discontinue his action, after the defendant or defendants shall have appeared; or if judgment shall
be given upon any verdict or demurrer against the plaintiff, the
defendant or defendants shall and may recover double costs, and Double costs.
have the like remedy for the same, as any defendant or defend-

ants

ants hath or have in other cafes by law for recovery of his or their cofts.

CAP. XXIII.

An act for enabling his Majefty to raife the fum of one million, for the ufes and purpofes therein mentioned.

Moft gracious Sovereign,

WE your Majefty's moft dutiful and loyal fubjects, the commons of Great Britain in parliament affembled, having taken into our ferious confideration your Majefty's moft gracious meffage, fignifying your Majefty's defire to be enabled by your faithful commons, to defray any extraordinary expences of the war, incurred or to be incurred, for the fervice of the year one thoufand feven hundred and fifty feven, and to take all fuch meafures as may be neceffary to difappoint or defeat any enterprizes or defigns of your Majefty's enemies, and as the exigency of affairs may require, have refolved to give and

One million granted to his Majefty to defray extraordinary expences.

grant to your Majefty the fum of one million for that purpofe; and do therefore moft humbly befeech your Majefty, that it may be enacted; and be it enacted by the King's moft excellent majefty, by and with the advice and confent of the lords fpiritual and temporal, and commons, in this prefent parliament affembled, and by the authority of the fame, That it fhall and may be lawful to and

His Majefty by warrant under his fign manual may authorize the treafury to take in loans, or iffue exchequer bills for the faid fum,

for the King's moft excellent majefty, by warrant or warrants under his royal fign manual, to authorize and impower the commiffioners of his Majefty's treafury now or for the time being, or any three or more of them, or the lord high treafurer for the time being, at any time or times before the fifth day of *January* one thoufand feven hundred and fifty eight, to caufe or direct any loans to be taken or received at his Majefty's exchequer, from any perfon or perfons, natives or foreigners, body or bodies politick or corporate; or any number of exchequer bills to be made out there, for any fum or fums of money, not exceeding in loans and exchequer bills together, in the whole, the faid

in the fame manner as loans or exchequer bills are to be taken or made by the land tax act of this feffion.

fum of one million, in the fame or like manner, form and order, and according to the fame or like rules and directions, as in and by an act of this prefent feffion of parliament, intituled, *An act for granting an aid to his Majefty by a land tax to be raifed in* Great Britain *for the fervice of the year one thoufand feven hundred and fifty feven; and for difcharging certain arrears of land taxes incurred before the time therein mentioned; and for the more effectual collecting of arrears for the future,* are enacted and prefcribed concerning the loans or exchequer bills to be taken or made in purfuance of the faid act.

Claufes, &c. in the faid act relating to loans or exchequer bills therein, extended to fuch as fhall be

II. And be it further enacted by the authority aforefaid, That all and every the claufes, provifoes, powers, privileges, advantages, penalties, forfeitures and difablities, contained in the faid laft-mentioned act relating to the loans or exchequer bills authorized to be made by the fame act (except fuch claufes as do charge the fame on the taxes granted by the fame act) fhall be applied and extended to the loans and exchequer bills to be made in in purfuance of this act, as fully and effectually to all intents and purpofes, as if the fame loans or exchequer bills had been originally authorized by the faid laft-mentioned act, or as if the faid feveral claufes or provifoes had been particularly repeated and re-enacted in the body of this act.

made in pur-fuance of this act.

III. And be it declared and further enacted by the authority aforefaid, That it fhall and may be lawful for the governor and company of the bank of *England*, to advance or lend to his Majefty, in like manner, at the receipt of the exchequer, upon the credit of loan granted by this act, any fum or fums of money not exceeding in the whole, the fum of one million.; any thing in an act made in the fifth and fixth years of the reign of King *William* and Queen *Mary*, intituled, *An act for granting to their Majefties feveral rates and duties upon tonnage of fhips and veffels, and upon beer, ale, and other liquors, for fecuring certain recompences and advantages in the faid act mentioned, to fuch perfons as fhall voluntarily advance the fum of one million five hundred thoufand pounds towards carrying on the war againft* France, to the contrary thereof in any wife notwithftanding.

The bank im-powered to lend his Maje-fty the faid fum, on the credit of this act, notwithftand-ing act 5 & 6 W. & M.

IV. And be it further enacted by the authority aforefaid, That all fuch loans or exchequer bills, together with the intereft, premium, rate and charges incident to or attending the fame, fhall be and are hereby charged and chargeable upon, and fhall be repaid or borne by or out of the firft aids or fupplies which fhall be granted in the next feffion of parliament; and in cafe fufficient aids or fupplies for that purpofe fhall not be granted before the fifth day of *July* one thoufand feven hundred and fifty eight, then all the faid loans or exchequer bills, with the intereft, premium, rate and charges incident to or attending the fame, fhall be and are hereby charged and chargeable upon fuch monies, as at any time or times, at or after the faid fifth day of *July* one thoufand feven hundred and fifty eight, fhall be or remain in the receipt of the exchequer, of the furpluffes, exceffes, overplus monies, and other revenues, compofing the fund commonly called *The finking fund*, except fuch monies of the faid finking fund as are appropriated to any particular ufe or ufes by any act or acts of parliament in that behalf; and fuch monies of the faid finking fund fhall and may be iffued and applied, as foon as the fame can be regularly ftated and afcertained, for and towards paying off, cancelling and difcharging fuch loans or exchequer bills, intereft, premium, rate or charges, until the whole of them fhall be paid off, cancelled and difcharged, or money fufficient for that purpofe be kept and referved in the exchequer, to be payable on demand to the refpective proprietors thereof.

Loans, with the intereft, to be paid out of the firft fupplies;

and if none fhall be grant-ed before 5 July 1758. out of the finking fund;

V. Provided always, and be it enacted by the authority aforefaid, That whatever monies fhall be fo iffued out of the faid furpluffes, exceffes, overplus monies, or other revenues compofing the finking fund, fhall from time to time be replaced by and out of the firft fupplies to be then after granted in parliaments, any thing herein contained to the contrary notwithftanding.

and the mo-nies iffued to be replaced out of the firft fupplies.

CAP. XXIV.

*An act for the more effectual punishment of persons who shall
attain, or attempt to attain, possession of goods or money,
by false or untrue pretences ; for preventing the unlawful
pawning of goods ; for the easy redemption of goods pawned ;
and for preventing gaming in publick houses by journeymen,
labourers, servants and apprentices.*

WHEREAS *divers evil-disposed persons, to support their
profligate way of life, have by various subtle stratagems,
threats and devices, fraudulently obtained divers sums of money, goods,
wares and merchandizes, to the great injury of industrious families,
and to the manifest prejudice of trade and credit* ; therefore for the
punishing all such offenders, be it enacted by the King's most
excellent majesty, by and with the advice and consent of the lords
spiritual and temporal and commons in this present parliament
assembled, and by the authority of the same, That from and after
the twenty ninth day of *September* one thousand seven hundred
and fifty seven, all persons who knowingly and designedly, by
false pretence or pretences, shall obtain from any person or persons, money, goods, wares or merchandizes, with intent to
cheat or defraud any person or persons of the same ; or shall
knowingly send or deliver any letter or writing, with or without
a name or names subscribed thereto, or signed with a fictitious
name or names, letter or letters, threatning to accuse any person of any crime punishable by law with death, transportation,
pillory, or any other infamous punishment, with a view or intent to extort or gain money, goods, wares or merchandizes
from the person or persons so threatened to be accused, shall be
deemed offenders against law and the publick peace ; and the
court before whom such offender or offenders shall be tried,
shall in case he, she or they shall be convicted of any of the said
offences, order such offender or offenders to be fined and imprisoned, or to be put in the pillory, or publickly whipped, or
to be transported, as soon as conveniently may be (according to
the laws made for transportation of felons) to some of his Majesty's colonies or plantations in *America*, for the term of seven
years, as the court in which any such offender or offenders shall
be convicted shall think fit and order.

II. And be it further enacted by the authority aforesaid, That
any justice or justices of the peace of the county, riding, division,
city, liberty or place, before whom any person or persons charged on oath, by any credible person or persons, with having committed any of the offences intended by this act to be punished,
shall be brought, shall examine by oath (which oath every such
justice or justices is and are hereby impowered and required to
administer) and such other lawful means as to any such justice
or justices shall seem meet, touching the matters complained of,
and deal with the offender or offenders according to law ; and if
the party or parties charged as being the offender or offenders, shall
be

*Persons con-
victed of ob-
taining money
or goods by
false pre-
tences, or of
sending
threatening
letters in order
to extort mo-
ney or goods,*

*may be pu-
nished by fine
and imprison-
ment, or by
pillory, whip-
ping or transf-
portation.*

*Where a
charge is
made of any
of the said of-
fences, justice
to enquire
therein upon
oath,*

*and to bind
over the com-
plainant, to ap-*

be committed to prison, or be admitted to bail, to answer the matters complained of at the next general or quarter sessions of the peace, or next sessions of *Oyer* and *Terminer*, which shall be held for the county, riding, division, city, liberty or place wherein the offence shall be charged, on oath, to have been committed, then such justice or justices shall bind over the prosecutor and prosecutors of every such offender or offenders to appear at the next general or quarter sessions of the peace, or next sessions of *Oyer* and *Terminer* which shall be held for the county, riding, division, city, liberty or place wherein the offence shall be charged to have been committed, by recognizance, in such reasonable sum of money as to such justice or justices shall seem requisite, to prosecute such offender and offenders with effect; and if any money, goods, wares or merchandizes fraudulently obtained, shall appear to such justice or justices to exceed the amount or value of twenty pounds, then the recognizance to be taken in that behalf from the prosecutor or prosecutors, shall be in not less than double the amount or value the same shall appear before any such justice or justices to be worth. *pear and prosecute; and his recognizance to be in proportion to the fraud.*

III. *And whereas divers of his Majesty's subjects suffer great inconveniencies and frequent losses, by persons pawning or unlawfully disposing of the goods and chattels of others, and the persons so pawning or unlawfully disposing of the goods or chattels of others, from the meanness of their circumstances, are seldom able to make restitution or recompence to the parties injured, and the laws now in being are insufficient to punish such offenders;* be it therefore further enacted by the authority aforesaid, That from and after the said twenty ninth day of *September* one thousand seven hundred and fifty seven, if any person or persons shall knowingly and designedly pawn or exchange, or unlawfully dispose of the goods or chattels of any other person or persons, not being employed or authorized by the owner or owners thereof so to do, and shall be thereof convicted by the oath of any credible witness or witnesses, or by the confession of the person or persons charged with such offence, before any such justice or justices of the peace as aforesaid (which oath every such justice as aforesaid is hereby impowered and required to administer) every such offender shall, for every such offence, forfeit the sum of twenty shillings; and in case the said forfeiture shall not be forthwith paid, the justice or justices of the peace as aforesaid, before whom such conviction shall be had, shall commit the party or parties so convicted to the house of correction, or some other publick prison of the county, riding, division, city or place wherein the offender or offenders shall reside or be convicted, there to remain and be kept to hard labour for the space of fourteen days, unless the said forfeiture shall be sooner paid; and if within three days before the expiration of the said fourteen days, the said forfeiture shall not be paid, the said justice or justices is and are hereby required to order, upon the application of the prosecutor or prosecutors, the person or persons so convicted to be publickly whipped in the house of correction or prison to which the offender *Penalty of 20s. on pawning, exchanging, or disposing of goods without leave of the owner; and on nonpayment, to be committed for 14 days to hard labour, and if not paid within that time, to be whipped, on application of the prosecutor.*

fender

fender or offenders shall be committed, or in some open publick place of the city, riding, division, town or place wherein the offence shall have been committed, as to such justice or justices shall seem proper ; and the said respective forfeitures when recovered, shall be applied towards making satisfaction thereout to the party or parties injured, and defraying the costs of the prosecution, as shall be adjudged reasonable by the justice or justices before whom such conviction shall be had ; but if the party or parties injured shall decline to accept of such satisfaction and costs ; or if there shall be any overplus of the said respective forfeitures, after making such satisfaction, and paying such costs as aforesaid, then such respective forfeitures, or the overplus thereof (as the case shall happen) shall be paid and applied to and for the use of the poor of the parish or place where the offence shall have been committed, and shall be paid to the overseers of the poor of such parish for that purpose.

Application of the forfeitures

IV. And be it further enacted by the authority aforesaid, That all and every person and persons who, from and after the twenty ninth day of *September* one thousand seven hundred and fifty seven, shall take by way of pawn, pledge or exchange, of or from any person or persons whomsoever, any goods or chattels, of what kind soever the same shall be, shall forthwith enter or cause to be entered, in a fair or regular manner, in a book or books to be kept for that purpose, a description of the goods or chattels which he, she or they shall receive in pawn, pledge or exchange ; and also the sum of money advanced or paid thereon, with the day of the month and year on which, and the name and place of abode of the person or persons by whom such goods or chattels were so pawned, pledged or exchanged, and also the name and place of abode of the owner or owners thereof, according to the information of the person pawning or pledging, or exchanging the same ; and shall at the same time give a duplicate or copy thereof to the person or persons so pawning, pledging or exchanging the said goods or chattels, if required ; for which the person or persons giving such duplicate or copy, shall be paid by the person or persons who shall so pawn, pledge or exchange such goods or chattels, the sum of one half-penny, on goods and chattels pawned for less than twenty shillings ; and one penny on goods or chattels pawned for twenty shillings, and not exceeding five pounds, and for every such duplicate upon goods or chattels pawned for any larger sum, the sum of two pence, and no more ; and in default of making such entry, and giving such duplicate or copy, if required as aforesaid, he, she or they shall respectively for every offence forfeit the sum of five pounds, to be levied by distress and sale of the goods and chattels of the offender or offenders, by warrant under the hand and seal, or hands and seals of any justice or justices of the peace of the county, riding, division, city, liberty or place where the offence shall be committed ; which respective forfeitures when levied, shall be paid and

Pawnbroker to make entry of goods pawned, pledged or exchanged,

and a duplicate, if required, to be given thereof to the pawner, upon paying for the same.

Penalty 5l. on default of making such entry, and giving such duplicate.

and applied to the ufe of the poor of the parifh or place wherein the offence fhall be committed.

V. *And whereas it fometimes happens that the goods or chattels pledged and pawned as aforefaid, are fpoiled and damaged, or rendered of lefs value than when the fame were pledged or pawned, through the neglect, default, or misbehaviour of the perfon or perfons to whom the fame were fo pledged or pawned, his, her or their agents or fervants, either by wearing or ufing thereof, or by letting the fame out to hire;* be it therefore enacted by the authority aforefaid, That if in the courfe of any of the aforefaid proceedings, before any juftice or juftices of the peace, in purfuance of, or under this act, it fhall appear or be proved to the fatisfaction of the juftice or juftices upon oath or folemn affirmation as aforefaid, that any of the goods or chattels fo pawned as aforefaid, are become or have been rendered of lefs value than the fame were at the time of pawning or pledging thereof, by or through the default, neglect, or wilful misbehaviour of the perfon or perfons to whom the fame were fo pledged or pawned, his, her or their executors, adminiftrators or affigns, agents or fervants, then, and in any fuch cafe, it fhall be lawful, and every fuch juftice or juftices is and are hereby required to allow or award a reafonable fatisfaction to the owner or owners of fuch goods or chattels, in refpect of fuch damage; and the fum or fums of money fo allowed or awarded fhall be deducted out of the principal and intereft, and allowance for warehoufe-room, which fhall appear to be due to any perfon or perfons, to whom the fame were fo pledged or pawned, his, her or their executors, adminiftrators or affigns; and in all cafes where the goods and chattels pawned as aforefaid, fhall have been damaged as aforefaid, it fhall be fufficient for the pawner or pawners, his, her or their executors, adminiftrators or affigns, to pay or tender the money upon the balance, after deducting out of the principal and intereft, and money payable for warehoufe-room as aforefaid, for the goods or chattels pawned, fuch reafonable fatisfaction in refpect to fuch damage, as any fuch juftice or juftices fhall order or award; and upon fo doing, the juftice or juftices fhall proceed as if the pawner or pawners, his, her or their executors, adminiftrators or affigns, had paid or tendered the whole money due for the principal, intereft, and warehoufe-room as aforefaid.

Where goods pawned fhall be damaged thro' neglect of the pawn-broker,

VI. And be it enacted by the authority aforefaid, That from and after the faid twenty ninth day of *September* one thoufand feven hundred and fifty feven, if any perfon or perfons fhall knowingly buy or take in as a pledge, any linen or apparel, intrufted to any other perfon or perfons to wafh, fcour, iron, mend or make up, and fhall be convicted of the fame, on the oath of one credible witnefs, or on confeffion of the party, before one or more juftice or juftices, every fuch perfon or perfons fhall forfeit double the fum given for or lent on the fame, to be paid to the poor of the parifh where the offence is committed, to be recovered in the manner other forfeitures are by

Perfons buying or taking in pledge, linen or apparel, intrufted to others to wafh or mend, &c. to forfeit double the fum,

this

and restore the goods.

this act directed to be recovered; and shall likewise be obliged to restore the said goods to the owner in the presence of the said justice or justices.

Persons offering goods to sale, pawn or exchange, not giving a good account of themselves,

may be detained, and carried before a justice.

VII. And be it further enacted by the authority aforesaid, That in case any person or persons, who shall offer by way of pawn, pledge, exchange or sale, any goods or chattels, shall not be able, or shall refuse, to give a satisfactory account of himself, herself or themselves, or of the means by which he, she or they, became possessed of such goods or chattels; or if there shall be any other reason to suspect that such goods or chattels are stolen, or otherwise illegally or clandestinely obtained; it shall and may be lawful for any person or persons, his, her or their servants or agents, to whom such goods or chattels shall be so offered, to seize and detain such person or persons, and the said goods or chattels, and to deliver such person or persons, as soon as conveniently may be, into the custody of the constable, or other peace officer, who shall, and is hereby required, immediately to convey such person or persons, and the said goods or chattels, before some justice or justices of the peace of the county, riding, division, city, liberty or place, wherein the offence shall be committed; and if such justice or justices shall, upon examination and enquiry, have cause to suspect that the said goods or chattels were stolen, or illegally or clandestinely obtained, it shall and may be lawful for such justice or justices to commit such person or persons into safe custody, for any time not exceeding the space of six days, in order to be further examined; and if upon either of the said examinations, it shall appear to the satisfaction of such justice or justices, that the said goods or chattels were stolen, or illegally or clandestinely obtained, the said justice or justices is and are hereby authorized and required to commit the party or parties offending to the common gaol or house of correction of the county, riding, division, city, liberty or place, wherein the offence shall be committed, there to be dealt with according to law.

Justice, may commit the party.

The persons detaining the party and goods, indemnified for so doing.

VIII. Provided nevertheless, and be it further enacted, That in case such goods or chattels so seized and detained as aforesaid, shall afterwards appear to be the property of the person or persons who offered the same to be pawned, pledged, exchanged or sold, or that he, she or they, was or were authorized by the owner or owners thereof to pawn, pledge, exchange, or sell the same, then and in such case, the person or persons who shall so seize or detain the party or parties who offered the said goods or chattels, shall be, and he, she and they, is and are by this act indemnified for having so done.

Justice, upon oath of the owner, to issue

IX. And, for the better enabling all persons to recover their goods or chattels, which after the said twenty ninth day of September one thousand seven hundred and fifty seven, shall be unlawfully pawned or pledged to, or exchanged with, any person or persons whatsoever; be it further enacted by the authority aforesaid, That if the owner or owners of any goods or chattels, unlawfully pawned, pledged or exchanged, shall make out, either on his, her or their oath,

oath, or by the oath of any credible witnefs, or (being one of the people called *Quakers*) by folemn affirmation before any juftice or juftices of the peace, within his or their jurifdiction, that fuch owner or owners, has or have had, his, her or their goods and chattels unlawfully obtained or taken from him, her or them, and that there is juft caufe to fufpect that any perfon or perfons, within the jurifdiction of any fuch juftice or juftices hath or have knowingly and unlawfully taken to pawn, or by way of pledge, or in exchange, any goods or chattels of fuch owner or owners, and without the privity of, or authority from fuch owner or owners thereof; and fhall make appear to the fatisfaction of any fuch juftice or juftices, probable grounds for fuch the fufpicion of the owner or owners thereof, then and in any fuch cafe, any juftice or juftices of the peace, within his or their jurifdiction, may iffue his or their warrant for fearching, in the day-time, the houfe, warehoufe or other place, of any fuch perfon or perfons, who fhall be charged on oath or affirmation, as aforefaid, as fufpected to have knowingly and unlawfully received or taken to pawn, or by way of pledge, or in exchange, any fuch goods or chattels, without the privity of, or authority from the owner or owners thereof; and if the occupier or occupiers of any houfe, warehoufe or other place, wherein any fuch goods or chattels fhall, on oath or affirmation as aforefaid, be charged or fufpected to be, fhall after the faid twenty ninth day of *September* one thoufand feven hundred and fifty feven, on requeft made to him, her or them, to open the fame, by any peace officer authorized to fearch there, by warrant from a juftice or juftices of the peace, for the county, riding, divifion, city, liberty, town or place, in which fuch houfe, warehoufe or other place fhall be fituate, refufe to open the fame, and permit the fame to be fearched, it fhall be lawful for any fuch peace officer to break open any fuch houfe, warehoufe or other place, in the day-time, and to fearch as he fhall think fit therein, for the goods or chattels fufpected to be there, doing no wilful damage; and if any perfon or perfons fhall oppofe or hinder any fuch fearch, and fhall be thereof convicted before any fuch juftice or juftices, by the oath of one or more credible witnefs or witneffes, every perfon fo offending in the premiffes fhall forfeit for every fuch offence the fum of five pounds; and in cafe fuch forfeiture be not immediately paid down, or within the fpace of twenty four hours, the juftice or juftices, before whom fuch conviction fhall be had, fhall commit the party or parties fo convicted to the houfe of correction, or fome other publick prifon of fuch county, riding, divifion, city, liberty, town or place, there to be kept to hard labour for any time not exceeding one month, nor lefs than five days, unlefs in the mean time fuch forfeiture fhall be paid; and fuch forfeiture, when recovered, fhall forthwith go and be applied to and for the ufe of the poor of the parifh wherein fuch offence fhall have been committed; and if upon the fearch of the houfe, warehoufe, or other place, of any fuch fufpected perfon or perfons, as aforefaid, any

a warrant to fearch the fufpected perfon's houfe.

Upon refufal of admittance officer may break open the door.

Perfons hindering fuch fearch, forfeit 5 l.

and on non-payment, are to be committed to hard labour.

The goods found to be reftored to the ufe of owner.

I 4

of the goods or chattels which fhall have been fo knowingly and unlawfully pawned, pledged or exchanged, as aforefaid, fhall be found, and the property of the owner or owners from whom the fame fhall have been unlawfully obtained or taken, fhall be made out, to the fatisfaction of any fuch juftice or juftices, by the oath of one or more credible witnefs or witneffes, or (if any fuch witnefs or witneffes be of the people called *Quakers*) by folemn affirmation, or by the confeffion of the perfon or perfons charged with any fuch offence, any fuch juftice or juftices fhall thereupon caufe the goods and chattels found on any fuch fearch, and unlawfully pawned, pledged or exchanged, as aforefaid, to be forthwith reftored to the owner or owners thereof.

X. *And whereas goods and chattels are often pawned or pledged for fecuring the payment of money lent thereon, and the intereft thereof; and although when the money becomes due, the borrowers, or their reprefentatives, are defirous to repay the fame, and the intereft due thereon, and make tender thereof to the perfon or perfons with whom the fame are fo pawned or pledged, they are frequently under great difficulties to get back the goods and chattels fo pawned, and are often under neceffity to commence fuits at law for the recovery thereof, to their great expence; for remedy whereof,* be it enacted by the authority aforefaid, That from and after the faid twenty ninth day of *September* one thoufand feven hundred and fifty feven, if any goods or chattels fhall be pawned or pledged for fecuring any money lent thereon, not exceeding in the whole the principal fum of ten pounds, and the intereft thereof; and if within two years after the pawning or pledging thereof, proof having been made on oath, by one or more credible witnefs or witneffes, or by producing a duplicate of the entry directed to be given by this act as aforefaid, before any fuch juftice or juftices, or by folemn affirmation (if the perfon be of the people called *Quakers*) to the fatisfaction of any fuch juftice or juftices, of the pawning or pledging of any fuch goods or chattels within the faid fpace of two years, any fuch pawner or pawners who was or were the real owner or owners of fuch goods or chattels at the time of the pawning or pledging thereof, his, her or their executors, adminiftrators or affigns, fhall tender unto the perfon or perfons who lent on the fecurity of the goods or chattels pawned, his executors, adminiftrators or affigns, the principal money borrowed thereon, and all intereft due for the fame, together with fuch charges for the warehoufe-room of the goods or chattels pawned, as fhall be agreed on at the time of the pawning of fuch goods and chattels; and the perfon who took fuch goods or chattels in pawn, his executors, adminiftrators or affigns, fhall thereupon neglect or refufe to deliver back the goods or chattels fo pawned, for any fum or fums of money not exceeding the faid principal fum of ten pounds, to the perfon or perfons who borrowed the money thereon, his, her or their executors, adminiftrators or affigns; then and in any fuch cafe, on oath, or (if the perfon or perfons be of the people called *Quakers*

Goods pawned for a fum not exceeding 10 l. may be recovered within 2 years.

Juftice, on complaint of pawnbroker

Quakers) on solemn affirmation thereof made by the pawner or refusing to de-
pawners thereof, his, her or their executors, administrators or liver goods to
assigns, or some other credible person, any justice or justices of summon and
the peace of the county, riding, division, city, liberty or place, examine the
where the person or persons who took such pawn as aforesaid, parties;
his executors, administrators or assigns, shall dwell on the application of the borrower or borrowers, his, her or their executors, administrators or assigns, is and are hereby required to
cause such person or persons who took such pawn, his, her or
their executors, administrators or assigns, within the jurisdiction of the justice or justices, to come before such justice or justices; and such justice or justices is and are hereby authorized
and required to examine on oath, or solemn affirmation, as the
case may require, the parties themselves, and such other credible persons as shall appear before him or them, touching the
premises; and if tender of the principal money due, and all and proof be-
interest thereof, together with charges for warehouse-room, ing made of
as aforesaid, shall be proved by oath or affirmation, as aforesaid, payment of
to have been made, such principal money not exceeding the said the principal,
sum of ten pounds, to the lender or lenders thereof, his, her interest and
or their executors, administrators or assigns, by the borrower charges;
or borrowers of such principal money, his, her or their executors,
administrators or assigns, within the said space of two years after or tender be-
the said pawning or pledging of the goods or chattels, then on ing then also
payment by the borrower or borrowers, his, her or their exe- made, and
cutors, administrators or assigns, of such principal money, and refused;
the interest due thereon, together with such charges for warehouse-room of the goods or chattels so pawned or pledged as
aforesaid, to the lender or lenders, his, her or their executors,
administrators or assigns; and in case the lender or lenders, his, Justice to
her or their executors, administrators or assigns, shall refuse to make an order
accept thereof, on tender thereof to him, her or them made, for the imme-
by the borrower or borrowers thereof, his, her or their execu- diate delivery
tors, administrators or assigns, before any such justice or justices, of the goods,
such justice or justices shall thereupon, by order under his hand, or
their hands, direct the goods or chattels so pawned, forthwith to be
delivered up to the pawner or pawners thereof, his, her or their
executors, administrators or assigns: and if the person or persons on refusal, to
who shall have lent any principal sum or sums of money, not commit the
exceeding in the whole the said sum of ten pounds, on any pawnbroker
goods or chattels pawned, his, her or their executors, admini- till satisfaction
strators or assigns, shall neglect or refuse to deliver up or make be made.
satisfaction for the goods or chattels, which shall be proved to
the satisfaction of such justice or justices as aforesaid, to have
been so pawned, as any such justice or justices of the peace,
as aforesaid, shall order and direct, then any such justice or justices shall, and is and are hereby authorized and required to
commit the party or parties so refusing to deliver up or make satisfaction for the same, to the house of correction, or some other
publick prison of the county, riding, division, city or place,
wherein the offender or offenders shall reside, or be convicted;
                                                              there

there to remain without bail or mainprize, until he, fhe or they, fhall deliver up the goods or chattels fo pawned, and continuing redeemable, as aforefaid, according to the order of fuch faid juftice or juftices, or make fatisfaction or compenfation for the value thereof, to the party or parties intitled to the redemption of fuch goods or chattels fo pawned, and continuing redeemable as aforefaid.

XI. And be it further enacted by the authority aforefaid, That if any pawn or pledge of goods or chattels, of what kind foever, made by or for the proprietor or propriotors thereof, fhall remain unredeemed for the fpace of two years, then every fuch pawn or pledge fhall be forfeited ; and it fhall and may be lawful to and for every fuch perfon or perfons, to whom fuch goods or chattels have been pawned or pledged, to fell the fame ; any law, ftatute, cuftom or ufage, to the contrary thereof notwithftanding ; fubject neverthelefs to account for the overplus, if any fhall be, of the produce of all fuch goods or chattels which have been pledged for two pounds and upwards, as by this act is directed.

Goods remaining unredeemed for 2 years, are forfeited, and may be fold ;

Overplus to be accounted for.

XII. Provided always, and be it further enacted by the authority aforefaid, That every perfon or perfons to whom any goods or chattels fhall have been pawned or pledged, fhall from time to time enter in a book or books to be kept for that purpofe, a true and juft account of the fale of all goods and chattels pawned to him, her or them, for two pounds, or upwards, which fhall be fold by any fuch perfon or perfons, expreffing the day when, the money for which, and the name and place of abode of the perfon to whom, fuch goods or effects pawned were fold ; and in cafe any fuch goods or effects fhall be fold for more than the principal money, with intereft, and the charge of warehoufe-room, as aforefaid, due thereon at the time of fuch fale, the overplus fhall by every fuch perfon or perfons be paid on demand to the perfon by or on whofe account fuch goods or chattels were pawned, his, her or their executors, adminiftrators or affigns ; and fuch perfon or perfons who pawned or pledged fuch goods or chattels, his, her or their executors, adminiftrators or affigns, fhall, for his, her or their fatisfaction in this matter, be permitted to infpect the entry to be made as aforefaid of every fuch fale, paying for fuch infpection the fum of one penny, and no more ; and in cafe any perfon or perfons fhall refufe to permit any fuch perfon or perfons, who pawned or pledged fuch goods or chattels, to infpect fuch entry as aforefaid in any fuch book or books, fuch perfon or perfons, if an executor or executors, adminiftrator or adminiftrators, or affignee or affignees, at fuch time producing his, her or their letters teftamentary, letters of adminiftration or affignment ; or in cafe the goods or effects were fold for more than the fum entered in any fuch book or books ; or if any fuch perfon or perfons fhall not make fuch entry, or fhall not have *bona fide* fold the goods or chattels pawned for the beft price that he, fhe or they might have reafonably had or got for the fame, without his, her or their wilful default ;

Entry to be made of fale of goods pawned for 2l. or upwards.

Overplus arising from the fale, to be paid on demand, to the owner ;

On refufal of infpection,

or the goods being fold for more than entered, &c.

or

or shall refuse to pay such overplus, for the same, without his, her or their wilful default, or shall refuse to pay such overplus, upon demand, to the pawner or pawners, his, her or their executors, administrators or assigns; he or they producing such their letters testamentary, letters of administration or assignment, every such person or persons so offending shall for every such offence forfeit treble the value of such goods and chattels to the person or persons by whom, or on whose account, such goods or chattels were pawned, his, her or their executors, administrators or assigns, to be recovered by action of debt, bill, plaint or information, in any of his Majesty's courts of record at *Westminster*. Pawnbroker to forfeit treble the value.

XIII. Provided always, and be it further enacted by the authority aforesaid, That no fee or gratuity whatsoever shall be had, taken or received, for any summons or summonses, warrant or warrants, granted by any justice or justices of the peace, in pursuance of this act, so far as the same relates to goods and chattels pawned, pledged, taken in exchange, or unlawfully disposed of. Summonses and warrants to be issued without fee.

XIV. *And whereas the occupiers of many licensed publick houses, and of other houses wherein wines and liquors are sold, frequently suffer gaming therein, and journeyman, labourers, servants and apprentices, by means of such gaming therein, not only mis-spend their time, but are often reduced to poverty and great distress*; be it therefore further enacted by the authority aforesaid, That from and after the said twenty ninth day of *September* one thousand seven hundred and fifty seven, if any person or persons licensed to sell any sorts of liquors, or who shall sell, or suffer the same to be sold, in his, her or their house or houses, or in any outhouses, ground or apartments thereto belonging, shall knowingly suffer any gaming with cards, dice, draughts, shuffle boards, mississippi or billiard tables, skittles, nine pins, or with any other implement of gaming, in his, her or their houses, outhouses, ground or apartments thereto belonging, by any such journeymen, labourers, servants or apprentices: and shall be convicted of the said offence on their own confession, or on the oaths of one or more credible witness or witnesses, before any justice or justices of the peace for the county, riding, division, city, liberty or place, wherein the offence shall be committed, within six days after any such offence shall be committed, he, she or they so offending, shall for every such offence forfeit and pay the sum of forty shillings; and for every like offence which he, she or they shall afterwards be convicted of, before any such justice or justices of the peace, he, she or they so offending, shall forfeit the sum of ten pounds; all which sums of money, so forfeited, shall be levied by distress and sale of the offenders goods and chattels, by warrant from the justice or justices before whom such offender or offenders shall be convicted; and which warrant every such justice or justices is and are hereby required and authorized to grant; and three fourths of all sums which shall be so forfeited shall, on the recovery thereof, be paid to the churchwardens of the parish in which the offence shall be committed, for the use of the poor of such parish; and the other fourth Publicans permitting journeymen, &c. to game in their houses, forfeit 40s. and for every subsequent offence, 10l. to be levied by distress and sale.

fourth part thereof fhall be paid to the perfon or perfons on whofe information the party or parties offending fhall have been convicted of the offence.

On complaint of journeymen &c. gaming in publick houfes, juftice to iffue his warrant for apprehending them,

XV. And be it further enacted by the authority aforefaid, That from and after the faid twenty ninth day of *September* one thoufand feven hundred and fifty feven, if any journeyman, labourer, apprentice or fervant, fhall game in any houfe, outhoufe, ground or apartments thereto belonging, wherein any liquors fhall be fold, and complaint thereof fhall be made on oath before any juftice or juftices of the peace for the county, riding, divifion, city, liberty or place, where the offence fhall have been committed, every fuch juftice or juftices fhall thereupon iffue his or their warrant to fome conftable, tythingman, headborough or other peace officer of the parifh, precinct or place, wherein the offence fhall be charged to have been committed, or where the offender fhall refide, to apprehend and carry every fuch offender before fome juftice or juftices of the peace acting for the county, riding, divifion, city, liberty or place, where the offence fhall be committed, or where the offender fhall refide;

who upon conviction, are to forfeit not exceeding 20s. nor lefs than 5s.

and if the perfon who fhall be apprehended fhall be convicted of the faid offence by the oath of one or more credible witnefs or witneffes, or on his own confeffion, every fuch offender fhall forfeit any fum not exceeding twenty fhillings, nor lefs than five fhillings, as the juftice or juftices before whom any fuch offender or offenders fhall be convicted fhall think fit and order, every time he fhall fo offend, and be convicted as aforefaid; and one fourth of all fuch money fo forfeited fhall, on the conviction of any fuch offender or offenders, be paid to the perfon or perfons on whofe information the party or parties offending fhall be convicted, and the other three fourths thereof fhall be applied for the ufe of the poor of the parifh wherein the offence fhall have been committed, and fhall be paid to the overfeers of the poor of fuch parifh for that purpofe;

Offender not paying the forfeiture, to be committed to hard labour.

and if the party who fhall be convicted of the offence laft-mentioned, fhall not forthwith pay down the faid fum fo forfeited by him, any fuch juftice or juftices fhall, by warrant under his hand, or their hands, commit every fuch offender to the houfe of correction, or fome other prifon, of the county, riding, divifion, city, liberty or place, in which he fhall be apprehended; there to remain and be kept to hard labour for any time not exceeding the fpace of one month, or until he fhall pay the fum of money fo forfeited.

Juftice, upon complaint, to iffue his warrant for bringing the offenders before him,

XVI. And be it further enacted by the authority aforefaid, That it fhall and may be lawful to and for any juftice or juftices of the peace of any county, riding, divifion, city, liberty, town or place, and he and they is and are hereby required, upon complaint made to him upon oath of any offence committed againft this act, within the fame county, riding, divifion, city, liberty, town or place, to iffue his warrant for bringing before him, or fome other juftice or juftices of the peace of any county, riding, divifion, city, liberty, town or place, the perfon or perfons charged

charged with such offence, and the justice or justices before whom such person or persons shall be brought, is hereby authorized and required to hear and determine the matter of every such complaint, and to proceed to judgment and conviction thereupon, as by this act is directed; and if it shall appear by oath of any credible person or persons, to the satisfaction of any such justice or justices, that any person or persons within the jurisdiction of such justice or justices can give or offer material evidence on behalf of the prosecutor, against any offender or offenders against the true intent and meaning of this act, or on behalf of the person accused, and who will not voluntarily appear before such justice or justices to be examined, and give his, her or their evidence, concerning the premisses; every such justice or justices and may summon witnesses. is and are hereby authorized and required to issue his or their summons to convene every such person or persons within his or their jurisdiction before him or them, to be examined upon oath concerning the premisses; and if any person so summoned shall neglect or refuse to appear on such summons, and no just excuse shall be offered for such neglect or refusal, then, (after proof by oath of such summons having been duly served upon him, her or them for that purpose) any such justice or justices is and are hereby authorized and required to issue his or their warrant to bring every such witness and witnesses, within his or their jurisdiction, before him or them; and on the appearance of any such witness before any such justice or justices, any such justice or justices is and are hereby authorized and impowered to examine upon oath every such witness; and if any and if the witness refuses to give evidence, he may be committed to hard labour. such witness, on his or her appearance, or being brought before any such justice or justices, shall refuse to be examined on oath concerning the premisses, without offering any just cause for such refusal, it shall be lawful for any such justice or justices, by warrant under his or their hand and seal, or hands and seals, to commit every person so refusing to the publick prison of the county, riding, division, city or place, in which the person or persons so refusing to be examined on oath, shall be brought before any such justice or justices, there to remain for any time not exceeding three months, as any such justice or justices shall direct; and if, on such examination, any such justice or justices shall deem the evidence of any such witness or Material witness may be bound over to give evidence before a court. witnesses to be material, any such justice or justices may bind over any such witness, unless a feme covert, or one under the age of twenty one years, by recognizance, in a reasonable penalty, to appear and give evidence at the next general or quarter sessions of the peace, or sessions of Oyer and Terminer, as in such recognizance shall be mentioned.

XVII. And be it further enacted by the authority aforesaid, Offenders not to be admitted to bail, till due notice has been given to the prosecutor, &c. That no persons charged on oath with being guilty of any of the offences punishable by this act, and which shall require bail, shall be admitted to bail before twenty four hours notice, at least, shall be proved by oath to have been given in writing to the prosecutor, of the names and places of abode of the persons proposed to be bail for any such offender or offenders, unless the

bail

Offender to be tried at the next session, unless the court put off the trial.

bail offered shall be well known to the justice or justices, and he and they shall approve of them ; and every such offender and offenders who shall be bound over to the general quarter sessions of the peace, or gaol delivery of the county, city or town wherein the offence charged on him shall have been committed, to answer any such offences punishable by this act, shall be tried at such general quarter sessions of the peace, or sessions of *Oyer* and *Terminer* and gaol delivery which shall be held next after his, her or their being apprehended, unless the court shall think fit to put off the trial on just cause made out to them.

Inhabitants where the offence is committed, deemed competent witnesses.

XVIII. Provided always, and be it enacted by the authority aforesaid, That in all actions, suits, trials and other proceedings in pursuance of this act, or in relation to any matter or thing herein contained, any inhabitant of the parish, town or place, in which any offence or offences shall be committed, contrary to the true intent and meaning of this act, shall be admitted to give evidence, and shall be deemed a competent witness, notwithstanding his, her or their being an inhabitant or inhabitants of the parish, town or place wherein any such offence or offences shall have been committed.

Conviction to be drawn up in the following form ;

XIX. And be it further enacted by the authority aforesaid, That the justice or justices before whom any person shall be convicted, in manner prescribed by this act, shall cause such respective conviction to be drawn up in the form or to the effect following ; that is to say,

To wit. { BE it remembered, *That on this* day of *in the* year of his *Majesty's reign, A. B. is convicted before of his Majesty's justices of the peace, for the said county of* or for the *riding or division of the said county of* or for the *city, liberty or town of* (as the case shall happen to be) *for* and the said *do adjudge him or her to pay and forfeit for the same, the sum of*

Given under the day and year aforesaid.

and to be written on parchment, and transmitted to the quarter sessions to be filed.
Justices at the quarter sessions to determine appeals.

And the said justice or justices, before whom such conviction shall be had, shall cause the same so drawn up, in the form aforesaid, to be fairly written upon parchment, and transmitted to the next general quarter session of the peace to be held for the county, riding, division, city, town, liberty or place wherein such conviction was had, to be filed and kept amongst the records of the said general or quarter sessions ; and in case any person or persons so convicted, shall appeal from the judgment of the said justice or justices, to the said general or quarter sessions, the justices in such general or quarter sessions are hereby requir-

required upon receiving the said conviction, drawn up in the form aforesaid, to proceed to the hearing and determination of the matter of the said appeal, according to the directions of this act; any law or usage to the contrary notwithstanding.

XX. And be it further enacted by the authority aforesaid, That no *Certiorari* shall be granted to remove any indictment, conviction or other proceedings had thereon in pursuance of this act.

XXI. Provided always, and it is hereby further enacted by the authority aforesaid, That if any person convicted of any offences punishable by this act, shall think him or herself aggrieved by the judgment of the justice or justices before whom he or she shall have been convicted, such persons shall have liberty to appeal to the justices at the next general or quarter sessions of the peace which shall be held for the county, riding, division, city, liberty, town or place, where such judgment shall have been given; and that the execution of the said judgment shall, in such case, be suspended, the person so convicted entering into a recognizance at the time of such conviction, with two sufficient sureties, in double the sum which such person shall have been adjudged to pay or forfeit, upon conviction to prosecute such appeal with effect, and to be forth coming, to abide the judgment and determination of the justices in their said next general or quarter sessions; which recognizance the said justice or justices before whom such conviction shall be had, is hereby impowered and required to take; and the justices in the said general or quarter sessions are hereby authorized and required to hear and finally determine the matter of the said appeal, and to award such costs as to them shall appear just and reasonable to be paid by either party; and if, upon the hearing of the said appeal, the judgment of the justice or justices before whom the appellant shall have been convicted, shall be affirmed, such appellant shall immediately pay the sum which he or she shall have been adjudged to forfeit, together with such costs as the justices in the said general or quarter sessions shall award to be paid, for defraying the expences sustained by the defendant or defendants in such appeal; or in default of making such payments, shall suffer the respective pains and penalties by this act inflicted upon persons respectively, who shall neglect to pay, or shall not pay the respective sums or forfeitures by this act to be paid by, or imposed upon, persons respectively, who shall be convicted by virtue of this act.

XXII. And be it further enacted by the authority aforesaid, That no person, who, by virtue of this act, shall be punished for any offence or offences by him, her or them committed, shall be punished for the same offence or offences, under any other law or statute; and that if any action or suit shall be commenced against any person or persons for any thing done in pursuance of this act, the defendant or defendants in any such action or suit, may plead the general issue, and give this act and the special matter in evidence, at any trial to be had thereupon, and

2

and that the same was done in purfuance and by the authority of this act; and if it fhall appear fo to have been done, or a verdict fhall be recorded for the defendant or defendants: and if the plaintiff fhall be nonfuited or difcontinue his action, after the defendant or defendants fhall have appeared; or if judgment fhall be given upon any verdict or demurrer againft the plaintiff, the defendant or defendants fhall and may recover

Double cofts. double cofts, and have the like remedy for the fame, as any defendant or defendants hath or have in other cafes by law, for recovery of his or their cofts.

Clause in act 24 G. 2. c. 44. extended to juftices acting under this act. XXIII. And be it further enacted by the authority aforefaid, That the ftatute made in the twenty fourth year of his prefent Majefty's reign, intituled, *An act for the rendering the juftices of the peace more fafe in the execution of their office, and for indemnifying conftables and others acting in obedience to their warrant,* fo far as the faid act relates to the rendering the juftices more fafe in the execution of their office, fhall extend and be conftrued to extend to the juftice or juftices of the peace acting under the authority or in execution of this act; and no action or fuit fhall be had

Notice to be given to peace officer, before commencing fuit againft him. or commenced againft, or writ iffued out, or copy of writ ferved upon any peace officer or officers, for any thing done in the execution of this act, until notice in writing fhall have been given to him or them, or left at his or their ufual place of abode, by the attorney for the party commencing fuch action, or fuing out or ferving the copy of the faid writ; which faid notice in writing fhall contain the name and place of abode of the perfon who is to bring fuch action, together with the caufe of action or complaint; and the name and place of abode of the faid attorney fhall be under-wrote or indorfed thereon; and any peace

Tender of amends may be made by him, officer or officers fhall be at liberty, and may by virtue of this act, at any time within fourteen days after fuch notice, tender or caufe to be tendered any fum or fums of money, as amends for the injury complained of, to the party complaining, or to

and pleaded in bar of the action. the faid attorney; and if the fame is not accepted of, the defendant or defendants, in fuch action or actions, may plead fuch tender in bar of fuch action or actions, together with the general iffue, or any other plea, with leave of the court; and if upon iffue joined upon fuch tender, the jury fhall find the amends tendered to have been fufficient, the faid jury fhall find a verdict for the defendant or defendants; and in fuch cafe, or if the plaintiff fhall become nonfuit or difcontinue his action, or if judgment fhall be given for the defendant or defendants upon demurrer, the defendant or defendants fhall be intitled to his

If none, or infufficient tender has been made, plaintiff, upon a verdict, to recover. and their cofts; and if the jury fhall find that no fuch tender was made, or that the amends tendered were not fufficient, and alfo fhall find againft the defendant or defendants on fuch other plea or pleas by them pleaded, the faid jury fhall give a verdict for the plaintiff, and fuch damages as they fhall think proper, for which the plaintiff fhall have judgment, together with his, her or their full cofts.

CAP.

CAP. XXV.

An act for the better ordering of the militia forces in the several counties of that part of Great Britain *called* England.

WHEREAS *a well ordered and well-disciplined militia is essentially necessary to the safety, peace and prosperity of this kingdom: and whereas the laws now in being for the regulation of the militia are defective and ineffectual*; be it enacted by the King's most excellent majesty, by and with the advice and consent of the lords spiritual and temporal and commons in parliament assembled, That from and after the first day of *May* one thousand seven hundred and fifty seven, his Majesty, his heirs and successors, may and shall issue forth commissions of lieutenancy for the respective counties, ridings and places herein after mentioned ; and the respective lieutenants thereby appointed shall have full power and authority to call together all such persons, and to arm and array them at such times and in such manner as is herein after expressed ; and such respective lieutenants shall from time to time constitute and appoint such persons as they shall think fit, qualified as is herein after directed, and living within their respective counties, ridings and places, to be their deputy lieutenants ; the names of such persons having been first presented to and approved by his Majesty, his heirs or successors ; and shall give commissions to a proper number of colonels, lieutenant colonels, majors and other officers, also qualified as is herein after directed to train and discipline the persons so to be armed and arrayed, according to the rules, orders and directions herein after provided ; and shall certify to his Majesty, his heirs and successors, the names of such commission officers, within one month after they shall be so appointed, and shall have accepted their respective commissions.

The King to issue forth letters of lieutenancy for the respective counties.

The lieutenants to assemble and arm the militia.

II. Provided always, and be it enacted, That nothing herein contained shall be construed to vacate any commission of lieutenancy already granted by his Majesty, nor any deputations granted to deputy lieutenants ; but that the same shall continue in full force and vigour for the purposes of this act, so as the said deputy lieutenants be qualified as is herein after directed.

Commissions of lieutenancy and deputations already granted to stand good.

III. And be it enacted, That his Majesty's lieutenant of every county, riding or place shall have the chief command of the militia thereof, which shall be raised by virtue of this act ; and in every county, riding or place in *England* and *Wales* (except as is herein after excepted) there shall be appointed twenty or more deputy lieutenants, if so many persons, qualified as is herein before and after expressed, can be therein found ; and if twenty persons so qualified cannot be therein found, then there shall be appointed so many persons as can be therein found ; and each person so to be appointed a deputy lieutenant or colonel,

Lieutenants to have the chief command of the militia. Number of deputy lieutenants in each county.

Deputy lieutenant or colonel to have 400l. per ann. or be heir to 800l. per ann. shall be seised or possessed, either in law or equity, for his own use and benefit, in possession of a freehold, copyhold or customary estate for life, or for some greater estate, or of an estate for some long term of years, determinable on one or more life or lives, in manors, messuages, lands, tenements or hereditaments in *England*, *Wales* or the town of *Berwick* upon *Tweed*, of the yearly value of four hundred pounds, or shall be heir apparent of some person who shall be in like manner seised or possessed of a like estate as aforesaid, of the yearly value of eight hundred pounds; and each person so to be appointed a lieutenant colonel Lieutenant colonel or major 300l. per ann. or major, shall be, in like manner, seised or possessed of a like estate as aforesaid, of the yearly value of three hundred pounds, or shall be heir apparent of some person who shall be, in like manner, seised or possessed of a like estate as aforesaid, of the yearly value of six hundred pounds; and Captain 200l. per annum, each person so to be appointed a captain, shall be, in like manner, seised or possessed of a like estate as aforesaid, of the yearly value of two hundred pounds, or shall be heir apparent of some person who shall be, in like manner, seised or possessed of a like estate as aforesaid, of the yearly value of four hundred pounds, or shall be a younger son of some person who shall be, or, at the time of his death, was in like manner seised or possessed of a like estate as aforesaid, of the yearly value of six hundred pounds; and that each person so to be appointed a lieutenant, Lieutenant 100l. per annum. shall be, in like manner, seised or possessed of a like estate as aforesaid, of the yearly value of one hundred pounds, or shall be son of some person who shall be, or, at the time of his death, was in like manner seised or possessed of a like estate as aforesaid, of the yearly value of two hundred pounds; and each person so to Ensign 50l. per annum. be appointed an ensign, shall be, in like manner, seised or possessed of a like estate as aforesaid, of the yearly value of fifty pounds, or shall be son of some person who shall be, or, at the time of his death, was in like manner seised or possessed of a like estate as aforesaid, of the yearly value of one hundred pounds; One moiety of the estates to be within the county for which they serve. one moiety of which said estates, required as qualifications for each deputy lieutenant, colonel, lieutenant colonel, major, captain, lieutenant and ensign respectively, shall be situate or arising within such respective county or riding in which he shall be so appointed to serve.

What shall be deemed equal to an estate of 100l. IV. Provided always, and be it enacted, That for the purposes of the respective qualifications required by this act, the immediate reversion or remainder of and in manors, messuages, lands, tenements or hereditaments which are leased for one, two or three life or lives, or for any term of years determinable upon the death of one, two or three life or lives on reserved rents, and which are to the lessee or lessees of the clear yearly value of three hundred pounds, shall be deemed equal to an estate herein before described as a qualification of the yearly value of one hundred pounds, and so in proportion, be the said qualifications of a greater or less degree; any thing in this act contained to the contrary notwithstanding.

V. Pro-

V. Provided always, and be it enacted, That any officer may be promoted on account of merit in the said militia, when called out and assembled, in case of actual invasion, or upon imminent danger thereof, or in case of rebellion, by the lieutenant of any county, riding or place, from a lower to an higher commission, inclusive of that of lieutenant colonel, notwithstanding he should not have the qualifications requisite for his first admittance into such higher rank of the militia. *(Officers may be promoted, in extraordinary occasions, on account of merit,)*

VI. Provided, That no person, not having the qualification herein before directed for a captain, shall be promoted to an higher rank than that of captain. *(but none higher than captains, who want a qualification for that rank.)*

VII. Provided also, That the qualifications above recited, to enable any person to be a deputy lieutenant, lieutenant colonel, major, captain, lieutenant or ensign, shall not extend to such commissions as shall be granted by his Majesty's constable of the *tower*, or lieutenant of the *tower hamlets*. *(Recited qualifications not to extend to the tower or tower hamlets.)*

VIII. Provided always, and be it enacted, That his Majesty, his heirs and successors shall from time to time, as he and they shall think fit, signify his and their pleasure to his and their lieutenants of any county, riding or place, to displace all or any such deputy lieutenants and officers; and thereupon his Majesty's respective lieutenants shall appoint others within the same county, riding or place, under the like qualifications, to serve in their stead. *(Deputy lieutenants and officers may be displaced at his Majesty's pleasure.)*

IX. Provided always, and be it enacted, That every deputy lieutenant and commission officer in the militia shall, within six months next after he shall have accepted his commission, leave with the clerk of the peace of the county, riding or place, in and for which he shall be so appointed, his qualification in writing, signed by himself; and such clerk of the peace is hereby required to enter the same upon a roll to be kept for that purpose; and every deputy lieutenant and commission officer shall, at some general quarter sessions holden for the county, riding or place for which he shall be so appointed, or in one of his Majesty's courts of record at *Westminster*, within six months after he shall have accepted his commission, take the oaths appointed to be taken in and by an act passed in the first year of the reign of his late majesty King *George*, intituled, *An act for the further security of his Majesty's person and government; and the succession of the crown in the heirs of the late princess Sophia, being protestants; and for extinguishing the hopes of the pretended prince of Wales, and his open and secret abettors*; and shall also make, repeat and subscribe the declaration in the said act mentioned. *(Their qualifications to be left with the clerk of the peace, and filed. They are to take the oaths, &c. appointed by 1 G. 1. st. 2. c. 13.)*

X. And be it enacted, That if any person shall execute any of the powers hereby conferred on deputy lieutenants, colonels, lieutenant colonels or majors (not being qualified as aforesaid) or shall not, within the time herein before limited, deliver in such qualification, and take the oaths, and make, repeat and subscribe the declaration aforesaid, every such person shall forfeit and pay the sum of two hundred pounds; and if any person shall execute any of the powers hereby conferred on captains, *(200l. penalty on deputy lieutenants, and all above the degree of captains;)*

and 100l. on
captains, and
thofe under,
acting if not
qualified, &c.

lieutenants or enfigns (not being qualified as aforefaid) and fhall not, within the time herein before limited, deliver in fuch qualification, and take the oaths, and make, repeat and fubfcribe the declaration aforefaid, every fuch perfon fhall forfeit and pay the fum of one hundred pounds; fuch feveral penalties to be recovered by action of debt, bill, plaint or information, in any of his Majefty's courts of record at *Weftminfter*, wherein no effoin, wager of law or protection, or more than one imparlance fhall be allowed; one moiety whereof fhall go to the ufe of the perfon who fhall fue for the fame, and the other moiety to the ufes herein after directed.

Peers exempted ferving; but they and their heirs apparent may be appointed deputy lieutenants or commiffion officers.

XI. Provided always, and be it enacted, That nothing in this act contained fhall extend, or be deemed or conftrued to extend to oblige any peer of this realm to ferve in the militia perfonally, or by fubftitute; or to reftrain his Majefty's lieutenant of any county, riding or place from appointing any peer of this realm, or heir apparent of any fuch peer, to be a deputy lieutenant or commiffion officer in the militia within the county, riding or place where fuch peer or heir apparent of fuch peer fhall refpectively have fome place of refidence; or to oblige any peer of this realm, or heir apparent of fuch peer (fo appointed a deputy lieutenant or commiffion officer refpectively) to leave with the clerk of the peace for the county, riding or place for which he fhall be fo appointed, any qualification in writing as aforefaid; but it fhall be lawful for every peer of this realm, or heir apparent of fuch peer fo appointed and taking the oaths, and making, repeating and fubfcribing the declaration aforefaid, to act as a deputy lieutenant or commiffion officer refpectively, although he fhall not be feifed or poffeffed of any fuch eftate in manors, meffuages, lands, tenements or hereditaments, as is required by this act; any thing herein contained to the contrary notwithftanding.

A commiffion does not vacate a feat in parliament.
At the end of 4 years, fuch a number of officers to be difcharged.

XII. Provided always, and be it enacted, That the acceptance of a commiffion in the militia fhall not vacate the feat of any member returned to ferve in parliament.

XIII. And be it enacted, That his Majefty's lieutenant, together with three or more deputy lieutenants of any county, riding or place, and on the death, or in the abfence of his Majefty's lieutenant, any five or more of them fhall, at the end of every four years, at their annual meeting, difcharge fuch a number of the officers of the militia (not exceeding one field officer of each regiment or battalion, and one third part of the whole number of officers of each inferior rank refpectively) as fhall be equal to the number of perfons who fhall be fit and willing to ferve as officers in the militia of fuch county, riding or place, and fhall be duly qualified for fuch ranks according to the directions of this act; and fuch lieutenant fhall appoint fuch perfons to ferve as officers in the room of the officers fo difcharged as aforefaid.

XIV. And be it enacted, That his Majefty, his heirs and fucceffors may and fhall appoint one proper perfon, who fhall

6   have

have ferved, or fhall, at the time of fuch appointment, actually ferve in fome of his Majefty's other forces, to be an adjutant to each regiment or battalion of militia in each county, riding or place refpectively; and fuch adjutant fhall, during his fervice in the faid militia, preferve his rank in the army in the fame manner as if he had continued in that fervice; and his Majefty, his heirs and fucceffors may and fhall alfo appoint, according to the proportion of one ferjeant to twenty private men, two or more proper perfons to be ferjeants to every company in the faid militia, out of and from his Majefty's other forces, fuch perfons having ferved in the faid forces for the fpace of three years next preceding their appointment to be ferjeants as aforefaid, or may appoint fuch other perfons to be ferjeants as aforefaid, as have formerly ferved for the fpace of three years in his Majefty's faid forces; and the fervice in the militia of fuch perfons fo appointed out of his Majefty's faid forces, fhall intitle them to the benefit of *Chelfea hofpital*, in the fame manner as if they had continued to ferve in the faid forces; and every perfon appointed to be a ferjeant as aforefaid, out of the penfioners on the eftablifhment of *Chelfea hofpital*, fhall be intitled to be put again upon the faid eftablifhment after he fhall be difcharged from the fervice of the militia, provided he brings a certificate of his good behaviour, under the hand of the colonel or commanding officer of the regiment or battalion in which he fhall have ferved as aforefaid.

(marginal notes: Adjutant from the King's forces to be appointed to each regiment; Serjeants to be appointed out of the army; and to be intitled to Chelfea hofpital. Serjeants appointed from thence, to be re-admitted.)

XV. And be it enacted, That no perfon who fhall keep any houfe of publick entertainment, or who fhall fell any ale, wine, brandy or other fpirituous liquors by retail, fhall be capable of being or continuing a ferjeant in the militia. *(Ale-houfe-keepers, &c. difqualified from being ferjeants.)*

XVI. And be it enacted, That the number of private men to be raifed by virtue of this act, in that part of *Great Britain*, called *England*, the dominion of *Wales* and town of *Berwick* upon *Tweed* (exclufive of the places herein after excepted) fhall be *(Number of private men to be raifed in each county.)*

For the county of *Bedford*, four hundred.
For the county of *Berks*, five hundred and fixty.
For the county of *Bucks*, five hundred and fixty.
For the county of *Cambridge*, four hundred and eighty.
For the county of *Chefter*, with the city and county of the city of *Chefter*, five hundred and fixty.
For the county of *Cornwall*, fix hundred and forty.
For the county of *Cumberland*, three hundred and twenty.
For the county of *Derby*, five hundred and fixty.
For the county of *Devon*, with the city and county of the city of *Exeter*, one thoufand fix hundred.
For the county of *Dorfet*, with the town and county of the town of *Poole*, fix hundred and forty.
For the county of *Durham*, four hundred.
For the county of *Effex*, nine hundred and fixty.
For the county of *Gloucefter*, with the city and county of the

city of *Gloucester*, and the city and county of the city of *Bristol*, nine hundred and sixty.

For the county of *Hereford*, four hundred and eighty.

For the county of *Hertford*, five hundred and sixty.

For the county of *Huntingdon*, three hundred and twenty.

For the county of *Kent*, with the city and county of the city of *Canterbury*, nine hundred and sixty.

For the county of *Lancaster*, eight hundred.

For the county of *Leicester*, five hundred and sixty.

For the county of *Lincoln*, with the city and county of the city of *Lincoln*, one thousand two hundred.

For the *tower division* in the county of *Middlesex*, commonly called *the Tower Hamlets*, one thousand one hundred and sixty.

And for the rest of the county of *Middlesex*, one thousand six hundred.

For the county of *Monmouth*, two hundred and forty.

For the county of *Norfolk*, with the city and county of the city of *Norwich*, nine hundred and sixty.

For the county of *Northampton*, six hundred and forty.

For the county of *Northumberland*, with the town and county of the town of *Newcastle upon Tyne*, and the town of *Berwick*, five hundred and sixty.

For the county of *Nottingham*, with the town and county of the town of *Nottingham*, four hundred and eighty.

For the county of *Oxford*, five hundred and sixty.

For the county of *Rutland*, one hundred and twenty.

For the county of *Salop*, six hundred and forty.

For the county of *Somerset*, eight hundred and forty.

For the county of *Southampton*, with the town and county of the town of *Southampton*, nine hundred and sixty.

For the county of *Stafford*, with the city and county of the city of *Litchfield*, five hundred and sixty.

For the county of *Suffolk*, nine hundred and sixty.

For the county of *Surry*, eight hundred.

For the county of *Sussex*, eight hundred.

For the county of *Warwick*, with the city and county of the city of *Coventry*, six hundred and forty.

For the county of *Westmoreland*, two hundred and forty.

For the county of *Worcester*, with the city and county of the city of *Worcester*, five hundred and sixty.

For the county of *Wilts*, eight hundred.

For the west riding of the county of *York*, with the city and county of the city of *York*, one thousand two hundred and forty.

For the north riding of the said county, seven hundred and twenty.

And for the east riding of the said county, with the town and county of the town of *Kingston upon Hull*, four hundred.

For the county of *Anglesea*, eighty.

For the county of *Brecknock*, one hundred and sixty.

For the county of *Cardigan*, one hundred and twenty.

For

For the county of *Caermarthen*, with the county borough of Caermarthen, two hundred.

For the county of *Carnarven*, eighty.

For the county of *Denbigh*, two hundred and eighty.

For the county of *Flint*, one hundred and twenty.

For the county of *Glamorgan*, three hundred and sixty.

For the county of *Merioneth*, eighty.

For the county of *Montgomery*, two hundred and forty.

For the county of *Pembroke*, with the town and county of the town of *Haverford West*, one hundred and sixty.

For the county of *Radnor*, one hundred and twenty.

XVII. Provided, That there shall not be more than three commission officers (that is to say) one captain, one lieutenant, and one ensign, to eighty private men; and so in proportion, as near as may be, to any greater or lesser number of private men.

Three officers allowed to 80 private men.

XVIII. Provided always, and be it enacted, That if his Majesty's lieutenant of any county, riding or place, shall think that too large a proportion of private men is by this act directed to be raised for such county, riding or place, it shall be lawful for his Majesty's privy council, upon application made to them by any such lieutenant, to fix as near as may be, the number of private men, which shall be furnished from the list of that county, riding or place so complaining, by the proportion which the whole number returned in all the lists bears to the whole number of the militia by this act directed to be raised; all which lists his Majesty's lieutenants of each county, riding or place respectively, are hereby required to transmit to his Majesty's privy council.

Where too large a proportion of men is directed, the privy council is to regulate the same.

XIX. And be it enacted, That his Majesty's lieutenants, together with any two or more deputy lieutenants, and on the death or removal, or in the absence of his Majesty's lieutenants, the deputy lieutenants, or any three or more of them, shall meet once in every year at some city or principal town of the county, riding or place for which they shall be commissioned, or oftener, if they shall think fit, there to concert such measures as shall be most conducive to the faithful execution of this act; the first of which meetings for the year one thousand seven hundred and fifty seven shall be on the twelfth day of *July*, and for every subsequent year on the first *Tuesday* in *June*; and shall at their first meeting, issue out their orders to the chief constable, and where there is no chief constable, to some other officer of the several hundreds, rapes, laths, wapentakes, or other divisions within their respective counties, ridings or places, to return to them upon a day, and at a place therein to be mentioned, fair and true lists in writing of all men usually, and at that time, dwelling within their respective hundreds, rapes, laths, wapentakes, or other divisions, between the ages of eighteen and fifty years (all peers of this realm; all persons who shall serve or act as deputy lieutenants, or commission officers in the militia; all persons ex-

Lieutenants and deputy lieutenants to meet annually or oftener.

First meeting to be on 12 July, and for subsequent years on first Tuesday in June.

Orders to be then issued to the constables to make returns of all men, between the ages of 18 and 50 years.

Persons excepted.

persons actually serving as commission officers in any regiment, troop or company in his Majesty's other forces, or in any of his Majesty's castles or forts; all persons being members of either of the universities, clergymen, teachers and preachers of separate congregations, constables, and other peace officers, and parish officers; articled clerks, apprentices, seamen and sea-faring men excepted) distinguishing the numbers in each parish, tything or place, and which of the persons so returned labour under any infirmities incapacitating them from serving as militia men;

Chief constables to order the parish officers to make such returns. for which purpose such chief constables, or other officers, and every of them, are hereby authorized and required, by order under their hands, to require the constable, tythingman, headborough, or other officer of each parish, tything or place within their respective hundreds, rapes, laths, wapentakes, or other divisions, to return to them upon a day, and at a place in such order to be mentioned, fair and true lists in writing of all such men as aforesaid, usually and at that time dwelling within their respective parishes, tythings or places, with the distinctions before described, having first affixed a true copy thereof on the

Copy to be affixed on the door of the church, the Sunday before the return is made. door of the church or chapel belonging to such parish, tything or place; and if any place, being extraparochial, shall have no church or chapel belonging thereto, on the door of the church or chapel of some parish or place thereunto adjoining, on the *Sunday* morning before they shall make such return; and his

Lieutenants and deputy lieutenants to meet and appoint the number of men to serve. Majesty's lieutenants, together with any two or more deputy lieutenants, or in the absence of his Majesty's said lieutenant, any three or more deputy lieutenants, shall on the day, and at the place on which they shall have so ordered such lists to be returned, meet and appoint what number of persons in each respective hundred, rape, lath, wapentake, or other division as aforesaid, shall serve in the said militia, towards raising the number of militia men hereby ordered and directed to be raised for such respective county, riding or place, in proportion to the whole number contained in such lists; and the said deputy lieu-

Deputy lieutenants to subdivide, and meet in their subdivisions within a month; tenants shall afterwards subdivide themselves; and any three or more deputy lieutenants, or in case three deputy lieutenants shall not meet, then any two deputy lieutenants, together with any one justice of the peace for such county, riding or place, or any one deputy lieutenant, together with any two such justices of the peace, shall within one month after the said second general meeting, meet within the respective subdivisions, at a time and place to be appointed by the said deputy lieutenants, or one of them, and the said deputy lieutenants, or any one or more of them, shall before such meeting issue out an order to the chief constables or other officers of the respective hundreds, rapes, laths, wapentakes, or other divisions, to return upon the day and at the place of meeting so appointed, true copies of the lists so by them returned, to his Majesty's said lieutenant, and the said deputy lieutenants, at their second general meeting as aforesaid; and the said deputy lieutenants, or any three or more of them, or any two deputy lieutenants, together with any one

justice

justice of the peace, or any one deputy lieutenant, together with any two justices of the peace so assembled in the said subdivisions, shall (after hearing any person who shall think himself aggrieved by having his name inserted in such lists, or by any others being omitted) direct such lists to be amended, and appoint what number of men in each respective parish, tything or place, shall serve in the said militia, in proportion to the whole number contained in the lists for such hundreds, rapes, laths, wapentakes, or other divisions, as aforesaid; and shall immediately cause them to be chosen by lot out of the whole number of men liable to serve for each respective parish, tything or place; and the said deputy lieutenants, or any one or more of them, shall appoint another meeting to be held within three weeks in the same subdivision, and shall issue out an order to the chief constables or other officers of the respective hundreds, rapes, laths, wapentakes, or other divisions, to direct the constable, tythingman, headborough or other officer of each parish, tything or place, to give notice to every man so chosen to serve in the militia, to appear at such meeting; which notice shall be given or left at his place of abode at least seven days before such meeting; and every person so chosen by lot, shall upon such notice appear at such meeting, and there take the oaths directed to be taken, and make, repeat and subscribe the declaration mentioned in and by the said act passed in the first year of his late majesty King *George*; which oaths and declaration any one deputy lieutenant is hereby authorized then and there to administer; and shall be inrolled to serve in the militia of such respective county, riding or place, as a private militia man, for the space of three years, in a roll to be then and there prepared for that purpose, or shall provide a fit person (to be approved by the said deputy lieutenants, or any three or more of them, or any two deputy lieutenants, together with any one justice of the peace, or any one deputy lieutenant, together with any two justices of the peace then met) to serve as his substitute; which substitute so provided and approved, shall take the said oaths, and make, repeat and subscribe the said declaration, and sign his consent on the said roll, to serve as his substitute during the said term; and if any person so chosen by lot to serve in the said militia (not being one of the people called *Quakers*) shall refuse or neglect to take the oaths, and make, repeat and subscribe the declaration aforesaid, and to serve in the said militia, or to provide a substitute to be approved as aforesaid, who shall take the oaths, and make, repeat and subscribe the said declaration, and sign his consent to serve as his substitute; every such person shall forfeit and pay the sum of ten pounds, and at the end of three years be appointed to serve again.

XX. And be it enacted, That the said deputy lieutenants, or any three or more of them, or any two deputy lieutenants, together with any one justice of the peace, or any one deputy lieutenant, together with any two justices of the peace, shall meet in the several sub-divisions, from time to time, as often as they

[Marginal notes: and after setling the lists, and number of men to serve, they are to cause them to be chosen by lot. Anothermeeting within three weeks after, and notice to the persons chosen to attend; who are then to take the oaths, &c. according to 1 Geo. 1. stat. 2. c. 13. and are to be inrolled to serve as private men for three years, or provide fit substitutes. Persons refusing to serve, &c. forfeit 10l. and at the end of three years are liable to serve again. Deputy lieutenants to meet occasionally, and annually on the Tuesday before Michael-]

mas; to grant discharges to such as have a right thereto,

and to fill up by lot all vacancies.

Persons chosen are to take the oaths, &c. and be inrolled.

they shall think necessary, for the due execution of this act, and one of the said meetings in every shall be on *Tuesday* in the week before *Michaelmas* day; and if any man serving in the said militia, being of the age of thirty five years or upwards, and having served two years in the militia, shall desire his discharge; or if any person whatsoever shall shew any just cause for his discharge; it may and shall be lawful for the said deputy lieutenants, or any three or more of them, or any two deputy lieutenants, together with any one justice of the peace, or any one deputy lieutenant, together with any two justices of the peace, at their said annual meetings for the respective subdivisions, to discharge such person from serving in the said militia; and in the stead of the persons so discharged, and also if there shall be any other vacancy by death, or otherwise, such deputy lieutenants, or any three or more of them, or any two deputy lieutenants, together with any one justice of the peace, or any one deputy lieutenant, together with any two justices of the peace, shall cause a like number of other persons to be chosen by lot out of the lists of such parishes, tythings or places where such vacancies shall happen, unless the person by whom any such vacancy shall be made, served as a substitute; in which case the person for whom he served shall himself serve, or provide another substitute for the remainder of the three years unexpired from his having provided his first substitute; which persons so chosen, or substitutes so provided and approved as aforesaid, shall take the said oaths, and make, repeat and subscribe the said declaration; and every person so chosen shall be inrolled, and every substitute so provided shall subscribe his consent to serve, and shall serve in the said militia for the space of three years, or for the remainder of the three years unexpired, subject to the directions, provisions and penalties in this act contained.

Private man, changing his residence, to serve in the place he removes to, and to give previous notice of his removal to the deputy lieutenant.

XXI. Provided always, and be it enacted, That every militia man shall, if he change the place of his abode, continue actually bound to serve in the militia of the parish, tything or place to which he shall so have removed, until his three years service shall be completed; and if the quota to the militia of the parish, tything or place to which he shall so have removed, be full, he shall, on the first vacancy, be inrolled to serve in the militia thereof, until the whole term of three years actual service be completed; and every such militia man shall, before he change the place of his abode, give notice thereof to any three or more deputy lieutenants, or to any two deputy lieutenants, together with any one justice of the peace, or to any one deputy lieutenant, together with any two justices of the peace, at some publick meeting, or to one deputy lieutenant, who shall give to such militia man a certificate of the time he shall have served in the militia of the respective parish, tything or place, from his inrollment to serve in the same; and if such certificate shall have been given by one deputy lieutenant only, such deputy lieutenant shall certify the same to the deputy lieutenants and justices of the peace at their next meeting within such subdivision; and if any

militia

militia man fo changing the place of his abode, fhall not give notice as aforefaid, fuch militia man fo neglecting, and thereof convicted on oath before one or more juftice or juftices of the peace, fhall forfeit and pay the fum of twenty fhillings; and if fuch offender fhall refufe immediately to pay fuch penalty, it fhall be levied by diftrefs and fale of his goods and chattels, by warrant under the hand and feal, or hands and feals of fuch juftice or juftices, rendering the overplus (if any) on demand, after deducting the charges of fuch diftrefs and fale to fuch offender, upon whom fuch diftrefs fhall have been made as aforefaid; and for want of fuch diftrefs, fuch juftice or juftices fhall commit fuch offender to the houfe of correction, there to be kept to hard labour for the fpace of one month.

On neglect of giving fuch notice, he forfeits 20 s.

XXII. And be it enacted, That the faid deputy lieutenants, or any three or more of them, or any two deputy lieutenants, together with any one juftice of the peace, or any one deputy lieutenant, together with any two juftices of the peace in the feveral fubdivifions, fhall yearly caufe new lifts in the feveral parifhes, tythings or places within the fame, to be made as is before directed, and to be returned to them at their faid annual meetings in the feveral fubdivifions; and fhall in every third year appoint what number of perfons fhall ferve for each parifh, tything or place; and fhall caufe a fufficient number of perfons to be chofen by lot, in the room of fuch perfons as fhall have ferved three years, and of thofe who fhall have been difcharged, which perfons fo chofen fhall take the faid oaths, make, repeat and fubfcribe the faid declaration, and be inrolled in manner aforefaid, fo that by rotation all perfons not excepted by this act, living in fuch parifhes, tythings or places, may ferve perfonally or by fubftitute, for the fpace of three years; and fhall be fubject to, and under the directions, provifions and penalties in this act contained; and no militia man having ferved as a fubftitute, fhall by fuch fervice be excufed from ferving for himfelf, when he fhall be chofen by lot as aforefaid; and the faid deputy lieutenants, or any three or more of them, or any two deputy lieutenants, together with any one juftice of the peace, or any one deputy lieutenant, together with any two juftices of the peace, fhall tranfmit to his Majefty's lieutenant true copies of the faid rolls, within fourteen days after their refpective meetings for that purpofe; and if any chief conftable, or other officer of any hundred, rape, lath, wapentake, or other divifion, or any conftable, tythingman, headborough, or other officer, of any parifh, tything or place, fhall refufe or neglect to return fuch lifts from time to time, or to comply with fuch orders and directions as he fhall from time to time receive from his Majefty's lieutenant, and the faid deputy lieutenants, or any three or more of them, or any two deputy lieutenants, together with any one juftice of the peace, or any one deputy lieutenant, together with any two juftices of the peace, in purfuance of this act, or fhall in making fuch return, be guilty of any fraud or wilful partiality, any three or more deputy lieutenants, or any two deputy lieutenants, together

New lifts to be made out, and returned to the deputy lieutenants at their annual meetings; and every third year, the number of men to ferve is to be appointed, and chofen by lot, &c.

No fubftitute to be excufed from ferving for himfelf. Copies of the rolls to be tranfmitted to the lieutenant.

Conftables or other officers neglecting their duty, or guilty of fraud,

gether with any one juftice of the peace, or any one deputy lieutenant, together with any two juftices of the peace, are hereby
impowered and required to imprifon in the common gaol of the
may be impri- refpective county or place, fuch chief conftable or other officer
foned for one of any hundred, rape, lath, wapentake, or other divifion; or
month, or fin- fuch conftable, tythingman, headborough, or other officer of any
ed, not ex- parifh, tything or place; there to be kept without bail or main-
ceeding 5 l. prize for the fpace of one month; or at their difcretion, to fine
nor under 40s. fuch officer in any fum not exceeding five pounds, nor under
forty fhillings; fuch fine to be levied by diftrefs and fale of the
offender's goods and chattels, by warrant under the hands and
feals of any three or more deputy lieutenants, or of any two deputy lieutenants, together with any one juftice of the peace, or
of any one deputy lieutenant, together with any two juftices of
the peace, rendering the overplus (if any) on demand, after
deducting the charge of fuch diftrefs and fale, to fuch officer upon
whom fuch diftrefs fhall have been made as aforefaid.

Private man XXIII. Provided always, and be it enacted, That no private
ferving for man, perfonally ferving for himfelf in the faid militia, during
himfelf is ex- the time of his ferving as a militia man, fhall be liable to do
empted from perfonally any highway duty, commonly called *ftatute work*, or
feveral duties to ferve as a peace officer or parifh officer; nor fhall fuch private
and offices. man be liable to ferve in any of his Majefty's land forces, by
virtue of any act for recruiting his Majefty's land forces, unlefs
he fhall confent thereto.

None having XXIV. Provided always, That no perfon having perfonally
ferved three or by fubftitute ferved three years in the militia, fhall be obliged
years, is liable to ferve again, until by rotation it comes to his turn.
to ferve again
but in rota- XXV. And be it enacted, That every man having perfonally
tion. ferved in the militia, when called out and affembled in cafe of
The fame li- actual invafion, or upon imminent danger thereof, or in cafe of
berty granted rebellion, and being a married man, may fet up and exercife any
to married- fuch trade as he is apt and able for, in any town or place within
men, if called the kingdoms of *Great Britain* and *Ireland*, without any let, fuit or
out in cafes of moleftation, of any perfon or perfons whatfoever, for or by
publick dan- reafon of the ufing of fuch trade, as freely, and with the fame
ger, to fet up provifions, and under the fame regulations, and with the like
trades, exception in refpect to the two univerfities of that part of *Great
Britain* called *England*, as any mariner or foldier may do, by an
as by 22 Geo. act paffed in the twenty fecond year of his Majefty's reign,
2, c. 44. is intituled, *An act to enable fuch officers, mariners and foldiers, as*
granted to *have been in his Majefty's fervice fince his acceffion to the throne, to*
mariners or *exercife trades.*
foldiers.
XXVI. And be it enacted, That if any perfon, being one of
If a Quaker be the people called *Quakers*, fhall be chofen by lot to ferve in the
chofen and re- militia, and fhall refufe or neglect to appear and take the oaths,
fufe to ferve, and make, repeat and fubfcribe the declaration aforefaid, and to
or provide a ferve in the faid militia, or to provide a fubftitute, to be appoint-
fubftitute, ed as aforefaid, who fhall take the faid oaths, make, repeat and
fubfcribe the faid declaration, and fubfcribe his confent to ferve
as the fubftitute of fuch *Quaker*; then and in every fuch cafe,
any

any three deputy lieutenants, or any two deputy lieutenants, together with any one justice of the peace, or any one deputy lieutenant, together with any two justices of the peace, shall, upon as reasonable terms as may be, provide and hire a fit person, who shall take the said oaths, make, repeat and subscribe the said declaration, and subscribe his consent to serve in the said militia for the space of three years, as the substitute of such *Quaker*; and any three deputy lieutenants, or any two deputy lieutenants, together with any one justice of the peace, or any one deputy lieutenant, together with any two justices of the peace, are hereby impowered and required to levy by distress and sale of the goods and chattels of such *Quaker*, by warrant under the hands and seals of any three deputy lieutenants, or any two deputy lieutenants, together with any one justice of the peace, or any one deputy lieutenant, together with any two justices of the peace, such sum or sums as shall be necessary to defray the expence of providing and hiring such person to serve in the said militia for the space of three years, as the substitute of such *Quaker* so refusing or neglecting as aforesaid, rendering the overplus, if any, after deducting the charges of such distress and sale, to such *Quaker*, upon whom such distress shall have been made as aforesaid; and in case any measures shall be used in making distress as aforesaid, which may be by any such *Quaker* thought oppressive, it shall be lawful for such *Quaker* to complain thereof to the deputy lieutenants and justices of the peace at their next meeting, who are hereby impowered and required to hear and finally determine the same.

Deputy lieutenants are to provide one, and levy the expence by distress and sale.

If oppressive measures be used in making the distress, Quaker upon complaint, to be redressed.

XXVII. And be it enacted, That within one month after the said rolls are so returned from the deputy lieutenants, and justices of the peace as aforesaid, his Majesty's lieutenant, together with any two or more deputy lieutenants, or in the absence of the said lieutenant, any three or more deputy lieutenants shall meet together, and form and order the militia for their respective counties, ridings or places, into regiments, consisting, where the number of militia men will admit the same, of twelve, but in no case of less than seven companies, of forty men each at the least, of persons living as near to each other as conveniently can be; and shall post to each company proper officers commissioned and qualified as aforesaid, and other proper non-commission officers; and the militia so formed and ordered shall be trained and exercised in manner following; that is to say, In half companies on the first *Monday* in the months of *March*, *April*, *May*, *June*, *July*, *August*, *September*, and *October*, and in companies on the third *Monday* in the said months, at each place of exercise, or so many, not amounting to half companies or companies respectively, living within the distances herein after mentioned, as can be conveniently brought together; and in regiments or by battalions on the *Tuesday*, *Wednesday*, *Thursday* and *Friday* in *Whitsun* week, in every year, at places of exercise to be appointed within the respective counties, ridings or places by his Majesty's lieutenant, together with any two or more deputy

Within one month after return of the rolls, the lieutenant and deputy lieutenants are to meet, and form the militia into regiments;

and post proper officers to each company.

Manner of training and exercising the militia.

puty

deputy lieutenants, or in the absence of the said lieutenant, by any three or more deputy lieutenants, as convenient with regard to the respective abodes of the militia men as may be, and so as such militia men may not be obliged to go above six miles from home to perform such exercise in half companies or companies;

Notice of the places of exercise is to be sent to the chief constables, &c. and by them to the parish officers, who are to fix the same on the church doors.

and notice of the several places of exercise to which the militia men of each parish, tything or place are to resort, shall be sent to the chief constables, or other officers of the several hundreds, rapes, laths, wapentakes, or other divisions, with directions to forward the same to the constables, tythingmen, headboroughs, or other officers of the several parishes, tythings or places within their respective hundreds, rapes, laths, wapentakes, or other divisions; which constables, tythingmen, headboroughs, or other parish officers, shall cause such notice to be fixed on the the doors of the churches or chapels belonging to their respective parishes, tythings or places; or if any place being extraparochial, shall have no church or chapel belonging thereto, on the door of the church or chapel of some parish, tything or place thereunto adjoining; and all such militia men shall duly attend

A clerk, serjeant major, and drum major to be appointed to each regiment.

on the days herein before mentioned, at the times and places of exercise so to be appointed; and his Majesty's lieutenant shall, from time to time as occasion shall require, appoint a clerk, and also a serjeant major out of the serjeants, and a drum major out of the drummers, to each regiment or battalion.

If it is inconvenient on account of fairs or markets to exercise the militia on the day set by this act,

XXVIII. Provided always, That if the principal inhabitants of any parish, town or place, or any five or more of them, shall represent to the lieutenant, or any three or more deputy lieutenants, or any two deputy lieutenants, together with any one justice of the peace, or to any one deputy lieutenant, together with any two justices of the peace, at any meeting in their subdivision, in which such parish, town or place is situate, that it is upon account of fairs or markets inconvenient to exercise the militia men on the day appointed by this act, it shall be lawful

they may be exercised on any other day in that week but Sunday.

for any three deputy lieutenants, or any two deputy lieutenants, together with any one justice of the peace, or any one deputy lieutenant, together with any two justices of the peace, to order and direct the militia men within such parish, town or place, to be exercised upon any other day within that week, *Sunday* excepted.

Where the numbers are insufficient to be regimented, they are to be formed into a battalion,

XXIX. Provided also, That in any county, riding or place, where the number of men to be raised, shall not amount to seven companies, and therefore not be sufficient to form a regiment, such companies shall be formed into a battalion, and shall be under the command of his Majesty's lieutenant of such county, riding or place, and one field officer, one adjutant (who shall not be of higher rank in the army than a subaltern) one serjeant major, one drum major, and one clerk, shall be

and are to be exercised for four days in Whitsun week annually.

appointed for the battalion of militia of such county, riding or place; and the whole militia of such county, riding or place, shall on the *Tuesday, Wednesday, Thursday* and *Friday* in *Whitsun* week in every year, be trained and exercised in the same manner,

as

as regiments in other counties are by this act directed to be brought together, trained and exercifed.

XXX. Provided alfo, That where by reafon of the diftance from the appointed place of exercife, a whole company, or half company of militia men, cannot be got together, his Majefty's lieutenant, together with any one or more deputy lieutenants, or in the abfence of his Majefty's lieutenant, any two or more deputy lieutenants, fhall order fuch fmaller numbers to be trained and exercifed by fuch perfon or perfons, and in fuch place or places as they fhall think fit. *Smaller bodies of men to be exercifed as fhall be thought fit by the lieutenant, &c.*

XXXI. And be it enacted, That one commiffion officer in every company fhall attend the exercife of his men, when in companies or in half companies, as often as convenient, and fhall then infpect the ftate of their arms, clothes and accoutrements, a report whereof he fhall forthwith tranfmit in writing to his Majefty's lieutenant, or to the commanding officer of the regiment or battalion. *Commiffion officer to attend the exercife of companies or half companies.*

XXXII. And be it enacted, That the captain of each company of militia fhall keep in his own cuftody, or leave and depofit with the feveral ferjeants belonging to his company, or with fuch perfons as the faid captain fhall appoint for that purpofe, the arms, clothes, and accoutrements provided for his company of militia; and the churchwardens of every parifh or place where the faid arms, clothes and accoutrements, are fo depofited, or one of them, is and are hereby required to provide, at the expence of fuch parifh or place, a cheft, in which fuch captain, ferjeant, or other perfon fo appointed as aforefaid, fhall keep the faid arms in fome dry part of his houfe or dwelling, under lock and key, and another cheft, in which he fhall keep under lock and key, the faid clothes and accoutrements; and the ferjeant, or fuch other perfon as fhall be appointed to train and difcipline the men, is hereby required to take care, that after exercife every militia man cleans and returns his arms, clothes and accoutrements, to his captain, or to fuch perfon as fhall be appointed as aforefaid to receive the fame. *Captain to have the charge of the arms and clothes, &c. of his company; and churchwardens to provide chefts.*

XXXIII. Provided always, and be it enacted, That his Majefty's lieutenant of any county, riding or place, or the colonel of any regiment of militia, is hereby authorized, by warrant under his hand and feal, to employ fuch perfon or perfons as he fhall think fit, to feize and remove the arms, clothes and accoutrements, belonging to the militia, whenever his Majefty's faid lieutenant, or the faid colonel, fhall judge it neceffary to the peace of the kingdom, and to deliver the faid arms, clothes and accoutrements, into the cuftody of fuch perfon or perfons as his Majefty's faid lieutenant, or the faid colonel, fhall appoint to receive the fame, for the purpofes of this act. *The King's lieutenant, or the colonel, may feize and remove the arms, &c. when neceffary to the publick peace.*

XXXIV. And be it enacted, That if any ferjeant, or any other perfon intrufted by the captain with the cuftody of any arms, clothes or accoutrements, belonging to the militia, fhall deliver out any fuch arms, clothes or accoutrements, unlefs for exercifing the men, or by the command of his fuperior officer, or by the order of any juftice of the peace under his hand and feal, *Perfon intrufted with cuftody of the arms, &c. delivering out the fame, unlefs for exercife, or by*

proper com-
mand, may be
committed for
6 months.

feal, it may and fhall be lawful for any two or more juftices of
the peace to commit fuch offender to the common gaol of the
county, riding or place, where the offence fhall be committed,
there to remain without bail or mainprize, for any time not exceeding fix months.

No pay, arms,
or clothing, to
be iffued, nor
adjutant or
ferjeant to be
appointed till
four fifths of
the men, and
officers, have
been appoint-
ed, &c.

XXXV. And be it further enacted by the authority aforefaid,
That no pay, arms, accoutrements or clothing, fhall be iffued,
and that no adjutant or ferjeants fhall be appointed for the militia of any county, riding or place, till it fhall appear by a return figned by his Majefty's lieutenant, or, in his abfence, by
three deputy lieutenants, that four fifths of the militia men of
the faid county, riding or place, have been chofen ; and that
four fifths of the commiffion officers have been appointed ; and
that they have taken out their commiffions and entered their
qualifications.

Names of the
men to be
called over at
exercife,
and a return
made to a ju-
ftice, of the
abfentees,
and of fuch as
be difobedi-
ent.

XXXVI. And be it enacted, That the ferjeant, or fuch other
perfon as fhall be appointed to train and difcipline the men, fhall
call over the names of the militia men fo appointed to be exercifed ; and within one week after every fuch exercife, fhall
certify in writing to fome neighbouring juftice of the peace, the
names of the militia men abfent from exercife, with the reafons
of their abfence, if known to him ; and the faid ferjeant, or
other perfon appointed to train and difcipline the men, fhall
alfo certify at the fame time, if any of the faid militia men be
difobedient, or otherwife mifbehave themfelves ; and fuch juftice

And the ju-
ftice may fine
fuch abfentee
for the 1ft of-
fence 2 s.

of the peace is hereby impowered and required, upon proof
then made upon oath, to fine every fuch abfent militia man,
whofe excufe he fhall not allow of, for the firft time of his being fo abfent, two fhillings ; and if fuch militia man fhall refufe
immediately to pay fuch fine, fuch militia man fhall, by order
of the faid juftice, be fet in the ftocks for the fpace of one hour ;

for the 2d of-
fence 4 s.

and for the fecond offence, fuch militia man fo convicted as
aforefaid, fhall forfeit and pay four fhillings ; and if fuch militia man fhall refufe immediately to pay fuch penalty, the juftice
of the peace before whom fuch militia man fhall be fo convicted
as aforefaid, fhall by warrant commit fuch militia man to the

for the 3d, and
every other
offence 6 s.

houfe of correction for the fpace of four days ; and for the third
and every other offence, fuch militia man fo convicted fhall forfeit and pay fix fhillings ; and if fuch militia man fhall refufe
immediately to pay fuch penalty, the juftice of the peace before
whom fuch militia man fhall be fo convicted as aforefaid, fhall,
by warrant, commit fuch militia man to the houfe of correction
for any time not exceeding one month, or until fuch penalty

and if any mi-
litia man fhall
be drunk on
his duty, he
forfeits 10 s.

fhall be paid ; and if any militia man fhall be drunk at the time
of his exercifing, fuch militia man, being thereof convicted on
oath before fome juftice of the peace, fhall forfeit and pay ten
fhillings ; and if fuch militia man fhall refufe immediately to
pay fuch penalty, fuch militia man fhall be, by order of fuch

if difobedient,
for the 1ft of-
fence 2 s. 6d.

juftice, fet in the ftocks for one hour ; and if any militia man
fhall be difobedient or infolent to his officer, and be convicted
thereof as aforefaid, fuch militia man fhall, for the firft offence,

forfeit.

forfeit and pay two shillings and six pence; and if such militia man shall refuse immediately to pay such penalty, the justice of the peace before whom such militia man shall be so convicted as aforesaid, shall, by warrant, commit such militia man to the house of correction for the space of four days; and, for the second offence, such militia man so convicted as aforesaid, shall forfeit and pay five shillings; and if such militia man shall refuse immediately to pay such penalty, the justice of the peace before whom such militia man shall be so convicted as aforesaid, shall, by warrant, commit such militia man to the house of correction for the space of seven days; and for the third and every other offence such militia man so convicted as aforesaid, shall forfeit and pay forty shillings; and if such militia man shall refuse immediately to pay such penalty, the justice of the peace before whom such militia man shall be so convicted as aforesaid, shall, by warrant, commit such militia man to the house of correction, for any time not less than fourteen days, nor exceeding one month: and if any militia man shall sell, pawn or lose, any of his arms, clothes or accoutrements, such militia man, being thereof convicted in manner aforesaid, shall forfeit and pay a sum not exceeding three pounds; and if such militia man shall refuse immediately to pay such penalty, the justice of the peace before whom such militia man shall be so convicted as aforesaid, shall, by warrant, commit such militia man to the house of correction for the space of one month, and until satisfaction be made for the same; and if he shall not be of ability to make such satisfaction, then for the space of three months: and if any militia man shall refuse or neglect to return his arms, clothes and accoutrements, in good order, to his captain, or to such person as shall be appointed as aforesaid to receive the same, on the day of exercise, or the next day, such militia man, being thereof convicted as aforesaid, shall, for every such offence, forfeit and pay two shillings and six pence; and if such militia man shall refuse immediately to pay such penalty, the justice of the peace before whom such militia man shall be so convicted as aforesaid, shall, by warrant, commit such militia man to the house of correction for the space of seven days; and if any militia man shall refuse or neglect to return his arms, clothes and accoutrements, in good order, to his captain, or to such person as shall be appointed as aforesaid to receive the same, on or before the *Monday* after *Whitsun* week, and be thereof convicted as aforesaid, such militia man shall forfeit and pay five shillings; and if such militia man shall refuse immediately to pay such penalty, the justice of the peace before whom such militia man shall be so convicted as aforesaid, shall, by warrant, commit such militia man to the house of correction for the space of fourteen days.

XXXVII. And be it enacted, That if the serjeant or other person appointed by any captain of the militia, to receive and keep in his custody the arms, clothes and accoutrements, thereto belonging, shall refuse or neglect to complain within three days

Marginal notes:
for the 2d offence 5 s.

and for the 3d and every other offence 40 s.

and if he sell, pawn, or lose his arms, clothes, &c. he forfeits 3 l.

if he neglect to return his arms, &c. he forfeits 2 s. 6 d.

and if he neglect to return them by Monday after Whitsun week, 5 s.

If the person entrusted therewith, shall not complain to a justice within

days to some neighbouring justice of the peace of any militia man's not having returned his arms, clothes and accoutrements, as before directed, such serjeant or other person appointed as aforesaid, being thereof convicted on oath before one of his Majesty's justices of the peace, shall forfeit and pay the sum of twenty shillings; which penalty, if the offender shall refuse immediately to pay the same, shall be levied by distress and sale of the offender's goods and chattels, by warrant under the hand and seal of the justice of the peace before whom such offender shall be so convicted as aforesaid, rendering the overplus, if any, on demand, after deducting the charges of such distress and sale, to such offender, upon whom such distress shall have been made as aforesaid.

XXXVIII. And be it enacted, That if any non-commission officer of the militia, or private militia man, shall be absent from the annual meeting of the militia, to which he shall belong, without just cause shewn, such non-commission officer or private militia man, being thereof convicted upon oath, before one or more justice or justices of the peace, shall forfeit and pay ten shillings for each day of such absence; and if such non-commission officer or private militia man, shall refuse immediately to pay such penalty, the justice or justices of the peace before whom such non-commission officer or private militia man shall be so convicted, shall, by warrant, commit such non-commission officer or private militia man to the house of correction for the space of one month.

XXXIX. And be it enacted, That if any non-commission officer shall be negligent in his duty, or insolent, or disobedient to the orders of the adjutant, or other his superior officer, and be thereof convicted as aforesaid upon the oath of the adjutant, or other superior officer, before one or more justice or justices of the peace, such non-commission officer shall forfeit and pay any sum not exceeding thirty shillings, at the discretion of such justice or justices; and if such non-commission officer shall refuse immediately to pay such penalty, the justice or justices of the peace before whom such non-commission officer shall be so convicted as aforesaid, shall, by warrant, commit such non-commission officer to the house of correction for the space of fourteen days, and his Majesty's lieutenant may discharge such non-commission officer out of the militia, if he shall think fit.

XL. And be it enacted, That if any person shall knowingly and willingly buy, take in exchange, conceal or otherwise receive, contrary to the true intent and meaning of this act, any arms, clothes or accoutrements, belonging to the militia, upon any account or pretence whatsoever, the person so offending, being convicted thereof upon oath before one or more justice or justices of the peace, shall forfeit and pay for every such offence, the sum of five pounds; and if such offender shall refuse immediately to pay such penalty, the justice or justices of the peace before whom such offender shall be so convicted as aforesaid, shall, by warrant under the hand and seal, or hands and seals,

of

of such justice or justices, levy the same by distress and sale of the offender's goods and chattels, rendering the overplus (if any) on demand, after deducting the charges of such distress and sale, to such offender upon whom such distress shall have been made as aforesaid; and for want of such distress, shall commit such offender to the common gaol of the county, riding or place, where the offence shall have been committed, there to remain, without bail or mainprize, for the space of three months, or shall cause such offender to be publickly whipt, at the discretion of such justice or justices.

XLI. Provided always, and be it enacted, That no officer of the militia, or private militia man, shall be liable to any penalty for or on account of his absence during the time he shall be going to vote at any election of a member to serve in parliament, or during the time he shall be returning from such election.

None liable to penalty for absence, during the time of going to vote for a member, or returning.

XLII. And be it enacted, That all the muskets delivered for the service of the militia, shall be marked distinctly in some visible place, with the letter M, and the name of the county, riding or place, to which they belong.

Muskets to be marked with an (M) and the name of county, &c.

XLIII. And be it enacted, That the several serjeants shall receive all their military orders, with respect to the training the militia men under their care, from the adjutant, and their superior officers; and are hereby required to report, from time to time, all crimes and misdemeanors of the several militia men under their command to their adjutant, or superior officers, or to some civil magistrate, as the case shall require.

Serjeants to receive orders from the adjutant, &c. and to report to him, &c. the misdemeanors of the men.

XLIV. Provided always, and be it enacted, That all chief constables, petty constables, tythingmen, headboroughs, and other officers of hundreds, rapes, laths, wapentakes, parishes, tythings and places, within that part of *Great Britain* called *England*, and the dominion of *Wales*, shall, and they are hereby required to be aiding and assisting to the justices of the peace, and to his Majesty's said respective lieutenants, and their deputy lieutenants, and to any of them, and to all to whom any power or authority is by this act given, in the execution of the premisses.

All constables, and other peace officers, required to be assisting in execution of the premisses.

XLV. And be it enacted, That in case of actual invasion, or upon imminent danger thereof, or in case of rebellion, it may and shall be lawful for his Majesty, his heirs and successors (the occasion being first communicated to parliament, if the parliament shall be then sitting, or declared in council, and notified by proclamation, if no parliament shall be then sitting or in being) to order and direct his lieutenants, and on their death or removal, or in their absence from their respective counties, ridings or places, any three or more deputy lieutenants, with all convenient speed, to draw out and embody all the regiments and battallions of militia of their respective counties, ridings or places, herein appointed to be raised and trained, or so many of them as his Majesty, his heirs, and successors shall in his or their great wisdom judge necessary, in such manner as shall be best adapted to the circumstances of the danger; and to put the

In case of invasion or rebellion, &c. the King may order the militia to be drawn out and embodied.

said

and put them under the command of general officers,

and direct them to be led to any parts of the kingdom; and they are to receive like pay as the King's forces.

and their officers to have equal rank with the officers in the army;

and they are to be subject to like rules and articles of war;

and being maimed or wounded are equally intitled to Chelsea hospital.

Private men not appearing, or refusing to march according to such order forfeit 40l.

In case of invasion, or rebellion, the parliament is to be summoned to meet, &c.

said forces under the command of such general officers as his Majesty, his heirs and successors shall be pleased to appoint over them; and to direct them to be led by their respective officers into any parts of this kingdom, for the suppression of such invasions and rebellions: and the said officers of the militia, and private militia men, shall, from the time of their being drawn out and embodied as aforesaid, and until they shall be returned again, by order of their commanding officers, to their respective parishes or places of abode, remain under the command of such general officers, and shall be intitled to the same pay as the officers and private men in his Majesty's other regiments of foot receive, and no other; and the officers of the militia shall, during such time as aforesaid, rank with the officers of his Majesty's other forces of equal degree with them as the youngest of their rank; and the officers of the militia, and private militia men, shall be hereby, during such time as aforesaid, subjected and made liable to all such articles of war, rules and regulations, as shall be then by act of parliament in force, for the discipline and good government of any of his Majesty's forces in *Great Britain*; any thing herein contained to the contrary notwithstanding; and when they shall be returned again to their respective parishes or places of abode, they shall be under the same orders and directions only, as they were before they were drawn out and embodied as aforesaid: and if any non-commission officer of the militia, or private militia man, shall be maimed or wounded in actual service, he shall be equally intitled to the benefit of *Chelsea Hospital*, with any non-commission officer, or private soldier, belonging to his Majesty's other forces: and if any militia man so ordered to be drawn out and embodied as aforesaid (not labouring under any infirmity incapacitating him to serve as a militia man) shall not appear and march in pursuance of such order, every such militia man, being convicted thereof upon oath, before two or more justices of the peace, shall forfeit and pay the sum of forty pounds; and if such militia man shall refuse immediately to pay such penalty, the justices of the peace before whom such militia man shall be so convicted, shall, by warrant, commit such militia man to the common gaol of the county, riding or place, where he shall have been so convicted, there to remain without bail or mainprize for the space of twelve months, or until he shall have paid the penalty aforesaid.

XLVI. And be it further enacted, That if at any time (in case of actual invasion, or upon imminent danger thereof, or in case of rebellion) the parliament shall happen to be separated by such adjournment or prorogation as will not expire within fourteen days, it shall be lawful for his Majesty, his heirs and successors, to issue a proclamation for the meeting of the parliament, upon such day as he or they shall thereby appoint, giving fourteen days notice of such appointment; and the parliament shall accordingly meet upon such day, and continue to sit and act in like

man-

manner to all intents and purposes, as if it had stood adjourned or prorogued to the same day.

XLVII. And be it enacted, That no officer serving in the militia, when called out into actual service, shall sit in any court martial upon the trial of any officer or soldier serving in any of his Majesty's other forces; nor shall any officer serving in any of his Majesty's other forces, sit in any court-martial upon the trial of any officer or private man serving in the militia.

Officers in the militia and army, are not to sit indiscriminately on trials for offences committed by the different corps.

XLVIII. And be it enacted, That it may and shall be lawful for the mayors, bailiffs, constables, tythingmen, headboroughs, and other chief magistrates, and officers of cities, towns, parishes, tythings, villages and other places, within that part of *Great Britain* called *England*, the dominion of *Wales*, and the town of *Berwick* upon *Tweed*, and in their default or absence, for any one justice of the peace inhabiting in or near any such city, town, parish, tything, village or place, and for no others, and they are hereby required to quarter and billet the officers and private men serving in the militia, at the times when they shall be called out to their annual exercise, in inns, livery stables, ale-houses, victualling-houses, and all houses of persons selling brandy, strong waters, cyder or metheglin by retail.

Officers and private men, when called out to their annual exercise, are to be quartered on publick houses, &c.

XLIX. And be it enacted, That in case of actual invasion, or upon imminent danger thereof, or in case of rebellion as aforesaid, it may and shall be lawful for any justice of the peace of any county, riding or place, being duly thereunto required by an order from his Majesty, or from his Majesty's lieutenant, or from any deputy lieutenant of the county, riding or place, or from the colonel, or other chief commission officer upon the place, of any regiment, company or detachment of militia, to issue out his warrant under his hand, to the chief constables of hundreds, rapes, laths, wapentakes or divisions, or to the constables, tythingmen, headboroughs or other officers of the parishes, tythings or places, from, through, near, or to which, any such regiment or company of militia men, or any detachment or troop thereof, shall be ordered to march, requiring such chief constables, tythingmen, headboroughs or other officers, to make such provision for carriages of the arms, clothes, accoutrements, powder, match, bullets or other warlike materials, with able men to drive such carriages, as is and are mentioned in the said order; but in case such sufficient carriages and men cannot be provided within any such county, riding, hundred, rape, lath, wapentake, division, parish, tything or place, then the next justice or justices of the peace shall, upon such order as aforesaid being shewn unto him or them, issue his or their warrant to the chief constables, constables, tythingmen, headboroughs or other such officers, of the next county, riding, hundred, rape, lath, wapentake, division, parish, tything or place, for the purposes aforesaid, to make up such deficiency of carriages; and such lieutenant, deputy lieutenant, colonel or other chief commission officer upon the place, who, by virtue of the

In case of invasion, or rebellion, justices, upon order from the King, or commanding officer, &c. are to issue warrants for carriages for the troops.

Officer is to pay for the use of such carriages;

the aforefaid warrant from the faid juftice of the peace, fhall demand fuch carriages of fuch chief conftable, conftable, tythingman, headborough, or other officer, is and are hereby required at the fame time to pay down in hand to the faid chief conftable, conftable, tythingman, headborough, or other officer, for the ufe of the perfon who fhall provide fuch carriages and men, the fum of one fhilling for every mile any waggon with five horfes fhall travel; and the fum of one fhilling for every mile any wain with fix oxen, or with four oxen and two horfes fhall travel; and the fum of nine pence for every mile any cart with

for which a receipt is to be given him, four horfes fhall travel; and fo in proportion for carriages drawn by a lefs number of horfes or oxen; for which refpective fums fo received, the faid chief conftable, conftable, tythingman, headborough, or other officer, is hereby required to give a receipt in writing, to the perfon or perfons paying the fame; and

and the conftables are to order carriages to be furnifhed accordingly; fuch chief conftable, conftable, tythingman, headborough, or other officer, fhall order and appoint fuch perfon or perfons, having carriages within their refpective hundreds, rapes, laths, wapentakes, parifhes, tythings or places, as they fhall think proper, to provide and furnifh fuch carriages and men according to the warrant aforefaid; which perfons fo ordered, are

for 1 day's journey; hereby required to provide and furnifh the fame accordingly, for one day's journey, and no more; and in cafe the faid chief con-

Additional expences to be repaid out of the county ftock. ftables, conftables, tythingmen, headboroughs, or other officers, fhall be at any charges for fuch carriages over and above what is fo received by them of his Majefty's faid lieutenant, the faid deputy lieutenant, colonel, or other chief officer as aforefaid, fuch overplus fhall be borne by each county, riding or place, where fuch additional expence fhall be incurred, and be repaid to them without fee or reward, by the treafurer of each refpective county, riding or place, out of the publick ftock.

Conftables, &c. neglecting their duty forfeit not exceeding 40s. nor lefs than 20s. L. And be it enacted, That if any fuch chief conftable, conftable, tythingman, headborough, or other officer, fhall wilfully neglect or refufe to execute any fuch warrant of any juftice of the peace; or if any perfon appointed by fuch chief conftable, conftable, tythingman, headborough, or other officer, to provide or furnifh any fuch carriage and man, fhall wilfully neglect or refufe to provide the fame, every fuch offender fhall forfeit a fum not exceeding forty fhillings, nor lefs than twenty fhillings, to the ufe of the poor of the parifh, tything or place, where fuch offence fhall be committed, and every fuch offence fhall and may be heard and determined by two juftices of the peace within the county, riding or place, where fuch offence fhall be committed; which juftices fhall, by warrant under their hands and feals, caufe the faid penalty to be levied by diftrefs and fale of the offender's goods and chattels, rendering the overplus (if any) on demand, after deducting the charges of fuch diftrefs and fale, to fuch offender upon whom fuch diftrefs fhall have been made as aforefaid.

Militia not liable to be LI. Provided always, and be it enacted, That neither this act, nor any matter or thing herein contained, fhall be deemed

£

or

or construed to extend to the giving or declaring any power for the transporting any of the militia of this realm, or any way of compelling them to march out of this kingdom. *marched out of the king-dom.*

LII. Provided always, and be it enacted, That his Majesty's lieutenants of the several counties of *Cumberland, Huntingdon, Monmouth, Westmoreland* and *Rutland,* and of every county and place in the dominion of *Wales,* shall respectively have the chief command of the militia thereof, which shall be raised by virtue of this act; and in all the said counties of *Cumberland, Huntingdon, Monmouth, Westmoreland* and *Rutland,* and in every county and place within the dominion of *Wales* respectively, there shall be five or more deputy lieutenants appointed (if so many qualified as herein after expressed can be therein found) and the estates requisite for the qualification of the respective deputy lieutenants and officers of the militia therein, shall be as follows; that is to say, They shall be seised or possessed of such an estate as is in this act mentioned, as a qualification for a deputy lieutenant, colonel or other officer of the militia, in that part of *Great Britain* called *England,* in the proportions following: A deputy lieutenant or colonel shall be in like manner seised or possessed of a like estate as aforesaid of the yearly value of three hundred pounds, or shall be heir apparent of a person who shall be in like manner seised or possessed of a like estate as aforesaid, of the yearly value of five hundred pounds; a lieutenant colonel or major shall be in like manner seised or possessed of a like estate as aforesaid, of the yearly value of two hundred pounds, or shall be heir apparent of a person who shall be in like manner seised or possessed of a like estate as aforesaid, of the yearly value of four hundred pounds; a captain shall be in like manner seised or possessed of a like estate as aforesaid, of the yearly value of one hundred and fifty pounds, or shall be son of a person who shall be, or, at the time of his death, was in like manner seised or possessed of a like estate as aforesaid, of the yearly value of three hundred pounds; a lieutenant shall be in like manner seised or possessed of a like estate as aforesaid, of the yearly value of one hundred pounds, or shall be son of a person who shall be, or, at the time of his death, was in like manner seised or possessed of a like estate as aforesaid, of the yearly value of two hundred pounds; an ensign shall be in like manner seised or possessed of a like estate as aforesaid, of the yearly value of fifty pounds, or shall be son of a person who shall be, or at the time of his death was, in like manner seised or possessed of a like estate as aforesaid, of the yearly value of one hundred pounds; one half of all which respective estates shall be situate or arising within the said counties and places respectively: and in all the said counties of *Cumberland, Huntingdon, Monmouth, Westmoreland* and *Rutland,* and in all the said several counties and places within the said dominion of *Wales* respectively, the penalties for acting not being duly qualified, or not having delivered in such qualification and taken the oaths, and made, repeated and subscribed the declaration aforesaid, shall be,

Lieutenants for Cumberland, Huntingdon, Monmouth, Westmoreland, Rutland and counties in Wales, to have command of the militia there. Number of deputy lieutenants.

Deputy lieutenant or colonel, to have 300l. per annum.

Lieutenant colonel, or major, 200l. per annum.

Captain 100l.

Lieutenant 100l. per annum.

Ensign 50l. per annum.

A moiety of the estates to lie in the county for which they act.

Penalties for acting, not being qualified, &c. for a deputy lieute-

L 4

nant, or field
officer 100l.
and for all
under, 50l.

be, for a deputy lieutenant or field officer one hundred pounds;
and for a captain, lieutenant or ensign fifty pounds; such several penalties to be recovered by action of bill, plaint or information, in any of his Majesty's courts of record at *Westminster*, wherein no essoin, wager of law or protection, or more
than one imparlance shall be allowed; one moiety whereof shall
go to the use of the person who shall sue for the same, and the

other moiety to the uses herein after directed; and any two or more
deputy lieutenants within the said counties of *Cumberland*, *Huntingdon*, *Monmouth*, *Westmoreland* and *Rutland*, and within all
the said several counties and places within the said dominion of
Wales respectively, shall have and exercise all and every the
powers conferred by this act on any three deputy lieutenants, or
on any two deputy lieutenants, together with any one justice of
the peace, or on any one deputy lieutenant, together with any
two justices of the peace, of any county, riding or place within
that part of *Great Britain* called *England*.

LIII. And whereas the ordering the militia in the isle of
Wight, has always been in the governor or lieutenant governor
of the said island: and whereas from the length of time since
the militia thereof was raised, the raising the same in manner
heretofore accustomed, may be attended with many difficulties;

Governor of
the isle of
Wight is to
appoint his
officers,
to act as lieu-
tenants of
counties,
and appoint
deputies;
who are to be
qualified and
act as like of-
ficers for
Wales;
and the mili-
tia is to be
raised as in the
county of
Southampton,
and deemed a
part thereof,
&c.

be it enacted, That the governor of the said island shall appoint
the officers of the militia to be raised in the said island, and
shall and is hereby impowered and required to act, in the execution of this act, in the same manner as his Majesty's lieutenants
of counties are hereby impowered and required to act; and shall
appoint five or more deputies to act with him in and for the said
island; which deputies and officers of the militia shall be qualified in the same manner, and are hereby impowered and required to act, in the execution of this act, in the same manner, and
under the same directions, provisions and penalties, as deputy
lieutenants and officers of the militia in the several counties
within the dominion of *Wales* are by this act subject to; and
the militia of the said island shall be raised in the same manner
as the militia of the county of *Southampton*, and shall be deemed a part of the militia of the said county; and after the same
shall be so raised, the said governor, lieutenant governor, and
deputies, shall order and direct the training and exercising the
said militia within the said island, in the same manner as his
Majesty's lieutenants, and the deputy lieutenants, are by this
act authorized and directed to do in any county within that part
of *Great Britain* called *England*.

LIV. Provided always, and be it enacted, That the militia

Militia of
Purbeck is to
be separate
from that of
the county of
Dorset;
and 80 men
are to be
raised therein,

of the island of *Purbeck* shall remain separate from that of the
county of *Dorset*, as heretofore has been used; and the number of militia men to be raised for the said island, shall be eighty, part of six hundred and forty appointed by this act to be
raised for the county of *Dorset*, with the county of the town of
Poole, with a field officer, and other proper officers; and the
said island shall, as to all the purposes of this act, be considered

a3

as if it were a distinct county of itself; and all the powers given with a field officer, &c.

as if it were a distinct county of itself; and all the powers given and provisions made by this act with respect to counties, and the militia thereof, shall take place and be in force with respect to the said island and the militia thereof, except only as to the several particulars herein expressed, and otherwise provided for; that is to say, The number of deputy lieutenants to be appointed for the said island shall be three, or more (if so many duly qualified can be therein found) any two of which said deputy lieutenants shall have and exercise all the powers conferred by this act on any three deputy lieutenants of any county, or on any two deputy lieutenants, together with any one justice of the peace, or on any one deputy lieutenant, together with any two justices of the peace, of any county; and the estates requisite for the qualification of the deputy lieutenants and officers of the militia in the said island, shall be as follows; a deputy lieutenant and field officer shall be seised or possessed of such an estate, and in like manner, as is in this act before mentioned, as a qualification for a deputy lieutenant, colonel or other officer of the militia, of the yearly value of two hundred pounds; a captain shall be in like manner seised or possessed of a like estate as aforesaid, of the yearly value of one hundred pounds, or be heir apparent of a person who shall be in like manner seised or possessed of a like estate as aforesaid, of the yearly value of two hundred pounds; a lieutenant or ensign shall be in like manner seised or possessed of a like estate as aforesaid, of the yearly value of fifty pounds, or be son of a person who shall be, or at the time of his death was, in like manner seised or possessed of a like estate as aforesaid, of the yearly value of one hundred pounds; one half of all which estates respectively shall be situate or arising within the said island; and the penalties for acting as deputy lieutenants, and other officers, of the militia of the said island, not being duly qualified, or not having delivered in their qualification, and taken the oaths, and made, repeated and subscribed, the declaration as aforesaid, shall be, for a deputy lieutenant, or field officer, sixty pounds; and for a captain, lieutenant or ensign, thirty pounds; such several penalties to be recovered by action of debt, bill, plaint or information, in any of his Majesty's courts of record at *Westminster*, wherein no essoin, wager of law, protection, or more than one imparlance, shall be allowed; one moiety whereof shall go to the use of the person who shall sue for the same, and the other moiety to the uses herein after directed.

Marginal notes: Three or more deputy lieutenants; Deputy lieutenants or field officer to have 200l. per annum. Captain 100l. per annum. Lieutenant or ensign 50l. per annum. Penalties for acting, not being qualified, &c. are, for a deputy lieutenant or field officer 60 l. for all under, 30l.

LV. Provided always, and be it enacted, That in all cities or towns which are counties within themselves, and have heretofore been impowered by law, or ancient usage, to raise and train a separate militia within their several precincts and liberties, and which are by this act united with and made part of any county or counties for the purposes of this act only, his Majesty's lieutenants of such cities or towns, or where there is no lieutenant appointed by his Majesty, the chief magistrate of such city or town shall appoint five or more deputy lieutenants

Marginal note: The lieutenants of cities and towns which are counties within themselves, or the chief magistrate, is to appoint deputy lieutenants and officers, &c.

(if

(if so many persons qualified as is herein after expressed, can therein be found) and shall also appoint officers of the militia, whose number and rank shall be proportionable to the number of militia men which such city or town shall raise, as their quota towards the militia of the county to which such city or town is by this act united for the purposes aforesaid, the qualification of which officers respectively shall be as is herein after mentioned; and all powers given and provisions made by this act, with respect to counties at large, and the militia thereof, and the registering the qualifications of deputy lieutenants and officers, shall take place and be in force with respect to the said cities and towns, and the militia thereof, and the registering the said qualifications, except only as to the particulars herein expressed and otherwise provided for; that is to say, after the number of persons which such city or town is to furnish to the militia shall have been appointed as aforesaid by his Majesty's lieutenant, and the deputy lieutenants, or by the deputy lieutenants of the county at large, of the militia, whereof the militia of such city or town is by this act made a part, any two or more of the deputy lieutenants within such city or town shall have and exercise all the powers conferred by this act on any three deputy lieutenants, or on any two deputy lieutenants, together with any one justice of the peace, or any one deputy lieutenant, together with any two justices of the peace of any county at large: and the value of the respective qualifications of the deputy lieutenants and officers of the militia of such cities or towns, shall be as follows;

Deputy lieutenant and field officer, to have 300l. per ann or 5000l. personal estate. every deputy lieutenant and field officer shall respectively be seised or possessed of such an estate, and in like manner as is in this act before mentioned, as a qualification for a deputy lieutenant, colonel, or other officer of the militia, in manors, messuages, lands, tenements or hereditaments, in *England*, *Wales*, or the town of *Berwick* upon *Tweed*, of the yearly value of three hundred pounds, or shall be possessed of a personal estate alone, to

Captain 150l. per ann. or 2500l. personal estate. the amount or value of five thousand pounds; and the qualification of a captain shall be a like estate as aforesaid, of the yearly value of one hundred and fifty pounds, in manors, messuages, lands, tenements or hereditaments, or personal estate alone, to the

Lieutenant or ensign 50l. or 750l. personal estate. amount or value of two thousand five hundred pounds; and the qualification of a lieutenant or ensign shall be a like estate as aforesaid, of the yearly value of fifty pounds, in manors, messuages, lands, tenements or hereditaments, or personal estate alone, to the amount or value of seven hundred and fifty pounds; one half of all which real estates respectively shall be situate or arising within such city or town, or within the county at large to which such city or town is by this act united for the purposes aforesaid; and in all such cities and towns, the penalties for

Penalties for acting if not qualified, &c. acting not being duly qualified, or not having delivered in such qualification, or not having taken the oaths, and made, repeated and subscribed the declaration aforesaid, shall be, for a de-

for a deputy lieutenant or field officer puty lieutenant or field officer, one hundred pounds; and for a captain, lieutenant or ensign, fifty pounds; such several penalties
ties

ties to be recovered by action of debt, bill, plaint or informa- 100l. for all
tion, in any of his Majesty's courts of record at *Westminster*, under 50l.
wherein no effoin, wager of law, or protection, or more than
one imparlance shall be allowed; one moiety whereof shall go
to the use of the person who shall sue for the same, and the other
moiety to the uses herein after directed; and his Majesty's lieu- Lieutenants
tenants, and the chief magistrates of such cities or towns, being and chief ma-
counties in themselves respectively, shall, and they are hereby giftrates to ex-
required to put the powers conferred by this act, for raising and within the faid
training the militia within such cities or towns, into execution; cities and
but the militia of such cities and towns as aforesaid, being by towns; but
this act declared to be part of the militia of the counties to the militia is
which such cities and towns are united for the purposes afore- the county at
faid, the militia of such cities or towns shall annually join the the general ex-
militia of the county to which such cities or towns are so united ercise in Whit-
for the purposes aforesaid, and the whole militia so joined toge- fun week.
ther, shall be exercised together at the general annual exercise in
Whitfun week, and shall then, and also in time of actual service,
be deemed the militia of the county to which such cities or towns
are so united for the purposes aforesaid.

LVI. And be it enacted, That all fines, penalties and forfei- Recovery of
tures by this act imposed, the manner or recovery whereof is not penalties not
in this act particularly provided for, shall on proof upon oath of otherwise pro-
the offence before any justice of the peace of the county, riding vided for.
or place where the offence shall be committed, be levied by di-
strefs and sale of the offender's goods and chattels, by warrant
under the hand and seal of such justice, rendering the overplus
(if any) on demand, after deducting the charges of such diftrefs
and sale, to the offender upon whom such diftrefs shall have
been made; and where the goods and chattels of such offender
shall not be sufficient to answer such diftrefs, such justice is hereby
required to commit such offender to the common gaol of the
county, riding or place where the offence shall have been committed, for any time not exceeding three months: and all fines,
penalties and forfeitures by this act imposed, the application Fines and pe-
whereof is not otherwise particularly provided for, shall be paid nalties not o-
to the clerk of the regiment or battalion, and shall be made a vided for, to
common stock in each subdivision wherein the same shall so be paid to the
arise; and the said clerk shall give a particular account thereof, clerk of the re-
as it shall arise, to any three deputy lieutenants, or to any two made a com-
deputy lieutenants, together with any one justice of the peace, or mon stock,
to any one deputy lieutenant, together with any two justices of
the peace at their next meeting within the several subdivisions;
and the said deputy lieutenants, or any three of them, or any two and to be ap-
deputy lieutenants, together with any one justice of the peace, or plied in erect-
any one deputy lieutenant, together with any two justices of ing butts, and
the peace, shall cause butts to be erected in some convenient providing
place or places, and shall direct the clerk of the regiment or ball,
battalion to buy and provide, with some part of the money so
arising, a proper quantity of gunpowder and ball, to be used at
proper times by the militia men in shooting at marks, and to
ap-

and in prizes to the best marksmen,

apply and dispose of such other part of the money aforesaid, as they shall think reasonable, in some prize or prizes to be given to such militia man or men as shall, by the commanding officer then present, be adjudged to be the best marksman or marksmen, and to apply the residue thereof to other contingencies relating to the militia within such subdivision; and that in all cases when any person shall be committed to the house of correction by virtue of this act, he shall during the time of such commitment, be kept to hard labour in such house of correction.

Persons committed to the house of correction to be kept to hard labour.

LVII. And be it enacted, That in every action, suit or information, brought against any person for acting as a deputy lieutenant, colonel, lieutenant colonel, major, captain, lieutenant or ensign, not being qualified as herein before is directed, the proof of this qualification shall lie upon such person against whom the same is brought.

Proof of qualification, in all suits, is to be on the defendant.

LVIII. Provided also, and be it enacted, That no order made by any of his Majesty's lieutenants, or by any one or more deputy lieutenants, or by any two deputy lieutenants, together with any one justice of the peace, or by any one deputy lieutenant, together with any two justices of the peace, or by any justice or justices of the peace, by virtue of this act, shall be removed by certiorari out of the county, riding, division, place, city or town wherein such order was made, into any court; and that no writ or writs of certiorari shall supersede execution or other proceedings, upon any such order so made in pursuance of this act, but that execution and other proceedings shall and may be had and made thereupon; any such writ or writs, or allowance thereof notwithstanding.

Orders of the lieutenants, &c. not removeable by certiorari,

nor execution, to be superseded thereby,

LIX. Provided always, and be it enacted, That where any parish shall lie in more counties or ridings than one, the inhabitants of such parish shall serve in the militia of that county or riding wherein the church belonging to such parish is situated.

Provision where a parish lies in two counties.

LX. Provided always, and be it enacted, That the inhabitants of the town and parish of Wokingham shall serve in, and be trained and exercised with the militia of the county of Berks.

Inhabitants of Wokingham to be trained with the militia of Berks;

LXI. Provided always, and be it enacted, That the inhabitants of the township of Filey, shall serve in the militia of the east riding of the county of York; any thing herein contained to the contrary notwithstanding.

of Filey, to serve in the east riding of York,

LXII. Provided always, and be it enacted, That the inhabitants of Threapwood shall serve in the militia of the county of Flint, and shall be trained and exercised with the militia of the parish of Worthenbury within the said county.

of Threapwood, in Flint, and to be exercised with that of Worthenbury; and

LXIII. Provided always, and be it enacted, That the inhabitants of and in the parish of saint Martin, called Stamford Baron in the suburbs of the borough and town of Stamford, on the south side of the waters there called Welland, shall serve in the militia of the county of Lincoln.

of saint Martin, Stamford Baron, &c. to serve in that of Lincoln.

LXIV. Provided always, and be it enacted, That nothing in this act contained shall extend to the tinners in the counties of Devon and Cornwall, but the lord warden of the stannaries for the

The tinners in Devon and Cornwall to be

the time being, in purfuance of his Majefty's commiffion in that under lord warden of th ftannaries.
behalf, and fuch as he fhall commiffionate and authorize under him,
may and fhall have and ufe the like powers, and array, affefs, arm,
mufter and exercife the faid tinners within the faid counties, and
either of them, as hath been heretofore ufed, and according to
the ancient privileges and cuftoms of the faid ftannaries.

LXV. Provided always, and be it enacted, That his Majefty's Lieutenants for London to lift and levy trained bands as heretofore.
lieutenants who are or fhall be commiffioned for the militia of
the city of *London*, may and fhall continue to lift and levy the
trained bands and auxiliaries of the faid city in manner as
heretofore.

LXVI. *Provided alfo, and be it enacted, That whereas the militia
of the* Tower *divifion in the county of* Middlefex, *commonly known
by the name of the* Tower Hamlets, *is and always have been under the
command of his Majefty's conftable of the* Tower, *or lieutenant of the*
Tower Hamlets, *for the fervice and prefervation of that royal fort ;*
it fhall be lawful for his Majefty's faid conftable or lieutenant for Militia of the Tower Hamlets to be under the conftable of the tower, who is to appoint his deputy lieutenants, &c.
the time being, from time to time to appoint his deputy lieute-
nants, and to give commiffions to a proper number of officers,
to train and difcipline the militia to be raifed within and for the
faid divifion or hamlets, purfuant to this act ; and to form the
fame into two regiments of feven companies each, in fuch manner as the faid conftable or lieutenant hath ufed to do ; and to
appoint a ferjeant major, a drum major, and a clerk, for the faid
militia ; and alfo that for defraying the neceffary charge of trophies and other incident expences of the militia of the fame
divifion or hamlets, it fhall be lawful for his Majefty's faid
conftable or lieutenant, to continue to raife in every year, the
proportion of a fourth part of one month's affeffment of trophy
money within the faid divifion or hamlets, in fuch manner as he
hath ufed to do by virtue and in purfuance of an act of the thir-
teenth and fourteenth years of the reign of King *Charles* the Se- 13 & 14 Car. 2. c. 3.
cond, intituled, *An act for ordering the forces in the feveral counties
of this kingdom ;* any thing in this act contained to the contrary
in any wife notwithftanding.

LXVII. And be it further enacted, That his Majefty's faid and to appoint a treafurer of the trophy money.
conftable of the *Tower*, or lieutenant of the *Tower Hamlets*, fhall
appoint a treafurer of the faid trophy money, for receiving and
paying fuch monies as fhall be levied by virtue thereof, which
faid treafurer fhall yearly account in writing, and upon oath for
the fame, to the faid lieutenant, or his deputy lieutenants, or any
three or more of them, which oath they fhall have power to
adminifter ; and which accounts for the fame fhall be certified
to the juftices of the peace for the faid divifion at their next
general or quarter feffions ; and that the faid lieutenant fhall not
iffue warrants for raifing any trophy money, until the juftices of
the peace, or the major part of them at fuch feffions, fhall have
examined, ftated and allowed the accounts of the trophy money
raifed, levied and collected for the preceding year, and certified
the fame under the hands and feals of four or more fuch juftices,

un-

unless in case where it shall appear to such justices, that by reason of the death of such treasurer, or otherwise such accounts cannot be passed.

Powers granted by former acts to the lord warden of the cinque ports, and his lieutenants, reserved;

LXVIII. Provided always, and be it enacted, That the lord warden of the cinque ports, two ancient towns, and their members, and in his absence his lieutenant or lieutenants, may and shall put in execution within the said ports, towns and members, all the powers and authorities given and granted by any former act or acts; and may and shall execute and perform all and every the things therein contained, in like manner as his Majesty's respective lieutenants of counties and their deputy lieutenants may do; and may keep up and continue the usual number of soldiers in the said ports, towns and members, unless he or they find cause

and the militia of the said ports to remain separate from that of the county.

to lessen the same; and the militia of the said ports, towns and members, shall remain separate from the militia of the several counties within which the said ports, towns and members are situate; any thing herein contained to the contrary notwithstanding.

Persons doing duty in the King's docks exempted.

LXIX. Provided always, and be it enacted, That nothing in this act contained shall extend, or be construed to extend, to subject any persons mustered, trained and doing duty in any of his Majesty's docks for the defence thereof, to the service in the militia; any thing herein contained to the contrary notwithstanding.

Repeal of all former acts for raising of the militia.

LXX. And be it enacted, That all former acts relating to the raising of the militia within that part of *Great Britain* called *England*, and the dominion of *Wales*, shall from and after the first day of *May* one thousand seven hundred and fifty seven, be repealed, except in such cases as are herein specially directed to be subject to the provisions of the said former acts, or any of them.

On death of a lieutenant, deputy is to act till a new one is appointed.

LXXI. Provided always, and be it enacted, That on the death of any of his Majesty's lieutenants, his deputy lieutenants shall continue to act and exercise all the authorities by this act committed to them, until his Majesty shall have appointed another lieutenant, and until commissions of deputy lieutenancy shall be by him issued.

Limitation of actions.

LXXII. Provided always, and be it enacted, That if any suit or suits shall be brought or commenced against any person or persons for any thing done in pursuance of this act, the action shall be laid in the county where such action did arise, and not elsewhere; and the defendant or defendants in such action or actions to be brought, may plead the general issue, and give this

General issue.

act and the special matter in evidence; and if the jury shall find for the defendant or defendants in such action or actions, or if the plaintiff or plaintiffs shall be nonsuited, or discontinue his or their action or actions, after the defendant or defendants shall have appeared; or if upon demurrer, judgment shall be given

Treble costs.

against the plaintiff or plaintiffs, the defendant or defendants shall have treble costs, and have the like remedy for the same as any defendant or defendants hath or have in other cases to recover costs by law.

LXXIII. Pro-

LXXIII. Provided always, and be it enacted by the authority aforesaid, That this act shall continue and be in force for the space of five years, and from thence to the end of the then next session of parliament, and no longer.

CAP. XXVI.

An act for granting to his Majesty certain sums of money out of the sinking fund; and applying certain monies remaining in the exchequer, and the savings out of the monies granted in this session of parliament for the pay of the troops of Hanover, for the service of the year one thousand seven hundred and fifty seven; and for further appropriating the supplies granted in this session of parliament; and for relief of Claud Johnson, with respect to a bond entered into by him, for securing the duties on tobacco imported by George Buchanan and William Hamilton.

WE your Majesty's most dutiful and loyal subjects the commons of Great Britain *in parliament assembled, being desirous to raise* the residue of the necessary supplies which we have chearfully granted to your Majesty in this session of parliament, by ways and means the least burthensome to your Majesty's subjects, have resolved to give and grant to your Majesty the sums herein after mentioned; and do therefore most humbly beseech your Majesty, that it may be enacted; and be it enacted by the King's most excellent majesty, by and with the advice and consent of the lords spiritual and temporal and commons in this present parliament assembled, and by the authority of the same, That by or out of such monies as have arisen, or shall or may arise, and be and remain in the receipt of the exchequer, of the surplusses, excesses, overplus monies, and other revenues composing the fund, commonly called the *Sinking Fund* (after paying or reserving sufficient to pay, all such sums of money as have been directed by any former act or acts of parliament to be paid out of the same) there shall and may be issued and applied a sum, not exceeding three hundred thousand pounds, for and towards the supply granted to his Majesty for the service of the year one thousand seven hundred and fifty seven; and the commissioners of his Majesty's treasury or any three or more of them now being, or the high treasurer, or any three or more of the commissioners of the treasury for the time being, are hereby authorized and impowered to issue and apply the same accordingly.

Towards the supplies in general, granted for the service of the year 1757.

300,000l. is to be issued out the sinking fund.

II. And be it further enacted by the authority aforesaid, That the sum of fifty thousand four hundred ninety one pounds seventeen shillings and eight pence half penny, remaining in the receipt of the exchequer, disposeable by parliament for the publick service, of the income of the surplusses, excesses, overplus monies, and other revenues composing the said fund commonly called the *Sinking Fund,* for the quarter ended the fifth day of *April*

50,491l. 17s. 8d. ¾q. surplus remaining in the exchequer of the said fund on 5 April 1757.

one

one thousand seven hundred and fifty seven, shall and may be in like manner issued and applied at the said receipt for and towards the said supply.

III. And be it further enacted by the authority aforesaid, That by or out of such monies as shall thereafter from time to time be and remain in the receipt of the exchequer, of the surplusses, excesses, overplus monies, and other revenues composing the said fund commonly called the *Sinking Fund*, after paying or reserving sufficient to pay all such sums of money as have been directed by any former act or acts of parliament to be paid out of the same, there shall and may in like manner be issued and applied a farther sum not exceeding eight hundred forty nine thousand five hundred eight pounds two shillings and three pence half penny, for and towards the said supply.

IV. And be it further enacted by the authority aforesaid, That the sum of sixteen thousand one hundred and ninety pounds five shillings and three pence remaining in the receipt of the exchequer, on the tenth day of *October* one thousand seven hundred and fifty six, of the surplus of the duties on licences for retailing spirituous liquors; and also the sum of one hundred forty thousand five hundred sixty eight pounds five shillings and two pence half penny remaining in the receipt of the exchequer, being the overplus of the grants for the service of the year one thousand seven hundred and fifty six; and also the sum of nineteen thousand four hundred and sixteen pounds fourteen shillings and nine pence half penny, being the savings out of the monies granted in this session of parliament, for the pay of the troops of *Hanover* in the pay of *Great Britain*, shall and may be in like manner issued and applied at the said receipt for and towards the said supply.

V. *And whereas it may so happen that there may be a want of money for carrying on the current service of the year one thousand seven hundred and fifty seven, before monies sufficient may have arisen into the exchequer from the said surplusses, excesses or overplus monies commonly called* The Sinking Fund, *to satisfy and pay the said sum of eight hundred forty nine thousand five hundred and eight pounds two shillings and three pence half penny by this act granted;* in such case, It shall and may be lawful to and for the said commissioners of his Majesty's treasury, or any three or more of them now being, or the high treasurer, or any three or more of the commissioners of the treasury for the time being, by warrant or warrants under his or their hands, to permit and suffer any person or persons, or body or bodies politic or corporate, to advance and lend unto his Majesty, at the receipt of his exchequer, so much money as, together with the monies then remaining in the said exchequer, of the said surplusses, excesses or overplus monies, shall be wanting to compleat the said sum of eight hundred forty nine thousand five hundred eight pounds two shillings and three pence half penny, upon credit of the growing produce of the said surplusses, excesses or overplus monies, and to be repaid out

of

Margin notes:

849,508l. 2s. 3d. 2q. as the same shall arise into the exchequer out of the said fund.

16,190l. 5s. 3d. surplus remaining in the exchequer of the duties on licences for retailing spirituous liquors.

140,568l. 5s. 2d. 2q. overplus remaining in the exchequer of the grants for 1756.

19,416l. 14s. 9d. 2d. savings in the pay of the troops of Hanover.

On want of money to pay the sum of 849,508l. 2s. 3d. 2d. treasury may take in loans on the credit of the sinking fund to compleat the said sum;

of the fame as they fhall quarterly afterwards arife, together the fame to be with intereft for the forbearance thereof, in the mean time; repaid quarterly. any thing herein contained to the contrary notwithftanding.

VI. Provided always, and it is hereby enacted by the authority aforefaid, That all the monies coming into the exchequer, either by loans or exchequer bills, upon one act of this feffion of parliament, intituled, *An act for granting an aid to his Majefty by a land tax to be raifed in* Great Britain, *for the fervice of the year one thoufand feven hundred and fifty feven; and for difcharging certain arrears of land taxes incurred before the time therein mentioned; and for the more effectual collecting of arrears for the future*; and fo much money, if any fuch be, of the tax thereby granted, as fhall arife or remain after all the loans or exchequer bills made or to be made on the fame act, and all the intereft, premium, rate and charges thereon; and the charges thereby allowable for raifing the faid land tax, fhall be fatisfied, or money fufficient fhall be referved in the exchequer, to fatisfy and difcharge the fame; and alfo all the monies coming into the exchequer, either by loans or exchequer bills, upon one other act of parliament of this feffion of parliament, intituled, *An act* Malt tax, c. 4. *for continuing and granting to his Majefty certain duties upon malt, mum, cyder and perry, for the fervice of the year one thoufand feven hundred and fifty feven*; and concerning the intereft to be paid for monies to be borrowed, as well on the credit of this act, as on the credit of an act of this feffion of parliament, for granting an aid to his Majefty by a land tax; and fo much money, if any fuch be, of the duties thereby granted, as fhall arife or remain after all the loans or exchequer bills made or to be made on the fame act; and all the intereft, premium, rate and charges thereon; and the charges thereby allowable for raifing the faid duties, fhall be fatisfied, or money fufficient referved in the exchequer, to fatisfy and difcharge the fame; and alfo all the monies coming into the exchequer, by contributions to a lottery, granted by one other act of this feffion of parliament, intituled, *An act for* Lottery act, *granting to his Majefty a fum not exceeding one million fifty thoufand* c. 5. *five pounds and five fhillings, to be raifed by way of lottery*; and alfo all the monies coming into the exchequer by contributions for annuities, granted by one other act of this feffion of parliament, intituled, *An act for granting to his Majefty feveral rates and duties* Stamp duties, *upon indentures, leafes, bonds and other deeds; and upon news papers,* c. 19. *advertifements, and almanacks; and upon licences for retailing wine; and upon coals exported into foreign parts; and for applying, from a certain time, the fums of money arifing from the furplus of the duties on licences for retailing fpirituous liquors; and for raifing the fum of three millions, by annuities, to be charged on the faid rates, duties, and fums of money; and for making perpetual an act made in the fecond year of the reign of his prefent Majefty, intituled,* An act for the better regulation of attornies and folicitors; *and for enlarging the time for filing affidavits of the execution of contracts of clerks to attornies and folicitors; and alfo the time for payment of the duties omitted to be paid for the indentures and contracts of clerks and appren-*

Appropriation of the fupplies in general. The monies arifing by the land tax, c. 3.

tices; and also a sum not exceeding one million, granted by one other act of this session of parliament, intituled, *An act for enabling his Majesty to raise the sum of one million for the uses and purposes therein mentioned;* and also the several and respective sums

and other sums remaining in the exchequer, &c. by this act granted, shall be further appropriated, and are hereby appropriated for and towards the several uses and purposes herein after expressed; that is to say, it is hereby enacted and declared

Viz. Out of the aids in general, 3,283,939l. 7s. 7d. towards naval services, herein specified. by the authority-aforesaid, That out of all or any the aids or supplies provided as aforesaid, there shall and may be issued and applied, any sum or sums of money, not exceeding three millions two hundred eighty three thousand nine hundred thirty nine pounds seven shillings and seven pence, for and towards the naval services herein after particularly expressed; that is to say, for or towards victuals, wages, wear and tear of the navy, and the victualling thereof, performed and to be performed; and for or towards sea services, in the office of ordnance, performed and to be performed; and for and towards defraying the ordinary of his Majesty's navy; and for half pay to sea officers; and for or towards maintaining eleven thousand four hundred and nineteen marines; and for or towards the buildings, re-buildings, and repairs, of his Majesty's ships, for the said year.

200,000l. towards paying off the navy debt. VII. And it is hereby also enacted by the authority aforesaid, That out of all or any of the aids or supplies aforesaid, there shall and may be issued and applied any sum or sums of money, not exceeding two hundred thousand pounds, towards paying off and discharging the debt of the navy.

10,000l. for the hospital near Plymouth. VIII. And it is hereby also enacted by the authority aforesaid, That out of all or any the aids or supplies aforesaid, there shall and may be issued and applied any sum or sums of money, not exceeding ten thousand pounds, for or towards purchasing of land near *Plymouth,* and carrying on the works of an hospital intended to be erected thereon, for the reception of sick and wounded men belonging to his Majesty's fleet.

10,000l. towards the support of Greenwich hospital. IX. And it is hereby enacted by the authority aforesaid, That out of all or any the aids or supplies aforesaid, there shall and may be issued and applied any sum or sums of money, not exceeding ten thousand pounds, upon account, towards the support of the royal hospital at *Greenwich,* for the better maintenance of the seamen of the said hospital, worn out and become decrepit in the service of their country.

437,620l. 8s. 9d. towards the office of ordnance for land service. X. And it is hereby also enacted by the authority aforesaid, That out of all or any the aids or supplies aforesaid, there shall and may be issued and applied any sum or sums of money, not exceeding four hundred thirty seven thousand six hundred twenty pounds eight shillings and nine pence, for the charge of the office of ordnance for land service for the year one thousand seven hundred and fifty seven, performed and to be performed, and for defraying the extraordinary expence of the office of ordnance for land service, for the year one thousand seven hundred and fifty six, not provided for by parliament.

XI. And

XI. And it is hereby also enacted by the authority aforesaid, That out of all or any the aids or supplies provided as aforesaid, there shall and may be issued and applied any sum or sums of money, not exceeding two millions five hundred sixteen thousand one hundred eighteen pounds eleven shillings and a half penny, for and towards maintaining his Majesty's land forces, and other services herein after more particular expressed; that is to say, Any sum or sums of money, not exceeding one million two hundred thirteen thousand seven hundred forty six pounds three shillings and nine pence, for defraying the charge of forty nine thousand seven hundred and forty nine effective men, including commission and non-commission officers; and also four thousand and eight invalids, for guards, garrisons, and other his Majesty's land forces in *Great Britain, Guernsey* and *Jersey,* for the year one thousand seven hundred and fifty seven; and any sum or sums of money, not exceeding four hundred twenty three thousand nine hundred sixty three pounds sixteen shillings and ten pence, for maintaining his Majesty's forces and garrisons in the plantations, and *Gibraltar,* and for provisions for the garrisons in *Nova Scotia, Newfoundland, Gibraltar,* and *Providence,* for the year one thousand seven hundred and fifty seven; and any sum or sums of money, not exceeding forty seven thousand sixty pounds fifteen shillings and ten pence, for the pay of the general and general staff officers, and officers of the hospitals for his Majesty's land forces, for the year one thousand seven hundred and fifty seven; and any sum or sums of money, not exceeding thirty thousand pounds, upon account, for out-pensioners of *Chelsea hospital,* for the year one thousand seven hundred and fifty seven; and any sum or sums of money, not exceeding forty six thousand twenty two pounds and five shillings, for defraying the charge of two highland battalions of foot, raised or to be raised for his Majesty's service, for the year one thousand seven hundred and fifty seven; and any sum or sums of money, not exceeding two thousand three hundred and fifty pounds, for paying of pensions to the widows of such reduced officers of his Majesty's land forces and marines, as died upon the establishment of half pay in *Great Britain,* and who were married to them before the twenty fifth day of *December* one thousand seven hundred and sixteen, for the year one thousand seven hundred and fifty seven; which said sum of two thousand three hundred and fifty pounds shall be issued to such person or persons as his Majesty shall by warrant or warrants under his royal sign manual direct and appoint to receive the same, to be by him or them paid over to such widows of half pay officers, or their assigns, according to such establishments, lists or other directions, and with and subject to such conditions, qualifications, and other allowances for the same, as his Majesty by such and the like warrant or warrants shall be graciously pleased to direct and appoint; and any sum or sums of money, not exceeding three thousand three hundred twenty one pounds sixteen shillings and three pence, for

M 2

Marginal notes:

2,516,118 l. 11 s. ½d. towards the land forces in general;

of which 1,213,746 l. 3 s. 9d. for guards and garrisons &c. in Great Britain, Guernsey, and Jersey.

423,963 l. 16 s. 10 d. for guards and garrisons, &c. in the plantations, Gibraltar, Nova Scotia, Newfoundland and Providence.

47,060 l. 15 s. 10d. for the staff officers and officers of hospitals of his Majesty's land forces.

30,000 l. for the out pensioners of Chelsea hospital.

46,022 l. 5 s. for 2 highland battalions of foot.

2,350 l. for the pensions of officers widows, &c.

to be issued by order under his Majesty's sign manual.

3,321 l. 16 s. 3d. to the officers and gentlemen of horse guards &c. reduced.

for defraying the charge for allowances to the feveral officers and private gentlemen of the two troops of horfe guards, and regiment of horfe reduced, and to the fuperannuated gentlemen of the four troops of horfe guards, for the year one thoufand feven hundred and fifty feven; and any fum or fums of money, not exceeding

33,000l. to the reduced officers of the land forces and marines.

thirty three thoufand pounds, upon account, for the reduced officers of his Majefty's land forces and marines, for the year one thoufand feven hundred and fifty feven; and any fum or fums of money, not exceeding five hundred feventeen pounds

517l. 11. 8d. to half pay ftaff officers of the late garrifon at Minorca.

one fhilling and eight pence, for defraying the charge of half pay to certain ftaff officers of the late garrifon at *Minorca*, *videlicet*, To the fecretaries to the governor of the ifland of *Minorca*, the captain of the ports there, the lieutenant governor of *fort faint Philip*, and the furgeon of the garrifon of *fort faint Philip*, for the

48,926l. 2s. 6d. for troops ferving in North America, and the Eaft Indies.

year one thoufand feven hundred and fifty feven; and any fum or fums of money, not exceeding forty eight thoufand nine hundred twenty fix pounds two fhillings and fix pence, for defraying the charge of four regiments of foot, on the Irifh eftablifhment ferving in *North America* and the *Eaft Indies*, and augmenting major general *Offarrell's* regiment of foot, for the year one thoufand feven hundred and fifty feven; and any fum

111,570l. 19s. 7d. 2q. for extraordinary expences of land forces and other fervices in 1756.

or fums of money, not exceeding one hundred eleven thoufand five hundred feventy pounds nineteen fhillings and feven pence half penny, for defraying the extraordinary expences of his Majefty's land forces, and other fervices, incurred in the year one thoufand feven hundred and fifty fix, and not provided for by parliament; and any fum or fums of money, not exceeding

57,963l. 7s. 1d. for troops hired from the landgrave of Heffe Caffel.

fifty feven thoufand nine hundred fixty three pounds feven fhillings and one penny, for defraying the charge of fix thoufand five hundred and forty four foot, with the general and ftaff officers, and train of artillery, the troops of the landgrave of *Heffe Caffel*, in the pay of *Great Britain*, from the twenty fifth day of *December* one thoufand feven hundred and fifty fix, to the twenty feventh day of *May* one thoufand feven hundred and fifty feven, both inclufive; and any fum or fums of money,

155,840l. 10s. for German pay to the troops of Heffe Caffel.

not exceeding one hundred fifty five thoufand eight hundred forty pounds and ten fhillings, towards defraying the charge of German pay, for fix thoufand fix hundred foot, with the general and ftaff officers, and train of artillery, the troops of the landgrave of *Heffe Caffel*, in the pay of *Great Britain*, from the twenty eighth day of *May* to the twenty fourth day of *December* one thoufand feven hundred and fifty feven, both inclufive; towards defraying the charge of *German* pay, for one thoufand and four hundred horfe, with the officers of the hofpital, the troops of the faid landgrave in the pay of *Great Britain*, from the twenty feventh day of *April* to the twenty fourth day of *December* one thoufand feven hundred and fifty feven, both inclufive; towards defraying the charge of *German* pay for three thoufand three hundred foot, with the general and ftaff officers and train of artillery, the troops of the faid landgrave, in the pay of *Great Bri-*

Britain, from the twenty second day of *April* to the twenty fourth day of *December* one thousand seven hundred and fifty seven, both inclusive; for defraying the charge of *German* pay for seven hundred horse, the troops of the said landgrave of *Hesse Cassel*, in the pay of *Great Britain*, from the twenty third day of *August* to the twenty fourth day of *December* one thousand seven hundred and fifty seven, both inclusive; for defraying the charge of remount and levy money for seven hundred horse, and three thousand three hundred foot, the troops of the said landgrave in the pay of *Great Britain*, pursuant to treaty; and for defraying the charge of the remaining moiety of remount money for one thousand four hundred horse pursuant to treaty, payable the twenty seventh day of *April* one thousand seven hundred and fifty seven, the supposed day when the cavalry took the field; and any sum or sums of money, not exceeding sixty thousand seven hundred sixty six pounds one shilling, to enable his Majesty to make good his engagements with the landgrave of *Hesse Cassel*, pursuant to treaty; and any sum or sums of money, not exceeding twenty six thousand and seven pounds five shillings and six pence half penny, for defraying the charge of an' advanced subsidy, at the rate of one hundred and fifty thousand crowns a year, due to the landgrave of *Hesse Cassel*, pursuant to treaty, from the sixth day of *August* one thousand seven hundred and fifty six, to the twenty seventh day of *April* one thousand seven hundred and fifty seven, the day when the cavalry enters into the pay of *Great Britain*; and any sum or sums of money, not exceeding fifty five thousand sixty two pounds five shillings and eleven pence half penny, for defraying the charge of eight thousand six hundred and five foot, with the general and staff officers, the train of artillery, and officers of the hospital, the troops of *Hanover*, in the pay of *Great Britain*, from the twenty fifth day of *December* one thousand seven hundred and fifty six, to the twenty sixth day of *March* one thousand seven hundred and fifty seven, both inclusive; and of five thousand seven hundred and twenty six foot, with the general and staff officers, the train of artillery, and officers of the hospital, the troops of *Hanover*, in the pay of *Great Britain*, from the twenty fifth day of *February* one thousand seven hundred and fifty seven, to the twenty sixth day of *March* following, both inclusive; and for defraying the expences of the march in *Germany* of the said troops, both at their coming here, and their return back; and any sum or sums of money, not exceeding two hundred thousand pounds, to assist his Majesty in forming and maintaining, during the present year, an army of observation for the just and necessary defence and preservation of his Majesty's electoral dominions, and those of his allies, and towards enabling his Majesty to fulfil his engagements with the king of *Prussia*, for the security of the empire against the irruption of foreign armies; and for the support of the common cause.

[Marginal notes: 60,766l. 1s. to the landgrave of Hesse Cassel, pursuant to treaty; and 26,007l. 5s. 6d. 2q. an advanced subsidy to the said landgrave pursuant to treaty.

55062l. 5s. 11d 2q. for pay of the troops hired from Hanover.

200,000l. towards forming an army of observation in Germany, &c.]

XII. And it is hereby also enacted by the authority aforesaid, That out of all or any the aids or supplies provided as aforesaid,

M 3   there

there shall and may be issued and applied, any sum or sums of money, not exceeding seven hundred thousand pounds, to enable his Majesty to discharge the like sum raised in pursuance of an act made in the last session of parliament, and charged upon the first aids or supplies to be granted in this session of parliament.

700,000l. to defray the like sum borrowed on a vote of credit of last session.

XIII. And it is hereby also enacted by the authority aforesaid, That out of all or any the aids or supplies provided as aforesaid, there shall and may be issued and applied any sum or sums of money, not exceeding one million upon account, to enable his Majesty to defray any extraordinary expences of the war incurred, or to be incurred, for the service of the year one thousand seven hundred and fifty seven ; and to take all such measures as may be necessary to disappoint or defeat any enterprizes or designs of his enemies, and as the exigency of affairs may require.

1,000,000l. upon account, to defray extraordinary expences of the war.

XIV. And it is hereby also enacted by the authority aforesaid, That out of all or any the aids or supplies provided as aforesaid, there shall and may be issued and applied any sum or sums of money, not exceeding twenty eight thousand seven hundred eighty nine pounds five shillings and one penny, upon account, for supporting and maintaining the settlement of his Majesty's colony of *Nova Scotia*, for the year one thousand seven hundred and fifty seven ; and any sum or sums of money not exceeding fifteen thousand three hundred eighty one pounds and four shillings, upon account, for defraying the charges incurred by supporting and maintaining the settlement of his Majesty's colony of *Nova Scotia* in the year one thousand seven hundred and fifty five, and not provided for by parliament ; and any sum or sums of money not exceeding three thousand five hundred fifty seven pounds and ten shillings, upon account, for defraying the charges of the civil establishment of his Majesty's colony of *Georgia*, and other incidental expences attending the same from the twenty fourth day of *June* one thousand seven hundred and fifty six, to the twenty fourth day of *June* one thousand seven hundred and fifty seven ; and any sum or sums of money, not exceeding ten thousand pounds, to be employed in maintaining and supporting the *British* forts and settlements, upon the coast of *Africa* ; and any sum or sums of money, not exceeding twenty thousand pounds, upon account, to be paid to the united company of merchants of *England*, trading to the *East Indies*, towards enabling them to defray the expence of a military force in their settlements, to be maintained by them in lieu of the battalion of his Majesty's forces, withdrawn from those settlements ; and any sum or sums of money, not exceeding fifty thousand pounds, upon account, to be paid to such persons, and in such manner, and by such proportions as his Majesty shall direct, for the use and relief of his Majesty's subjects in his several provinces of *North* and *South Carolina*, and *Virginia*, in *America*, in recompence for such services, as with the approbation of the commander in chief of his Majesty's forces in *America* they respectively shall have performed, or shall perform,

28,789l. 5 s. 1 d. upon account, for supporting the colony of Nova Scotia; and 15,381 l. 4 s charges incurred in 1755, for supporting the said colony, not provided for.
3,557 l. 10 s. on account for defraying the civil establishment of Georgia.
10,000 l. towards maintaining the forts and settlements in Africa; and 20,000 l. to the East India company, in lieu of the King's troops withdrawn from thence.
50,000 l. on account to the provinces of N. and S Carolina, and Virginia, for services performed and to be performed by them.

Anno tricesimo GEORGII II. c. 26.

form, either by putting the said provinces in a state of defence, or by acting with vigour against the enemy; and any sum or sums of money not exceeding ten thousand pounds, towards the further enabling the commissioners for building a bridge cross the river *Thames*, from the city of *Westminster* to the opposite shore in the county of *Surry*, to purchase houses and grounds for the widening the ways, and making more safe and commodious the streets, avenues and passages, leading from *Charing Cross* to the two houses of parliament, the courts of justice, and *Westminster Bridge*; and any sum or sums of money not exceeding two thousand five hundred pounds, to enable the said commissioners to widen the street or passage leading from *Cockspur Street* to the passage in *Spring Garden* leading to Saint *James's Park*; and any sum or sums of money not exceeding three thousand pounds, upon account, for repairing and finishing a road proper for the passage of troops and carriages, from the city of *Carlisle* to the town of *Newcastle upon Tyne*, whereof the sum of five hundred pounds to be paid to the commissioners and trustees acting within and for the county of *Cumberland*, and the sum of two thousand five hundred pounds, the residue of the said sum of three thousand pounds, to be paid to the commissioners and trustees acting within and for the county of *Northumberland*; and any sum or sums of money not exceeding thirty thousand pounds, towards enabling the governors and guardians of the hospital for the maintenance and education of exposed and deserted young children, to receive all such children under a certain age to be by them limited, as shall be brought to the said hospital before the first day of *January* one thousand seven hundred and fifty eight; and also towards enabling them to maintain and educate such children as are now under their care, and to continue to carry into execution the good purposes for which they were incorporated.

XV. And it is hereby further enacted by the authority aforesaid, That the said aids and supplies provided as aforesaid, shall not be issued or applied to any use, intent or purpose whatsoever, other than the uses and purposes before mentioned, or for the several deficiencies or other payments directed to be satisfied thereout, by any act or acts, or any particular clause or clauses for that purpose contained in any other act or acts of this present session of parliament.

XVI. And as to the said sum of thirty three thousand pounds, by this act appropriated, on account of half-pay as aforesaid, it is hereby enacted and declared by the authority aforesaid, That the rules herein after prescribed shall be duly observed in the application of the said half-pay; that is to say, That no person shall have or receive any part of the same, who was a minor and under the age of sixteen years, at the time when the regiment, troop or company, in which he served, was reduced; that no person shall have or receive any part of the same, except such persons who did actual service in some regiment, troop or company; that no person having any other place or employment

Marginal notes:

10,000 l. for purchasing houses and grounds to widen the streets, &c. leading from Charing cross, to both houses of parliament, &c.

2,500 l. to widen the passage from Cockspur street to the park.

3,000 l. on account for making the road from Carlisle to Newcastle.

30,000 l. to the Foundling hospital.

These aids to be applied to no other uses.

Rules to be observed in the application of the half-pay.

M 4 of

of profit, civil or military, under his Majefty, fhall have or receive any part of the faid half-pay; that no chaplain of any
garrifon or regiment, who has any ecclefiaftical benefice in
Great Britain or *Ireland*, fhall have or receive any part of the
faid half-pay; that no perfon fhall have or receive any part of
the fame, who has refigned his commiffion, and has had no
commiffion fince; that no part of the fame fhall be allowed to
any perfon by virtue of any warrant or appointment, except to
fuch perfons as would have been otherwife intitled to the fame
as reduced officers; and that no part of the fame fhall be allowed to any of the officers of the five regiments of dragoons
and eight regiments of foot, lately difbanded in *Ireland*, except
to fuch as were lately taken off the eftablifhment of half-pay in
Great Britain.

Claufe in an
act of 29 Geo.
2. c. 29. f. 10.

XVII. And whereas by an act of parliament made and paffed
in the twenty ninth year of his Majefty's reign, intituled, *An
act for enabling his Majefty to raife one million, for the purpofe
therein mentioned; and for further appropriating the fupplies granted in this feffion of parliament,* the feveral fupplies which had
been granted to his Majefty, as is therein mentioned, were appropriated to the feveral ufes and purpofes therein expreffed; a-
mongft which any fum or fums of money not exceeding thirty
eight thoufand pounds, was appropriated to be paid to the reduced officers of his Majefty's land forces and marines; fubject
neverthelefs to fuch rules to be obferved in the application of
the faid half-pay, as in and by the aforefaid act were prefcribed
in that behalf: now it is hereby provided, enacted and declared,
by the authority aforefaid, That fo much of the faid fum of

Application of
the favings
out of the fum
of 38,000l.
granted the
laft feffion to-
wards half-
pay.

thirty eight thoufand pounds, as is, or fhall be, more than fufficient to fatisfy the faid reduced officers, according to the rules
prefcribed by the faid act, to be obferved in the application thereof, or any part of fuch overplus, fhall and may be difpofed of
to fuch officers who were maimed or loft their limbs in the late
wars, or fuch others as by reafon of their long fervice or otherwife, his Majefty fhall judge to be proper objects of charity, or
to the widows or children of fuch officers, according to fuch
warrant or warrants under his Majefty's royal fign manual, as
fhall be figned in that behalf; any thing in this act, or the faid
former act, to the contrary notwithftanding.

XVIII. *And whereas* Claud Johnfon *of* London, *merchant, did
on or about the twenty eighth day of* September *one thoufand feven
hundred and fifty one, at the fpecial inftance and requeft of* George
Buchanan *and* William Hamilton, *become bound for them in a
bond, conditioned for the payment of five thoufand fix hundred and
feven pounds twelve fhillings and nine pence halfpenny, or thereabouts,
being the duties of two hundred and fifty thoufand pounds weight of
tobacco imported by the faid* George Buchanan *and* William Hamilton; *and the faid* George Buchanan *and* William Hamilton,
*as an indemnification to him, againft the faid bond, did, on or about
the fixth day of* February *one thoufand feven hundred and fifty two,
affign to him two hundred hogsheads of tobacco, the marks and numbers*

bers of which were specified on the back of such assignment; and the said two hundred hogsheads of tobacco were, soon after the date of the said assignment, conveyed away by the said George Buchanan and William Hamilton, and sold and exported by them as their property; and they did afterwards replace ninety nine hogsheads of tobacco, with different marks and numbers, as part of the said two hundred: and whereas the said George Buchanan and William Hamilton, did, on or about the twenty first day of April one thousand seven hundred and fifty two, assign forty two hogsheads of tobacco to the said Claud Johnson, as a further indemnification to him against the said bond, the marks and numbers of which hogsheads were also specified upon the back of such last assignment: and whereas, on or about the twenty seventh day of April one thousand seven hundred and fifty two, an extent was issued at the suit of the crown against the effects of the said George Buchanan and William Hamilton, for duties on tobacco imported by them; and an inquisition being taken on or about the thirtieth day of April one thousand seven hundred and fifty two, one hundred and thirty five hogsheads of tobacco were seized as the property of the said George Buchanan and William Hamilton; forty two hogsheads of which were the tobacco last assigned to the said Claud Johnson, and the remaining ninety three were part of the said ninety nine hogsheads replaced as aforesaid, the other six hogsheads being seised by the warehouse-keeper for rent; and the said George Buchanan and William Hamilton soon after becoming bankrupts, the said Claud Johnson entered his claim to the said one hundred and thirty five hogsheads in the court of exchequer; and, upon a trial in the year one thousand seven hundred and fifty two, a verdict was found for his Majesty, as to the said ninety three hogsheads, because the marks and numbers thereof did not correspond with the marks and numbers indorsed on the said first assignment, and for the claimant, as to the said forty two hogsheads: and whereas the commissioners of the customs, in consideration of the payment of a certain sum by the assignees of the said bankruptcy, as a satisfaction for the monies due from the said bankrupts to the crown, allowed the said assignees all the effects seised upon the said inquisition; but the said bond was not included in such agreement, the same not being then due: and whereas the said Claud Johnson has paid three thousand one hundred seventy three pounds and seven pence, or thereabouts, in part of the said five thousand six hundred seven pounds, twelve shillings and nine pence halfpenny, and the said ninety three hogsheads of tobacco were sold for the sum of two thousand six hundred fifty five pounds eight shillings and eight pence: and whereas there is great reason to believe that if the said George Buchanan and William Hamilton had continued in credit, no part of the said bond would have been paid in money, but have been discharged by debentures taken out upon the exportation of tobacco; and as the said ninety three hogsheads were part of the effects which were allowed by the commissioners of his Majesty's customs to the said assignees, in consideration of a certain sum to be paid by them, whereby the revenue received an advantage, and the said Claud Johnson sustained a loss more than adequate to the principal money now due upon the said bond;

be

be it therefore enacted by the authority aforesaid, That it shall be lawful for the high treasurer, or any three or more of the commissioners of his Majesty's treasury for the time being, and he or they is and are hereby authorized and impowered to exonerate, acquit and discharge the said *Claud Johnson* of and from the penalty mentioned in, and the payment of, any sum or sums of money conditioned to be paid by the said bond, dated on or about the said twenty eighth day of *September* one thousand seven hundred and fifty one, and all interest due thereupon; and to discharge and vacate the said bond, in such manner as to him or them shall seem expedient; any act or acts of parliament to the contrary notwithstanding.

CAP. XXVII.

An act for enlarging the times for the first meetings of commissioners or trustees for putting in execution certain acts of this session of parliament.

WHEREAS *by several acts of this present session of parliament, the first meeting of the commissioners or trustees for putting such acts, or any part or parts thereof in execution, hath been, or may be appointed or directed to be held before, or upon the day of the passing of such acts respectively, whereby several doubts and difficulties may arise with respect to the due execution of the said acts;* be it therefore enacted by the King's most excellent majesty, by and with the advice and consent of the lords spiritual and temporal and commons in this present parliament assembled, and by the authority of the same, That in case any act of parliament hath passed, or doth or shall pass, at any time whatsoever during this present session of parliament, upon or after the day specified in any such act for the first meeting of the commissioners or trustees appointed to put the same, or any part thereof in execution, in each and every such case, such commissioners or trustees respectively or the same number of such respective commissioners or trustees as is or shall be, authorized to hold such first meeting, or any greater number of them, shall and may hold their first meeting upon the fourteenth day after the passing of this act, at such places as were respectively appointed in such acts for holding the first meetings on the days therein specified; and all such commissioners or trustees, or any number of them as aforesaid, being so assembled respectively on the said fourteenth day after the passing of this act, shall and may proceed to the execution of such acts respectively; and then, and from time to time afterwards adjourn, and do and perform all such matters and things, and execute all the powers and authorities granted to them in the said acts respectively, in the same manner, and as fully and effectually to all intents and purposes, as if such commissioners or trustees had been assembled, in pursuance of, and on the respective days specified or appointed in such acts for holding the first meeting of such commissioners or trustees; any thing therein contained to the contrary notwithstanding.

CAP.

CAP. XXVIII.

An act to render more effectual the several laws now in being for the amendment and preservation of the publick highways and turnpike roads of this kingdom.

WHEREAS it hath been found that the use of broad wheels does very much contribute to the improvement and preservation of the turnpike roads of that part of Great Britain called England, and using heavy carriages with narrow wheels, is very ruinous and destructive to the same; for remedy whereof; be it enacted by the King's most excellent majesty, by and with the advice and consent of the lords spiritual and temporal, and commons, in this present parliament assembled, and by the authority of the same, That during the time of seven years, to be computed from the twenty fourth day of *June* one thousand seven hundred and fifty eight, the trustees appointed or to be appointed by virtue or under the authority of any act of parliament made, or to be made, for making, repairing or amending, turnpike roads, or such person or persons as are or shall be authorized by them, shall and may, and they are hereby required to demand and take for every waggon, wain, cart or carriage, having the fellies of the wheels thereof of less breadth or gage than nine inches from side to side, at the least, at the bottom or sole thereof, or for the horses or beasts of draught drawing the same, one half more than the tolls or duties which are or shall be payable for the same respectively, by any act or acts of parliament made, or to be made, for making, amending or repairing turnpike roads, before any such waggon, wain, cart or carriage, respectively, shall be permitted to pass through any turnpike gate or gates, bar or bars, where tolls shall be payable by virtue of any of the said acts.

[marginal: Trustees for turnpikes to take, for 7 years, one half more than the tolls for waggons and carts, having the fellies of their wheels of less breadth than 9 inches.]

II. Provided, That nothing in this act shall extend, or be construed to extend, to carts or carriages drawn by one horse, or two oxen, and no more.

[marginal: Carts drawn by one horse, or two oxen, excepted.]

III. Provided always, and be it enacted by the authority aforesaid, That during the time aforesaid, it shall and may be lawful to and for any cart or carriage drawn by two horses, or four oxen, and no more, having the fellies of the wheels thereof of the breadth or gage of six inches at the bottom, from side to side, to pass upon any turnpike road, and through any turnpike gate or bar, paying the tolls or duties required to be paid by any of the said acts respectively.

[marginal: Carts with two horses, or four oxen, and fellies six inches broad, to pay only the common tolls.]

IV. *And whereas there are in several acts of parliament, made for making, amending and repairing turnpike roads, exemptions allowed from payment of tolls, in particular cases therein respectively mentioned, and liberties are allowed, in particular cases, to pay lesser tolls than are charged upon other waggons, carts and carriages, passing through turnpike gates or bars: and whereas it will tend to the advantage and preservation of turnpike roads, to confine such exemptions,*

[marginal: No carriage to be exempted from tolls, or pay lesser tolls, unless the fellies are 9 inches broad.]

tions, liberties, privileges and advantages, to carriages with wheels of the breadth or gage of nine inches as, aforesaid; be it therefore enacted by the authority aforesaid, That during the time aforesaid, no person shall, by virtue of any of the said acts of parliament, have, claim or take, the benefit or advantage of any exemption from tolls, or part of tolls, or to pay lesser toll, for or in respect of any waggon, wain, cart or other carriage, or horses drawing the same, than other carriages of the like nature ought to pay, unless such waggon, wain, cart or carriage, have

Exception.

fellies of the wheels thereof of the breadth or gage of nine inches as aforesaid; other than and except carts and carriages drawn by one horse or two oxen, and no more; and other than and except carts and carriages drawn by two horses or four oxen, and no more, having the fellies of the wheels thereof of the

but the additional and ordinary tolls are to be paid.

breadth or gage of six inches as aforesaid; but that the toll, together with the additional toll hereby enacted, for or in respect of every such waggon, wain, cart or other carriage having the fellies of the wheels thereof of less breadth or gage than nine inches as aforesaid; or for or in respect of horses or beasts of draught drawing the same (except as before excepted) required by the said acts respectively, shall be paid in the same manner, to all intents and purposes, as if no exemption or lesser toll had been enacted or allowed by any of the said acts respectively, and as fully as all other waggons, wains, carts and carriages and horses drawing the same, ought respectively to pay, which are not intitled to any exemption from toll in the whole or in part, or to pay a lesser toll than other waggons, wains, carts and carriages; any law or statute to the contrary notwithstanding.

Waggons, &c. with broad wheels to pay half the tolls within 100 miles of London;

V. And be it further enacted by the authority aforesaid, That during the time aforesaid, the trustees appointed or to be appointed by virtue or under the authority of any act of parliament made or to be made for making, repairing or amending turnpike roads, and such person and persons as shall be authorized by them, shall and may, and they are hereby required to permit and suffer all waggons, wains, carts and carriages having the fellies of the wheels thereof of the breadth or gage of nine inches from side to side at the bottom or sole thereof, and drawn according to law, to pass through any turnpike gate or gates, bar or bars, within one hundred miles from *London*, paying only so much toll or duty as shall not exceed one half of the full toll or duty payable for such waggons, wains, carts and carriages respectively, or for the horses or beasts of draught drawing the same, by virtue of any act or acts of parliament made or to be made for making, repairing or amending turnpike roads.

VI. *And whereas great damage is done to turnpike roads by waggons and wains with broad wheels drawn by horses or beasts of draught at length, and not in pairs:* for remedy whereof, be it enacted by

but such waggons are not to pass, unless drawn by horses in pairs,

the authority aforesaid, That during the time aforesaid it shall not be lawful for any waggon or wain, having fellies of the wheels thereof of the breadth or gage of nine inches as aforesaid, to pass upon any turnpike road, or through any turnpike gate or bar, unless the same be drawn by horses or beasts of draught in

pairs;

pairs; provided that where there is an odd horfe or beaft of and not at draught belonging to fuch waggon or wain, it fhall be lawful length; for fuch odd horfe or beaft of draught to draw fuch waggon or wain, together with the other horfes or beafts of draught drawing in pairs as aforefaid; provided that fuch horfes or beafts of draught do not in the whole exceed the number of horfes or beafts of draught allowed by law.

VII. *And whereas great damage is done to turnpike roads by wag-* narrow wheel *gons and wains with narrow wheels, drawn by horfes or beafts of* carriages are *draught in pairs, and not drawn by oxen:* for remedy whereof, be not to pafs it enacted by the authority aforefaid, That during the time if drawn in aforefaid it fhall not be lawful for any waggon or wain, having pairs, unlefs the fellies of the wheels thereof of lefs breadth or gage than nine by oxen. inches, to pafs upon any turnpike road, or through any turnpike gate or bar, if the fame be drawn by horfes or beafts of draught in pairs, and not by oxen.

VIII. And be it enacted by the authority aforefaid, That Perfons driv- if any perfon or perfons fhall, during the time aforefaid, drive ing prohibit- or caufe to be driven on any turnpike road any common ftage ed waggons, waggon, prohibited by this act to pafs along any turnpike road, or an unlaw- or fhall drive or caufe to be driven any waggon, wain, cart or ful number of horfes, carriage on any turnpike road, with any greater number of horfes or beafts of draught than is allowed by law, or in any wife contrary to the true intent and meaning of this act, every perfon and perfons fo offending, and every mafter or owner of fuch waggon, wain, cart or carriage fo driven, fhall be deemed to be guilty of a common nufance and mifdemeanor, and fhall be may be pu- punifhed for the fame by indictment or information, or fhall, nifhed by in- at the election of the profecutor or informer, for every fuch of- dictment, or fence, be fubject and liable to fuch and the fame penalties and information, forfeitures as the owners of the waggons and carriages, having &c. the fellies of the wheels of lefs breadth or gage than nine inches from fide to fide, are made fubject and liable to, by virtue of an Act 26 Geo.2 act made in the twenty fixth year of the reign of his prefent Ma- c. 30. jefty, intituled, *An act for the amendment and prefervation of the publick highways and turnpike roads of this kingdom; and for the more effectual execution of the laws relating thereto;* to be paid and applied to fuch ufes and purpofes, and to be levied and recovered as is thereby directed.

IX. And be it enacted by the authority aforefaid, That No compofi- during the time aforefaid it fhall not be lawful for any truftees tion for tolls of any turnpike road, to make any compofition for tolls for or may be made in refpect of any waggon, wain, cart or carriage, or horfes or for narrow beafts of draught drawing the fame (except as before excepted) wheel car- unlefs fuch waggons, wains, carts and carriages have the fellies riages. of the wheels thereof of the breadth or gage of nine inches as Exception. aforefaid.

X. *And whereas by an act made in the twenty eighth year of the reign of his prefent Majefty, it is, amongft other things, enacted,* 28 G. 2. c. 1 *That from and after the faid twenty fourth day of* June *it fhall* f. 2. & f 3. *and may be lawful for all waggons having the fellies of the wheels* repealed. *thereof*

thereof of the breadth or gage of fix inches from fide to fide, at the leaft, at the fole or bottom of the wheel, to pafs through all and every turnpike gate or gates, bar or bars, with fix horfes; and all carts and other carriages having the fellies thereof of the breadth or gage of fix inches from fide to fide at the leaft, at the fole or bottom of the wheel, with four horfes, without paying any more toll or duty than is paid for waggons now drawn by four, and carts drawn by three horfes, or for the horfes drawing the fame: and whereas by another claufe in the laft-mentioned act it is enacted, That from and after the faid twenty fourth day of June all waggons, wains and other four wheel carriages, not being common ftage waggons or carriages (though the fellies of the wheels are not of the breadth of nine inches or fix inches) may travel, pafs or be driven upon any turnpike road, with any number of horfes not exceeding five horfes or beafts of draught: and if any owner or driver of any fuch waggon, wain or other four wheel carriage fhall travel, pafs or drive any fuch waggon or other four wheel carriage with more than five horfes or beafts of draught, every fuch owner fo offending fhall, for every fuch offence, forfeit and pay the fum of five pounds; which faid penalty fhall be recovered and levied by diftrefs and fale of the offender's goods and chattels, by warrant or warrants under the hands and feals of the truftees, or any three or more of them, of fuch diftrict, or any one or more juftice or juftices of the peace, in or near to the place or places where the offence fhall be committed, or by action of debt, bill, plaint or information in any of his Majefty's courts of record at Weftminfter; where no effoin, protection or wager of law, or more than one imparlance fhall be allowed; and in cafe any driver of any waggon, wain or other carriage as aforefaid, fhall act contrary to the true intent and meaning hereof, fuch juftice or juftices fhall, by warrant or warrants under his or their hands and feals, commit fuch driver to the houfe of correction for the fpace of one month, there to remain without bail or mainprize; be it enacted by the authority aforefaid, That the said recited claufes in the laft-mentioned recited act fhall, from and after the faid twenty fourth day of *June* one thoufand feven hundred and fifty eight, be repealed.

XI. And be it further enacted by the authority aforefaid,

That from and after the time aforefaid no waggon having the fellies of the wheels thereof of the breadth or gage of nine inches at the bottom, fhall pafs along any turnpike road, which fhall be wider than five feet fix inches from the middle of the fellies of the wheels on one fide of fuch waggon, to the middle of the fellies of the wheels on the other fide of fuch waggon; and the furveyor or furveyors, gate-keeper or gate-keepers of any turnpike road, is and are hereby authorized and required, at any turnpike or toll-gate, or at any other place upon the turnpike road, to meafure every fuch waggon from the middle of the fellies of the wheels on one fide of fuch waggons, to the middle of the fellies of the wheels on the other fide thereof; and if any mafter or driver of any waggon fhall hinder or refufe to permit fuch furveyor or furveyors, gate-keeper or gate-keepers, to meafure fuch waggon as aforefaid, it fhall be unlawful

for

for every such waggon, not permitted to be measured as aforesaid, to pass along any turnpike road.

XII. And be it enacted by the authority aforesaid, That if any action or suit shall be commenced against any person or persons, for any thing done or acted in pursuance of this act, then and in every such case, such action or suit shall be commenced or prosecuted within six calendar months next after the fact committed, and not afterwards; and the same, and every such action or suit, shall be brought in the county, riding or place where the person against whom such action or suit shall be commenced doth ordinarily inhabit and reside, or in the county or riding where the fact was committed, and not elsewhere; and the defendant or defendants in every such action or suit shall and may plead the general issue, and give this act and the special matter in evidence, at any trial to be had thereupon, and that the same was done in pursuance of and by authority of this present act; and if the same shall appear to have been so done, or if any such action or suit shall be brought after the time herein before limited for bringing the same, or be brought or laid in any other county, riding or place than as afore-mentioned, then the jury shall find for the defendant or defendants;' or if the plaintiff or plaintiffs shall become nonsuited or discontinue his, her or their action, after the defendant or defendants shall have appeared; or if, upon demurrer, judgment shall be given against the plaintiff or plaintiffs, the defendant or defendants shall and may recover treble costs, and have the like remedy for recovery thereof, as any defendant or defendants hath or have in any other cases by law.

Limitation of actions.

General issue.

Treble costs.

XIII. And whereas some doubts have arisen concerning the meaning of the words Common Stage Waggons, it is hereby declared, That every waggon, wain, cart or carriage travelling with or carrying goods for hire, is and shall be deemed to be a common stage waggon, within the true intent and meaning of an act made in the twenty eighth year of the reign of his present Majesty, intituled, An act to amend an act in the twenty sixth year of the reign of his present Majesty, intituled, An act for the amendment and preservation of the publick highways and turnpike roads of this kingdom; and for the more effectual execution of the laws relating thereto.

What shall be deemed a common stage waggon. 28 G. 2. c. 17.

XIV. Whereas it is in and by an act of the twenty eighth year of his present Majesty amongst other things enacted and declared, That if any collector or receiver of the toll or duties at any gate or turnpike, where to or near to which any crane, machine or engine for weighing of carriages shall be built or erected, shall permit any cart, waggon or carriage, within the descriptions therein mentioned, to pass or repass through any such gate or turnpike without weighing the same, such collector or receiver shall, upon conviction, as by the said act is directed, be liable to be committed to the house of correction, and there to be kept to hard labour for the space of one month: and whereas doubts have arisen whether such collector or receiver is not by the said act obliged to weigh all carriages whatsoever, whether loaded

Clause in act 28 G. 2. c. 17 s. 7.

loaded or unloaded; and many difficulties have arisen thereupon; for obviating whereof it is hereby enacted and declared, That from and after the twenty ninth day of *September* one thousand seven hundred and fifty seven, any collector or receiver of any tolls at any turnpike or turnpikes erected or to be erected by virtue of any act of parliament, shall and may permit all and every person or persons going or travelling through any turnpike with an empty cart, waggon or other carriage, to pass and repass through the same, without weighing such empty cart, waggon, or other carriage, and without incurring the penalty aforesaid; and that such collector or receiver shall not be obliged to weigh any cart, waggon or other carriage, but those only which shall be laden; the said last abovementioned act, or any law now in force to the contrary notwithstanding.

C A P. XXIX.

An act to indemnify persons who have been guilty of the un-
lawful importing, landing, or running of prohibited, un-
customed, or other goods or merchandize, upon certain
terms therein mentioned.

WHEREAS *there is a great want of seamen for the com-*
pleatly manning of his Majesty's royal navy: and whereas
there are are many sailors, mariners, and other sea-faring persons,
subjects of his Majesty, at this time in parts beyond the seas, and in
several of the gaols of this kingdom, on account of sundry offences by
them committed in breach of the laws of the customs and excise; and
likewise several persons who have been or may be charged with riding
with fire arms, contrary to the acts passed in the eighth year of the

8 G. 1. c. 18.
9 G. 2. c. 35.
19 G. 2. c. 34.

reign of his late majesty King George the First, and the ninth year
of his present Majesty, as well as other acts now in force, and who
have neglected to take the benefit of the late act of indemnity, and are
capable and may be inclined, or by grace and clemency induced, to serve
on board his Majesty's ships of war, provided they were certain of
their being indemnified for their several offences and past misdemean-
ors; be it therefore enacted by the King's most excellent maje-
sty, by and with the advice and consent of the lords spiritual and temporal, and commons, in this present parliament assembled, and by the authority of the same, That every person, who be-

Smugglers,
&c. indemni-
fied from of-
fences com-
mitted before
1 May 1757.

fore the first day of *May* one thousand seven hundred and fifty seven, shall have been guilty of illegal running, landing, un-shipping, concealing, receiving or carrying any wool, prohibited goods, wares or merchandizes, or any foreign goods liable to the payment of the duties of customs or excise, the same duties not having been paid or secured, or of aiding or assisting there-in; or shall have been armed with fire-arms, or other offensive arms or weapons, in order to be aiding or assisting any such offenders, or have been guilty of rescuing such goods, wares or merchandizes as aforesaid where duties had not been paid or secured after seizure from the officers of the customs or excise, or of any act or matter whatsoever whereby persons may be deemed and taken to be runners of foreign goods and commodities

ilities within the intent and meaning of any law now in force; or of hindering, opposing, obstructing, wounding or beating any officer or officers of the customs or excise, in the execution of his or their office or duty, or of aiding or affisting therein, shall be and are by the authority of this present act, acquitted, indemnified, released and discharged against the King's majesty, his heirs and successors, and any officer or officers of the customs or excise, and every of them, and all and every other person or persons, of and from all and every the said offences, concerning which no suit, information or indictment shall have been commenced, filed or found, or composition made before the said first day of *May* one thousand seven hundred and fifty seven, upon the following terms and conditions; that is to say, That he do, before he shall be apprehended or prosecuted for the same, and before the first day of *December* one thousand seven hundred and fifty seven, enter himself with some commission officer of his Majesty's fleet to serve as a common sailor in the said fleet, and do for three years at least from the time of such entry, unless he shall be sooner duly discharged from the service, actually and *bona fide* serve and do duty as such in the said fleet; and shall also before the said first day of *December* one thousand seven hundred and fifty seven, register his name, employment, and usual place of abode, with the clerk of the peace of the county, riding or division where he resides, in a book which is hereby directed to be kept by the said clerk, among the records of the sessions for the said county, riding or division for this purpose; and shall sign such register, signifying that he claims the benefit of this act, and that he has entered himself with a certain commission officer by name, of his Majesty's fleet, to serve as a common sailor, which entry shall be made in the following form,

provided, before they are prosecuted, and before a December next, they enter and serve on board the navy, and register their names, &c. with the clerk of the peace.

A. B. of   claims
the benefit of an act of the thirtieth year of the reign of his majesty King George the Second, and has entered himself with a commission officer of his Majesty's fleet, and has registered his name in the book kept by the clerk of the peace of this county, riding or division, this   day of   pursuant to the directions of the said act.

For which entry or register there shall be paid to the clerk of the peace of such county, riding or division, one shilling, and no more; and that the said clerk of the peace shall immediately after the said first day of *May* one thousand seven hundred and fifty seven, from time to time, transmit to the commissioners of the customs and excise, an exact account of all the persons who have, by such entry or register as aforesaid, intitled themselves to claim the benefit of this act.

Clerk's fee 1s. who is to transmit an account of the claimants to the commissioners of the customs and excise.

II. Provided always, and be it enacted by the authority aforesaid, That every person who shall make such entry, and claim the benefit of this present act as aforesaid, and shall afterwards

The said persons being guilty of the like offences afterwards, or deferting, or unduly procuring their difcharge, liable to profecution for the former, as well as fuch new offences.

be guilty of, or commit any of the like offences as thofe herein before mentioned, or hereby intended to be acquitted, releafed or difcharged, or fhall at any time after defert from the faid fervice, or within the faid three years unduly procure his difcharge therefrom, fhall be fubject and liable to be profecuted, not only for or in refpect of fuch new offence, but fhall alfo be fubject and liable to all the fame pains, penalties and forfeitures as he would have incurred or been fubject or liable to in cafe this indemnity had never been given; any thing herein contained to the contrary notwithftanding.

Officer permitting any fuch perfon to avoid actual fervice, forfeits 500l. and fuch perfon lofes the benefit of the act. Perfons fo entering themfelves are difabled from bringing any action againft the King's officers, &c. for offences intended to be difcharged by this act.

III. Provided alfo, That if any officer of his Majefty's navy fhall by falfe mufter or certificate, or in confideration of a gratuity of any kind, or by any other collufive or evafive ways or means whatfoever, fuffer or permit fuch perfon to avoid the actual fervice as aforefaid, fuch perfon fhall not only lofe the benefit of this act, but every fuch officer fhall fuffer the penalty of five hundred pounds.

IV. Provided alfo, and be it enacted by the authority aforefaid, That no perfon who fhall have made fuch entry with the clerk of the peace as aforefaid, or receive or be intitled to any benefit or advantage by virtue of this prefent act of indemnity, fhall be capable of maintaining any action brought or to be brought by him, againft any officer of his Majefty's cuftoms or excife, or againft any perfon or perfons who fhall or may have been aiding or affifting to any officer for or concerning any matter, caufe or thing done or committed by fuch officer, or by any perfon or perfons aiding and affifting him on occafion, or for any other matter or thing by this act intended to be acquitted, indemnified, releafed and difcharged; but fuch claim is and fhall be deemed an abfolute difcharge and releafe to fuch officer, who

General iffue.

may plead the general iffue, and give a copy of fuch claim fo as aforefaid entered with the faid clerk of the peace, and give this act in evidence, on fuch action or profecution.

Prohibition of fuits againft perfons entering themfelves.

V. Provided alfo, and it is hereby further enacted by the authority aforefaid, That no perfon, who fhall duly enter himfelf to ferve as a common failor in his Majefty's fleet for the term of three years at leaft in purfuance of this act, fhall during fuch term of three years (unlefs he fhall within fuch fpace of time defert or withdraw from fuch fervice) be liable to be apprehended or imprifoned, or to be fued or profecuted in any manner whatfoever, for or on account of any of the offences intended to be releafed by this act.

C A P. XXX.

An act for allowing a further bounty on veffels employed in the white herring fifhery; for giving liberty to alter the prefent form and fize of the nets ufed in the faid fifhery; and for other purpofes therein mentioned.

23 Geo. 2. c. 24. fect. 11 & 12.

WHEREAS by an act made in the twenty third year of the reign of his prefent Majefty, intituled, An act for the encouragecouragement of the *British* white herring fishery; *it is amongst other things enacted, That as an encouragement to all persons whatsoever, as well bodies politick and corporate, as others, and also the persons who should be incorporated by virtue of and under the said act, to engage in the said white herring fisheries, that a bounty of thirty shillings* per *ton should be paid annually out of such sums as should be produced out of his Majesty's customs to the owner or owners of all decked vessels, from twenty to eighty tons burthen, which should be built after the commencement of the said act, for the use of the said fisheries, and fitted out and employed in the said fisheries, in manner and under the regulations in the said act after-mentioned; such bounty of thirty shillings* per *ton to be paid yearly during the space of fourteen years from the commencement of the said act, and no longer, upon conforming to the regulations of the said act; in which said act it is, amongst other things enacted, That every buss or vessel of the burthen of seventy tons, and designed for the said fishery, should on her proceeding to sea, have on board one fleet of fifty nets, each net to be thirty yards full upon the rope, and seven fathoms deep, and so in proportion for any vessels of a greater or lesser tonnage; and should be provided with one other fleet of fifty like nets on board a jagger or tender to attend the said fishery, or left on shore in a proper place for the use of the said buss or vessel: and whereas pursuant to the power by the said act given to his said Majesty, a society, by the name of the society of* The free *British* fishery, *hath been incorporated by charter bearing date the eleventh day of* October *one thousand seven hundred and fifty: and whereas by another act made in the twenty eighth year of the reign of his said Majesty,* For further explaining, amending and rendering more effectual the said first mentioned act; and for giving further encouragement for the carrying on the said fishery; and for other purposes therein mentioned; *it is enacted, That the several allowances of three pounds* per centum per annum, *and the said bounty of thirty shillings* per *ton granted by the said first mentioned act for the respective terms therein mentioned, should be continued for the further term of three years, to be computed immediately from and after the expiration of the said respective terms, in manner in the said act of the twenty eighth year of his said present Majesty mentioned: and whereas the bounty of thirty shillings* per *ton hath not been found a sufficient bounty on the tonnage of the vessels employed in the said fisheries, and the nets by the said first mentioned act directed to be employed in the said fisheries, have been found by experience, both in their form and depth, to be very inconvenient and unfit for the said fisheries; and it may tend greatly to the support of the said fisheries, if the vessels employed therein were permitted, during the intervals of the two fishing seasons called* The Shetland and Yarmouth *fisheries, to be otherwise employed;* therefore be it enacted and declared, and it is hereby enacted and declared by the King's most excellent majesty, by and with the advice and consent of the lords spiritual and temporal, and commons, in this present parliament assembled, and by the authority of the same, That the said bounty of thirty shillings *per* ton by the said two several acts granted and con-

28 G. 2. c. 14

The former bounty to cease,

continued for the respective terms of years therein respectively mentioned, shall from henceforth cease, determine and be at an end; and that in lieu thereof, a bounty of fifty shillings *per* ton on the vessels employed in the said fisheries, shall be paid and payable for such term and terms of years to the said society, and such other persons as would have been intitled to the said bounty of thirty shillings *per* ton by virtue of, or under the said two several acts herein before recited, or either of them, in case this act had not been made; and that such bounty of fifty shillings *per* ton shall be paid and payable at such times, in such manner, and by such person and persons, and out of such monies as the said bounty of thirty shillings *per* ton is by the said two several acts, or either of them, directed to be paid.

and in lieu thereof, 50s. per ton allowed on vessels employed in the fishery.

II. And be it further enacted by the authority aforesaid, That it shall and may be lawful to and for the said society, and to and for all other person and persons employed in the said fisheries, in lieu of the nets by the said first mentioned act directed to be employed in the said fisheries, to make use of such nets in the white herring fisheries as they shall find best adapted to the said fisheries.

Liberty given to use such nets as are best adapted to the fisheries;

III. Provided always, That each buss or vessel do carry to sea the like quantity of netting in the whole as such buss or vessel is now bound to carry by the said first mentioned act.

so as the like quantity be carried on board each buss.

IV. And it is further enacted by the authority aforesaid, That in all cases where it shall happen that the nets to be employed in the said fisheries shall, by virtue of the liberty and power in and by this present act given and allowed for that purpose, vary from the size and form of the nets in and by the said first-mentioned act directed to be employed in the said fisheries, that so much of the certificate in and by the said first mentioned act directed to be given by the officer or officers who shall be appointed to examine the busses or vessels to be employed in the said white herring fisheries as relates to the fishing nets on board each buss or vessel; and also so much of the oath by the said act directed to be made by the owner or owners, or agent appointed by them, or of a proper officer or agent of the said society, and of the master or chief officer of such vessel, as relates to the nets on board such vessel; may and shall from henceforth be varied and made conformable to such alterations as may be made in such nets so employed in the said fisheries, by virtue of the liberty and power herein before for that purpose given.

Certificates given by the inspectors,

and the oath made by the owners, agents and masters, are to be varied conformable to the size and form of the nets made use of.

V. And be it further enacted by the authority aforesaid, That after the two fisheries called *The Shetland* and *Yarmouth fisheries* shall be over in every year, it shall and may be lawful to and for the said society, in the mean time, and until the commencement of the next ensuing fishing season, to use and employ in any other business not prohibited by law, such of their busses or vessels, and no others, as shall have been really and *bona fide* employed in the said two fisheries then last preceding, during the whole time of such two fisheries; any thing in the said

Liberty given to employ the vessels in the intervals of the fisheries.

said first mentioned act, or in the charter of the said society to the contrary notwithstanding.

VI. And whereas by an act made in the twenty ninth year of his said Majesty, intituled, *An act for encouraging the fisheries in that part of* Great Britain *called* Scotland, it is amongst other things enacted, That from and after the twenty fifth day of *June* one thousand seven hundred and fifty eight, the staves of all barrels in which white herrings and wet white fish, in that part of *Great Britain* called *Scotland* shall be packed or put up, shall be at least one half part of an inch in thickness throughout, under such penalty as in the said act is mentioned: and whereas the said society, and other persons following the said fisheries, have at a very great expence provided a large quantity of barrels for the packing their fish, and no inconvenience hath arisen from the make of such barrels; be it therefore enacted and declared by the authority aforesaid, That so much of the said act of the twenty ninth year of his said Majesty, as relates to the thickness of the barrels to be used in the packing and putting up of white herrings and wet white fish, shall not extend, or be deemed or construed to extend, to barrels made use of, or to be made use of by the said society, or by any other person or persons following the said white herring fisheries, by virtue of or under the said act of the twenty third year of his said present Majesty; any thing in the said act of the twenty ninth year of his said Majesty to the contrary thereof in any wise notwithstanding.

29 Geo. 2. c. 23.

Regulation of the thickness of barrel staves not to extend to barrels used in the herring fishery.

VII. And be it further enacted by the authority aforesaid, That the said society, and all and every person or persons employed in the said fisheries, shall have and exercise the free use of all ports, harbours, shores and forelands in *Great Britain,* or the islands belonging to the crown of *Great Britain,* below the highest high water mark, and for the space of one hundred yards on any waste or uncultivated land beyond such mark within the land, for landing their nets, casks and other materials, utensils and stores, and for erecting tents, huts and stages, and for the landing, pickling, curing and reloading their fish, and in drying their nets without paying any foreland or other dues, or any other sum or sums of money, or other consideration whatsoever for such liberty (except as herein after is excepted) any law, statute or custom whatsoever to the contrary notwithstanding: and if any person or persons shall presume to demand or receive any dues, sums of money, or other consideration whatsoever for the use of any such ports, harbours, shores or forelands within the limits aforesaid, or shall obstruct the fishermen or other persons employed in the taking or curing of fish, or drying their nets in the use of the same, every person so offending shall for every such offence forfeit the sum of one hundred pounds, to be recovered and levied in manner herein after directed.

Free use of all ports and shores, &c. below high water mark, and 100 yards above, on any waste grounds, for landing and drying nets.

Persons obstructing such use, forfeit 100l.

VIII. Provided always, That nothing in this act contained shall extend to exempt the vessels or boats employed in the said fish-

Where harbour or pier dues are demandable by law, the

fishing vessels are to pay the same. fisheries from the payment of such harbour or pier dues as are and by law ought to be demanded for ships, vessels or boats, in piers or harbour which are built or artificially made; but that such harbour or pier dues shall be paid in like manner as the same were liable to be paid before the passing of this act.

Penalty where and how to be sued for. IX. And be it further enacted by the authority aforesaid, That the penalty herein before mentioned shall and may be prosecuted and determined by bill, plaint or information, in any of his Majesty's courts of record at *Westminster*, or in the court of *exchequer* in *Scotland* respectively, wherein no essoin, protection, privilege, wager of law, or more than one imparlance shall be allowed; and one moiety of such penalty shall be to the use of his Majesty, and the other moiety to such person or persons as will sue for or prosecute the same.

The tonnage bounty is not to be paid, till a certificate be produced of the duty payable to Greenwich hospital being duly paid. X. Provided always, and be it further enacted and declared by the authority aforesaid, That the said bounty of fifty shillings *per* ton herein before given and granted to vessels employed in the said fishery, shall not be paid or payable in respect of any such vessels, until it shall have been made appear to the satisfaction of the commissioners of his Majesty's customs, by one or more certificate or certificates, receipt or receipts, from the receiver or collector for the time being of the duty of six pence *per* man *per* month, payable out of seamens wages, for the support of the royal hospital at *Greenwich*, that all monies payable on account of such duty from any vessel, in respect whereof such bounty of fifty shillings *per* ton shall be demanded, hath been fully paid and discharged; any thing herein before contained to the contrary thereof in any wise notwithstanding.

CAP. XXXI.

An act to explain, amend and render more effectual an act passed in the twenty eighth year of the reign of his present Majesty, intituled, *An act to enable the churchwardens, overseers and inhabitants of the parish of Saint Saviour in the borough of Southwark in the county of Surry, to hold a market within the said parish, not interfering with the high street in the said borough.*

28 Geo. 2. c. 23.   The ground described in the recited act, ascertained. The bishop of Rochester may grant separate leases of Rochester yard, to the churchwardens and inhabitants of the parish, and to John Howell, esquire. The said leases, and reservations of rent declared to be valid. Where other persons refuse to treat, notice to be given them, that the value of their lands will be settled by a jury. Precepts to be issued accordingly for returning a jury; who are to assess the damage and recompence, on oath. Jury may be challenged. Verdict of the jury, and judgment of the commissioners thereon, to be conclusive, and to be filed among the records of the quarter-sessions. All contracts and sales deemed valid, and to bar all dower, and estate, &c. The further sum of 2000l. may be borrowed for the purposes of the act, on annuity for lives, at the rate of 8l. per cent. per an. to be charged on the rents and profits of the market. Rate to be made for making good deficiencies in the said fund, to be allowed and signed by the justices, and collected quarterly; and may be levied by distress and sale. Persons aggrieved by the rate, may appeal to the quarter sessions. Collector to pay over the monies to the churchwardens, or to their order; and to account before the justices yearly, or oftener, and pay over the balance on making up his accounts. Penalty on per-

persons selling, or exposing meat to sale, in any house, &c. except their own. Penalty on persons hawking or exposing to sale, meat, or other provisions, within 1000 yards of the market, except in their own shops, &c. in market time. Forfeitures may be levied by distress and sale; and for want of sufficient distress, offender to be committed. Persons aggrieved, by order of justices may appeal. Powers of the recited act confirmed, and extended to this act. Charges of this act to be paid out of the first monies raised. Publick act.

CAP. XXXII.

An act for draining and preserving certain marsh and fen lands and low grounds in the parish of Wiggenhall Saint Mary Magdalen, in the county of Norfolk.

Commissioners appointed. Penalty on persons acting, if not qualified. Commissioners power to make banks, &c. and to erect engines, paying for the damage; and if the parties cannot agree, the same to be adjudged by the justices in session. Time and place of trustees meeting. Commissioners may make orders, &c. choose officers. Officers may be removed. To give security. Commissioners to lay an equal acre-tax, not exceeding 2s. per acre each year. Highlands not to be charged. Justices to determine differences. Commissioners to borrow money on the tax. Money not to be borrowed but at a publick meeting, and not by less than 7 commissioners. Application of the money. Commissioners may distrain for taxes. Distress may be appraised and sold, after 5 days. Tenants to pay the rates, and deduct the same out of the rents. Person neglecting to pay the rates, for 2 months after demand, forfeits 5s. for every 20s. he shall be in arrear; to be levied by distress and sale; if no distress be found, the lands to remain a security for the tax, &c. Rates liable to the payment of the money borrowed, &c. Creditors may distrain for interest, if not paid half-yearly, or within three months after. Assignments transferrable without stamp. Persons maliciously destroying the works, guilty of felony. Persons maliciously stopping up, &c. any drain, &c. shall forfeit 10l. or be kept to hard labour. Penalty for making places for watering in the mill-drains. Accounts how to be kept and entered. Commissioners to take the accounts upon oath. Directions concerning dykes and drains, bridges and tunnels. If owners neglect, commissioners may order drains, &c. to be made and scoured. Penalty per rod. Money so expended to be levied with charges. Commissioners not to prejudice the navigation of the Ouze. Limitation of actions. General issue. Treble costs. Publick act.

CAP. XXXIII.

An act for draining and preserving certain fen lands and low grounds in the several parishes of Ramsey, Bury, Wistow, Warboys, Farceitt, Standground and Water-newton in the county of Huntingdon, and of Doddington in the isle of Ely and county of Cambridge.

Lands divided into six districts. Commissioners for the first district; for the second district; for the third district; for the fourth district; for the fifth district; for the sixth district. Perpetual commissioners. Commissioners to be elected annually. Commissioners dying, &c. others to be chosen. Qualification of commissioners. Penalty on persons acting, if not qualified. Meetings of commissioners. Commissioners to make and maintain works. Waters passing from highlands, &c in first and second districts, not to be excluded from the proper outlets, &c. Satisfaction to be made. In case of difference, damages to be settled at the quarter sessions. If any private mill is taken down, commissioners to make satisfaction to the owner. Commissioners may appoint officers, and allow them salaries. Officers to give security. Commissioners not to hold a place of profit. The acre tax for the respective districts. Ramsey Hern, &c. exempt from all taxes. Taxes to be levied by distress and sale. Tenants may pay taxes, and deduct them from their rent; except where there is a lease of three years to come. Grounds unoccupied to remain a security for the taxes. The quantity of rateable lands to be given in by the owners. Highlands not to be charged. Manner of determining which are highlands. Mr. Wyldbore's lands not to be taxed while the banks are supported. Taxes may be assigned for money borrowed. Mortgages may be assigned; and assignments transferred. The sums to be borrowed in each respective district. Taxes to be security for monies borrowed. Application of the monies. Charges of the act to be paid in equal parts by each district. Annual meetings for passing accounts. Officers to account on oath. Certain owners may erect stanches. A mill or mills to be placed at the opening of Ash drain into forty foot river. Ash drain and Willow fen drain to be kept open with consent of the corporation of Bedford level. Northey bank may be repaired. Ramsey Hern to be imbanked. Commissioners may build a bridge. Outring and division dikes to be kept open by the proprietors. No cut to be made in whole lands. Exception. Penalty on making sockdikes, &c. All mills to discharge the water either into Bevill's river, river Nene or Whittlesea meer. Certain works to be drained separately. Delph dike to remain dammed up. Lands which shall not be cut. No trees to be planted within 20 poles of any mill. Persons discharging water by any engine, except into the river Nene, &c. shall forfeit 50l. No private bank, &c. to be altered, till new ones are made. Allowance to be made from the 4th to the 5th district. Persons damaging the works, to forfeit 100l. and for want of distress, to be committed. Persons destroying mills, &c. to suffer as felons. Mills to be insured. Allowances for catching moles. Proceedings to be entered in books; books may be produced and read in evidence in cases of appeals. Quorum of commissioners of the several districts. No order made by the commissioners shall be altered, &c. unless 10 days notice be first given. All proceedings to be at a meeting. Penalties and forfeitures how to be recovered and applied. This act not to interfere with the conservators of Bedford level. 15 Car. 2. c. 17. Reservation of rights to commissioners for preserving the navigation of Salter's load sluice, &c. 27 Geo. 2. c. 12. Reservation of rights to lords of manors. Limitation of actions. General issue. Double costs. Publick act.

CAP. XXXIV.

An act to enable the commissioners for building Westminster *Bridge, to widen the street or avenue leading from* Cockspur *Street, to the passage in* Spring Garden, *near Saint* James's *park.*

WHEREAS *commissioners for building a bridge cross the river* Thames, *from the* Woolstaple, *or thereabouts, in the parish of* Saint Magaret, *in the city of* Westminster, *to the opposite shore in the county of* Surry, *are by virtue of several former acts of parliament passed in the reign of his present Majesty, or by virtue of some or one of them, impowered to make, open, design, assign, and lay out, such new ways, streets and passages, as they shall find proper to be opened and made on each side the river* Thames, *to and from the said bridge, the courts of justice, both houses of parliament, and the parts adjacent; and to agree for and purchase such houses and grounds as they shall find necessary for them to be possessed of, and to be removed, rebuilt, pulled down, or employed for those purposes, comprized within certain bounds and limits particularly mentioned and described in the said respective acts, or some or one of them: and whereas the way, street or avenue, leading from* Cockspur Street, *in the parish of* Saint Martin in the Fields, *in the liberty of* Westminster, *to the passage in* Spring Gardens *leading to* Saint James's*

park,*

park, and from thence to both houses of parliament, Westminster
Hall, and the courts of justice, and Westminster Bridge, might be
rendered more open, safe and commodious, for the ease of passengers
and the publick benefit, than the same now is, in case the said commissioners were enabled to open and widen the said way, street or
avenue, and to purchase, pull down and remove, such buildings and
houses, and to take possession of such grounds and estates, as they shall
think proper and necessary for those purposes; wherefore, for the
promoting a design so useful and beneficial to the publick, may it please
your most excellent Majesty, that it may be enacted; and be it enacted by the King's most excellent majesty, by and with the advice and consent of the lords spiritual and temporal and commons, in this present parliament assembled, and by the authority
of the same, That the said commissioners, or any five or more
of them, shall have full power and authority to open and widen
the way, street or avenue, now leading from *Cockspur Street*, in the
parish of Saint *Martin in the Fields*, in the liberty of *Westminster*,
to the passage in *Spring Garden*, leading to Saint *James's* park, in
such manner as they shall think proper.

Commiffion-
ers impowered
to widen the
avenues lead-
ing from
Cockspur
street, to the
passage in
Spring Gar-
den;

II. And for the better performance and execution thereof, be
it further enacted by the authority aforesaid, That the said
commissioners, or any five or more of them, shall have full power
and authority to agree with the owner or owners, and occupier
or occupiers, for the purchase of the freehold and inheritance of all
and every such building or buildings, house or houses, grounds
and estates, as they the said commissioners, or any five or more
of them, shall think necessary for them to be possessed of, or
to be removed, rebuilt, pulled down, disposed of, or employed, for the purposes of this act, comprized within the bounds
and limits following; that is to say, situate, standing, lying or
being upon, near or adjoining to the said way, street or avenue,
on the east side thereof, as far as a certain messuage or building,
messuages or buildings, now in the occupation of *Robert Taylor*
statuary, his undertenants or assigns, and abutting north on
Cockspur Street, and south on *Spring Gardens*; and also to purchase
and become possessed of the freehold and inheritance of all such
buildings, houses, grounds and estates, and of all rent charges,
annuities, mortgages, terms of years, or incumbrances whatsoever affecting the same; any thing in the said several former acts
of parliament, or any of them, contained to the contrary thereof in any wise notwithstanding.

and to pur-
chase houses
and grounds
to be made
use of for that
purpose;

III. And whereas it may happen, that some person or persons,
bodies politick, corporate or collegiate, corporations aggregate or sole,
femes covert, and their husbands in the right of such femes covert
respectively, trustees or feoffees in trust, guardians, and committees
for lunaticks and ideots, executors and administrators, or other trustees
or guardians for femes covert, infants, issue unborn, or other cestuique trusts, or for some charitable or other use or uses, or others who
are themselves, or whose respective wards or cestuique trusts, are seised,
possessed of, or intitled unto, some of the buildings, houses, grounds,
or estates, which may be thought necessary to be purchased, removed,
pulled

*pulled down, disposed of, or employed by the said commissioners, with-
in the bounds and limits, and for the purposes mentioned and prescribed in and by this act, or of some estate or interest therein, or of
some charge or incumbrance affecting the same, may be willing to
treat for and agree to sell such buildings, houses, grounds or estates,
in order to perfect the useful and beneficial works intended by this act,
but are incapable of granting or conveying the same, by reason of some
disability, or not being under any disability may refuse to treat, agree
for, or sell the same;* be it therefore enacted by the authority a-

foresaid, That the said commissioners, or any five or more of
them, shall and may, in order to purchase and become possessed of the several buildings, houses, grounds and estates, to be
purchased by virtue of, and under this act, take, use and follow,
all or any such ways, means, methods and proceedings, and observe such rules and directions, as by any act or acts of parliament heretofore passed in the reign of his present Majesty, they
are enabled to take, use, follow, and observe, in order to be
purchased, or be possessed of any other houses, grounds and
estates; and that all and every the powers and authorities, clauses,
rules, forms and directions, prescribed, mentioned, expressed
and contained, in each and every of the said act and acts of
parliament heretofore passed in the reign of his present Majesty, in any wise relating to the said commissioners purchasing or
becoming possessed of any other houses, grounds or estates whatsoever, or to any body or bodies politick, corporate or collegiate,
corporations aggregate or sole, or any other person or persons
whatsoever, selling, disposing of, or conveying any houses,
grounds or estates, by any of the said last mentioned act or acts
directed to be sold, purchased and conveyed; or for obliging
the high bailiff of *Westminster* to summon juries, and for obliging such juries to assess the value of any such houses, grounds
or estates, or any interest therein, in case any person or persons
having or claiming to have any such estate or interest, shall refuse to sell or convey the same to the said commissioners, or to
manifest a sufficient title thereto; or in case the person or persons intitled to any such estate or interest therein, cannot be
found, or to the disposal, paying, depositing, or vesting of any
sum or sums of money thereby directed to be disposed of,
paid, deposited, or vested, as the considerations for the purchase
of, or value assessed for any of the said houses, grounds or
estates, or to the obliging persons to produce title deeds, books,
papers or writings, for inspection and perusal, or to the obliging any persons to appear, and be examined on oath as witnesses; and every other rule, clause, matter and thing, in each and
every of the said last-mentioned act and acts of parliament mentioned and contained, and now being in force, shall and are
hereby declared to be of full force and effect, to all intents and
purposes, for enabling the said commissioners, or any five or
more of them, to purchase the freehold and inheritance, and
to become possessed of, and to pull down, and remove any of
the buildings, houses, grounds and estates within the bounds
and

Side note left of paragraph: and in order
thereto, they
may take such
measures, as by
any former
acts they are
impowered to
do in like
cases.

Side note lower left: Clauses in the
several former
acts still in
force, extend-
ed to the pur-
chases, &c. to
be made under
this act.

and limits mentioned and prefcribed in this prefent act; and
fhall extend, and be in all refpects deemed and conftrued to extend, to all and every the faid laft-mentioned buildings, houfes,
grounds and eftates, and to all bodies politick, corporate and
collegiate, corporations aggregate and fole, femes covert, and
their hufbands, truftees, and feoffees in truft, guardians and
committees for lunaticks and ideots, executors, adminiftrators,
and all other truftees and guardians, whether for femes covert,
infants, iffue unborn, or other ceftuique trufts, or for any charitable or other ufe or ufes; and to all other perfons whatfoever
having or claiming to have, either in their own right or otherwife howfoever, any eftate, right, title or intereft, in, to or out
of the faid laft-mentioned buildings, houfes, grounds and eftates;
and to the methods and proceedings, for conveying and abfolutely iffuing the fame to the faid commiffioners or their truftees,
with good titles, ufual and reafonable covenants, and free from
incumbrances; and for barring, docking, and cutting off all
eftates tail, dower, and right of dower; and alfo to bar the
right of all and every perfon and perfons, who fhall not enter
their faid claim or claims, and profecute the fame with effect,
in the manner, and within the times prefcribed and limited by
the faid acts of parliament, or fome or one of them, as fully
and effectually as if the faid powers and authorities, rules, forms,
directions, claufes, matters and things, mentioned and contained in each of the faid acts of parliament heretofore paffed
in the reign of his prefent Majefty, were particularly and at
large repeated and enacted in the body of this prefent act.

IV. *And whereas by means of the purchafes which the faid commiffioners are hereby impowered to make, they may be poffeffed of one
or more piece or pieces of ground, over and above what may be neceffary for the opening and widening the way, ftreet or avenue*; be it
further enacted by the authority aforefaid, That it fhall and may
be lawful to and for the faid commiffioners, or any five or more
of them, to lett, fell or difpofe of any fuch piece or pieces of
ground, either together or in parcels, as they fhall find moft advantageous and convenient, to any perfon or perfons who fhall
be willing to contract, agree for, or purchafe the fame; that it
fhall and may alfo be lawful to and for the faid commiffioners,
or any five or more of them, to defign, affign and lay out, in
what manner any new houfes fhall be erected and built on any
of the faid piece or pieces of ground which they may be poffeffed of as aforefaid, over and above what may be neceffary for
the opening and widening of the faid way, ftreet or avenue; and
likewife of what breadth and extent fuch way, ftreet or avenue
fhall be; and alfo to fell and difpofe of the materials of fuch houfe
or houfes, building or buildings, as they the faid commiffioners,
or any five or more of them, fhall purchafe and caufe to be pulled down by virtue of this act.

They may alfo lett or difpofe of any piece of ground purchafed by them, not neceffary for widening the ftreet, and defign in what manner any new houfes fhall be built thereon; and the breadth and extent of the ftreet; and fell the old materials.

V. Provided always, That the money arifing by the fale or
letting of fuch grounds, and felling the materials of the houfes
and buildings to be purchafed and pulled down as aforefaid, fhall
be

Money arifing thereby to be applied in defraying the charges of the truft.

be employed, paid and disposed of, by the said commissioners, or any five or more of them, towards defraying the charges and expences of executing the powers and trusts hereby in them reposed.

VI. *And in order to preserve the said way, street or avenue, hereby intended to be opened and widened, when the same shall be so opened and widened; and also the houses and buildings that shall be erected on any of the grounds which shall be let or sold by the said commissioners, by virtue of this act, free from nuisances and annoyances; and to preserve the uniformity and beauty thereof;* be it further enacted by the authority aforesaid, That a certain act of parliament passed in the eighteenth year of the reign of his present Majesty, intituled, *An act for granting further powers to the commissioners for building a bridge cross the river* Thames, *from the city of* Westminster, *to the opposite shore in the county of* Surry; *and for the better enabling them to finish the said bridge, and to perform the other trust reposed in them;* and all and every the powers, authorities, clauses, matters and things, therein mentioned and contained, which are now in force, shall extend to and be deemed and taken to be to all intents and purposes in full force, with respect to the said last-mentioned way, street or avenue, when the same shall be so opened and widened as aforesaid; and to the owners and occupiers of such houses and buildings, as shall be let or sold by the said commissioners by virtue of this act, for effectually impowering and enabling them the said commissioners, or any five or more of them, from time to time, to perform, use and exercise all and every the like powers and authorities for preserving the said way, street or avenue, and the said last-mentioned houses and buildings, free from nuisances and annoyances, or for abating any such nuisances, and for preserving the uniformity and beauty of such houses and buildings; and for a better and more effectual enforcing the covenants, conditions, agreements, limitations and restrictions, under which the said commissioners shall let or sell any pieces of ground or buildings by virtue of this act, as are expressed and contained in the said act of the eighteenth year of the reign of his present Majesty, with respect to the several streets and premisses therein mentioned, as fully as if the said several powers, authorities, clauses, matters and things, in that act mentioned and contained, were particularly and at large repeated and reenacted in the body of this present act.

VII. And be it further enacted by the authority aforesaid, That out of all or any of the aids or supplies granted to his Majesty, for the service of the year one thousand seven hundred and fifty seven, there may and shall be applied and paid to the said commissioners for building the said bridge, or any five or more of them, or to such person or persons as shall be appointed under the hands and seals of the said commissioners, or any five or more of them, to receive the same, the sum of two thousand five hundred pounds without account (other than as is herein after directed) to be applied towards purchasing houses and grounds

Margin notes

Powers and clauses in act 18Geo.2. c.29. extended to the street to be widened under this act,

for keeping the same free from nuisances,

and preserving the uniformity and beauty of the buildings, &c.

2,500l. granted to the commissioners for the purposes aforesaid.

grounds for widening the said way, street or avenue, and for making the same more commodious and useful to the publick, and for the payment of other incidental charges and expences attending the execution of this act, in such manner, and at such times, as the said commissioners, or any five or more of them, shall from time to time direct.

VIII. And be it also enacted by the authority aforesaid, That the said commissioners for building the said bridge, shall lay an account of the application, as well of the said sum of two thousand five hundred pounds, as of all other monies raised by virtue of this and the said former acts, and by them applied and expended, before both houses of parliament, within twenty days after the opening of every session of parliament, in the same manner as they are directed to do by the said former acts.

Account of the application thereof, &c. to be laid before the parliament.

IX. And be it further enacted by the authority aforesaid, That all such costs and charges as shall be expended in obtaining, or by reason of passing this present act, and such monies as shall become due to any person or persons employed in pursuance hereof, shall be paid out of the monies to be raised by virtue hereof.

Charges of passing this act to be paid out of the said monies.

X. *And whereas part of the lands and grounds intended to be purchased by virtue of this act, are the freehold and inheritance of the right reverend doctor* Zachary Pearce, *the present lord bishop of* Rochester: *and whereas a surety and estimate of the value of the said lands and grounds, and of the buildings and erections thereon, has been had and made by two indifferent persons, with the consent of the said lord bishop, who have valued and estimated the same at the sum of one thousand three hundred and forty five pounds: and whereas the said lord bishop is willing to accept of the said sum of one thousand three hundred and forty five pounds, in full satisfaction for all his right, title, and interest whatsoever, in the same, and the street adjoining;* be it therefore enacted by the authority aforesaid, That if the said lord bishop of *Rochester*, or the person or persons who shall be respectively intitled to the said lands and grounds, with the buildings and erections thereon, now belonging to the said lord bishop of *Rochester*, shall, on or before the first day of *August* one thousand seven hundred and fifty seven, signify to the said commissioners, in writing, his, her or their consent, to accept the said sum of one thousand three hundred and forty five pounds, for his, her or their interest in the said premisses, and shall do, perform and execute, all and every matter and thing as shall be necessary and required by the said commissioners, or any five or more of them, for compleating and perfecting his, her or their title to the said premisses, and for conveying the same to the said commissioners, in such manner as they, or any five or more of them, shall direct and appoint; then, and in such case, the said commissioners, or any five or more of them, shall, and they are hereby impowered and required, out of the said sum of two thousand five hundred pounds, to pay and apply the sum of one thousand three hundred and forty five pounds, to the said lord bishop of *Rochester*, or to the such person or persons as shall be respectively intitled to the said premisses, in such and the like man-

The commissioners to pay to the bishop of Rochester 1,345l. for the purchase of lands, &c. his property, on his making out a title, and proper conveyance.

manner, as any fum or fums agreed for by the faid commiffioners are directed to be paid by virtue of any former acts.

The foot way of the ftreets to be raifed fix inches above the carriage way, and to be paved with flagg ftone.

XI. Provided always, and be it enacted, That when the faid way, ftreet or avenue, fhall be opened and widened, the foot way on the weft fide thereof fhall be raifed fix inches at leaft, above the carriage way, and be paved with good flagg ftone, and be made in the narroweft part, not lefs than nine feet wide ; and that the faid carriage way fhall not thereafter be altered, fo as to raife the fame nearer the furface of the faid foot way, than the fame fhall be left, when finifhed, in purfuance of this act.

Lights of the cellar ftory not to be obftructed thereby.

XII. Provided alfo, That in the making the faid foot way, care be taken not to obftruct the lights of the cellar ftory adjoining to the faid foot way.

Commiffioners and perfons acting under them, indemnified for what they fhall do.

XIII. And be it further enacted by the authority aforefaid, That the faid commiffioners, and each and every other perfon or perfons authorized by the faid commiffioners, or any five or more of them, to do any act in execution of any of the powers intended to be hereby vefted in the faid commiffioners, are and fhall be hereby indemnified for what they fhall do in purfuance of this act; and that if any action fhall be brought, or fuit commenced, againft any perfon or perfons, for any thing done in purfuance of this act, or in relation to the premiffes herein before mentioned, every fuch action or fuit fhall be laid or brought within fix calendar months after the fact done; and fuch action

Limitation of actions.

General iffue.

fhall be laid in the county of *Middlefex*, and not elfewhere; and the defendant or defendants in fuch action or fuit, fhall and may be at liberty to plead the general iffue, and give this act and the fpecial matter in evidence without fpecially pleading thefame.

CAP. XXXV.

An act for draining and preferving certain fen lands lying in the South Level, part of the great level of the fens, commonly called Bedford Level, between Brandon River and Sams's Cut Drain ; and for impowering the governor, bailiffs and commonalty, of the company of confervators of the faid great level, to fell certain lands within the faid limits, commonly called Invefted Lands.

Who fhall be commiffioners for putting the act in execution. Firft commiffioners for Feltwel, Helgay, Southery and Methwold. Proprietors to meet in March annually, to chufe commiffioners. If no election fhall be made in any year, the commiffioners for the preceeding year to be continued. Qualification of commiffioners. Commiffioners to meet half yearly, or oftener. Their firft general meeting to be held at Feltwell. Subfequent meetings where. Commiffioners to make orders for draining, &c. and to appoint proper officers. Collectors to give fecurity. 1s. to be paid to each commiffioner for his attendance at any meeting. Commiffioners impowered to fcour and make cuts, drains, and other works. The waters to be thrown off into the Oufe and Brandon. Satisfaction to be made for damages done in erecting new works. Differences to be fettled by the juftices at their quarter feffions. Acre rates to be made for defraying the expences. Highlands not fubject to be rated. Hod and turf pools not rateable for feven years. Decoy of Robert Clough may be inbanked, and is not rateable. Two perfons to be appointed to fet out the commiffioners portion of common, to be enjoyed in feveralty, and to veft in the commiffioners in truft, &c. The fen reeves neglecting, the juftices are to appoint a proper perfon. Commiffioners may borrow money on the rates, with intereft. Application of the money borrowed. Principal not to exceed 4000l. Rates

charg-

charged with the principal and interest, and on non-payment to vest in the creditors. Assignments may be transferred. Entry to be made thereof. Rates on non-payment, after notice, may be levied by distress and sale. Tenants to pay the rates, and deduct the same out the rent. Exception. Where no distress can be found, the lands are to remain a security; and if lands shall be dug up into hods or turf, taxes are to be levied on owner's goods wheresoever found. Horse mills and other engines may be erected on arable lands, to drain the same. Owners neglecting to rode, &c. the leading dikes and lay proper tunnels, collectors to cause the same to be done, and levy the expence. Penalty on persons making watering places for cattle in milldrains, or driving waggons on the banks. Penalty of destroying the banks, or other works, &c. Accounts of receipts and disbursements to be audited annually; and the vouchers to be produced, &c. Accounts when allowed to be entered in 3 books, &c. Rights of the conservators of Bedford Level reserved to them. 15 Car. 2. c. 17, 20 Car. 2. c. 8. The corporation's receiver is to pay out of the taxes of the south and middle levels, the rates chargeable hereby on the invested lands, until the said lands are sold. Commissioners to be appointed annually for the invested lands. The said lands may be sold by auction, giving notice of such sale. Corporation to make a conveyance thereof to the purchasers. The said lands are liable to be rated after sale, as they were before. Limitation of actions. General issue. Treble costs. Publick act.

C A P. XXXVI.

An act for draining and preserving certain fen lands, low grounds and commons in the townships or hamlets of March and Wimblington, and in the parish of Upwell in the isle of Ely and county of Cambridge.

Lands to be divided into six districts: The first district. Second district. Third district. Fourth district. Fifth district. Sixth district. Commissioners for 1st, 3d, 5th and 6th districts. Commissioners intitled but to one vote. Commissioners for the second district. Fourth district. Election of commissioners for fourth district. Qualification. Agents may be appointed. For qualifying persons jointly possessed of estates. Meetings for the respective districts. Where to be held. Commissioners to make and maintain works; making satisfaction. Officers to be appointed. Taxes on several lands. The quantity of rateable lands to be given in by the owners. Taxes on common rights; how to be apportioned, and raised. Separate collectors. Certain lots exempted. Highlands not to be charged. Manner of determining which are highlands. Exemption in 2d district. Money to be borrowed. And assignments transferred. The sums to be borrowed in each respective district. Taxes not to be under a certain rate when money is owing. Taxes to be security for monies borrowed. Application of the monies. Charges of the act to be paid in equal parts by each district. Taxes to be levied by distress and sale. Tenants may pay taxes, and deduct them from their rent; except where there is a lease of three years to come. Taxes upon Estepher farm, &c. to be paid by the tenants. Grounds unoccupied to remain a security for the taxes. No order made by the commissioners shall be altered, &c. unless 10 days notice be first given. All orders to be made at meetings. Persons destroying mills, &c. to suffer as felons. Persons damaging the works, to forfeit 100l. Penalty on working horse mills, &c. Accounts how to be settled. Proceedings to be entered in books; books may be produced and read in evidence in cases of appeals. Satisfaction to be made for private mills. Allowance to be made in the 4th district for private banks. Private works not to be altered until the mills are ready to work. Directing bridges and tunnels to be erected and made. Penalty on making watering places and sock dikes, &c. A bank to be made on the west side of Plant Water, Owner's of Barber's Lot may maintain the bank to the gravel bank. Mr. Collier to support his bank. Outring ditch next to Mr. Collier's lands to be cleansed How waters are to be drained from 1st and 2d district. No trees to be planted within 20 poles of any mill. Drains not to be made thro' Mr. Brown's lands. Penalty on neglecting to cleanse dikes, &c. Notice of meetings for the second district. Saving of rights to the corporation of Bedford Level. 15 Car.

s. c. 17. Refervation of rights to commiffioners for preferving the navigation of Salter's Load Sluice, &c. 27 Geo. 2. c. 22. Limitation of actions. General iffue. Treble cofts. Public act.

CAP. XXXVII.

An act for enlarging the times limited for executing and performing feveral provifions, powers and directions in certain acts of this feffion of parliament.

WHEREAS *by certain acts of this prefent feffion of parliament, feveral provifions, powers and authorities therein contained, have been or may be required, directed or authorized to be executed on or before the day of the paffing of fuch acts refpectively, whereby feveral doubts and difficulties may arife with refpect to the execution of the faid acts, and the good purpofes thereby intended may be defeated;* be it therefore enacted by the King's moft excellent majefty, by and with the advice and confent of the lords fpiritual and temporal and commons in this prefent parliament affembled, and by the authority of the fame, That in cafe any act of parliament hath paffed, or doth or fhall pafs, at any time whatfoever during this prefent feffion of parliament, whereby any provifion, power or authority, or any matter or thing hath been, is or fhall be directed, required or authorized to be executed, done or performed, on or before any day which hath been, is or fhall be the day of the paffing, or which hath, is or fhall have elapfed, before the paffing of any fuch act refpectively; in each and every fuch cafe, all fuch provifions, powers, authorities, matters and things, as have been, are or fhall be directed or required to be executed, done or performed, on or before the days refpectively limited in every fuch act, fhall be and are hereby directed and required to be executed, done or performed, on or before the fourteenth day after the day of paffing this act, by the perfons refpectively, who in every fuch act refpectively have been, are or fhall be directed or required to execute, do or perform the fame, on or before the days therein limited; and all fuch provifions, powers, authorities, matters and things, as have been, are or fhall be authorized to be executed, done or performed, on or before the refpective days limited in every fuch act refpectively, may be and are hereby authorized to be executed, done and performed, on or before the faid fourteenth day after the day of paffing of this act, by the perfons refpectively who have been, are or fhall be authorized to execute, do or perform the fame; and all fuch provifions, powers, authorities, matters and things fo executed, done and performed, on or before the faid fourteenth day after the day of paffing this act, fhall be as valid and effectual, and be deemed and taken, to all intents and purpofes, as if the fame had been executed, done and performed, on or before the days limited in every fuch act refpectively; any thing therein contained to the contrary notwithstanding.

Where any provifions, powers, &c. are directed to be executed by any act of this feffion, before the day, &c. on which fuch act fhall happen to have paffed, the fame may be executed on or before the 14th day after paffing this act;

and the matters fo done declared to be valid.

CAP. XXXVIII.

An act for amending, widening, and keeping in repair, feveral roads in and near to the town of Tenbury in the counties of Salop, Worcefter and Hereford.

CAP.

CAP. XXXIX.

An act for repairing and widening several roads leading to, through and from the town of Frome in the county of Somerfet; and for giving further powers to the truftees in an act paffed in the twenty fifth year of his prefent Majefty's reign, for repairing the roads from the town of Warminfter in the county of Wilts, to the city of Bath in the county of Somerfet, and other roads therein mentioned.

CAP. XL.

An act for enlarging the terms and powers granted by two acts of parliament, one paffed in the third, and the other in the feventeenth year of the reign of his prefent Majefty, for repairing the road leading from a gate called Shipfton Toll-gate at Bridgetown in the parifh of Old Stratford in the county of Warwick, through Alderminfter and Shipfton upon Stower, to the top of Long Compton Hill in the faid county of Warwick; and alfo for repairing the road leading from the firft mile ftone ftanding on the faid Shipfton road, through a lane called Clifford Lane, and thro' Mickleton and Chipping Campden, to a place called Andover's Ford, in the county of Gloucefter.

CAP. XLI.

An act for amending, widening, and keeping in repair, the road from the turnpike road at the bottom of Shaw Hill in the parifh of Melkfham, through Googes Lane, Corfham, Biddefton and Weft Yatton, to the turnpike road at Upper Combe in the parifh of Caftlecombe in the county of Wilts.

CAP. XLII.

An act for the afcertaining and collecting the poor's rates; and for the better ordering and regulating the poor in the parifh of faint Luke in the county of Middlefex.

CAP. XLIII.

An act for amending, widening, and keeping in repair, the road from the town of Hitchin in the county of Hertford, through the town of Shefford and Carrington Cotton End, to a lane oppofite a farm houfe called faint Leonard's, leading into the turnpike road from St. Alban's to the town of Bedford; and alfo the road from the turning out of the aforefaid road into Henlow Field to Gerford Bridge; and alfo the road from the town of Henlow, over Henlow bridge, to Arlefey in the county of Bedford.

CAP. XLIV.

An act for amending, widening, and keeping in repair, the road leading from Burleigh Bridge in the town of Loughborough, to Afhby de la Zouch in the county of Leicefter.

CAP. XLV.

An act for amending, widening, and keeping in repair, the roads from the eaft end of the town of Hertford in the county of Hertford, through Watton to Broadwater; and from the town of Ware, through Watton, to the north end of the towns of Walkern in the faid county.

CAP. XLVI.

An act for amending, widening, making commodious, and keeping in repair, the road from the Crofs Keys, otherwife Brickers Barn in the parifh of Corfham in the county of Wilts, to Bath Eafton Bridge in the county of Somerfet.

CAP. XLVII.

An act for making the river Blyth navigable from Halefworth Bridge in the county of Suffolk, into the haven of Southwould.

CAP. XLVIII.

An act for repairing and widening the road from Towcefter, through Silverfton and Brackley in the county of Northampton, and Ardley and

VOL. XXII.   O   Mid-

Middleton Stoney, to Weston gate in the parish of Weston on the Green in the county of Oxford.

CAP. XLIX.

An act for repairing and widening the road from Markfield turnpike in the county of Leicester, over Charley, otherwise Charnwood forest, thro' the town of Whitwick; and from thence through Talbot Lane, to where the road leading from the town of Loughborough, to the town of Ashby de la Zouch in the said county, comes in from Ryley Lane, near to a place called Snape Gate.

CAP. L.

An act for amending, widening, and keeping in repair, the roads leading from the village of Milford in the county of Surry, through Petworth, to the top of Duncketon Hill, and from Petworth, to Stopham Bridge in the county of Sussex.

CAP. LI.

An act for explaining and amending several acts of parliament for repairing the roads between a place called the White Post, on Alconbury Hill and Wansford Bridge in the county of Huntingdon, and between Norman Cross Hill in the said county, and the city of Peterborough, with respect to the elections of new trustees, the power of compelling persons employed by the trustees in the execution of such acts, to deliver up such books and papers relating thereto as are in their custody, and also to the manner of summoning and holding the meetings of the trustees.

CAP. LII.

An act for enlarging the term and powers granted by an act passed in the twentieth year of the reign of his present Majesty, for repairing the high road leading from the north end of the Cow Cawsey, near the town of Newcastle upon Tyne, to the town of Belford; and from thence to Buckton Burn in the county of Northumberland; and for making the same more effectual.

CAP. LIII.

An act for enlarging the term and powers granted by two acts of parliament, one passed in the fourth year of the reign of his late majesty King George, and the other in the ninth year of the reign of his present Majesty, for repairing the highways from Crown Corner in the town of Reading, leading by and through the several parishes of Shinfield and Heckfield in the several counties of Berks, Wilts and Southampton, to Basingstoke in the county of Southampton.

CAP. LIV.

An act for enlarging the terms and powers granted by two several acts passed in the fourteenth year of his present Majesty, the one for repairing the roads from a place called the Red House near Doncaster, to Wakefield, and through the said town of Wakefield by Dewsbury, Hightown and Lightcliff, to the town of Halifax in the West Riding of the county of York; and the other for repairing the road from Wakefield to Pontefract, and from thence to a place called Weeland in the township of Hensall; and from Pontefract to Wentbridge in the township of Darrington in the west riding of the county of York.

CAP. LV.

An act for rebuilding the bridge over the river Ribble, between the townships of Preston and Penwortham, near a place called The Fish House in the county palatine of Lancaster.

CAP. LVI.

An act for rebuilding and keeping in repair the shire hall of the county of Warwick.

CAP.

CAP. LVII.

An act for enlarging the term and powers granted by an act passed in the twenty sixth year of the reign of his present Majesty, intituled, *An act for repairing several roads leading into the city of* Glasgow, *so far as the same* relates to certain roads mentioned in the said act; and also to enlarge the term and powers granted by an act passed in the twenty seventh year of the reign of his present Majesty, intituled, *An act to explain, amend, and render more effectual an act passed in the twenty sixth year of the reign of his present Majesty,* intituled, An act for repairing several roads leading into the city of Glasgow; and to repair several other roads leading into the said city; and for building a bridge cross the river of Inchinnan.

CAP. LVIII.

An act for enlarging the term, and amending and altering several powers granted by an act made in the twentieth year of his present Majesty's reign, for opening, cleansing, repairing and improving the haven of Southwould in the county of Suffolk.

CAP. LIX.

An act for building a bridge over the river Lea, at or near a place called Jeremy's Ferry; and for making, repairing, and widening roads from thence into the great roads at Snaresbrook in the county of Essex, and at Clapton in the county of Middlesex.

CAP. LX.

An act for repairing and widening the road from the north end of Dapdon Wharf in the parish of Stoke, next Guldeford, through Guldeford to Andrew's Cross, and to Alford Bars in the county of Surry, and from thence to Saint Mary's Gate in Arundel in the county of Sussex.

CAP. LXI.

An act for repairing the road from a place called The Golden Farmer, near Bagshot in the county of Surrey, to Hertfordbridge hill in the county of Southampton.

CAP. LXII.

An act for making the river Ivel, and the branches thereof navigable, from the river Ouze at Tempsford in the county of Bedford, to Shotling Mill, otherwise called Burnt Mill in the parish of Hitchin in the county of Hertford; and to Black Horse Mill in the parish of Bygrave in the said county of Hertford; and to the south and north bridges in the town of Shefford in the said county of Bedford.

CAP. LXIII.

An act for building a bridge or bridges cross the river of Thames, from a certain place in Old Brentford in the parish of Ealing in the county of Middlesex, known by the name of Smith or Smith's Hill, to the opposite shore in the county of Surry.

CAP. LXIV.

An act for enlarging the terms and powers granted by two acts of parliament of the first and seventeenth years of the reign of his present Majesty, for repairing and amending several roads leading to and from the Borough of Evesham in the county of Worcester; and for explaining and making more effectual the said acts; and also for amending, widening and keeping in repair, several other roads in the counties of Worcester, Warwick and Gloucester.

CAP. LXV.

An act for cleansing, paving and lightening the streets of the city of Bath, and liberties thereof; and for regulating chairmen; and also for the keeping a sufficient and well regulated watch in the night time, in the

said

faid city and liberties; and to oblige all owners of houfes, and other buildings within the faid city and liberties, to bring down the water from the roofs of their houfes, and other buildings, by proper pipes, down the fides or walls of fuch houfes and buildings; and alfo to oblige all coal carriages to pafs by the borough walls of the faid city during the night feafon.

CAP. LXVI.

An act to explain, amend, aud render more effectual, an act made in the laft feffion of parliament, *For repairing and widening feveral roads leading from a gate called* Poole Gate *in the town and county of* Poole.

CAP. LXVII.

An act for enlarging the terms and powers granted by an act paffed in the twelfth year of the reign of his prefent Majefty, for repairing and enlarging the highways between the top of Kingfdown Hill and the city of Bath, and for amending feveral other highways therein mentioned, leading to the faid city; and alfo for repairing feveral other roads therein mentioned.

CAP. LXVIII.

An act for repairing and widening the roads leading from Spalding High Bridge, through Littleworth, and by Froguall, and over James Deeping Stone Bridge in the county of Lincoln, to Maxey Outgang in the county of Northampton, adjoining the high road there.

CAP. LXIX.

An act for amending, widening, and keeping in repair, the roads from the town of Wrexham in the county of Denbigh, to Pentre Bridge in the county of Flint; and from the town of Mold, to Northopp, Holywell and Rhuddlan in the fame county; and from thence to the Ferry Houfe oppofite to the town of Conway in the county of Carnarvon; and from Ruthin to the faid town of Mold.

Anno Regni GEORGII II. Regis Magnæ Britanniæ, Franciæ, & Hiberniæ, tricefimo primo.

AT the parliament begun and holden at Weftminfter, *the thirty-firft day of* May, Anno Dom. *one thoufand feven hundred and fifty four, in the twenty feventh year of the reign of our fovereign lord* George *the Second, by the grace of God, of* Great Britain, France, *and* Ireland, *King, defender of the faith,* &c. *And from thence continued by feveral prorogations to the firft day of* December *one thoufand feven hundred and fifty feven, being the fifth feffion of this prefent parliament.*

CAP. I.

An act for continuing certain laws made in the laft feffion of parliament, for prohibiting the exportation of corn, malt, meal,

meal, flour, bread, bifcuit, and ftarch; and for prohibit-
ing the making of low wines and fpirits, from wheat,
barley, malt, or any other fort of grain, or from meal or
flour; and to allow the tranfportation of wheat, barley,
oats, meal, and flour, to the Ifle *of Man, for the ufe of*
the inhabitants there; and for reviving and continuing an
act made in the fame feffion, for difcontinuing the duties
upon corn and flour imported, and upon corn, grain, meal,
bread, bifcuit, and flour, taken from the enemy; and to
permit the importation of corn and flour into Great Britain
and Ireland, *in neutral fhips; and to authorize his Ma-*
jefty, with the advice of his privy council, to order and
permit the exportation of fuch quantities of the commodi-
ties aforefaid, as may be neceffary for the fuftentation of
any forces in the pay of Great Britain, *or of thofe of his*
Majefty's allies acting in fupport of the common caufe;
and to prohibit the payment of any bounty upon the expor-
tation of any of the faid commodities to be made during
the continuance of this act.

WHEREAS the laws herein after-mentioned are near ex- Preamble.
piring, and it is expedient that the fame fhould be further continued; may it therefore pleafe your Majefty that it
may be enacted, and be it enacted by the King's moft excellent
majefty, by and with the advice and confent of the lords fpiritual and temporal, and commons, in this prefent parliament
affembled, and by the authority of the fame, That an act made 2 acts of 30
in the laft feffion of parliament, intituled, *An act to prohibit, for* Geo. 2.
a time to be limited, the exportation of corn, malt, meal, flour, bread,
bifcuit, and ftarch; and alfo an act made in the fame feffion, intituled, *An act to prohibit, for a limited time, the making of low*
wines and fpirits from wheat, barley, malt, or any other fort of
grain, or from any meal or flour; fhall be, and the fame are here- continued to
by further continued, from the expiration thereof refpectively, 24 Dec. 1758.
until the twenty fourth day of *December,* one thoufand feven
hundred and fifty eight.

II. Provided always, and be it enacted by the authority a- Corn may be
forefaid, That the faid act, intituled, *An act to prohibit, for a* exported from
time to be limited, the exportation of corn, malt, meal, flour, bread, Southampton
bifcuit, and ftarch, or any thing therein contained, fhall not ex- and Exeter, to
tend to any wheat, barley, oats, meal, or flour, to be tranfport- the Ifle of
ed out of or from the ports of *Southampton* or *Exeter* only, unto Man, for the
the *Ifle of Man,* for the only ufe of the inhabitants of that ifland, ufe of the in-
fo as the exporter, before the lading of fuch wheat, barley, oats, habitants
meal, or flour, or laying the fame on board, do become bound there,
with other fufficient fecurity (which the cuftomer or comptroller the exporter
of either of the faid ports refpectively, hath hereby power to take giving fecuri-
in his Majefty's name, and to his Majefty's ufe, and for which ty.

security no fee or reward shall be given, or taken) that such wheat, barley, oats, meal, or flour, shall be landed in the said *Isle of Man* (the danger of the seas only excepted) for the use of the inhabitants there, and shall not be landed or sold in any other parts whatsoever, and to return the like certificates of the landing the same there, as are by the said act required on the exportation of the said commodities to the *British* colonies in *America*, and within the time for that purpose therein mentioned, and so as the whole quantity of wheat, barley, oats, meal, or flour, which at any time or times after the passing of this act, and before the said twenty fourth day of *December*, shall be shipped at both the said ports for the said *Isle of Man* as aforesaid, shall not exceed in the whole, two thousand five hundred quarters, one moiety whereof to be exported at the said port of *Southampton*, and the other moiety thereof to be exported at the said port of *Exeter*; any thing in the said act, or any other act to the contrary notwithstanding.

Quantity exported not to exceed 2,500 quarters in the whole.

III. And whereas an act made in the last session of parliament, intituled, *An act to discontinue, for a limited time, the duties upon corn and flour imported, and also upon such corn, grain, meal, bread, biscuit, and flour, as have been or shall be taken from the enemy, and brought into this kingdom,* is expired, and it is necessary that the same should be revived and continued; be it therefore enacted by the authority aforesaid, That the said act shall be, and the same is hereby revived, and shall continue and be in force, until the twenty fourth day of *December*, one thousand seven hundred and fifty eight.

Act of 30 Geo. 2. continued to 24 Dec. 1758;

IV. And be it further enacted by the authority aforesaid, That it shall be lawful, during the continuance of the said act, and under the regulations therein mentioned, for any person or persons whatsoever, to import and bring into this kingdom, in any ship or vessel belonging to *Great Britain*, or to any kingdom or state in amity with his Majesty, his heirs, or successors, from any part or place whatsoever, corn and flour duty-free; and that it shall be lawful at any time or times before the said twenty fourth day of *December*, for any person or persons whatsoever, to import and bring into the kingdom of *Ireland*, in any ship or vessel belonging to any kingdom or state in amity with his Majesty, his heirs, or successors, corn and flour from any port or place whatsoever; any act or acts of parliament to the contrary notwithstanding.

during which time, corn and flour may be imported into Great Britain or Ireland duty-free, from foreign states in amity with the King.

V. And whereas it may become necessary, in case of exigency, to export certain quantities of the commodities aforesaid, for the supply and sustentation of any forces in the pay of *Great Britain*, or of those of his Majesty's allies, acting in support of the common cause; be it provided and enacted by the authority aforesaid, That, in case of such exigency, it shall and may be lawful to and for his Majesty, at any time during the continuance of this act, by and with the advice of his privy council, from time to time, to order and permit to be exported from *Great Britain* or *Ireland*, for the only use, supply, and sustentation

In case of exigency, the King may permit corn, &c. to be exported for the supply of for-

tation of the faid forces, fuch quantities of the aforefaid com- ces in his pay,
modities as fhall be neceffary for that purpofe, and in fuch or thofe of his
manner, as his Majefty fhall think fit to direct; any thing in allies.
this or any other act to the contrary in any wife notwithftanding.

VI. Provided always, That, during the continuance of this No bounty to
act, the bounty or bounties granted by any law upon the expor- be paid on
tation of any of the commodities before-mentioned, fhall not be corn, &c. ex-
allowed or paid to any perfon upon the exportation thereof out ported.
of this kingdom to any place whatfoever, or by whatfoever authority the fame may be exported; any thing in this or any
other act of parliament to the contrary notwithftanding.

CAP. II.

An act for continuing and granting to his Majefty certain duties upon
malt, mum, cyder, and perry, for the fervice of the year one thoufand feven hundred and fifty eight.

CAP. III.

An act for allowing the importation of fuch fine Italian or-
ganzine filk into this kingdom from any port or place what-
foever, as fhall have been fhipped on or before the day
therein mentioned.

WHEREAS by an act paffed the laft feffion of parlia- Preamble, re-
ment, intituled, *An act for the importation of fine organ-* citing claufe
zined Italian *thrown filk*; it was (among other things) enacted, in act 30 G. 2.
that it fhould and might be lawful for any perfon or perfons to
import or bring into this kingdom from any port or place, or
in any fhip or veffel whatfoever until the firft day of *December*,
one thoufand feven hundred and fifty feven, organzined thrown
filk of the growth or production of *Italy*; and that all fuch organzined thrown filk as was allowed to be imported by the faid
act, wherefoever landed, fhould be brought to his Majefty's
cuftom-houfe at *London*, to the intent that no other fort of
thrown filk might be imported than that allowed by the faid
act: and whereas, in purfuance of the faid act, large quantities
of fuch filk were bought and fent over land through *Germany*,
and in all probability would have arrived at *London* fome time
before the expiration of the faid act, if the carriage thereof by
land had not been protracted by rains and inundations in *Italy*;
and if the faid filk, when fhipped, had not been detained in
port by ftorm and contrary winds, fo that the faid filk could not
poffibly arrive before the time limited by the faid act: and
whereas the greateft part of the faid filk is, fince that time, arrived in the river of *Thames*: and whereas, if the fame is not
admitted to be entered, the perfons, whofe property the faid
filk is, will be great fufferers; be it therefore enacted by the
King's moft excellent majefty, by and with the advice and confent of the lords fpiritual and temporal, and commons, in this
prefent parliament affembled, and by the authority of the fame,

Importation
allowed of
such fine Ita-
lian organzine
silk, as was
shipped on or
before 30 Nov.
1757, under
the regulati-
ons in the re-
cited act.

That it shall and may be lawful to and for any person or persons to import and bring into this kingdom from any port or
place, and in any ship or vessel whatsoever, all such fine organzine thrown silk of the growth or production of *Italy*, and
of the quality described by the said act, as shall appear by the
several bills of lading, and the oaths of the respective captains,
to have been shipped on or before the thirtieth day of *November*, one thousand seven hundred and fifty seven, under, and
subject to, such penalties and forfeitures as are in the said act
mentioned; any thing in the said recited act, or any other law
or statute, to the contrary notwithstanding.

C A P. IV.

An act for granting an aid to his Majesty by a land tax, to be raised in
Great Britain, for the service of the year one thousand seven hundred
and fifty eight; and for inforcing the payment of the rates to be assessed upon Somerset House in the Strand. *Four shillings in the pound.*

C A P. V.

An act for punishing mutiny and desertion; and for the better payment
of the army and their quarters.

C A P. VI.

An act for the regulation of his Majesty's marine forces while on shore.

C A P. VII.

An act for appointing commissioners for putting in execution an act of
this session of parliament, intituled, *An act for granting an aid to his Majesty, by a land tax to be raised in Great Britain, for the service of the year
one thousand seven hundred and fifty eight ; and for enforcing the payment of
the rates to be assessed upon Somerset House in the Strand*; and for rectifying
a mistake in the said act; and for allowing farther time to the receivers
of certain aids, for setting *insuper* for monies in arrear.

C A P. VIII.

*An act for enlarging the terms and powers granted and con-
tinued by several acts of parliament, for repairing the
harbour of* Dover *in the county of* Kent.

WHEREAS by an act of parliament made and passed in
the eleventh and twelfth years of the reign of his late
majesty King *William* the Third, intituled, *An act for the repair
of* Dover *harbour*, several rates and duties were charged upon
coals, and upon ships and vessels, in order to raise a sum, not
exceeding thirty thousand one hundred pounds, to be applied
for repairing and perfecting the said harbour of *Dover*, under
such rates and directions, and with such penalties and other
provisions for the levying and recovering the same, as are therein mentioned, inserted, and contained; and which rates, duties, and provisions, were to take place and commence from the
first day of *May*, one thousand seven hundred, and to continue
and be in force, until the first day of *May*, one thousand seven
hundred and nine; and by two subsequent acts, one of them
made

made in the second year of the reign of her late majesty Queen 2 Annæ.
Anne, and the other of them in the fourth year of the reign of 4 Geo. 1
his late majesty King *George* the First, were continued, and declared to be in force, until the first day of *May*, one thousand
seven hundred and twenty seven: and whereas by an act made and
passed in the ninth year of his late majesty King *George* the First, 9 Geo. 1
intituled, *An act for compleating the repairs of the harbour of Do-*
ver in the county of Kent; *and for restoring the harbour of* Rye *in*
the county of Sussex *to its ancient goodness*; after taking notice of
the said former acts relating to the harbour of *Dover*, and that
it was found that the said sum of thirty thousand one hundred
pounds was not sufficient for the purposes of the said former
acts; and that unless a further sum was raised, the said harbour
could not be effectually repaired and secured, according to the
intent of the said former acts; but that the useful works then
begun and carried on for the benefit of the publick, would be
wholly lost, and the said harbour again fall to decay, and the
town itself be in danger of being utterly lost and destroyed; and
also reciting, that the ancient harbour of *Rye* was formerly of
great use and benefit to trade and navigation, but the same was
then choaked up, and that it was necessary to open the same in
such manner as should be found most proper and expedient to
restore the said harbour; it was therefore enacted, That the
said acts respectively made in the eleventh and twelfth years of
the reign of King *William* the Third, and the second year of the
reign of Queen *Anne*, for the repair of *Dover* harbour, and every
clause, matter, or thing, in them, or either of them, contained,
and not altered by the said act of the ninth year of King *George*
the First, should continue, and be in full force and virtue, till
the first day of *May*, one thousand seven hundred and forty
four, for the purposes in that and the said former acts mentioned; and that the duty of three pence *per* ton, granted by the
said act of the eleventh and twelfth years of King *William* the
third, for the repair of *Dover* harbour, upon all ships and vessels therein described, should, from the first day of *May*, one
thousand seven hundred and twenty three, be collected and received, in such manner, and by such officers and persons respectively, as in and by the said act of the eleventh and twelfth
of King *William* the Third, was directed and appointed; and
should be appropriated, divided, and paid, for the benefit of the
said harbour of *Dover* and *Rye* respectively, in manner following; that is to say, one third thereof to the treasurer for *Dover*
harbour for the time being, to be applied to such uses and purposes as in and by the said former acts are directed; and the
other two thirds to the treasurer for the harbour of *Rye*, to be
appointed as therein after is directed: and whereas by an act 11 Geo.
made in the eleventh year of the reign of his present Majesty,
the said recited acts, and all the clauses, powers, penalties, and
forfeitures, authorities, articles, rules, and directions, therein
contained and prescribed, and then in force, should continue and
be in full force, and executed, from and after the expiration of
the

the term continued and granted by the said act of the ninth
year of the reign of his said late majesty King *George* the First,
for and during the further term of twenty one years, which term
will expire the first day of *May* one thousand seven hundred and
sixty five, old stile: and whereas the commissioners or trustees
acting under the authority of the former acts for the harbour of
Dover, did borrow upon the credit of the same acts the sum of
three thousand pounds, which hath been applied pursuant to
the directions and for the purposes of the said former acts, and
for the repayment thereof with interest, the rates and duties so
granted were charged and made a security to the person and
persons who advanced and lent the said sum, and the same doth
still remain due, and owing, and unsatisfied: and whereas great
progress hath been made in the works intended for the preservation and improvement of the harbour of *Dover*, but the works
proposed and directed to be done for that purpose have not been
perfected and compleated: and whereas it would tend greatly
to the preservation of his Majesty's ships of war, and the protection and encouragement of the trade of this kingdom, that
the said harbour of *Dover* should be effectually repaired, and
put in good order and condition, but the money arising by the
rates and duties granted and appropriated by the said former
act of the ninth year of the reign of King *George* the First, for
the repair of *Dover* harbour, will not be sufficient for that purpose, and for discharging the said sum of three thousand pounds
borrowed upon the credit of the former acts as aforesaid, unless
the terms for which the said rates and duties are granted by the
said former acts be enlarged, or some other provision be made
in that behalf: may it therefore please your Majesty that it may
be enacted, and be it enacted by the King's most excellent majesty, by and with the advice and consent of the lords spiritual
and temporal, and commons, in this present parliament assem-

A moiety of bled, and by the authority of the same, That from and after
the rates the expiration of the terms continued and granted by the said
granted by act passed in the ninth year of the reign of his late Majesty, and
former acts, by the said act of the eleventh year of his present Majesty, one
continued for moiety of the rates and duties granted and continued by the said
21 years. former acts, shall be granted and continued for the term of
twenty one years, and shall be collected and received in such
manner, and by such officers and persons respectively, as was
directed by the said act of King *William* the Third, with respect
Application to the duties thereby granted; and shall be applied for the be-
thereof. nefit and support of the harbour of *Dover*, and for the discharging the said sum of three thousand pounds, and such other money
as shall hereafter be borrowed and taken up upon any mortgage
for security to be made of the duties applicable for the benefit
The powers of the same harbour; and that all the provisions, powers, pe-
and regula- nalties and forfeitures contained in the said former acts of King
tions of the *William* the Third, King *George* the First, and his present Ma-
former acts, jesty, so far as they relate to the harbour of *Dover* (excepting
continued and only what concerns the rate of the duties to be collected, and
extended for the

the division of them into two parts, which is herein before other- the purpofes
wife provided for) fhall be and continue in as full force as they of this act.
now are, by virtue of the faid acts, for and during the faid
term of twenty one years, to commence from the expiration of
of the faid former terms granted and continued by the faid
acts.

II. And be it further enacted by the authority aforefaid, That Publick act.
this prefent act fhall be deemed, adjudged, and taken to be a
publick act, and be judicially taken notice of as fuch by all
judges, juftices, and other perfons whatfoever, without fpecially
pleading the fame.

CAP. IX.

An act to indemnify perfons who have omitted to qualify themfelves for
offices and employments; and to indemnify juftices of the peace, and
others, who have omitted to regifter their qualifications within the time
limited by law; and for giving further time for thofe purpofes, and the
filing of affidavits of articles of clerkfhip.

Preamble, reciting the feveral qualifying acts of 1 Geo. 1. 13 Car. 2.
15 Car. 2. 13 Car. 2. 18 Geo. 2. 30 Geo. 2. Further time, to 28 Nov.
1758, allowed to perfons who have omitted to qualify themfelves, as the
faid laws direct. Perfons qualifying themfelves in manner and within the
time appointed, recapacitated and indemnified. Further time allowed for
providing and ftamping admiffions into civil offices. Officers thereupon
recapacitated, and indemnified. Offices, &c. already avoided by judgement of a court, and filled up, confirmed. Provifo.

CAP. X.

An act for the encouragement of feamen employed in the royal
navy; and for eftablifhing a regular method for the punctual,
frequent, and certain payment of their wages; and for enabling them more eafily and readily to remit the fame for
the fupport of their wives and families; and for preventing frauds and abufes attending fuch payments.

WHEREAS the encouragement of feamen employed in the Preamble.
royal navy, will greatly tend to augment the marine force of
this realm, whereon, under the good providence and protection of God,
the fecurity of thefe kingdoms, and the fupport and prefervation of
their trade and commerce, do moft immediately depend: and whereas
by an act made in the firft year of the reign of his prefent Majefty, Act 1 Geo. 2.
intituled, An act for granting an aid to his Majefty, of five hundred thoufand pounds, towards difcharging wages due to feamen; and for the conftant, regular, and punctual payment of
feamens wages for the future; and for appropriating the fupplies granted in this prefent feffion of parliament; and for difpofing of the furplus of the money granted for half pay, for the
year one thoufand feven hnndred and twenty feven; and by ano-
ther act alfo made in the firft year of the reign of his prefent Majefty, Act 1 Geo. 2.
intituled, An act for encouraging feamen to enter into his Ma-
jefty's fervice; feveral provifions and regulations were enacted and
prefcribed, for the benefit and encouragement of the feamen employed
in the royal navy, and for preventing frauds and abufes in purchafing
of their wages or pay; which provifions and regulations, from various.

ous difficulties in carrying the same into execution, have been found, in a great measure, ineffectual to answer the purposes thereby intended: and whereas the establishing a regular method for the punctual, frequent, and certain payment of the wages or pay due to inferior officers and seamen employed in the royal navy; the enabling such officers and seamen more easily and readily to obtain such payments, and to allot and remit any part thereof for the support and relief of their wives and families; and the preventing, as far as may be, the unwary, the ignorant, or the necessitous, from being defrauded and injured by the extortion and usury of wicked and evil-designing persons, are of the utmost consequence to the publick service; therefore, for effectuating these important and compassionate purposes, be it enacted by the King's most excellent majesty, by and with the advice and consent of the lords spiritual and temporal, and commons, in this present parliament assembled, and by the authority of the same, That from and after the first day of *November*, one thousand seven hundred and fifty eight, if any seaman, or able-bodied landman, shall freely and voluntarily come before and enter his name with any commission officer or officers of the fleet, to be appointed for entering such volunteers, in order to serve in, or on board, any of the ships or vessels of his Majesty, his heirs, or successors, then fitting out for sea, or that shall be in want of men, and shall receive a certificate of his so doing from such commission officer or officers (who is or are hereby directed and required to make out and give such certificates, without fee or reward, and duly to date the same) and if such person shall forthwith proceed towards such ship or vessel, and shall make his personal appearance on board the same, within the space of fourteen days from the day of the date of such certificate, inclusive of the day of the date thereof, if the place where he so enters his name be not above one hundred miles distant from the port where such ship or vessel lies; or within the space of twenty days, if it be at a greater distance; or within the space of thirty days, if the place where he so enters his name be above two hundred miles distant; then, and in such case, every such person shall be and is hereby declared to be, intitled to wages from the day of the date of such certificate, inclusive of the day of the date thereof, and shall also be allowed the usual conduct money, and shall be paid an advance of two months wages at the first fitting out of such ship or vessel, and before such ship or vessel in which he shall serve shall proceed to sea.

Volunteer, entering his name with a proper officer,

and receiving a certificate thereof,

and appearing within a limited time on board the ship in which he is to serve, is intitled to wages from the date of his certificate; and to be paid conduct money, and an advance of two months wages.

II. *And for remedying the many inconveniencies, mistakes, and hardships, which arise from bearing any seamen or able-bodied landmen on board of his Majesty's ships, for any length of time, as supernumeraries, for victuals only*, be it further enacted by the authority aforesaid, That from and after the said first day of *November*, every seaman, or able-bodied landman, who shall be entered on the books of any ship or vessel belonging to his Majesty, his heirs, or successors, as supernumerary to the complement of such ship or vessel, shall be borne for, and intitled to, his wages,

Men borne on any ship's books as supernumeraries, are intitled to wages, &c.

wages, upon the books of the first, and of every other ship or vessel in which he shall serve for the space of ten days, and shall receive all other benefits and advantages as if he were part of the complement thereof.

on board the first and every other ship they shall serve in for 10 days, &c.

III. Provided always, That where such seaman, or able-bodied landman, shall have been lent from any ship or vessel belonging to his Majesty, his heirs, or successors, to any other such ship or vessel, such seaman, or able-bodied landman, shall continue to be borne for, and intitled to, his wages, upon the books of such ship or vessel from which he shall have been so lent, until he shall be regularly discharged from thence, and in no other; any thing herein contained to the contrary notwithstanding.

Men lent from one ship to another, are to be borne on the ship's books they were lent from, till discharged.

IV. And be it further enacted by the authority aforesaid, That from and after the said first day of *November*, in case any inferior officer or seaman shall be turned over from one ship or vessel in the service of his Majesty, his heirs, or successors, into any other such ship or vessel, either by order from the lord high admiral of *Great Britain*, or from the commissioners for executing the office of lord high admiral of *Great Britain*, or any three or more of them, or by order from any commander in chief of any squadron of such ships or vessels, in any port of *Great Britain*, or on the coast of the same, every such officer and seaman, in case such ship or vessel, into which he shall be so turned over, shall be in or shall come into any port of *Great Britain* where any commissioner of the navy shall be or reside, shall be paid, by proper pay lists to be made out, all the wages which shall appear to be due to him in the ship or vessel from which he shall be so turned over, before the ship or vessel, into which he shall be turned over, shall proceed to sea; unless it shall be otherwise directed by special order from the lord high admiral of *Great Britain*, or from the commissioners for executing the office of lord high admiral of *Great Britain*, or any three or more of them, in cases of the greatest exigency only: and if such ship or vessel, in pursuance of the said order, shall proceed to sea before such payment can possibly be made, then the said wages shall be paid as soon as ever such ship or vessel shall come again into any such port of *Great Britain* where any commissioner of the navy shall be or reside as aforesaid.

Inferior officer or seaman turned over to another ship, if such ship shall be or come into any port of Great Britain, where a commissioner of the navy shall be, is to be paid the wages due to him before such ship goes to sea, unless by the admiralty it be otherwise directed; in which case, he is to be paid as soon as the ship returns into port again.

V. Provided always, and be it further enacted by the authority aforesaid, That in case any officer or seaman shall be turned over from one ship or vessel in the service of his Majesty, his heirs or successors, into any other such ship or vessel; then, and in such case, such officer or seaman, so turned over, shall not serve or be rated in a worse quality, or lower degree or station, than he served in or was rated for in the ship or vessel from which he was turned over; and shall receive, over and above such wages as shall then be due to him, an advance of two months wages, before the ship or vessel into which he shall be so turned over shall proceed to sea, in case he shall not have received such advance

Persons turned over, are to be rated, and serve, as in the former ship; and to be paid their wages then due, and two months pay in advance, if none be received before.

vance in any of the ships or veffels from which he shall be fo turned over.

VI. *And, to the intent that all arrears of feamens wages, and their growing wages, may be conftantly, regularly, and punctually paid;* be it further enacted by the authority aforefaid, That from and out of fuch monies as have been or shall be granted in this feffion of parliament, for the fervice of the navy; and alfo from and out of all fuch fupplies as shall be hereafter granted in parliament, for any naval fervices, fuch fums of money shall, in the firft place, be appropriated, and shall, from time to time, be iffued and applied, as shall be fufficient for the conftant, regular, and punctual payment of all tickets that shall be made out in the manner herein after directed, for the wages or pay due to any officer or feaman; and alfo for the conftant, regular, and punctual difcharge of all wages or pay now due, or to grow due, upon any ship's books, to any officer or feaman employed in the royal navy, in manner following; that is to fay, That from time to time, and at all times, from and after the faid firft day of *November*, when and fo often as any of the ships or veffels of his Majefty, his heirs, or fucceffors, shall have been in fea pay twelve whole months, or more, if fuch ship or veffel shall then be, or shall arrive, in any port of *Great Britain*, or on the coaft thereof, the captain or commander of fuch ship or veffel shall immediately make out, or caufe to be made out, five complete pay books for all the officers and feamen belonging to the faid ship or veffel, for all the time that fuch ship or veffel shall have been in fea pay, except the laft fix months; to which time, *videlicet*, the laft fix months, the wages due upon all fuch ships or veffels are hereby intended to be cleared; and shall forthwith fend or tranfmit, by the firft fafe opportunity, fuch pay books, together with three alphabets, and a flop book, to the commiffioners of the navy, at their board; and whenfoever or as foon as any fuch ship or veffel, having been twelve whole months or more in fea pay as aforefaid, shall be or arrive in any port of *Great Britain* where any commiffioner of the navy shall be or refide, the faid commiffioners of the navy, at their board, are hereby ftrictly directed and required to follicit fuch fums of money as shall be fufficient, and as foon as the fame shall be iffued, to caufe immediate payment to be made of all the wages due upon the faid pay books as aforefaid, to all fuch officers and feamen, their executors or adminiftrators, or to the refpective attorney or attornies of fuch officers or feamen, their executors or adminiftrators duly authorized as is herein after directed, deducting thereout whatever monies shall have been paid before by way of advance, or that shall ftand againft them in the books of fuch ships or veffels, on account of any defalcation; leaving always fix months wages, and no more, due to fuch officers and feamen for their fervice in fuch ship or veffel, unpaid and in arrear: and whenever any of the ships or veffels of his Majefty, his heirs, or fucceffors, shall return home in order to be laid up, all the wages due to the officers and feamen ferving on

board

Marginal notes

Monies are to be appropriated and iffued, in the firft place, out of the grants for naval fervices, fufficient for the regular payment of feamens tickets,

viz. If a ship shall be in fea pay twelve months, or more, and lie in port, or on the coaft of Great Britain, the captain is to make out 5 pay books (except for the laft 6 months)

and tranfmit them, with 3 alphabets, and a flop book, to the navy board.

On the ship's arrival where a commiffioner is, money is to be follicited, and payment immediately to be made,

deducting advance money and defalcation.

Ships laid up are to be paid off within 2 months.

board of any such ship or vessel, shall be entirely paid off as soon as may be, or within two months at farthest after the arrival of such ship or vessel in the port where the same is designed to be laid up: and it is hereby declared, That the computation of the said month's wages shall be by reckoning twenty eight days to the month, according to the usual course or practice of the navy.

Month to consist of 28 days.

VII. *And whereas inferior officers and seamen are frequently absent, either with the leave of the commanding officer, or upon duty, at the time of the payment of the ship or vessel to which they belong;* therefore, for enabling such officers or seamen to receive their wages or pay with as little delay as possible; be it enacted by the authority aforesaid, That from and after the said first day of *November,* whensoever and as often as any application shall be made to the commissioners of the navy, at their board, by any such inferior officer or seaman, who shall then be in the service of his Majesty, his heirs, or successors, and who shall have been so absent at the payment of the ship or vessel whereunto he did belong as aforesaid, or from the captain or commander of any ship or vessel of his Majesty, his heirs, or successors, on board of which such officer or seaman shall then serve, in case such ship or vessel shall be in any port where any commissioner of the navy shall be or reside; then the commissioners of the navy, at their board, shall immediately, upon such application, cause the pay books of such ship or vessel so paid, or pay lists for such officers and seamen so unpaid made out from them, to be sent, without any delay, to the commissioner of the navy at the port where such ship or vessel shall be to which such officers or seamen shall then belong; and such commissioner of the navy shall forthwith cause payment to be made to the said officers and seamen of the wages or pay which they were entitled to receive on the payment of such ship or vessel, as aforesaid.

Upon application to the navy board, the pay books are to be sent down to a commissioner, for paying off such men then in the service as shall have been absent at the payment of the ship.

VIII. *And whereas many inconveniencies and frauds have arisen for want of a proper regulation with respect to making out, and to the payment of, the tickets of inferior officers and seamen;* be it therefore enacted by the authority aforesaid, That from and after the said first day of *November,* if any inferior officer or seaman shall die in the service of his Majesty, his heirs, or successors, the captain or commander of the ship or vessel in which such officer or seaman served at the time of his death, shall, as soon as may be after his death, make out a ticket for the wages or pay due to such officer or seaman at the time of his death; which ticket the said captain or commander shall sign himself, and shall cause to be signed by the proper signing officers of such ship or vessel, and shall send or transmit the said ticket so made out and signed as aforesaid, by the first safe opportunity, to the commissioners of the navy, at their board, for the use of the executors or administrators of such officer or seaman: and the said commissioners of the navy shall immediately cause the day of the receipt of such ticket to be indorsed thereon; and such ticket shall be forthwith examined and shall, by three or

Upon the death of an inferior officer or seaman, the captain is to make out a ticket for his pay, and transmit the same to the navy board; for the use of the executors.

Day of receipt to be indorsed thereon; and the ticket to be more examined, and

more of the said commissioners of the navy, be assigned for
payment as soon as may be, or within one mouth at farthest, to
be computed from the day of the making such indorsement;

and to be de-
livered to the
executors,

and the said ticket being so assigned for payment, shall, without
any fee or reward whatsoever, be delivered, upon demand, to
the executors or administrators of such officer or seaman, or to
their respective attorney or attornies, to be duly authorized as is
herein after directed;

and the money due thereon shall, with-
out any fee or reward whatsoever, be paid to such executors or
administrators, or to their respective attorney or attornies as
aforesaid, as soon as such ticket shall be brought to the pay office of the navy.

Captain to re-
port inferior
officer or sea-
man fit to be
discharged as
unserviceable;

IX. And be it further enacted by the authority aforesaid,
That from and after the said first day of *November*, when and
so often as any inferior officer or seaman, in the service of his
Majesty, his heirs, or successors, shall, by wounds, sickness, or
any other manifest infirmity, be disabled and rendered unserviceable, in case such officer or seaman shall be on board of any ship
or vessel which shall then be in any port of *Great Britain*, or
on the coast thereof, or which shall belong to any squadron of
his Majesty's ships or vessels which shall not be in any port of
Great Britain, or on the coast thereof, the captain or commander
of such ship or vessel, shall represent the same to the commander
in chief of any squadron of his Majesty's ships or vessels, who
is hereby directed carefully to inquire into, and to examine the
same; and if he shall be fully satisfied thereof, such commander
in chief shall order such captain or commander to discharge such
officer or seaman, and to make out and sign, in the usual form,
a ticket for the wages or pay then due to such officer or seaman;

and upon dis-
charge grant-
ed, to make
out a ticket
for his pay,
&c.

or if such ship or vessel shall not be in any port of *Great Britain*,
or on the coast thereof, and shall not belong to any squadron of
ships or vessels of his Majesty, his heirs, or successors, or shall
be separated from the commander in chief of any squadron to
which such ship or vessel shall belong, then the captain or commander of such ship or vessel, being fully satisfied of such disability, shall discharge such officer or seaman, and shall make out
such ticket without the direction of any such commander in
chief, and shall sign the same himself, and cause it to be signed
by the proper signing officers, as aforesaid: and whenever any
such officer or seaman, so disabled and rendered unserviceable,
shall be discharged, and such ticket shall be so made out for such
officer or seaman, and shall be signed in the manner herein be-

and deliver to
him a certifi-
cate of his
discharge,

fore directed, such captain or commander shall, at the same
time, grant and deliver to such officer or seaman, without fee or
reward, a certificate of his discharge, containing an exact copy
of the said ticket, and a description of the person for whom such
ticket was so made out; which ticket shall not, upon any account or pretence whatsoever, be delivered to such officer or

seaman, but such captain or commander shall send or transmit
the same, by the first safe opportunity, to the commissioners of
the navy, at their board, for the use of such officer or seaman;
and

and the said commissioners shall immediately cause the day when they shall receive such ticket to be endorsed thereon, and such ticket shall be forthwith examined, and shall, by three or more of the said commissioners, be assigned for payment, as soon as may be, or within one month at farthest from the day of the making of such endorsement : and in case such officer or seaman shall present the said certificate of his discharge at the navy office, the said commissioners of the navy, or any of them, shall forthwith examine the said certificate, and the person presenting the same, and being satisfied that the said certificate was made out for the said person, and that he is rendered unserviceable, shall sign and testify the same on such certificate ; and the said ticket, being so assigned for payment, shall, without any fee or reward whatsoever, be immediately delivered to such officer or seaman to whom such certificate of discharge shall have been granted as aforesaid, and to no other person whatsoever, and the money due thereon shall, without any fee or reward, be paid to such officer or seaman, and to no other person whatsoever, as soon as such ticket shall be brought to the pay office of the navy ; or if the said ticket shall not have been transmitted to, and received by the said commissioners of the navy, at their board, then the said certificate shall be forthwith examined as aforesaid, and the money appearing to be due on the said ticket, by the copy thereof contained in the said certificate, shall be paid to the person producing the same, as aforesaid, and to no other person whatsoever, in like manner as if the said original ticket had been transmitted and received : and in case any officer or seaman, so discharged, shall be desirous to receive his wages or pay at any port of *Great Britain* where a commissioner of the navy shall be or reside, and shall present to such commissioner the certificate of his discharge ; the said commissioner upon examining such certificate, and the person so presenting the same, and being satisfied that the said certificate was made out for the said person, and that he is rendered unserviceable, shall sign and testify the same on such certificate, and transmit such certificate to the commissioners of the navy, at their board, who are hereby strictly charged and required, within four days after the receipt of such certificate, to cause the ticket made out and transmitted to them for such officer or seaman, and assigned for payment as aforesaid ; or if such ticket shall not have been transmitted to, and received by them, then the said certificate, containing a copy of the said ticket, instead thereof ; to be sent to the said commissioner of the navy at such port, who shall cause the money due thereon to be immediately paid at such port, to such officer or seaman applying for the same, and intitled thereto, without any fee, reward, or deduction whatsoever ; and the commissioner of the navy at such port where such certificate shall be so presented, shall send such officer or seaman, so presenting the same, with an order to the nearest hospital, who shall receive such officer or seaman, and victual him from the time

Marginal notes:

who are to endorse the day of receipt thereon, and examine the ticket, and assign it for payment ; and if presentment be made of the certificate, they are to examine, and sign the same, if satisfied therewith ; and deliver the ticket thereupon to the owner, and the money to be paid.

If the ticket be not transmitted or received, the certificate alone, when examined, &c. is sufficient.

If the certificate be presented to a commissioner in any of the ports in Great Britain, he is to examine and sign the same, if satisfied therewith, and transmit it to the navy board, &c. who are to order payment to be made thereupon at such port,

and the commissioner is to send such disabled man, with an order, to the nearest hospital, till

Payment of his wages.

time he shall present such certificate, until he shall be so paid the wages or pay due to him as aforesaid.

If the certificate should be lost or destroyed,

X. Provided always, and it is hereby further enacted by the authority aforesaid, That in case any such certificate herein before directed to be granted and delivered to such inferior officer or seaman, so discharged, on account of being rendered unserviceable, as aforesaid, should happen to be lost or destroyed; or if

or the person not appear, and present the same,

any such officer or seaman should not appear in person, and present the same to the commissioners of the navy, at their board, or to the commissioner of the navy at any such port in *Great Britain*, as aforesaid; in either of which cases, the wages or pay due to such officer or seaman, would not be payable by virtue

or the money due on the ticket be not paid before the general payment of the ship; the ticket is to be cancelled, and the wages to be paid to the executors, &c.

of the said ticket so made out for him; or if the wages or pay due upon such ticket, shall not be paid before the general payment of the ship's company; then, and in every such case, the said commissioners of the navy, at their board, shall cause such ticket to be cancelled, and all such wages or pay shall accrue and become payable to such officer or seaman, his executors or administrators, or to the respective attorney or attornies of such officer or seaman, his executors or administrators, demanding the same, and duly authorized as is herein after directed, when the wages or pay due upon such ship or vessel shall be paid, in the manner prescribed by this act; and as if such ticket and certificate had never been made out or granted; any thing herein contained, or any law or usage to the contrary, notwithstanding.

Captain to make out sick tickets for those set ashore, and transmit the same with the sick persons to the hospital;

XI. And be it further enacted by the authority aforesaid, That from and after the said first day of *November*, when and so often as any inferior officer or seaman belonging to any ship or vessel of his Majesty, his heirs, or successors, shall, by order of the captain or commander of such ship or vessel, be set sick ashore, and be sent into any hospital, or sick quarters, for his recovery, such captain or commander shall, at the same time, make out a sick ticket for the wages or pay then due to such officer or seaman, and shall sign the same himself, and cause it to be signed by the proper signing officers as aforesaid; which sick ticket being so made out, and signed, shall be transmitted along with such officer or seaman to such hospital or sick quarters: and if such officer or seaman not being cured in such hospital, or sick quarters, shall be regularly discharged from thence

and if any be discharged as unserviceable, a certificate thereof, with the sick ticket annex'd, is to be granted him; which being presented to a commissioner, is to be signed by him, if satisfied there-

as unserviceable, then a certificate of such discharge, together with the said sick ticket annexed thereunto, shall be granted and delivered to him; and in case he shall present the same to the commissioner of the navy that shall be or reside at any port in *Great Britain*, such commissioner of the navy, upon examining the person presenting the same, and being duly satisfied that he is rendered unserviceable, shall sign and testify the same on such certificate, and shall forthwith transmit such certificate, together with the said sick ticket annexed thereunto, to the commissioners of the navy, at their board, who are hereby strictly charged and required immediately to cause the day when they shall receive the same to be indorsed thereon, and such certificate and sick

ticket

ticket annexed thereunto, to be examined by the muster books, if received, and a proper ticket or pay list, in the usual form, to be made out within four days after the receipt of such certificate and sick ticket, for the payment of all wages or pay due to such officer or seaman; and shall send such ticket or pay list without any delay to the said commissioner of the navy at such port, who shall, without any fee or reward whatsoever, cause the money due thereon to be immediately paid to such officer or seaman applying for the same, and intitled thereunto; who notwithstanding such discharge, shall be kept and maintained in such hospital, or sick quarters, from the time he shall present such certificate and sick ticket annexed thereunto, until he shall be so paid the wages or pay due to him, as aforesaid.

with, and transmitted with the ticket to the navy board, who are to examine and indorse the same, and make out a pay list,

and the party is to be kept in sick quarters till payment.

XII. Provided always, and it is hereby further enacted by the authority aforesaid, That in case the muster books or pay books for any such ship or vessel shall not be regularly transmitted to, and received by, the commissioners of the navy, in the manner herein before prescribed, yet the payment of the tickets, or certificates containing copies thereof, or pay lists, herein before directed to be made out or granted, shall not be delayed or postponed for such omission; but if any error, to the detriment of the publick treasure, shall be made in any such ticket, or certificate containing a copy thereof, or pay lists, by the captain or commander issuing or making out the same, the loss arising by such error shall be made good and compensated out of any wages or pay due or to grow due to such captain or commander by whom such ticket, or certificate, or pay list, was so made out or granted as aforesaid.

Payment of tickets, certificates, or pay lists, not to be delayed, for want of the muster or pay books not being duly sent to the navy board. If error be made in any ticket, the loss is to be made good out of the captain's wages.

XIII. And, in order to enable inferior officers and seamen employed abroad to remit any part of their wages or pay for the support of their wives and families, without any expence or delay, and free from usurious oppressions; be it further enacted by the authority aforesaid, That from and after the said first day of *November*, when and so often as any such ship or vessel which shall not be in any port of *Great Britain*, or on the coast thereof, shall have twelve months wages or pay due, the captain or commander of such ship or vessel shall read over, or cause to be read over, in a distinct audible manner, the names of all the inferior officers and seamen belonging to such ship or vessel, and shall cause every such officer and seaman to answer to his name; and shall do the same, from time to time, at the end of every six months, as long as such ship or vessel shall have twelve months, or more, wages or pay due as aforesaid: and if any such officer or seaman shall thereupon declare by word of mouth, or deliver in writing, the name and place of abode of his wife, father, or mother, and desire that the whole, or any part, of his wages or pay then due (except the wages or pay that shall be due for the last six months of his service on board such ship or vessel) should be allotted and paid to his said wife, father, or mother, by the receiver general of the land tax for any county, riding, or city, in *Great Britain*, or by the collector of the customs

If a ship, not on the coast, or in a port of Great Britain, shall be in sea pay twelve months, the captain is to cause the ship's crew to be called over, and if any shall desire to remit his wages to his wife or parents,

the captain is to direct proper lists of such persons to be made out,

toms for any port, or collector of the excise for any collection in *Great Britain*, or by the clerk of the cheque at any of his Majesty's dock yards; then, and in such case, the captain or commander of such ship or vessel is hereby strictly required and enjoined to cause four lists to be made out, which shall contain the names of all such inferior officers and seamen as shall be desirous to remit to their wives, fathers, or mothers, the whole, or any part, of their wages or pay, except for the last six months of their service as aforesaid; in which lists, the amount of the wages or pay so desired to be paid, the name and place of abode of such officer or seaman's wife, father, or mother, to whom such wages or pay are to be remitted and paid, and the receiver-general of the land tax, collector of the customs, collector of the excise, or clerk of the cheque, by whom such wages are to be made payable, shall be specified and described in three separate distinct columns, opposite to the name of such

which are to be signed by them, and the proper officers, and transmitted to the navy board,

officer or seaman, in the said lists; and every such officer or seaman who shall so desire that any such part of his wages or pay may be allotted and paid to his wife, father, or mother, shall write his name, or make his mark, in a separate distinct column in the said lists; which lists shall be forthwith compleated, and signed by the captain or commander, and proper signing officers of such ship or vessel; and such captain or commander shall transmit the said lists, by the first safe opportunity, without any neglect or delay whatsoever, to the commissioners of the navy, at their board: and the said commissioners, upon receiving such lists wherein any such allotment shall be made by any such inferior officer or seaman, of any such part of his wages or pay, to

who are to make out two bills, duplicates, for such allotments,

his wife, father, or mother, shall immediately make out, or cause to be made out, two bills for every such allotment; which bills shall be duplicates, and joined together with oblique lines, flourishes, or devices, in such manner as the said commissioners, or

which are to be made, payable according to the appointment in the lists,

any three or more of them, shall think proper; and shall be made payable to the wife, father, or mother, respectively, of such inferior officer or seaman, by the receiver general of the land tax, collector of the customs, collector of the excise, or clerk of the cheque, respectively, according to the appointment

and signed by three commissioners.

in such lists; and the said bills, being numbered and dated, shall be signed by any three commissioners of the navy, and be written or printed according to the following form:

A. N° I.   Navy Office.

SIR,   *day of*

The form.

P AY *to* B. D. *of*   *in the county*

of { wife father mother } *of* E. D. { inferior officer, seaman, } *belonging*

to his Majesty's ship   *upon* { his her } *producing the duplicate hereof, together with a certificate, under the hands of the minister and churchwardens, or, in that part of* Great Britain *called* Scotland, *under the hands of the minister and two elders of the parish*

rish where the said B. D. $\left\{ \substack{\text{was married,} \\ \text{or resides,}} \right\}$ *that the said* B. D. *to the best of their knowledge and belief, is the* $\left\{ \substack{\text{wife} \\ \text{father} \\ \text{mother}} \right\}$ *of the said* E. D. *the sum of*   *being on account of the wages of the said* E. D. *if the same shall be demanded within six calendar months from the date hereof; otherwise you are to return this bill to the treasurer of the navy, at the pay office of the navy.*

To $\left\{ \begin{array}{l} \text{The receiver gene-} \\ \text{ral of the land} \\ \text{tax of the county} \\ \text{of} \\ \text{The collector of the} \\ \text{customs at the} \\ \text{port of} \\ \text{The collector of the} \\ \text{excise at} \\ \text{The clerk of the} \\ \text{cheque at} \end{array} \right.$ *Signed,* $\left\{ \begin{array}{l} \text{O. P.} \\ \text{Q. R.} \\ \text{S. T.} \end{array} \right\}$ $\substack{\textit{Commissioners} \\ \textit{of} \\ \textit{the navy.}}$

By virtue of the act of the thirty first George *the Second.*

N. B. *The personating or falsely assuming the name and character of the wife or relation of any inferior officer or seaman, or procuring any other to do the same, in order to receive wages due to such officer or seaman, is made felony without benefit of clergy, by thirty first* George *the Second.*

And as soon as the said bills shall be so made out and signed, the said commissioners of the navy shall cause them to be cut asunder, indentwise, through the oblique lines, flourishes, or devices; and shall cause one of the said bills to be transmitted forthwith to the person nominated and specified in such lists as the wife, father, or mother, of such officer or seaman, and the other of the said bills to be transmitted forthwith to the said receiver general of the land tax, collector of the customs, collector of the excise, or clerk of the cheque, on whom such bill shall be so drawn as aforesaid: and the said receiver general of the land tax, collector of the customs, collector of the excise, and clerk of the cheque, if the said duplicates of such bill shall be produced and delivered to either of them respectively within six calendar months from the date thereof, are hereby required and enjoined to examine such duplicate, together with the certificate to be produced as aforesaid; and to enquire into the truth thereof, by the oath of the person producing the same; which oath they are hereby respectively authorized and directed to administer; and upon being duly satisfied of the truth of such certificate, to testify the same on the back of such bill; and shall immediately pay to the wife, father, or mother, of such officer or seaman, without fee or reward on any pretence whatsoever, the sum con-

The bills to be cut out indentwise; and one to be sent to the person specified in the list, and the other to the person on whom the bill is drawn. Upon present-ment of the duplicate and certificate within six months, and examination of the truth certified on the back of the bill, the mo-ney to be paid;

tained

tained in such bill, taking his or her receipt for the same on the back thereof; which bill so paid, upon being produced and delivered, together with the duplicate thereof, at the navy office, shall be immediately assigned for payment by three or more commissioners of the navy; and shall be immediately repaid by the treasurer of the navy, to such receiver general of the land tax, collector of the customs, collector of the excise, clerk of the cheque, or to the order of any such receiver general, collector of the customs, collector of the excise, or clerk of the cheque respectively: but in case the duplicate of such bill shall not be produced and delivered, and the payment thereof be demanded, within six calendar months from the date thereof, or if a proper certificate of the person claiming to be the wife, father, or mother, of such officer or seaman, be not likewise produced, then the said receiver general, collector of the customs, collector of the excise, or clerk of the cheque, shall return such bill to the treasurer of the navy, at the pay office of the navy, who shall cause such bill to be immediately cancelled; and from and after the cancelling thereof, the sum contained in such bill shall accrue and become payable to such inferior officer or seaman for whose wages or pay it was made out, or to his executors or administrators, or to the respective attorney or attornies of such officer or seaman, his executors or administrators, demanding the same, and duly authorized as is herein after directed, without any fee, reward, or deduction whatsoever, when the wages or pay due upon such ship or vessel shall be paid, in the manner prescribed by this act.

XIV. And, for the better enabling inferior officers and seamen, upon payment being made to them of their wages or pay in the manner hereby before directed, to remit any part thereof to their wives, children, or parents, or to such other person as they shall judge proper; be it further enacted by the authority aforesaid, That from and after the said first day of *November*, when and so often as any wages or pay due to such inferior officer or seaman shall be paid at the pay office of the navy, or at any of the out ports, in the manner before prescribed, if such officer or seaman shall desire to receive a bill for the whole, or for any part of his said wages or pay, to be drawn upon the receiver general of the land tax for any county, riding, or city, in *Great Britain*, or upon any collector of the customs for any port, or collector of the excise for any collection in *Great Britain*, or upon the clerk of the cheque at any of his Majesty's dock yards; then, and in such case, two bills, being duplicates, and joined together with oblique lines, flourishes, or devices, as aforesaid, shall be immediately made out, numbered, and dated, by the clerk of the treasurer of the navy, appointed to pay such wages, and be signed, if made out at the pay office of the navy, by the commissioners of the navy comptrolling the payment when such bills shall be so made out; or if made out at any of the out ports, by the commissioner of the navy comptrolling such payment there; and such bills shall be attested at the foot thereof,

Marginal notes:

and the bill and duplicate to be returned to the navy board, and repaid by the treasurer.

If the duplicate and certificate be not tender'd, &c. within six months,

the bill is to be returned to the treasurer of the navy, and cancelled; and the money to be paid to the seaman, &c. when the ship is paid.

Bills to be made out, &c. in like manner, if a seaman, at the time of receiving his pay, shall desire to remit any part thereof to his wife, children, or parents, &c.

thereof, by the firſt clerk of the treaſurer of the navy at ſuch pay office or out port ; and the ſaid bills ſhall be made payable to ſuch perſon or perſons only, and by ſuch receiver general, collector of the cuſtoms, collector of the excise, or clerk of the cheque, as ſhall then be named by ſuch inferior officer or ſeaman, and inſerted in ſuch bills ; which ſhall be written or printed according to the following form :

A. Nº L.   day of

SIR,

PAY to B. C. of   on $\left\{ \begin{array}{c} his \\ her \\ theirs \end{array} \right\}$ producing and

, delivering the duplicate hereof, the ſum of being on account of the wages of D. E. mariner, on board of his Majeſty's ſhip the   if the ſame be demanded within ſix calendar months from the date hereof ; otherwiſe you are to return this bill to the treaſurer of the navy at the pay office of the navy.

Form of the bills.

To $\left\{ \begin{array}{l} \text{The receiver ge-} \\ \text{neral of the} \\ \text{land tax for} \\ \text{the county of} \\ \\ \text{The collector of} \\ \text{the cuſtoms at} \\ \text{the port of} \\ \text{The collector of} \\ \text{the exciſe at} \\ \text{The clerk of the} \\ \text{cheque at} \end{array} \right.$

Signed, $\left\{ \begin{array}{l} \text{F. G. Commiſ-} \\ \textit{ſioner of the} \\ \textit{navy.} \end{array} \right.$

Atteſted, $\left\{ \begin{array}{l} \text{H. J. Clerk to} \\ \textit{the treaſurer of} \\ \textit{the navy.} \end{array} \right.$

By virtue of the act of the thirty firſt of George the Second.

And ſo ſoon as the ſaid bill ſhall be made out, aſſigned, and atteſted, the ſaid commiſſioner of the navy ſhall cauſe them to be cut aſunder, indentwiſe through the oblique lines, flouriſhes, or devices, and ſhall cauſe one of the ſaid bills to be delivered to ſuch officer or ſeaman, and the other to be forthwith tranſmitted to the ſaid receiver general of the land tax, collector of the cuſtoms, collector of the exciſe, or clerk of the cheque, on whom ſuch bill ſhall be drawn as aforeſaid : and the ſaid receiver general of the land tax, collector of the cuſtoms, collector of the exciſe, or clerk of the cheque, are hereby ſtrictly required and enjoined, if the duplicate of ſuch bill ſhall, within ſix calendar months from the date thereof, be produced and delivered to either of them reſpectively, by the perſon or perſons to whom ſuch bill is payable, to pay to ſuch perſon or perſons immediately, without fee or reward on any pretence whatſoever, the ſum contained therein, taking his, her, or their receipt for the ſame, on the

Bills to be cut indentwiſe, and one to be delivered to the ſeaman, and the other to be remitted to the perſon on whom it is drawn. Upon producing the duplicate within ſix months, the bill to be paid ;

and upon returning the same, &c. to the navy office, the money to be reimbursed, &c. If the duplicate be not produced, and payment demanded, within six months, the bill is to be returned to the treasurer of the navy, and cancelled; and the money to be paid to the seaman, or his executors, &c.

back of the said bill; which bill, so paid, upon being produced and delivered, together with the duplicate thereof, at the navy office, shall be immediately assigned for payment by three or more commissioners of the navy, and shall be immediately repaid by the treasurer of the navy to such receiver general of the land tax, collector of the customs, collector of the excise, or clerk of the cheque, or to the order of any such receiver general, collector of the customs, collector of the excise, or clerk of the cheque; but in case the duplicate of such bill shall not be produced and delivered, and the payment of the same be demanded, within six calendar months from the date thereof, then the said receiver general, collector of the customs, collector of the excise, or clerk of the cheque, shall return such bill to the treasurer of the navy at the pay office of the navy, who shall cause such bill, or the duplicate thereof, so delivered to such officer or seaman, if the same shall be returned, to be immediately cancelled; and from and after the return and cancelling of such bill, or of the duplicate thereof, such part of the wages or pay for which such bill was so made out, shall be immediately paid to such inferior officer or seaman, or his executors or administrators, or to the respective attorney or attornies of such officer or seaman, his executors or administrators, demanding the same, and duly authorized as is herein after directed, without any fee, reward, or deduction, whatsoever.

if the duplicate be not paid when tender'd, the cause of refusal or delay, and the time when tendered, to be indorsed thereon,

and a future day of payment to be appointed, &c.

If payment has been unnecessarily delayed,

or any fee, on account of payment, hath been taken,

XV. Provided always, and it is hereby further enacted by the authority aforesaid, That if any such receiver general, collector of the customs, collector of the excise, or clerk of the cheque, to whom the duplicate of any of the bills herein before directed to be made out, shall be tendered for payment by the wife, father, or mother, of any such officer or seaman, shall not then have in his hands publick money sufficient to answer the same, and shall refuse or delay the immediate payment thereof, such receiver general, collector of the customs, collector of the excise, or clerk of the cheque, shall immediately indorse on the back of the said duplicate, the day of its being so tendered to him, and the cause of his refusal or delay to pay the same; and shall appoint thereon for the payment of such bill, some future day, within the space of two months at the farthest from the day of its having been first tendered to him, as aforesaid; which duplicate, with the indorsement thereon, shall immediately be delivered back to the person presenting the same: and if, upon complaint to be made to the respective commissioners appointed by his Majesty, his heirs, or successors, to manage the said several duties of the land tax, customs, or excise, or to the commissioners of the navy if the person complained of be a clerk of the cheque, it shall appear that such receiver general, collector of the customs, collector of the excise, or clerk of the cheque, hath unnecessarily and wilfully refused or delayed the payment of such bill; or that such receiver general, collector of the customs, collector of the excise, or clerk of the cheque, or any person employed by or under any of them, hath directly or indirectly

directly received or taken any fee, reward, gratuity, discount, or deduction whatsoever, on account of the payment of the said bill; it shall and may be lawful to and for any three or more of the said commissioners to convict and fine any such offender under their respective direction, in any sum not exceeding fifty pounds, according to the nature and degree of the offence; which conviction shall be made by such respective commissioners, and such fine shall be levied and recovered, in such and the same manner, to all intents and purposes, as any conviction may be made, and any penalty may be levied or recovered, for any offence against any law by which any custom or excise is imposed or laid; and the said fine, when recovered, shall be paid to the informer or informers against such offender or offenders. *the offender to forfeit 50l.*

to the informer.

XVI. Provided always, That this act, or any thing herein contained, shall not extend to or be construed to invalidate or make void any indenture or indentures, whereby any master is or shall be intitled to have or receive the wages, pay, or other allowances of money, earned by his apprentice, but such wages, pay, or other allowances, shall be paid by the treasurer of the navy for the time being, or by his direction, according to such indenture or indentures, as has been usual in such cases; unless such apprentice shall be above the age of eighteen years at the time when such indenture or indentures were made and executed, or unless such apprentice shall have been hired and rated as a servant to any commission or warrant officer belonging to any of the ships or vessels of his Majesty, his heirs, or successors, such apprenticeship not being then known to such officer; in which case, the wages or pay of such servant shall be due and payable to such commission or warrant officer, according to the usual practice of the navy, until such officer shall be informed of such apprenticeship: and in either of the cases herein before mentioned, the master of such apprentice shall not be intitled to receive any wages, pay, or allowances, by virtue of any such indenture; any thing herein contained, or any law, statute, or usage, to the contrary thereof, in any wise notwithstanding. *Wages of apprentice to be paid to his master,*

unless he be above the age of eighteen when the indentures were executed; or be rated as servant to some officer, to whom such apprenticeship was unknown.

XVII. *And whereas it is of great importance to the carrying on of the payments in the manner herein before directed, that all the captains and commanders of the ships and vessels of his Majesty, his heirs or successors, should regularly transmit to the commissioners of the navy, by the first safe opportunity, all such complete pay books, and all such lists and tickets, to be so made out as aforesaid, and should also regularly transmit to the commissioners of the navy, once in every two months from the time any such ships or vessels shall have been entered into sea pay, muster books for every such ship or vessel, according to the method now prescribed and required, or which shall at any time hereafter be prescribed and required, by the lord high admiral of Great Britain, or by the commissioners for executing the office of lord high admiral of Great Britain;* be it therefore enacted by the authority aforesaid, That from and after the said first day of November, every captain and commander of every ship or vessel *Captains to transmit regularly to the* navy board pay books, and lists of tickets to be made out ;

and also once in 2 months the ship's muster book, properly sign'd, &c.

and in default, &c.

(except in cases of necessity, to be made appear to the lords of the admiralty)

to forfeit all their wages to the chest at Chatham,

and to suffer moreover, as a court martial shall adjudge.

The tickets, pay lists, and bills, deemed sufficient vouchers to the treasurer of the navy for money paid thereon.

Captains issuing tickets

fel of his Majesty, his heirs or successors, shall and do, from time to time, regularly and duly send or transmit to the commissioners of the navy, at their board, by the first safe opportunity, all and every such complete pay books, and all and every such list or lists, ticket or tickets, to be so made out as aforesaid; and also shall and do regularly and duly send and transmit, once in every two months, to the commissioners of the navy, at their board, one complete muster book for such ship or vessel, signed by himself and the proper officers, not only for the said two months, but for the whole time which such ship or vessel shall have been in commission, or from the time to which such ship or vessel was last paid : and in case such captain or commander shall be guilty of any failure or neglect in any part hereof, the said commissioners of the navy are hereby strictly directed and required not to grant to any such captain or commander the general certificate, to intitle him to his wages or pay for such ship or vessel, unless thereto required by particular order from the lord high admiral of *Great Britain*, or from the commissioners for executing the office of lord high admiral of *Great Britain*, or any three or more of such commissioners, in cases of necessity, and on its being made appear to their satisfaction, that the directions herein before given in this behalf have been complied with as far as the nature of the service would admit, and that the said complete pay books, lists, tickets and muster books, had been actually sent to the said commissioners of the navy, as often as any proper and safe opportunities offered : and in case such captain or commander shall not sufficiently exculpate himself from such neglect or failure, in the manner hereby prescribed, before the lord high admiral of *Great Britain*, or the commissioners for executing the office of lord high admiral of *Great Britain*, or any three or more of such commissioners, within twelve calendar months after the arrival of such captain or commander in *Great Britain*; then such captain or commander shall lose and forfeit all the wages due to him for his service on board such ship or vessel, which are hereby directed to be paid and applied to and for the use of the chest at *Chatham*; and such captain or commander, being tried for and convicted of such offence by a court-martial, shall be liable to such farther censure or punishment, not extending to loss of life or limb, as such court-martial shall adjudge.

XVIII. And be it further enacted by the authority aforesaid, That all and every such ticket and tickets, certificate and certificates, pay list and pay lists, bill and bills, herein before directed to be made out and paid as aforesaid, shall be deemed and taken as good and sufficient vouchers for the treasurer of the navy, for so much money as shall have been so directed to be paid upon all or any such tickets, certificates, pay lists, or bills respectively, and as shall have been paid by him thereon, and shall be allowed as such in passing his accounts.

XIX. And be it further enacted by the authority aforesaid, That if, after the said first day of *November*, any captain or com-

Commander of any of the ships or vessels of his Majesty, his otherwise than the act directs, heirs or successors, shall make out, or cause to be made out, and issued, any ticket or tickets for wages or pay to any inferior officer or seaman, under any pretence whatsoever, other than and except in the manner, and under the regulations, herein before directed concerning the same, every such captain or commander so offending shall, for every such offence, lose and for- to forfeit for each offence, feit the sum of fifty pounds of lawful money of *Great Britain*; 50 l. one moiety whereof shall be forfeited and paid to the person who One moiety to to the inform- shall inform or sue for the same, and the other moiety shall be er, and the paid and applied to and for the use of the chest at *Chatham*; other to the which forfeiture shall be sued for and recovered in any of his chest at Chat- Majesty's courts of record at *Westminster*, by action of debt, ham. bill, plaint or information, in which no essoin, protection, privilege, wager of law, or more than one imparlance, shall be allowed; and the court shall award such costs to the parties as shall be just: and in all cases where judgement or sentence shall The court, be given against any such offender, the court where such judge- where judge- ment or sentence shall be given shall, with all convenient speed, ment shall be certify the same to the lord high admiral of *Great Britain*, or to given, to cer- the commissioners for executing the office of lord high admiral tify the same of *Great Britain*; and as a further punishment, such offender to the admi- shall, upon such certificate, lose and forfeit all the wages or pay ralty; due to him for his service in such ship or vessel; which wages and the of- or pay the lord high admiral, or commissioners for executing the fender there- office of lord high admiral of *Great Britain*, or any three or upon to for- more of such commissioners, shall direct and order to be paid feit also all his and applied to and for the use of the chest at *Chatham*. wages to the chest at Chatham.

XX. Provided always, That no captain or commander of Captain not any ship or vessel shall be liable to any penalty, upon account of liable to forfeit any offence which shall be committed against this act before the on this act, first day of *June*, one thousand seven hundred and fifty nine, before 1 June unless, before the time of his committing such offence, he shall 1759, unless he have received the abstract of the provisions and regulations of hath previous- this act, herein after directed to be delivered to the captain or ly received an commander of every ship or vessel of his Majesty, his heirs and abstract there- successors. of.

XXI. And, for establishing a proper method for making and attesting letters of attorney; be it further enacted by the autho- Method to be rity aforesaid, That from and after the said first day of *Novem-* observed in *ber*, one thousand seven hundred and fifty eight, no letter of at- making and torney made by any inferior officer or seaman in the service of attesting let- his Majesty, his heirs or successors, or by the executors or ad- ters of attor- ministrators of any such officer or seaman, in order to impower ney. or intitle any person or persons to receive any wages, pay or allowances of money of any kind, due or to grow due for such service, shall be good and valid, or sufficient for that purpose, unless such letter of such attorney shall be made and declared to be revocable by the express words thereof; and unless such letter of attorney, if made by any such officer or seaman then in the service of his Majesty, his heirs or successors, shall be signed before

before and attested by the captain or commander, and one other of the signing officers of the ship to which such inferior officer or seaman shall belong, or by the clerk of the cheque at some of the dock yards; and unless such letter of attorney, if made by any such officer or seaman who shall have been discharged from the service of his Majesty, his heirs or successors, shall be signed before and attested by the mayor or chief magistrate of the town or place where such officer or seaman shall then reside; or if made by the executors or administrators of any such officer or seaman, unless such letter of attorney shall be signed before and attested by the minister and churchwardens, or, in that part of *Great Britain* called *Scotland*, by the minister and two elders of the parish where such executors or administrators shall respectively reside.

Letters of attorney otherwise made and attested than the act directs, and all bargains, &c. concerning wages, made after 1 Nov. 1758, declared null;

XXII. And be it further enacted and declared by the authority aforesaid, That all letters of attorney, other than such as shall be made and attested in manner aforesaid, and all bargains, sales, bills of sale, contracts, agreements and assignments, whatsoever, of, for, or concerning any wages, pay or allowances of money of any kind, due or to grow due to any such inferior officer or seaman in the service of his Majesty, his heirs or successors, for such service made or entered into from and after the said first day of *November*, shall be and are hereby declared to be void and of no effect, to all intents and purposes whatsoever; any law, statute, custom, or usage, to the contrary thereof in any wise notwithstanding: and the treasurer of the navy for the time being is hereby authorized, directed, and required, to pay, or cause to be paid, to every such inferior officer or seaman as shall appear in person at the pay table, or, in his absence, to his lawful attorney impowered by him in the manner herein before directed, or to the executors or administrators of such officer or seaman, or to their respective attorney or attornies, duly authorized in such manner as is herein before directed, the respective wages, pay, or allowances of money of any kind due, to him or them, without regard to any such letter of attorney, bargain, sale, bill of sale, contract, agreement, or assignment, whatsoever, made or to be made of, for, or concerning any such wages, pay or allowances of money of any kind.

and the wages due to be paid the seaman himself, appearing at the pay table, or to his lawful attorney, &c.

Fees of court for probate of wills, viz.

1s. for goods under 20 l.

XXIII. And be it further enacted by the authority aforesaid, That from and after the said first day of *November*, no ecclesiastical court, or any person or persons whatsoever, under any pretence, shall take or receive any more than the sum of one shilling for the seal, parchment, writing, and suing forth of the probate of any will, or any letters of administration, granted to the widow or children, father or mother, brother or sister, of any inferior officer, seaman, or marine whatsoever, dying in the pay of his Majesty's navy, and for the pains, trouble, and expence, attending the suing forth of such probate, or letters of administration, unless the goods and chattels of such officer, seaman, or marine, do amount to the value of twenty pounds; nor more

than

than the sum of two shillings, unless the goods and chattels of such officer, seaman, or marine, do amount to the value of forty pounds; nor more than the sum of three shillings, unless the goods and chattels of such officer, seaman, or marine, do amount to the value of sixty pounds: and in all cases where it shall be necessary to issue commissions, to swear the widows or children, father or mother, brother or sister, being executors or administrators, of such inferior officers, seamen, or marines, no ecclesiastical court, nor any person or persons whatsoever, under any pretence, shall take or receive more than the sum of one shilling for the seal, parchment, writing, and suing forth of any such commission, and for the pains, trouble, and expence, attending the same, unless the goods and chattels of such officer, seaman, or marine, do amount to the value of twenty pounds; nor more than the sum of two shillings, unless the goods and chattels of such officer, seaman, or marine, do amount to the value of forty pounds; nor more than the sum of three shillings, unless the goods and chattels of such officer, seaman, or marine, do amount to the value of sixty pounds: and if any officer or officers, or any other person or persons, shall presume to take any more than the said sums of one shilling, two shillings, or three shillings, respectively, for the seal, parchment, writing, and suing forth of the probate of any such will, or any such letters of administration, and for the pains, trouble, and expence attending the same; or for the seal, parchment, writing, and suing forth of any such commission as aforesaid, and for the pains, trouble, and expence, attending the same; the person or persons so offending shall forfeit to the party aggrieved the sum of fifty pounds; to be recovered, with full costs of suit, by action of debt, bill, plaint, or information, in any of his Majesty's courts of record at *Westminster*, or elsewhere.

XXIV. *And whereas divers wicked practices have been carried on, by personating and falsely assuming the names and characters of officers, seamen, and others, intitled, or supposed to be intitled, to wages, pay, or other allowances of money, or prize money, for serving on board of ships or vessels of the royal navy, and by forging and counterfeiting letters of attorney, bills, tickets, assignments, last wills, and other authorities and powers, from such officers and seamen, and by falsely taking out probate of wills, and letters of administration, to such officers and seamen;* be it therefore enacted by the authority aforesaid, That from and after the said first day of *November*, whosoever willingly and knowingly shall personate, or falsely assume the name or character of, or procure any other to personate, or falsely to assume the name or character of, any officer, seaman, or other person, intitled, or supposed to be intitled, to any wages, pay, or other allowances of money, or prize money, for service done on board of any ship or vessel of his Majesty, his heirs, or successors; or the executor or administrator, wife, relation, or creditor, of any such officer or seaman, or other person, in order to receive any wages, pay, or other allowances of money, or prize money, due, or supposed to be due or payable,

for

Marginal notes:

2s. under 40l.

3s. under 60l.

and for issuing commissions, 1s. under 20l.

2s. under 40l.

3s. under 60l.

No greater fees to be taken, under penalty of 50l.

Penalty of personating an officer, or seaman, supposed to have wages due to him,

or his executor, relation, or creditor,

for or on account of the fervices of any fuch officer or feaman, or other perfon as aforefaid; or fhall forge or counterfeit, or procure to be forged or counterfeited, any letter of attorney, bill, ticket, certificate, affignment, laft will, or any other power or authority whatfoever, in order to receive any fuch wages, pay, or other allowances of money, or prize money, due, or fuppofed to be due, to any fuch officer or feaman, or other perfon as aforefaid; or fhall willingly and knowingly take a falfe oath, or procure any other perfon to take a falfe oath, to obtain the probate of any will or wills, or to obtain letters of adminiftration, in order to receive the payment of any wages, pay, or other allowances of money, or prize money, due, or that were fuppofed to be due, to any fuch officer, feaman, or other perfon, as aforefaid, who has really ferved, or was fuppofed to have ferved, on board of any fhip or veffel of his Majefty, his heirs, or fucceffors; every fuch perfon fo offending, being lawfully convicted of any fuch offence or offences, fhall be deemed guilty of felony, and fhall fuffer death as a felon, without benefit of clergy.

XXV. And be it further enacted by the authority aforefaid, That from and after the faid firft day of *November*, when and fo often as any of the pay books of the fhips or veffels of his Majefty, his heirs, or fucceffors, fhall be clofed, fuch feamen as fhall not then receive, or have received, the wages, pay, or other allowances of money, due to them, fhall, upon application made by them to the commiffioners of the navy, at their board, have or. receive tickets made out to them to the value of the faid wages, pay, or other allowances, due to them refpectively; and the faid commiffioners are hereby directed and required to make out the faid tickets accordingly, and to caufe the fame to be dated, numbered, regiftered and paid in courfe, once a month.

XXVI. And be it further enacted by the authority aforefaid, That the governors, minifters, and confuls, appointed, or that fhall be appointed, by his Majefty, his heirs, or fucceffors, in foreign parts, and refiding there, or where none fuch are refident, any two or more *Britifh* merchants then and there refiding, fhall, from and after the faid firft day of *November*, be, and are hereby authorized, directed, and required, to fend and provide for all feafaring men and boys, fubjects of *Great Britain*, that fhall by fhipwreck, capture, or other unavoidable accident, be driven or caft away to, or that fhall be difcharged as unferviceable from any of the fhips or veffels of the royal navy at fuch foreign parts or places, where fuch governors, minifters, confuls, or merchants refide; and the faid governors, minifters, confuls, and merchants, are hereby required to provide for and fubfift fuch feafaring men and boys, at or after the rate of fix pence *per diem* each; and to fend bills of their feveral disburfements upon fuch occafions, together with proper vouchers for the fame, to the commiffioners of the navy, at their board, who are hereby directed and required to caufe immediate payment to be made of fuch bills and disburfements, after due examination of the faid vouchers; and the faid governors, minifters, confuls, and

mer-

merchants, shall put or send the said men or boys on board the first ship belonging to his Majesty, his heirs, or successors, that shall arrive at the parts or places where they reside, or any other parts or places, being near or within a convenient distance for that purpose; or in case no ship of war shall be then in such parts or places, or within a convenient distance, they shall send such men or boys on board such merchant ships or vessels as are bound for any port of *Great Britain*, and are in want of men to make up their complement; but if neither case happens within a convenient time, then they shall provide and order a passage homeward for such men and boys, in the first merchant ship or vessel bound for *Great Britain*: and every master or person having charge of a merchant ship or vessel, that shall arrive in such foreign parts, and be homeward bound from thence to any port in *Great Britain*, shall be, and is hereby required to take on board such and so many of such seafaring men or boys, as the said governors, ministers, consuls, or merchants, shall direct, not exceeding four for each one hundred tons of which his ship consists.

The men to be sent home on board the first King's ship, or merchant ship, bound to Great Britain.

Master of such ships to receive the said men and boys on board;

XXVII. *And, for an encouragement for such masters of such ships or vessels to take such seamen or boys aboard, and bring them to* Great Britain; be it further enacted by the authority aforesaid, That every such master or person having charge of a ship or vessel, who shall produce a certificate under the hands of the said governors, ministers, consuls, or merchants, or any of them, certifying the number and names of the men or boys taken on board by their direction, and the time of taking them on board, and shall make an affidavit at his return, setting forth the time during which he subsisted such men or boys, and that he did not, during that time, want of his own complement of men, or how many he did want of such complement, and for what time, shall receive, and the commissioners of the navy, at their board, are hereby required to cause to be paid to such master, or other person as aforesaid, six pence *per diem* for the passage and provisions of each man and boy, from the day of their embarkation homewards to the day of their arrival in *Great Britain*, or being put into some ship or vessel of his Majesty, his heirs, or successors; six pence *per diem* only being deducted for such time, and for so many persons, as such master, or other person as aforesaid, wanted of the complement of his ship or vessel, during the voyage.

and to be allowed 6d per diem, for all such as shall be above his complement; upon producing a certificate, and making a proper affidavit.

XXVIII. *And, to prevent for the future, as far as may be, any unjust or fraudulent arrests upon seamen actually belonging to any of the ships of his Majesty, his heirs, or successors*; be it also enacted by the authority aforesaid, That from and after the said first day of *November*, no person whatsoever, who shall list and enter himself to serve as a seaman on board any of the ships or vessels of his Majesty, his heirs, or successors, shall be liable to be taken out of the service of his Majesty, his heirs, or successors, by any process or execution whatsoever, either in *Great Britain*, *Ireland*, or any other part of his Majesty's dominions, other than for some criminal matter; unless such process or execution be for a real

Seamen not liable to be taken out of the service, except for some criminal matter, or a real debt of the value of 10l.

real debt, or other juft caufe of action, and unlefs before the taking out of fuch procefs or execution, not being for a criminal matter, the plaintiff or plaintiffs therein, or fome other perfon or

persons on his or their behalf, fhall make affidavit before one or more judge or judges of the court of record, or other court, out of which fuch procefs or execution fhall iffue, or before fome perfon authorized to take affidavits in fuch courts, that to his or their knowledge the fum juftly due and owing to the plaintiff or plaintiffs, from the defendant or defendants in the action or caufe of action on which fuch procefs fhall iffue, or the debt or damage and coft for which fuch execution fhall be iffued out, amounts

to the value of twenty pounds at the leaft; a memorandum of which oath fhall be marked on the back of fuch procefs or writ, for which memorandum or oath no fee fhall be taken; and if

any perfon be neverthelefs arrefted, contrary to the intent of this act, it fhall and may be lawful for one or more judge or judges of fuch court, upon complaint made thereof by the party himfelf, or by any one of his fuperior officers, to examine into the fame, by the oath of the parties, or otherwife, and, by warrant under his or their hands and feals, to difcharge fuch feamen fo arrefted contrary to the intent of this act, without paying any fee or fees, upon due proof made before him or them, that fuch feamen fo arrefted were actually belonging to one of the fhips or veffels of his Majefty, his heirs, or succeffors, and arrefted contrary to the intent of this act, and alfo to award to the party fo

complaining fuch cofts as fuch judge or judges fhall think reafonable; for the recovery whereof, he fhall have the like remedy that the perfon who takes out the faid execution might have had for his cofts, or the plaintiff in the faid action might have had for the recovery of his cofts, in cafe judgment had been given for him with cofts againft the defendant in the faid action.

XXIX. *And, to the end that bonefit creditors, who aim only at the recovery of their juft debts due to them from fuch feamen as are actually belonging to fome of the fhips or veffels of his Majefty, his heirs, or fucceffors, may not be hindered from fuing for the fame, but on the contrary, may be affifted and forwarded in their fuits; and that, inftead of proceeding by an arreft, which may hurt the fervice, and occafion a great expence and delay to themfelves, they may be enabled to proceed in a more fpeedy and eafy method;* be it further

enacted by the authority aforefaid, That it fhall be lawful for any plaintiff or plaintiffs, upon notice firft given in writing of the caufe of action to fuch feaman or feamen belonging to the royal navy, or left at his or their laft place of refidence before his or their entering into the fervice of his Majefty, his heirs, or fucceffors, to file a common appearance in any action to be

brought for or upon account of any debt whatfoever, fo as to intitle fuch plaintiff or plaintiffs to proceed therein to judgment and outlawry, and to have an execution thereupon, other than againft the body or bodies of him or them fo actually belonging to any fhip or veffel of his Majefty, his heirs, or fucceffors, as

afore-

affectibly this act, or any thing herein, or any former law or statute, to the contrary notwithstanding.

XXX. And, *to prevent extortion by persons employed in the receiving of seamens wages, and other monies;* be it further enacted by the authority aforesaid, That no person or persons whatsoever who shall be employed in the receiving of any wages, pay, prize money, or any other monies, due, or becoming due, for or upon account of the service of any officer, seaman, or other person, in the royal navy, shall be intitled to take or retain more than six pence in the pound for or upon account of receiving thereof, and for paying the same to the person or persons by whom he or they shall be employed, or according to the direction and appointment of such person or persons, and for all his and their trouble and attendance in relation thereto : and if any person or persons so employed shall, directly or indirectly, demand, take, or retain, or cause or procure, or knowingly and willingly permit or suffer, to be demanded, taken or retained, any allowance, gratuity, reward, or valuable consideration, exceeding in the whole the sum of six pence in the pound, for the monies so received as aforesaid, every such person shall, for every such offence, forfeit the sum of fifty pounds, to be recovered, with full costs of suit, to any person or persons who will sue for the same in any of his Majesty's courts of record at *Westminster*, by action of debt, bill, plaint, or information, in which no essoin, protection, privilege, wager of law, or more than one imparlance shall be allowed : and if any such offender shall be a clerk, officer, or servant in any office belonging or relating to the navy, he shall, upon conviction, over and above the said penalty of fifty pounds, to be recovered as aforesaid, forfeit and lose his place, and be for ever thereafter incapable of holding any place of profit in any such office.

No more than 6d. in the pound to be deducted for receiving and paying seamens wages, or prize money;

under penalty of 50l.

and if the offender belong to any office in the navy, to lose his place also.

XXXI. And be it further enacted by the authority aforesaid, That if any clerk, officer, or servant, in any office belonging or relating to the navy, shall, directly or indirectly, demand, take, or retain, or cause or procure, or knowingly and willingly permit or suffer, to be demanded, taken, or retained, any fee, gratuity, compensation, or valuable consideration (not being authorized so to do by this act) of or from any person or persons whatsoever, for or under pretence of the doing or performing any matter or thing hereby directed or authorized to be done or performed, or which shall be in execution hereof, every such clerk, officer, or servant, shall be subject to the same forfeitures, costs, and incapacities, as is herein before mentioned with respect to the taking more than six pence in the pound for the receiving of seamens wages.

Clerks, officers, or servants belonging to any office in the navy taking other fees than the act allows,

subject to the same forfeitures.

XXXII. And be it further enacted by the authority aforesaid, That from and after the said first day of *November*, so much of an act made in the ninth and tenth year of the reign of King *William* the Third, intituled, *An act for the better preventing the imbezzlement of his Majesty's stores of war, and preventing cheats, frauds, and abuses, in paying seamens wages,* as relates to the taking

Part of the several acts of 9 & 10 Wil. 3.

ing up more than the sum of one shilling for suing forth any
letters of administration to the wife or children of any seaman
dying in the pay of his Majesty's navy, unless the goods and
chattels of such seaman do amount to the sum of twenty pounds:
and also so much of an act made in the fourth year of the reign
of Queen *Anne*, intituled, *An act for the encouragement and increase
of seamen, and for the better and speedier manning of her Majesty's
fleet*, as relates to the payment of the wages due to seamen turned
over from one ship to another : and so much of an act made in
the first year of the reign of his present Majesty (intituled, *An act
for granting an aid to his Majesty of five hundred thousand pounds,
towards discharging wages due to seamen; and for the constant, regular, and punctual payment of seamens wages for the future; and for
appropriating the supplies granted in this present session of parliament;
and for disposing of the surplus of the money granted for half pay for
the year one thousand seven hundred and twenty seven*), as contains
any provisions relative to his Majesty's royal navy, or the commissioners thereof, or to the captains, commanders, seamen, or
other persons serving therein, or to the payment of the wages
due for such service : and also an act made in the first year of
the reign of his present Majesty, intituled, *An act for encouraging
seamen to enter into his Majesty's service*; shall be and are hereby
repealed.

XXXIII. And be it further enacted by the authority aforesaid,
That the lord high admiral of *Great Britain*, or the commissioners for executing the office of lord high admiral of *Great Britain*,
shall direct an abstract of the provisions and regulations herein
contained, for the benefit of seamen belonging to the ships and
vessels of his Majesty, his heirs, and successors, together with
the articles of war, to be printed; and that a competent number
of the copies thereof be delivered to the captain or commander
of every such ship or vessel; and such captain or commander, as
soon as the ship or vessel by him commanded shall be put into
sea pay, shall cause one of the said printed abstracts, together
with the articles of war, to be hung up and affixed to the most
publick place of such ship or vessel, and shall cause the same to
be constantly kept up and renewed, so that they may be at all
times accessible to the inferior officers and seamen on board of
such ship or vessel; and every such captain or commander shall
cause such abstract to be audibly and distinctly read over once in
every month, in the presence of the officers and seamen of such
ship or vessel, immediately after the articles of war are read; and
the reading both of the articles of war, and of this abstract, and
the days when read, shall be attested by the captain or commander, and the usual signing officers, of such ship or vessel, at the foot
of the muster books for such ship or vessel, before they are transmitted to the commissioners of the navy : and the said commissioners are hereby charged and directed strictly to inquire whether
the directions hereby given for hanging up and affixing the said
abstract and articles of war, and for the reading of the same, as
aforesaid, have been duly observed by the captain or commander
of

Margin notes:

4 Annæ.

1 Geo. 2.

1 Geo. 2.
repealed.

An abstract
of this act, to-
gether with
the articles of
war, to be
printed;

and copies de-
livered to all
captains.
One to be
kept constant-
ly hung in the
most publick
place of the
ship;

and to be read
to the ship's
company, af-
ter the articles,
once a month;
of which, pro-
per attestation
is to be made at
the foot of the
muster books.
Commissioners
of the navy
to inquire
whether these
directions are
complied with;

of such ship or vessel, and not to grant to such captain or commander his general certificate, until they are fully satisfied thereof; to the end and intent that every seaman employed in the royal navy of *Great Britain* may, at one and the same time, hear and know the forfeitures and punishments he is liable to for any neglect or disobedience, and likewise the encouragements and benefits to which he is intitled by a due and faithful performance of his duty; and that, upon suffering any oppression or injury in such service, he may be the better enabled to lay his complaint before the lord high admiral of *Great Britain*, or the commissioners for executing the office of lord high admiral of *Great Britain*, who are hereby respectively charged and directed, upon any such complaint being laid, strictly to enquire into the circumstances of the same, and to grant immediate redress therein, if such complaint shall be justly founded; and to take special and constant care that this act, and all the provisions and regulations therein, be fully complied with, and punctually carried into execution. *to the end that seamen may both know their duty, and their rights, and how to seek redress for injuries.*

XXXIV. And be it further enacted by the authority aforesaid, That the abstract herein before directed, shall be in the following words; that is to say, *Form of the abstract.*

Abstract of an act of parliament made in the thirty first year of the reign of King George *the Second, intituled,* An act for the encouragement of seamen employed in the royal navy; and for establishing a regular method for the punctual, frequent, and certain payment of their wages; and for enabling them more easily and readily to remit the same for the support of their wives and families; and for preventing frauds and abuses attending such payments.

I. EVERY volunteer entering his name with a commission officer, appointed for entering volunteers on board any ship in the royal navy, shall receive a certificate thereof *gratis*; and be intitled to wages from the date of such certificate, including the day of the date thereof, in case he appears on board within fourteen days, if the place where he enters is not above one hundred miles from the ship; within twenty days, if above one hundred miles; or within thirty days, if above two hundred miles; and shall be allowed the usual conduct money, and also two months wages advance, at the first fitting out of the ship, and before the ship proceeds to sea.

II. Every supernumerary man serving ten days in any ship, shall be borne for and intitled to his wages upon the books of such ship, and to all other benefits, as if he was part of the complement of such ship; but men lent from one ship into another, shall continue to be borne for and intitled to their wages upon the books of the ship from which they were lent, until they shall be regularly discharged from thence, and in no other.

Q 2   III. Every

III. Every inferior officer or feaman, who fhall be turned over from one fhip to another (in cafe the fhip into which he is turned over, is then or fhall come into a port of *Great Britain* where there is a commiffioner of the navy) fhall be paid, by proper pay lifts, all the wages due to him in the fhip from which he was fo turned over, before the fhip into which he fhall be turned over proceeds to fea, unlefs it fhall be otherwife directed by fpecial order from the admiralty, in cafes of the greateft exigency only; and if the fhip, in purfuance of fuch order, proceeds to fea before fuch payment can poffibly be made, the wages fhall be paid as foon as fuch fhip fhall come again into any port of *Great Britain* where there is a commiffioner of the navy.

IV. Every officer or feaman who fhall be turned over from one fhip to another, fhall not ferve or be rated in a worfe quality, or lower degree, than he ferved in or was rated for in the former fhip; and fhall have an advance of two months wages before the fhip into which he is turned over proceeds to fea, in cafe he fhall not have received fuch advance before.

V. Such fums of money fhall in the firft place be appropriated, and fhall, from time to time, be iffued and applied out of the fupplies granted, or to be granted, for any naval fervices, as fhall be fufficient for the regular payment of all tickets made out purfuant to the act, and for the regular difcharge of all wages due, or to grow due, in manner following; that is to fay, As often as any fhip which fhall have been in fea pay twelve months, or more, fhall be or arrive in any port of *Great Britain*, or on the coaft thereof, the captain or commander fhall immediately caufe five complete pay books to be made out, for all the time fuch fhip fhall have been in pay, except the laft fix months; and fhall forthwith tranfmit, by the firft fafe opportunity, fuch books, together with three alphabets, and a flop book, to the commiffioners of the navy, at their board: and as foon as fuch fhip fhall be or arrive in any port of *Great Britain* where there is a commiffioner of the navy, the faid commiffioners of the navy fhall folicit the neceffary fums of money, and fhall caufe immediate payment to be made of the wages due, deducting the advance money, and all defalcations; leaving always fix months wages unpaid, and no more: and all the wages due upon any fhip fhall be paid as foon as may be, or within two months at fartheft, after the arrival of fuch fhip in port to be laid up.

VI. The month fhall confift of twenty eight days.

VII. Upon application to the commiffioners of the navy, at their board, by an inferior officer or feaman who fhall then be in the fervice, and was abfent at the payment of the fhip to which he did belong, or from the captain or commander of any fhip in which fuch officer or feaman fhall then ferve, in cafe fuch fhip fhall be in any port of *Great Britain* where there is a commiffioner of the navy, the commiffioners of the navy, at their board, fhall immediately fend the pay books, or pay lifts made out from them, to fuch commiffioner, who fhall forthwith caufe the wages to be paid to fuch officer or feaman.

2

VII. The

VIII. The captain or commander, shall make out a ticket upon the death of every inferior officer and seaman, and shall transmit the same, by the first safe opportunity, to the commissioners of the navy, at their board, who are to assign the same for payment within one month after the receipt thereof; and the same shall be delivered, and payment thereon made, without fee or reward, to the executors or administrators of such officer or seaman, or to the attorney of such executors or administrators.

IX. The captain or commander, shall make out a ticket for every inferior officer or seaman who shall be discharged as unserviceable, pursuant to the directions of the act, and shall send such ticket, by the first safe opportunity, to the commissioners of the navy, at their board. The captain or commander, shall not deliver such ticket to such officer or seaman, but shall give him a certificate of such discharge, containing an exact copy of the ticket, and a description of his person. The said commissioners of the navy shall immediately cause the day when such ticket was received to be indorsed thereon, and shall assign the same for payment within one month at farthest from the day of making such indorsement. And if any such officer or seaman shall present such certificate at the navy office, the said commissioners of the navy are forthwith to examine such certificate, and the person presenting the same; and being satisfied that the certificate was made out for such person, and that he is rendered unserviceable, they shall testify the same on such certificate. The said ticket being so assigned, shall be immediately delivered, and payment made at the pay office of the navy, to such officer or seaman, without fee or reward, and to no other person whatsoever. If the ticket shall not have been transmitted to, and received by, the commissioners of the navy, the money appearing to be due by the copy of the ticket in the certificate, shall be paid in like manner as if the ticket had been received. Such officer or seaman being desirous to receive his wages at any port in *Great Britain* where a commissioner of the navy resides, may produce his certificate to such commissioner of the navy, who, being satisfied that such certificate was made out for such person, and that he is rendered unserviceable, shall sign and transmit the same to the commissioners of the navy, at their board; who, within four days after the receipt of such certificate, are to send the ticket for such officer or seaman, or if such ticket shall not have been transmitted to and received by them, then the said certificate, containing a copy of the said ticket instead thereof, to the commissioner at such port; who shall cause immediate payment thereon to be made, without fee or reward: and such commissioner shall send such officer or seaman to the nearest hospital, where he is to be received and victualled, from the time of presenting such certificate until payment is made. If any such certificate shall be lost or destroyed, or such officer or seaman shall not present the same in person, or the money due on any such ticket shall not be paid before the general payment of the ship's company, the ticket shall be cancelled, and the wages be

pay-

payable as if such ticket and certificate had not been made out.

X. When any inferior officer or seaman shall, by order of the captain, or commander, be set sick ashore, and be sent into any hospital, or sick quarters, such captain or commander shall make out a sick ticket, for the wages due to such officer or seaman, and transmit the same with such officer or seaman to the hospital, or sick quarters; and if such officer or seaman shall be regularly discharged from thence as unserviceable, a certificate of his discharge, with the sick ticket annexed thereto, shall be delivered to him : and if he shall present the same to a commissioner at any port in *Great Britain*, such commissioner being satisfied that such officer or seaman is unserviceable, shall sign the same on the certificate, and forthwith transmit such certificate, and sick ticket, to the commissioners of the navy, at their board, who, within four days after the receipt thereof, are required to cause a proper ticket, or pay list, to be made out for the wages due to such officer or seaman, and to send such ticket, or pay list, without delay, to the commissioner at such port, who shall cause immediate payment of the wages to be made, without fee or reward, to such officer or seaman; who, notwithstanding such discharge, shall be maintained in such hospital, or sick quarters, from the time he shall present the certificate, and sick ticket, until the payment shall be made.

XI. The payment of tickets, certificates, or pay lists, shall not be delayed, though the muster or pay books be not regularly sent to and received by the commissioners of the navy; but if any error shall be made in any ticket, certificate, or pay list, the loss shall be made good out of the wages of the captain, or commander, by whom such ticket, certificate, or pay list, was made out.

XII. As often as any ship which shall not be in a port of *Great Britain*, or on the coast thereof, shall have twelve months wages due, the captain, or commander, shall cause the names of all the inferior officers and seamen to be called over, and each to answer to his name, and shall do the same at the end of every six months, when twelve months, or more, wages, shall be due: and if any such officer or seaman shall then declare, or deliver in writing, the name and place of abode of his wife, father, or mother, and desire that the whole or any part of his wages then due, except the wages due for the last six months, should be paid to such wife, father, or mother, by the receiver general of the land tax for any county, riding, or city, or collector of the customs for any port, or collector of the excise for any collection in *Great Britain*, or the clerk of the cheque at any dock yard ; the captain, or commander, is strictly required to cause four lists to be made out of the persons so desiring to make such remittances, and shall transmit such lists, by the first safe opportunity, without delay, to the commissioners of the navy, at their board, who, on receipt thereof, shall immediately make out two bills pursuant to the directions of the act, for the payment of the wages so allotted by each person ; one

of

of which bills shall be sent to the persons respectively specified in each lists, and the other to such receiver, collector, or clerk of the cheque; and if the person to whom any such bill is sent, shall, within six months from the date thereof, produce and deliver the same to such receiver, collector, or clerk of the cheque, together with a certificate that such person is the wife, father, or mother, of such officer or seaman respectively, under the hands of the minister and churchwardens, or, in *Scotland*, of the minister and two elders, of the parish where such person was married, or resides; such receiver, collector, or clerk of cheque, upon being satisfied of the truth of such certificate, is immediately, without fee or reward, to pay the sum mentioned in such bill, taking a receipt. Such bill, together with the duplicate thereof, being produced at the navy office, shall be immediately assigned for payment by the commissioners of the navy, and repaid by the treasurer of the navy, to such receiver, collector, or clerk of the cheque, or their order respectively; but if payment of the said bill be not demanded of such receiver, collector, or clerk of the cheque, and the duplicate of the said bill, together with a proper certificate, be not produced and delivered to them respectively, within six months from the date thereof, the bill is to be returned and cancelled, and the sum contained therein is to become payable to such inferior officer or seaman when the ship shall be paid.

XIII. In like manner, when wages shall be paid at the pay office, or at any of the out ports, if any inferior officer or seaman shall be desirous to remit the whole or part of his wages to his wife, children, parents, or any other person, and to have a bill for the same drawn upon any such receiver, collector, or clerk of the cheque, two bills are to be made out, one of which is to be delivered to such officer or seaman, and the other to be sent to such receiver, collector, or clerk of the cheque, who is to pay immediately the sum therein mentioned, without any fee or reward, taking a receipt. Such bill, together with the duplicate thereof, being produced at the navy office, shall be immediately assigned for payment by the commissioners of the navy, and be repaid, by the treasurer of the navy, to such receiver, collector, or clerk of the cheque, or their order respectively: but if payment of the said bill be not demanded of such receiver, collector, or clerk of the cheque, and the duplicate of the said bill shall not be produced and delivered to them respectively within six calendar months from the date thereof, the bill is to be returned and cancelled, and the sum contained therein is to be immediately paid to such officer or seaman, or other person duly authorized to receive the same.

XIV. If any such receiver, collector, or clerk of the cheque, shall not have in his hands money to answer any bill tendered by such wife, father, or mother, aforesaid, and shall refuse or delay the immediate payment thereof he is immediately to indorse on such bill the cause of his refusal or delay, and appoint for payment some day within two months after such tender; and if,

upon

upon complaint to the commissioners, respectively, appointed to manage the land tax, customs, or excise, or to the commissioners of the navy, respectively, it shall appear, that any such receiver, collector, or clerk of the cheque, hath unnecessarily and wilfully refused or delayed payment, or that he, or any person employed by or under him, hath taken any fee, reward, gratuity, discount, or deduction, on account of payment of any such bill, such commissioners may fine such offender in any sum not exceeding fifty pounds.

XV. The wages, pay, and allowances, earned by any indentured apprentice, shall be paid to his master, as hath been usual, unless such apprentice was above eighteen years of age when his indentures were executed, or shall be rated as a servant to any officer to whom such apprenticeship is not known; in which case, such officer shall be intitled to the pay and wages of such servant, according to the usual practice of the navy, until such officer shall be informed of such apprenticeship.

XVI. Captains or commanders of ships are to transmit from time to time to the commissioners of the navy, at their board, complete pay books, lists, and tickets, and also once in every two months complete muster books, under the penalty of forfeiting all their wages to the chest at *Chatham*, and of being liable to such further punishment as a court-martial shall inflict; except in cases of necessity, to be made appear to the satisfaction of the lord high admiral, or commissioners of the admiralty.

XVII. The tickets, certificates, pay lists, and bills, shall be sufficient vouchers to the treasurer of the navy for the payments thereon.

XVIII. Captains, or commanders, issuing any tickets other than such as are directed by the act, shall be subject to a penalty of fifty pounds for every ticket, and shall forfeit all their wages to the chest at *Chatham*.

XIX. No captain, or commander, shall be liable to any penalty for any offence against the act before the first of *June*, one thousand seven hundred and fifty nine, unless he hath previously received this abstract.

XX. No letters of attorney made by inferior officers or seamen, or their executors or administrators, for receiving wages or allowances of money, shall be valid, unless declared therein to be revocable; and unless the same, if made by any such officer or seaman then in the service, be signed before, and attested by, the commander and one other of the signing officers of the ship, or by a clerk of the cheque: and if made by any such officer or seaman after his discharge from the service, unless the same be signed before, and attested by, the mayor or chief magistrate of the town or place where such officer or seaman shall then reside; or unless the letter of attorney, if made by such executors or administrators, be signed before, and attested by, the minister and churchwardens, or, in *Scotland*, by the minister and two elders, of the parish where such executors or administrators reside.

XXI. All

XXI. All letters of attorney, other than such as are made in manner aforesaid, and all bargains, sales, bills of sale, contracts, agreements, and assignments, concerning wages or money to inferior officers or seamen, shall be null and void.

XXII. No more than one shilling shall be taken by any ecclesiastical court, or other person, for the probate of any will, or letters of administration, granted to the widows, children, fathers, mothers, brothers, or sisters, of inferior officers, seamen, or marines, dying in the service, and for the pains, trouble, and expence, attending the same, unless the goods and chattels are of the value of twenty pounds ; nor more than two shillings, unless such goods and chattels are of the value of forty pounds ; nor more than three shillings, unless such goods and chattels are of the value of sixty pounds : nor more than one shilling for issuing commissions to swear such widows, children, fathers, mothers, brothers, or sisters, being executors or administrators to inferior officers, seamen, or marines, and for the pains, trouble, and expence, attending the same, unless the goods and chattels are of the value of twenty pounds ; nor more than two shillings, unless the goods and chattels are of the value of forty pounds ; nor more than three shillings, unless the goods and chattels are of the value of sixty pounds ; under the penalty of fifty pounds, to be paid by the offender to the party aggrieved.

XXIII. Whoever willingly and knowingly shall personate, or falsely assume, the name or character of, or procure any other to personate, or falsely to assume, the name or character of any officer, seaman, or other person, intitled to wages, pay, allowances, or prize money, for service done on board of any ship of the royal navy, or the executor, administrator, wife, relation, or creditor, of any such officer, seaman, or other person, in order to receive any wages, pay, allowances, or prize money, or shall forge or counterfeit, or procure to be forged or counterfeited, any letter of attorney, or other power or authority whatsoever, in order to receive any wages, pay, allowances, or prize money, or shall willingly and knowingly take a false oath, or procure a false oath to be taken, to obtain the probate of a will, or letters of administration, in order to receive any wages, pay, allowances, or prize money, shall be guilty of felony, and suffer death.

XXIV. When the pay books are closed, tickets shall be made out at the navy office to the seamen who shall not have received their wages, and such tickets shall be paid in course once a month.

XXV. *British* governors, ministers, and consuls, residing at foreign parts, or where no such are present, any two *British* merchants, are required to provide for seafaring men and boys, subjects of *Great Britain*, who, by shipwreck, capture, or other unavoidable accident, shall be in foreign parts, or who shall be discharged there as unserviceable from the royal navy, and subsist them at six pence *per diem* each ; and send them home as

soon

soon as conveniently may be, in any ship belonging to the royal navy, or in any merchant ship.

XXVI. Masters of ships shall be allowed six pence *per diem* for all such men and boys as shall exceed their complement.

XXVII. Seamen shall not be taken out of the service for any debt under twenty pounds :

XXVIII. But creditors may file a common appearance, so as to intitle them to proceed to judgement and outlawry, and to have an execution thereupon, except against the bodies of such seamen.

XXIX. Receivers of seamens wages taking more than six pence in the pound, shall, for every offence, forfeit fifty pounds; and if any such offender be a clerk, officer, or servant, in an office belonging to the navy, he shall also lose his place, and be incapable of holding any place of profit in any such office.

XXX. Clerks, officers, and servants, in offices belonging to the navy, taking fees (not allowed by the act) for doing any thing directed by the act, shall be subject to the same forfeitures.

XXXI. Part of several acts made in the ninth and tenth years of King *William* the Third, and in the fourth year of Queen *Anne*, and in the first year of King *George* the Second, and also another act made in the said first year of King *George* the Second, relating to seamen, are repealed.

XXXII. This abstract, together with the articles of war, shall be printed, and kept hung up in the most publick place of every ship of the royal navy, that it may be accessible to all inferior officers and seamen ; and every captain and commander, shall cause the same to be read over once in every month after the articles of war are read ; and the reading the same shall be attested by the captain, or commander, and signing officers, at the foot of the muster books : to the end that every seaman in the royal navy may know the punishments he is liable to for any neglect or disobedience, and the encouragements he is intitled to by the performance of his duty ; and that upon suffering any injury, he may be enabled to lay his complaint before the lord high admiral, or the commissioners of the admiralty, who are by the act directed to enquire into the same, and to grant redress, if such complaint be justly founded ; and to take especial care that this act be punctually carried into execution.

CAP. XI.

An act to amend an act made in third year of the reign of King William and Queen Mary, intituled, An act for the better explanation, and supplying the defects of the former laws for the settlement of the poor, so far as the same relates to apprentices gaining a settlement by indenture; and also to impower justices of the peace to determine differences between masters and mistresses and their servants in husbandry, touching their wages, though such servants are hired for less time than a year.

WHEREAS *by an act made in the third year of the reign of* King William *and* Queen Mary, *intituled,* An act for the better explanation, and supplying the defects of the former laws for the settlement of the poor, *it is enacted, That if any person should be bound an apprentice by indenture, and inhabit in any town or parish, such binding and inhabitation shall be adjudged a good settlement: and whereas since the making the said act, great numbers of persons have been unwarily bound apprentices by certain deeds, writings, or contracts, not indented, by which binding many of them have suffered great loss and damage, on account of their having been refused a settlement in such town or parish, where they have been so bound and resided forty days, and have been removed to the parish or place where their last legal settlement was before such apprenticeship, where they have had no encouragement to exercise their trades, or opportunity to gain a livelihood by their said trades to which they were so bound apprentices:* for relief therefore of such apprentices, and for preventing the like mischief for the future; be it enacted by the King's most excellent majesty, by and with the advice and consent of the lords spiritual and temporal, and commons, in this present parliament assembled, and by the authority of the same, That no person who shall have been bound an apprentice, or who shall hereafter be bound an apprentice, by any deed, writing, or contract, not indented, being first legally stamped, shall be liable to be removed from the town, parish, or place, where he or she shall have been so bound an apprentice, and resident forty days, by virtue of any order of removal, granted by two justices of the peace, of any county, riding, division, city, borough, town corporate, or place; or by virtue of any order of the justices at their general or quarter sessions, by reason or on account of such deed, writing, or contract, not being indented only.

II. Provided nevertheless, That nothing herein before enacted, shall extend, or be construed to extend, to set aside or make void, any judgement, order, or decree, which shall have been made as aforesaid, before the first day of *May*, one thousand seven hundred and fifty eight.

III. *And whereas by an act passed in the twentieth year of his present Majesty's reign, intituled,* An act for the better adjusting and more easy recovery of the wages of certain servants, and for the

better

better regulation of fuch fervants, and of certain apprentices ; it is enacted, That from and after the twenty fifth day of *March*, one thoufand feven hundred and forty feven, all complaints, differences and difputes, which fhall arife between mafters or miftreffes, and fervants in hufbandry, who fhall be hired for one year or longer, or which fhall happen or arife between mafters and miftreffes and artificers, handicraftfmen, miners, colliers, keelmen, pitmen, glaffmen, potters, and other labourers, employed for any certain time, or in any other manner, fhall be heard or determined by one or more juftice or juftices of the peace, for the place where fuch mafter or miftrefs fhall inhabit : and whereas doubts have arifen whether the words any labourers employed for any certain time, or in any other manner, extend to fervants in hufbandry hired for a lefs time than one year ; for obviating the faid doubts, be it enacted by the authority aforefaid, That the faid act, and all and every claufe and matter therein contained, fhall from and after the faid firft day of *May*, one thoufand feven hundred and fifty eight, be deemed and conftrued to extend to all fervants employed in hufbandry, though hired for a lefs time than one year ; any thing in the faid recited act of the twentieth year of his prefent Majefty's reign, or any other act contained to the contrary notwithftanding.

Recited act extended to fervants employed in hufbandry, though hired for a lefs time than a year.

CAP. XII.

An act to encourage the growth and cultivation of madder in that part of Great Britain *called* England, *by afcertaining the tithe thereof there.*

Preamble.

WHEREAS madder is an ingredient effentially neceffary in dyeing and callicoe printing, and of great confequence to the trade and manufactures of this kingdom ; and may be raifed therein equal in goodnefs, if not fuperior, to any foreign madder : and whereas the encouraging of the growth thereof in this kingdom, will be a faving of a very large fum of money, which is now paid for that commodity imported duty free from abroad ; and will alfo be a means of employing great numbers of poor in the winter months : and whereas the afcertaining of the tithe of madder will be the greateft means of encouraging the growth of that commodity in this kingdom : may it therefore pleafe your Majefty, that it may be enacted ; and be it enacted by the King's moft excellent majefty, by and with the advice and confent of the lords fpiritual and temporal, and commons, in this prefent parliament affembled, and by the authority of the fame, That from and after the firft day of *Auguft*, which will be in the year of our Lord one thoufand feven hundred and fifty eight, all and every perfon and perfons who fhall plant, grow, raife, or cultivate, or caufe to be planted, grown, raifed, or cultivated, any madder in any parifh or place within that part of *Great Britain* called *England*, fhall pay, or caufe to be paid, to every parfon, vicar, curate, or impropriator of any fuch parifh or place, the fum of five fhillings, and no more, yearly, and every year, for each acre of

Madder to pay 5 s. per acre, tithe,

madder

madder so planted, grown, raised, or cultivated, and so proportionably for more or less ground so planted or cultivated, in lieu
of all manner of tithe of madder; for the recovery of which
sum or sums of money, the parson, vicar, or impropriator, shall
have the common and usual remedy allowed of by the laws of
this realm.

II. Provided always, and be it enacted by the authority a-
foresaid, That no madder shall be carried off the ground on
which it grows, before the sum or sums of money herein before
directed to be taken in lieu of tithes, be paid to the person or
persons respectively intitled to receive the same.

and not to be removed till tithe be paid.

III. Provided also, That this act, or any thing herein contained, shall not extend to charge any lands discharged by any
Modus Decimandi, ancient composition, or other discharge of
tithes by law.

Act not to ex-tend to lands discharged of tithes, &c.

IV. Provided always, and be it enacted by the authority a-
foresaid, That this act shall continue and be in force for the
space of fourteen years, and from thence to the end of the then
next session of parliament, and no longer.

and to be in force 14 years.

CAP. XIII.

*An act for allowing a further time for holding the first meet-
ings of commissioners or trustees for putting in execution
certain acts made in the last session of parliament.*

WHEREAS by an act passed in the last session of parliament,
intituled, An act for enlarging the times for the first meetings of commissioners or trustees for putting in execution certain
acts of this session of parliament; it was enacted, That in case
any act of parliament had passed, or did, or should pass, at any time
whatsoever, during that session of parliament, upon or after the day
specified in any such act for the first meeting of the commissioners or
trustees appointed to put the same, or any part thereof, in execution;
in each and every such case, such commissioners or trustees respectively,
or the same number of such respective commissioners or trustees, as
was, or should be authorized to hold such first meeting, or any greater
number of them, should and might hold their first meeting, upon the
fourteenth day after the passing of the said first above recited act,
and proceed to the execution of such acts respectively, as effectually as
if they had been assembled on the respective days appointed in such acts
for holding their first meeting: and whereas the said fourteen days
have been found in experience too short a time for the holding the first
meeting in some of the cases aforesaid, in a proper manner, whereby several doubts and difficulties have arisen, with respect to the due execution of some of the said acts; be it therefore enacted by the
King's most excellent majesty, by and with the advice and consent of the lords spiritual and temporal, and commons, in this
present parliament assembled, and by the authority of the same,
That such commissioners or trustees for putting such acts as a-
foresaid, or any part or parts thereof, in execution respectively,
or the same number of such respective commissioners or trustees

Preamble, re-citing act 30 Geo. 2.

Commission-ers for certain acts of the last session, are to

as

as was or were authorized to hold such first meeting, or any greater number of them, shall and may hold a meeting on the twenty first day after the day of the passing of this act, at such places as were respectively appointed in such acts, for holding the first meetings on the days therein specified; and all such commissioners or trustees, or any sufficient number of them, as aforesaid, being so assembled respectively, on the said twenty first day after the day of the passing of this act, shall and may proceed to the execution of such acts respectively, and then, and from time to time afterwards, adjourn, and do and perform all such matters and things, and execute all such powers and authorities, as are mentioned or granted to them respectively in the said acts, in the same manner, and as fully and effectually to all intents and purposes, as if such commissioners or trustees had been assembled, in pursuance of, and on the respective days specified or appointed in such respective acts for holding the first meeting of such commissioners or trustees; any thing in the said acts or any of them contained to the contrary notwithstanding.

(margin: meet on 21st day after passing this act, and put the same then in execution.*)*

CAP. XIV.

An act for further explaining the laws touching the electors of knights of the shire to serve in parliament for that part of Great Britain *called* England.

(margin: Preamble.*)*

WHEREAS *by an act made in the eighteenth year of the reign of his present Majesty, intituled,* An act to explain and amend the laws touching the elections of knights of the shire to serve in parliament for that part of Great Britain called England; *it is enacted,* That no person shall vote at the election of any knight or knights of a shire within that part of Great Britain called England, or principality of Wales, without having a freehold estate in the county for which he votes, of the clear yearly value of forty shillings, over and above all rents and charges payable out of or in respect of the same: *and whereas, notwithstanding the said act, certain persons who hold their estates by copy of court roll, pretend to have a right to vote, and have, at certain times, taken upon them to vote at such elections;* be it therefore enacted by the King's most excellent majesty, by and with the advice and consent of the lords spiritual and temporal, and commons, in this present parliament assembled, and by the authority of the same, That from and after the twenty fourth day of *June*, one thousand seven hundred and fifty eight, no person, who holds his estate by copy of court roll, shall be intitled thereby to vote at the election of any knight or knights of a shire within that part of *Great Britain* called *England*, or principality of *Wales*: and if any person shall vote in any such election, contrary to the true intent and meaning hereof, every such vote shall be void to all intents and purposes whatsoever; and every person so voting shall forfeit to any candidate for whom such vote shall not have been given, and who shall first sue for the same, the sum of fifty pounds, to be recovered by him or them, his, her, or their

(margin: Copyholders disabled from voting for knights of the shire;*)*

(margin: their vote void, and they to forfeit 50l.*)*

ex-

executors and administrators, together with full costs of suit, *with full costs of suit.*
by action of debt in any of his Majesty's courts of record at
Westminster, wherein no essoin, protection, wager of law, privi- *Onus probandi.*
lege, or imparlance shall be admitted or allowed; and in every
such action the proof shall lie on the person against whom such
action shall be brought.

II. And be it further enacted by the authority aforesaid, That *Plaintiff's plea in the action upon the case.*
it shall and may be sufficient for the plaintiff in any such action
of debt to set forth in the declaration or bill, that the defendant
is indebted to him in the sum of fifty pounds, and to alledge
the offence for which the action or suit is brought, and that the
defendant hath acted contrary to this act, without mentioning
the writ of summons to parliament, or the return thereof; and
upon trial of any issue in any such action or suit, the plaintiff
shall not be obliged to prove the writ of summons to parliament,
or the return thereof, or any warrant or authority to the sheriff
grounded upon any such writ of summons.

III. Provided always, That every such action or suit shall be *Limitation of actions.*
commenced within the space of nine calendar months next after
the fact, upon which the same is grounded, shall have been
committed.

IV. And be it further enacted by the authority aforesaid, *Statutes of jeofails, &c. extended to such suits.*
That all the statutes of jeofails, and amendments of the law
whatsoever, shall and may be construed to extend to all proceedings in any such action or suit.

V. Provided always, and be it further enacted by the autho- *Plaintiff nonsuited, &c. to pay treble costs.*
rity aforesaid, That in case the plaintiff in any such action or
suit, shall discontinue the same, or be nonsuited, or judgement
be otherwise given against him, then, and in any of the said
cases, the defendant, against whom such action or suit shall
have been brought, shall recover his treble costs.

CAP. XV.

An act for the encouragement of the exportation of culm to Lisbon, in the kingdom of Portugal.

WHEREAS since the late dreadful earthquake at Lisbon, a *Preamble.*
considerable demand hath arisen for culm to be there used, in
the burning or calcining of lime, for the purpose of rebuilding of the
said city, and the exportation of culm to Lisbon, under a small duty,
will greatly contribute to the more speedy and effectual rebuilding of
the said city, as well as to the encouragement of the trade and navigation of this kingdom; may it therefore please your Majesty that
it may be enacted; and be it enacted by the King's most excellent majesty, by and with the advice and consent of the lords
spiritual and temporal, and commons, in this present parliament
assembled, and by the authority of the same, That from and *Culm may be exported for 15 years,*
after the twenty fifth day of *March*, one thousand seven hundred
and fifty eight, it shall be lawful for any person or persons, for
and during the term of fifteen years, and from thence to the
end of the then next session of parliament, to export any quantity

upon payment of 1s. per chalder duty; and the exporter giving security thereof,

tity or quantities of culm to the city of *Lifbon*, in the kingdom of *Portugal*, upon payment of a duty of one shilling for every chalder (*Newcaftle-meafure*) of culm so exported, and no more, and after that rate for any greater or lesser quantity; so as the exporter shall, before the lading of such culm, or laying the same on board, become bound with other sufficient security in treble the value thereof, to the commissioners or chief officer or officers of his Majesty's customs, belonging to the port or place where such culm shall be shipped or put on board (who hath or have hereby power to take such security in his Majesty's name, and to his Majesty's use, and for which security no fee or reward shall be given or taken) that such culm shall be landed at *Lifbon*, in the kingdom of *Portugal*, and not elsewhere; and that a certificate under the hand and seal of the *British* consul general, or deputy consul residing at *Lifbon*, shall, within twelve calendar months from the date of the said bonds (the danger of the seas and enemies excepted) be returned to the officers who took the said bonds, that such culm hath been landed at *Lifbon*; and in case the ship or vessel on which any culm shall be put on board, for which such security ought to be given, shall depart or go out of port before such security is given, in every such case the ship or vessel, and the culm therein, or the value thereof, shall be forfeited, and shall and may be recovered, to wit, one moiety thereof to the use of the King, and the other moiety thereof to the person or persons who will seize, inform, or sue for the same.

of landing the same at Lifbon only, and returning a certificate thereof within 12 months. Ship and culm otherwise to be forfeited.

Duty to be levied, &c. as the duty upon coals.

II. And be it further enacted by the authority aforesaid, That the said duty on culm exported to *Lifbon* shall be raised, collected, levied, recovered, and paid, in the same manner, and under such penalties and forfeitures, and by such rules, ways, and methods, as the duties payable to his Majesty upon the exportation of coals are, by virtue of any law or statute now in force, to be raised, collected, levied, or recovered.

Limitation of actions.

III. And be it further enacted by the authority aforesaid, That if any action or suit shall be commenced against any person or persons for any thing done in pursuance of this act, the defendant or defendants in any such action or suit, may plead

General issue.

the general issue, and give this act, and the special matter, in evidence, at any trial to be had thereupon; and that the same was done in pursuance, and by the authority, of this act: and if it shall appear so to have been done, the jury shall find for the defendant or defendants; and if the plaintiff shall be nonsuit, or discontinue his action, after the defendant or defendants shall have appeared; or if judgement shall be given upon any verdict or demurrer against the plaintiff, the defendant and defendants

Treble costs.

shall and may recover treble costs, and have the like remedy for the same as the defendant or defendants hath or have in other cases by law.

CAP.

CAP. XVI.

An act to enforce and render more effectual an act made in the twenty fifth year of his present Majesty's reign, intituled, An act for annexing certain forfeited estates in Scotland to the crown unalienably; and for making satisfaction to the lawful creditors thereupon; and to establish a method of managing the same, and applying the rents and profits thereof, for the better civilizing and improving the highlands of Scotland, and preventing disorders there for the future.

WHEREAS *the lands, lordships, baronies, patronages, tythes, fishings, and other like heretages of* Donald Cameron *of* Lochiel, Charles Stewart *of* Ardsheil, Donal Mack Donald *of* Kinlochmoydart, Evan Macpherson *of* Clunie, Francis Buchanan *of* Arnprior, Donald Mack Donald *of* Lochgarry, Allan Cameron *of* Callart, Francis Farquharson *of* Monaltree, *and* Alexander Mack Donald *of* Keppoch, *by their attainders of high treason for their being engaged in the late unnatural and wicked rebellion, became forfeited and vested in his Majesty, by virtue of an act made in the twentieth year of his Majesty's reign, intituled,* An act for vesting in his Majesty the estates of certain traitors, and for more effectually discovering the same, and applying the produce thereof to the use of his Majesty, and for ascertaining and satisfying the lawful debts and claims thereupon: *and whereas by an act made in the twenty fifth year of his Majesty's reign, intituled,* An act for annexing certain forfeited estates in *Scotland* to the crown unalienably; and for making satisfaction to the lawful creditors thereupon; and to establish a method of managing the same, and applying the rents and profits thereof, for the better civilizing and improving the highlands of *Scotland,* and preventing disorders there for the future; *reciting, That the lands and estates of the said* Donald Cameron *of* Lochiel, *and the several other persons therein before-mentioned, which by virtue of the before-mentioned act of the twentieth year of his Majesty's reign, and of the said persons attainder of high treason, became vested in his Majesty, were holden of subject superiors, who had entered claims in the court of session to the property thereof; it is amongst other things, enacted, That it shall and may be lawful for his Majesty, his heirs and successors, by proper persons to be appointed for that purpose, under his or their sign manual, to transact or compound with such subject superiors, concerning their claims to the property of the said forfeited estates held of them respectively: and whereas his Majesty has been pleased, by his royal sign manual dated the twentieth day of* March, *one thousand seven hundred and fifty five, to appoint* James West *and* Nicholas Harding, *esquires; to transact and compound with the said subject superiors, and considerable progress has been made therein: and whereas claims have been entered in the*

Preamble, reciting clauses in act,

20 Geo. 1.

25 Geo. 2.

court of feffion, in terms of the faid act of the twentieth year of his Majefty's reign, by fundry crediters of the faid forfeiting perfons, upon the faid forfeited eftates: and whereas the faid tranfactions and compofitions cannot be concluded, and the price to be paid to the fubject fuperiors afcertained, until the faid claims, entered in the court of feffion by the crediters of the faid forfeiting perfons, are enquired into, and the extent of them afcertained, which cannot be done without the authority and interpofition of parliament: for remedy whereof, and for rendering effectual the good and valuable purpofes intended by the faid in part recited act made in the twenty fifth year of his Majefty's reign; be it enacted by the King's moft excellent majefty, by and with the advice and confent of the lords fpiritual and temporal, and commons, in this prefent parliament affembled, and by the authority of the fame, That the court of feffion in *Scotland*, fhall, and is hereby authorized and required to proceed upon and determine all claims entered, or that fhall be entered, by virtue of and in terms of the beforementioned act of the twentieth year of his Majefty's reign, by the crediters of the faid *Donald Cameron* of *Lochiel, Charles Stewart* of *Ardfheil, Donald Mack Donald* of *Kinlochmoydart, Evan Macpherfon* of *Clunie, Francis Buchanan* of *Amprior, Donald Mack Donald* of *Lochgarry, Allan Cameron* of *Callart, Francis Farquharfon* of *Monaltry,* and *Alexander Mack Donald* of *Keppoch,* upon the lands and eftates of the faid forfeiting perfons, or upon any other lands and eftates vefted in his Majefty by the aforefaid act of the twentieth year of his Majefty's reign, held of fubject fuperiors, according to the rules and regulations, and in the manner and form prefcribed by the above-mentioned act of the twentieth year of his Majefty's reign, for determining claims entered upon the eftates of forfeiting perfons holding of the crown.

Court of feffion to proceed on and determine all claims entered by the crediters of the forfeited eftates.

II. *And whereas it is neceffary to determine and afcertain the annual produce or value of the faid eftates;* be it further enacted by the authority aforefaid, That actions may be brought before the court of feffion, at the inftance of his Majefty's advocate, for proving the faid annual value and rental, and alfo the value of the faid lands and real eftates; which actions fhall be ferved againft the defendants, and fhall otherways be proceeded in before the court of feffion, in the fame way and manner, and agreable to the rules and regulations prefcribed by the faid act of the twenty fifth year of his Majefty's reign, concerning the valuation of the other forfeited eftates annexed to the crown.

Actions may be brought before the court for proving the annual rental and value.

III. And be it further enacted by the authority aforefaid, That every decree or determination of the court of feffion in the faid matters and things, fhall be final and binding upon the fubject fuperiors, and all other perfons and parties concerned, in cafe application for reverfing or amending fuch decrees is not duly made in the manner prefcribed, and within the time limited, by the faid laft-mentioned act of the twenty fifth year of his Majefty's reign.

Decree of the court to be final, unlefs application for reverfing the fame be made within a limited time.

IV. And, *to the end that the intereft of the fubject fuperiors may*

no

no ways be prejudged, it is hereby further enacted by the authority aforesaid, That it shall and may be lawful to the said subject superiors, by themselves, or by their counsel, to appear in
the said court when the claims entered upon the said estates respectively held of them, or when the said actions of valuation
are heard and determined, and to object thereto as they shall
see cause.

  · V. Provided always, and be it enacted by the authority aforesaid, That nothing in this act shall be construed to hurt or prejudice the right accruing to his Majesty, by the forfeiture of the
foresaid persons, or to invalidate or destroy the claim of the said
subject superiors duly entered in the court of session to the property of the said estates.

*Subject supe-
riors may ap-
pear in court,
and object,
when the
claims are en-
tered, or ac-
tions of valua-
tion heard.
Rights of the
crown and of
the subject
superiors re-
served.*

CAP. XVII.

*An act to explain, amend, and render more effectual an act
passed in the twenty ninth year of the reign of his present
Majesty, intituled,* An act for appointing a sufficient
number of constables for the service of the city and liberty of *Westminster* ; and to compel proper persons to
take upon them the office of jurymen, to present nu-
sances and other offences, within the said city and
liberty.

WHEREAS *an act passed in the twenty ninth year of the
reign of his present Majesty, intituled,* An act for appointing a sufficient number of constables for the service of the city
and liberty of *Westminster* ; and to compel proper persons to take
upon them the office of jurymen, to prevent nuisances and
other offences within the said city and liberty : *and whereas difficulties have arisen in ascertaining, who ought, in many cases, to repair pavements and remove annoyances, and the said act hath in other
respects been found insufficient to answer the several purposes thereby
intended :* therefore, to render the same more effectual ; be it
enacted by the King's most excellent majesty, by and with the
advice and consent of the lords spiritual and temporal, and commons, in this present parliament assembled, and by the authority
of the same, That all pavements, within the said city and liberty, belonging or opposite to churches, or other publick
buildings or grounds, which are the property of any parish, and
which of right ought to be repaired by such parish, shall, from time
to time be repaired, and kept in repair, and also all annoyances
belonging thereto be removed, by the churchwardens of such
parish for the time being ; and all pavements belonging or opposite to markets, shall be repaired and kept in repair, and all
annoyances belonging thereto be removed, by the proprietors of
such markets, their agents or lessees ; and all pavements belonging or opposite to hospitals, alms-houses, charitable foundations,
and all other publick buildings, not being the property of any
parish, shall be repaired, and all annoyances belonging thereto

*Preamble, re-
citing the act
29 Geo. 2.*

*Repairs of
pavements,
and removal
of annoy-
ances, belong-
ing to parish
churches, pub-
lick buildings,
or grounds, to
be done by
the church-
wardens ;
if belonging
to markets, by
the proprie-
tors, &c.
to hospitals,
alms-houses,
charitable*

be

foundations, &c. by the principal officer thereof; and to private grounds, by the owners.

be removed, by the principal officer or person residing in such buildings respectively, who are hereby declared to be the occupier or occupiers thereof; and all pavements belonging or opposite to lands and grounds, or adjoining to any wall or fence, where no houses are erected or built shall be repaired, and all annoyances belonging thereto be removed, by the owners of such lands and grounds, or other person or persons, who of right ought to repair such pavements, or remove such annoyances, as the case shall be: and it shall be lawful for the said annoyance jury appointed by the said recited act, and qualified as therein is directed, or any twelve or more of them, and they are hereby required to present all bad and defective pavements, and all annoyances belonging or opposite to all such buildings, places, and grounds, as aforesaid, first leaving notice in writing with such churchwardens, proprietors of markets, their agents or lessees, principal officers, or persons residing in such buildings, or owners of such grounds, as aforesaid, or affixing the same upon some publick part of such buildings, or on the walls or fences of such grounds, where any defective pavements or annoyances shall be found of their intention to present the same;

Annoyance jury may present bad pavements and annoyances, first giving notice of their intention to the proper persons;

and if the same be not amended, or removed within 14 days, may amerce the said persons according to the nature of the offence.

and in case such churchwardens, proprietors of markets, their agents or lessees, principal officers, or persons residing in such buildings, or owners of grounds, as aforesaid, shall not within fourteen days next after such notice given, cause such pavements to be amended, and annoyances to be removed, then the said jury shall amerce the said churchwardens, proprietors of markets, their agents or lessees, principal officers, or persons aforesaid, in such sum or sums of money as they shall think proper, according to the nature of the offence, not exceeding forty shillings for any one offence.

Occupiers of houses are to repair the pavements, and deduct the charges out of their rent;

II. And be it further enacted by the authority aforesaid, That all tenants or occupiers of houses, buildings, or grounds, in all places within the said city and liberty, shall be subject and liable to repair the pavements belonging or opposite to any such houses, buildings, or grounds; and it shall be lawful for all tenants to deduct and detain out of their rent due or to grow due, all and every such sum and sums of money as they shall have expended in repairing such pavements, according to notice to be given for that purpose by the annoyance jury, as aforesaid, (except in such cases only where tenants are by any covenant, contract, or agreement, to keep such pavements in repair at their own expence) any law or usage to the contrary notwithstanding.

except where they are by contract, to keep the same in repair.

Pavements broken up by persons belonging to any company of water works, are to be re-

III. *And whereas the pavements within the limits aforesaid are frequently broken up and damaged by persons belonging to the several proprietors of water works, and are often relaid with bad materials, or in an improper manner*; be it therefore further enacted by the authority aforesaid, That when and as often as any paviour, agent, servant, or other person, belonging to or employed by any of the proprietors of water works, or any other person employed by them, or any of them, shall break, take up, or otherwise damage any pavement within the said city and liberty,

such

fuch paviour, agent, fervant, or other perfon, fhall caufe the *laid by them* fame to be relaid or repaired as foon as conveniently may be, *in a fubftantial* with good durable ftone and gravel, and in a fubftantial and *manner, and* workman-like manner; and in cafe they fhall not relay or re- *in a conveni-* pair fuch pavement with all convenient fpeed, and to the fatis- *ent time.* faction of the perfon to whom the fame belongs, fuch perfon *In default, the* may at any time within fourteen days next after fuch pavement *annoyance* fhall have been broken up or damaged, as aforefaid, apply to *jury, upon* the foreman, or to any one of the annoyance jurymen of the *complaint,* divifion for the parifh wherein fuch pavement fhall be, who, *thereof,* upon fuch application, is hereby required, together with fix or more of the jurymen for that divifion, to view the premiffes in queftion; and if upon their view it fhall appear to them that *may direct the* fuch pavement hath not been relaid in due time, or in the man- *proprietor to* ner before directed, the faid jurymen fhall direct the perfon to *relay the fame,* whom fuch pavement belongs, or who is liable to repair the fame, to caufe the fame to be relaid or repaired in a proper man- ner; and when fuch pavement fhall have been relaid or repair- *and upon his* ed, according to the direction of the faid jurymen, the perfon *application* to whom fuch pavement belongs, and who fhall have caufed *to the court,* fuch pavement to be relaid or repaired, as aforefaid, may apply *the charges,* to a court, to be held by the dean of *Weftminfter* for the time being; or the high fteward of the city and liberty of *Weftminfter* for the time being, or his deputy; the two chief burgeffes of *Weftminfter*, and the other burgeffes, or any five or more of them, whereof the faid dean, high fteward, or his deputy, or one of the faid two chief burgeffes, to be one; and upon fuch application made, the faid court are hereby required to examine into the premiffes, upon oath (which oath they are hereby im- powered to adminifter to any perfon or perfons for that purpofe;) *the jury are to* and the faid jury, or any twelve or more of them, fhall at the *amerce the* faid court amerce any collector, paviour, agent, fervant, or any *company's* other perfon belonging to or employed by any of the proprietors *agent in the* of water works, upon whofe account fuch pavement fhall have *fame,* been broken up or otherwife damaged, and which fhall not have been relaid or repaired as before directed, in fo much money, as fhall, upon fuch examination, appear to the faid court to have been juftly expended in relaying or repairing fuch pavements; and alfo in a further fum not exceeding forty fhillings, nor lefs *and alfo in a* than twenty fhillings, for every fuch neglect or offence; which *fum not ex-* money fo expended in relaying or repairing fuch pavement, fhall, *nor lefs than* when recovered, be forthwith paid by the faid court, to the per- *20 s. for fuch* fon who fhall have caufed fuch pavement to be relaid or repair- *neglect.* ed, according to the direction of the faid jurymen, as aforefaid.

IV. Provided always, That no fuch amerciament fhall be fet *But the court* or impofed upon any fuch collector, paviour, agent, fervant, *is to give no-* or perfon aforefaid, unlefs three days notice in writing fhall have *tice to the a-* firft been given by the faid court to fuch collector, paviour, agent, *amerciament* fervant, or other perfon aforefaid. *be impofed.*

V. Provided always, and be it further enacted by the autho- *Paviour be-* rity aforefaid, That no paviour, or other perfon or perfons be- *longing to*
long- *water works,* *before he*

breaks up any pavement, is to give notice to what company he belongs,

longing to any company of water works, fhall break or take up, or otherwife damage, any pavement within the faid city and liberty, without firft giving notice, in writing, by what company of water works he or they are employed, to the proprietor or occupier of the houfe, ground, wall, or building, to which fuch pavement fhall belong or appertain, or by affixing fuch notice upon fome confpicuous part of fuch houfe, ground, wall, or building, where the proprietor or occupier cannot be found;

under penalty of 40 s.

any law or ufage to the contrary notwithftanding : and in cafe any fuch paviour, or other perfon or perfons aforefaid, fhall break up or damage any pavement as aforefaid, without giving fuch notice as aforefaid, every fuch perfon fhall be amerced by the faid jury in any fum not exceeding forty fhillings for every offence.

VI. *And whereas the long time allowed by the faid recited act, for removing annoyances, in fome cafes hath been found inconvenient :* for remedy whereof, be it enacted by the authority aforefaid, That

Annoyance jury where requifite may order the fpeedy removal of any annoyances or obftructions ;

when and as often as the faid annoyance jury fhall, upon their own view and knowledge, find any annoyances, obftructions, or encroachments, upon any of the publick ways, ftreets, or paffages, within the faid city and liberty, of fuch a nature as to require as fpeedy removal as may be, or which can be removed within a lefs time than fourteen days, it fhall be lawful for the faid jury, by an order in writing, left at the houfe of the perfon who fhall have caufed or fuffered fuch annoyance, obftruction, or encroachment, to direct fuch perfon to remove the fame within a reafonable time to be fpecified in fuch notice ; and if

and if not complied with, may amerce the offender in a fum not exceeding 40 s.

all fuch annoyances, obftructions, or encroachments, fhall not be removed within fuch reafonable time as by the faid notice fhall be directed, then the faid jury fhall amerce the perfon or perfons caufing fuch annoyance, obftruction, or encroachment, in fuch fum as they fhall think proper, not exceeding forty fhillings for any one offence.

No hourd or fence to be fet up in the ftreets, without a licence firft had from the court.

VII. And be it further enacted by the authority aforefaid, That no builder, or other perfon fhall erect or fet up, or caufe to be erected or fet up, in any of the publick ftreets, lanes, or paffages, within the faid city and liberty, any hourd or fence whatfoever, without a licence under the common feal of the faid court firft had and obtained ; in which licence fhall be expreffed the length and breadth of fuch hourd or fence, and alfo the time the fame fhall be allowed to continue ; which licences the faid court are hereby required to grant to all perfons applying for the fame, under fuch reftrictions and limitations, as aforefaid, at the difcretion of the faid court ; and no more than five fhillings

Fee payable for the licence.

fhall be paid for each licence : and if any perfon fhall erect, or caufe to be erected, any hourd or fence within the limits aforefaid, without fuch licence, or which fhall not be agreeable to the directions thereof, or fhall fuffer any materials for building to remain on the outfide of any hourd or fence above the fpace

Penalty.

of forty eight hours, every perfon offending in any of the cafes
afore-

aforesaid, shall be amerced by the said jury in a sum not exceeding forty shillings for every such offence.

VIII. Provided always, That such licences shall not be construed to extend to be a defence to any prosecution for a nui-
sance.

· IX. *And whereas by the said recited act the said annoyance jury
are impowered to destroy all unlawful weights, balances, and measures, of persons dealing by weight or measure within the limits aforesaid; and a doubt having arisen upon the construction of such part of
the said act as relates thereto :* for obviating whereof, be it enacted and declared by the authority aforesaid, That all weights and
measures made use of by persons dealing by weight or measure,
within the said city and liberty, shall be sized and sealed by the
standards belonging to the said city, and also marked with a port-
cullis by the officer already appointed for that purpose, or by such
other officer as may hereafter be appointed by the said dean, high
steward, or his deputy, the two chief burgesses, and the other
burgesses, of *Westminster*, or any five or more of them, whereof
the said dean, high steward, or his deputy always to be one, at
a court to be held for that purpose (and by no other person or
persons whatsoever) which officer appointed, or to be appointed,
is hereby required, upon application to him made for that purpose, to seal and mark, in manner aforesaid, all weights and
measures which shall be brought to him for that purpose, and
which shall be agreeable to the standards belonging to the said
city; and the said officer shall demand and receive, for each
weight and measure so by him sealed and marked, as aforesaid,
for his pains and trouble therein, the fees following, and no
more; that is to say, for every bushel, four pence; for every
half bushel, two pence; for every peck, half peck, and quarter
peck, one penny; for all half pecks, or quarter pecks, *per* dozen,
ten pence; for every sack two pence; for every ale and beer
measure, one farthing; for every hundred weight, four pence;
for every half hundred weight, two pence; for all pound weights,
and all other weights under half a hundred weight, one half-
penny; for all ounce weights, and all other weights under a
pound, one farthing: and all weights and measures belonging
to persons dealing by weight or measure within the said city and
liberty, which shall not be sealed and marked in manner before
directed, shall be deemed unlawful; and it shall and may be
lawful for the said annoyance jury, or any twelve or more of
them, and they are hereby authorized and required, to destroy
all such unlawful weights and measures, and to amerce the owner or owners thereof, or the person in whose possession the same
shall be found, in any sum or sums of money not exceeding
forty shillings for any one offence.

X. And be it further enacted by the authority aforesaid, That
the officer already appointed, or hereafter to be appointed as a-
foresaid, after all necessary charges and expences attending the
sizing, scaling, and marking such weights and measures as aforesaid, shall have been first deducted, shall, and he is hereby di-

rected

Sealing officer
to pay half-
yearly to the
deputy stew-
ard a moiety
of his profits.
rected and required half-yearly, within one calendar month next after the twenty fifth day of *March*, and the twenty ninth day of *September*, in every year, to pay, or caufe to be paid to the deputy fteward of *Weftminfter* for the time being, on account of his trouble and expence in attending his office of deputy steward of *Weftminfter*, one moiety of the clear money arifing from or on account of fuch fizing, fealing, and marking as aforefaid.

Court, upon
complaint,
may amerce
annoyance
juryman, for
non-executi-
on of his of-
fice.
XI. And, for the better executing the purpofes of the faid recited act, and this prefent act; be it further enacted by the authority aforefaid, That if any annoyance juryman fhall in any manner neglect or refufe to execute the duty of his office of juryman, it fhall be lawful for the faid court, upon complaint to them made of any fuch neglect or refufal to fine fuch juryman for every fuch offence, in any fum not exceeding forty fhillings.

High confta-
ble to obey the
orders of the
court,

and petty con-
ftables to be
affifting to
him;
under penalty
of being a-
merced by the
court.
XII. And be it further enacted by the authority aforefaid, That the high conftable for the faid city and liberty is hereby required to obey all lawful orders which he fhall from time to time receive from the faid dean, high fteward, or his deputy, at any court to be holden for the faid city and liberty; and all petty conftables are required to be aiding and affifting to the high conftable in the execution of all fuch orders and directions; and if the faid high conftable, or any petty conftable, fhall refufe or neglect to obey fuch orders, or in any other manner mifbehave in their refpective offices, the faid court fhall and may fine any high and petty conftable, fo offending, in any fum not exceeding forty fhillings for every fuch offence.

Aged perfons
exempted
from ferving
as conftables,
or as leet or
annoyance
jurymen.
XIII. And be it further enacted by the authority aforefaid, That no perfon within the faid city or liberty of *Weftminfter*, fhall be liable or compelled to ferve as a conftable, or to find a perfon to ferve in his ftead, who is of the age of fixty three years, or upwards; nor fhall any perfon be liable or compelled to ferve either as a leet or annoyance juryman, who is of the age of feventy years, or upwards; any thing in the faid recited act, or this prefent act, contained to the contrary notwithftanding.

Adjourn-
ments of the
court leet.
XIV. And be it further enacted by the authority aforefaid, That the faid dean, high fteward, or his deputy, fhall, and are hereby authorized and impowered to adjourn the court leet held for faid city and liberty, from time to time, as often as fhall be convenient; any law or ufage to the contrary notwithftanding: and if any leet juryman appointed, or to be appointed by virtue
Court may
amerce jury-
men for non-
attendance, or
other neglect.
of the faid recited act, fhall neglect or refufe to attend the faid court leet as often as thereunto required by the faid court, or in any other manner neglect or refufe to execute the duty of his office of juryman, it fhall be lawful for the faid court leet to fine fuch juryman for every fuch offence, in any fum not exceeding forty fhillings.

High bailiff,
or his deputy,
to execute all
warrants of
the court leet,
or court of
burgeffes,
XV. And be it further enacted by the authority aforefaid, That the faid high bailiff, or his deputy or deputies, is and are hereby directed and required forthwith to execute all warrants which he or they have already received, or may hereafter receive, for levying any fine fet or impofed, or to be fet or impofed,

pofed, for any offences againft the faid recited act, or this prefent act, from the faid court leet, or from the faid court of burgeffes, or from any juftice of the peace before whom any perfon fhall have been, or may be convicted for any offence againft the faid acts, or either of them; and in cafe the faid high bailiff, or his deputy or deputies, fhall refufe or neglect to execute any fuch warrant or warrants, as aforefaid, according to the true intent and meaning thereof, or to pay over all fuch fines as he **and to pay** fhall, from time to time, receive by virtue of any fuch warrant **over the fums** or warrants, according to the true intent and meaning of the **received, on** faid recited act, or this prefent act, it fhall and may be lawful **penalty of be-** for the faid court leet, or court of burgeffes refpectively, and **ing fined by** they are hereby authorized and impowered to fine fuch high **the court.** bailiff, or his deputy or deputies, fo offending, in any fum not exceeding five pounds for every fuch offence; and if any fine or **Fines impofed** fines fet or impofed upon the faid high bailiff, or his deputy or **on the high** deputies, by the faid court leet, or court of burgeffes, as afore- **bailiff, &c. for** faid, fhall remain unpaid for the fpace of one calendar month **default in the** next after the fame fhall have been fo fet or impofed, the high **premiffes,** conftable of the city and liberty of *Weftminfter*, is hereby autho- **to be levied by** rized and required by any warrant or warrants from the faid **the high con-** court leet, or court of burgeffes refpectively, directed to him for **ftable, by di-** that purpofe, to levy all and every fuch fine and fines, fo to be **ftrefs and fale.** fet or impofed on the faid high bailiff, or his deputy or deputies, as aforefaid, by diftrefs of the goods and chattles of the faid high bailiff, or his deputy or deputies, and to caufe fale to be made thereof, in cafe they fhall not be redeemed within five days next after fuch diftrefs made, rendering the overplus, if any, to the owner upon demand, after deducting the reafonable charges of making fuch diftrefs and fale, as aforefaid.

XVI. And be it further enacted by the authority aforefaid, **High bailiff to** That it fhall and may be lawful for the faid high bailiff, or his **retain a fourth** deputy or deputies, to retain in his or their hand or hands, one **of the fines** fourth part of the feveral fums of money that fhall be levied by **levied by him;** him or them, for the refpective fines fet by virtue of this or the faid recited act, in confideration of his or their trouble and expence in levying the fame.

XVII. Provided always, and be it declared and enacted by **and pay over** the authority aforefaid, That the remaining three fourth parts of **the remainder** the faid fines fhall be paid over by the faid high bailiff, his de- **to the over-** puty or deputies, to the refpective overfeers of the feveral pa- **feers of the** rifhes in *Weftminfter*, within the like time, and applied by them **parifh, to be** to the fame ufes and purpofes, as are directed by the faid recited **applied as the** act, with refpect to the whole of fuch fines. **former act di-** **rects.**

XVIII. And be it further enacted by the authority aforefaid, **Fines and a-** That all fines and amerciaments which fhall be fet or impofed **merciaments** upon any perfon by virtue or in purfuance of this act, fhall and **in general, ex-** may be levied, recovered, and applied, except where the fame **cept where** are directed to be otherwife levied, recovered, applied, or dif- **otherwife di-** pofed of by this act, in the fame manner as the fines and amer- **rected, to be** ciaments **levied and ap-** **plied as the** **former act** **directs.**

eiaments fet or impofed by the faid recited act, are thereby directed to be levied, recovered, and applied.

High bailiff to tranfmit an account thereof to the court of burgeffes,

to be entered, together with the licence fees for hoards, &c. and their application, in proper books,

which may be infpected by the overfeers; and copies taken thereof.

XIX. And be it enacted by the authority aforefaid, That the faid high bailiff, or his deputy or deputies, fhall, from time to time, tranfmit to the faid court of burgeffes, an account in writing of all fines and amerciaments by him levied or received, in purfuance of this, or the faid recited act; and that the clerk of the faid court of burgeffes, fhall, in a book to be kept for that purpofe, make a juft and due entry of all fines and amerciaments fet or impofed by virtue of this, or the faid recited act, and likewife an account of all monies received in purfuance thereof, or on account of licences granted for erecting hoards, by virtue of this act, and the application of the feveral fums fo received; which account the refpective overfeers of the feveral parifhes in *Weftminfter*, for the time being, fhall have liberty to infpect at all feafonable and convenient times, upon application to the faid clerk, and take copies thereof fo far as relates to the faid fines.

Commencement and continuance of this act.

XX. And be it further enacted by the authority aforefaid, That this act and all the powers and authorities herein contained, fhall commence and have continuance from and after the twenty ninth day of *September*, in the year of our Lord one thoufand feven hundred and fifty eight.

Limitation of actions.

General iffue.

Treble cofts.

XXI. And be it further enacted by the authority aforefaid, That if any fuit fhall be brought or commenced againft any perfon or perfons, for any thing done in purfuance of this act, or in relation to the premiffes, that in every fuch cafe, the action fhall be commenced within fix months next after the fact committed, and not afterwards; and fhall be laid and brought in the county of *Middlefex*, and not elfewhere, except fuch perfon or perfons againft whom fuch action fhall be brought, fhall remove into and refide in the city of *London*, in which cafe the faid action fhall be laid and brought in the faid city of *London*; and the defendant and defendants in fuch action or actions to be brought, may plead the general iffue, and give this act, and the fpecial matter, in evidence, at any trial to be had thereupon, and that the fame was done in purfuance and by the authority hereof; and if it fhall appear fo to be done, or if any fuch action or fuit fhall be brought after the time before limited for bringing the fame, or fhall be brought in any other county, city, or place, than the county of *Middlefex* (except in fuch cafe as aforefaid) that then and in fuch cafe, the jury fhall find for the defendant or defendants; and if upon fuch verdict, or if the plaintiff or plaintiffs fhall become nonfuit, or difcontinue his, her, or their action or actions; or if a verdict fhall pafs againft the plaintiff or plaintiffs; or if, upon demurrer, judgement fhall be given againft the plaintiff or plaintiffs; the defendant or defendants fhall and may recover treble cofts, and have the like remedy for the fame, as any defendant or defendants hath or have for cofts of fuit, in other cafes by law.

Places and

XXII. Provided always, That this act, or any thing or matter

ter herein contained, shall not extend to the church or college of
Westminster, nor to the close of *Westminster,* nor to any person
or persons inhabiting within the site, circuit, or precinct of the
said church, college, or close, for any offence or misgovern-
ment to be committed by them, or any of them, within the
site, circuit, or precinct of the said church, college, or close.

CAP. XVIII.

An act for draining and preserving certain fen lands and low grounds in
the isle of Ely and county of Cambridge, between the Cam, otherwise
Grant, Ouse, and Mildenhall rivers, and bounded on the south east by
the hard lands of Isleham, Fordham, Soham, and Wicken; and for impowering the governor, bailiffs, and commonalty of the company of
conservators of the great level of the fens, called Bedford Level, to sell
certain lands within the said limits, commonly called Invested Lands.

Preamble. Certain persons appointed commissioners, with others, to be
chosen for the several places, to execute the act. An agent to be appointed for every 200 hundred acres any commissioner shall be possessed of,
more than is required for his own qualification. Lords and ladies to appoint agents in like manner. The first commissioners for the several places.
Their continuance. Future commissioners to be chosen annually. Commissioners dying, or becoming disqualified, others to be chosen. Penalty on commissioners acting, if not qualified. Exception. Commissioners
to meet twice in every year, or oftner, if necessary. First general meeting when to be held. Allowance to be made to commissioners for their
attendance. Commissioners impowered to raise and strengthen the banks
of the rivers Cam, Ouze, &c. and of the several drains; and to lay proper
tunnels and bridges; and to repair the same, &c. Invested lands not to
be meddled with, without consent of the corporation. Power of making
orders. Satisfaction to be made to private owners for damages done to
their grounds. To be determined, in case of difference, by the justices
at the quarter sessions. Navigation of the rivers not to be obstructed, &c.
Commissioners to appoint collectors, and other officers; who are to be removable, and to give security. An acre rate to be laid on the lands for
raising money for carrying on the purposes of this act. Lands exempted from
tax. Such lands only as are subject to inundations, are to be taxed. Hod
or turf pools not taxable for 4 years. Common grounds belonging to the
poor, to pay only half the tax charged on other lands. Commissioners
may sever so much of the common lands, and let the same, as shall be sufficient to pay the taxes charged on the rest. Taxes how to be levied in
default of payment. Tax to be paid by the tenants, and deducted out
of their rent. In case of a lease, tenant to pay in proportion. Person
not paying the taxes within two months after demand, to forfeit 2s. for every 20s. he shall be in arrear. Lands unoccupied, to remain a security for
payment of the tax. Commissioners may take up money at interest for
carrying on the works, and assign the rates as a security for the same.
Charges of this act to be paid thereout. Rates chargeable with the monies borrowed thereon, and upon default of payment to vest in the creditors.
Assignments may be transferred. Assignments to be entered in a book.
Penalty upon persons cutting down or destroying banks or other works.
Offender may be transported. Persons convicted of destroying, stopping,
or damming up the drains, forfeit 50l. and convicted of throwing rubbish
or other obstruction, 5l. For want of distress the offender to be commited. 10s. penalty on making or continuing the use of watering places for
cattle, after notice given to the contrary; or of driving carriages
over the banks. Outring or division dykes, to be kept of a certain width
and depth, and effectually roded and scoured; bridges and tunnels to be
also laid, &c. where the commissioners shall judge necessary, under certain
penalties; commissioners may cause the same to be done, and levy the
charges, with the penalty. Application of the penalties. Regulations to
be observed in laying tunnels; penalty 5l. Rates and assessments to be
enter-

entered in proper books; and also accounts of receipts and disbursements. Accounts to be audited on oath half-yearly; at which times the collectors and receivers are to attend with their vouchers, &c. Accounts, after they are passed, to be entered in 2 sets of books, &c. Moles in lands adjoining to banks to be destroyed by the owners of the said lands; or the charges thereof to be levied on them. No trees, holts, or buildings, to be suffered to stand near any mill or engine. Commissioners impowered to erect staunches for keeping up a head of water at proper places, in the drains leading from the skirt lands. Mills may be erected for draining arable lands which produce winter crops. Mills to be erected, &c. by the commissioners for draining the tract of land principally belonging to lord Townshend, &c. General reservation of rights. Rights of the conservators of the great level reserved. Recital of clauses in act 15 Car. 2. & 20 Car. 2. The corporation's receiver to pay to the commissioners collector the rates charged on the invested lands, until the same be sold. Conservators to appoint annually a commissioner for every 200 acres of the invested lands taxed by this act. Sale may be made of the invested lands; giving one month's publick notice thereof. The same to be discharged of all former taxes; but not from taxes liable to be assessed thereon after such sale. Particular lands exempted from taxes. Disputes concerning the exemption of lands herein omitted to be exempted, to be determined by view of 9 commissioners on oath. Two copies to be made of such determinations, &c. Limitation of actions. General issue. Treble costs. Publick act.

CAP. XIX.

An act for draining and preserving certain fen lands, low grounds, and commons, in the parishes of Chatteris and Doddington, in the isle of Ely, in the county of Cambridge.

Preamble. The fen and low grounds before described, divided into two districts. Certain persons appointed commissioners, with others, to be chosen for the several places, to execute the act. An agent to be appointed for 20 acres any commissioner shall be possessed of. Joint owners of lands sufficient for a qualification, &c. may act as commissioners, and appoint agents. Persons disqualified from acting as commissioners. Commissioners to meet twice in every year. First general meeting when to be held. Adjournments, and other meetings of the commissioners. Sums allowed to be expended at half-yearly and other meetings. Meetings where to be held. Commissioners impowered to cut drains, and perform all other works proper for draining the lands. Satisfaction to be made to private owners for damages done to their grounds; to be determined, in case of difference, by 4 commissioners, who are to choose an umpire. Commissioners to appoint collectors, and other officers; who are to be removable, and to give security. An acre rate to be laid on the lands for raising money for carrying on the purposes of this act. Proviso. Lands exempted from tax. Quantities of land to be taxed, to be given in to commissioners. Penalty on neglect. Such lands only as are subject to inundations, are to be taxed. Commissioners may sever so much of the common lands, and let the same, as shall be sufficient to pay the taxes charged on the rest. Commissioners may take up money at interest for carrying on the works, and assign the rates as a security for the same. Assignments may be transferred. Assignments to be entered in a book. Limitation of the sum to be borrowed. Rates chargeable with the monies borrowed thereon, and upon default of payment to vest in the creditors. Application of the assessments, &c. Charges of passing this act to be first paid. Taxes how to be levied in default of payment. Tax to be paid by the tenants, and deducted out of their rent. No order made by the commissioners to be repealed, unless 5 consent. Penalty upon persons cutting down or destroying banks or other works. Offender may be transported. Persons convicted of destroying, stopping, or damming up the drains, forfeit 50l. For want of distress the offender to be committed. Allowance to be made out of the taxes for destroying moles. Satisfaction to be made for damages done to the banks, by burning of the grounds.

Penalty

Penalty of throwing the waters upon another perſon's lands, and not immediately into the publick drains. Accounts to be audited on oath yearly; at which times the collectors and receivers are to attend with their vouchers, &c. Accounts, after they are paſſed, to be entered in 2 ſets of books, &c. Proceedings of commiſſioners to be entered in books, and ſigned, and may be produced, and read in evidence. Penalty of cutting turf within a certain diſtance of the banks ; and of making or continuing the uſe of watering places for cattle; and of making any ſock-dike, &c. near the banks ; the ſaid penalties how to be recovered. Tunnel to be laid under Wimblington-Leam, &c. unleſs a mill be erected for anſwering the purpoſe thereof. Charges thereof to be paid by the firſt diſtrict. Sufficient drains to be made in the ſecond diſtrict, in particular parts thereof; and proper bridges and tunnels, to be defrayed by the ſecond diſtrict. Fences to be erected for each diſtrict. Proprietors of lands in Normore, to maintain ſuch parts of the bank on the weſt ſide of the Sixteen Foot, as adjoin to the ſaid lands. Tenants repairing the ſame, or the charge thereof being levied on them, are to be reimburſed. Diſputes relating to ſuch charges how to be determined. No trees or holts to be ſuffered to ſtand near any mill. Penalty on occupiers neglecting to rode and ſcour, &c. the outring and diviſion dikes. Collectors may cauſe the ſame to be done &c. and levy the charge. Mills to be inſured againſt fire. Rights of the conſervators of the great level reſerved. General reſervation of rights. Limitation of actions. General iſſue. Treble coſts. Publick act.

CAP. XX.

An act for applying a ſum of money granted in this ſeſſion of parliament, for rebuilding London Bridge; *and for rendering more effectual an act paſſed in the twenty ninth year of his preſent Majeſty's reign, intituled,* An act to improve, widen, and enlarge the paſſage over and through *London Bridge.*

WHEREAS *by an act paſſed in the twenty ninth year of the reign of his preſent Majeſty, intituled,* An act to improve, widen, and enlarge the paſſage over and through *London Bridge ; certain tolls* Preamble, re-citing part of the act 29 Geo. 2. *and ſums of money, from and after the twenty fourth day of* June *one thouſand ſeven hundred and fifty ſix, were thereby reſerved and made payable, for or upon account of every horſe, coach, chariot, hearſe, berlin, landau, calaſh, chaiſe, or chair, paſſing over the ſaid bridge, and alſo by the owner or owners of every hoy, barge, veſſel, lighter, or other craft, having any goods on board, except as therein is excepted, every time ſuch hoy, barge, veſſel, lighter, or other craft, ſhould paſs through any of the arches of the ſaid bridge, and ſuch tolls or ſums of money were veſted in the mayor and commonalty, and citizens of the city of* London, *for the purpoſes of the ſaid act : and whereas in purſuance of the powers given by the ſaid act a conſiderable progreſs hath been made in taking down the houſes on the ſaid bridge, and two of the arches under the ſame, in order to lay them into one ; and alſo a temporary wooden bridge was at a great expence erected to preſerve a publick paſſage to and from the ſaid city, which ſaid wooden bridge hath been entirely conſumed by fire, and muſt neceſſarily be re-built, at a further conſiderable expence : and whereas it hath been found by experience that the ſaid tolls, or ſums of money, will not be ſufficient for effecting the ends and purpoſes for which the ſame were granted and made payable : and whereas a*

ſum

sum not exceeding fifteen thousand pounds hath been granted to his Majesty this session of parliament, to be applied for rebuilding of London Bridge: may it therefore please your most excellent Majesty, that it may be enacted; and be it enacted by the King's most excellent majesty, by and with the advice and consent of the lords spiritual and temporal, and commons, in this present

15,000 l. to be paid out of the supplies granted for the year 1758, into the chamber of London.

parliament assembled, and by the authority of the same, That out of all or any of the aids or supplies granted to his Majesty for the service of the year one thousand seven hundred and fifty eight, there may and shall be applied and paid into the chamber of the city of *London*, the sum of fifteen thousand pounds, without account, to be applied for rebuilding the said bridge.

Tolls granted by the former act to continue to 24 June next, and no longer.

II. Provided always, That all and every the said tolls or sums of money made payable by the said recited act, shall continue and be in force until the twenty fourth day of *June*, one thousand seven hundred and fifty eight, and no longer; any thing in the said recited act contained to the contrary thereof in any wise notwithstanding.

Charges of passing this act how to be paid.

III. And be it further enacted by the authority aforesaid, That the charges and expences of obtaining and passing this present act, shall be paid out of any money which has been or shall be raised and received by virtue of the said former and this act.

Continuation of such powers, &c. of the former act, as are not hereby discontinued or altered.

IV. And it is hereby further enacted, That all and every the powers, clauses, provisoes, matters, and things, contained in the said former act, except such as are hereby discontinued or altered, shall remain, continue, and be in full force, and be executed, as well for the purposes of this act, as of the said former act, as amply and effectually as if the same were in and by this act, expresly re-enacted and declared to take effect and be in force.

Commencement of this act.

V. And be it further enacted by the authority aforesaid, That this act and all the powers and authorities herein contained, shall commence from and after the twenty first day of *April*, one thousand seven hundred and fifty eight.

Penalty of wilfully damaging or destroying the bridge, or any of the works thereof.

VI. And for the more effectually preventing any person or persons, from burning or destroying the said bridge; be it enacted by the authority aforesaid, That if any person or persons shall unlawfully, wilfully, and maliciously set fire to, burn, blow up, pull down, or destroy the said bridge, or any part thereof, or any works or buildings which now do or shall belong thereto, or in any wise direct or procure the same to be done, every such offender or offenders being lawfully convicted, shall be

Death.

deemed guilty of felony, and shall suffer death as a felon, without benefit of clergy.

Account of the application of the monies received to be laid annually before parliament.

VII. And be it also enacted by the authority aforesaid, That the chamberlain of the city of *London*, shall lay an account of the application, as well of the said sum of fifteen thousand pounds, as of all other monies received by virtue of this and the said former act, before both houses of parliament, within twenty days next after the opening of every session of parliament, in the same manner as is directed by the said former act.

VIII. And

VIII. And be it enacted by the authority aforesaid, That if any action shall be brought, or suit commenced, against any person or persons for any thing done in pursuance of this act, or in relation to the premisses, or any of them, such action or suit shall be laid or brought within six months next after the fact done, and shall be laid or brought in the city of *London* or county of *Surry*, and not elsewhere; and the defendant or defendants in such action, may plead the general issue, and give this act and the special matter in evidence, at any trial to be had thereupon; and that the same was done in pursuance and by authority of this act; and if the same shall appear to have been so done, or if any such action or suit shall not be brought within the time before limited, or shall be brought in any other county or place than as aforesaid, then the jury shall find for the defendant or defendants; or if the plaintiff or plaintiffs shall become nonsuited, or suffer a discontinuance of his, her, or their action or actions; or if a verdict shall pass against the plaintiff or plaintiffs; or if upon demurrer, judgement shall be given against the plaintiff or plaintiffs, the said defendant or defendants shall have treble costs, and shall have such remedy for recovering the same, as any defendant or defendants hath or have for costs in other cases by law.

Limitation of actions.

General issue.

Treble costs.

IX. And it is hereby further enacted, That this act shall be deemed a publick act; and shall be taken notice of as such, by all judges, justices, and other persons whatsoever, without specially pleading the same.

Publick act.

CAP. XXI.

An act for allowing further time for inrolment of deeds and wills made by papists; and for relief of protestant purchasers.

WHEREAS by a clause in an act of parliament passed in the third year of his late Majesty's reign, intituled, An act for explaining an act passed in the last session of parliament, intituled, *An act to oblige papists to register their names and real estates, and for enlarging the time for such registering; and for securing purchases made by protestants;* it was enacted, That from and after the twenty ninth day of September, in the year of our Lord one thousand seven hundred and seventeen, no manors, lands, tenements, hereditaments, or any interest therein, or rent or profit thereout, should pass, alter, or change, from any papist, or person professing the popish religion, by any deed or will, except such deed, within six months after the date, and such will, within six months after the death of the testator, should be inrolled in one of the King's courts of record at Westminster, or else within the same county or counties wherein the manors, lands, and tenements lie, in such manner as therein for that purpose is particularly directed: and whereas by several acts of parliament made in the tenth year of his said late Majesty's reign, and in the third, sixth, ninth, eleventh, twelfth, sixteenth, and nineteenth years of the reign of his present Majesty, it was enacted, That every deed and will which had been then made since the

Preamble, reciting the acts 3 Geo. 1.

twenty

twenty ninth day of September, one thousand seven hundred and seventeen, in order to pass, alter, or change, any manors, lands, tenements, or hereditaments, or any interest therein, or rent or profit thereout, from any papist or person professing the popish religion, though not then inrolled, should be as good and effectual in the law, as the same would have been in case the said deeds and wills had been inrolled within the time limited, by the said clause in the said first-mentioned act, for inrollment thereof, provided the said deeds and wills should be inrolled on or before the respective times in the said several acts respectively mentioned, in such manner as by the said first-mentioned act was directed: and whereas by another act made in the twenty sixth year of the reign of his present Majesty, it was enacted, That every deed and will made since the first day of December, one thousand seven hundred and forty six, in order to pass, alter, or change, any manors, lands, tenements, or hereditaments, or any interest therein, or any rent or profit thereout, from any papist or person professing the popish religion, to any protestant or protestants, or by reason of which deed or will any protestant or protestants may claim or derive any legal, equitable, or other interest whatsoever, to his, her, or their use, for his, her, or their benefit, or to the use or benefit of any other protestant or protestants, though not inrolled, or not inrolled in due time, should be as good and effectual in the law, as the same would have been in case the said deeds and wills had been inrolled within the times limited by the said clauses, in the said acts for the inrolment thereof, provided the same deeds and wills should be inrolled on or before the first day of January, one thousand seven hundred and fifty four, in such manner as by the said clause in the said first-mentioned act is directed: and whereas by an act made in the twenty eighth year of the reign of his present Majesty, it was enacted, That every deed and will made since the twenty ninth day of September, one thousand seven hundred and seventeen, in order to pass, alter, or change, any manors, lands, tenements, or hereditaments, or any interest therein, or any rent or profit thereout, from any papist or person professing the popish religion, to any protestant or protestants, or by or by reason of which deed or will, any protestant or protestants may claim or derive any legal, equitable, or other interest whatsoever, to his, her, or their use, for his, her, or their benefit, or to the use, or benefit of any other protestant or protestants, though not inrolled in due time, should be as good and effectual in the law, as the same would have been in case the said deeds and wills had been inrolled within the times limited by the said clauses, in the said acts for the inrollment thereof, provided the same deeds and wills should be inrolled on or before the first day of January, one thousand seven hundred and fifty six, in such manner as by the said clause in the said first-mentioned act is directed; be it enacted by the King's most excellent majesty, by and with the advice and consent of the lords spiritual and temporal, and commons, in this present parliament assembled, and by the authority of the same, That every deed and will made since the twenty ninth day of September, one thousand seven hundred and seventeen, in order to pass, alter, or change, any manors, lands, tenements, or hereditaments, or any

26 Geo. 2.

and 28 Geo. 2.

Further time given for inrolling deeds and wills of papists till 1 Jan. 1759.

interest

interest therein, or any rent or profit thereout, from any papist or person professing the popish religion, to any protestant or protestants, or by or by reason of which deed or will, any protestant or protestants may claim or derive any legal, equitable, or other interest whatsoever, to his, her, or their use, for his, her, or their benefit, or to the use or benefit of any other protestant or protestants, though not inrolled, or not inrolled in due time, shall be as good and effectual in the law, as the same would have been in case the said deeds and wills had been inrolled within the times limited by the said clauses, in the said acts for the inrollment thereof, provided the same deeds and wills shall be inrolled on or before the first day of *January*, one thousand seven hundred and fifty nine, in such manner as by the said clause in the said first-mentioned act is directed.

II. Provided always, That nothing herein contained shall extend, or be construed to extend, to make good any such deed, will, or lease, already made and not inrolled, of the want of inrolment whereof advantage shall have been taken, on or before the first day of *January* one thousand seven hundred and fifty eight, but every such deed, will, or lease, shall remain of such force and effect only, as the same would have had if this act had never been made, and of none other force and effect.
No deed, will, or lease made good hereby, whereof advantage has been taken of the non-inrolment thereof before 1 Jan. 1758.

III. And whereas many purchases made by protestants, may be in danger of being impeached or called in question, in regard that some deeds or wills, through which the title thereto is derived, ought to have been inrolled according to the said acts, but have not been so inrolled; be it therefore further enacted by the authority aforesaid, That no purchase made for full and valuable consideration of any manors, messuages, lands, tenements, or hereditaments, or of any interest therein, by any protestant or protestants, and meerly and only for the benefit of the protestants, shall be impeached or avoided, for or by reason that any deed or will through which the title thereto is derived, hath not been inrolled as required by the said acts, so as no advantage was taken of inrollment thereof, before such purchase was made, and so as no decree or judgement hath been obtained for want of the inrolment of such deeds or wills.
Purchases made by protestants shall stand good, if no advantage has been taken for non-inrolment.

IV. Provided also, That nothing herein contained, shall extend or be construed to extend, to make good any grant, lease, or mortgage, of the advowson, or right of presentation, collation, nomination, or donation, of and to any benefice, prebend, or ecclesiastical living, school, hospital, or donative, or any avoidance thereof, made by any papist or person professing the popish religion, in trust, directly or indirectly, mediately or immediately, by or for any such papist or person professing the popish religion, whether such trust hath been declared by writing or not.
No grant, lease, or mortgage of the advowson, or right of presentation to a living, &c. made by any papist in trust &c. to be hereby deemed good.

CAP. XXII.

An act for granting to his Majesty several rates and duties upon offices and pensions; and upon houses; and upon windows or lights; and for raising the sum of five millions by annuities, and a lottery, to be charged on the said rates and duties.

Most gracious Sovereign,

Preamble.

WE, your Majesty's most dutiful and loyal subjects, the commons of *Great Britain*, in parliament assembled, being desirous, by the most easy and effectual ways and means, to raise such supplies as are necessary for the prosecution of the present war, and for enabling your Majesty, at the end thereof, to establish a good and lasting peace, have, for that end and purpose, given and granted, and, by this present act, do give and grant, unto your Majesty, the several and respective duties, impositions, and sums of money, following, as well for and upon all salaries, fees, and perquisites, of offices and employments in *Great Britain*, and on all pensions and other gratuities payable out of any revenues belonging to your Majesty in *Great Britain*, exceeding the value of one hundred pounds *per annum*, as for and upon such houses, and windows or lights, as are herein after mentioned; and do most humbly beseech your Majesty that it may be enacted; and be it enacted by the King's most excellent Majesty, by and with the advice and consent of the lords spiritual and temporal, and commons, in this present parliament assembled, and by the authority of the same, That from and after the fifth day of *April*, one thousand seven hundred and fifty eight, there shall be yearly raised, levied, and paid, unto his Majesty, his heirs, and successors, the sum of one shilling, over and above all other duties already charged or payable, for every twenty shillings of the yearly value or amount of all salaries, fees, and perquisites, incident unto, or received for or in respect of, all offices and employments of profit in *Great Britain*; and the like sum of one shilling for every twenty shillings, of all pensions and other gratuities payable out of any revenue belonging to his Majesty in *Great Britain*, exceeding the value of one hundred pounds *per annum*.

Employments of profit, pensions, and gratuities, exceeding 100l. *per annum*, to pay 1s. *per* pound.

Duty on such as are payable at the exchequer, to be deducted and kept by the officers there.

II. And for the better raising, levying, and receiving, the said several sums of money and duties hereby charged for and upon the said offices and employments of profit; and for, and upon the pensions and gratuities aforesaid; and for the more effectual putting of this act in execution in reference to the same, it is hereby declared and enacted, That a deduction shall be made of the said sum of one shilling out of every twenty shillings, payable for, or in respect of, the salary, wages, or fees, of any offices and employments payable by the crown in *Great Britain*, which exceed one hundred pounds *per annum*; and for or in respect of any pension or gratuity which is or shall be payable out of any revenue belonging to his Majesty in *Great Britain* exceeding the value of one hundred pounds *per annum*, and that the money

money so deducted by the officers of his Majesty's exchequer in *England*, shall remain there for the purposes herein after declared; and such part of the said money as shall be so deducted by any officer or officers of the dutchies of *Lancaster* and *Cornwall*, or by any other commissioners, officers, and persons, by whom the said salaries, wages, fees, pensions, and gratuities, are or shall be respectively payable in *England*, shall be by them paid into the receipt of his Majesty's exchequer at *Westminster*; and such part of the said money as shall be so deducted by any of the officers of the court of exchequer in *Scotland*, or by any commissioners, officers, or other persons, by whom the said salaries, wages, fees, pensions, and gratuities, are or shall be respectively payable in *Scotland*, shall be paid at the city of *Edinburgh*, to such person or persons as the commissioners of the treasury, or the high treasurer of *Great Britain* for the time being, shall constitute and appoint to be receiver-general, or receivers thereof, for his Majesty's use; which said general receiver or receivers shall pay the same into the receipt of his Majesty's exchequer at *Westminster*; and the officers of the exchequer are hereby directed and required to keep separate and distinct accounts of all sums of money by them respectively retained or received, for or in respect of the said duty on offices, and on pensions and other gratuities, by virtue of this act, in order that the same may be applied to the purposes in this act mentioned, and to and for no other use or purpose whatsoever.

(margin: and such as shall be deducted at other publick offices, to be paid over into the exchequer; and such as shall be deducted in Scotland, to be paid to the receiver-general in Edinburgh, and by him into the exchequer at Westminster. Officers of the exchequer to keep a separate and distinct account of the money retained and received by them.)

III. *And whereas the profits of several offices and employments in Great Britain, arise in the whole, or in part, from perquisites, which are due and payable in the course of office;* it is hereby further enacted, That such part of the sums of money hereby granted, as are payable for or in respect of the profits of any office or employment, in any part of *England, Wales,* and *Berwick upon Tweed,* which arise from such perquisites, shall be computed, raised, levied, and paid, according to the annual value at which such profits stand valued and rated in the last assessment to the land tax.

(margin: Profits of offices to be computed and pay as they were rated to the last land tax.)

IV. Provided always, That such profits arising from such perquisites as aforesaid, shall be deemed and taken to have been valued and rated in such last assessment to the land tax, at so much only, as the entire sum, at which any such office was valued and rated in the said assessment, does exceed the amount of the salary, wages, or fees, payable as aforesaid, in respect of the same office.

(margin: Profits to be deemed rated to the land tax, at so much only, as the entire sum charged exceeds the salary.)

V. And be it further enacted by the authority aforesaid, That for the better rating, ordering, levying, and collecting, of the duty by this act charged, upon such perquisites of such of the said offices or employments as are in that part of *Great Britain* called *England, Wales,* and *Berwick* upon *Tweed*; and for the more effectual putting of this act in execution, in reference to the same; the commissioners of the land tax for the time being, within the several counties, cities, boroughs, cinque ports, towns, and places, of *England, Wales,* and town of *Berwick* upon *Tweed*, shall be commissioners for putting so much of this

(margin: Commissioners of the land tax to put so much of this act in execution as relates to the duties upon perquisites of offices.)

act

act in execution, as relates to the duty hereby charged upon the perquisites of offices.

Commissioners to meet on or before 3d July yearly;

VI. And be it further enacted and declared, That the several commissioners aforesaid, shall meet together at the most usual and common places of meeting within each of the said counties, ridings, cities, boroughs, cinque ports, towns, and places respectively, within *England*, *Wales*, and town of *Berwick* upon *Tweed*, for which they are appointed commissioners as aforesaid, yearly on or before the third day of *July*, and afterwards in like manner, as often as it shall be necessary for putting so much of this act in execution, as is hereby committed to their care and charge; and the said commissioners, or so many of them as shall be present at such meeting or meetings, or the major part of them, are hereby authorized and required, to put so much as aforesaid, of this present act in execution, and shall also, if they see cause, subdivide and distribute themselves, and the other commissioners not then present, into less numbers, so as three or more of the said commissioners may be appointed for the service of each hundred, lathe, wapentake, rape, ward, or other division, as may best conduce to the carrying on his Majesty's services, hereby required; nevertheless, not thereby to restrain the said commissioners, or any of them, from acting as commissioners in any other part of the county or place for which they are appointed: and the said commissioners, within the several hundreds, lathes, wapentakes, rapes, wards, or other divisions, in *England*, *Wales*, and *Berwick* upon *Tweed*, or any two or more of them, are hereby authorized and required at such general meeting, or within eight days after, according to the best of their judgements and discretions, to ascertain and set down in writing, in a rate to be prepared by them for that purpose, the amount of the said duty of one shilling in the pound, to be paid in pursuance of this act, by all commissioners or other officers, their clerks, agents, secondaries, substitutes, and other inferior ministers and persons whatsoever, having, using, or exercising any of the said offices or employments, the salary, wages, fees, and perquisites whereof, exceed the value of one hundred pounds *per annum*, within their respective hundreds, lathes, wapentakes, rapes, wards, or other divisions, in proportion to the annual value, at which the profits of such offices or employments respectively stand valued and rated, in the last assessment to the land tax, for the said respective hundreds and divisions respectively: and to the end the aforesaid duty on such perquisites of offices and employments may be duly collected, and true accounts thereof made, the said commissioners, or any three or more of them, are hereby required and ordered, within the time above limited, to sign and seal two duplicates of the said rates hereby directed to be made by them, and one of them to deliver, or cause to be delivered, to such persons as shall then be collectors of the land tax for each parish and place, or to such other two or more honest and responsible persons, which the said commissioners shall at their discretion nominate and appoint, to
be

(margin notes)

and subdivide themselves, &c.

Commissioners at their general meeting, or within eight days after, to rate the amount of the duty payable on all offices and employments of profit, in proportion to the value at which they stand rated to the last land tax.

Duplicates thereof to be signed, &c. by them, and one delivered to the collectors, &c. with warrant for collecting.

be collectors of this present duty, for each parish or place, with warrant to the collectors to collect the sums contained in such rates, respectively payable as aforesaid, so as the said several sums may be paid to the receiver general at the respective times herein limited; and if any person or persons shall think himself or themselves aggrieved, by being over-rated by the said commissioners, it shall and may be lawful to and for such person or persons, to appeal from the same to the barons of his Majesty's court of *Exchequer*, and the barons of the said court, or any one or more of them, is and are hereby authorized and required to hear and determine all such appeals, on or before the last day of *Michaelmas* term yearly; and the said collectors are hereby required, upon the application of any person or persons who shall think himself or themselves over-rated to the said rates, to permit such person or persons, or their stewards or bailiffs, or other proper representatives, to inspect the duplicates of such rates, upon the division or district of which he is collector, at all seasonable times in the day, without any fee or reward for the same; and every person so intending to appeal to the said barons, shall, and he is hereby required to give notice thereof in writing, to one or more of the collectors of the parish wherein he is rated, of such his intention to appeal; and it is hereby declared, that all appeals once heard and determined by the said barons, or any one or more of them, shall be final, without any further appeal upon any pretence whatsoever: and the said commissioners are hereby required to deliver, or cause to be delivered, a schedule or duplicate in parchment, under their hands and seals, fairly written, containing the whole sum rated within each parish or place, unto the receiver general of each county, riding, city, borough, town, and place respectively, in *England*, *Wales*, and *Berwick* upon *Tweed*, or his deputy; and shall transmit, or cause to be transmitted, a like schedule or duplicate into the King's remembrancer's office of the exchequer; and this the said commissioners shall cause to be done, upon or before the first day of *Hilary Term*, or within twenty days after (all appeals being first determined) for which duplicates the remembrancer, or his deputy, shall give to the person who brings the same, a receipt in writing *gratis*.

Persons aggrieved by being over rated, may appeal to the barons of the exchequer

Collectors to permit inspection of the rates.

Notice to be given them of intention to appeal.

Appeals once heard and determined to be final.

A duplicate in parchment of the rate to be delivered to the receiver general; and one to the remembrancer's office,

by the first day of Hilary Term, or 20 days after (all appeals first determined)

VII. And be it enacted by the authority aforesaid, That the said duty by this act imposed upon offices or employments within that part of the kingdom of *Great Britain* called *England*, *Wales*, and *Berwick* upon *Tweed*, as aforesaid, shall in all respects, (save as is herein otherwise enacted and provided) be raised, levied, collected, and paid into his Majesty's exchequer, for the purpose in this act expressed, in such and in like form and manner, and with such allowances, and under such penalties, forfeitures, and disabilities, and according to such rules, methods, and directions, as are prescribed or appointed for raising, levying, collecting, and paying the aid commonly called *The Land Tax* within *England*, *Wales*, and *Berwick* upon *Tweed*, in and by an act of parliament made and passed in this present

Duty to be raised, collected, and paid, in like manner, and with such allowances, and under such penalties, &c. as the land tax of this session.

session

feffion of parliament, intituled, *An act for granting an aid to his Majefty by a land tax, to be raifed in* Great Britain, *for the fervice of the year one thoufand feven hundred and fifty eight;* and for enforcing the payment of the rates to be affeffed upon Somerfet Houfe in the Strand; and all and every the powers, authorities, rules, directions, penalties, forfeitures, claufes, matters, and things contained in the faid act, for the raifing, levying, collecting, and paying the rates or duties thereby granted, within *England, Wales*, or *Berwick* upon *Tweed*, (fo far forth as the fame are not with refpect to the duties granted by this prefent act varied and altered) fhall be in full force, and be duly obferved, practifed, and put in execution, for raifing, levying, collecting, and paying the faid duty by this act impofed on offices and employments, within *England, Wales*, and *Berwick* upon *Tweed*, as fully and effectually to all intents and purpofes, as if the fame or the like powers, authorities, rules, directions, penalties, forfeitures, claufes, matters, and things, were particularly repeated and re-enacted in the body of this prefent act.

Their royal highneffes the princefs dowager of Wales, and prince of Wales, not chargeable,

nor their officers or fervants;

VIII. Provided always, and it is hereby declared, That this act, or any thing herein contained, fhall not charge or be conftrued to charge her royal highnefs the princefs dowager of *Wales*, or his royal highnefs the prince of *Wales*, with the above mentioned duty or payment of one fhilling out of every twenty fhillings, by the year, for or in refpect of any fums of money or annuities given or granted by his Majefty to their faid royal highneffes, or the officers or fervants attending their perfons; but that fuch fums of money and annuities, and their royal highneffes, and their treafurers, or receivers general for the time being, fhall be free and clear of all taxes, impofitions, and other publick charges whatfoever; any thing in this or any former act to the contrary in any wife notwithftanding.

nor his royal highnefs the duke of Cumberland, nor the princefs royal, nor princefs Amelia.

IX. And be it further enacted by the authority aforefaid, That this act, or any thing herein contained, fhall not charge or be conftrued, deemed, or taken, to charge his royal highnefs the duke of *Cumberland*, or her royal highnefs the princefs royal, or her royal highnefs the princefs *Amelia*, or the officers or fervants attending their perfons, with the above mentioned duty or payment of one fhilling out of every twenty fhillings, by the year, for or in refpect of any annuities or yearly payments granted or to be granted by his Majefty to their faid royal highneffes, and their fervants, for the time being, in refpect of the fame; but that fuch fums of money or annuities, fhall be free and clear from all taxes, impofitions, and other charges whatfoever.

Perquifites of offices and employments to pay where laft affeffed.

X. Provided always, and be it further enacted and declared by the authority aforefaid, That for the avoiding all obftructions and delays in collecting the duty by this act to be rated upon the perquifites of any offices or employments, the fame fhall pay and be rated in fuch county, hundred, rape, wapentake, conftablewick, divifion, or place of allotment, within *England, Wales*, and *Berwick upon Tweed*, in which the fame were laft affeffed, and not elfewhere.

XI. And

XI. And be it further enacted, That the first half-yearly payment of the said assessments for *England*, *Wales*, and town of *Berwick upon Tweed*, shall be levied, collected, and paid unto the receivers general of the said several counties, cities, and other places, who shall be appointed as aforesaid, on or before the tenth day of *October* yearly; and the last of the said half yearly payments, on or before the fifth day of *April* yearly.

First half yearly payment to be made on or before 10 October, and the last on or before 5 April yearly.

XII. And be it further enacted by the authority aforesaid, That every receiver general in *England*, *Wales*, and *Berwick upon Tweed*, from time to time, within the space of one month next after he shall have received the full sum that shall be charged within any hundred or division, for such particular payment that is to be made to such receiver general by virtue of this act, shall give to such commissioners as shall act in such division or hundred, a receipt under his hand and seal, acknowledging the receipt of the full sum charged within such hundred or division, for such particular payments; which receipt shall be a full discharge to each hundred or division, for such particular payment, against his Majesty, his heirs, and successors; which said receiver general are hereby required forthwith, or at furthest within twenty days after the receipt of any money of the taxes or duties by this act granted, to transmit or cause to be paid the money by them received into the receipt of his Majesty's exchequer.

Receiver general within a month after receiving the full sum charged, to give the commissioners a receipt.

which shall be a full discharge for payment; Receivers general within 20 days to pay the monies into the exchequer.

XIII. And be it further enacted, That if any collector of any parish or place in *England*, *Wales*, or *Berwick upon Tweed*, shall keep in his hands any part of the money by him collected for any longer time than is by this act directed (other than the allowance made unto him by this act) or shall pay any part thereof to any person or persons other than the receiver general of such county or place, or to his respective deputy, that every such collector shall forfeit for every such offence, the sum of forty pounds; and in case any receiver general of any part of *England*, *Wales*, or *Berwick upon Tweed*, or his deputy, shall pay any part of the monies paid to him or them by any collector by virtue of this act, to any person or persons whatsoever, other than into the receipt of his Majesty's exchequer, and at or within the respective times limited by this act; or in case any such receiver general of any part of *England*, *Wales*, or *Berwick upon Tweed*, or his deputy, shall pay any part of the said monies by any warrant of the high treasurer, commissioners of the treasury, or under treasurer, for the time being, or upon any tally of pro, or tally of anticipation, or other way or device whatsoever, whereby to divert or hinder the actual payment thereof into the receipt of the exchequer, as aforesaid, then every such receiver general shall, for every such offence of himself, or his deputy, forfeit the sum of five hundred pounds to him or them that shall sue for the same in any court of record, by bill, plaint, or information; wherein no essoin, protection, or wager of law, is to be allowed.

Collectors keeping the money in their hands, or paying it otherwise than to the receiver general forfeit 40l.

Receiver general, or his deputy, paying the money otherwise than into the exchequer, forfeit 500l.

XIV. And be it further enacted by the authority aforesaid, That the commissioners of the supply for the time being, for

put-

Commissioners of the land tax in Scotland, to put this act in execution there;

putting in execution any act for raising the aid commonly called *The Cess* or *Land Tax*, within the several shires of *Scotland*, or such of them who have qualified, or shall qualify themselves, according to the laws of *Scotland* in that behalf, shall be commissioners for ordering, raising, and levying, the duty hereby granted on the perquisites of offices and employments, exercised within the same shires, or within any boroughs within the same respectively; which said commissioners shall put in execution this present act, and the powers therein contained, within and for the same shires and boroughs respectively; and the said commissioners have hereby power to chuse their own clerk, and to do every thing concerning the said supply, as is prescribed and

according to the cess act of 6 Nov. 1706, &c.

appointed by the cess act of the sixth of *November*, one thousand seven hundred and six, and other acts made in any former parliament of *Scotland*, to which the said act of the sixth of *November*, one thousand seven hundred and six, doth relate, holding the same as if herein repeated.

Execution to be done as by the said acts is prescribed.
First meeting to be at the head burghs on the second Monday in July yearly, &c.

XV. And it is hereby further enacted, That execution shall be done in *Scotland* for bringing the said duty to be raised there, as is provided by the same acts in all points not altered by this act; and that the first meeting of the said commissioners for shires in *Scotland*, shall be at the respective head burghs thereof, the second *Monday* in *July* in every year; and that the sheriffs, or their deputies, do intimate the same to the said commissioners of their shires, with power to the said commissioners, to appoint the subsequent diets of their meetings, and their convenors, from time to time; and also to appoint collectors, with such caution as they shall think fit.

All clauses in former acts relating to the bringing in the cess, &c. to be in force as to the supply herein granted

XVI. And be it further enacted by the authority aforesaid, That all clauses contained in former acts of parliament of *Scotland*, and convention of estates there, in relation to the bringing in of the cess, and quartering, and touching riding money, shall stand in full force, as to the supply now imposed upon *Scotland*, as if they were herein expressed, and as they were observed before the making this act.

Clerks of the sheriff's court to deliver yearly, on or before 10 June, to the commissioners, lists of all offices of profit in each shire; and a duplicate thereof to the deputy remembrancer of the exchequer; on penalty of 50l.

XVII. And it is hereby further enacted, That the clerk of the *sheriff's court* in each shire in *Scotland*, shall yearly on or before the tenth day of *June*, deliver to the said commissioners of supply for such shire, a true and exact list of all and every office of employment of profit, exercised in such shire, and every burgh within the same; and also do, and shall, within the time aforesaid, deliver, or cause to be delivered, a duplicate of such list, to the deputy remembrancer of his Majesty's court of *Exchequer* in *Scotland*; and in case any clerk of the *sheriff's court* shall neglect to deliver such list, or the duplicate thereof, within the time herein before mentioned, or shall wilfully omit out of such lists, or the duplicate thereof, any office or employment that ought to have been inserted therein, he shall, for every such offence, forfeit the sum of fifty pounds sterling.

XVIII. And it is further enacted, That the said commissioners in their respective shires do, and shall yearly on or before the

tenth

tenth day of *July*, according to the best of their judgments and discretions, ascertain, and set down in writing, in a rate or assessment to be prepared by them for that purpose, the annual value of all and every office and employment, exercised in such shire, and in every burgh within the same; and do therein rate and assess the said sum of one shilling for every twenty shillings of the annual value thereof, on the officers and persons who then do, or shall execute any such office or employment, the salary, fees, and perquisites of office whereof, exceed one hundred pounds *per annum*; and in case the said commissioners of supply for any shire in *Scotland*, shall neglect to make such rate and assessment, within the time herein before limited for that purpose, in that case, the sheriff depute of the county, shall, and is hereby required, on or before the twenty fifth day of *July*, yearly, according to the best of his judgment and discretion, to make and perfect such rate or assessment in writing; and a note of the said respective rates or assessments, shall, within six days after the making and perfecting thereof, be lodged by the clerk of the commissioners, or the said sheriff depute respectively, in the hands of the collector of the cess or land tax, for the time being, for each county or burgh within *Scotland*, who shall be, and is hereby appointed, impowered, and required, to be collector thereof; and every such collector of the cess or land tax, and his cautioners, or security, shall be bound *ipso facto*, by virtue of this act, for the due and faithful performance by such collector, of all parts of the duty of the office hereby committed to him in respect of the said rates and assessments, and that under the penalty of one hundred pounds sterling; and that every such collector of the cess, shall be intitled to have an allowance from the receiver general of the sum of three pence *per* pound of the money by him collected and paid over to such receiver general; and the persons so rated and charged with the said duty on their respective offices and employments, shall, by themselves, or others for their behoof, pay in the duty with which they were charged, on or before the tenth day of *October*, yearly, for the half year betwixt *Whitsunday* and *Martinmas*, and on or before the fifth day of *April*, yearly, for the half year betwixt *Martinmas* and *Whitsunday*, to the collector of the cess, personally, or at his office by him held for the receiving the land tax; unless such person shall enter an appeal against the assessment made, in which case such appeal shall be discussed before payment, in manner herein after provided; and in case of appeal, such payment shall be made within ten days after discussing or dismissing such appeal, in the manner herein after provided; and that every person so rated and assessed, shall, in case of his not paying in the duties with which he is charged, to the collector of the cess, upon the day upon which he is hereby appointed to pay the same, or within three days after, forfeit treble the value and extent of the duty with which he stands charged.

XIX. And be it further enacted, That it shall be in the power of the persons liable to, and assessed for, the duty aforesaid,
in

Commissioners on or before 10 July yearly, to rate the annual value of all offices and employments, and assess in 1s. per pound, all such as shall exceed 100l. per annum.

On commissioners neglect, sheriff depute to make such rate.

Note of the rate, within 6 days after the making, to be delivered to the collector of the land tax.

Collector bound in 100l. penalty for the faithful performance of his duty.

Collectors to have 3d. in the pound for their trouble.

Duty to be paid half yearly, on or before 10 October, and 5 April, except in cases of appeal,

and then within 10 days after hearing the same;

on forfeiture of treble value.

Appeal may be made in behalf of the

in case they shall conceive themselves to be injured by the assessment and charge made upon them by the said commissioners of supply or sheriff depute; or to the collectors, or any other officer of the crown, if he shall judge the crown to be lessed by the assessment or charge made; to appeal to the barons of the court of *exchequer* in *Scotland*, who are to determine finally all such appeals on or before the last day of term of *Martinmas* yearly; and every such appellant shall, within the space of ten days after the note in writing of his charge being delivered to him, or left at his house, by the collector by himself, or some other person acting on his behalf, deliver, or cause to be delivered, to the collector of the cess, at his office, a note in writing of the wrong or grievance of which such person complains, and whereof he shall be minded to seek redress by appeal; and such collector is hereby to make an entry, to be kept by him for that purpose, of all such notices given to him.

subject, or of the crown, to the barons of the exchequer.

All appeals to be determined on or before the last day of Martinmas term.

Notice to be given to collector of the intention and cause of appeal; who is to make an entry thereof.

XX. And be it further enacted, That in case the party giving such notice of an appeal or complaint, shall neglect to insist thereon before the said barons within the time before limited, then and in that case such complaint or appeal shall be held to be fallen from, and the charge or assessment therein referred to shall stand in full force; and in all cases of appeals fallen from, or upon hearing whereof the said barons shall not vary the rate, the barons shall and may order the appellant to pay to the collector any sum not exceeding twenty shillings sterling, as they shall think proper, as and for the costs he may have been at by reason of such appeal.

Appeal if not prosecuted within due time,

or if the assessment be affirmed,

appellant forfeits to the collector 20s.

XXI. And it is hereby enacted by the authority aforesaid, That every person rated or assessed for any office or employment in *Scotland*, shall be rated, and pay for his said office or employment in the shire where the same shall be exercised, although the revenue or profits arising by such office or employment are payable elsewhere.

Duty to be paid where the offices are exercised;

XXII. And it is hereby declared and enacted by the authority aforesaid, That the money imposed on offices and employments in *Scotland*, be raised in *Scotland* in the respective shires, stewartries, cities, and boroughs, free of all charges to his Majesty, save as is herein before mentioned; and shall in like manner be paid at the city of *Edinburgh*, to such person or persons as the commissioners of the treasury, or the high treasurer of *Great Britain* for the time being, shall constitute and appoint to be receiver general or receivers thereof, for his Majesty's use; which said general receiver or receivers shall be answerable and accountable for the same to his Majesty in the exchequer.

and to be raised free of all charges, other than as before allowed, and to be paid to the receiver general at Edinburgh,

and by him into the exchequer.

XXIII. Provided always, and it is hereby enacted, That where any person shall have, use, or exercise, two or more offices or employments in any part of *Great Britain*, the salary and perquisites whereof together exceed the sum of one hundred pounds a year, that such person shall be rated and liable to pay the said sum of one shilling in the pound for the profits of such offices and employments, notwithstanding the salary and perquisites of

Where two or more offices, exceeding together 100l. per ann. are exercised by one person, such person is to pay 1s. per

no

no one of the faid offices are of the value of one hundred pounds *pound for the* per annum. *fame.*

XXIV. Provided always, That nothing in this act contained *Military offi-* fhall extend, or be conftrued to extend, to the pay of com- *cers, &c. of the* miffion or non-commiffion officers or private men ferving in the *army or navy,* navy or army. *exempted*

XXV. Provided always, That no commiffioner of the land *from paying.* tax in *England, Wales,* or *Berwick upon Tweed,* or commiffioner *Commiffioners* of the fupply in *Scotland,* who fhall be poffeffed of any office or *holding offices* employment fubject and liable to the duty hereby impofed, fhall *liable to be* fit, or act, or any way interfere in rating his own office or em- *rated, to with-* ployment, but fhall withdraw until the rating thereof be fettled *draw, &c.; till* and determined by the reft of the commiffioners then prefent; *the rating* and in default thereof the reft of the commiffioners then prefent *thereof be* fhall have power, and are hereby required to impofe fuch fine *fettled by the* or fines as to them fhall be thought fit, upon fuch commiffioner *reft of the* fo refufing to withdraw, or acting in his own caufe, not exceeding *commiffioners;* one hundred pounds fterling; and caufe the fame to be levied *on penalty of* and paid as other fines and forfeitures to be impofed by virtue *100l.* of this act are to be levied and paid in *England* and *Scotland* re- fpectively.

XXVI. And be it enacted, That in all cafes where any fees, falaries, wages, or other allowances or profits on any offices or *Duty on fees,* employments of profit charged by this act, fhall be payable at the *falaries, &c.* receipt of the exchequer, or by the cofferer of his Majefty's houf- *not paid, may* hold, or out of any other publick office, or by any of his Majefty's *be ftopt at the* receivers or paymafters in *Great Britain,* the duty or payment *publick offices.* which, in purfuance of this act, fhall be charged for or in refpect of fuch offices or employments, fhall and may (in cafe of non- payment thereof) be detained and ftopped out of the fame, or out of any money which fhall be paid upon fuch fees, falaries, wages, allowances, or profits, or for arrears thereof, and be ap- *A true account* plied to the fatisfaction of the duties not otherwife paid as *to be kept of* aforefaid; and the proper officers in the faid exchequer, and *the money* other the publick offices aforefaid, fhall keep true accounts of all *ftopt, and co-* monies ftopped, and (upon requeft) fhall give copies of fuch *pies thereof to* accounts to the proper collectors of fuch monies for the refpective *be given to the* parifhes or places where the faid monies are rated by this act. *collectors, if* *required.*

XXVII. *And whereas divers offices and employments of profit chargeable by this act are executed by deputy, and the principal officers living in places remote from the divifion, parifh, or place, where fuch offices or employments are taxable, the rates and affeffments for fuch particular offices and employments cannot be recovered without great charge and difficulty;* be it therefore enacted by the authority *Deputies to* aforefaid, That where any office or employment of profit *pay for prin-* chargeable by this act, is or fhall be executed by deputy, fuch *cipals; and on* deputy fhall pay fuch affeffment as fhall be charged thereon, and *nonpayment* deduct the fame out of the profits of fuch office or employment; *are liable to* and in cafe of refufal or non-payment thereof, fuch deputy fhall *diftrefs.* be liable to fuch diftrefs, as by this act is prefcribed againft any perfon having and enjoying any office or employment of profit,

and

and to all other remedies and penalties therein respectively contained.

XXVIII. Provided always, and be it further enacted by the authority aforesaid, That there shall be provided and kept in his Majesty's exchequer (that is to say) in the office of the auditor of the receipt, one book of register, in which all the money that shall be paid into the exchequer for the duties on offices and pensions hereby granted, shall be entered and registered apart and distinct from all other monies paid and payable to his Majesty.

XXIX. And be it further enacted, That all penalties, treble values, and forfeitures, incurred by virtue of this act in *Scotland*, shall be recovered at the suit of the respective collectors by distraining or poynding, according to the forms of the law of *Scotland*, upon warrants to be granted and subscribed by any two of the commissioners for supply, or by the sheriff, or depute sheriff, of the county from whom such warrant shall be required; and they are hereby respectively required to grant the same under the penalty of ten pounds sterling *toties quoties*, upon certificate made to them, or either of them, by the collector of the cess, that such penalties or forfeitures are incurred, and such duties resting and not duly paid; which warrants shall be executed by

the constables or sheriff officers of the county; and the goods or effects so poynded or distrained shall be valued and appraised by any two persons to be appointed by the sheriff officer, or constable, to value and appraise such goods; which two persons shall be obliged to value the same, under the penalty of forty shillings sterling for each neglect or refusal; and which valuation shall be made upon the ground, or at the house, where the same were poynded and distrained, and may and shall be sold and disposed of at the value by the officer or constable who does poynd or distrain the same; and the value to be applied, in the first place,

to the satisfaction and payment of the duty, triple value, or penalty, owing by the person whose goods are so poynded; and, in the second place, to the payment for the trouble of the officer or constable so poynding, at the rate of two shillings *per* pound of the triple value, penalty, or forfeitures, for which the goods shall be poynded or distrained, unless the owner from whom the

same were poynded or distrained, shall redeem the same by payment of the appraised value within the space of four days after the poynding and valuation, to the officer who poynded the

same; and in case any surplus shall remain of the price or value, after payment of the penalty incurred, and after payment of what is allowed to be retained by the officer or constable in manner herein directed, such surplus shall be returned to the owner from

whom the goods were distrained; and in case no purchaser or buyer do appear at the said sale, that the said goods or effects so poynded or distrained shall be consigned and lodged in the hands of the sheriff depute of the county, or his substitute; and if not redeemed by the owner within the space of four days after the consignment of the hands of the said sheriff, that the same shall

be

be rouped, fold, and difposed of, by order of the fheriff, in fuch manner, and at fuch time and place, as he fhall appoint; he always being liable to the payment of the triple value of the penalty or penalties incurred, to the collector of the cefs, and to the officer or conftable who fhall have poynded the fame, for their trouble and expence as above ftated, in cafe the value of the goods fo fold fhall amount to the extent of the penalties incurred, and to the fees due to the officer or conftable; and fhall be in the third place, intitled to one fhilling *per* pound of the value of the goods fo difpofed of, for his own pains and trouble, after preference and allowance of the penalties, and of what is appointed to be paid to the officer or conftable fo poynding, the expence of preferving or maintaining the goods or cattle fo poynded, during the four days allowed to the owner to redeem them, and the expence of the fale; and in like manner the expence fhall be allowed to the fheriff for preferving and maintaining the goods or cattle diftrained, during the four days that the owner is allowed to redeem after confignment in his hands, as alfo the expence of the fale.

(margin: who is accountable to the collector and conftable for the penalties and fees.)

(margin: 1s. per pound allowed to the fheriff for his trouble and expence.)

XXX. And be it further enacted, That the officer or conftable who fhall difpofe of fuch goods or cattle fo poynded, diftrained, and fold, fhall be bound to pay in the fums arifing from the fale, in fo far as extends to the penalties for which the fame were poynded by the collector of the cefs or land tax, within ten days after the receipt of the price, allowing always what is above allowed for his own pains and expence; and that, in like manner, if the goods or cattle diftrained fhall be difpofed of by the fheriff, as before directed, he fhall, within four days after receipt of the price, be obliged to pay in the fame to the collector of the cefs, after deduction of what is appointed to be paid to the officer or conftable who made the poynding, and after deduction of what is above allowed to be retained by him for his own pains and expence, and fhall remain liable to the collector of the cefs, until payment, and fubject to be poynded and diftrained therefore, in the fame manner as is above provided with regard to any perfon liable to penalties in virtue of this act.

(margin: Conftable to pay over the money arifing by the fale of the diftrefs, within 10 days; and the fheriff within 4 days after receipt thereof.)

XXXI. And be it further enacted by the authority aforefaid, That from and after the fifth day of *April* one thoufand feven hundred and fifty eight, there fhall be charged, raifed, levied, and paid, unto his Majefty, his heirs, and fuccefors, the feveral rates and duties upon houfes, windows, or lights, herein aftermentioned; that is to fay,

(margin: Rates charged upon houfes, windows, or lights.)

For and upon every dwelling-houfe inhabited, which now is, or hereafter fhall be, erected within that part of *Great Britain* called *England*, the yearly fum of one fhilling, over and above the yearly fum of two fhillings already charged upon every fuch dwelling houfe.

And for and upon every dwelling-houfe inhabited, which now is, or hereafter fhall be, erected within that part of *Great Britain* called *Scotland*, the yearly fum of one fhilling.

(margin: viz. 1s. additional duty upon every dwelling-houfe in England, and 1s. upon every dwelling houfe in Scotland;)

And

and 6d. additional duty for every window or light in every dwelling house containing 15 windows, or more.

And for every window or light in every dwelling-houfe inhabited, or to be inhabited, within and throughout the whole kingdom of *Great Britain*, which fhall contain fifteen windows or lights, or upwards, the yearly fum of fix pence for each window or light in fuch houfe, over and above, and by way of addition to, the feveral and refpective duties chargeable thereupon; by virtue of former acts of parliament made in that behalf.

The faid duties to be raifed, levied, collected, and paid, as the 3 feveral acts of

XXXII. And be it enacted by the authority aforefaid, That the faid feveral duties by this act impofed, within and throughout the faid kingdom of *Great Britain*, for and upon fuch houfes, and fuch windows or lights as aforefaid, fhall be raifed, levied, collected, and paid, into his Majefty's exchequer, for the purpofes in this act expreffed, in fuch and like form and manner, and with fuch allowances, and under fuch penalties, forfeitures, and difabilities, and according to fuch rules, methods, and directions, as are prefcribed or appointed for raifing, levying, collecting, and paying, the duties on houfes, windows, or lights, in and by two feveral acts of parliament made in the twentieth

20 Geo. 2.

year of his prefent Majefty's reign, the one, intituled, *An act for repealing the feveral rates and duties upon houfes, windows and lights; and for granting to his Majefty other rates and duties upon houfes, windows, or lights; and for raifing the fum of four millions four hundred thoufand pounds by annuities, to be charged on the faid rates or duties*; and the other intituled, *An act to enforce the execution of an act of this feffion of parliament, for granting to his Majefty feveral rates and duties upon houfes, windows, or lights*;

and 21 Geo. 2. prefcribe with refpect to the duties thereby granted.

and in and by a certain other act of parliament, intituled, *An act for explaining, amending, and further enforcing the execution of an act paffed in the laft feffion of parliament, intituled,* An act for repealing the feveral rates and duties upon houfes, windows, and lights; and for granting to his Majefty other rates and duties upon houfes, windows, or lights; and for raifing the fum of four millions four hundred thoufand pounds by annuities, to be charged on the faid rates or duties; and all and every the powers, authorities, rules, directions, penalties, forfeitures, claufes, matters, and things now in force, contained in the faid three feveral acts of parliament, or any of them, for the raifing, levying, collecting, and paying, the rates or duties thereby granted, fhall be in full force, and be duly obferved, practifed, and put in execution, within and throughout the whole kingdom of *Great Britain*, for raifing, levying, collecting and paying the feveral rates and duties upon houfes, windows, or lights, by this act granted, as fully and effectually to all intents and purpofes, as if the fame or the like powers, authorities, rules, directions, penalties, forfeitures, claufes, matters, and things, were particularly repeated and re-enacted in the body of this prefent act.

Houfes in Scotland not having more than 5 windows exempted from the duty on houfes.

XXXIII. Provided always, That no houfe or cottage in that part of *Great Britain* called *Scotland*, that has not more than five windows or lights, fhall pay or be liable to pay the duty of one fhilling impofed on each houfe by this prefent act.

XXXIV. And

XXXIV. And be it further enacted by the authority aforesaid, That the commissioners authorized for putting in execution the three said former acts, or either of them, for all and every the respective counties, shires, stewartries, ridings, cities, boroughs, cinque ports, towns, and places respectively, within *Great Britain,* shall meet together at the most usual and common place of meeting, within such counties, shires, stewartries, ridings, cities, boroughs, cinque ports, towns, and places respectively, within *Great Britain,* on or before the twenty ninth day of *July* one thousand, seven hundred and fifty eight; and shall then divide themselves to act in separate districts, and proceed in the execution of this present act, for assessing, raising, levying, and collecting the duties hereby granted, in such and the same manner, to all intents and purposes, as is prescribed by the three former acts, or either of them, with respect to the rates and duties thereby imposed.

The commissioners for executing the said 3 acts, are to meet on or before 29 July, for putting this act in execution.

XXXV. And be it further enacted by the authority aforesaid, That the several annuities which by this act shall be granted and made payable, with respect to the principal sum of five millions, to be raised in manner and form as is hereafter directed, shall be charged and chargeable upon, and payable out of, the several additional and new rates and duties by this act imposed upon offices and pensions, and upon houses and windows or lights; and the said several additional and new rates and duties, are hereby appropriated for that purpose accordingly.

Annuities payable on the monies to be raised by this act, charged on the several additional and new duties.

XXXVI. *And whereas several persons, natives or foreigners, and bodies politick or corporate, have, in books opened at the bank of* England *for that purpose, subscribed towards the said sum of five millions; four millions five hundred thousand pounds, part thereof, to be attended with annuities after the rate of three pounds ten shillings per centum per annum; and five hundred thousand pounds residue thereof, to be raised by a lottery, and attended with annuities after the rate of three pounds per centum per annum; and the said subscribers or contributers have in pursuance of the resolutions of the commons of* Great Britain *in parliament assembled, deposited with, or paid to the cashier or cashiers of the governor and company of the bank of* England *for the time being, the sum of ten pounds per centum, in part of the sums by them subscribed respectively, and are desirous to pay the remaining principal sums by them subscribed as aforesaid, at the times and in the manner herein after appointed in that behalf;* be it therefore enacted by the authority aforesaid, That it shall and may be lawful to and for all such respective contributors who have already deposited with, or paid to the said cashier or cashiers of the said governor and company of the bank of *England,* the sum of ten pounds for every one hundred pounds by them subscribed respectively, to advance and pay unto the said cashier or cashiers, who is and are hereby appointed the receiver and receivers of such contributions (without any further or other warrant to be sued for, had, or obtained in that behalf) the remainder of the several sums so subscribed, at or before the respective days or times, and in the proportions in this act limited in that behalf.

Contributors who have already deposited 10l. per cent. of their subscriptions, to the cashier of the bank, may pay the remainder at the times and in the proportions limited in the act.

XXXVII. *And whereas it is intended that all such contributors to the said sum of five millions, who shall have subscribed for five hundred*

pounds,

pounds, shall be intitled to four hundred and fifty pounds in annuities, after the rate of three pounds ten shillings per centum per annum, transferrable at the bank of England, *subject to such reduction as is hereafter mentioned; and to fifty pounds in lottery tickets, to be attended with annuities (transferrable also at the bank of* England) *after the rate of three pounds per centum per annum, and so in proportion for a greater or less sum;* be it enacted by the authority aforesaid,

That all such contributors who have so made the said deposit of ten pounds *per centum*, in part of the sums by them severally subscribed, as a security for making their future payments, shall make the same accordingly, at or before the respective days or times, and in the proportions in this act limited in that behalf; that is to say, In respect of their proportional share of the said sum of four millions five hundred thousand pounds, fifteen pounds *per centum*, on or before the thirtieth day of *May* one thousand seven hundred and fifty eight; fifteen pounds *per centum*, on or before the twenty eighth day of *June* then next ensuing; fifteen pounds *per centum*, on or before the twenty seventh day of *July* then next ensuing; fifteen pounds *per centum*, on or before the thirtieth day of *August* then next ensuing; fifteen pounds *per centum*, on or before the twenty seventh day of *September* then next ensuing; and the remaining fifteen pounds *per centum*, on or before the twenty sixth day of *October* then next ensuing: and in respect of their proportional share of the said

sum of five hundred thousand pounds, twenty pounds *per centum*, on or before the tenth day of *June* one thousand seven hundred and fifty eight; fifteen pounds *per centum*, on or before the tenth day of *July* then next ensuing; fifteen pounds *per centum*, on or before the nineteenth day of *August* then next ensuing; twenty pounds *per centum*, on or before the ninth day of *September* then next ensuing; and the remaining twenty pounds *per centum*, on or before the ninth day of *October* then next following: and that

all such contributors for or in respect of nine equal tenth parts of the sums so by them subscribed, shall be intitled to their proportional share of annuities after the rate of three pounds ten shillings *per centum per annum*, subject as aforesaid; and for and in respect of the remaining one tenth of the sum so subscribed, to as many lottery tickets as the said tenth part of the sum so subscribed shall

purchase, after the rate of ten pounds for each ticket; and that every such contributor or adventurer for every sum of ten pounds so advanced, for the purchase of a lottery ticket, shall be intitled to such lot, and to such annuity, after the rate of three pounds *per centum per annum*, as is herein after directed and appointed.

XXXVIII. And be it further enacted by the authority aforesaid, That the several contributors, their executors, administrators, successors, and assigns, in respect of the said sum of four millions five hundred thousand pounds, part of the said principal sum of five millions, shall be intitled to annuities after the rate of three pounds ten shillings *per centum per annum*, for the term of twenty four years, to commence and be computed from the fifth day of *July*, one thousand seven hundred and fif-

ty

ty eight; and from and after the end and expiration of the said term of twenty four years, to annuities after the rate of three pounds *per centum per annum*, until redemption thereof by parliament, in manner herein after mentioned; and that such annuities shall be paid half-yearly, on the fifth day of *January*, and the fifth day of *July*, by even and equal portions; and that the annuities which shall become due and payable to the said contributors, their executors, administrators, successors, and assigns, at the rate of three pounds *per centum per annum*, in respect of the said principal sum of five hundred thousand pounds, residue of the said principal sum of five millions, shall commence and be computed from the fifth day of *January*, which shall be in the year of our Lord one thousand seven hundred and fifty nine, and shall, from time to time, be paid half-yearly, on the fifth day of *July*, and the fifth day of *January*, by equal and even portions; the first payment thereof to be due and payable for the half year ended the fifth day of *July*, which shall be in the year of our Lord one thousand seven hundred and fifty nine.

First payment of interest to be on 5 Jan. 1759, and payable half-yearly. Interest on lottery tickets to commence on 5 Jan. 1759, and afterwards to be paid half-yearly.

XXXIX. And be it further enacted by the authority aforesaid, That the said cashier or cashiers who shall have received or shall receive any part of the sums so paid by way of deposit, or otherwise, in respect of the said annuities, after the rate of three pounds ten shillings *per centum per annum*, shall forthwith give receipts in writing signed by himself or themselves, to every such contributor, for all such sums; and that the receipts to be given for any sums paid in respect of the said annuities, after the rate of three pounds ten shillings *per centum per annum*, shall be assignable, by indorsement thereupon made, at any time before the thirtieth day of *October*, one thousand seven hundred and fifty eight, and no longer.

Cashier to give receipts for money paid in, the same made assignable.

XL. Provided always, That such cashier or cashiers shall give security, to the good liking of any three or more of the commissioners of the treasury now being, or the high treasurer, or any three or more of the commissioners of the treasury for the time being, for duly answering and paying into the receipt of his Majesty's exchequer, for the publick use, all the monies which they shall have already received by way of deposit, or otherwise, or shall hereafter receive from time to time, of or for the said sum of five millions, and for accounting duly for the same, and for performance of the trusts hereby in them reposed; and shall from time to time so pay all such monies as soon as they shall receive the same, or any part thereof, or within five days afterwards at the farthest, and shall account for all monies so received by him or them, in the exchequer, according to the due course thereof, deducting thereout such sums as shall have been paid by him or them in pursuance of this act, in manner herein after mentioned; for which sums so paid, allowance shall be made in his or their accounts.

Cashier to give security; and to pay in the monies into the exchequer.

XLI. And be it further enacted by the authority aforesaid, That it shall and may be lawful to and for the commissioners of

Treasury to apply the monies to the ser-

vices voted by the commons.

his Majesty's treasury now being, or the high treasurer, or any three or more of the commissioners of the treasury, from time to time, to issue and apply all such sums of money as shall so be paid into the receipt of his Majesty's exchequer by the said cashier or cashiers, to such services as shall then have been voted by the commons of *Great Britain* in this session of parliament, and not otherwise.

Contributors names to be entered in a book;

the same to be inspected gratis.

XLII. And be it further enacted by the authority aforesaid, That in the office of the accountant general of the said governor and company of the bank of *England* for the time being, there shall be provided and kept a book or books, in which shall be fairly entered the names of all such contributors as aforesaid; and it shall and may be lawful to and for the said respective contributors, their executors, administrators, successors, and assigns, from time to time, at all seasonable times, to have resort to and inspect the said book or books, without any fee or charge: and that the said accomptant general for the time being shall, on or before the twenty fifth day of *March*, one thousand seven hundred and sixty, transmit an attested duplicate, fairly written on paper, of the said book or books, into the office of the auditor of the receipt of his Majesty's exchequer, there to remain for ever.

Duplicate thereof to be transmitted to the exchequer.

Contributors making good their payments, to have sure estates in the annuities.

XLIII. And it is hereby enacted by the authority aforesaid, That all such contributors duly paying the whole sums by them respectively subscribed at or before the respective days and times in this act before limited in that behalf, their respective executors, administrators, successors, and assigns, shall have, receive, and enjoy their proportional share of the respective annuities of three pounds ten shillings *per centum per annum*, and three pounds *per centum per annum*, out of the monies by this act herein after appropriated for payment thereof, and shall have good and sure estates and interests therein for ever; subject nevertheless to the terms and provisoes of reduction and redemption in this act herein contained concerning the same respectively.

Contributors making their payments previous to the times limited,

to be allowed interest for the same, &c.

XLIV. And be it further enacted by the authority aforesaid, That all such contributors, their executors, administrators, successors, and assigns, paying in the whole or any part of the sums by them subscribed respectively, previous to the days appointed for the respective payments herein before directed, as well in respect to their proportional share of the said sum of four millions five hundred thousand pounds, as of the said sum of five hundred thousand pounds, shall be intitled to an allowance of so much money as the interest of the several sums so previously paid after the rate of three pounds *per centum per annum*, shall amount to, from the days on which such previous payments shall have been actually made, to the respective times on which such payments are directed to be made; such allowance to be paid, by the said cashier or cashiers out of the monies contributed towards the said sum of five millions, as soon as such respective contributors, their executors, administrators, successors, and assigns, shall have completed their payments herein before directed to be made; and that as soon as any contributors, their

6

exe-

executors, administrators, successors, and assigns, shall have completed their payments of the whole purchase money payable by them respectively for any such annuities, after the rate of three pounds, ten shillings, *per centum per annum*, the principal sum or sums by them subscribed and paid for the purchase of such annuities, shall forthwith be placed to the credit of the said contributors, their executors, administrators, successors, and assigns, completing the said payments, and made transferrable in the books of the bank of *England*, to be kept for that purpose; and that after any contributors, their executors, administrators, successors, and assigns, shall have completed their payments of the whole purchase money payable by them respectively for any such annuities, after the rate of three pounds *per centum per annum*, lottery tickets to the amount of the principal sum or sums by them subscribed and paid for the purchase thereof, at the rate of ten pounds for each ticket, shall, as soon as they can conveniently be made out, be delivered to such contributors, their executors, administrators, successors, and assigns.

XLV. Provided always, That in case any such contributors *Contributors* who have already deposited with or paid to the said cashier or *not making* cashiers, any sum or sums of money, at the times and in the *good their* manner before mentioned, in part of the sums so by them sub-*payments* scribed, or their respective executors, administrators, successors, *within the* or assigns, do not advance and pay to the said cashier or cashiers, *times limited,* the residue of the sums so by them subscribed, at the times and *to forfeit their* in the manner before mentioned; then and in every such case, *deposits.* so much of the sum so subscribed as shall have been actually paid in part thereof, to the said cashier or cashiers, shall be forfeited for the benefit of the publick; any thing in this act contained to the contrary thereof in any wise notwithstanding.

XLVI. And be it further enacted by the authority aforesaid, *Annuities, &c.* That all the several annuities which by this act are granted and *charged on the* made payable, until redemption thereof by parliament, in man-*sinking fund.* ner herein after mentioned, shall be charged and chargeable upon, and payable out of, such fund or funds as are by this act established for payment thereof; and if at any time or times it shall happen that the produce of the fund or funds so established for payment of the said several annuities, shall not be sufficient to pay and discharge the several and respective annuities, and other charges, directed to be paid thereout at the end of any or either of the respective half-yearly days of payment, at which the same are hereby directed to be paid, then and so often, and in every such case, such deficiency or deficiencies shall and may be supplied out of any of the monies which at any time or times shall be or remain in the receipt of the exchequer, of the surplusses, excesses, overplus monies, and other revenues, composing the fund commonly called *The sinking fund* (except such monies of the said sinking fund as are appropriated to any particular use or uses by any former act or acts of parliament, in that behalf) and such monies of the said sinking fund shall and may be, from time to time, issued and applied accordingly; and

it

if at any time or times before any monies of the feveral rates and duties and fums of money hereby granted, fhall be brought into the exchequer as aforefaid, there fhall happen to be a want of money for paying the feveral annuities as aforefaid, which fhall be actually incurred, and grown due at any of the half-yearly days of payment before mentioned, that then and in every fuch cafe, the money fo wanted fhall and may be fupplied out of the monies of the finking fund (except as before excepted) and be iffued accordingly.

Sinking fund to be replaced out of the firft fupplies. XLVII. Provided always, and be it enacted by the authority aforefaid, That whatever monies fhall be iffued out of the finking fund, fhall, from time to time, be replaced by and out of the firft fupplies to be then after granted in parliament.

Annuities,&c. charged on the finking fund. XLVIII. Provided always, and be it enacted by the authority aforefaid, That in cafe there fhall be any furplus or remainder of the monies arifing by the faid fund or funds by this act eftablifhed for payment of the faid annuities, after the faid feveral and refpective annuities and all arrears thereof are fatisfied, or money fufficient fhall be referved for that purpofe, fuch furplus or remainder fhall, from time to time, be referved for the difpofition of parliament, and fhall not be iffued but by the authority of parliament, and as fhall be directed by future act or acts of parliament; any thing in any former or other act or acts of parliament to the contrary notwithftanding.

Managers and directors of the lottery to be appointed by the treafury. XLIX. And, for eftablifhing a proper method for drawing the faid lottery, be it further enacted by the authority aforefaid, That fuch perfons as the commiffioners of his Majefty's treafury, or any three or more of them now being, or the high treafurer, or any three or more of the commiffioners of the treafury, for the time being, fhall appoint, fhall be managers and directors for preparing and delivering out tickets, and to overfee the drawing of lots, and to order, do, and perform, fuch other matters and things, as are hereafter in and by this act directed and appointed by fuch managers and directors to be done and performed; and that fuch managers and directors fhall meet together from time to time, at fome publick office or place, for the execution of the powers and trufts in them repofed by this act; and that the faid managers and directors, or fo many of them as fhall be prefent at any fuch meeting, or the major part of them, **Books to be prepared with 3 columns, in each of which 50,000 tickets to be printed.** fhall caufe books to be prepared, in which every leaf fhall be divided or diftinguifhed into three columns; and upon the innermoft of the faid three columns, there fhall be printed fifty thoufand tickets, hereby intended to be made forth, to be numbered, one, two, three, and fo onward, in an arithmetical progreffion, where the common excefs is to be one, until they rife to and for the number of fifty thoufand; and upon the middle column in every of the faid books, fhall be printed fifty thoufand tickets of the fame breadth and form, and numbered in like manner; and in the extream column of the faid books, there fhall be printed a third rank or feries of tickets, of the fame number with thofe of the other two columns; which tickets
fhall

shall severally be of an oblong figure; and in the said books shall be joined with oblique lines, flourishes, or devices, in such manner as the said managers and directors, or the major part of them, shall think most safe and convenient; and that every ticket in the third or extream column of the said books shall have written or printed thereupon (besides the number of such ticket, and the present year of our Lord Christ) words to this effect:

Tickets to be of an oblong form, and joined with oblique lines, &c.

Tickets in the 3d column to have the words following printed on them.

T H E *bearer hereof is intitled to six pounds, part of the joint stock of annuities after the rate of three pounds per centum per annum, transferrable at the bank of* England, *or to a better chance.*

L. And it is hereby enacted, That the said managers and directors, or so many of them as shall be present at such meeting, or the major part of them then present, shall carefully examine all the said books, with the tickets therein, and that the same be contrived, numbered, and made, according to the true intent and meaning of this act, and shall deliver or cause to be delivered the same books, and every or any of them, as they shall be examined, to the said cashier or cashiers, taking from such cashier or cashiers, an acknowledgement in writing under his or their hands, importing his or their receipt of such book or books, and so many tickets therein as shall be delivered to him or them; and the said cashier or cashiers is and are hereby directed and required, upon his and their receiving every or any intire sum of ten pounds, in full payment of a ticket, from any person or persons contributing or adventuring as aforesaid, to cut out of the said book or books so to be put into his or their custody, through the said oblique lines, flourishes, or devices, indentwise, one of the tickets in the said extream columns, which the said cashier or cashiers shall sign with his or their own name or names; and such cashier or cashiers shall permit the contributors or adventurers, if it be desired, to write his or her name or mark on the corresponding ticket in the same book; and at the same time the cashier or cashiers shall deliver to the said contributor or adventurer the ticket so cut off, which he, she, or they, are to keep and use for the better ascertaining and securing of the interest which he, she, or they, his, her, or their executors, administrators, successors, or assigns, shall or may have in the said fund, for the monies so contributed or adventured, until redemption thereof, in manner herein after mentioned.

Managers to examine the books with the tickets, and deliver them to the cashier,

and take a receipt for the same.

Cashier to give a ticket for every sum of 10 l. paid in,

and permit the adventurer to write his name on the corresponding ticket.

LI. And be it further enacted by the authority aforesaid, That the said cashier or cashiers, on or before the fourteenth day of *October*, one thousand seven hundred and fifty eight, shall re-deliver to the said managers and directors, at their said office or place of meeting, all the said books, and therein all the tickets which the said cashier or cashiers shall not have cut out and delivered to the contributors or adventurers for their monies as

Cashier to re-deliver the books to the managers, by 14 October, 1758, and account for the fums received.

aforefaid; and fhall then and there alfo deliver to the faid managers and directors, a true and juft account in writing under his or their hands, of all fums of money accrued or come to the hands of fuch cafhier or cafhiers, by or for the tickets delivered or to be delivered out purfuant to this act, and how the fame, or how much thereof, fhall have been actually paid by fuch cafhier or cafhiers, into the receipt of the exchequer, for the purpofes in this act expreffed; and that the faid managers and directors, or the major part of them, which fhall be prefent at a meeting as aforefaid, fhall forthwith caufe all the tickets of the faid outermoft columns which fhall not have been delivered to the contributors as aforefaid, if any fuch be, to be delivered into the receipt of his Majefty's exchequer, there to be retained and kept as cafh, to be iffued, fold, and difpofed of, for raifing money for the purpofes in this act mentioned, as the commiffioners of his Majefty's treafury, or the high treafurer, for the time being, fhall judge reafonable and fitting.

Tickets undifpofed of to be returned into the exchequer.

Tickets of the middle column to be rolled up, and tied;

LII. And be it further enacted, That the faid managers and directors, or the major part of them, which fhall be prefent at a meeting as aforefaid, fhall caufe all the tickets, of the middle columns in the books made out in three columns as aforefaid, which fhall be delivered back to them by or from the faid cafhier or cafhiers as aforefaid, to be carefully rolled up and made faft with thread or filk; and the faid managers or directors, or the major part of them as aforefaid, fhall, in their prefence, and in the prefence of fuch contributors or adventurers as will be there, caufe all the faid tickets which are to be fo rolled up and made faft as aforefaid, to be cut off indentwife through the faid oblique lines, flourifhes or devices, into a box to be prepared for that purpofe, and to be marked with the letter (A) which is prefently to be put into another ftrong box, and to be locked up with feven different locks and keys, to be kept by as many of the faid managers, and fealed with their feals, or the feals of fome of them, until the faid tickets are to be drawn, as is herein after mentioned; and that the tickets in the firft or innermoft columns of the faid books fhall remain ftill in the books for difcovering any miftake or fraud (if any fuch fhould happen to be committed) contrary to the true meaning of this act.

and cut off indentwife into a box marked with the letter (A)

Box to be locked up and fealed.

Books to be prepared with 2 columns, on each of which 50,000 tickets to be printed.

LIII. And be it further enacted by the authority aforefaid, That the faid managers and directors, or the major part of them, which fhall be prefent at any meeting as aforefaid, fhall alfo prepare, or caufe to be prepared, other books, in which every leaf fhall be divided or diftinguifhed into two columns, and upon the innermoft of thofe two columns, there fhall be printed fifty thoufand tickets, and upon the outermoft of the faid two columns there fhall be printed fifty thoufand tickets; all which fhall be of equal length and breadth as near as may be; which two columns in the faid books, fhall be joined with fome flourifh or device, through which the outermoft tickets may be cut off indentwife, and that fix thoufand five hundred tickets, part of those to be contained in the outermost columns of the books last-mentioned, shall be, and be called, the fortunate tickets, to which extraordinary benefits shall belong, as is herein after-mentioned; and the said managers and directors, or the major part of them, or such of them as shall be present at a meeting as aforesaid, shall cause the said fortunate tickets to be written upon or otherwise expressed, as well in figures as in words at length, in manner following; that is to say, upon two of them **The number** severally, ten thousand pounds principal money; upon three **and value of** of them severally, five thousand pounds principal money; upon **the fortunate** six of them severally, two thousand pounds principal money; **tickets.** upon seventeen of them severally, one thousand pounds principal money; upon every one of twenty nine of them severally, five hundred pounds principal money; upon every one of one hundred forty two of them severally, one hundred pounds principal money; upon every one of six hundred and twenty six of them severally, fifty pounds principal money; upon every one of five thousand six hundred and seventy five of them severally, twenty pounds principal money; which principal sums so to be written, or otherwise expressed, upon the said fortunate tickets, together with five hundred pounds principal money to be allowed to the **500 l. to the** owner of the first drawn ticket, and one thousand pounds prin- **first drawn** cipal money to the owner of the last drawn ticket, besides the **ticket, and** benefits which may happen to belong to the two last-mentioned **last drawn.** tickets, will amount in the whole to the principal sum of two hundred thirty nine thousand pounds; which sum being added to the sum of two hundred sixty one thousand pounds (which will be the principal payable according to the intent and mean-ing of this act, on the remaining forty three thousand five hun-dred blank or unfortunate tickets, computed at the rate of six **43,500 blank** pounds for each blank or unfortunate ticket) do amount toge- **tickets, at the** ther to the principal sum of five hundred thousand pounds, be- **rate of 6 l.** ing the total principal sum to be converted into annuities in pursuance of this act, in respect of the said lottery tickets; and the said managers and directors, or the major part of them, **Tickets of the** who shall be present at a meeting as aforesaid, shall cause all **outermost co-** the said tickets contained in the outermost columns of the last- **lumns to be** mentioned books, to be, in the presence of the said managers **rolled up and** and directors, or the major part of them, which shall be present **tied,** at a meeting as aforesaid, and in the presence of such contribu-tors or adventurers as will then be there, carefully rolled up and **and cut out** fastened with thread or silk, and carefully cut out indentwise **indentwise,** through the said flourish or device, into another box to be pre- **into a box** pared for this purpose, and to be marked with the letter (B) **marked with** which box shall be presently put into another strong box, and **the letter (B)** locked up with seven different locks and keys, to be kept by as **Box to be** many of the said managers, and sealed up with their seals, or **locked up and** the seals of some of them, until those tickets shall also be drawn, **sealed.** in the manner and form herein after-mentioned; and that the whole business of rolling up and cutting off, and putting into the said boxes the said tickets, and locking up and sealing the

T 4   said

faid boxes, fhall be performed by the faid managers and directors, or fuch of them as aforefaid, within fix days at leaft before the drawing of the faid lottery fhall begin; and to the end every perfon concerned may be well affured that the counterpart of the fame number with his or her ticket, is put into the box marked with the letter (A) from whence the fame may be

Publick notice to be given of times of cutting the tickets into the boxes.

drawn, and that other matters are done as hereby directed, fome publick notification in print fhall be given of the precife time or times of cutting the faid tickets into the faid boxes, to the end that fuch adventurers as fhall be minded to fee the fame done, may be prefent at the doing thereof.

Lottery to begin drawing on 13 Nov. 1758.

LIV. And be it further enacted by the authority aforefaid, That on or before the thirteenth day of *November*, one thoufand feven hundred and fifty eight, the faid managers and directors fhall caufe the faid feveral boxes, with all the tickets therein, to be brought into the guildhall of the city of *London* by nine of the clock in the forenoon of the fame day, and placed on a table

Method to be obferved in drawing, &c.

there for that purpofe, and fhall then and there feverally attend this fervice, and caufe the two boxes containing the faid tickets, to be feverally taken out of the other two boxes, in which they fhall have been locked up; and the tickets of lots in the refpective innermoft boxes being, in the prefence of the faid managers and directors, or fuch of them as fhall be then prefent, and of fuch adventurers as will be there for the fatisfaction of themfelves, well fhaken and mingled in each box diftinctly; and fome one indifferent and fit perfon, to be appointed and directed by the managers aforefaid, or the major part of them, or fuch of them as fhall be then prefent, fhall take out and draw one ticket from the box where the faid numbered tickets fhall be as aforefaid put; and one other indifferent and fit perfon, to be appointed and directed in like manner, fhall prefently take out a ticket or lot from the box where the faid fix thoufand five hundred fortunate, and forty three thoufand five hundred blank tickets fhall be promifcuoufly put as aforefaid; and immediately both the tickets fo drawn fhall be opened, and the number, as well of the fortunate as the blank ticket, fhall be named aloud; and if the ticket taken or drawn from the box containing the fortunate and blank lots fhall appear to be a blank, then the numbered ticket fo drawn with the faid blank at the fame time, fhall both be put upon one file; and if the ticket fo drawn or taken from the box containing the fortunate and blank lots, fhall appear to be one of the fortunate tickets, then the principal fum written upon fuch fortunate ticket, whatever it be, fhall be entered by a clerk, which the faid managers, or the major part of them as aforefaid, fhall employ and overfee for this purpofe, into a book to be kept for entering the numbers coming up with the faid fortunate tickets, and the principal fums whereunto they fhall be intitled refpectively, and two of the faid managers fhall fet their names as witneffes to fuch entries; and the faid fortunate and numbered tickets fo drawn together, fhall be put upon another file; and fo the faid drawing of the tickets

fhall

shall continue, by taking one ticket at a time out of each box, and with opening, naming aloud, and filing the same, and by entering the fortunate lots in such method as is before mentioned, until the whole number of six thousand five hundred fortunate tickets, and one more for the last drawn as aforesaid, shall be compleatly drawn; and if the same cannot be performed in one day's time, the said managers and directors shall cause the boxes to be locked up and sealed in manner as aforesaid, and adjourn till the next day, and so from day to day, and every day, (except *Sundays*, *Christmas*, and fast days appointed by particular acts of parliament, or by the King's proclamation) and then open the same, and proceed as above till the said whole number of six thousand five hundred fortunate tickets, and one more, shall be compleatly drawn as aforesaid; and afterwards the said numbered tickets so drawn, with the fortunate tickets drawn against the same, shall be and remain in a strong box locked up as aforesaid, and under the custody of the said managers, until they shall take them out to examine, adjust, and settle the property thereof.

After each day's drawing, the boxes to be locked up and sealed.

LV. And, to the end the fortunate may know, whether absent or present to what degree they have been so; be it enacted, That as soon as the drawing is over, the said managers are hereby required, as soon as conveniently may be, to cause to be printed and published the number of the tickets drawn against each fortunate ticket, and the principal sum written on the same; and if any contention or dispute shall arise in adjusting the property of the said fortunate tickets, the major part of the said managers, agreeing therein, shall determine to whom it doth or ought to belong: and if any person or persons shall forge or counterfeit any ticket or tickets, certificate or certificates, to be made forth in pursuance of this act, or made forth, or to be made forth, on any former lottery act, or alter any the numbers thereof, or utter, vend, barter, or dispose of, or offer to dispose of, any false, altered, forged or counterfeited ticket or tickets, certificate or certificates, or bring any forged or counterfeit ticket or certificate, or any ticket or certificate the number whereof is altered (knowing the same to be such) to the said managers, or any of them, or the said governor and company of the bank of *England*, or their cashier or cashiers, or accomptant general for the time being, or to any other person or persons whatsoever, to the intent to defraud his Majesty, or any contributor or adventurer, or the executors, administrators, successors, or assigns, of any contributor or adventurer upon this act, with a fraudulent intention; then every such person, being thereof convicted in due form of law, shall be adjudged a felon, and shall suffer death as in cases of felony, without benefit of clergy: and the said managers and directors, or any two or more of them, are hereby authorized and required to cause any person or persons bringing or uttering such forged or counterfeit ticket or tickets, certificate or certificates, as aforesaid, to be apprehended, and to commit him, her, or them, to his Majesty's gaol of *Newgate*, or to the

Numbers of the fortunate tickets, and the sums, to be printed.

Disputes relating thereto, to be adjusted by the managers.

Penalty of forging tickets or certificates.

Felony.

com-

common gaol of the county or place where such person or persons shall be so apprehended, to be proceeded against for the said felony according to law.

Managers to be sworn.

LVI. Provided always, and it is hereby enacted by the authority aforesaid, That every person who shall be appointed as aforesaid to be a manager and director for putting this act in execution, before his acting in such commission, shall take the oath following; that is to say,

The oath.

I *A. B. do swear, That I will faithfully execute the trust reposed in me; and that I will not use any indirect art or means, or permit or direct any person to use any indirect art or means, to obtain a prize or fortunate lot, for myself, or any other person whatsoever; and that I will, to the best of my judgement, declare to whom any prize, lot, or ticket, of right does belong, according to the true intent and meaning of the act of parliament made in the twenty ninth year of his Majesty's reign in that behalf.*

Which said oath shall and may be administered by any two or more of the other managers and directors.

LVII. Provided always, That it shall and may be lawful to and for the said cashier or cashiers, having given security as aforesaid, at any time or times before such cashier or cashiers shall have received any book or books from the said managers comprehending the said fifty thousand tickets as aforesaid, in three columns as aforesaid, to receive from any person or persons who will voluntarily offer, contribute, and advance, the residue of any sum of ten pounds, or several sums of ten pounds, upon this act as aforesaid, the sums so offered to be contributed or advanced, at one entire payment, or in such proportions and manner as aforesaid, before such cashier or cashiers shall have received such book or books; and the said cashier or cashiers shall give a note or receipt, under his or their hand or hands, for the sum or sums so contributed, and shall be obliged thereby, and by this act, to give the bearer of every such note or receipt, a ticket or tickets of the extream column of the three columns book or books aforesaid, for every ten pounds so contributed, paid, or answered, as soon as he or they shall be enabled thereunto by delivery of any such book or books to him or them from the said managers as aforesaid; any thing herein contained to the contrary notwithstanding.

Adventurer not paying his whole consideration-money by the times limited, shall lose the advanced money.

LVIII. Provided also, That in case any such contributor or adventurer aforesaid, who shall have advanced and paid down to such cashier or cashiers a proportion of his, her or their consideration-money, his, her, or their executors, administrators, successors, or assigns, do not advance and pay unto such cashier or cashiers the remaining part of his, her, or their consideration-money, so to be paid in full for such tickets as aforesaid, on or before the times for paying thereof as aforesaid; that then, and in every such case, every such contributor or adventurer shall forfeit and lose to his Majesty, for the use of the publick,

lick, the proportion of his, her, or their purchafe-money which he, fhe, or they fhall have fo paid down as aforefaid; and in fuch cafe no ticket or tickets fhall be delivered out by the faid cafhier or cafhiers to fuch contributor or contributors making fuch default, but the ticket and tickets which fhould have been delivered to fuch contributor and contributors, had they paid the full money for the fame, fhall be returned and delivered to the faid managers and directors by the faid cafhier or cafhiers, together with the other tickets (if any) in the outermoft column of the book and books firft herein mentioned and directed to be prepared, which fhall not have been difpofed of to contributors as aforefaid; and fuch ticket and tickets, upon and for which defaults of payments fhall have been made as aforefaid, fhall be delivered into the receipt of his Majefty's exchequer with other the faid undifpofed tickets (if any) there to be retained and kept as cafh, and to be iffued, fold, and difpofed of, for the purpofes, and in the manner, herein before directed and appointed with refpect to the faid undifpofed tickets; and the faid contributor and contributors making fuch default, fhall not have or receive, or be intitled to have or receive, any benefit or advantage for or in refpect of the money which he, fhe, or they fhall have paid for or towards the purchafe of fuch ticket or tickets; any thing herein contained to the contrary notwithftanding.

Tickets to be difpofed of, fhall be delivered into the exchequer.

LIX. Provided alfo, and it is hereby enacted by the authority aforefaid, That out of the monies to arife by the faid contributions to the lottery as aforefaid, it fhall and may be lawful to and for any three or more of the commiffioners of the treafury, or the high treafurer for the time being, to reward the faid managers and directors, and the clerks and officers to be employed by and under them, and any other officers and perfons that fhall and may be any ways employed in this affair, for their labour and pains; alfo to difcharge all incident expences as fhall neceffarily attend the execution of this act, in fuch manner as any three or more of the commiffioners of the treafury, or the high treafurer for the time being, fhall, from time to time, think fit and reafonable in that behalf; any thing in this act contained to the contrary notwithftanding.

Managers, &c. to be paid by the commiffioners of the treafury out of the lottery money.

LX. And be it further enacted, That it fhall and may be lawful for any guardian or truftee having the difpofition of the money of any infant, for the ufe and behoof of fuch infant, to contribute and pay, for or towards advancing the faid fum of five millions, any fums of the monies of fuch infant, and fuch infant, upon payment of fuch fum or fums, fhall become a contributor within the meaning of this act, and be intitled to have and receive fuch payment in refpect thereof, and in fuch like manner as any other contributor; and the faid guardian and truftee, as to the faid fum or fums fo advanced, is hereby difcharged, fo as the name of fuch infant be expreffed in the receipt or receipts for fuch money; and alfo upon the ticket or tickets that fhall be delivered out for the fame, that fo it may apppear

Guardians may adventure infants money in the lottery.

appear that fuch infant or infants was or were the contributor or contributors.

LXI. And be it further enacted by the authority aforefaid, That no perfon or perfons, in *Great Britain* or *Ireland*, fhall fell the chance or chances of any ticket or tickets in the faid lottery, or any fhare or fhares in any ticket or tickets in the faid lottery, for a day, or part of a day, or for a longer time lefs than the whole time of drawing the lottery then to come, or fhall receive any money whatfoever in confideration of the repayment of any fum or fums of money, in cafe any ticket or tickets in the faid lottery fhall prove fortunate; or fhall lay any wager relating to the drawing of any ticket or tickets in the faid lottery, either as to the time of fuch ticket or tickets being drawn, or whether fuch ticket or tickets be drawn fortunate or unfortunate; and all and every perfon and perfons who fhall offend in any of the above-mentioned matters, fhall forfeit and pay treble the fum and fums of money which fhall have been received by fuch perfon or perfons, contrary to the true intent and meaning of this act; to be recovered by action of debt, bill, plaint, or information, in any of his Majefty's courts of record at *Weftminfter* or *Dublin* refpectively; on which no effoin, protection, privilege, or wager of law, or more than one imparlance, fhall be allowed; one moiety whereof to be for the ufe of his Majefty, his heirs, or fucceffors, and the other moiety to be paid to the perfon or perfons who fhall fue for the fame; and every fuch wager or contract, and every agreement relating thereto, fhall be, and is hereby declared to be null and void.

LXII. And be it further enacted by the authority aforefaid, That if any perfon or perfons, in *Great Britain* or *Ireland*, fhall keep any office or offices, or fhall print or publifh any fcheme or propofal, for receiving any fum or fums of money in confideration of an intereft to be granted for the fame, any ticket, or number of tickets, in the faid lottery, whereof fuch perfon or perfons fhall not then be actually poffeffed, or in confideration of any fum or fums of money to be repaid in cafe any ticket or number of tickets, in the faid lottery, which fhall not be in the actual poffeffion of fuch perfon or perfons, fhall prove fortunate, all and every fuch perfon and perfons fhall forfeit and pay the fum of five hundred pounds; to be recovered by action of debt, bill, plaint, or information, in any of his Majefty's courts of record at *Weftminfter* or *Dublin* refpectively; in which no effoin, protection, or wager of law, or more than one imparlance, fhall be allowed; one moiety thereof to be for the ufe of his Majefty, his heirs or fucceffors, and the other moiety to be paid to the perfon or perfons who fhall fue for the fame; and alfo fhall fuffer three months imprifonment without bail or mainprize.

LXIII. And be it further enacted by the authority aforefaid, That if any offence againft any of the acts of parliament made in this kingdom, for preventing private and unlawful lotteries, fhall be committed in *Ireland*, the offender fhall incur the like penalty

Marginal notes: Limitation of fale of chances, &c. Penalty. Perfons felling fhares in tickets of which they are not poffeffed, to forfeit 500l. Offences committed in Ireland againft acts for preventing un-

penalty and punishment, to be inflicted in like manner as if the offence was committed in this kingdom; and that such penalties as, by any of the said acts, are directed to be recovered in any of his Majesty's courts of record at *Westminster*, shall, in case of offences committed against any of the said acts in *Ireland*, be recovered in any of his Majesty's courts of record at *Dublin*. *lawful lotteries, declared to be punishable, and may be sued for in Dublin.*

LXIV. *And to the end that all the payments as well upon the fortunate as upon the unfortunate tickets, may be more easily ascertained, settled, and adjusted, for the persons who shall be and become intitled thereunto;* be it further enacted by the authority aforesaid, That as soon as conveniently may be after the drawing of the said lottery shall be completed and ended, all the said tickets, as well those contained in the books with three columns, as those contained in the books with two columns, to be given out as aforesaid, shall be exchanged for certificates to be signed by such of the said managers, as shall be appointed for that purpose. *After the drawing of the lottery, the tickets to be exchanged for certificates.*

LXV. And be it further enacted, That such of the said managers, as any three or more of the comissioners of the treasury now being, or the high treasurer for the time being, shall appoint to take in the said tickets, and deliver out the said certificates for and in lieu thereof, shall give timely notice, by advertisement to be printed and published in manner as they shall think fit, of the days and times for taking in the said tickets, and delivering out the said certificates, for and in lieu of the same; and every person's certificate shall be numbered in course, according to their bringing their tickets to the said officer or officers so to be appointed for exchanging the same; to which purpose such officer or officers shall enter or cause to be entered in a book or books to be by him or them kept for that purpose, the name of every person who brings any ticket or tickets to be exchanged for such certificate or certificates, and the number or numbers of the ticket or tickets which shall be so brought by such person or persons, the value in principal money payable thereupon, and the day of the month, and the year of our Lord, when the same was so brought, which book and books shall lie open in the office to be appointed for taking in the said tickets to be exchanged for such certificates, for all persons concerned to peruse; all which certificates shall be signed by the officer or officers so to be appointed, or the major part of them, and be directed to the accountant general of the bank of *England* for the time being. *Managers to give notice of the time for taking in the tickets, and delivering out the certificates, &c. Book to be kept for entering persons names, and the number of their tickets, &c.*

LXVI. And be it further enacted by the authority aforesaid, That the said accountant general of the bank of *England* for the time being, to whom the said certificates are to be directed as aforesaid, shall upon receiving and taking the said certificates, or any of them, give credit to the persons named therein, in a book or books, in manner herein before directed, to be by him provided and kept for that purpose, for the principal sums contained in every such certificate; and the persons to whose credit such principal sums shall be entered in the said book or books, his, her, or their executors, administrators, successors, and assigns, *Certificates to be signed, &c. Accomptant general to give credit for the principal sums in the certificates.*

signs, shall and may have power to assign and transfer the same, or any part, share, or proportion thereof, to any other person or persons, bodies politick or corporate whatsoever, in other books to be prepared and kept by the said accountant general for that purpose; and the principal sums so assigned or transferred, shall carry the said annuity of three pounds *per centum per annum*, and shall be taken and deemed to be stock transferrable by virtue of this act, until the redemption thereof, in manner herein after mentioned; and the said accountant general of the bank of *England* for the time being, is hereby authorized and directed to cancel and file the certificates, as they shall from time to time be received and taken in by him, and to give the persons bringing the same, a note under his hand, testifying the principal money for which they have credit in the said book or books, by reason or means of the certificates so received, taken in, and cancelled, as aforesaid, and of the annuities attending the same.

margin: Assignments may be made of the said sums, &c.

margin: Certificates to be filed and cancelled, and notes to be given in lieu thereof.

LXVII. *And, for the more easy and sure payment as well of said annuities after the rate of three pounds* per centum per annum, *as of the said annuities after the rate of three pounds* per centum per annum; be it enacted by the authority aforesaid, That the said governor and company of the bank of *England*, and their successors, shall, from time to time, until the said respective annuities shall be redeemed according to this act, appoint and employ one or more sufficient person or persons within their office in the city of *London*, to be the first or chief cashier or cashiers, and one other sufficient person in the said office to be their accountant general; and that so much of the monies by this act appropriated for this purpose, as shall be sufficient from time to time to answer the said several and respective annuities and other payments herein directed to be made out of the said monies, shall, by order of the commissioners of the treasury, or any three or more of them now being, or the high treasurer, or any three or more of the commissioners of the treasury, for the time being, without any further or other warrant to be sued for, had, or obtained, in that behalf, from time to time, at the respective days of payment in this act before appointed for payment thereof, to be issued and paid at the receipt of his Majesty's exchequer, to the said first or chief cashier or cashiers by way of imprest, and upon account, for the payment of the said several and respective annuities payable by virtue of this act; and that all and every such cashier or cashiers, to whom the said monies shall, from time to time, be issued, shall from time to time, without delay, pay the same accordingly, and render his or their accounts thereof, according to the due course of the exchequer.

margin: A chief cashier, and accountant general, to be appointed by the bank for paying the annuities.

margin: Treasury to issue money for that purpose to the said cashier,

margin: who is to account for the same.

LXVIII. And it is hereby also enacted, That the said accountant general for the time being, shall, from time to time, inspect and examine all receipts and payments of the said cashier or cashiers, and the vouchers relating thereunto, in order to prevent any fraud, negligence, or delay; and that all persons who shall be intitled to any of the said several and respective annuities, and all persons lawfully claiming under them, shall be pos-

margin: Accountant general to examine the receipts and payments of the cashier. Annuities deemed a personal estate, possessed thereof as of a personal estate, and that the same shall &c. and to be not be descendable to the heir, and shall be free from all taxes, tax free. charges, and impositions whatsoever, and shall not be liable to any foreign attachment by the custom of *London*, or otherwise; any law, statute, or custom, to the contrary in any wise notstanding.

LXIX. And be it further enacted by the authority aforesaid, The 3 and That the said sum of four millions five hundred thousand half per cent. pounds, part of the said sum of five millions, shall be deemed annuities one capital or joint stock; and that all persons and corporations deemed a joint whatsoever, in proportion to the monies by them severally ad- stock; vanced, for the purchase of the said annuities, after the rate of three pounds, ten shillings *per centum per annum*, or such other annuities to which they shall become intitled by virtue of this act, shall have and be deemed to have a proportional interest and share in the said stock, and in the annuities attending the same, at the rates aforesaid; and that the said whole capital or and made joint stock, or any share or interest therein, and the propor- transferrable. tional annuity attending the same, shall be assignable and transferrable as this act directs, and not otherwise.

LXX. And be it further enacted by the authority aforesaid, The 3l. per That all the monies to which any person or persons shall become cent. annuities intitled by virtue of this act, in respect of any sum advanced to be made a or contributed towards the said sum of five hundred thousand joint stock pounds, on which the said annuities after the rate of three pounds with annuities *per centum per annum*, shall be attending, shall be added to the of like value, joint stock of annuities transferrable at the bank of *England*, in- by acts 5 Geo 2. to which the several sums carrying an interest at the rate of three pounds *per centum per annum*, were by an act made in the twenty fifth year of the reign of his present Majesty converted, and shall be deemed part of the said joint stock of annuities, subject nevertheless to a redemption by parliament, in such manner, and upon such notice, as is in the said act directed, in respect of the several and respective annuities, redeemable by virtue of the said act; and that all and every person or persons and corporations whatsoever, in proportion to the money to which he, she, or they shall become intitled as aforesaid, by virtue of this act, shall have and be deemed to have a proportional interest and share in the said joint stock of annuities, at the rate aforesaid.

LXXI. And be it further enacted by the authority aforesaid, Transfer That there shall be constantly kept by the accountant general books to be for the time being, books, wherein all assignments of the sums kept by the advanced or contributed towards the said sum of four millions accountant five hundred thousand pounds, and also all assignments or general. transfers of all sums advanced and contributed towards the said sum of five hundred thousand pounds, shall at all seasonable times be entered and registered; which entries shall be Method of conceived in proper words for that purpose, and shall be signed transferring by the parties making such assignments or transfers; or if such stock. parties be absent, by their respective attorney or attornies, thereunto lawfully authorized in writing under their hands and seals,

to

to be attested by two or more credible witnesses, and the several persons to whom such transfers shall be made, do respectively underwrite their acceptance thereof; and that no other method of assigning and transferring the said several annuities, or any part thereof, or any interest, shall be good or available in law.

LXXII. Provided always, That all persons possessed of any share or interest in either of the said joint stocks of annuities, of any estate or interest therein, may devise the same by will in writing, attested by two or more credible witnesses, but that no payment shall be made upon any such devise till so much of the said will as relates to the said joint stocks of annuities, be entered in the said office; and in default of such transfer or devise, such share or interest in the said joint stock of annuities, shall go to the executors or administrators; and that no stamp duties whatsoever, shall be charged upon the said transfers, or any of them; any other law or statute to the contrary notwithstanding.

LXXIII. Provided always, and be it enacted by the authority aforesaid, That out of the monies arising from the contribution towards raising the said sum of five millions, the commissioners of the treasury, or any three or more of them now being, or the high treasurer, or any three or more of the commissioners of the treasury for the time being, shall have power to discharge all such incident charges as shall necessarily attend the execution of this act, in such manner as to them shall seem just and reasonable; and also to settle and appoint such allowances as they shall see just and reasonable, for the service, pains, and labour of the said cashier or cashiers, for receiving, paying, and accounting for the said contributions; and also shall have power to take out of the said sinking fund such further allowances as they shall think just and reasonable, for the service, pains, and labour of the cashier or cashiers of the governor and company of the bank of *England*, for receiving, paying, and accounting for the several and respective annuities payable by virtue of this act, and also for the service, pains, and labour of the accountant general of the said governor and company for performing the duty and trust incumbent on him by this act; all which allowances hereby impowered to be made as aforesaid, in respect to the service, pains, and labour of any officer or officers of the said governor and company, shall be for the use and benefit of the said governor and company, and at their disposal only; any thing herein contained to the contrary notwithstanding.

LXXIV. And be it hereby enacted by the authority aforesaid, That no fee or gratuity shall be demanded or taken of any of his Majesty's subjects for receiving or paying the said contribution-monies, or any of them, or for any tallies or receipts concerning the same, or for issuing the monies for paying the said several annuities, or any of them; and that no fee or gratuity shall be demanded or taken for any transfer great or small, to be made in pursuance of this act, upon pain that the officer or person offending by taking or demanding any such fee or gratui-

ty,

[margin notes:]

Annuities deviseable by will.

Entry to be made of such clause in the will.
Transfer not liable to stamp duties.

Treasury to pay all incident charges attending the execution of this act;

and to make an allowance to the cashier, and accountant general;

to be at the disposal of the governor and company of the bank.

Officers taking any fee or gratuity in the course of their business, forfeit 10 s.

ty, contrary to this act, shall forfeit the sum of twenty pounds to the party grieved, to be recovered with full costs of suit, in any of his Majesty's courts of record at *Westminster*.

LXXV. Provided also, and it is hereby enacted by the authority aforesaid, That at any time after the expiration of twenty four years, to be computed from the fifth day of *July*, one thousand seven hundred and fifty eight, and not sooner, upon six months notice to be printed in the *London Gazette*, and affixed upon the *Royal Exchange* in *London*, by authority of parliament; and upon repayment by parliament of the whole principal sum of four millions five hundred thousand pounds, for which the said annuities, after the rate of three pounds ten shillings *per centum per annum*, are payable to such respective persons or corporations as shall be intitled to the same annuities; or upon the like repayment by parliament of any part of the said sum of four millions five hundred thousand pounds, so as such part of the sum so paid at any one time be not less than five hundred thousand pounds; and also upon full payment of all arrearages of the same annuities; then, and not till then, the said annuities shall cease and determine, and be understood to be redeemed; and that any vote or resolution of the house of commons, signified by the speaker in writing, to be inserted in the *London Gazette*, and affixed on the *Royal Exchange* in *London* as aforesaid, shall be deemed and adjudged to be sufficient notice within the words and meaning of this act.

LXXVI. Provided always, and it is hereby enacted by the authority aforesaid, That the said governor and company of the bank of *England*, and their successors, notwithstanding the redemption of all or any their own funds, in pursuance of the acts for establishing the same, or any of them, shall continue a corporation, till all the said several annuities shall be redeemed by parliament, according to the provisoes herein before contained in that behalf; and that the said governor and company, or any member thereof, shall not incur any disability, for or by reason of their doing any matter or thing in pursuance of this act.

LXXVII. *And whereas doubts may arise, whether the punishment inflicted in and by an act of parliament made and passed in the eighth year of the reign of his late majesty King* George *the First, intituled,* An act to prevent the mischiefs by foreign powers, to transfer such stocks, or to receive such annuities or dividends as are therein mentioned; or by fraudulently personating the true owners thereof; and to rectify mistakes of the late managers for taking subscriptions for increasing the capital stock of the South Sea company, and in the instruments founded thereupon, *on persons guilty of the several species of forgery, and other offences therein mentioned, extends to the commission of the like forgery and offences in relation to such capital stocks and funds as have been established by the authority of parliament, since the passing of the said act, and may be hereafter established;* be it therefore enacted by the authority aforesaid, That if any person or persons whatsoever, from and after the first day of *July*, one thousand seven hundred and

The annuities at 3l. 10s per cent. not redeemable till after the expiration of 24 years, &c.

Bank to continue a corporation till these annuities be redeemed, &c.

Act 8 Geo. 1.

Penalty in the recited act of forging or counterfeiting

letters of attorney, in order to fell, or transfer ftock in any of the funds, &c. or to receive any dividends or annuities thereon, &c. extended to this act, &c.

and fifty eight, fhall forge or counterfeit, or procure to be forged or counterfeited, or knowingly and wilfully act or affift in the forging or counterfeiting any letter of attorney, or other authority or inftrument, to transfer, affign, fell, or convey any fhare or fhares, or any part of any fhare or fhares, of or in any fuch capital ftock or funds of any body or bodies politick or corporate eftablifhed, or which fhall be eftablifhed, by any act or acts of parliament; or to receive any dividend or dividends attending any fhare or fhares, or any part of any fhare or fhares, of, or in, any fuch capital ftock or funds as aforefaid; or to receive any annuity or annuities, in refpect whereof any proprietor or proprietors have or fhall have any transferrable fhare or fhares of or in any capital ftock or ftocks which now are, or hereafter fhall be, eftablifhed by any act or acts of parliament, in proportion to their refpective annuities; or fhall forge or counterfeit, or procure to be forged or counterfeited, or knowingly and wilfully act or affift in the forging or counterfeiting any the name or names of any the proprietors of any fuch fhare or fhares in ftock, or of any the perfons intitled to any fuch annuity or annuities, dividend or dividends, as aforefaid, in or to any fuch pretended letter of attorney, inftrument, or authority; or fhall knowingly or fraudulently demand, or endeavour to have, any fuch fhare or fhares in ftock, or any part thereof, transferred, affigned, fold, or conveyed, or fuch annuity or annuities, dividend or dividends, or any part thereof, to be received by virtue of any fuch counterfeit or forged letter of attorney, authority or inftrument; or fhall falfely and deceitfully perfonate any true and real proprietors of the faid fhares in ftock annuities and dividends, or any of them, or any part thereof, and thereby transferring or endeavouring to transfer the ftock, or receiving or endeavouring to receive the money, of fuch true and lawful proprietor, as if fuch offender were the true and lawful owner thereof; then, and in every or any fuch cafe, all and every fuch perfon and perfons, being thereof lawfully convicted in due form of law, fhall be deemed guilty of felony, and fuffer death as a felon, without benefit of clergy.

LXXVIII. *And whereas doubts may arife whether the punifhment inflicted in and by an act of parliament made and paffed in the fecond* Penalty in the act of 2 Geo. 2. *year of the reign of his prefent Majefty, intituled,* An act for the more effectual preventing and further punifhment of forgery, perjury, and fubornation of perjury; and to make it felony to fteal bonds, notes, or other fecurities for payment of money, *on perfons guilty of the feveral fpecies of forgery therein mentioned, extends to the commiffion of the like forgeries with an intention to defraud any corporation:* be it therefore enacted by the authority aforefaid, That if any perfon from and after the firft day of July, one thoufand feven hundred and fifty eight, fhall falfely make, forge, or counterfeit, or caufe or procure to be falfly made, forged, or counterfeited, or willingly act or affift in the falfe making, forging, or counterfeiting, any deed, will, teftament, bond, writing obligatory bill of exchange, promiffory note for payment of money,

of forging or publifhing any deed, will, obligation, acquittance, &c with intent to defraud any corporation, extended to this act.

indorfe-indorsement or assignment of any bill of exchange, or promissory note for payment of money, or any acquittance or receipt either for money or goods, with an intention to defraud any corporation whatsoever; or shall utter or publish as true, any false, forged, or counterfeited deed, will, testament, bond, writing, obligatory bill of exchange, promissory note for payment of money, indorsement, or assigment of any bill of exchange, or promissory note for payment of money, acquittance or receipt either for money or goods, with intention to defraud any corporation, knowing the same to be false, forged, or counterfeited; then every such person, being thereof lawfully convicted according to the due course of law, shall be deemed guilty of felony, and suffer death as a felon, without benefit of clergy.

LXXIX. And it is hereby enacted by the authority aforesaid, *Limitation of* That if any person or persons shall, at any time or times, be *actions.* sued or prosecuted for any thing by him or them done or executed in pursuance of this act, or of any matter or thing in this act contained, such person or persons shall and may plead the general issue, and give the special matter in evidence for his or *General issue.* their defence; and if upon trial a verdict shall pass for the defendant or defendants, or the plaintiff or plaintiffs shall become *Treble costs.* nonsuited, then such defendant or defendants shall have treble costs to him or them awarded against such plaintiff or plaintiffs.

CAP. XXIII.

An act for the more easy and speedy recovery of small debts within the western division of the hundred of Brixton, in the county of Surry.

CAP. XXIV.

An act for the more easy and speedy recovery of small debts within the borough of Great Yarmouth, and the liberties thereof.

CAP. XXV.

An act for establishing a free market for the sale of corn and grain, within the city or liberty of Westminster.

WHEREAS *the establishing a free market for the sale of corn and grain, within the city or liberty of* Westminster, *would* Preamble. *be very advantageous to the inhabitants of the said city and liberty, as well as the adjacent parts, but such market cannot be established without the aid of parliament :* may it therefore please your Majesty, that it may be enacted; and be it enacted by the King's most excellent majesty, by and with the advice and consent of the lords spiritual and temporal, and commons, in this present parliament assembled, and by the authority of the same, That there shall A free market be a free and open market held within the city or liberty of *West-* for sale of *minster,* for all sorts of corn and grain whatsoever; and that it corn and shall and may be lawful for any person or persons to buy or sell grain to be any sort of corn and grain, feed, malt, meal, and flour, in the held in West-said market, without any disturbance or molestation whatsoever, minster. nevertheless yielding and paying such sums as are herein after mentioned.

U 2 II. *And*

II. *And to end the faid intended market may be erected, eftablifhed,
and maintained, under fuch rules and regulations, as are by this act
herein after directed and prefcribed*; be it further enacted by the
authority aforefaid, That the honourable major general *Edward
Cornwallis*, Sir *John Croffe* baronet, and the reprefentatives in
parliament for the city of *Weftminfter* for the time being; Sir
William Beauchamp Proctor baronet, *George Cooke* efquire, and the
reprefentatives in parliament for the county of *Middlefex* for the
time being; the honourable *Charles Cavendifh* efquire, commonly called lord *Charles Cavendifh*; the right honourable
lord *Carpenter* in the kingdom of *Ireland*, Sir *Richard Grofvenor*,
Sir *Matthew Lambe* baronets; *George Onflow*, *John Wilkes*, *John
Little*, *Nathaniel Curzon*, *Samuel Threfher*, *John Olmius*, *John
Goodchild*, *John Drummond*, *Edward Byron*, *John Pudfey*, *Saun-
ders Welch*,   *Clutterbuck*, *John Walfh*, *Henry Col-
lett*, *Thomas Gilpin*, efquires; *John Wright* coachmaker,
Giffard, *John Machin* timber merchant,   *Latham*
diftiller, *Thomas Chamberlain* pewterer, *Kemp Bridges* laceman,
                          Morris woollen draper, *Thomas Bedwell* iron-
monger, *Samuel Peirfon*, *Nicholas Spencer*, *Roger Jackfon*, *Richard
Lane*, *Thomas Brooke*, and *Nathaniel Bever*, gentlemen; fhall,
from and immediately after the paffing of this act, be, and they
are hereby appointed truftees for putting this act in execution.

III. And be it further enacted by the authority aforefaid,
That it fhall and may be lawful to and for the faid truftees, or
any five or more of them, or any perfon or perfons authorized
by them, to fet out ground proper for holding the faid market
at fome convenient place within the faid city or liberty; and alfo
to purchafe fuch ground, together with any buildings erected
thereupon, or upon any part thereof, and all or any eftate, term,
or intereft, fubfifting therein, and to convert the faid ground
into a market; in truft neverthelefs, to and for the feveral ufes,
intents, and purpofes, as are herein after declared concerning
the fame.

IV. And be it further enacted by the authority aforefaid,
That it fhall and may be lawful to and for all perfons whatfoever, bodies politick, corporate, or collegiate, corporations aggregate or fole, femes covert who are or fhall be feifed or interefted in their own right, truftees and feoffees in truft, guardians
and committees for lunaticks and ideots, executors, adminiftrators, and guardians whatfoever, not only in behalf of themfelves, their heirs and fucceffors, but alfo for and in behalf of
their ceftuique trufts, whether infants or iffue unborn, lunaticks,
ideots, femes covert, or other perfons whatfoever, who are or
fhall be feifed or poffeffed of, or interefted in, any lands, meffuages, or tenements, which fhall be within the bounds and limits fo to be fet out by the faid truftees, as aforefaid, or any five
or more of them, for the holding the faid market thereon, to
contract for, fell, convey, or furrender to the faid truftees, or
any five or more of them, or to any perfon or perfons they fhall
appoint in truft for them, all or any fuch meffuages, lands, tenements,

nements, or hereditaments, or any part thereof, or any terms for years, or any estate or interest therein; and that all such contracts, agreements, bargains, sale, assignments, surrenders, and other conveyances, which shall be so made as aforesaid, shall be good and valid in law to all intents and purposes whatsoever, not only to convey the estate and interest of the person or persons conveying, but also all right, estate, interest, use, property, claim, and demand whatsoever, of their several and respective cestuique trusts, whether infants or issue unborn, lunaticks, ideots, femes covert, or other persons whatsoever, and all persons claiming, or to claim, by, from, or under them; any law, statute, or usage, to the contrary thereof in any wise notwithstanding.

Such sale, and conveyance, deemed good in law.

V. Provided always, and be it enacted by the authority aforesaid, That all and every sum and sums of money which shall be paid by the said trustees, for the purchase of such messuages, lands, tenements, and hereditaments, or any estate therein, to any person or persons whatsoever, bodies politick, corporate, or collegiate, corporations aggregate or sole, femes covert, trustees or feoffees in trust, guardians or committees for lunaticks or ideots, executors, administrators, or guardians whatsoever, either as aforesaid, or in manner herein after directed, shall be laid out again in the purchase of other messuages, lands, tenements, or hereditaments, or of such estate therein, as the vender or venders had in the premisses, from the sale of which the said purchase money arose; and the messuages, lands, tenements, hereditaments, or other premisses, which shall be purchased with the said money, shall be settled, conveyed, and assured, to the same uses, and stand charged with, and be liable to, the same charge or charges, as the messuages, lands, tenements, or hereditaments, from the sale of which the purchase money shall arise, were liable to, and chargeable with, before the same were so sold to the said trustees.

Where such lands, &c. shall be held in trust, the money is to be laid out in purchases of other lands, &c. of equal value, to be settled and applied to like uses as declared in such trusts.

VI. And be it further enacted by the authority aforesaid, That if it shall happen that any person or persons, bodies politick corporate or collegiate, or other person or persons whatsoever, who are hereby enabled to convey as aforesaid, shall refuse to treat and agree with the said trustees, or to convey as aforesaid, then, and in such case, it shall and may be lawful to and for the said trustees, or any five or more of them, to issue out a warrant or warrants, precept or precepts, to the high bailiff of *Westminster* (who is hereby authorized and directed to obey the same) to impanel and return a competent number of substantial and disinterested persons qualified to serve on juries, not less than forty eight, nor more than seventy two; and out of such persons so to be impannelled, summoned, and returned, a jury of twelve persons shall be drawn by the said trustees, or any five or more of them, or some person to be by them, or any five or more of them, appointed; in such manner as juries for the trial of issues joined in his Majesty's courts at *Westminster*, by an act made in the third year of the reign of his present Majesty (intituled,

If the parties interested shall refuse to treat,

Trustees are to issue their warrant to the high bailiff, to impanel and return a jury;

who are to be drawn as juries for the trials of issues joined, by act of 3 Geo. 2. are directed.

tituled, *An act for the better regulation of juries*) are drawn ; which persons so to be impanelled, summoned, and returned, are hereby required to come and appear before the said trustees, or any five or more of them, at such time and place as in such warrant or warrants, precept or precepts, shall be directed and appoint-

Jurors may be challenged. ed ; and all parties concerned shall and may have their lawful challenges against any of the said jurymen ; and the said trustees, or any five or more of them, are hereby authorized and impowered by warrant or warrants under their hands and seals, from time to time, as occasion shall require, to call before them all and every person or persons whatsoever, who shall be thought proper and necessary to be examined as witnesses before them, touching

Trustees may summon and examine witnesses on oath; and order evidences and documents of the estates to be produced. or concerning the premisses, and to require any person or persons who shall have any books, papers, deeds, or writings, which may tend to discover the value of the premisses, or the title or titles of the persons claiming any estate or interest therein, to produce the same to the said trustees, or any five or more of them, or such person or persons as they shall appoint to inspect the same ; and the said trustees, or any five or more of them, shall, and are hereby impowered to administer oaths, as well to the parties concerned, as to others, for the discovery of the truth of the value of the premisses, or of the title of the person or persons claiming any estate or interest in the premisses ; and shall

Jury to view the place in question, and assess the damage and recompence on oath. and may authorize the said jury to view the place or places, or matters in question, in case the said trustees, or any five or more of them, shall think fit so to do ; and the said jury upon their oaths (which oaths shall also be administered by the said trustees, or any five or more of them) shall inquire of, and assess such damages and recompence, as they shall judge fit to be awarded to the owners and occupiers of such houses, ground, or other estate or interest, or either of them, for their respective estates and interests therein, and which the said trustees shall adjudge neces-

Trustees to give judgement thereupon ; which is to be final and binding. sary to be purchased for the purpose aforesaid ; and the said trustees, or any five or more of them, assembled together, shall and may give judgment for such sum or sums so assessed by such jury or juries respectively ; which said verdict or verdicts, and the judgment, decree, or determination, thereupon declared and pronounced by the said trustees, or any five or more of them, assembled together ; and the value and recompence so to be as-

Notice of the meeting of the jury to be given to the party in possession, &c. sessed and declared (notice in writing being first given of the time and place and intent of the meeting of the said trustees, at least twenty days before such meeting, to any person who is in possession of any estate or interest, then to be valued and assessed ; or in case such person or persons cannot be found to be personally served therewith, such notice being left at the dwelling-house or usual place of abode of such person or persons so interested as aforesaid, or with some tenant or occupier of the

er, if untenanted, to be published in the Gazette. messuages, lands, tenements, or premisses, so to be valued and assessed, or any of them, or if wholly untenanted, then publication thereof being made in the *London Gazette*) shall be binding and conclusive to all intents and purposes whatsoever, against all and

and every perfon or perfons whatfoever, bodies politic or corporate, claiming any right, title, truft, or intereft, in, to, or out of, the faid houfes, grounds, tenements, and premiffes, to be affected by this act, either in poffeffion, reverfion, remainder, or expectancy, as well infants, lunaticks, ideots, femes covert, tenants in tail, tenants for life, terms of years, or at will, his, her, and their heirs, fucceffors, executors, and adminiftrators; and the faid verdicts, judgments, orders, and other proceedings of the faid truftees, or any five or more of them, which concern fuch lands, tenements, and hereditaments, fhall be tranfmitted to, and entered or docquetted in, the regifter's office for the county of *Middlefex*, and fhall be deemed and taken to be records to all intents and purpofes whatfoever; and all perfons may have recourfe to the fame *gratis*, and take copies thereof, paying for the copies a fum not exceeding fix pence for every two hundred words; and fo proportionably for any greater number of words.

Verdict, and judgment thereupon, to be tranfmitted to, and entered in, the regifter's office. Recourfe may be had thereto, and copies taken thereof.

VII. And it is hereby further enacted and declared, That upon payment of fuch fum or fums of money fo to be adjudged for the purchafe of the premiffes, or any part thereof, the perfon or perfons intitled thereto fhall make and execute, or procure to be made and executed, good, valid, and legal conveyances, affignments, and affurances in the law, to the faid truftees and their fucceffors, of the faid premiffes, for which fuch fum or fums of money were fo awarded, and fhall do all fuch acts, matters and things neceffary or requifite to make a good, real, and perfect title thereto; and fuch conveyances, affignments, and affurances, fhall contain all fuch reafonable and ufual covenants as fhall, on behalf of the faid truftees and their fucceffors, be required; and in cafe any perfon or perfons to whom fuch money fhall be awarded as aforefaid, fhall not evince a title to the faid premiffes to the faid truftees, and make, or procure to be made, good and legal conveyances thereof, or fhall refufe fo to do, being thereunto required, fuch fum and fums of money fo awarded as aforefaid, being ready to be paid to him, her or them, on making fuch title, and tendered for that purpofe; or in cafe any perfon or perfons intitled to the premiffes for which fum or fums of money fhall be fo awarded as aforefaid, cannot be found within the city or liberty of *Weftminfter* or county of *Middlefex*; or in cafe that by reafon of difputes depending in any court of law or equity, or for defect of evidence, it fhall not appear to the faid truftees, or any five or more of them, what perfon or perfons is or are intitled to the premiffes in queftion, that then, and in all and every or any fuch cafe and cafes as aforefaid, it fhall and may be lawful to and for the faid truftees, or any five or more of them, to order fuch fum or fums of money fo awarded as aforefaid, as the value of and purchafe money for the faid premiffes, to be paid into the bank of *England* for the ufe of the parties interefted in the faid premiffes, to be paid to them, and each and every of them, according to their refpective eftates and interefts in the faid premiffes, at fuch times as the faid truftees, or any five or more of them, fhall, by warrant or warrants under

Upon payment of the fum affeffed, conveyance to be made and executed of the premiffes.

Where a title fhall not be evinced, or fhall be refufed to be made,

or the proprietor cannot be found;

or it fhall be doubtful who is the right owner;

the truftees are to lodge the money, payable for the premiffes, in the bank;

U 4   their

their hands, order and direct; and the cashier and cashiers of the bank of *England*, who shall receive such sum and sums, is

receipt to be given for the money,

and are hereby required to give a receipt or receipts for such sum and sums mentioning and specifying for what premisses, and for whose use the same is or are received, to such person or persons as shall pay such sum or sums into the bank of *England* as aforesaid; which receipt or receipts shall be transmitted to, and en-

and to be transmitted to, and entered in, the register's office;

tered or docquetted in the register's office of the county of *Middlesex*, in manner aforesaid, and shall be deemed and taken to be records to all intents and purposes whatsoever; and immediately on such payment and registry all the estate, right, title, use,

after which, all right in the premisses to vest in the trustees.

trust, property, equity of redemption, claim and demand in law and equity, of all and every person and persons for whose use such money was paid, of, in, to, from, and out of the said premisses, or any part thereof, shall vest in the said trustees and their successors, and they the said trustees, and their successors, shall be deemed in law to be in the actual possession thereof, and to be seized thereof in fee-simple, freed and discharged from all claims, demands, and equity of redemption either at law or in equity, to all intents and purposes, as fully and effectually, as if all and every person and persons, having any estate, right, title, trust, interest, or equity of redemption, of, in, to, from, or out of the said premisses, had actually conveyed the same by lease and release, bargain and sale, inrolled feoffment, with livery of seisin, fine and recovery, or any other conveyance whatsoever; and such payment shall not only bar all right, title, interest, equity of redemption, claim, and demand, of the person or persons to whose use such payment was made; but also shall extend to and be deemed and construed to bar the dower and dowers of the wife or wives of such person or persons, and all estates tail, and remainders, as fully and effectually as a fine or recovery would do, or would have done, if levied or suffered by proper parties in due form of law.

After payment of the purchase-money, trustees may enter on the premisses, and convert the same into a market.

VIII. And be it further enacted by the authority aforesaid, That from and immediately after payment made for the lands and hereditaments so to be purchased as aforesaid, it shall and may be lawful for the said trustees and their successors to enter upon the premisses so purchased, and every part thereof, and to convert the same to be used as a free market as aforesaid.

Trustees may borrow money for the purposes of this act;

and build sheds and stands in the market;

IX. *And, for raising a sum of money sufficient for the payment of the purchase of such lands and hereditaments, and other the purposes of this act*; be it further enacted by the authority aforesaid, That it shall and may be lawful to and for the said trustees, or any nine or more of them, and they are hereby authorized and impowered to raise, borrow, take, and receive, of and from any person or persons whomsoever, or any body or bodies corporate or politick whatsoever, who are willing to lend and advance the same, any sum or sums of money not exceeding in the whole the sum of three thousand pounds for the payment of such purchase money, and for other the purposes of this act; and to set up and build upon such lands so to be purchased, all such sheds,

stands,

ftands, ftalls, and other erections, as fhall be found neceffary
for conftituting the faid market; or in eafe it fhall be found to
be more convenient and beneficial to let out fuch ground upon a
building leafe or leafes for the purpofes aforefaid, it fhall and
may be lawful for the faid truftees, or any nine or more of them,
and they are hereby authorized and impowered to fet and let out
fuch ground for the beft rent that can be gotten for the fame,
payable quarterly, or otherwife, upon a leafe or leafes, for any
term or terms not exceeding fixty one years, to any perfon or
perfons who fhall be willing to contract for and take the fame,
with proper covenants binding him or them to build and fet up
all neceffary erections thereupon for coverting the fame into a
market as aforefaid. *or let the ground on a building leafe.*

X. Provided always, and it is hereby declared, That no money fhall be borrowed on the credit of this act by the faid truftees, unlefs notice in the *London Gazette* fhall be firft given there-
of at leaft twenty days before the borrowing of fuch money. *Previous notice to be given in the Gazette before the borrowing money.*

XI. *And, for difcharging the debt to be incurred as aforefaid*, be
it further enacted by the authority aforefaid, That it fhall and
may be lawful to and for any perfon or perfons to contribute,
advance, and pay into the hands of the faid truftees, or any five
or more of them, or their treafurer for the time being, any fum
or fums of money not exceeding in the whole, the fum of three
thoufand pounds, for the abfolute purchafe of one or more annuity or annuities, to be paid and payable during the full term of
the natural life of fuch contributor or contributors refpectively,
or the natural life of fuch other perfon or perfons as fhall be
nominated by and on the behalf of fuch refpective contributor
or contributors, at the time of payment of his or their refpective
contribution monies; which annuity or annuities fhall not exceed the rate of eight pounds *per centum per annum*, for every
one hundred pounds, and fo in proportion for any greater or
lefs fum to be advanced and paid as aforefaid; all which annuities fo to be purchafed, fhall not exceed in the whole, the fum
of two hundred and forty pounds *per annum*, and fhall be payable and paid by the faid truftees, or any five or more of them,
in fuch place within the faid city or liberty of *Weftminfter*, as
they, or any five or more of them, fhall for that purpofe appoint, by quarterly payments, the firft payment to begin and be
made, to the refpective purchafer or purchafers, and his or their
affigns, at the expiration of three months after payment of their
refpective purchafe monies; which annuities fhall be publickly
fold by the faid truftees, to the beft bidder for the fame. *3000l. may be advanced for the purchafe of life annuities, after the rate of 8l per cent. per annum. and to be paid quarterly. Annuities to be fold to the beft bidder.*

XII. And it is hereby enacted, That there fhall be provided
by the faid truftees, and kept in fuch place within the faid city
or liberty of *Weftminfter*, as they, or any five or more of them,
fhall appoint, a book or books in which fhall be fairly written
in words at length, the names and furnames, with the proper
additions and places of abode, of all fuch perfons who fhall be
proprietors of any of the annuities aforefaid, and of all perfons
by whofe hands the faid purchafers fhall pay in any fum or fums *Names and abode of the purchafers, the fums when and by whom paid, &c. to be enter'd in proper books*

6   of

of money upon the credit of this act, and also the sum so paid for the purchase of such annuities, and the respective days of payment thereof; to which book and books, it shall be lawful for the said respective purchasers, and their assigns, and to and for any other person or persons, at all seasonable times, to have recourse to and inspect the same, without fee or reward.

to which recourse may be had gratis.

XIII. And it is hereby further enacted, That all and every the contributor and contributors upon the credit of this act, duly paying the consideration or purchase-money at the rate aforesaid, for any such annuity or annuities as aforesaid, or such person or persons as he, she, or they, shall appoint, his, her, or their respective assigns, shall have, receive, and enjoy the respective annuity or annuities so to be purchased, during the term of the natural life of the person to be nominated by each such purchaser or contributor, as above mentioned; and that all and every such purchaser, and purchasers, and their assigns respectively, shall have good, sure, absolute, and indefeazable estates and interest in the annuities so by them respectively to be purchased, according to the tenor and true meaning of this act; and that none of the said annuities shall be subject or liable to any tax assessed upon land by authority of parliament; and that every contributor upon the credit of this act for the purchase of any such annuity or annuities as aforesaid, his, her, or their assigns, upon payment of the consideration or purchase-money for the same, at the rate aforesaid, or any part or proportion thereof, into the hands of the said trustees, or any five or more of them, or their treasurer for the time being, shall have one or more receipt or receipts, importing the receipt of so much purchase-money as shall be so paid; and upon payment of all the purchase-money for any such annuity or annuities, every such contributor, his, her, or their assigns respectively, shall have an order on parchment or vellum for payment of the said annuity or annuities, for and during the natural life of such person as shall be nominated by such contributor or purchaser, as aforesaid; which order shall be signed by the said trustees, or any five or more of them, and after signing thereof, the same shall be firm, good, valid, and effectual, in the law, according to the purport and meaning thereof, and of this act.

Annuities ensured to the purchasers,

and to be tax free.

Receipts to be given to contributors for the money paid in by them;

and upon completing their payments, an order is to be given them on vellum or parchment, signed by the trustees, for payment of their annuities.

XIV. And be it further enacted by the authority aforesaid, That it shall and may be lawful to and for any purchaser or purchasers of any such annuity or annuities as aforesaid, and his, her, and their executors, administrators, or assigns, at any time or times, by writing under his, her, or their hands and seals (without any stamp thereupon) to assign such annuity or annuities, or any part thereof, or any interest therein, to any person or persons whatsoever, and so *toties quoties*; and a memorandum or entry of all such assignments, shall be made in a book, which is hereby required to be kept for that purpose at the charge of the said trustees, as aforesaid; which entry or memorandum, shall be made *gratis*.

Annuities may be assigned.

Entry to be made thereof.

XV. And be it further enacted by the authority aforesaid,
That

Annuities charged upon

That all and every the annuities fo to be purchafed under and the rents and by virtue of this act, fhall be, and are hereby charged upon, and profits of the fhall be paid and payable from time to time, upon all monies market. arifing by the rents and profits of the fheds, ftalls, ftands, and all other buildings and erections, to be fet up in and upon the ground to be fet out and appointed for the fcite of the faid market, and all other the profits whatfoever, arifing or accruing by or from the faid market, to the faid truftees, and their fucceffors.

XVI. And be it further enacted by the authority aforefaid, That all the lands, tenements, and hereditaments, to be pur- The grounds, chafed by virtue and under the authority of this act, for the buildings, fcite of the faid market as aforefaid, and all fheds, ftalls, ftands, rents and pro- fits of the and other erections to be built or fet up thereupon, and the market, vefted rents and profits arifing from the fame, fhall be and are hereby in the truftees, vefted in the faid truftees, and their fucceffors, for ever; and for the ufes that they fhall ftand feized thereof in truft, for the feveral ufes, herein decla- intents, and purpofes, herein after mentioned and declared, con- red. cerning the fame; that is to fay, The faid truftees, and their fucceffors, or any five or more of them, fhall, out of the firft monies to be borrowed or arifing by granting of leafes, or the fale of annuities, as aforefaid, or by any other ways and means under the authority of this act, pay and difcharge the reafonable expences of obtaining and paffing this act of parliament; and fhall in the next place pay off and difcharge all debts that fhall be incurred by the purchafe of the ground whereon the faid market fhall or may be erected, and all fuch charges and ex- pences as fhall neceffarily attend the erecting and conftituting the fame; and the rents, produce, and profits, arifing thereby, fhall be applied in paying the annuity or annuities to be granted to fuch purchafer or purchafers, as aforefaid, fo long as any of them fhall live; and all fuch favings as fhall from time to time be made by the death of any fuch annuitants, fhall, after the dif- charge of all debts accrued for effecting the purpofes of this act, be appropriated in manner herein after mentioned.

XVII. And be it further enacted by the authority aforefaid, Tolls to be That there fhall be paid to the faid truftees, or fuch other per- paid for corn fon or perfons as the faid truftees, or any five or more of them, fold in the fhall, from time to time, appoint to receive the fame, the fol- market. lowing fums, by all and every perfon and perfons felling any fort of corn or grain, feed, malt, meal, or flour, in the faid market; that is to fay,

One penny for every fack of corn, grain, malt, meal, or The tolls; flour; and, One half-penny for every bufhel of feed.

Which faid feveral fums fhall, and they are hereby declared to they are vefted be vefted in the faid truftees, and their fucceffors; and the fame, in the truftees and every part thereof, fhall be paid, applied, and difpofed of, pofes of this and affigned to and for the feveral ufes, intents, and purpofes, act; and

and in such manner, as by this act is directed; and it shall and may be lawful to and for the said trustees, or any five or more of them, or such person or persons as they, or any five or more of them, under their hands and seals, shall, at a general meeting, nominate and appoint, to demand and take the sums hereby granted and made payable; and to levy the same upon any person or persons, who shall, after demand thereof made, neglect or refuse to pay such sums, as aforesaid, by distress of any goods or chattels belonging to the person or persons who by this act are made liable to the payment of the same, and to keep such goods and chattels so distrained, until such sums, with the reasonable charges of such distress, shall be paid; and such person or persons so distraining, after the space of three days after such distress made and taken, shall and may sell the goods or chattels so distrained, returning the overplus (if any be) upon demand, to the owner thereof, after such sums, and the reasonable charges for distraining, keeping, and selling the same, shall be deducted and paid.

and may be levied by distress and sale.

XVIII. And be it further enacted by the authority aforesaid, That the said trustees, or any nine or more of them, shall and may, at the first or any succeeding general meeting, by writing under their hands and seals, make rules and regulations for the government of the said market; and shall and may chuse and appoint one or more fit person or persons to be collector or collectors of the sums aforesaid, and shall also appoint one or more treasurer or treasurers, and all other necessary officers as to them shall appear proper, for the better execution of the powers contained in this act, allowing to such person or persons so by them appointed, such salaries or other rewards for their trouble, as to the said trustees, or any nine or more of them, shall appear just and reasonable; and the said trustees, or any nine or more of them, shall and they are hereby impowered, to remove or displace such treasurer or treasurers, collector or collectors, or other person or persons whatsoever, so by them from time to time appointed, and to place others in their stead; and the person or persons so appointed to collect and receive the said sum or sums, and also such treasurer or treasurers so appointed as aforesaid, shall, before the said trustees, or any five or more of them, upon the first *Monday* in every month, or oftener, if thereunto required by the said trustees as aforesaid, give in a true, exact, and perfect account in writing, under their respective hands, of all the monies which he or they, and every or any of them, shall to such time have received, paid, and disbursed, by virtue of this act, by reason of their respective offices, and produce vouchers for the same, and shall pay over the balance to such person or persons as the said trustees, or any five or more of them, shall at such meeting direct; and in case such treasurer or treasurers, collector or collectors, shall refuse to give in such account, or to pay such balance as aforesaid, as often as required by the said trustees, or any five or more of them, at a general meeting, such person or persons so refusing shall be committed to the common gaol

Trustees to make regulations for the government of the market; and appoint collectors, treasurers, and other officers,

with salaries, &c.

Collectors and treasurers to account to the trustees monthly, or oftener, if required;

under pain of commitment,

gaol of the said city and liberty of *Westminster*, by warrant under the hand and seal of any one of his Majesty's justices of the peace for the said city and liberty, upon application made to him by any two of the said trustees, there to remain without bail or mainprize, until he or they shall make or render in, a true, exact, and perfect account, of their receipts and disbursements, by virtue of this act, and shall have produced and delivered up all vouchers relating thereto, and shall have likewise paid over the money due on such account, to such person or persons as the said trustees, or any five or more of them, shall direct and appoint to receive the same, or shall have made such composition as the said trustees, or any five or more of them, shall approve; which composition the said trustees, or any five or more of them, are hereby impowered to make and accept. *till payment or composition be made.*

XIX. And be it further enacted by the authority aforesaid, That the said trustees, or any five or more of them, are hereby authorized and required, to take such security from the treasurer or treasurers to be appointed for the purposes of this act, for the due execution of his and their said office and offices, as to the said trustees, or any five or more of them, shall seem meet. *Treasurer to give security.*

XX. And be it further enacted by the authority aforesaid, That the said trustees, or any five or more of them, shall yearly and every year, within six weeks next after the twenty fifth day of *December*, make and deliver in to the justices of the peace for the said city and liberty of *Westminster*, at the general quarter sessions, or any adjournment thereof assembled, a just, true, and perfect account in writing, fairly entered in a book or books to be kept for that purpose, and signed by the said trustees, or any five or more of them, of all and every sum and sums of money, which they shall know to have been received or disbursed under the authority of this act, during the preceding year, with the balance (if any) remaining in the hands of the said trustees; and such accounts shall be kept by the clerk of the said sessions among the records thereof, to be inspected by any person or persons desiring the same, upon payment of one shilling to the said clerk; and if any surplus of the said sums, shall remain in the hands of the said trustees, the same is hereby appropriated to, and shall be applied, yearly and every year, by them, within twelve months next after the delivering of such accounts to the said justices as aforesaid, to the treasurer for the time being of *Westminster Infirmary*. for the benefit of the said charity. *Trustees to render an account annually to the justices of their receipts and disbursements. Account to be kept amongst the records of the sessions; and the surplus monies to be paid over, for the benefit of the Westminster Infirmary.*

XXI. And be it further enacted by the authority aforesaid, That it shall and may be lawful to and for any corn chandler, or other person or persons whatsoever, who shall buy any corn or grain, seed, malt, meal, or flour, in the said market, to sell the same again in any other place or places within the said city or liberty of *Westminster*, or elsewhere, without any let or disturbance from any person or persons whatsoever for so doing; any law or statute to the contrary thereof in any wise notwithstanding. *Corn, &c. bought by the corn chandlers in the market, may be sold again by them in any other place within the city and liberty.*

XXII. *And whereas by an act passed in the twenty second year of* *Clause in act his 22 Geo. 2.*

his Majefty's reign, intituled, An act for making a free market for the fale of fifh, in the city of *Weftminfter ;* and for preventing the forestalling and monopolizing of fifh, and for allowing the fale of fifh under the dimensions mentioned in a claufe contained in an act of the firft year of his late Majefty's reign, in cafe the fame are taken with a hook, *the commiffioners for building a bridge crofs the river* Thames, *from the New Palace Yard, in the city of* Weftminfter, *to the oppofite fhore in the county of* Surry, *were impowered to make a grant to the truftees appointed by the faid act of the twenty fecond year of his Majefty's reign, of a piece of ground near* Common Row, *in the faid city of* Weftminfter, *which was conveniently fituated for holding the faid intended market, which grant has been fince made for the purpofes of the faid act : and whereas the faid piece of ground may be found convenient for holding the faid corn market, in common with the faid fifh market ;* be it therefore enacted by the authority aforefaid, That in cafe the truftees herein before appointed by this act, or any nine or more of them, fhall find the faid piece of ground to be proper and convenient for holding the faid market for the fale of corn and grain, that then it fhall and may be lawful to and for the truftees, appointed to put the faid act of the twenty fecond year of his Majefty's reign in execution, or any five or more of them, to contract and agree with the truftees for putting this act in execution, to permit and fuffer the faid piece of ground to be ufed as a free and open market for all forts of corn and grain, feed, malt, meal, and flour whatfoever, in common with the faid market for the fale of fifh ; and the faid truftees appointed by the faid act of the twenty fecond year of his prefent Majefty's reign, are hereby authorized and impowered, in cafe fuch agreement fhall take place, to ufe and apply the faid piece of ground for the holding of a market for all forts of corn and grain, feed, malt, meal, and flour, in common with the faid market for the fale of fifh ; any thing in the faid act of the twenty fecond year of his prefent Majefty, or any other act contained to the contrary notwithftanding.

If the fcite of the fifh market fhall be convenient for holding the corn market in common with it, the truftees of the recited and this act, are impowered to agree to permit fuch ufe to be made thereof.

XXIII. Provided always, in cafe fuch agreement fhall take place, that then from and immediately after the execution thereof, all the powers and authorities vefted by this act in the truftees herein named, fhall ceafe and determine ; and that then and from thenceforth, the truftees appointed to put in execution the faid act of the twenty fecond year of his prefent Majefty, fhall be, and they are hereby declared to be, truftees for putting this act in execution, and fhall be, and are hereby declared to be, invefted with all and every the powers and authorities in this act contained, in as full and ample manner, to all intents and purpofes as if they had been originally nominated and appointed as truftees for putting this act in execution.

If fuch agreement take place, the powers vefted in the truftees named in this act, are to ceafe; and are to veft in truftees named in the recited act;

XXIV. And be it further enacted by the authority aforefaid, That it fhall and may be lawful to and for the faid truftees appointed to put the faid act of the twenty fecond year of his prefent Majefty's reign in execution, or any five or more of them,

and the leffees of the premiffes are to be impowered by them, to per-

in

in case such agreement shall take place as aforesaid, to impower *mit the hou-* the lessee or lessees of the said premisses for the time being, his, *ses, &c. there-* her, or their executors, administrators, or assigns, to permit or *in, to be used* suffer any person or persons whatsoever, to inhabit, dwell in, or *for the pur-* occupy, any messuage, dwelling-house, shop, or other building *ing and selling* whatsoever, which shall be erected or built, in or upon any part *corn.* of the said premisses, for the exercising or carrying on therein, any occupation, trade, or business, which shall relate to the buying or selling of corn and grain, seed, malt, meal, and flour; any law or statute to the contrary notwithstanding.

XXV. Provided always, and be it further enacted by the au- *Trustees may* thority aforesaid, That it shall and may be lawful to and for the *suspend the* said trustees, or any nine or more of them, if they shall think fit, *payment of* to suffer corn and grain, seed, malt, meal, and flour, to be sold for *the tolls for* any time not exceeding the space of three years from the open- *three years;* ing of the said market, without the payment of any toll; and *and may also* also to reduce or lessen the toll, from time to time, as to them, *reduce the* or any nine or more of them, at a publick meeting assembled, *same.* shall appear reasonable (notice of which meeting shall be given in the *London Gazette*, one week at least before such meeting) any thing in this act contained to the contrary notwithstanding.

XXVI. Provided always, and be it further enacted and de- *Trustees disa-* clared, That no person or persons appointed or to be appointed *bled from* by this act a trustee or trustees for putting the same in execution, *holding any* shall have or accept of any place of profit, arising out of or by *place of profit* reason of any sums by this act laid or granted, but such person *under this act.* or persons shall be incapable of acting as a trustee or trustees, from the time of his accepting, and during the enjoyment of such place of profit as aforesaid.

XXVII. And, for continuing a sufficient number of trustees, for putting this act in execution; be it further enacted by the *Election of* authority aforesaid, That when and as often as any trustee or *new trustees.* trustees, shall die, or by writing under his or their hand refuse to act, it shall and may be lawful for such of the said trustees as shall survive or remain, or any nine or more of them, at any general meeting, by any writing or writings under their hands and seals, to elect, nominate, and appoint, one or more fit per- son or persons, in the room or place of such trustee or trustees so dying or refusing to act as aforesaid; and such person or per- sons so elected, nominated, or appointed, shall be joined with such surviving or remaining trustees, in the execution of all and every the powers in them reposed by virtue of this act.

XXVIII. And be it further enacted by the authority aforesaid, *First meeting* That the first meeting of the said trustees, shall be on the first *of the tru-* *Tuesday* in *July*, one thousand seven hundred and fifty eight, at *stees.* the house known by the name of the *King's Arms Tavern* in *New Palace Yard*, within the said city of *Westminster*; and they shall *Power of ad-* have power to adjourn their succeeding meetings, from time to *journment.* time, and to such places within the said city or liberty, as they shall think fit.

XXIX. And be it further enacted by the authority aforesaid, *Limitation of* That *actions.*

That if any action, plaint, suit, or information, shall be commenced or prosecuted against any person or persons for what he or they shall do in pursuance or execution of this act, the same shall be commenced within six months after the offence committed; and such person or persons so sued in any court whatsoever, shall and may plead the general issue not guilty, and upon any issue joined, may give this act and the special matter in evidence; and if the plaintiff or prosecutor shall become non-suit, or forbear further prosecution, or suffer a discontinuance; or if a verdict pass against him, the defendant shall recover treble costs, for which he shall have the like remedy, as in any case where costs by the law are given to defendants.

XXX. And be it further enacted by the authority aforesaid, That this act shall be deemed, adjudged, and taken to be a publick act, and be judicially taken notice of as such by all judges, justices, and other persons whatsoever, without specially pleading the same.

Margin notes:
- General issue.
- Treble costs.
- Publick act.

CAP. XXVI.

An act to explain, amend, and enforce an act made in the last session of parliament, intituled, An act for the better ordering of the militia forces in the several counties of that part of Great Britain called England.

Margin note: Preamble.

WHEREAS *several doubts have arisen, and difficulties have occurred, in carrying into execution an act passed in the last session of parliament, intituled,* An act for the better ordering of the militia forces in the several counties of that part of *Great Britain* called *England: and whereas it has been found, that some farther provisions are necessary, in order to enforce the execution of the said act;* be it therefore enacted by the King's most excellent majesty, by and with the advice and consent of the lords spiritual and temporal, and commons, in parliament assembled, and by the authority of the same, That in all counties, ridings, or places, wherein nothing has been done towards carrying the said act into execution, his Majesty's lieutenant for every such county, riding, or place, shall immediately proceed to put in execution the said recited act, and this present act; and that his Majesty's lieutenants, and all other persons concerned in such execution, shall, in all points, conform themselves to the directions of the said former act so far only as they are not either amended or repealed by this present act; and in all counties, ridings, or places, where some progress has been made towards the execution of the said former act, but not sufficient to enable them to chuse the men by lot out of the lists already returned, his Majesty's lieutenant of every such county, riding, or place, and all other persons concerned as aforesaid, shall begin with and proceed in the execution of the said former act, and of this present act, in like manner, to all intents and purposes, as if nothing had been hitherto done in such county, riding, or place, towards the execution of the said former act; and that in all counties, ridings,

Margin note: Renewal of the former direction to lieutenants to execute the militia acts, conforming to the former act where unrepealed by this act, and to the new provisions of this. In counties where they have not proceeded so far as to be able to chuse by lot out of the lists returned, such counties to begin the whole execution of the two acts *de novo.*

or

or places where the militia men have been actually chosen by lot, or where they can now be chosen out of the lists already returned, either for the whole county, or for any subdivision thereof, his Majesty's lieutenant, and all other persons concerned in the execution of the said former act, and of this present act, within such county, riding, or place, shall proceed to execute the remaining provisions of the said former act (which have not been yet executed in all or any of the subdivisions within such county, riding, or place) as the same are amended, supplied, or enforced, by the provisions of this act.

In counties where the men can be chose by lot out of the lists returned, the remainder of the former act to be executed, as amended by this.

II. And be it enacted, That his Majesty's lieutenant of every county, riding, or place, shall, and he is hereby required to appoint a proper number of commission officers to train and discipline the militia of his respective county, riding, or place, before the times appointed for holding the second meetings of the deputy lieutenants and justices of the peace within their respective subdivisions, for chusing by lot the persons to serve in the militia for such county, riding, or place.

Direction to appoint the officers of the militia before the second meeting of the deputy lieutenants in their subdivisions.

III. And whereas in the said recited act passed in the last session of parliament, there is contained a proviso, That there shall not be more than three commission officers (that is to say) one captain, one lieutenant, and one ensign, to eighty private men, and so in proportion, as near as may be, to any greater or lesser number of private men, which has been found inconvenient; be it therefore enacted and declared, That the said proviso shall be and is hereby repealed.

Repeal of the clause in the former act prescribing that there shall not be more than 3 officers to 80 private men, and so in proportion.

IV. And be it enacted, That a person seised or possessed, either in law or equity, for his own use and benefit, in possession of an estate for a certain term originally granted for twenty one years or more, and renewable, of an annual value, over and above all rents and charges payable out of or in respect of, the same, equal to the annual value of such an estate as is required by the said recited act for the qualification of a deputy lieutenant and commission officer of the militia respectively, and situate as in the said recited act required, shall be, and is hereby deemed and declared to be, duly and sufficiently qualified to act and serve under such respective commission; any thing in the said recited act, or in this act, contained to the contrary notwithstanding.

A leasehold estate originally granted for 21 years renewable, shall be deemed a qualification for deputy lieutenants and officers.

V. And be it enacted, That in such counties where twenty deputy lieutenants cannot be found, who are seised or possessed of an estate of the yearly value of three hundred pounds, as is required by the said recited act, and this act, it may and shall be lawful for his Majesty's lieutenant of any such county, to appoint such number of persons to be deputy lieutenants as he shall think fit, who shall respectively be seised or possessed of a like estate of the yearly value of two hundred pounds, and situate as in the said recited act is required; provided that the persons so appointed shall not make the whole number of deputy lieutenants for the said county to exceed the number of twenty; and every such person shall be, and is hereby deemed and declared

That in those counties where 20 deputy lieutenants cannot be found with 300l. qualification, the lieutenant may appoint persons with 200l. qualification.

to be, duly and fufficiently qualified to act and ferve under fuch refpective commiffion; any thing in the faid recited act, or this act, contained to the contrary notwithftanding.

VI. And be it enacted, That the captain of every company of militia may and fhall appoint two perfons to be drummers to his company, and may and fhall appoint corporals out of the private men of his company, in the proportion of one corporal to twenty men, and may difplace fuch drummers and corporals refpectively for mifbehaviour, and appoint others in their room, from time to time, as he fhall fee occafion; and may and fhall appoint, with the approbation of his Majefty's lieutenant, fer-jeants out the private men of his company, to fill up fuch vacan-cies of ferjeants as may happen therein; and every fuch appoint-ment fhall be deemed an actual difcharge of the perfon fo ap-pointed from ferving in the militia as a private militia man; and that it fhall be lawful for the colonel, or, in his abfence, for the commanding officer of any battalion of militia, to difplace, upon the application of the captain, any perfon fo appointed a ferjeant out of the private militia men.

VII. Provided always, and be it enacted and declared, That it is and fhall be lawful for any deputy lieutenant, or juftice of the peace, to act in the execution of this act in any and every fub-divifion within the county, riding, or place, for which he is or fhall be commiffioned; and that each and every fuch deputy lieutenant and juftice of the peace, hath, and fhall have, the fame power and authority therein, as is by the faid recited act, or by this act, given to any deputy lieutenant or juftice of the peace, within the fubdivifion to which he is or fhall be particu-larly appointed; any thing in the faid recited act, or in this act, to the contrary notwithftanding.

VIII. And be it enacted, That his Majefty's lieutenant for any county, riding, or place, may and fhall appoint a clerk for the general meetings within fuch county, riding, or place, and may difplace fuch clerk, if he fhall think fit, and appoint ano-ther in his room; and the deputy lieutenants, at their firft meet-ing within their refpective fubdivifions, or the major part of them prefent, may and fhall appoint a clerk for their fubdivifi-on, and may, at any other meeting within their fubdivifion, difplace fuch clerk, if they, or the major part of them prefent, fhall think fit, and appoint another in his room.

IX. And be it enacted by the authority aforefaid, That in every county, riding, or place, in which commiffions for the field officers, and captain of any one battallion of the militia of fuch county, riding, or place, have not already been given and accepted in purfuance of the faid recited act, his Majefty's lieu-tenant fhall, within fourteen days after the paffing of this act, or as foon after as may be, by an advertifement inferted in the *Lon-don Gazette*, and alfo in fome one or more of the weekly news papers (if any fuch there be) publifhed or ufually circulated with-in fuch county, riding, or place, fummon a meeting of all per-fons qualified according to the directions of the faid recited act,

and

and of this act, to serve as officers in the militia of such county, riding, or place, and willing to accept such commissions, to be holden on some certain day with one month after the publication of such advertisement; and at some certain place within such county, riding, or place; in order that every person so qualified as aforesaid, and willing to accept any such commission, may, at such meeting, deliver his name in writing, or cause it to be delivered to his Majesty's said lieutenant, or in case of his absence, to such person as shall be authorized by such lieutenant to receive the same, specifying also the rank in which he is willing to serve; and that if his Majesty's said lieutenant shall not be able to find, within one month after such meeting, so many persons qualified and willing to accept the commissions of field officers and captains respectively, as shall be equal to the number of field officers and captains requisite for any one battalion of the militia of such county, riding, or place, then, and in such case, it shall be lawful for his Majesty's said lieutenant, upon notice thereof published by him in the *London Gazette*, and such other papers as aforesaid, to suspend all farther proceedings in the execution of the provisions of the said recited act, and of this act, within such county, riding, or place, until the following year; and that whensoever and as often as such execution shall have been so suspended, his Majesty's said lieutenant shall, on or before the twenty fifth day of *March* next following, summon, in like manner, and with like notice, a meeting within such county, riding, or place, of all persons so qualified and willing to serve as aforesaid; and his Majesty's said lieutenant, and all other persons, shall proceed thereupon, and also in the farther execution of the provisions of the said recited act, and of this act, in like manner, to all intents and purposes, as he and they respectively ought to have done, in case a sufficient number of persons so qualified and willing to serve as aforesaid, had been found in the year one thousand seven hundred and fifty eight.

where they are to deliver in their names, and rank they are willing to serve in;

and if at such meeting, or within one month after, a sufficient number of persons duly qualified shall not be found to accept commissions, the lieutenant is, by like public notice, to suspend all farther proceeding, till March following, when like summons and notice is to be given, and the provisions in the former and this act, are then to be carried into full execution.

X. Provided always, That no commission shall be granted to any person to be an officer of the militia of any county, riding, or place, until the lieutenant of such county, riding, or place, shall have certified the name of such person to his Majesty, his heirs, or successors (which such lieutenant is required to do) and in case his Majesty, his heirs, or successors, shall, within one month after such certificate laid before his Majesty, his heirs, or successors, signify his or their disapprobation of such person to be such officer in the said militia, his Majesty's said lieutenant shall not grant such commission to such person.

The names of persons intended for officers are to be certified to his Majesty, before commissions be granted them; and if he shall signify, within a month, his disapprobation of any such, no commission is to be granted to such person.

XI. And be it enacted, That the method for carrying into execution the said recited act, and this act, to be observed in the year one thousand seven hundred and fifty eight, shall be as followeth; that is to say, His Majesty's lieutenant for each county, riding, or place, together with any two or more deputy lieutenants, and on the death or removal, or in the absence of his Majesty's lieutenant, the deputy lieutenants, or any three or more of them, shall meet at some city or principal town of the county, riding, or place,

General directions for carrying the former and this act into present execu-

tion, viz. a general meeting to be had of the lieutenants and deputy lieutenants in their respective counties, &c. in August, for appointing the subdivisions of the deputy lieutenants, and their first meetings therein, and also the second general meeting.

Orders to be then issued to the constables, to return on a day appointed, to the deputy lieutenants.

Lists of the inhabitants between 18 and 50 years of age, distinguishing each person.

Copy of the list to be affixed on the door of the church on the Sunday before the return is made.

Deputy lieutenants, assisted by the justice, on the day of the returns, after hearing particular grievances, are to amend the lists; and then appoint a second meeting The lists so amended, to be returned to the next general meeting; when orders are to be given for copies of the said lists to be made out, and returned to the deputy lieutenants at their second meetings in

place, for which they shall be commissioned, on the third *Tuesday* in *August*, and shall, at their first general meeting, appoint subdivisions of the deputy lieutenants within their respective counties, ridings, and places, and the times and places for their first meetings within the said subdivisions respectively, and the time and place for a second general meeting; and shall issue out their orders to the chief constable, and where there is no chief constable, to some other officer of the several hundreds, rapes, laths, wapentakes, or other divisions, within their respective counties, ridings, or places, to require, by orders under their hands, the constable, tythingman, headborough, or other officer, of each parish, tything, or place, within their respective hundreds, rapes, laths, wapentakes, or other divisions, to return to the deputy lieutenants within their respective subdivisions, at the place and on the day appointed at the said first general meeting, fair and true lists in writing, of all the men usually and at that time dwelling within their respective parishes, tythings, and places; between the ages of eighteen and fifty years, distinguishing their respective ranks and occupations, and which of the persons so returned, labour under any infirmities incapacitating them from serving as militia men, having first affixed a true copy of such list on the door of the church or chapel belonging to such parish, tything, or place; and if any place, being extraparochial, shall have no church or chapel belonging thereto, on the door of the church or chapel of some parish or place thereto adjoining on the *Sunday* morning before they shall make such return; and on the day, and at the place, so respectively appointed as aforesaid, for the returns of the lists, the said deputy lieutenants, or any three or more of them, or any two deputy lieutenants, together with any one justice of the peace, or any one deputy lieutenant, together with any two justices of the peace, so assembled in their subdivisions, shall (after hearing any person who shall think himself aggrieved by having his name inserted in such lists, or by any others being omitted) direct such lists to be amended, as the case shall require, and also the names of all persons by this act respectively excepted, to be struck out of the said lists, and shall appoint the times and places for their second meetings within their respective subdivisions, and shall return to the second general meeting all the lists for the several parishes, tythings, and places, so amended; at which said second general meeting, his Majesty's lieutenant, together with any two or more deputy lieutenants, or, in the absence of his Majesty's said lieutenant, any three or more deputy lieutenants, shall order copies to be made of all the said lists, and such copies to be returned to the deputy lieutenants at their second meetings within their subdivisions, wherein the parishes, tythings, and places, for which such lists are made and returned, are respectively situate; and shall appoint what number of men in each respective hundred, rape, lath, wapentake, or other division, shall serve in the said militia, towards raising the number of militia men, by the said recited act ordered and directed to be raised for such respective county,

county, riding, or place, in proportion to the whole number their fubdivi-
contained in fuch lifts; and the faid deputy lieutenants, or any fions;
three or more of them, or any two deputy lieutenants, together and the num-
with any one juftice of the peace, or any one deputy lieutenant, ber of men
together with any two juftices of the peace, affembled at their each hundred,
faid fecond meetings within the faid fubdivifions, fhall caufe the nifh, is to be
number of men appointed at the faid fecond general meeting to afcertained;
ferve for each refpective hundred, rape, lath, wapentake, or other at the faid fe-
divifion, to be chofen by lot out of the lifts of the feveral parifhes, cond meetings
tythings, and places, within the fame; and the faid deputy fuch number
lieutenants, or any one or more of them, fhall appoint another is to be chofen
meeting to be held within three weeks in the fame fubdivifion, by lot, out of
and fhall iffue out an order to the chief conftable, or other officers the faid lifts.
of the refpective hundreds, rapes, laths, wapentakes, or other A meeting is
divifions, to direct the conftable, tythingman, headborough, or then to be ap-
other officer of each parifh, tything, or place, to give notice to pointed to be
every man fo chofen to ferve in the militia, to appear at fuch held within 3
meeting; which notice fhall be given or left at his place of abode, weeks after,
at leaft feven days before fuch meeting; and every perfon fo and orders if-
chofen by lot, fhall, upon fuch notice, appear at fuch meeting, fued for fum-
and there take the oath by this act directed to be taken (which moning the
oath any one deputy lieutenant is hereby authorized then and men chofen, to
there to adminifter) and fhall be inrolled to ferve in the militia appear thereof fuch refpective county, riding, or place, as a private militia at;
man, for the fpace of three years, in a roll to be then and there the men to ap-
prepared for that purpofe, or fhall provide a fit perfon (to be pear accord-
approved by the faid deputy lieutenants, or any three or more of ingly, and be
them, or by any two deputy lieutenants, together with any one fworn and in-
juftice of the peace, or by any one deputy lieutenant, together rolled, to ferve
with any two juftices of the peace then met) to ferve as his fub- for 3 years;
ftitute; which fubftitute fo provided, fhall take the faid oath, and or provide
fign on the faid roll his confent to ferve as his fubftitute, during proper fubfti-
the faid term; and if any perfon fo chofen by lot to ferve in the tutes;
militia (not being one of the people called *Quakers*) fhall refufe who are to be
or neglect to take the faid oath, and ferve in the militia, or to fworn, and fign
provide a fubftitute to be approved as aforefaid, who fhall take on the roll
the faid oath, and fign his confent to ferve as his fubftitute, every their confent
fuch perfon fo refufing or neglecting, fhall forfeit and pay the to ferve for the
fum of ten pounds, and at the end of three years be appointed to faid term;
ferve again. on penalty of
10l. and being
liable to ferve
at the end of
3 years.

XII. Provided always, That no peer of this realm, nor any Specification
perfon who fhall ferve as a commiffion officer in any regiment, of perfons ex-
troop, or company, in his Majefty's other forces, or in any one empted from
of his Majefty's caftles or forts, nor any noncommiffion officer ferving in the
or private man, ferving in any of his Majefty's other forces, nor militia.
any commiffion officer ferving in the militia, nor any perfon
being a member of either of the univerfities, nor any clergyman,
nor any teacher of any feparate congregation, nor any conftable
or other peace officer, nor any articled clerk, apprentice, feaman,
or feafaring man, fhall ferve perfonally, or provide a fubftitute
to ferve in the militia.

Persons that
are free of the
watermen's
company not
liable to serve.

XIII. *And whereas the members of the company of watermen of
the river* Thames, *are liable at all times under certain penalties to
serve in the royal navy of* Great Britain, *when summoned for that
purpose*; be it therefore enacted, That no person free of the said
company, shall serve personally, or provide a substitute to serve
in the militia.

Deputy lieute-
nants and pa-
rish officers to
be returned in
the lists, and
liable to serve.

XIV. And be it enacted, That all deputy lieutenants and
parish officers shall be liable to serve in the militia, and the
constable, tythingman, headborough, or other officers of every
parish, tything, or place, is and are hereby required to insert the
names of such deputy lieutenants and parish officers, in the list
to be returned to the lieutenants and deputy lieutenants of persons
liable to serve in the militia, for such parish, tything, or place,
according to the directions of the said recited act, and this act;
any thing therein or herein contained to the contrary notwithstanding.

Deputy lieute-
nants are an-
nually to tranf-
mit to the
lieutenant true
copies of the
roll for their
respective fub-
divisions; and
a general meet-
ing for form-
ing and order-
ing the mili-
tia, to be held
within 3 weeks
after.

XV. And be it enacted, That the deputy lieutenants and
justices of the peace, shall every year, within fourteen days after
their respective meetings in their subdivisions for administering
the oaths to, and inrolling, the private militia men, transmit to
his Majesty's lieutenant true copies of the rolls for their respective
subdivisions: and that a general meeting of his Majesty's lieutenant, and the deputy lieutenants, or of the deputy lieutenants,
for the forming and ordering the militia of the respective counties, ridings, and places, into regiments, and for the posting
officers to each company, shall be held within three weeks after
the said rolls shall have been transmitted to his Majesty's lieutenant as aforesaid; any thing in the said recited act, or this act,
to the contrary notwithstanding.

The lists of
two or more
parishes may
be united, and
proceeded on,
as if they had
been returned
for one parish.

XVI. And be it enacted, That it shall be lawful for any three
or more deputy lieutenants, or any two deputy lieutenants, together with any one justice of the peace, or any one deputy
lieutenant, together with any two justices of the peace, within
their respective subdivisions, to add together, whensoever they
shall think necessary, the lists for two or more parishes, tythings,
or places, and proceed upon such lists thus added together, in
like manner as if they had been originally returned for one parish, tything, or place, so as to make the choice of militia men
by lot, within such subdivision, as equal and impartial as possible.

Parishes may
offer, and de-
puty lieute-
nants accept
volunteers;
in which case,
so many men
only as shall
then be want-
ing of the
quota of such
parish are to
be chosen by
lot of the lists.

XVII. Provided always, and be it enacted, That if the churchwardens or overseers, or churchwarden or overseer, of any parish,
tything, or place, or of two or more parishes, tythings, or places,
so added together, as aforesaid, shall provide and produce to the
said deputy lieutenants, or any three or more of them, or to any
two deputy lieutenants, together with any one justice of the
peace, or to any one deputy lieutenant, together with any two
justices of the peace, at their meetings within their respective
subdivisions for chusing the militia men any number of volunteers, not being seamen or seafaring men, and such volunteers
shall be approved by the said deputy lieutenants and justices so
met as aforesaid, the said deputy lieutenants and justices within
their respective subdivisions, shall cause only such a number of

per-

persons to be chosen by lot out of the list returned for such parish, tything, or place, or parishes, tythings, or places as aforesaid, as shall be wanted, after the acceptance of the said volunteers, to make up the whole number to serve for such parish, tything, or place, or parishes, tythings, or places as aforesaid; and in case *If such volunteers shall not* all or any such volunteers shall not, at the next meeting of the *appear at the* said deputy lieutenants, or any three or more of them, or of any *next meeting,* two deputy lieutenants, together with any one justice of the peace, *and serve;* or of any one deputy lieutenant, together with any two justices of the peace, appear, and be sworn and inrolled to serve in the militia for such parish, tything, or place, or parishes, tythings, or places as aforesaid, the churchwardens and overseers, or church-*the church-* warden and overseer, of such parish, tything, or place, or parishes, *wardens are* tythings, or places as aforesaid, shall find one or more fit person *to find other* or persons in the room of such volunteer or volunteers, or forfeit *persons to* and pay the sum of ten pounds for every volunteer not appearing *serve in their* as aforesaid; such penalty to be recovered and applied in the *stead,* same manner as the penalty of ten pounds laid upon any person *or forfeit 10l.* for refusing or neglecting to appear, and be sworn and inrolled *a man.* to serve in the militia, is, by the said recited act, and this act, *Application of* directed to be recovered and applied; and the said churchwarden *Churchward-* and overseer, and churchwardens and overseers, shall be reim-*ens to be re-* bursed the said penalty out of the rates to be made for the relief *same out of* of the poor within such parish, tything, or place, or parishes, *the poors* tythings, or places as aforesaid. *rate.*

XVIII. And be it enacted, That every person who shall be *The following* chosen by lot to serve in the militia, or the person provided to *oath to be ta-* serve as a substitute, instead of taking the oaths, and making, *ken instead of* repeating, and subscribing the declaration, in the said recited act *the oaths and* mentioned, shall, at the time and place appointed by the said *declaration* recited act for taking the said oaths, and making, repeating, and *be made and* subscribing the said declaration, take the oath following; that is *subscribed by* to say, *the former act,*

I A. B. *do sincerely promise and swear, That I will be faithful, and* **The oath;** *bear true allegiance, to his majesty King* George, *his heirs, and successors; and I do swear, that I am a protestant, and that I will faithfully serve in the militia within the kingdom of* Great Britain, *for the defence of the same, during the time for which I am inrolled, unless I shall be sooner discharged.*

Which oath any one deputy lieutenant is hereby authorized to *to be admini-* administer: and in case any such person shall refuse or neglect *stered by the* to take the said last mentioned oath, he shall be subject and lia-*deputy lieute-* ble to the same penalties as are inflicted in and by the said recited *nant.* act, for refusing to take the oaths, and to make, repeat, and *Penalty of re-* subscribe the declaration therein mentioned; to be recovered *fusing to take* and applied in the same manner as the said penalties are therein *the same.* directed to be recovered and applied.

XIX. And be it enacted, That it may and shall be lawful for the said deputy lieutenants, or any three or more of them,

or

Discharges may be granted, and vacancies filled up, at any meeting of the deputy lieutenants in their subdivisions.
A vacancy upon the death of a substitute; or his entering into the King's service; or upon his promotion in the militia; or upon his discharge for just cause; to be filled up by lot.

or any two deputy lieutenants, together with any one justice of the peace, or any one deputy lieutenant, together with any two justices of the peace, at any of their meetings within their respective subdivisions, as well as at their annual meetings in the week before *Michaelmas* day, to discharge persons from serving in the militia, and also to fill up all vacancies, according to the directions of the said recited act, and this act.

XX. Provided always, That when any substitute shall, after having been approved of by any three deputy lieutenants, or by any two deputy lieutenants, together with any one justice of the peace, or by any one deputy lieutenant, together with any two justices of the peace, and before the expiration of the term for which he was to serve, die, or enter into any of his Majesty's land or sea forces, or be appointed a serjeant in the militia, or be discharged for any other just cause, the person for whom he served as substitute shall not be obliged to serve himself, or to find another substitute; but such vacancy shall be filled up in like manner as is directed by the said recited act, and by this act, in case of vacancies occasioned by the death or discharge of persons serving for themselves.

XXI. *And whereas it is found by the returns of the numbers of persons contained in the lists for the parishes, tythings, and places, within the several counties, ridings, and places, in that part of* Great Britain *called* England, *out of which lists the private militia men are by the said recited act passed in the last session of parliament directed to be raised, that the numbers of private militia men so directed to be raised in the said several counties, ridings, and places, do not bear so just a proportion to each other, in making up the whole number of private militia men, by the said act directed to be raised, within that part of* Great Britain *aforesaid, as in justice they ought*; be it enacted, That after all the said lists shall have been returned to, and amended by, the respective deputy lieutenants and justices of the peace, and transmitted to his Majesty's privy council, as they are by the said recited act, and by this act, directed to be, it shall be lawful for the said council, and they are hereby required to fix and settle, as near as may be, the number of private militia men, who shall for the future serve for each county, riding, or place, within the part of *Great Britain* aforesaid, by the proportion which the number returned in all the lists for the parishes, tythings, and places therein, bears to the whole number of private militia men by the said recited act directed to be raised, within the part of *Great Britain* aforesaid; and forthwith to transmit accounts of the numbers so fixed and settled to all his Majesty's lieutenants of counties, ridings, and places, within the part of *Great Britain* aforesaid respectively: and where the number of private militia men so fixed and settled as aforesaid, shall be respectively greater than the number of private militia men who shall have been, by virtue of the said recited act, appointed to serve for any county, riding, or place, then, and in such case, his Majesty's lieutenants, together with any two or more deputy lieutenants, or, in the absence of his Majesty's

The privy council upon receiving the corrected lists ordered to be transmitted to them, are to settle the quota of men to serve for each county, according to the proportion the returns for each county bear to the whole number to be raised throughout the kingdom; and are forthwith to transmit accounts of the numbers so settled, to the respective lieutenants; and if the

sty's

sty's lieutenant, any three or more deputy lieutenants, shall, at a general meeting to be held for that purpose, appoint what number of private militia men shall serve for each respective hundred, rape, lath, wapentake, or other division, within the county, riding, or place, to which they belong; and the additional number of private militia men to make up the whole number so fixed and settled as aforesaid, shall be chosen by lot, in the same manner as all other private militia men are by this act directed to be chosen; and all the additional men so chosen, or their substitutes (to be appointed as substitutes are required to be by this act) shall take the oath by this act required to be taken, and shall respectively be inrolled, or sign their consent to serve in the militia in the same manner as is directed, and shall be subject, in case of refusal, to the same penalties as are in like cases inflicted by this act: and where the number of private militia men so fixed and settled as aforesaid, shall be respectively less than the number of private militia men who shall have been, by virtue of the said recited act, appointed to serve for any county, riding, or place, then, and in such case, his Majesty's lieutenant, together with any two or more deputy lieutenants, or, in the absence of his said Majesty's lieutenant, any three or more deputy lieutenants, shall at a general meeting to be held for that purpose, discharge by lot proportionably out of each respective hundred, rape, lath, wapentake, or other division, so many private militia men as shall exceed the number so fixed and settled as aforesaid.

number shall be greater than was required by the former act, a general meeting is to held. and the additional men are to be then chosen by lot;

and if less, a proportional number is to be discharged by lot.

XXII. And be it enacted, That in case it shall at any time appear to his Majesty's lieutenant, and any two or more deputy lieutenants, or on the death or removal, or in the absence of his Majesty's lieutenant, to any three or more deputy lieutenants of any county, riding, or place, at their general meeting, that the distribution by them made of the whole number of militia men charged upon such county, riding, or place, among the several hundreds, rapes, lathes, wapentakes, or other divisions, was either unequally and erroneously made, or, from any subsequent alteration of circumstances, is become unequal and disproportionable, it shall be lawful for his Majesty's said lieutenant, and any two or more deputy lieutenants, or on the death or removal, or in the absence of his Majesty's lieutenant, for any three or more deputy lieutenants, to make a new and more equal distribution of such number as aforesaid, among the said several hundreds, rapes, lathes, wapentakes, or other divisions, according to the method prescribed by this act for making the original distribution for the year one thousand seven hundred and fifty eight; and to cause such additional number of men to be chosen by lot, or such number to be discharged out of those before chosen, for each respective hundred, rape, lathe, wapentake, or other division, as shall become necessary in consequence of such new distribution, in like manner as is by this act prescribed to be done, where the same shall become necessary in consequence of the accounts transmitted from his Majesty's privy council.

Where the number to be raised in any county, shall be unequally or erroneously apportioned amongst the hundreds or divisions thereof; the lieutenant and deputy lieutenants are to make a new and more equal distribution;

and raise, and discharge men conformable thereto.

XXIII. And

Persons tampering with the constables to make false returns, or to erase the name of any person out of the lists, forfeit 50 l.

XXIII. And be it enacted, That any person who shall, by gratuity, gift, or reward, or by promise thereof, or of any indemnification, or by menaces, endeavour to prevail on any chief constable, or any constable, tythingman, headborough, or other officer, of any parish, tything, or place, to make a false return of any list for any parish, tything, or place, or to erase or leave out of any such list, the name of any such person as ought to be returned, shall, for every such offence, forfeit and pay the sum of fifty pounds, to be recovered by action of debt, bill, plaint, or information, in any of his Majesty's courts of record at *Westminster*, wherein no essoin, wager of law, or protection, or more than one imparlance shall be allowed; all which penalty shall go to the use of the person who shall sue for the same.

Militia men exempted from statute-work; and from serving any parish office; and from being pressed into the King's service; and substitutes, having been in actual service, are equally intitled, with

XXIV. Provided always, and be it enacted, That no private man serving in the militia, either for himself, or as a substitute, shall, during the time of such service, be liable to do any highway duty commonly called *Statute-work*: or be appointed to serve as a peace officer or parish officer; nor shall such private militia man be liable to serve in any of his Majesty's land or sea forces, unless he shall consent thereto; and that every person having served as a substitute in the militia, when ordered out into actual service, and being a married man, shall have the like privilege in respect to setting up and exercising any trade, as by the said recited act is given to those who shall have personally served in the militia in the like circumstances, persons serving for themselves, to set up any trade.

Militia men to retain their regimentals at the end of 3 years service.

XXV. Provided also, That every such private militia man, who shall have served in the militia for the space of three years, shall be intitled to, and shall keep and retain to his own use, the cloathes provided for him as private militia man.

Militia man falling sick on a march, or at the place of annual exercise, is to be provided for by an order from the magistrate, or justice of the place; and the expence thereof to be reimbursed by his proper parish.

XXVI. And be it enacted, That in case any private man serving in the said militia shall, on the march, or at the place where he shall be called out to annual exercise, be disabled by sickness, it shall and may be lawful for any one justice of the peace of the county, or any mayor or chief magistrate of any city, town, or place, where such man shall then be, to order him such relief as he shall think reasonable, by warrant under his hand and seal; and the officers of the parish, tything, or place, for which such man shall serve as a militia man, shall reimburse the same to the officers of the parish where such militia man shall then receive such relief, which shall be allowed in their accounts, upon producing the above order: provided that such allowance shall not intitle such person to any settlement in the said parish or place where he shall receive such relief.

Every militia man to receive one guinea upon being ordered out into actual service.

XXVII. And be it enacted, That when the militia of any county, riding, or place, shall be ordered out into actual service, the receiver or receivers general of the land tax for such county, riding, or place, shall, and he or they is and are hereby required to pay, or cause to be paid, to the captain, or other commanding officer of each company of militia so ordered out for such county, riding, or place, one guinea for each private

militia,

militia man belonging to his company, to be paid over by such
captain, or other officer, to every such private militia man, on
or before the day appointed for marching; and such receiver or
receivers general shall be allowed the same in his or their accounts.

XXVIII. And be it enacted, That when any militia man
shall be ordered out into actual service, leaving a family not of
ability to support themselves during his absence, the overseer or
overseers of the parish where such family shall reside, shall, and
they are hereby required to allow to such family such weekly allowance for their support, until the return of such militia man,
as shall be ordered by any one justice of the peace; such allowance to be reimbursed out of the county stock by the treasurer
of the county; and such treasurer shall be allowed the same in
his accounts.

Weekly allowance to be made to the distress'd families of militia men in actual service which is to be reimbursed out of the county stock.

XXIX. And be it enacted, That all sums of money arising
by forfeitures paid by or levied upon persons refusing to serve in
the militia personally, or by substitute, shall be applied in the
first place, by any three deputy lieutenants, or by any two deputy lieutenants, together with any one justice of the peace, or
by any one deputy lieutenant, together with any two justices of
the peace, within their respective subdivisions, in providing a
substitute for the person who shall have paid such penalty; and
if any part of such penalty shall remain after such substitute shall
be provided, the same shall be paid into, and be applied as part
of, the regimental stock; any thing in the said recited act, or
this act, to the contary notwithstanding.

Fines for not serving to be applied in providing substitute in such person's room.

Surplus to go into the regimental stock.

XXX. *And whereas by the said recited act passed in the last
session of parliament, it is enacted, That the militia of every county,
riding, or place, shall be trained and exercised in half companies, on
the first* Monday *in the months of* March, April, May, June, July,
August, September, *and* October, *and in companies, on the third*
Monday *in the said months: and whereas the training and exercising
of the whole militia for any county, riding, or place, in half companies, or companies, in the week, on the same day, will render it im-
possible for the adjutant of any regiment or battalion to attend such half
companies, or companies, so often as the necessity of the service may
require*; be it enacted, That it shall be lawful for his Majesty's
lieutenant of any county, riding, or place, together with any
two or more deputy lieutenants, or, in the absence of the lieutenant, for any three or more deputy lieutenants, to change the
day of training and exercising any half company, or companies
of militia, from *Monday* to any other day of the week *(Sunday*
excepted) as shall appear to them to be best for the good of the
service, so that the whole militia for his or their respective county, riding, or place, be trained and exercised in half companies,
within the first week, and in whole companies, within the third
week; in each of the months aforesaid; any thing in the said recited act to the contrary notwithstanding.

The exercise in half and whole companies not confined to Monday, and the day left open to be appointed as shall be found best for the service; so as the men be exercised in half companies the first week, and in whole, the third week, in the months above recited.

XXXI. And be it enacted, That his Majesty's lieutenant,
together

6

The lieutenants may change the exercise from two days in a harvestmonth, to the Tuesday and Wednesday in Easter week.

together with any two or more deputy lieutenants, or on the death or removal, or in the absence of his Majesty's lieutenants, the deputy lieutenants, or any three or more of them, are hereby impowered to dispense with the training and exercising of the militia within their respective counties, ridings, or places, in any one month in the time of harvest, and to order and direct that the said militia shall be trained and exercised instead thereof on the *Tuesday* and *Wednesday* in *Easter* week; any thing in the said recited act, or this act, to the contrary notwithstanding.

The time the militia men may be kept to exercise.

XXXII. And be it enacted, That it may and shall be lawful for the officers of the militia, or, in the absence of an officer, for a non-commission officer, to detain the militia men, on the days of exercise, any time not exceeding six hours; provided they do not keep them above two hours under arms at any one time, without allowing them a proper time to refresh themselves.

Militia men to be furnished where they are quartered at a certain rate, viz.

Subalterns at 1 s. and private men at 4 d. per diem.

XXXIII. And be it enacted, That the officers and private men serving in the militia quartered and billeted according to the directions of the said recited act, shall be received and furnished with diet and small beer by the owners of the inns, alehouses, victualling-houses, and other houses in which they are allowed to be quartered and billeted, paying and allowing for the same the several rates herein after mentioned; that is to say, For one commission officer under the degree of a captain, for diet and small beer *per diem* one shilling; and for one private man's diet and small beer *per diem*, four pence.

When the pay, arms, cloaths, and accoutrements may be issued.

XXXIV. And be it enacted by the authority aforesaid, That pay, arms, accoutrements, and clothing, may be issued, and that an adjutant and serjeants may be appointed, for any regiment or battalion of militia of any county, riding, or place, when it shall appear, by a return signed by his Majesty's lieutenant, or in his absence by three deputy lieutenants, that three fifths of the militia men of any such regiment or battalion have been inrolled; and that three fifths of the commission officers have been appointed; and that they have taken out their commissions, and entered their qualifications; any thing in the said recited act to the contrary notwithstanding.

Attendance of constables enforced by like penalties, as are inflicted by the recited act for non-compliance with orders.

XXXV. And be it enacted, That it shall be lawful for the deputy lieutenants, or any three or more of them, or any two deputy lieutenants, together with any one justice of the peace, or any one deputy lieutenant, together with any two justices of the peace, within their respective subdivisions, from time to time, to issue out their order or warrant, under their hands and seals, commanding the attendance of the constable, tythingman, headborough, or other officer, of any parish, tything, or place, within their several subdivisions, at such times and places as in such order or warrant shall be expressed; and such constable, tythingman, headborough, or other officer, who shall refuse or neglect to appear according to such order or warrant, shall suffer all the like pains and penalties as are inflicted by the said

recited

recited act upon fuch officers, for not complying with any orders given in purfuance of the faid recited act.

XXXVI. And be it enacted, That whenfoever the militia fhall be ordered out into actual fervice, it fhall and may be lawful for the captain of any company of militia men to augment his company, by incorporating, with the confent of his Majefty's lieutenant, or, in the abfence of his Majefty's lieutenant, with the confent of two or more of the deputy lieutenants, any number of perfons who fhall offer themfelves as volunteers, and who fhall appear to him to be fufficiently trained and difciplined, and provided with proper cloaths, arms, and accoutrements, and who fhall take the oath appointed to be taken by this act, and fign their confent to ferve in the militia for the time of fuch actual fervice, and to fubmit to the fame rules and articles of war as militia men are by the faid recited act, and this act, liable to, during the time of their continuing in actual fervice. *Power to the captain, when the militia is called into actual fervice, to augment his company with volunteers, with the confent of the lieutenant.*

XXXVII. And be it enacted, That it fhall be lawful for any commiffion officer of the militia, being a juftice of the peace, and acting as fuch, upon his own view of any offence committed by any non-commiffion officer or private militia man under his command, punifhable by the faid recited act paffed in the laft feffion of parliament, to punifh fuch non-commiffion officer or private militia man refpectively, in the fame manner as any one juftice of the peace is impowered to do, upon proof thereof made according to the directions of the faid recited act. *A commiffion officer being a juftice of the peace, may, upon his own view, punifh a militia man guilty of any offence punifhable by the recited act.*

XXXVIII. And be it enacted, That any two deputy lieutenants, together with any one juftice of the peace, or any one deputy lieutenant, together with any two juftices of the peace, within the counties of *Cumberland*, *Huntingdon*, *Monmouth*, *Weftmorland*, and *Rutland*, and within all the feveral counties and places within the faid dominion of *Wales* refpectively, fhall have and exercife all and every the powers conferred by the faid recited act, and this act, on any three deputy lieutenants, or on any two deputy lieutenants, together with any one juftice of the peace, or on any one deputy lieutenant, together with any two juftices of the peace of any county, riding, or place, within that part of *Great Britain* called *England*; any thing therein or herein contained to the contrary notwithftanding. *Perfons required for the execution of this act in Cumberland, Huntingdon, &c.*

XXXIX. *And whereas by the faid recited act paffed in the laft feffion of parliament, it is enacted, That the number of private men to be raifed for the* Tower Divifion *in the county of* Middlefex, *commonly called* The Tower Hamlets, *fhall be one thoufand one hundred and fixty*; be it enacted, That fo much of the faid act as relates to the number of private militia men to be raifed within and for the faid divifion or hamlets, or to the levying, training, and exercifing the militia of the faid divifion or hamlets, or to the appointment of officers, or levying trophy money, within the fame, fhall be, and the fame is hereby repealed. *Claufe in the recited act refpecting the number and training of the militia of The Tower Hamlets, repealed.*

XL. Provided always, and be it enacted, That whereas the militia of the *Tower Divifion* in the county of *Middlefex*, commonly known by the name of *The Tower Hamlets*, is, and always has *Lieutenant of the Tower impowered to appoint deputy lieutenants,* and grant commissions, and regiment the militia of the said hamlets, as the act of 13 & 14 Car. 2. directs;

has been, under the command of his Majesty's constable of the *Tower*, or lieutenant of the *Tower Hamlets*, for the service and preservation of that royal fort; it shall be lawful for his Majesty's said constable, or lieutenant for the time being, from time to time, to appoint his deputy lieutenants, and to give commissions to a proper number of officers to train and discipline the militia to be raised within and for the said division or hamlets, pursuant to an act of the thirteenth and fourteenth years of the reign of King *Charles* the Second, intituled, *An act for ordering the forces of the several counties of this kingdom*; and to form the same into two regiments of eight companies each, in such manner as the said constable or lieutenant hath used to do;

and raise trophy money for defraying incident charges;

and also for defraying the necessary charge of trophies, and other incident expences of the militia of the same division or hamlets, it shall be lawful for his Majesty's said constable or lieutenant, to continue to raise in every year the proportion of a fourth part of one month's assessment of trophy money, within the said division or hamlets, in such manner as he hath used to do, by virtue and in pursuance of the said act of the thirteenth and fourteenth years of the reign of King *Charles* the Second.

and appoint a treasurer of the said monies,

XLI. And be it further enacted, That his Majesty's said constable of the *Tower*, or lieutenant of the *Tower Hamlets*, shall appoint a treasurer of the said trophy money, for receiving and paying such monies as shall be levied by virtue of the said act of the thirteenth and fourteenth years of the reign of King *Charles*

who is to account yearly upon oath. The said accounts to be certified to the justices at their sessions; and no warrant to be issued for raising trophy money, till the preceding year's accounts are settled.

the Second; which said treasurer shall yearly account in writing, and upon oath, for the same, to the said lieutenant, or his deputy lieutenants, or any three or more of them; which oath they shall have power to administer; and which accounts for the same shall be certified to the justices of the peace for the said division at their next general or quarter sessions; and that the said constable, or lieutenant, shall not issue out warrants for raising any trophy money, until the justices of the peace, or the major part of them at such sessions, shall have examined, stated, and allowed, the accounts of the trophy money raised, levied, and collected, for the preceding year, and certified the same under the hands and seals of four or more of such justices, unless in case where it shall appear to such justices, that by reason of the death of such treasurer, or otherwise, such accounts cannot be passed.

Provisions, &c. in the recited act with respect to Com' Northumberland, extended to Berwick upon Tweed; and the number of men to be chosen by

XLII. *And whereas from the peculiarity of the jurisdiction of the town of* Berwick upon Tweed, *the said recited act could not be carried into execution in that place without a particular provision*; be it therefore enacted, That all the powers given, and provisions made, by the said recited act, and this act, with respect to the county of *Northumberland*, and the militia thereof, shall, in like manner, take place, and be in force, with respect to the said town of *Berwick upon Tweed*, except only as to the particulars herein expressed, and otherwise provided for; and that out of the persons returned in the lists for the said town, a number of private militia men shall be chosen by lot to serve for the said

town,

town, in the same proportion with the private militia men appointed to serve for the other respective hundreds, wards, and other divisions, within the said county of *Northumberland*; and if persons can be found within the said town and liberties thereof, with such qualifications as are required for deputy lieutenants and officers within the cities and towns which are counties of themselves, the chief magistrate of the said town of *Berwick upon Tweed* shall appoint five deputy lieutenants, and such number of officers of the militia as shall be proportionable to the number of militia men which the said town shall raise, as their *Quota* towards the militia of the county of *Northumberland*; and the said lieutenants and officers are hereby required to put the powers conferred by the said recited act, and this act, for raising and training the militia, into execution, within the said town and liberties, subject to such penalties as are inflicted upon deputy lieutenants and officers of the militia for acting, not being duly qualified according to the directions of the said recited act, and this act; and that the said militia shall annually join the militia of the county of *Northumberland*, and be exercised together at the general annual exercise in *Whitsun* week, and shall then, and also in time of actual service, be deemed the militia of the county of *Northumberland* for the purposes aforesaid.

XLIII. *And whereas the separating the militia of the isle of Purbeck from the militia of the county of* Dorset, *is attended with many inconveniencies*; be it enacted, That the clause in the said recited act passed in the last session of parliament relative to the militia of the isle of *Purbeck* aforesaid, be and is hereby repealed; and that all the powers given and provisions made by any part of the said recited act unrepealed, and by this act, with respect to the said county of *Dorset*, and the militia thereof, shall take place and be in force with respect to the said isle; and that out of the persons to be returned in the lists for the several parishes, tythings, and places, within the said isle, a number of private militia men shall be chosen by lot to serve for the respective hundreds, liberties, and other divisions, within the said isle, in the same proportion with the private militia men appointed to serve for the other respective hundreds, liberties, and other divisions, within the said county of *Dorset*, with the town and county of the town of *Poole*; and that the number remaining out of the eighty private men, by the said clause in the said recited act directed to be raised for and in the said isle, shall be apportioned as equally as may be amongst all the hundreds, liberties, and other divisions, within the said county of *Dorset*, with the said town and county of the town of *Poole*.

XLIV. Provided always, That nothing in this act contained, shall in any wise extend to annul, or make void, any thing already done in pursuance of the said recited act, within any such county, riding, or place, or any such subdivision, where the militia men have been, or now can be, chosen out of the lists already returned; or to oblige his Majesty's lieutenant, or any other person concerned in the execution of the said recited act,

and

[marginal notes:] lot to serve for the said town, to be in proportion to the number appointed for the other hundreds, &c. within the said county. Chief magistrate to appoint 5 deputy lieutenants, if so many shall be found qualified, and a number of officers in proportion to the Quota of the men. Men to join the militia of the county at their general annual exercise.

Clause in the recited act relative to the militia in the isle of Purbeck repealed; and the militia thereof for the future to be chosen, &c. as is provided with respect to the other hundreds, &c. in the county of Dorset.

Nothing in this act shall make void what has been done in pursuance of the former act.

and of this act, within fuch county, riding, place, or fubdivifion, to put in execution any of the provifions contained in this act, except only fuch as relate to matters fubfequent, in order of time, to thofe provifions of the faid recited act, which they have already put in execution, within fuch county, riding, place, or fubdivifion; any thing in this act contained to the contrary notwithftanding.

Limitation of actions.   XLV. And be it enacted, That if any action or actions, fuit or fuits, fhall be brought or commenced againft any perfon or perfons, for any thing done in purfuance of the faid recited act or this act, fuch action or actions, fuit or fuits, fhall be commenced within fix calendar months after the fact committed, and not afterwards; and fhall be laid in the county or place where fuch action or actions, fuit or fuits, did arife, and not elfewhere; and the defendant or defendants in fuch action or

General iffue. actions, fuit or fuits, to be brought, may plead the general iffue, and give this act, and the fpecial matter, in evidence, and if fuch action or actions, fuit or fuits, fhall be brought after the time for bringing the fame; or if the jury fhall find for the defendant or defendants in fuch action or actions; or if the plaintiff or plaintiffs fhall be nonfuited, or difcontinue his or their action or actions, fuit or fuits, after the defendant or defendants fhall have appeared; or if, upon demurrer, judgement fhall be given againft the plaintiff or plaintiffs, the defendant

Treble cofts. or defendants fhall have treble cofts, and have the like remedy for the fame, as any defendant or defendants hath or have, in other cafes, to recover cofts by law.

Continuance of the act.   XLVI. Provided always, and be it enacted, That this act fhall continue and be in force, for and during the continuance of the faid recited act, and no longer.

CAP. XXVII.

An act for repealing an act made in the twenty fifth year of his prefent Majefty, to reftrain the making infurances on foreign fhips bound to or from the Eaft Indies.

Preamble, reciting certain claufes in act 25 Geo. 2.   WHEREAS *by an act made in the twenty fifth year of the reign of his prefent Majefty, intituled,* An act to reftrain the making infurances on foreign fhips bound to or from the *Eaft Indies; all and every perfon or perfons, bodies politick or corporate, being fubjects of his Majefty in* Great Britain *or* Ireland, *or elfewhere; and all other perfons whatfoever refiding within* Great Britain *or* Ireland, *are reftrained and prohibited from granting, figning, or underwriting, any policy or policies of affurance, or lending any money on bottomree or refpondentia, of or upon any foreign fhips trading or failing to or from the* Eaft Indies, *and other places beyond the* Cape of Good Hope, *within the limits of trade granted to the united company of merchants of* England *trading to the* Eaft Indies, *or to or from any ports or places within the faid limits;* be it enacted by the King's moft excellent majefty, by and with the advice and confent of the lords fpiritual and temporal, and

com-

ommons, in this present parliament assembled, and by the authority of the same, That the said act shall from and after the ifth day of *July*, one thousand seven hundred and fifty eight, be repealed ; any thing to the contrary thereof in any wise notwithstanding. *The recited act repealed.*

C A P. XXVIII.

An act to permit the importation of salted beef, pork, and butter, from Ireland, for a limited time.

WHEREAS the permitting the importation of salted beef, pork, and butter, into this kingdom from Ireland, for a limited time, may at this time, be of great advantage to both kingdoms ; be it therefore enacted by the King's most excellent majesty, by and with the advice and consent of the lords spiritual and temporal, and commons, in this present parliament assembled, and by the authority of the same, That from and after the twenty ourth day of *June*, one thousand seven hundred and fifty eight, he importation of all sorts of salted beef, pork, and butter, nto this kingdom from *Ireland*, shall be, and is hereby, permitted, allowed, and authorized, for and during the term of six months from thence next ensuing ; and that all persons shall be, and are hereby, exempted, freed, and discharged, from the payment of all subsidies, customs, rates, duties, or other impositions, and also from all penalties, forfeitures, payments, and punishments, for or upon account of importing or bringing salted beef, pork, and butter into this kingdom from *Ireland*, during the term aforesaid, other than such as herein after are mentioned in respect thereof ; any act or acts of parliament to the contrary notwithstanding. *Importation of salted beef, pork, and butter, allowed for 6 months ; without being subject to any penalties or forfeitures ;*

II. Provided always, and to the intent that the revenue arising from salt may not be prejudiced by such importation of salted beef, pork, and butter, from *Ireland* ; be it enacted, That after the said twenty fourth day of *June*, one thousand seven hundred and fifty eight, during the continuance of this act, there shall be paid to such officer as the commissioners for the duties on salt for the time being shall appoint, at the port in *England* into which any such salted beef, pork, or butter, shall, in pursuance of this act, be imported from *Ireland*, and before any part thereof shall be delivered out to the person or persons to whom the same shall belong or be consigned, the sum of one shilling and three pence for every hundred weight of all such salted beef or pork ; and the sum of four pence for every hundred weight of all such salted butter ; and so in proportion for any greater or lesser quantity than an hundred weight of any such salted beef, pork, or butter, as or for custom, or for duty, on or in respect thereof ; the money so arising by the importation of the said salted beef, pork, or butter, to be paid into his Majesty's exchequer as part of the duties on salt laid on by an act in the fifth year of his present Majesty's reign, and continued by several subsequent acts. *or other duties, on the landing thereof, than 1s. 3d. per C. wt. for beef or pork, and 4d. per C. wt. for butter ; the same to be paid into the exchequer, as part of the duties on salt, laid by the act of 5 Geo. 2.*

III. And be it enacted by the authority aforesaid, That if any

If any shall be landed before duty paid, the importer, besides the forfeiture of the said commodities, is to forfeit also 20 s. per barrel;

person or persons shall, after the said twenty fourth day of one thousand seven hundred and fifty eight, during the nuance of this act, land any such salted beef, pork, or h into this kingdom from *Ireland*, before payment of the d duties by this act specified and directed, the same shall b feited and lost, and twenty shillings *per* barrel for every thereof; and so in proportion for any greater or lesser qui to be recovered of the importer or proprietor thereof; an all such forfeitures and penalties shall be distributed in m

One moiety thereof to the King, the other to the Informer.

following; that is to say, one moiety thereof to the King heirs, and successors, and the other moiety thereof to the son or persons who shall seize, sue, or inform for the sam be recovered by action of debt, bill, plaint, or informatic any of his Majesty's courts of record at *Westminster*.

No bounty to be allowed on the exporting thereof from hence.

IV. Provided always, and it is hereby enacted, Th bounty shall be allowed or paid for any such salted beef or so imported into this kingdom from *Ireland*, and which sh exported from hence elsewhere.

General issue.

V. And be it further enacted by the authority afor That if any action or suit shall be commenced against any son or persons for any thing done in pursuance of this act, defendant or defendants in any such action or suit, may the general issue, and give this act, and the special matter evidence, at any trial to be had thereupon, and that the was done in pursuance, and by the authority of this act; if it shall appear so to have been done, the jury shall fine the defendant or defendants; and if the plaintiff shall be suited, or discontinue his action, after the defendant or def ants shall have appeared; or if judgement shall be given, u any verdict or demurrer, against the plaintiff, the defendan

Treble costs.

defendants shall and may recover treble costs, and have the remedy for the same, as any defendant or defendants hath or I in other cases by law.

CAP. XXIX.

An act for the due making of bread; and to regulate price and assize thereof; and to punish persons who a adulterate meal, flour, or bread.

Preamble, reciting act 51 Hen. 3.

and 8 Annæ.

WHEREAS by an act of parliament made in the one fiftieth year of the reign of King Henry the Third, institu Assisa Panis & Cervisiæ, provision was made, amongst other thin for settling the assize of bread: and whereas by an act of parliam made in the eighth year of the reign of her late majesty Queen An intituled, An act to regulate the price and assize of bread, so mu of the said act (intituled, Assisa Panis & Cervisiæ) as related to assize of bread, was repealed, annulled, and made void; and the s act made in the said eighth year of the reign of her said late maje Queen Ann, was only made to continue in force for three years, a from thence to the end of the then next session of parliament, but some subsequent acts of parliament, the said in part recited act m

said eighth year of her said majesty Queen Ann, with seve-
alterations and amendments thereto hath been continued until the
..rty fourth day of June, one thousand seven hundred and fifty
..n, and from thence to the end of the then next of session of par-
..ent: and whereas it is expedient to reduce into one act the several
..now in force relating to the due making, and to the price and as-
..of bread, and to make some alterations in, and amendments, to
..same; be it therefore enacted by the King's most excellent
..esty, by and with the advice and consent of the lords spiri-
..and temporal, and commons, in this present parliament
..nbled, and by the authority of the same, That the said
..made in the said eighth year of the reign of her said late
..esty Queen *Ann*, and all alterations and amendments made
..my acts of parliament subsequent thereto, for continuing,
..taining, or amending the same, is and are hereby further
..tinued from the expiration thereof, until the twenty ninth
..of *September*, one thousand seven hundred and fifty eight;
..that from and after the said twenty ninth day of *September*,
..thousand seven hundred and fifty eight, so much of the said
..ute (intituled *Assisa Panis & Cervisiæ*) as relates to the assize
..bread, and which would otherwise be revived, when the said
..ited act made in the said eighth year of her said late majesty
..een *Ann*, shall expire; and also the said act of parliament
..de in the said eighth year of the reign of her said late majesty
..een *Ann*, and all the alterations and amendments made by
..acts of parliament subsequent thereto, for continuing, ex-
..ning, or amending the same, shall be and are hereby repeal-
..annulled, and made void.

The recited act of 8 Ann. and other acts subsequent, and relating thereto, continued to 29 Sept. 1758; from which time so much of the act of 51 Hen. 3. as relates to the assize of bread, and act 8 Ann. and other acts, continuing, or amending, the same, are repealed.

II. *And, to the intent that from and after the said twenty ninth*
of September, a plain and constant rule and method may be duly
served and kept in the making and assizing of the several sorts of
bread which shall be made for sale in any place or places where an as-
..e of bread shall at any time be thought proper to be set in pursuance
this act, be it further enacted by the authority aforesaid, That
..m and after the said twenty ninth day of *September*, it shall be
..wful for the court, or person or persons herein after authoriz-
..by this act to set the assize of bread, to set, ascertain, and ap-
..int, in any place or places within their respective jurisdictions,
..assize and weight of all sorts of bread, which shall, in any
..ch place or places, be made for sale, or exposed to sale, and
..e price to be paid for the same respectively, when, and as oft-
.., from time to time, as any such court, or person or persons
..aforesaid, shall think proper; and that in every assize of bread
..hich shall be set in pursuance of this act, respect shall, from time
..time, be had by the court, person or persons as aforesaid,
..ho shall set the same, to the price which the grain, meal, or
..ur, whereof such bread shall be made, shall bear in the pub-
..k market or markets, in or near the place or places for which
..y such assize shall be so at any time set; and making, from
..ne to time, reasonable allowance to the makers of bread for
..le, where any such assize shall be so set, for their charges, la-

General ordinance for setting an assize and price of bread.

Assize to be regulated by the price the grain, meal, or flour bears in the market, and the profit to be allowed to the baker.

bour, pains, livelihood, and profit, as fuch court, or perfon
perfons as aforefaid refpectively, who fhall at any time th
fit to fet any fuch affize, fhall, from time to time, da
proper.

Where an af-
fize fhall be fet,
no fort of
bread (wheat-
en and houfe-
holdexcepted)
other than
what is there-
by allowed, is
to be made
for fale;

III. And be it further enacted by the authority aforeu
That from and after the faid twenty ninth day of Septems
where an affize of bread fhall at any time be thought propa
be fet for any place or places by virtue of this act, no perfon
perfons fhall there make for fale, or fell, or expofe to or for f
any fort of bread, except wheaten and houfhold, otherwife bra
bread, and fuch other fort or forts of bread, as in fuch plac
places fhall be publickly allowed to be made or fold by the ca
or perfon or perfons, who by this act are authorized to fet an
fize of bread for any fuch place or places; but where it hath b
ufual to make bread with the meal or flour of rye, barley, c
beans, or peafe, or with the meal or flour of any fuch diffe
forts of grain mixed together, or the court or perfon or pen
impowered to fet an affize of bread by virtue of this act,
at any time think fit to order or allow in any place or pl
within the limits of their refpective jurifdictions, bread t
made with rye, barley, oats, beans, or peafe, or with the f
or meal thereof, or with the meal or flour of any fuch diffe
forts of grain mixed together, fuch bread fhall and may be t
made and fold; and if any perfon fhall offend in the prem:

under penalty
of forfeiting
not exceeding
40s. nor lefs
than 20s.

and fhall be convicted of any fuch offence, either by his,
or their own confeffion, or by the oath of one or more cre
witnefs or witneffes, before any magiftrate or magiftrates
ftice or juftices of the peace, within the limits of his or
jurifdiction, every one fo offending, fhall, on every fuch
viction, forfeit and pay any fum not exceeding forty fhilli
nor lefs than twenty fhillings, as any fuch magiftrate or n
ftrates, juftice or juftices, fhall think fit and order.

Affize and
price of bread
to be fet ac-
cording to the
two follow-
ing tables
mark'd Nº I.
and Nº II.

IV. And be it alfo enacted by the authority aforefaid,
from and after the faid twenty ninth day of *September*, in e
place and places for which an affize of bread fhall at any
be thought proper to be fet by virtue of this act, the affize
weight of the feveral forts of bread which fhall be there mad
fale, or fold, or expofed to or for fale, and the price to be
for the fame refpectively, fhall be fett and afcertained accor
to the tables hereafter following, marked Nº. I. and II.

Nº. I. A TAB

e of Wheat, in Two Parts.

le,

14 s. 6 d. the Bushel, the Allowance of the Magistrate
Con eral Loaves: So that (for Example) if the Price of Wh
Jug, find 6 s. 6 d. in Column N° I. and even therewith, un
in he Allowance 1 s. then the Weight of the said Loaves
N
be if the Magistrates or Justices shall think fit to allow of
a Three-fourths of the Weight of the Wheaten Loaves

8 ½	0 6 ½	1 5	1 1	2 10	[illegible]	7
8 ¾	0 6 ¾	1 5 ½	1 1 ½	2 11 ¼	2 2 ¾	7
9 ¼	0 6 ¾	1 6 ¼	1 1 ¾	3 0 ½	2 3 ½	8
9 ½	0 7	1 7	1 2	3 2	2 4	8
9 ¾	0 7 ¼	1 7 ½	1 2 ½	3 3	2 5	8
10	0 7 ½	1 8	1 3	3 4	2 6	8
10 ¼	0 7 ¾	1 8 ½	1 3 ½	3 5	2 7	9
10 ½	0 8	1 9	1 3 ¾	3 6 ¼	2 7 ¾	9
10 ¾	0 8 ¼	1 9 ¾	1 4 ¼	3 7 ¼	2 8 ¾	9
11	0 8 ¼	1 10 ¼	1 4 ¾	3 8 ½	2 9 ½	9
11 ½	0 8 ½	1 11	1 5	3 10	2 10	10
11 ¾	0 8 ¾	1 11 ½	1 5 ½	3 11	2 11	10
0	0 9	2 0	1 6	4 0	3 0	10
0 ¼	0 9 ¼	2 0 ½	1 6 ½	4 1	3 1	10
0 ½	0 9 ½	2 1	1 7	4 2	3 2	11
0 ¾	0 9 ¾	2 1 ¾	1 7 ¼	4 3 ¼	3 2 ¾	11
1	0 10	2 2 ¼	1 7 ¾	4 4 ½	3 3 ½	11
1 ½	0 10	2 3	1 8	4 6	3 4	11
1 ¾	0 10 ¼	2 3 ½	1 8 ½	4 7	3 5	12
2	0 10 ½	2 4	1 9	4 8	3 6	12
2 ¼	0 10 ¾	2 4 ½	1 9 ½	4 9	3 7	12
2 ½	0 11	2 5	1 10	4 10	3 8	12
3	0 11 ¼	2 5 ¾	1 10 ¼	4 11 ½	3 8 ½	13
3 ¼	0 11 ¼	2 6 ½	1 10 ½	5 1	3 9	13
3 ½	0 11 ½	2 7	1 11	5 2	3 10	13
3 ¾	0 11 ¾	2 7 ½	1 11 ½	5 3	3 11	13
4	1 0	2 8	2 0	5 4	4 0	14
4 ½	1 0 ¼	2 8 ½	2 0 ½	5 5	4 1	14
5	1 0 ½	2 9	2 1	5 6	4 2	14

(To face Page 325.

S.

Magi
ice a
rew
La

allw
i La

under mentioned.

re adapted so as to serve either for the Winchester Bushel
nsisting of Two-thirds Wheat and One-third Rye; the
a Column N° I. or VII. the Weights which the several
(which are to weigh 17 lb. 6 oz. each) under N° VI.
r their respective Titles in the same Line will be found

here Bread is ordered to be made for Sale of a coarse
be set and fixed from the Barley Columns.

				N° VI.										N° VII.	
oaf.				Price of the Peck Loaf.										Price of the Bushel and Baking.	
	Maslin.			Rye.		Barley.		Oats.		Beans.		Maslin.			
d.	lb.	oz.	d.	s.	d.	s.	d.	s.	d.	s.	d.	s.	d.	s.	d.
0	52	8	0	0	4½	0	4¼	0	9	0	3¼	0	4	1	0
0	42	0	0	0	5½	0	5¼	0	11	0	4	0	5	1	3
0	34	15	8	0	6½	0	6¼	1	1¼	0	5	0	6	1	6
8	30	0	0	0	7¾	0	7¼	1	3¼	0	5¾	0	7	1	9
8	26	4	0	0	8¾	0	8¼	1	5¼	0	6¾	0	8	2	0
0	23	5	8	0	10	0	9¼	1	7¼	0	7½	0	9	2	3
0	21	0	0	0	11	0	10½	1	10	0	8¼	0	10	2	6
4	19	0	8	1	0	0	11½	2	1	0	9¼	0	11	2	9
8	17	7	12	1	1	1	0½	2	2½	0	10	1	0	3	0
0	16	2	0	1	2¼	1	1½	2	4¼	0	10¾	1	1	3	3
4	15	0	0	1	3¼	1	2¾	2	6½	0	11¼	1	2	3	6
2	13	15	8	1	4½	1	3¾	2	8¼	1	0½	1	3	3	9
4	13	2	0	1	5¾	1	4¾	2	11½	1	1¼	1	4	4	0
4	12	6	0	1	6¾	1	5¾	3	0¾	1	2¼	1	5	4	3
2	11	10	12	1	8	1	7	3	2½	1	3	1	6	4	6
4	11	1	0	1	8¾	1	8	3	5¼	1	3¾	1	7	4	9
0	10	8	0	1	10	1	9	3	8	1	4¾	1	8	5	0
4	9	15	12	1	11¼	1	10	3	11	1	5¾	1	9	5	3
0	9	8	4	2	0¼	1	11	4	1	1	7½	1	10	5	6
2	9	1	8	2	1¼	2	0	4	3	1	7¾	1	11	5	9
4	8	11	14	2	2¼	2	1	4	5½	1	8	2	0	6	0
8	8	6	4	2	3¼	2	2	4	7¼	1	8¼	2	1	6	3
8	8	1	0	2	5	2	3	4	9	1	9½	2	2	6	6
4	7	12	8	2	6	2	4	5	0	1	10½	2	3	6	9
0	7	8	0	2	7	2	5	5	1½	1	11¼	2	4	7	0

(To face Page 325.)

V. And be it further enacted by the authority aforesaid, that from and after the said twenty ninth day of *September*, one ousand seven hundred and fifty eight, every assize which shall, om time to time, be set in any city, town corporate, hundred, vision, liberty, rape, or wapentake, in pursuance of this act, all be always set in averdupois weight, of sixteen ounces to e pound, and not troy weight, and in the several proportions directed in or by the said tables above set forth, or as near the same may be, as to the several sorts of bread in this act specified; id that the said tables shall extend as well to such bread which all be made with the flour of wheat mixed with the flour of her grain, as also to bread which shall be made with the flour other grain or grains than wheat, which shall be publickly licensed and allowed to be made into bread, in any place or places pursuance of this act; and that the assize of all such mixed ead shall be set and ascertained as near as may be, according the said tables.

Assize to be set in averdupoise weight, and in the proportions directed by the tables, for the several forts of bread.

VI. And be it further enacted by the authority aforesaid, hat from and after the said twenty ninth day of *September*, the specttive prices which the several kinds of grain, meal, and our, fit and proper to make the different sorts of bread which all be allowed to be made in pursuance of this act, shall, from ne to time, *bona fide*, sell for in the markets or places in *London*, where such grain, meal, and flour, shall be openly and publickly sold during the whole market, and not at particular times ereof, or on particular contracts only, shall, from time to me, be given in and certified on oath, on some certain day in every week, as the court of mayor and aldermen of the city of *London* shall, from time to time, appoint, by the meal weighers the said city of *London*, or such other persons as the said court mayor and aldermen in *London*, shall, from time to time, direct; and shall also on some certain day in every week, to be appointed by the said court of mayor and aldermen in *London*, be itered by such meal weighers, or other persons to be appointed aforesaid, in writing under their hands, in some book to be for at purpose provided by the said city of *London*, and kept at the wn clerk's office in the said city: and the next day after every ch price shall be so given in and certified as aforesaid, the assize id weight of all sorts of bread to be sold or exposed to sale by ly person within the limits of their jurisdiction, and the price be paid for the same respectively, shall, from time to time, set by the said court of mayor and aldermen in *London*, if the id court shall then fit, and if such court shall not then fit, by e mayor of the said city for the time being; and that the assize bread which shall be so set in *London* shall take place from such ne as the said court shall order, and be in force for the said ty of *London* and the liberties thereof, and the weekly bills of ortality (the city of *Westminster* and liberties thereof, the borough of *Southwark*, and weekly bills of mortality in the county of *urry* excepted) until a new or other assize of bread in *London* all be set; and that after the fixing or setting of every such

Return to be made weekly to the court of mayor and aldermen of London, by the meal weighers, of the places which the several kinds of grain, meal, and flour, fit for bread, publickly sell for in the markets of the city; the prices to be entered by them on a certain day in a book to be kept in the town clerk's office; and the assize and price of bread to be set the next day;

and to take place according to order, and continue 'til a new assize be set;

     assize

affize of bread, by the faid court of mayor and aldermen of *London*, or the mayor of the faid city for the time being, when the faid court of mayor and aldermen of *London* fhall not fit, the affize fo from time to time fet, fhall, with all convenient speed after fetting thereof, be made public in fuch manner as the faid court of mayor and aldermen fhall order or direct : but before any advance or reduction fhall in any week be made by the faid court of mayor and aldermen, or the mayor of the faid city of *London* for the time being, in the price of bread, the meal weighers of the faid city of *London* for the time being, or fuch other perfons as the faid court of mayor and aldermen fhall from time to time appoint to return the price of grain, meal, and flour, fhall leave in writing at the common hall of the company of bakers in the faid city of *London*, a copy of every return of the price of grain, meal, and flour, which they fhall make, and enter in fuch book to be provided and kept at the town clerk's office as aforefaid, fome time of the fame day on which fuch meal weighers or other perfons fhall make every fuch return and entry as aforefaid ; to the intent that the faid company of bakers may the morning of the next day after every fuch return and entry fhall be made, and before any affize fhall be fet, from time to time, have an opportunity to offer to the faid court of mayor and aldermen, if fuch court fhall then fit, and if fuch court fhal not then fit, to the mayor of the faid city of *London* for the time being, all fuch objections as the faid company of bakers fhal have and think fit to offer againft any advance or reduction being that day made in *London* in the price of bread.

The court of mayor and aldermen, and magiftrates, &c. in other cities, towns, and boroughs, may, in like manner, caufe returns to be made them of the prices which the feveral forts of grain, meal, and flour, fit for bread, fhall be publickly fold at in the markets, within their jurifdictions.

VII. And be it further enacted by the authority aforefaid That from and after the faid twenty ninth day of *September*, the court of mayor and aldermen of every other city, where there fhall be any fuch court, and when fuch court fhall fit ; and where there fhall be no fuch court, or, there being any fuch, when the fame fhall not fit, the mayor, bailiffs, or other chief magiftrate or magiftrates of every fuch other refpective city ; and in town corporate, or boroughs, the mayor, bailiffs, aldermen, or other chief magiftrate or magiftrates for the time being of every fuch town corporate or borough ; or two or more juftices of the peace in fuch towns and places where there fhall be no fuch mayor, bailiffs, aldermen, or chief magiftrates ; fhall and may feverally and refpectively, from time to time, as there fhall be occafion, within their feveral and refpective jurifdictions, caufe the refpective prices with the feveral forts of grain, meal, and flour, fit and proper to make the different forts of bread which fhall be allowed to be made in every fuch other refpective city, town corporate, borough, town, or place, fhall, from time to time, *bona fide*, fell for, in the refpective publick markets in or near to every fuch other town corporate, borough, town, or place, during the whole market, and not at particular times thereof, or on particular contracts only, from time to time be given in and certified, upon oath, unto fuch court, mayor, bailiffs, aldermen, chief magiftrate or magiftrates, or juftices, as afore aforesaid respectively, within their several jurisdictions, in such manner, and by such person or persons, and on such day in every week, as any such respective court, mayor, bailiffs, aldermen, chief magistrate or magistrates, or justices, as aforesaid, within their respective jurisdictions, shall from time to time appoint; and the price which shall be so certified, shall, from time to time, be entered by the respective person or persons who shall certify the same in some book or books to be provided by such respective person or persons, and kept by him or them for that purpose: and within two days after every such price shall be so returned, the assize and weight of bread for every such other respective city, town corporate, borough, town, and place, and the price to be paid for the same, shall, from time to time, be set by the court of mayor and aldermen of every such other city where there shall be any such court, and when the same shall sit; and when such court shall not sit, by the mayor of every such other respective city; and where there shall be no such court of mayor and aldermen in any such other city, then by the mayor, bailiffs, or other chief magistrate or magistrates of every such other city; and in towns corporate, and boroughs, by the mayor, bailiffs, aldermen, or other chief magistrate or magistrates of every such town corporate, or borough; and by two or more justices of the peace in towns or places where there shall be no such mayor, bailiffs, aldermen, or chief magistrate or magistrates: and the assize and weight of bread, and price to be paid for the same, which shall be so from time to time set in every such other city, and in every town corporate, or borough, and in every town and place where there shall be no such mayor, bailiffs, aldermen, or chief magistrate or magistrates, as aforesaid, shall commence and take place on such day in every week, and be in force for such time, not exceeding seven days from the setting of every such assize, and shall be made publick in such manner, as such court of mayor and aldermen in every such other city where there shall be any such court, and when the same shall sit; and where there shall be no such court of mayor and aldermen, or there being any such, when the same shall not sit, as the mayor, bailiffs, or other chief magistrate or magistrates, as aforesaid, of every such other city; and as the mayor, bailiffs, aldermen, or other chief magistrate or magistrates, as aforesaid, of every such town corporate, or borough; and in towns and places where there shall be no such mayor, bailiffs, aldermen, or chief magistrate or magistrates, as aforesaid, as any such two justices, as aforesaid, shall, within their respective jurisdictions, from time to time direct.

the prices to be entered and certified in a proper book;

and the assize and price of bread, to be set within 2 days after;

and to take place, and continue (not exceeding 7 days) and to be published, as the court or magistrates shall direct.

VIII. And be it further enacted by the authority aforesaid, That from and after the said twenty ninth day of *September*, if any two or more justices of the peace of counties at large, ridings, or divisions, shall at any time think fit to set an assize of bread, for any place or places within the limits of their respective jurisdictions, then, and in any such case, it shall be lawful for any such two or more justices, within the limits of their respec-

Two or more justices within their jurisdictions, may set an assize of bread, and cause returns to be made by the clerks of the neighbour-

 ing markets of the price at which grain, meal, flour, fhall be there fold;

fpective jurifdictions, to caufe the price which grain, meal, and flour, fit to make the feveral forts of bread which fhall be made for fale in any fuch place or places, fhall, from time to time, *bona fide*, fell for in the refpective public corn market or corn markets, in or near any fuch place or places refpectively, during the whole market, and not at particular times thereof, or on fpecial contracts only, to be from time to time given, and certified on oath, to them at their refpective houfes or places of

the returns to be made on a certain day,

abode, in any fuch county, riding, or divifion, on fuch day in every week, as any fuch two or more juftices fhall for that purpofe fix on and appoint, by the refpective clerks of the market of the feveral markets in or near fuch refpective place or places, or fuch other perfon or perfons as any fuch two or more juftices as aforefaid refpectively, within their refpective jurifdictions, fhall

and to be entered and figned in a book to be kept for that purpofe; the affize and price of bread to be fet within 2 days after, and to continue (not exceeding 14 days) and to commence and be publifhed as fhall be ordered.

for that purpofe appoint; and that the price of grain, meal, and flour, which fhall be fo returned, fhall, from time to time, be entered by the refpective perfon or perfons who fhall fo return the fame, in fome book or books to be provided by him or them, and kept for that purpofe; and within two days after any fuch return of the price of grain, meal, and flour, fhall be made, to any fuch two or more juftices, as aforefaid, the price and affize of bread may be by them, or any two of them, fet for every fuch place or places, for any time not exceeding fourteen days from every fetting thereof: and the affize which fhall be fo from time to time fet, fhall commence and be in force, at fuch time after every fetting thereof, and be made public in fuch place or places for which the fame fhall be fo fet, in fuch manner as the juftices who fhall fet the fame, fhall order or direct.

Bakers may fee the returns, the day after the fame fhall be made,

IX. And be it further enacted by the authority aforefaid, That any maker of bread for fale in any fuch other city, town corporate, borough, or place, where the price and affize of bread, in purfuance of this act, fhall at any time be thought proper to be fet, fhall have liberty, at all feafonable times, in the day time, the next day after every return of the price of grain, meal, and flour, fhall be made for any fuch other city, town corporate, borough, town, or place, and entered in the proper book hereby directed to be provided and kept for that purpofe, to fee the entry which fhall be made in fuch book, of the price of grain,

that they may have time to object to the advance or reduction to be made in the price of bread, before the affize be fet.

meal, and flour, without paying any thing for the fame; to the intent that every fuch maker of bread for fale, may have an opportunity on the faid next day after any fuch entry as aforefaid fhall be made as hereby is directed, to offer to any fuch court, mayor, bailiffs, aldermen, or other chief magiftrate or magiftrates, or juftices, as aforefaid, who fhall think fit to fet any fuch affize of bread within their refpective jurifdictions, and before any fuch affize fhall be fet, fuch objections as any fuch maker of bread for fale can reafonably make againft any advance or reduction being at any time made in the affize or price of bread in any fuch other city, town corporate, borough, town, or place.

X. And be it further enacted by the authority aforefaid,

That

That no baker or maker of bread for fale fhall be liable or compellable to pay any fee, gratuity, or reward, to any perfon or perfons for, or by means of, any affize of bread being at any time fet, altered, or publifhed, by virtue of, or under this act. Baker not liable to pay fees on account of the affize of bread.

XI. And be it further enacted by the authority aforefaid, That the form of the return, or the certificate of the price of grain, meal, or flour, fhall, from time to time, be to the purport or effect as followeth; that is to fay, Form of the returns to be made of the price of grain, meal, or flour.

The prices of grain, meal, and flour, as fold in the corn market in   in the   of
                    the   day of   17

The beft wheat	– – – –	– at	by the bufhel.
The fecond	– – –	– at	by ditto.
The third	– – –	– at	by ditto.
The beft wheaten flour	–	– at	by the fack.
Houfhold flour	– –	– at	by ditto.
Rye	– – – –	– at	by the bufhel.
Rye meal, or flour,	– –	– at	by the bufhel.
Barley	– – – –	– at	by ditto.
Barley meal	– – –	– at	by ditto.
Oats	– – – –	– at	by ditto.
Oatmeal	– – – –	– at	by
White peas	– – –	– at	by the bufhel.
White pea flour, or meal,	–	– at	by
Beans	– – – –	– at	by the bufhel.
Bean meal, or flour,	– – –	– at	by

To every of which returns the perfon or perfons, who fhall be appointed to make the fame, fhall, from time to time, fign their refpective names or marks. Returns to be figned.

XII. And be it further enacted by the authority aforefaid, That when an affize of bread fhall at any time be fet in purfuance of this act, the fame fhall be made public in the form or to the effect following; that is to fay, Form of publication of the affize of bread.

To wit, The affize of bread, fet the   day of
                    for   to take place
on the   day of   now
next enfuing, and to be in force   for the
faid   of

And in places where penny, twopenny, fixpenny, twelvepenny, and eighteenpenny loaves, fhall be made, as followeth;

6   The

	lb.	oz.	dr.
The penny loaf wheaten is to weigh - -			
Ditto houfhold is to weigh - - -			
The twopenny loaf wheaten is to weigh -			
Ditto houfhold is to weigh - - -			
The fixpenny loaf wheaten is to weigh - -			
Ditto houfhold is to weigh - - -			
The twelvepenny loaf wheaten is to weigh - -			
Ditto houfhold is to weigh - - -			
The eighteenpenny loaf wheaten is to weigh +			
Ditto houfhold is to weigh - - -			

And in places where quartern, half peck, and peck loaves fhall be made, then as follows;

	lb.	oz.	dr.		s.	d.
The peck loaf wheaten is to weigh - -				and is to be fold for -		
Ditto houfhold is to weigh - - -				and is to be fold for -		

Half peck, and quartern loaves to weigh, and be fold, in due proportion to the peck loaf. Magiftrate to direct how the affize of rye, barley, or mixed bread, when order'd to be made, fhall be publifhed.

And the half peck and quarter of a peck loaves of wheaten and houfhold bread are to weigh, from time to time, in proportion to the weight a peck loaf of wheaten or houfhold bread ought to weigh, and are to be fold according to the price a peck loaf of wheaten or houfhold bread refpectively is to be fold; and whenever any bread fhall be ordered to be made by any fuch magiftrate or magiftrates, or juftices, within the limits of their jurifdiction, with the meal or flour of rye, barley, oats, peas, or beans, either alone, or mixed with the meal or flour of any other grain or grains, the affize of fuch bread fhall be made public in fuch manner as the faid magiftrate or magiftrates, or juftices, who fhall fet fuch affize, fhall, from time to time, direct.

Where bread of a certain denomination and value fhall be ordered, or allowed to be made, no bread of a different denomination is to be fold at the fame time, under penalty

XIII. And be it alfo enacted by the authority aforefaid, That in places where any fixpenny, twelvepenny, and eighteenpenny loaves fhall at any time be ordered or allowed to be made or fold, no peck, half-peck, or quarter of a peck loaves fhall be permitted or allowed at the fame time to be there made or fold; to the intent that one of thofe forts of loaves of bread may not be fold defignedly, or otherwife, for the other fort thereof, to the injury of unwary people; upon pain that every one who fhall offend in the premiffes, and fhall be thereof convicted in manner herein after prefcribed, fhall, for every fuch offence, forfeit a fum not exceeding forty fhillings, nor lefs than twenty fhillings, as
the

the magistrate or magistrates, justice or justices, before whom not exceeding 40s. nor less than 20s. for such offence. any such offender shall be convicted, shall from time to time think fit.

XIV. And be it further enacted by the authority aforesaid, That if, for the better carrying into execution this act, the justices of the peace of any county, riding, or division, shall, at any general or general quarter sessions of the peace to be held by them for any such county, riding, or division, think fit to ascertain or fix, that any hundred or hundreds, or other place or places, in any such county, riding, or division, ought to be estimated or considered, as of, or in, any one particular hundred, riding, or division, of any such county, riding, or division, in order that the assize of bread which shall be set for such particular hundred, place or places, may extend to or comprize such other hundred, place or places, then, and in any such case, it shall be lawful for them so to do; but by so doing thereof, no justice of the peace of any such county, riding, or division, shall be excluded or debarred from acting as a justice of the peace in any hundred, riding, or division of any such county in which any such particular towns, districts, or places shall lie, or the assize for them shall be set. The justices, at a general or quarter sessions, may fix the jurisdiction of any hundred or place within a certain district, so as the assize of bread set for the same may extend thereto.

XV. And be it likewise enacted by the authority aforesaid, That an entry shall, from time to time, be made by every clerk of the market, or other person or persons who, in pursuance of this act, shall be appointed to make such return and certificate as hereby is directed respectively, in some book or books to be provided and kept by them respectively for that purpose, of every return which shall be made, in pursuance of this act, by them respectively; and also of the rate at which the price, assize, and weight of bread shall, from time to time, be set or fixed within the jurisdiction of every such clerk of the market, or other persons who shall, in pursuance of this act, be appointed to make such return or certificate as aforesaid; which book or books any inhabitant of every such city, town corporate, borough, franchise, hundred, riding, division, liberty, lath, rape, or wapentake, shall, at all seasonable times in the day-time, have liberty to see and inspect, without any fee or reward being to be paid for the same. Entry to be made by every clerk of the market, &c. in proper books, of the returns made by him, and of the rate the assize and price of bread shall be set at from time to time, the said books to be open to the inspection of any inhabitant.

XVI. And be it also enacted by the authority aforesaid, That after an assize of bread shall, at any time after the said twenty ninth day of *September*, be set, no alteration shall be made therein in any subsequent week, either to rise the same higher, or to sink the same lower, unless and except when the price of wheat, or other grain, shall be returned as having rose three pence each bushel, more than the last return made, or having fallen three pence each bushel lower than the said last return; no provision being made by the said assize tables for altering any assize, when the variation in the price of wheat, or other grain, shall not in any week have amounted to, and have been returned three pence a bushel. No alteration is to be made in assize of bread, unless the price of wheat, or other grain, shall vary 3d. in the bushel from the last return.

XVII. And be it likewise enacted by the authority aforesaid, That

Any meal weigher, clerk of the market, &c. who shall neglect his duty, or make a false return;

and any peace officer, who shall disobey the warrant of any magistrate, or justice, or otherwise neglect his duty,

forfeit not exceeding 5l. nor less than 20s.

That if any meal weigher, clerk of any market, or other person or persons who shall be appointed to certify or return, as hereby is directed, the price of grain, meal, and flour, shall in any wise neglect, omit, or refuse to do, any matters or things by this act required or directed to be done by him or them respectively, or shall designedly or knowingly make any false certificate or return ; or if any constable headborough, or other peace officer, shall refuse or neglect to observe or obey any warrant in writing which shall be delivered to him under the hand and seal of any magistrate or justice of the peace, or to do any other act requisite to be done by him or them for the carrying this act, or any of the powers or authorities hereby given, into execution; then every person so offending in any of the premisses, on being convicted of any such offence, shall forfeit and pay for every such offence, any sum not exceeding five pounds, nor less than twenty shillings, as the magistrate or magistrates, justice or justices, before whom any such offender or offenders shall be convicted, shall think fit and order, every time he or they shall so offend and be convicted, as hereby is directed.

Any buyer, seller, or dealer, who shall refuse to disclose to the meal weighers in London, or clerks of the markets, &c. in other places, the true prices the several sorts of grain, meal, and flour, shall be bought or sold at in the publick market,

or shall give in a false or collusive price,

forfeit not exceeding 10l. nor less than 40s.

XVIII. And be it further enacted by the authority aforesaid, That in case any buyers or sellers of, or dealers in corn, grain, meal, or flour, at any time after the said twenty ninth day of *September*, on reasonable request to him, her, or them made by the meal weighers of the city of *London* in *London*, or by the respective clerks of the markets, or other persons, who, in pursuance of this act, shall be appointed to give in and certify, as hereby is directed, the prices of grain, meal, and flour, from the respective markets or places within their respective jurisdictions, shall refuse to disclose and make known to such meal weighers, clerks of the markets, or other persons, who shall be appointed to make such returns and certificates as hereby are directed respectively, and also shall request the same within their respective jurisdictions, the true real prices the several sorts of grain, meal, and flour, shall be *bona fide* bought at, or sold, by or for him, her, or them respectively, at any corn market or corn markets, or other place, where corn, grain, meal, or flour, is or shall be usually, openly, or publickly sold, within the jurisdiction of any such person or persons as aforesaid, who shall request any such account to be given to him or them; or shall knowingly give in to any such meal weigher, clerk of the market, or other person, who shall be appointed in pursuance of this act, to give in and certify the price of grain, meal, and flour, any false or untrue price or prices of any grain, meal, or flour, bought or sold, or agreed so to be, or any price which hath been made by any deceitful means; then, and in every such case, he, she, or they, so offending, on being convicted of any such offence by the oath of one or more credible witness or witnesses, or solemn affirmation of any credible witness or witnesses, being a *Quaker*, or on the confession of the party accused, shall forfeit any sum not exceeding ten pounds, nor less than forty shillings, as the magistrate or magistrates, justice or justices, before whom any such offen-

fen-

fender or offenders fhall be convicted, fhall think fit and order, every time he, fhe, or they, fhall fo offend, and be convicted of any fuch offence.

XIX. And be it further enacted by the authority aforefaid, That if any fuch court, magiftrate or magiftrates, juftice or juftices as aforefaid, who fhall have thought proper to have ordered any return to be made of the price of grain, meal, or flour, within their refpective jurifdictions, fhall, at any time within the fpace of three days after any fuch return fhall have been made, fufpect that the fame was not truly and *bona fide* made, then, and in any fuch cafe, it fhall be lawful for any fuch court, magiftrate or magiftrates, juftice or juftices, within their refpective jurifdictions, to fummon before them refpectively, any perfon or perfons who fhall have bought or fold, or fhall be fufpected to have bought or fold, or agreed to buy or fell, any grain, meal, or flour, within their refpective jurifdictions, or who fhall be thought to be likely to give any information concerning the premiffes, and to examine them refpectively upon their feveral oaths, touching the rates and prices the feveral forts of grain, meal, and flour, or any of them, were there really and *bona fide* bought at, or fold for, or agreed fo to be by him, her, or them refpectively, at any time or times within the fpace of feven days preceding the fummoning of him, her, or them refpectively: and if any perfon or perfons who fhall be fo fummoned as aforefaid, fhall neglect or refufe to appear on fuch fummons (and proof fhall be made on oath of fuch fummons having been duly ferved upon him, her, or them for that purpofe) or if any perfon or perfons fo fummoned fhall appear, and neglect or refufe to anfwer fuch lawful queftions touching the premiffes, as fhall be propofed to him, her, or them by any fuch court, magiftrate or magiftrates, juftice or juftices as aforefaid, within their refpective jurifdictions, without fome juft or reafonable excufe, to be allowed of by any fuch court, magiftrate or magiftrates, juftice or juftices as aforefaid, he, fhe, or they fo offending, on being convicted of any fuch offence, either by the oath of one or more credible witnefs or witneffes, or his, her, or their own confeffion, before any court, magiftrate or magiftrates, juftice or juftices, fhall, on every fuch conviction, forfeit and pay any fum not exceeding ten pounds, and not lefs than forty fhillings, as any fuch court, magiftrate or magiftrates, juftice or juftices, fhall think fit and order: and if any perfon, who fhall be fo examined on oath, fhall wilfully forfwear him or herfelf, every fuch perfon fhall be fubject and liable to be profecuted as for perjury, by indictment or information by due courfe of law; and, if convicted, fhall be liable to the penalties perfons convicted of wilful and corrupt perjury are fubject and liable to; provided that the party or parties fo fummoned be not obliged to travel above five miles from the place or places of his, her, or their above.

XX. And be it further enacted by the authority aforefaid, That whenever any court as aforefaid, magiftrate or magiftrates, or juftices of the peace, fhall order any bread to be made within

their

Marginal notes:

Where any falfe return fhall befufpected to be made, the court, magiftrate, or juftice, may, within 3 days, fummon any buyer, or feller, or other perfon, likely to give information.

and examine them upon oath, touching the prices of grain, meal, and flour, within 7 days before;

and any perfon who fhall not appear thereto, without juft caufe fhewn, or fhall refufe to give evidence,

forfeits not exceeding 10l. nor lefs than 40s. and forfwearing himfelf, incurs the penalties of perjury.

Party fummoned, not obliged to travel above 5 miles from the place of his abode.

When an order shall be made for making bread for sale of any other grain than wheat, or of mixed meal or flour,

their respective jurisdictions, of or with the flour or meal of any other grain or grains than wheat, or to be mixed with the flour of wheat, or to be made with the flour or meal of any other sort or sorts of grain or grains, either separate or mixed together, all persons who shall make any bread for sale, in any place where any such order or orders shall at any time be made, shall, from time to time, make bread with such mixed meal or flour, in every such place and places, in such manner as they shall be required and ordered by any such court, magistrate or magistrates, or justices as aforesaid, within their respective jurisdictions, and shall, from time to time, make the same of such weight and goodness, and shall sell the same at such prices, as any such court, magistrate or magistrates, or justices, within their respective jurisdictions, shall, from time to time, order or direct; upon pain that every person who shall at any time offend in the premisses, and shall be convicted of any such offence in the manner herein after prescribed by this act, shall forfeit any sum not exceeding five pounds, nor less than forty shillings, as the magistrate or magistrates before whom any such offender or offenders shall be convicted shall think fit and order, every time he, she, or they shall so offend and be convicted.

Bakers to conform to such order, and make the bread of such weight and goodness, and at such price, as shall therein be directed, on penalty of forfeiting not exceeding 5l. nor less than 40s.

The several sorts of bread made for sale, are to be always well made, and, in their degrees; according to the goodness of the sorts of meal or flour the same ought to be made of, without any adulteration or mixture, except the genuine meal or flour, salt, water, eggs, milk, yeast, and barm, or such leaven as shall be occasionally allowed; upon penalty of the offender forfeiting (not being the servant or journeyman) not exceeding 10l. nor less than 40s.

XXI. And be it further enacted by the authority aforesaid, That from and after the twenty fourth day of *June*, one thousand seven hundred and fifty eight, the several sorts of bread which shall be made for sale, or sold, or exposed to or for sale, in any place or places, shall always be well made, and in their several and respective degrees, according to the goodness of the several sorts of meal or flour whereof the same ought to be made; and that no allum, or preparation or mixture in which allum shall be an ingredient, or any other mixture or ingredient whatsoever (except only the genuine meal or flour which ought to be put therein, and common salt, pure water, eggs, milk, yeast, and barm, or such leaven as shall at any time be allowed to be put therein by the court, or person or persons who shall, by virtue of this act, have set an assize of bread, for the place or places where any such leaven shall be used, and where no such assize shall have been set, then such leaven as any magistrate or magistrates, justice or justices of the peace, within his or their jurisdiction, shall allow to be used in making of bread) shall be put into, or in any wise used in making dough, or any bread to be sold, or as or for leaven to ferment any dough, or on any other account, in the trade or mystery of making bread, under any colour or pretence whatsoever, upon pain that every person (other than a servant or journeyman) who shall knowingly offend in the premisses, and shall be convicted of any such offence, either by his, her, or their own confession, or by the oath of one or more credible witness or witnesses, before any such magistrate or magistrates, justice or justices of the peace, within the limits of his or their jurisdiction, shall, on every such conviction, forfeit and pay any sum of money not exceeding ten pounds, and not less than forty shillings; or shall, by warrant under the hand and seal, or hands and seals,

of

of any such magistrate or magistrates, justice or justices, within his or their respective jurisdiction, be apprehended and commited to the house of correction, or some prison of the county, city, town corporate, borough, riding, division, or place, where the offence shall have been committed, or the offender or offenders shall be apprehended, there to remain and be kept to hard labour for any time not exceeding one calendar month, nor less than ten days, from the time of such commitment, as any such magistrate or magistrates, justice or justices, shall think fit and order; and if any servant or journeyman baker shall knowingly offend in the premisses, and shall be convicted of any such offence, either by his, her, or their own confession, or by the oath of one or more credible witness or witnesses, before any such magistrate or magistrates, justice or justices of the peace, within the limits of his or their jurisdiction, he, she, or they who shall so offend, shall, on every such conviction, forfeit and pay any sum of money not exceeding five pounds, and not less than twenty shillings; or shall, by warrant under the hand and seal, or hands and seals, of any such magistrate or magistrates, justice or justices, within his or their respective jurisdiction, be apprehended and committed to the house of correction, or some prison of the county, city, town corporate, borough, riding, division, liberty, or place, where the offence shall have been committed, or the offender or offenders shall be apprehended, there to remain and be kept to hard labour for any time not exceeding one calendar month, nor less than ten days, from the time of every such commitment, as any such magistrate or magistrates, justice or justices, shall think fit and order; and it shall and may be lawful for the magistrate or magistrates, justice or justices, before whom any such offender shall be convicted, out of the money forfeited, when recovered, to cause the offender's name, place of abode, and offence, to be published in some news paper, which shall be printed or published in or near the county, city, or place, where any such offence shall have been committed.

XXII. And be it further enacted by the authority aforesaid, That from and after the said twenty ninth day of *September*, no person shall knowingly put into any corn, meal, or flour, which shall be ground, dressed, bolted or manufactured for sale, either at the time of grinding, dressing, bolting, or in any wise manufacturing the same, or at any other time or times, any ingredient, mixture, or thing whatsoever; or shall knowingly sell, offer, or expose to or for sale, any meal or flour of one sort of grain as or for the meal or flour of any other sort of grain, or any thing as or for, or mixed with, the meal or flour of any grain, which shall not be the real and genuine meal or flour of the grain the same shall import to be and ought to be, upon pain that every person who shall offend in the premisses, and shall be thereof convicted in manner herein after prescribed, shall forfeit and pay for every such offence, any sum not exceeding five pounds, nor less than forty shillings, as the magistrate or magistrates, justice

[Marginal notes:] or being committed, and kept to hard labour for any time not exceeding one month, nor less than 10 days;

and if the offender be a servant or journeyman, on penalty of his forfeiting not exceeding 5l. nor less than 20s.

or being committed, and kept to hard labour for any time not exceeding one month, nor less than 10 days;

and the magistrate may, out of the money of the forfeiture, publish in some news paper the offender's name, place of abode, and offence.

The penalty of adulterating corn, meal, or flour, whether at the time of grinding, dressing, or bolting, &c. or of selling the meal or flour of one sort of grain for another sort; or any thing mixed which shall not be of the genuine meal or flour of the grain the same is sold for;

is not to exceed 5l. nor be lefs than 40s.

stice or justices, before whom any such offender or offenders shall be convicted, shall think fit or order.

Where bread shall be of a different mixture of corn than what it imported to be of, or is allowed, or where the proportion of the mixture allowed of shall not be duly observed, or where any thing shall be sold as flour, which is not genuine, the offender is to forfeit not exceeding 5l. nor lefs than 20s.

XXIII. And be it further enacted by the authority aforesaid, That from and after the said ninth day of *September*, no perfon shall knowingly put into any bread which shall be made for sale, any mixture of meal or flour of any other sort of grain than of the grain the same shall import to be, and shall be allowed to be made of, in pursuance of this act; or shall put into any bread which shall be made for sale, any larger or other proportion of any other or different sort or sorts of grain, or the meal or flour thereof, than what shall be appointed or allowed to be put therein by this act; or any mixture or thing as for or in lieu of flour, which shall not really be the genuine flour the same shall import to be, and ought to be; upon pain that every perfon who shall offend in the premifies, and shall be convicted of any such offence in manner herein after prescribed, shall forfeit and pay any sum not exceeding five pounds, nor lefs than twenty shillings, as the magistrate or magistrates, justice or justices, before whom any such offender or offenders shall be convicted, shall think fit and order, every time he, she, or they, shall so offend, and be convicted.

Where bread shall be made under weight,

XXIV. And be it further enacted by the authority aforesaid, That if any perfon or perfons who shall make any bread for sale, or who send out, or fell, or expofe to or for sale, any bread, shall at any time from and after the said twenty ninth day of *September*, make, send out, fell, or expofe to or for sale, any bread which shall be deficient in weight, according to the affize which shall be set for any such bread, from time to time to be sold at, in pursuance of this act, he, she, or they, so offending in the premifies, and being thereof convicted in manner herein after prescribed of any such offence, shall forfeit and pay a sum not exceeding five shillings, nor lefs than one shilling, for every ounce of bread which shall at any time be wanting or deficient in the weight every such loaf ought to be of; and for every loaf of bread which shall be found wanting lefs than an ounce of the weight the same ought to be of, a sum not exceeding two shillings and six pence, nor lefs than six pence; as any such magistrate or magistrates, justice or justices, before whom any such bread which shall not be of the due weight the same ought to be, shall be brought, shall think fit or order, so as such bread which shall be complained of as wanting at any time in the weight the same ought to be of, in any city, town corporate, borough, liberty, or franchise, or the jurisdiction thereof, or within the weekly bills of mortality, shall from time to time be brought before some magistrate or magistrates, justice or justices, having jurisdiction in the premifies, and shall be weighed before such magistrate or magistrates, justice or justices, within twenty four hours after the same shall have been baked, fold, or expofed to or for sale; and so as such bread which shall be complained of as wanting at any time in the weight the same ought to be of, in any hundred, riding, division, liberty, rape, wapentake, or place, shall from

the offender forfeits not exceeding 5s nor lefs than 1s. for every oz. deficient, and if under an oz. not exceeding 2s. 6d. nor lefs than 6d.

provided such bread complained of, if in any city, town corporate, or borough, be weighed before the magistrate, within 24 hours after the same shall be baked, fold, or expofed to sale;

time

time to time be brought before some justice or justices of the peace of such hundred, riding, division, liberty, rape, or wapentake, or other place, and shall be weighed before such justice or justices within three days after the same shall have been baked, sold, or exposed to or for sale; unless it shall be made out to the satisfaction of any such magistrate or magistrates, justice or justices, by or on the behalf of the party or parties against whom any such complaint or information shall be made, that such deficiency in weight wholly arose from some unavoidable accident in baking, or otherwise, or was occasioned by or through some contrivance or confederacy. *and if in any hundred, riding, or division, &c. within 3 days of the baking, or sale thereof, unless such deficiency arose from some unavoidable accident, or by contrivance or confederacy.*

XXIV. And be it further enacted by the authority aforesaid, That from and after the said twenty ninth day of *September*, every person who shall make for sale, or sell, expose, or send out, to or for sale, any sort of bread whatsoever, shall, from time to time, cause to be fairly imprinted or marked on every loaf of each respective sort of bread which he, she, or they, shall make or sell, or carry out, or expose to or for sale, the roman letters herein after-mentioned; that is to say, Upon every loaf of bread which shall be made, sold, carried out, or exposed to or for sale, as wheaten bread, a large roman W; and upon every loaf of bread which shall be made, sold, carried out, or exposed to or for sale, as household or brown bread, a large roman H; and that every person who shall make for sale, or shall sell, carry out, or expose to or for sale, any loaf of any sort of bread, which shall be allowed to be made in pursuance of this act, which shall not be marked pursuant to the directions of this act, so as the same may, on the view thereof, be ascertained, from time to time, under what denomination or sort of bread every such loaf was made, and ought to be weighed (except as to such loaves which shall be rasped after the bespeaking or purchasing thereof, by the particular desire of any person who shall order the same to be so rasped, for his, her, or their own use or uses) shall, for every time he, she, or they, shall offend in the premisses, and be thereof convicted in manner herein after prescribed, forfeit and pay a sum not exceeding twenty shillings, nor less than five shillings, as any magistrate or magistrates, justice or justices, before whom the offender shall be convicted, shall direct, for every loaf of bread not marked as hereby is directed. *All bread made for sale, is to be fairly marked; the wheaten bread with a large roman W, and household with H, in order to ascertain under what denomination it was made, and ought to be weighed, under penalty not exceeding 20s. nor less than 5s.*

XXV. And be it further enacted by the authority aforesaid, That from and after the said twenty ninth day of *September*, no baker, or other person or persons, shall ask, demand, or take, for any bread which he, she, or they, shall sell, or expose to or for sale, any greater or higher price than such bread shall be ascertained to be sold for or at by the court, magistrate or magistrates, or justices, hereby authorized to set the price and assize of bread, within their respective jurisdictions; and that no baker, or other person who shall make any bread for sale, shall refuse or decline to sell any loaf or loaves of any of the sorts of bread which, in pursuance of this act, shall be allowed or ordered to be made, to any person or persons who shall tender ready money, *Bakers demanding or taking a higher price for bread than what the same shall be set at by the assize; or refusing to sell to any person any of the sorts allowed or ordered to be made;*

ney in payment for the same, at or for the price such bread, by the assize which shall have been set in respect thereof, shall be

fixed at, or ascertained to be sold for, when any such baker, or other person who shall make bread for sale, shall have any loaf of any such bread in his or their house, bakehouse, shop, or possession, to be sold, more than shall be requisite for the immediate necessary use of his, her, or their own family, or customers; and which it shall be incumbent on such baker, or other person who shall be complained of, for refusing or declining to sell any such bread, to prove before the magistrate or magistrates, justice or justices, to whom any such complaint shall be made, if thereunto required by the party or parties who shall

make any such complaint; upon pain that every person who shall be convicted of any such offence, in manner herein after prescribed, shall forfeit and pay a sum not exceeding forty shillings, nor less than ten shillings, as the magistrate or magistrates, justice or justices, before whom any such offender or offenders shall be convicted, shall think fit and order, every time he, she, or they, shall so offend and be convicted.

XXVI. Provided further, and it is hereby likewise enacted, That from and after the said twenty ninth day of *September*, no person shall sell, or offer to sale, any bread of an inferior quality to wheaten bread, at a higher price than household bread shall be set at by the assize; and if any person shall offend in the premisses, he shall forfeit and pay for every such offence, on being convicted thereof, either by his, her, or their confession, or by the oath of one or more credible witness or witnesses, before any magistrate or magistrates, justice or justices, within whose jurisdiction any such offence shall have been committed, the sum of twenty shillings.

XXVII. And, that the good design of this statute may be the more effectually accomplished, be it further enacted by the authority aforesaid, That from and after the said twenty ninth day of *September*, it shall be lawful for any magistrate or magistrates, justice or justices of the peace, within the limits of their respective jurisdictions, and also for any peace officer or officers, authorized by warrant under the hand and seal, or hands and seals, of any such magistrate or magistrates, justice or justices; and which warrant any such magistrate or magistrates, justice or justices, is and are hereby impowered to grant; at seasonable times in the day time, to enter into any house, shop, stall, bakehouse, warehouse, or outhouse, of or belonging to any baker, or seller of bread, to search for, view, weigh, and try, all or any the bread which shall be there found: and if any bread, on any such search, shall be found to be wanting either in the goodness of the

stuff whereof the same shall be made, or to be deficient in the due baking or working thereof, or shall be wanting in the due weight, or shall not be truly marked according to the directions of this act, or shall be of any other sort of bread than shall be allowed to be made by virtue of this act; any such magistrate or magistrates, justice or justices, peace officer or peace officers,

within

within the limits of their refpective jurifdictions, may feize the
fame; and any fuch magiftrate or magiftrates, juftice or juftices,
may difpofe thereof as he or they, in his or their difcretion,
fhall think fit.

XXVIII. And be it further enacted by the authority aforefaid,
That if, at any time after the faid twenty ninth of *September*,
information fhall be given, on oath, to any magiftrate or magiftrates, juftice or juftices of the peace, that there is reafonable
caufe to fufpect that any miller who grinds any grain for toll or
reward, or any perfon or perfons who doth or do drefs, bolt, or
in any wife manufacture any meal or flour for fale, or any maker of bread for fale, within the limits of the jurifdiction of any
fuch magiftrate or magiftrates, juftice or juftices, doth or do
mix up with, or put into, any meal or flour ground or manufactured for fale, any mixture, ingredient, or thing whatfoever,
not the genuine produce of the grain fuch meal or flour fhall
import and ought to be, or whereby the purity of any meal or
flour, in the poffeffion of any fuch miller, mealman, or baker,
is or fhall be in any wife adulterated; then, and in every fuch
cafe, it fhall be lawful for any fuch magiftrate or magiftrates,
juftice or juftices, and alfo for any peace officer or officers, authorized by warrant or warrants to him or them directed, under
the hand and feal, or hands and feals, of any magiftrate or magiftrates, juftice or juftices, within the limits of their refpective
jurifdictions: and which warrant or warrants every fuch magiftrate and magiftrates, juftice and juftices, is and are hereby impowered to grant; at all feafonable times in the day time, to
enter into any houfe, mill, fhop, bake-houfe, ftall, bolting-
houfe, paftry, warehoufe, or out-houfe, of or belonging to any
fuch miller, mealman, or baker, and to fearch and examine whether any mixture, ingredient, or thing, not the genuine produce
of the grain fuch meal or flour fhall import and ought to be,
fhall have been mixed up with, or put into, any meal or flour
in the poffeffion of any fuch miller, mealman, or baker, either
in the grinding of any grain at the mill, or in the dreffing, bolting, or manufacturing thereof, or whereby the purity of any
meal or flour is or fhall be in any wife adulterated; and if on any
fuch fearch it fhall appear that any offence hath been committed
in any mill, bolting-houfe or other place allowed to be fearched, contrary to the true intent of this act; then, and in every
fuch cafe, it fhall and may be lawful to and for any magiftrate
or magiftrates, juftice or juftices of the peace, officer or officers,
authorifed as aforefaid refpectively, within the limits of their
refpective jurifdiction, to feize and take any meal or flour which
fhall be deemed, on any fuch fearch, to have been adulterated,
and all mixtures and ingredients which fhall be found and deemed to have been ufed, or intended to be ufed, in or for any fuch
adulteration; and fuch thereof as fhall be feized by any peace
officer or officers authorifed as aforefaid, fhall, with all convenient fpeed, after feizure thereof, be carried to fome magiftrate
or magiftrates, juftice or juftices of the peace, within the limits

Side notes:

or of any dif-
ferent fort
than is allow-
ed of,
and difpofe
thereof at their
difcretion.
Where any
miller, meal-
man, or baker,
fhall be fuf-
pected of
adulterating
meal or flour,

the magiftrate
&c. upon in-
formation
made thereof
on oath, may
enter the pre-
miffes of fuch
fufpected per-
fon himfelf,
and make
fearch, or may
grant a fearch
warrant to
fome peace
officer;

and fuch meal
and flour as
fhall be deem-
ed to have
been adultera-
ted, may be
feized together
with the bafe
mixtures and
ingredients;
if feized by a
peace officer,
it is to be car-
ried before a
magiftrate;

of whose jurisdiction the same shall have been so seized: and if any magistrate or magistrates, justice or justices of the peace, who shall make any seizure in pursuance of this act, or to whom any thing seized under the authority of this act shall be brought, shall adjudge that any mixture or ingredients, not the genuine produce of the grain any such meal or flour which shall have been so seized, shall import and ought to be, shall have put into any such meal or flour, or that the purity of any such meal or flour so seized, was adulterated by any mixture or ingredient put therein; then, and in any such case, every such magistrate or, magistrates, justice or justices, is and are hereby required, within the limits of their respective jurisdiction, to dispose of the same as he or they, in his or their discretion, shall, from time to time, think proper.

if seized by the magistrate or adjudged by him to be adulterated.

he may dispose thereof as he thinks proper;

XXIX. And be it further enacted by the authority aforesaid, That every miller, mealman, baker, or seller of bread as aforesaid, in whose house, mill, shop, bake-house, stall, bolting-house, pastry, warehouse, out-house, or possession, any mixture or ingredient shall be found, which shall be adjudged by any magistrate or magistrates, justice or justices, to have been lodged there, with an intent to have adulterated the purity of meal, flour, or bread, shall, on being convicted of any such offence, either by his, her, or their own confession, or by the oath of one or more credible witness or witnesses, before any such magistrate or magistrates, justice or justices of the peace, within whose jurisdiction any such offence shall have been committed, forfeit and pay for every such offence, a sum not exceeding ten pounds, nor less than forty shillings, as the magistrate or magistrates, justice or justices, before whom any such offender or offenders shall be convicted, shall think fit and order; unless the party or parties charged with any such offence, shall make it appear to the satisfaction of the magistrate or magistrates, justice or justices, who shall find or seize any such mixture or ingredients, or before whom the same shall be brought, that such mixture or ingredients was or were not brought or lodged where the same was or were found or seized, with any design or intent to have been put into any meal or flour, or to have adulterated therewith the purity of any meal or flour, but that the same was in the place or places in which the same shall have been so found or seized as aforesaid, for some other lawful purpose: and it shall and may be lawful for the magistrate or magistrates, justice or justices, before whom any such offender shall be convicted, out of the money forfeited, when recovered, to cause the offender's name, place of abode, and offence, to be published in some news paper which shall be printed or published in or near the county, city, or place, where any such offence shall have been committed.

and the miller, mealman, or baker, in whose premisses such mixture or ingredients shall be found, and adjudged to be intended to be used in adulterating, is to forfeit upon conviction, not exceeding 10 l. nor less than 40 s.

unless it be made appear, that the same were not lodged there with such intention, but for some other lawful purpose;

and part of the forfeiture may be applied in publishing the offender's name, place of abode, and the offence.

XXX. And be it further enacted by the authority aforesaid, That if any person or persons shall wilfully obstruct or hinder any search as herein before is authorized to be made, or the seizure of any bread, or of any ingredients which shall be found

Persons obstructing or opposing any search or seizure as afore-

on

on any such search, and deemed to have been lodged with an intent to adulterate the purity or wholesomeness of meal, flour, or bread, or shall wilfully oppose or resist any such search being made, or the carrying away any such ingredients as aforesaid, or any bread which shall be seized, as not being made pursuant to this act, he, she, or they, so doing or offending in any of the cases aforesaid, shall, on being convicted thereof in manner herein after prescribed, forfeit and pay for every offence such sum, not exceeding five pounds, nor less than twenty shillings, as the magistrate or magistrates, justice or justices, before whom any such offender or offenders shall be convicted, shall think fit, and order. *[said, are to forfeit not exceeding 5 l. nor less than 20 s.]*

XXXI. Provided always, and be it further enacted by the authority aforesaid, That no person who shall follow, or be concerned in, the business of a miller, mealman, or baker, shall be capable of acting, or shall be allowed to act, as a magistrate, or justice of the peace, under this act, or in putting in execution any of the powers in or by this act granted; and if any miller, mealman, or baker, shall presume so to do, he or they so offending in the premisses, shall, for every such offence, forfeit and pay the sum of fifty pounds to any person or persons who will inform or sue for the same; to be recovered in any of his Majesty's courts of record at *Westminster*, by action of debt, bill, plaint, or information; wherein no essoin, wager of law, or more than one imparlance, shall be allowed; or by way of summary complaint before the court of session in that part of *Great Britain* called *Scotland*. *[Any miller, mealman, or baker, presuming to act as a magistrate or justice in the execution of this act, forfeits 50 l. to the informer. Method of recovery.]*

XXXII. Provided always, and be it also enacted by the authority aforesaid, That if any person who shall carry on or follow the trade of a baker, shall, at any time after the twenty ninth day of *September*, make complaint to any magistrate or magistrates, justice or justices of the peace, within their jurisdiction, and make appear to them, by the oath of any credible witness, that any offence, which any such person who shall so carry on or follow the said trade of a baker shall have been charged with, and shall have incurred and paid any penalty under this act, shall have been occasioned by or through the wilful neglect or default of any journeyman or other servant employed by or under any such person who shall so follow or carry on the said trade of a baker; then, and in any such case, any such magistrate or magistrates, justice or justices, may and are hereby required to issue out his or their warrant, under his or their respective hands and seals, for bringing any such journeyman or servant before any such magistrate or magistrates, justice or justices, or any magistrate or justice of the county, city, riding, division, or place, where the offender can be found; and, on any such journeyman or servant being thereupon apprehended, and brought before any such magistrate or magistrates, justice or justices, he or they, within their respective jurisdictions, is and are hereby authorized and required to examine into the matter of such complaint; and, on proof thereof being upon oath, to the satisfaction *[Where any baker shall, on complaint, make it appear, that the offence he was charged with, and paid the penalty of, was occasioned by the wilful default of his journeyman or servant, the magistrate shall issue his warrant for apprehending the party; and upon conviction of the]*

Z 3

offence, shall decree a reasonable recompence to be paid to the master;

tion of any such magistrate or magistrates, justice or justices of the peace, who shall hear such said complaint, then any such magistrate or magistrates, justice or justices, is and are hereby directed and authorized by any order under his or their respective hand or hands, to adjudge and order what reasonable sum of money shall be paid by any such journeyman or servant to his master or mistress, as or by way of recompence to him or her, for the money he or she shall have paid by reason of the wilful neglect or default of any such journeyman or servant: and if any

and on non-payment thereof, shall commit the offender;

such journeyman or servant shall neglect or refuse, on his conviction, to make immediate payment of the sum of money which any such magistrate or magistrates, justice or justices, shall order him to pay by reason of such his said wilful neglect or default; then any such magistrate or magistrates, justice or justices, within their respective jurisdictions, is and are hereby authorized and required, by warrant under his or their hands and seals, to

to be kept to hard labour for any time not exceeding one month, unless payment be sooner made.

cause every such journeyman or servant to be apprehended and committed to the house of correction, or some other prison of the county, riding, division, city, town corporate, borough, or place, in which any such journeyman or servant shall be apprehended or convicted, to be there kept to hard labour for any time not exceeding one calendar month from the time of such commitment, as to such magistrate or magistrates, justice or justices, shall seem reasonable, unless payment shall be made of the money ordered after such commitment, and before the expiration of the said term of one calendar month.

XXXIII. *And, for the better and more easy recovery of the several penalties and forfeitures to be incurred by disobedience to this act, and the powers herein contained, and disposing of the money which shall be forfeited by breach or non-observance of any part of this act;*

All offences against this act may be heard and determined in a summary way, by magistrates within their respective jurisdictions.

Offenders may be summoned;

be it further enacted by the authority aforesaid, That it shall and may be lawful to and for the mayor of the said city of *London* for the time being, or any alderman of the said city, within the said city or liberties thereof; and to and for any other of his Majesty's justices of the peace, or any one of them, within their respective counties, ridings, divisions, cities, towns corporate, boroughs, liberties, or jurisdictions, to hear and determine, in a summary way, all offences committed against the true intent and meaning of this act; and, for that purpose, to summon before them, or any of them, within their respective jurisdictions, any party or parties accused of being an offender or offenders

and not appearing thereto, or offering a reasonable excuse, may be apprehended.

against the true intent and meaning of this act: and in case the party accused shall not appear on such summons, or offer some reasonable excuse for his default; then, upon oath by any credible witness of any offence committed contrary to the true intent and meaning of this act, any such magistrate or magistrates, justice or justices, shall issue his or their warrant or warrants for apprehending the offender or offenders within the jurisdiction of any such magistrate or magistrates, justice or justices: and upon

Matter of the complaint to be enquired into upon

the appearance of the party or parties accused, or, in case he or they shall not appear, on notice being given to, or left for, him

2

of

or them, at his or their ufual place of abode, or if he or they cannot be apprehended on a warrant granted againft him or them as herein before is directed ; then, and in any fuch cafe, any fuch magiftrate or magiftrates, juftice or juftices, is and are hereby authorized and required to proceed to make inquiry touching the matters complained of, and to examine any witnefs or witneffes, who fhall be offered on either fide, on oath, as aforefaid, and which every fuch magiftrate or magiftrates, juftice or juftices, is and are hereby authorized, impowered, and required, to adminifter ; and, after hearing of the parties who fhall appear, and the witneffes who fhall be offered on either fide, fuch magiftrate or magiftrates, juftice or juftices, fhall convict, or acquit, the party or parties accufed : and if the penalty, or money forfeited, on any fuch conviction, fhall not be paid within the fpace of twenty four hours after any fuch conviction, every fuch magiftrate or magiftrates, juftice or juftices, fhall thereupon iffue a warrant or warrants under his hand and feal, or their hands and feals, refpectively, directed to any peace officer or officers within their refpective jurifdictions, impowering him or them to make diftrefs of the goods or chattels of the offender or offenders : and if any offender fhall convey away his goods out of the jurifdiction of any fuch magiftrate or magiftrates, juftice or juftices, before whom he was convicted, or fo much thereof that the penalty cannot be levied, then fome magiftrate or juftice within whofe jurifdiction the offender fhall have removed his goods, fhall back the warrant granted by any fuch magiftrate or juftice, magiftrates or juftices ; and thereupon the penalty forfeited, fhall be levied on the offender's goods and chattels, by diftrefs and fale thereof ; and if within five days from the diftrefs being taken, the money forfeited fhall not be paid, the goods feized fhall be appraifed and fold, rendering the overplus (if any) after deducting the penalty or forfeiture, and the cofts and charges of the profecution, diftrefs, and fale, to the owner ; which charges fhall be afcertained by the magiftrate or magiftrates, juftice or juftices, before whom any fuch offender or offenders fhall have been fo convicted, or by the magiftrate or juftice who backed the warrant, if either of them fhall continue alive ; and if not, by fome other magiftrate or juftice of the county, riding, divifion, city, or place, in which the offender fhall have been convicted ; and for want of fuch diftrefs, then every fuch magiftrate or juftice within whofe refpective jurifdiction any fuch offender or offenders fhall refide or be, fhall, on the application of any profecutor or profecutors, and proof made of the conviction and nonpayment of the penalty and charges, by warrant under his hand and feal, commit every fuch offender or offenders to the common gaol or houfe of correction of the city or county, riding, divifion, or place, where fuch offender or offenders fhall be found ; there to remain for the fpace of one calendar month from the time of fuch commitment, unlefs, after fuch commitment, payment fhall be made of the faid penalty or forfeiture, cofts and charges, before the expiration of the faid one

Marginal notes:

oath, and examination of witneffes ;

and the party to be convicted or acquitted thereupon. The penalty on nonpayment thereof within 24 hours,

is to be levied by diftrefs and fale ;

and if the goods and chattels of the party fhall be removed into another jurifdiction, the magiftrate thereof is to back the warrant of diftrefs, and the diftrefs, if not redeemed within five days, is to be appraifed and fold ; and all charges, after fettled by the magiftrate, to be deducted thereout ;

and for want of diftrefs the offender is to be committed for 1 month,

unlefs payment be fooner made,

calendar month; and all such penalties and forfeitures, when recovered, shall be paid to the informer.

Power to summon material evidences,

XXXIV. And be it further enacted by the authority aforesaid, That if it shall be made out by the oath of any credible person or persons to the satisfaction of any magistrate or magistrates, justice or justices, that any one within the jurisdiction of any such magistrate or magistrates, justice or justices, is likely to give or offer material evidence on behalf of the prosecutor of any offender or offenders against the true intent and meaning of this act, or on behalf of the person or persons accused, and will not voluntarily appear before such magistrate or magistrates, justice or justices, to be examined, and give his, her, or their evidence concerning the premisses, every such magistrate or magistrates, justice or justices, is and are hereby authorized and required to issue his or their summons to convene every such witness and witnesses before any such magistrate or magistrates, justice or justices, at such seasonable time as in such summons

and of compelling, by warrant, to appear, such as shall not appear upon summons.

shall be fixed; and if any person so summoned shall neglect or refuse to appear at the time by such summons appointed, and no just excuse shall be offered for such neglect or refusal, then (after proof by oath of such summons having been duly served upon the party or parties so summoned) every such magistrate and magistrates, justice and justices, is and are hereby authorized and required to issue his or their warrant under his hand and seal, or their hands and seals, to bring every such witness or witnesses before any such magistrate or magistrates, justice or

Witnesses to be examined on oath;

justices; and on the appearance of any such witness before any such magistrate or magistrates, justice or justices, every such magistrate or magistrates, justice or justices, is and are hereby authorized and impowered to examine upon oath every such witness: and if any such witness on his or her appearance, or on being brought before any such magistrate or magistrates, justice or justices, shall refuse to be examined on oath concerning the premisses, without offering any just excuse for such refusal, any

and on refusal, without just cause shewn,

such magistrate or magistrates, justice or justices, within the limits of his or their jurisdiction, may, by warrant under his hand and seal, or their hands and seals, commit any person or persons so refusing to be examined, to the public prison of the county, riding, division, city, liberty, or place, in which the person or persons so refusing to be examined shall be, there to

may be committed for 14 days, but not less than 3.

remain for any time not exceeding fourteen days, nor less than three days, as any such magistrate or magistrates, justice or justices, shall direct.

Conviction to be drawn up in the following form.

XXXV. And be it further enacted by the authority aforesaid, That the magistrate or magistrates, justice or justices, before whom any person shall be convicted, in manner prescribed by this act, shall cause such respective conviction to be drawn up in the form, or to the effect following (that is to say)

(*To wit*) BE it remembered, *That on this*   *day*
    of   *in the*   *year of the reign of*
     A. B. *is convicted before*   *Maje-*
jesty's justices of the peace for the said county of
    or for the   *riding or division of the said county of*
     or for the city, liberty, or town of
  (as the case shall happen to be) *for*   *and*
    do adjudge him, her (or them) *to pay and forfeit for*
the same, the sum of
       Given under   the day
      and year aforesaid.

XXXVI. And be it further enacted by the authority aforesaid, That no *Certiorari*, letters of advocation, or of suspension shall be granted to remove any conviction, or other proceedings had thereon in pursuance of this act. *[marginal: No conviction, or other proceedings, may be removed by Certiorari, &c.]*

XXXVII. Provided always, and it is hereby further enacted by the authority aforesaid, That if any person convicted of any offence punishable by this act, shall think him, her, or themselves, aggrieved by the judgement of the magistrate or magistrates, justice or justices, before whom he, she, or they, shall have been convicted, such person shall have liberty, from time to time, to appeal to the justices at the next general or quarter sessions of the peace, which shall be held for the county, riding, division, city, liberty, town, or place, where such judgement shall have been given, and that the execution of the said judgement, shall, in such case, be suspended; the person so convicted, entering into a recognizance at the time of such conviction, with two sufficient sureties in double the sum which such person shall have been adjudged to pay or forfeit, upon condition to prosecute such appeal with effect, and to be forthcoming to abide the judgement and determination of the justices at their said next general or general quarter sessions; which recognizance the magistrate or magistrates, justice or justices, before whom such conviction shall be had, is and are hereby impowered and required to take; and the justices in the said general or general quarter sessions are hereby authorized and required to hear and finally determine the matter of every such appeal, and to award such costs as to them shall appear just and reasonable to be paid by either party: and if, upon hearing the said appeal, the judgement of the magistrate or magistrates, justice or justices, before whom the appellant or appellants shall have been convicted, shall be affirmed, such appellant or appellants shall immediately pay down the sum he, she, or they, shall have been adjudged to forfeit, together with such costs, as the justices in their said general or general quarter sessions, shall award to be paid to the prosecutor or informer, for defraying the expences sustained by reason of any such appeal; and in default of the appellant's paying the same, any two such justices, or any one magistrate or justice of the peace, having jurisdiction in the place into which any such appellant or appellants shall escape, or where he, she,

[marginal: Persons aggrieved by the judgement of any magistrate or justice, may appeal to the next general or quarter sessions, and execution of judgement is to be thereupon suspended. Appellant is to enter into recognizance, and give security, to prosecute the appeal with effect, &c. and the justices in their said sessions are to hear and determine the matter thereof, and award costs thereupon. If the former judgement be affirmed, the appellant is to pay down the forfeiture and costs; and on default is to be committed.]

or

or they, shall reside, shall and may, by warrant under their hands and seals, or his hand and seal, commit every such appellant and appellants to the common gaol of the county, city, riding, division, or place, where he, she, or they, shall be apprehended, until he, she, or they, shall make payment of such penalty, and of the costs and charges which shall be adjudged on the conviction, to the informer; but if the appellant or appellants in any such appeal shall make good his, her, or their appeal, and be discharged of the said conviction, reasonable costs shall be awarded to the appellant or appellants against such informer or informers, who would (in case of such conviction) have been intitled to the penalty to have been recovered as aforesaid; and which costs shall and may be recovered by the appellant or appellants against any such informer or informers, in like manner as costs given at any general or general quarter sessions of the peace, are recoverable.

XXXVIII. Provided also, and be it further enacted by the authority aforesaid, That if any such conviction shall happen to be made within six days before any general or general quarter sessions of the peace which shall be held for the county, riding, division, city, town corporate, borough, or place, where such conviction shall have been made, then the party or parties who shall think him, her, or themselves aggrieved by any such conviction, shall and may, on entering into a recognizance in manner and for the purposes before directed, be at liberty to appeal either to the then next or the next following general or general quarter sessions of the peace, which shall be held for any such county, riding, division, city, town corporate, borough, liberty, or place, where any such conviction shall have been made.

XXXIX. And be it further enacted by the authority aforesaid, That every action or suit which shall be brought or commenced against any magistrate or magistrates, justice or justices, or any peace officer or officers, for any matter or thing done or committed by virtue of, or under this act, shall be commenced within six months next after the fact committed, and not afterwards; and shall be laid or brought in the county, city, or place, where the matter in dispute shall arise, and not elsewhere; and that the statute made in the twenty fourth year of his present Majesty's reign, intituled, *An act for rendering the justices of the peace more safe in the execution of their office; and for indemnifying constables, and others, acting in obedience to their warrants;* so far as the said act relates to the rendering the justices more safe in the execution of their office, shall extend and be construed to extend to the magistrate and magistrates, justice and justices of the peace, acting under the authority or in pursuance of this act; and that no action or suit shall be had or commenced against, nor shall any writ be sued out, or copy of any writ be served upon, any peace officer or officers, for any thing done in the execution of this act, until seven days after a notice in writing shall have been given to or left for him or them, at his or their usual place of abode, by the attorney for the party intending to
com-

commence such action; which notice in writing shall contain the name and place of abode of the person intending to bring such action, and also of his attorney, and likewise the cause of action or complaint: and any peace officer or officers shall be at liberty, and may, by virtue of this act, at any time within seven days after any such notice shall have been given to, or left for, him, tender, or cause to be tendered, any sum or sums of money, as amends for the injury complained of, to the party complaining, or to the attorney named in any such notice; and, if the same is not accepted of, the defendant or defendants in any such action or actions may plead such tender in bar of such action or actions, together with the general issue, or any other plea, with leave of the court in which the action shall be commenced; and if, upon issue joined on such tender, the jury shall find the amends tendered to have been sufficient, they shall find a verdict for the defendant or defendants: and in every such case, or if the plaintiff shall become nonsuit, or discontinue his action; or if judgement shall be given for the defendant or defendants upon demurrer; or if any action or suit shall be brought after the time limited by this act for bringing the same, or shall be brought in any other county or place than as aforesaid; then, and in any such case, the jury shall find for the defendant or defendants; and the defendant or defendants shall be intitled to his or their costs: but if the jury shall find, that no such tender was made, or that the amends tendered were not sufficient, or shall find against the defendant or defendants, on any plea or pleas by him or them pleaded; they shall then give a verdict for the plaintiff, and such damages as they shall think proper; and the plaintiff shall thereupon recover his costs against every such defendant and defendants.

Notice to contain the name and abode of the prosecutor and his attorney, and cause of action. Officer may thereupon make tender of amends; and plead the same, together with the general issue, &c. in bar of such action.

Defendant recovering to be allowed his costs. Plaintiff recovering, intitled to damages and costs.

XL. And be it further enacted by the authority aforesaid, That if any action or suit shall be commenced against any person or persons for any thing done in pursuance of this act, the defendant or defendants in any such action or suit may plead the general issue, and give this act, and the special matter, in evidence, at any trial to be had thereupon; and that the same was done in pursuance and by the authority of this act: and if it shall appear so to have been done, or if a verdict shall be recorded for the defendant or defendants; or if the plaintiff shall be nonsuited, or discontinue his action, after the defendant or defendants shall have appeared; or if judgement shall be given, upon a verdict or demurrer, against the plaintiff or plaintiffs; the defendant or defendants in every such action shall and may recover treble costs; and have the like remedy for the same as any defendant or defendants hath or have in other cases by law for recovery of his, her, or their costs.

Persons sued on this act, may plead the general issue; and obtaining a verdict, recover treble costs.

XLI. Provided always, That no person shall be convicted, in manner aforesaid, for any of the before-mentioned offences, unless the prosecution, in order to such conviction, be commenced within three days next after the offence committed.

Prosecution to be commenced within 3 days after the offence.

XLII. Pro-

XLII. Provided also, and be it enacted, That this act, or any thing herein contained, shall not extend to prejudice any right or custom of the city of *London*, or the practice there used, or any right or custom of any lord or lords of any leet, to set, inquire, and punish, the breach of assize of bread, within their respective leets or views of frank pledge, or the right of any clerk or clerks of the market in any place.

Reservation of
rights of the
dean and high
steward of
Westminster,
to set an assize
of bread, with-
in the city and
liberty of
Westminster;

XLIII. Provided further, and it is hereby likewise enacted, That neither this act, or any thing herein contained, shall extend, or be construed to extend, to prejudice the ancient right or custom of the dean of the collegiate church of *Saint Peter*, *Westminster*, or the high steward of the city of *Westminster*, and the liberties thereof, or his deputy, or any of them, to set, ascertain, and appoint, the assize and weight of all sorts of bread to be sold or exposed to sale within the said city of *Westminster*, and the liberties thereof; but they, and every of them, shall and may severally and respectively, from time to time, as there shall be occasion, set, ascertain, and appoint, within the said city of *Westminster*, and the liberties thereof, according to the true intent and meaning of this act, the assize and weight of all sorts of bread which shall be made, sold, or exposed to sale, by any person or persons within the limits of the said city of *Westminster*, and the liberties thereof; and shall and may inquire and punish the breach of every such assize and weight of bread, as fully and freely in all respects, as they, or any of them, have heretofore

been accustomed to do, and as if this act had never been made; any thing herein contained to the contrary thereof notwithstanding.

XLIV. Provided likewise, That neither this act, nor any thing herein contained, shall extend, or be construed to extend, to prejudice the ancient right or custom of the two universities of *Oxford* or *Cambridge*, or either of them, or of their or either of their clerks of the market, or the practice within the several jurisdictions of the said universities, or either of them, used, to set, ascertain, and appoint, the assize and weight of all sorts of bread to be sold or exposed to sale within their several jurisdictions; but that they, and every of them, shall and may severally and respectively, from time to time, as there shall be occasion, set, ascertain, and appoint, within their several and respective jurisdictions, the assize and weight of all sorts of bread to be sold or exposed to sale by any baker or other person whatsoever, within the limits of their several jurisdictions; and shall and may inquire and punish the breach thereof, as fully and freely in all respects as they used to do, and as if this act had never been made; any thing herein contained to the contrary thereof notwithstanding.

Reservation of
rights to the
universities of
Oxford and
Cambridge, to
set an assize of
bread within
their jurisdic-
tions;

CAP.

CAP. XXX.

An act for applying the money granted by parliament towards defraying the charge of pay and cloathing for the militia, for the year one thousand seven hundred and fifty eight; and for defraying the expences incurred on account of the militia, in the year one thousand seven hundred and fifty seven.

WHEREAS the sum of one hundred thousand pounds has been granted to his Majesty, upon account, towards defraying the charge of pay and cloathing for the militia, for the year one thousand seven hundred and fifty eight; and for defraying such expences as were actually incurred upon the account of the militia, in the year one thousand seven hundred and fifty seven; in order therefore that the said sum of one hundred thousand pounds may be regularly and properly applied; be it enacted by the King's most excellent majesty, by and with the advice and consent of the lords spiritual and temporal, and commons, in this present parliament assembled, and by the authority of the same, That within fourteen days after that his Majesty's lieutenant of any county, riding, or place, within that part of *Great Britain* called *England*, or, in his absence, three deputy lieutenants, shall have certified to the commissioners of his Majesty's treasury, or the high treasurer for the time being, that such proportion of the number of private militia men of any regiment or battalion of such county, riding, or place, has been chosen or inrolled, as is by law required to be chosen or inrolled, before any pay, arms, accoutrements, or cloathing for the militia, is allowed to be issued; and that the like proportion of the number of the commission officers of such regiment or battalion have been appointed, and have taken out their commissions and entered their qualifications; the said commissioners of his Majesty's treasury, or any three or more of them, or the said high treasurer, shall issue a warrant or order directed to the receiver or receivers general of the land tax for such county, riding, or place, to make the issues or payments following; that is to say,

Preamble.

Upon certificate of the lieutenant or deputy lieutenants of the county, to the treasury, of the actual inrollment of the proportion of men required to be inrolled, before pay, arms, or cloathing are to be issued, and that the officers also are appointed. Treasury is to issue an order to the receiver general of the county to make the payments according to the rates set down; viz. for cloathing;

The whole sum required for cloathing the militia for such county, riding, or place, at the rate of one pound one shilling for each private man or drummer; and at the rate of two pounds ten shillings for each serjeant.

And also for the pay of the said militia for four months in advance, at the rate of six shillings a day for each adjutant; and at the rate of one shilling a day for each serjeant, with the addition of two shillings and six pence a week for each serjeant major; and at the rate of six pence a day for each drummer, with the addition of three shillings and six pence a week for each drum major; and also at the rate of one shilling for each private man, with the addition of six pence to each corporal,

for pay of the militia for 4 months in advance;

for

for every day in which such private man or corporal shall be respectively employed in the militia.

And also half a year's salary for the clerk of each battalion of militia belonging to such county, riding, or place, at the rate of fifty pounds a year.

And also to pay the respective allowances to the clerk of the general meetings, and clerks of the several subdivision meetings, at the rates following ; that is to say,

To the clerk of the general meetings, at the rate of five pounds five shillings for each meeting.

And to the several clerks of the subdivision meetings, at the rate of one pound one shilling for each meeting.

All which said sums of money, except such as shall be due to the several clerks of the meetings aforesaid, shall be paid by the said receiver or receivers general into the hands of the clerk or clerks of the battalion or battalions of militia belonging to such county, riding, or place, upon his or their producing his or their warrant of appointment to such office, under the hand and seal of his Majesty's lieutenant for such county, riding, or place, according to the number of persons hereby intitled to receive pay, of which such battalion or battalions shall have been appointed to consist ; and also within fourteen days after the expiration of the third month from the time of the said first payment, to make a second payment for four months, in advance, for the pay of the militia, and clerks of battalions aforesaid, in the proportions before mentioned ; and the receipts of such clerk or clerks shall be a sufficient discharge to such receiver or receivers general, for the several sums of money so by him or them paid.

II. And be it enacted, That the clerk of each battalion of militia, shall forthwith, after the receipt of such sums of money as aforesaid, pay or cause to be paid, to the captain or commanding officer of each company belonging to such battalion, two months pay in advance for his respective company, and so from time to time so long as any money on that account, shall remain in his hands ; which pay the said captain or commanding officer is hereby required to distribute to each person belonging to his company, by this act intitled to receive the same, as it shall become due ; and shall give in to the clerk of the battalion to which such company shall belong, an account of the several payments he shall have made in pursuance of this act ; and shall pay back to the said clerk the surplus, if any, of the monies by him, from time to time, received, and then remaining in his hands.

III. And be it further enacted, That the said clerk may and shall retain to his own use out of the money so by him received, such sums as are herein before allowed for his salary, and shall also pay and discharge such sums of money as shall be due and owing for, or on account of the cloathing of the said militia, not

ex-

exceeding the rates herein before mentioned, to such person or persons as shall produce an order from his Majesty's lieutenant, or from the commanding officer of such battalion, for that purpose. *and to pay the bills for cloathing.*

IV. And be it enacted, That the said receiver or receivers general shall pay to the clerk of the general meetings his allowance at the rate of five pounds five shillings for each meeting, upon his producing an order or orders for that purpose from his Majesty's lieutenant, or three deputy lieutenants, assembled at some general meeting or meetings; and shall also pay to each and every the clerks of the subdivision meetings their several allowances, at the rate of one pound one shilling for each meeting, upon his or their producing an order or orders from one or more deputy lieutenant or deputy lieutenants, assembled in the several subdivision meetings; which said orders shall be to the said receiver or receivers general a sufficient discharge for the payment of such allowances, and be allowed in his or their account. *Allowance to be paid to the clerk of the general meetings, upon producing an order from the lieutenant, &c. to the clerks of the subdivision meetings, upon producing a like order from the deputy lieutenants. Orders to be a discharge to receivers general.*

V. Provided always, and be it enacted, That the clerk of each battalion of militia shall give security to the good liking of his Majesty's lieutenant of the county, riding, or place, to which such battalion shall belong, for duly answering and paying such sums as he shall from time to time have received, and for duly accounting for the same, and for performance of the trust hereby in him reposed; and shall, between the feast days of Saint *Michael* the Archangel and Saint *John* the Evangelist, in the year one thousand seven hundred and fifty eight, deliver to the receiver or receivers general of the land tax for the county, riding, or place, to which such battalion shall belong, a fair account in writing of all monies by him received and disbursed in pursuance of this act, with proper vouchers for the same; and shall pay back to the said receiver or receivers general any surplus that shall be then in his hands; which said accounts shall be signed by the said clerk, and transmitted by the said receiver or receivers general of the land tax into the office of the auditor of the receipt of his Majesty's exchequer. *Clerks of the militia to give security; and to deliver to the receivers general, between Michaelmas and 27 December, account of their receipts and disbursements, and pay back the surplus. Account to be transmitted into the auditor's office.*

VI. *And whereas in the course of the year one thousand seven hundred and fifty seven, several expences were incurred on account of the militia;* be it enacted, That his Majesty's lieutenant of any county, riding, or place, wherein any such expences have been incurred, shall be, and is hereby impowered and directed to satisfy such demands on that account, as to him shall appear reasonable; and to draw on the receiver or receivers general of the land tax for such county, riding, or place, for such sum of money, as shall have been paid, or shall be due on that account; which said draught shall be to the said receiver or receivers general a sufficient discharge for the payment of such sum of money, and be allowed in his or their account. *Lieutenants to pay the expences incurred the last year, on account of the militia; and to draw on the receivers general for the sums so paid, or due. Draughts to be a discharge for the same.*

VII. Provided also, and be it enacted, That no fee or gratuity whatsoever shall be given or paid for or upon account of any *No fee to be paid for issuing warrants or money.*

any warrant, or any sum of money which shall be issued in relation to, or in pursuance of, this act.

CAP. XXXI.

An act for granting to his Majesty certain sums of money out of the sinking fund, for the service of the year one thousand seven hundred and fifty eight; and for empowering the proper officers to make forth duplicates of exchequer bills, tickets, certificates, receipts, annuity orders, and other orders, in lieu of such as shall be lost, burnt, or otherwise destroyed; and for obliging the retailers of wines, commonly called Sweets, *or,* Made Wines, *to take out a wine licence.*

Most gracious Sovereign,

Preamble.

WE, your Majesty's most dutiful and loyal subjects, the commons of *Great Britain* in parliament assembled, being desirous to raise the residue of the necessary supplies which we have chearfully granted to your Majesty in this session of parliament, by ways and means the least burthensome to your Majesty's subjects, have resolved to give and grant to your Majesty the sums herein after mentioned; and do therefore most humbly beseech your Majesty, that it may be enacted; and be it enacted by the King's most excellent majesty, by and with the advice and consent of the lords spiritual and temporal, and commons, in this present parliament assembled, and by the authority of the same, That by or out of such monies as have arisen, or shall or may arise, and be and remain in the receipt of the exchequer, of the surplusses, excesses, overplus monies, and other revenues composing the fund, commonly called *The sinking fund,* (after paying or reserving sufficient to pay all such sums of money as have been directed by any former act or acts of parliament to be paid out of the same) there shall and may be issued and applied a sum not exceeding three hundred thousand pounds, for and towards the supply granted to his Majesty for the service of the year one thousand seven hundred and fifty eight; and the commissioners of his Majesty's treasury, or any three or more of them now being, or the high treasurer, or any three or more of the commissioners of the treasury for the time being, are hereby authorized and impowered to issue and apply the same accordingly.

300,000l. granted out of the surplusses of the sinking fund for the service of the year 1758, and to be issued by the treasury accordingly.

93,371l. 11s. 7d. 3q. surplus monies remaining in the exchequer of the said fund for the quarter ending 10 Oct.

II. And be it further enacted by the authority aforesaid, That the sum of ninety three thousand three hundred and seventy one pounds, eleven shillings, and seven pence three farthings, remaining in the receipt of the exchequer, disposeable by parliament for the public service, of the income of the surplusses, excesses, overplus monies, and other revenues, composing the said fund, commonly called *The sinking fund,* for the quarter ended the tenth day of *October,* one thousand seven hun-

hundred and fifty seven, shall and may be, in like manner, issued and applied at the said receipt, for and towards the said
supply.

III. And be it further enacted by the authority aforesaid,
That the sum of four hundred ninety two thousand and four
hundred pounds, eight shillings and three pence, remaining in
the receipt of the exchequer, disposeable by parliament for the
public service, of the income of the surplusses, excesses, overplus monies, and other revenues, composing the said fund, commonly called *The sinking fund*, for the quarter ended the fifth
day of *April*, one thousand seven hundred and fifty eight, shall and
may be in like manner issued and applied at the said receipt, for
and towards the said supply.

492,400l. 8s. 3d. like surplus remaining in the exchequer, for the quarter ending 5 April, 1758, to be issued towards the said supply.

IV. And be it further enacted by the authority aforesaid,
That by or out of such monies as shall thereafter, from time to
time, be and remain in the receipt of the exchequer, of the surplusses, excesses, overplus monies, and other revenues, composing the said fund, commonly called *The sinking fund*, after paying or
reserving sufficient to pay, all sums of money as have been directed by any former act or acts of parliament to be paid out of
the same, there shall and may in like manner be issued and applied, a further sum not exceeding one million six hundred and
six thousand and seventy six pounds, five shillings, and one penny farthing, for and towards the said supply.

1,606,076l. 5s. 1d. 1q. to be issued, in like manner, out of the growing produce of the sinking fund, towards the said supply.

V. *And whereas it may happen, that there may be a want of money for carrying on the current service of the year one thousand seven
hundred and fifty eight, before monies sufficient may have arisen into
the exchequer, from the said surplusses, excesses, or overplus monies,
commonly called* The sinking fund, *to satisfy and pay the said sum
of one million six hundred and six thousand and seventy six pounds,
five shillings, and one penny farthing, by this act granted;* in such
case it shall and may be lawful to and for the said commissioners
of his Majesty's treasury, or any three or more of them now
being, or the high treasurer, or any three or more of the commissioners of the treasury for the time being, by warrant or
warrants under his or their hands, to permit and suffer any person or persons, or body or bodies, politick or corporate, to advance and lend unto his Majesty, at the receipt of his exchequer, so much money, as, together with the monies then remaining in the said exchequer of the said surplusses, excesses, or
overplus monies, shall be wanting to compleat the said sum of
one million six hundred and six thousand and seventy six pounds,
five shillings, and one penny farthing, upon credit of the growing produce of the said surplusses, excesses, or overplus monies,
and to be repaid out of the same, as they shall quarterly afterwards arise, together with interest for the forbearance thereof in
the mean time; any thing herein before contained to the contrary notwithstanding.

In case of want, treasury may occasionally borrow money on the credit of the sinking fund,

and repay the same quarterly, with interest.

VI. *And whereas several bills commonly called* exchequer bills,
several tickets commonly called Lottery tickets, *several orders and certificates made forth in lieu of the said lottery tickets, and likewise*

for annuities of divers kinds, payable at or near the receipt of his Majesty's exchequer (as also several receipts of the cashiers of the governor and company of the bank of England, or some of them, for money contributed there for the purchase of annuities transferrable in the books of the said governor and company, have by casualty or mischance been lost, burnt, or otherwise destroyed, which exchequer bills, lottery tickets, certificates, receipts, annuity orders, and other orders, of the respective denominations aforesaid, were made forth by and in pursuance of several acts of parliament in that behalf; be it therefore enacted by the authority aforesaid, That in all cases where it shall appear by affidavit to be made, before any of the barons of the exchequer for the time being (who shall interrogate the deponent thereupon) to the satisfaction of such baron or barons, that any such exchequer bills, or any such tickets, certificates, receipts, annuity orders, or other orders, as aforesaid, before the first day of *August*, one thousand seven hundred and fifty eight, have been, or are lost, burnt, or otherwise destroyed, or that there be good reason to believe the same have been burnt, lost, or otherwise destroyed; it shall and may be lawful for the respective officers and persons appointed to issue or make forth such exchequer bills, tickets, certificates, receipts, annuity orders, or other orders, or to pay or discharge the same, or to issue any monies due or payable thereupon, upon producing a certificate from any of the said barons of such affidavit made before him (which affidavit the said barons, or any of them, is and are hereby authorized to take, and which certificate he or they are hereby required to make and grant without fee or reward) and on security given to the said respective officers and persons to their good liking, to indemnify them respectively against all other person whatsoever, for or concerning the monies specified in, or due upon, such respective bill or bills, ticket or tickets, certificate or certificates, receipt or receipts, order or orders, they the said persons respectively, shall, and are hereby required, to make forth duplicates of the said bills, tickets, certificates, receipts, and orders, at the request of the respective owners, and to pay and discharge the same, and all such interest as is or shall be due on any of them carrying interest, or to make forth stock or transferrable annuities in lieu of such receipts as he or they should have paid or discharged, or made forth on the said original bills, tickets, certificates, receipts, annuity orders, or other orders, if the same had been produced, and shall be allowed all such payments, sum or sums of money, in their respective accounts; and in all cases where the signing of the commissioners of his Majesty's treasury, or the lord high treasurer of *Great Britain* for the time being, is necessary for making the said duplicates, or any of them, effectual for the purposes aforesaid; it is hereby further enacted, That it shall and may be lawful to and for the said commissioners of his Majesty's treasury, or any three or more of them, or the lord high treasurer for the time being, to sign such duplicates accordingly.

VII. *And whereas by an act passed in the last session of parliament,*

[Marginal notes, left column]

Proper officers to make forth duplicates of exchequer bills, tickets, certificates, receipts, annuity orders, and other orders, in lieu of such as shall appear, upon affidavit before the barons of the exchequer, to have been lost, burnt, or destroyed; and to pay the monies due thereon; the persons intitled thereto, giving proper security of indemnification,

Commissioners of the treasury impowered to sign such duplicates.

ment, intituled, An act for granting to his Majesty several rates
and duties upon indentures, leases, bonds, and other deeds; and
upon news papers, advertisements, and almanacks; and upon
licences for retailing wine; and upon coals exported to foreign
parts; and for applying, from a certain time, the sums of money
arising from the surplus of the duties on licences for retailing spirituous liquors; and for raising the sum of three millions, by annuities, to be charged on the said rates, duties, and sums of money;
and for making perpetual an act made in the second year of the
reign of his present Majesty, intituled, *An act for the better regulation of attornies and solicitors;* and for enlarging the time for
filing affidavits of the execution of contracts of clerks to attornies and solicitors; and also the time for payment of the duties
omitted to be paid for the indentures and contracts of clerks
and apprentices; *it was among other things enacted, That from
and after the fifth day of* July, *one thousand seven hundred and
fifty seven, no person whatsoever, unless authorized and enabled by
taking out such licence as is therein prescribed, subject to the payment
of such duties as are therein respectively charged thereupon, should sell
or utter by retail (that is) by the pint, quart, pottle, or gallon, or by
any other greater or lesser retail measure, or in bottles, in any less
quantity than should be equal to the measure of the cask or vessel in
which the same should have been, or might lawfully be imported, any
kind of wine or wines, or any liquor called or reputed wine, upon
pain to forfeit for every such offence, the sum of one hundred pounds:
and whereas great frauds might easily be practised in case the retailers
of certain liquors made in this kingdom, commonly called* Sweets, *or*
Made Wines, *should not be equally with the retailers of other kinds
of wine, obliged to take out such licences as aforesaid, for retailing
wine;* be it therefore enacted by the authority aforesaid, That

Recital of clauses in act 30 Geo. 2.

from and after the fifth day of *July,* one thousand seven hundred and fifty eight, no person whatsoever, unless he be authorized and enabled by having taken out such licence as by the said
act is prescribed, subject to the payment of such duties as are
therein respectively charged upon such licences to sell wine by
retail, shall sell or utter by any retail measure, or in bottles, in
any quantity less than twenty five gallons, any kind of liquor made in *Great Britain,* by infusion, fermentation, or otherwise, from foreign fruit or sugar, or from *British* fruit or sugar,
or from fruit or sugar mixed with any other ingredients, commonly called *Sweets,* or *Made Wines;* or any kind of liquor
made in *Great Britain,* and known by the name of *Sweets,* or
Made Wines, of whatsoever materials, or in whatsoever manner, the same may be made, upon pain to forfeit for every such
offence, one hundred pounds; to be recovered and applied in
such manner, as the penalties for selling wine by retail, without
licence, are by the said act to be recovered and applied.

Retailers of wines called Sweets, or Made Wines, to take out a licence.

100l. penalty on retailing such wines without a li-cence.

CAP. XXXII.

An act for repealing the duty granted by an act made in the
sixth year of the reign of his late Majesty, on silver plate,
made, wrought, touched, assayed, or marked, in Great
Britain ; *and for granting a duty on licences, to be taken*
out by all persons dealing in gold or silver plate ; and for
discontinuing all drawbacks upon silver plate exported ;
and for more effectually preventing frauds and abuses in
the marking or stamping of gold or silver plate.

WHEREAS *by an act of parliament made in the sixth year*
of the reign of his late Majesty, intituled, An act for laying a duty upon wrought plate ; and for applying money arising
for the clear produce (by sale of the forfeited estates) towards
answering his Majesty's supply ; and for taking off the drawbacks
upon hops exported for *Ireland* ; and for payment of annuities
to be purchased after the rate of four pounds *per centum per an-*
num, at the *exchequer,* redeemable by parliament ; and for appropriating supplies granted in this session of parliament ; and
to prevent counterfeiting receipts and warrants of the officers
of the *South Sea* company ; and for explaining a late act concerning foreign salt, cellared and locked up, before the four and
twentieth day of *June,* one thousand seven hundred and nineteen ; and to give a further time for paying duties on certain
apprentices indentures ; and for relief of *Thomas Vernon* esquire,
in relation to a parcel of senna imported in the year one thousand seven hundred and sixteen ; *it was amongst other things en-*
acted, That there should be raised, levied, collected, answered, and
paid unto, and for the use of his Majesty, his heirs, and successors,
for ever (subject nevertheless to such redemption as in and by the said
act was afterwards provided in that behalf) for and upon all silver
plate which should be made or wrought in Great Britain, *or at any*
time or times from and after the first day of June, *one thousand*
seven hundred and twenty, should or ought to be touched, assayed, or
marked, in Great Britain, *as is before in the said act mentioned,*
a duty after the rate of six pence for every ounce troy, and propor-
tionally for any greater or lesser quantity, to be paid by the makers or
workers thereof respectively ; and divers provisions and directions are
contained in the said act for and in relation to the managing, securing,
ascertaining, collecting, recovering, levying, and paying, the said
duty for the uses and purposes therein mentioned: and whereas the
methods prescribed for ascertaining and collecting the said duty, and
for preventing frauds therein, have been found ineffectual to secure
the payment thereof, and the said duty hath, by reason of various
frauds and evasions, for some years past greatly decreased, and is now
insufficient to answer the purposes for which the same was granted ;
we, your Majesty's most dutiful and loyal subjects, the commons of *Great Britain* in parliament assembled, think it will be
for the advantage of the publick to repeal the said duty, and in
lieu

lieu thereof, to grant unto your Majesty the duty upon licences herein after mentioned: and therefore, do most humbly beseech your Majesty, that it may be enacted; and be it enacted by the King's most excellent majesty, by and with the advice and consent of the lords spiritual and temporal, and commons, in this present parliament assembled, and by the authority of the same, That from and after the first day of *June*, one thousand seven hundred and fifty eight, the said duty granted by the said act re- *Former duty on plate re-* made in the sixth year of his late Majesty's reign, of six pence *pealed;* *per* ounce troy, for and upon all silver plate made or wrought in *Great Britain*, or which ought to be touched, assayed, or marked, in *Great Britain*, shall cease, determine, and be no longer paid or payable; and, that then and from thenceforth all the *and all powers,* powers and authorities given and granted, and the rules and re- *&c. relating* gulations established and prescribed by the said recited act, or by *thereto;* any other act or acts of parliament, for or in relation to the managing, securing, ascertaining, collecting, recovering, levying, and paying, the said duty, and all penalties and forfeitures in respect thereof, shall also cease, determine, and be no longer *except with* put in execution, save only and except in all cases relating to the *respect to the* recovering any arrears which may at that time remain unpaid of *recovery of* the said duty, or to any penalty or forfeiture which shall have *arrears, and* been incurred upon or at any time before the said first day of *penalties in-* *June*, one thousand seven hundred and fifty eight; any thing *1 June, 1758.* herein before contained to the contrary notwithstanding.

II. And be it further enacted by the authority aforesaid, That *Duty on li-* in lieu of the said duty by this act repealed, there shall, from *cences granted* and after the fifth day of *July*, one thousand seven hundred and *in lieu thereof,* fifty eight, be paid unto his Majesty, his heirs and successors, a duty of forty shillings for every licence to be taken out in manner herein after mentioned, by each person trading in, selling, or vending gold or silver plate.

III. And be it further enacted by the authority aforesaid, That *Traders in,* from and after the fifth day of *July*, one thousand seven hundred *and venders* and fifty eight, no person or persons whatsoever, who now, or *of, plate, to* at any time or times hereafter, doth or shall trade in, vend, or *take out such* sell, any gold or silver plate, shall presume by him, her, or them- *licences;* selves, or by any other person or persons whatsoever, employed by him, her, or them, for his, her, or their benefit, either publickly or privately to trade in, vend, or sell, any gold or silver plate, without first taking out a licence for that purpose, in manner hereafter mentioned, before he, she, or they, shall trade in, vend, or sell, any such gold or silver plate, for which he, she, or they shall immediately, upon taking out thereof, pay down for such licence, the sum of forty shillings, in manner following; that is to say, If such licences be taken out in *London, Westmin-* *Licences with-* *ster*, or in any other parts within the limits or jurisdiction of the *in the limits* chief office of excise in *London*, then such licences shall be grant- *of the chief* ed under the hands and seals of two or more of his Majesty's *office of ex-* commissioners for the duty of excise for the time being; and the *cise in London,* duty for the same shall be paid at the chief office of excise in *to be granted* *by two of the* *commission-* A a 3 *Lon-* *ers, and the*

London, or at any other place, and to fuch perfon or perfons as the faid commiffioners for the time being fhall appoint to deliver out fuch licences, and to receive the faid duty; but if fuch licences fhall be taken out without the limits aforefaid, then fuch licences fhall be granted under the hands and feals of the feveral collectors and fupervifors of excife within their refpective collections and diftricts, and the duty for the fame fhall be paid by all and every the perfons fo taking out fuch licences at the office of excife next adjoining to the place where they refpectively refide or inhabit, or at any other place, and to fuch perfons as his Majefty's commiffioners of excife for the time being fhall appoint to deliver out fuch licences, and to receive the faid duty; and in cafe fuch licences be taken out within the limits of the city of Edinburgh, fuch licences fhall be granted under the hands and feals of two or more of his Majefty's commiffioners of excife in Scotland for the time being; and the duties for the fame fhall be paid at the chief office of excife in Edinburgh, in the fame manner as is herein before directed in regard to the licences to be taken out in London, Weftminfter, or in any other parts within the limits or jurifdiction of the chief office of excife in London; but if fuch licences fhall be taken out in any other part of Scotland, without the limits aforefaid, then fuch licences fhall be granted under the hands and feals of the feveral collectors and fupervifors of excife in Scotland, within their refpective collections and diftricts; and the duties for the fame fhall be paid in like manner as is herein before directed with regard to the licences to be taken out in England, without the limits or jurifdiction of the chief office of excife in London; and fuch refpective commiffioners of excife, and the perfons appointed by them refpectively, and alfo all fuch collectors and fupervifors, are hereby refpectively authorized and required to grant and deliver fuch licences to all perfons applying for the fame, upon their payment of forty fhillings for each licence.

IV. And be it further enacted by the authority aforefaid, That every perfon or perfons who fhall take out any fuch licence as aforefaid, is and are hereby required to take out a frefh licence ten days at leaft before the expiration of twelve calendar months after the taking out the firft licence, before he, fhe, or they do prefume to trade in, vend, or fell, any gold or filver plate, and in the fame manner to renew every fuch licence from year to year, paying down the like fum of forty fhillings for each and every new or renewed licence, at the places and at the times before mentioned; and if any perfon or perfons fhall, after the faid fifth day of July, one thoufand feven hundred and fifty eight, prefume, or offer to trade in, vend, or fell, any gold, or filver plate, without firft taking out fuch licence, and renewing the fame yearly, in manner aforefaid, he, fhe, or they fhall refpectively forfeit and lofe the fum of twenty pounds for each offence.

V. Provided always, and be it further enacted by the authority aforefaid, That from and after the faid firft day of June,
one

one thousand seven hundred and fifty eight, no duty shall be paid `not fit for use` for, or in respect of, any quantity of silver plate which hath `before 1 June` been, or shall be, entered upon the books of the excise officers, `1758.` and which shall not be finished and fit for use before the said first day of *June*; but that the persons in whose names such entries are or shall be made, shall be exonerated from all duty upon such plate, or so much thereof, as they shall produce to the officers of excise, after the said day, unfinished, and not fit for use.

VI. And be it further enacted by the authority aforesaid, That `Persons deem-` all persons using the trade of selling or vending gold or silver `ed traders in,` plate, or any goods or wares composed of gold or silver, or any `and venders` goods or wares in which any gold or silver is or shall be manu- `of plate, with-` factured; and also all persons employed to sell any gold or silver `in the act, and` plate, or any such goods or wares aforesaid, at any auction or `liable to take` publick sale, or by commission, shall respectively be deemed `out licences.` traders in, sellers or venders of gold or silver plate, within the intent and meaning of this act, and shall take out a licence for the same.

VII. Provided always, That persons in partnership, and car- `In copartner-` rying on their trade or business in one house, shop, or tenement `ships, where` only, shall not be obliged to take out more than one licence in `trade is carri-` any one year, for the carrying on such trade or business; and `ed on in one` that no licence for trading in, selling, or vending, gold or silver `house only,` plate, shall authorize and impower any person or persons to `one licence is` whom the same may be granted, and who shall sell such gold `sufficient.` or silver plate in shops, to trade in, sell, or vend, such gold or `Licence to` silver plate, in any other shop or place, except in such houses or `serve for the` places thereunto belonging, wherein he, she, or they, shall in- `house, &c. on-` habit and dwell, at the time of granting such licence, or in booths `ly for which` or stalls at fairs or markets. `it was grant-` `ed.`

VIII. And be it further enacted by the authority aforesaid, `Duties to be` That from and after the said fifth day of *July*, one thousand `paid over into` seven hundred and fifty eight, all the money arising by the said `the exche-` duty on licences (the necessary charges of raising and accounting `quer, separate` for the same excepted) shall, from time to time, be paid into `from all other` the receipt of his Majesty's exchequer at *Westminster*, separate `branches of` and apart from all other branches of the publick revenues; and `the publick` are hereby appropriated, and shall be applied to the same uses `revenues, and` and purposes, and in such manner, as the said duty hereby re- `to be applied` pealed is, by the said act made in the sixth year of his late Ma- `to the same` jesty's reign, appropriated unto and directed to be applied, sub- `uses as the` ject to such redemption as is mentioned in the said act with re- `duty on plate.` spect to the said duty; and if any surplus shall remain of the `Surplus mo-` produce of the said duty hereby granted, after such uses and `nies to be re-` purposes are answered and satisfied, or money sufficient shall be `served for the` reserved for that purpose, such surplus shall be reserved for the `future disposi-` future diposition of parliament. `tion of par-` `liament.`

IX. And be it further enacted by the authority aforesaid, `No drawback` That no drawback whatsoever shall be allowed or paid, upon, `to be allowed` for, or in respect of the exportation of any silver plate which `on exportati-` `shall on of plate.`

shall have been, or shall be, imported into, or made, wrought, or manufactured, in this kingdom, either before, on, or after the said first day of *June*, one thousand seven hundred and fifty eight, and which shall be entered for exportation after the said first day of *June*, one thousand seven hundred and fifty-eight; any former act or acts of parliament to the contrary notwithstanding.

Traders, &c. in gold or silver lace, silver wire, thread, or fringe, not obliged to take out licences.

X. Provided always, and be it further enacted by the authority aforesaid, That this act shall not extend to subject any person or persons to any penalty or forfeiture, for, or in respect of, his, her, or their trading in, selling, or vending, gold or silver lace, or gold or silver wire, thread, or fringe, without taking out such licence as aforesaid; nor to repeal or alter any drawbacks or allowances now payable upon the exportation of any such lace, wire, thread, or fringe; any thing herein before contained to the contrary notwithstanding.

Prosecutions for recovery of penalties,

XI. And be it further enacted by the authority aforesaid, That all prosecutions for the recovery of penalties and forfeitures, incurred for offences committed against this act, shall and may be heard, adjudged, and determined, either by bill, plaint, or information, in any of his Majesty's courts of record at *Westminster*, or in the court of *Exchequer* in *Scotland*, if such penalty or forfeiture shall be incurred there, or in such manner and form as hereafter is directed; that is to say, All prosecutions for recovery of penalties and forfeitures, incurred for offences committed against this act, within the limits or jurisdiction of the chief office of excise in *London*, shall and may be heard, adjudged, and determined, by any three or more of the commissioners of excise in *England* for the time being; and in case of appeal from the judgement of the said commissioners (and not otherwise) shall be heard, adjudged, and determined, by the commissioners for appeals for the time being, or the major part of them, whose judgement therein shall be final; and all prosecutions for recovery of penalties and forfeitures, incurred for offences committed within all or any other the counties, shires, stewartries, cities, towns, or places, within the kingdom of *Great Britain*, shall and may be heard, adjudged, and determined, by any two or more of the justices of the peace residing near to the place where such offence shall be committed; and if either the informers or defendants shall think themselves aggrieved by the judgement given by such justices, it shall and may be lawful for every such informer or defendant, to appeal to the justices of the peace at the next quarter session to be holden in and for the county, shire, stewartry, city, town, or place, where the penalty or forfeiture shall be incurred, who are hereby authorized and impowered to hear, adjudge, and determine the same, and whose judgement therein shall be final; and the said commissioners for excise, and commissioners for appeals (in case of appeal) and all justices of the peace aforesaid, respectively, are hereby authorized and required, upon complaint or information, upon oath, exhibited and brought before them respectively, as aforesaid,

if incurred within the limits of the chief office of excise of London, to be heard and determined by three of the commissioners, and in cases of appeals, by the commissioners for appeals. Prosecutions within other counties and places, to be heard and determined by two justices; and in cases of appeal, by the justices at their quarter session.

Commissioners and justices impowered to summon offenders;

said, of the commiffion of any offence againft this act (which oath the faid commiffioners, and juftices of the peace refpectively, are hereby authorized to adminifter) to fummon the party or parties accufed; and upon the appearance or contempt of any and upon their appearance, or contempt, perfon or perfons fo fummoned, to proceed to the examination of the matter of fact; and upon due proof made thereof, either to proceed to the examina- by the voluntary confeffion of the perfon or perfons fo fummoned, or by the oath of one or more credible witnefs or witneffes tion of the matter of fact, (which oath they the faid commiffioners and juftices refpectively have hereby power to adminifter) to give judgement or fentence and give judgment, thereupon, and to award and iffue out warrants under their hands refpectively, for the levying of fuch penalties or forfei- and award execution tures upon the goods and chattels of fuch perfon or perfons, thereupon; and to caufe fale to be made of fuch goods and chattels, if they fhall not be redeemed within fourteen days; rendering to fuch and for want perfon or perfons the overplus (if any be) and for want of fuf- of diftrefs, ficient diftrefs, to imprifon the party or parties offending, till to commit the satisfaction be made. party.

XII. And it is hereby further enacted, That all penalties and Application of forfeitures which fhall be recovered, for any offences committed the penalties againft this act (all neceffary charges for the recovery thereof and forfei- being firft deducted) fhall be diftributed, one moiety thereof for tures. the ufe of his Majefty, his heirs, and fucceffors, and the other moiety thereof to him, her, or them, who fhall inform or fue for the fame.

XIII. And be it further enacted by the authority aforefaid, Limitation of That if any action or fuit fhall be commenced againft any per- actions. fon or perfons, for any thing done in purfuance of this act, in that part of *Great Britain* called *England*, the defendant or defendants in any fuch action or fuit, may plead the general iffue, General iffue. and give the fpecial matter in evidence, at any trial to be had thereupon, and that the fame was done in purfuance and by the authority of this act; and if it fhall appear fo to have been done, the jury fhall find for the defendant or defendants; and if the plaintiff fhall be nonfuited, or difcontinue his action, after the defendant or defendants fhall have appeared; or if judgement fhall be given upon any verdict or demurrer againft the plaintiff, the defendant or defendants fhall and may recover treble Treble cofts. cofts, and have the like remedy for the fame, as any defendant or defendants hath or have in other cafes by law; and if fuch Defendants action or fuit fhall be commenced or profecuted in that part of plea in action *Great Britain* called *Scotland*, the court before whom fuch action brought in or fuit fhall be brought, fhall allow the defendant to plead this Scotland. act on his defence; and if the purfuer fhall not infift on his Defendant re- action; or if judgement fhall be given againft fuch purfuer, the covering, al- defender fhall and may recover the full and real expences he lowed his ex- may have been put to by any fuch action or fuit. pences.

XIV. *And whereas by a claufe in an act of parliament made in the* Recital of *twelfth year of his prefent Majefty's reign, intituled,* An act for the claufe in act better preventing frauds and abufes in gold and filver wares; 12 Geo. 2. *every perfon who fhould caft, forge, or counterfeit, any of the marks*

or

or stamps of the goldsmiths company in London, *or any of the marks or stamps appointed to be used for marking wrought plate at* York, Exeter, Bristol, Chester, Norwich, *or* Newcastle upon Tyne, *or any mark, stamp, or impression, to resemble any mark, stamp, or impression, to be made with any mark or stamp to be used by the said company in* London, *or by the wardens or assayers at any of the other places aforesaid, in pursuance of the said act, or any other acts of parliament then in force; or mark or stamp with any such counterfeit mark or stamp, any wrought plate of gold or silver, or any wares of brass, or other base metal, silvered or gilt over, and resembling plate of gold or silver; or transpose or remove from one piece of wrought plate to another, or to any vessel of such base metal, any of the marks, stamps, or impressions, made, or to be made, with any of the marks or stamps of the said company; or of the said wardens or assayers, used, or to be used, in pursuance of the said or any other act then in force; or cause to procure any of the said offences to be committed, or sell, exchange, or expose to sale, any manufacture of gold or silver, or export the same with any such forged, counterfeit, or transposed mark, stamp, or impression, knowing the same to be forged, counterfeited, or transposed, was made liable, for every offence, to the forfeiture of one hundred pounds; and for default of payment, to imprisonment, in manner therein mentioned: and whereas, notwithstanding the penalty or punishment inflicted by the said clause, great quantities of gold and silver plate of a base and inferior standard, with such forged, counterfeit, or transposed marks, stamps, and impressions, are now frequently vended in this kingdom, and also exported to foreign parts; and it is necessary that all persons guilty of such practices for the future, should be subjected to exemplary punishment, in order to deter, as far as may be, the commission of offences, manifestly tending to the detriment of the fair trader, and the diminution of the wealth, the credit, and the commerce of this kingdom;* be it therefore enacted by the authority aforesaid, That the said clause shall, from and after the fifth day of *July,* one thousand seven hundred and fifty eight, be, and is hereby repealed.

The recited clause repealed.

XV. And be it further enacted by the authority aforesaid, That if any person whatsoever, from and after the said fifth day of *July,* one thousand seven hundred and fifty eight, shall cast, forge, or counterfeit, or cause or procure to be cast, forged, or counterfeited, any mark or stamp used, or to be used, for making gold or silver plate in pursuance of the said act, or of any other act or acts of parliament now in force, by the company of goldsmiths in *London,* or by the wardens, or assayer or assayers, at *York, Exeter, Bristol, Chester, Norwich,* or *Newcastle upon Tyne,* or by any maker or worker of gold or silver plate, or any or either of them; or shall cast, forge, or counterfeit, or cause or procure to be cast, forged, or counterfeited, any mark, stamp, or impression, in imitation of, or to resemble any mark, stamp, or impression, made, or to be made, with any mark or stamp, used, or to be used, as aforesaid, by the said company of goldsmiths in *London,* or by the said wardens, or assayer or assayers, or by any maker or worker of gold or silver plate, or any or

Penalty of forging or counterfeiting the stamp used for marking plate, in pursuance of the recited act of 12 Geo. 2, &c. by the goldsmiths company, &c.

either

either of them; or shall mark or stamp, or cause or procure to be marked or stamped, any wrought plate of gold or silver, or any wares of brass, or other base metal, silvered or gilt over, and resembling plate of gold or silver, with any mark or stamp which hath been or shall be forged or counterfeited, at any time either before, on, or after, the said fifth day of *July*, in imitation of, or to resemble, any mark or stamp used, or to be used, as aforesaid, by the said company of goldsmiths in *London*, or by the said wardens, or assayer or assayers, or by any maker or worker of gold or silver plate, or any or either of them; or shall transpose or remove, or cause or procure to be transposed or removed, from one piece of wrought plate to another, or to any vessel of such base metal, as aforesaid, any mark, stamp, or impression, made, or to be made, by or with any mark or stamp used, or to be used, as aforesaid, by the said company of goldsmiths, in *London*, or by the said wardens, or assayer or assayers, or by any maker or worker of gold or silver plate, or any or either of them; or shall sell, exchange, or expose to sale, or export out of this kingdom, any wrought plate of gold or silver, or any vessel of such base metal, as aforesaid, with any such forged or counterfeit mark, stamp, or impression, thereon, or any mark, stamp, or impression, which hath been or shall be transposed or removed from any other piece of plate, at any time either before, on, or after, the said fifth day of *July*, knowing such mark, stamp, or impression, to be forged, counterfeited, or transposed, or removed, as aforesaid; or shall wilfully and knowingly have, or be possessed of, any mark or stamp which hath been or shall be forged or counterfeited, at any time, either before, on, or after, the said fifth day of *July*, in imitation of, or to resemble, any mark or stamp used, or to be used, as aforesaid, by the said company of goldsmiths in *London*, or by the said wardens, or assayer or assayers, or by any maker or worker of gold or silver plate, or any or either of them; every such person offending in any, each, or either of the cases aforesaid, being thereof lawfully convicted, shall be adjudged guilty of felony, and shall suffer death as a felon, without benefit of clergy.

[marginal notes: or of marking plate, &c. with a forged or counterfeited stamp; or of transposing the marks impressed from one vessel to another; or of selling or exporting plate with a forged, counterfeit or transposed mark; or of having any such stamp in possession; is felony, without benefit of clergy.]

CAP. XXXIII.

An act for enabling his Majesty to raise the sum of eight hundred thousand pounds, for the uses and purposes therein mentioned; and for further appropriating the supplies granted in this session of parliament.

Preamble. 800,000l. granted to his Majesty. His Majesty, by warrant under his royal sign manual, may, at any time before 5 Jan. 1759, authorize the commissioners of the treasury to raise the said sum, either by loans, or exchequer bills; in the same manner as is prescribed, concerning loans or exchequer bills, by the malt act of this session. All clauses, provisoes, and powers, &c. in the said act, relating to loans and exchequer bills, extended to this act. Exception. The money so raised, to be repaid out of the first supplies; and if none be granted before 5 July 1759, then to be paid out of the sinking fund; and the monies to be issued thereout accordingly. Monies issued out of the sinking fund, to be replaced out of the first supplies. Monies arising into the exchequer by the malt act, land tax, annuity and lottery act; and also the sum of 300,000l. granted out of the sinking fund, by an act of this session, and 93,371l. 11s. 7d. 3q, surplus remaining in the exchequer of the produce of the sinking fund,

for

for the quarter ended 10 October 1757; and 492,400l. 8s. 3d. surplus of the produce of the said fund, on 5 April, 1758; and 1,606,076l. 5s. 1d. 1q. directed to be issued out of the surplusses of the said fund; and 800,000l. by this act granted are appropriated in general; viz. out of all, or any the said supplies, any sum not exceeding 3,544,421l. 5s. 8d. for naval services herein expressed; 300,000l. towards paying off the debt of the navy; 10,000l. towards building the hospital for sick and wounded near Gosport. 10,000l. towards building the hospital for sick and wounded near Plymouth. 10,000l. upon account, towards the support of Greenwich hospital; 391,807l. 7s. 3d. for charge of the office of ordnance for land service; 4,032,772l. 3s. 9d. 1q. for land forces, &c. in general; viz. 1,253,368l. 18s. 6d. thereof, for charge of guards, garrisons, and land forces in Great Britain, Guernsey, and Jersey; 37,452l. 3s. 4d. for pay of the general, and general staff officers, &c. 623,704l. 0s. 2d. for the forces and garrisons in the plantations and Gibraltar; and provisions for the garrisons in Nova Scotia, Newfoundland, Gibraltar, and Providence; 43,968l. 4s. 2d. for the four regiments of foot on the Irish establishment serving in North America, and the East Indies; 35,602l. to the reduced officers of the land forces and marines; 3,098l. 17s. 11d. allowance to the officers and private gentlemen of the two troops of horse guards, and regiment of horse reduced, and superannuated gentlemen of the four troops of horse guards; 2,226l. for pay of widows pensions; 26,000l. upon account, for out-pensioners of Chelsea hospital; 145,454l. 15s. 1q. for extraordinary expences of the land forces, and other services incurred in 1757, not provided for; 38,360l. 19s. 10d. 3q. for troops of the landgrave of Hesse Cassel, in the pay of Great Britain, from 25 Dec. 1757, to 28 Feb. 1758; together with the subsidy for the said time, pursuant to treaty; 38,360l. 19s. 10d. 3q. for defraying the charge of the said troops, and payment of like subsidy, from 23 Feb. 1758, to 23 April following, 165,175l. 4s. 10d. 2q. for defraying the remaining charge of the said troops and subsidy, from 25 Dec. 1757, to 24 Dec. 1758, inclusive; 100,000l. upon account, towards subsisting and keeping together the armies formed last year in his Majesty's electoral dominions, employed in concert with the King of Prussia; 463,084l. 6s. 10d. for the troops of Hanover, Wolfenbuttle, Saxe Gotha, and count of Buckkeburgh, employed in concert with the King of Prussia; from 28 Nov. 1757, to 24 Dec. 1758, inclusive; to be issued in advance every two months; and the troops to be mustered by an English commissary, &c. 386,915l. 13s. 2d. in full for defraying all extraordinary charges and contingencies of his Majesty's army employed in concert with the King of Prussia, from 28 Nov. 1757, to 24 Dec. 1758, inclusive; the said sum to be issued as the pay of the said troops; 670,000l. to the King of Prussia pursuant to treaty. 800,000l. to discharge the like sum raised in pursuance of an act of the last session, and charged upon the first aids; 800,000l. upon account to his Majesty, to defray extraordinary expences of the war, &c. 9,902l. 5s. upon account, for supporting the colony of Nova Scotia; 6,626l. 9s. 9d. 2q. upon account, for defraying the charges incurred by supporting the said colony in 1756, not provided for; 3,557l. 10s. for defraying the charges of the civil establishment, &c. of the colony of Georgia, from 24 June, 1757, to 24 June 1758; 31,000l. to make good the like sum issued by his Majesty's orders, pursuant to an address of the house; 40,000l. to the Foundling hospital; to be paid without any fee or deduction; 284,802l. 1s. 3q. to make good the deficiency of the grants for the year 1757; 15,000l. towards rebuilding London bridge; 100,000l. upon account, for pay and cloathing for the militia for 1758, and expences incurred in 1757; 10,000l. towards fortifying the harbour of Milford; 27,380l. 19s. 11d. 2q. for reimbursing to the province of Massachuset's bay, the expences in furnishing provisions and stores to the troops raised there in 1756; 13,736l. 17s. 7d. for reimbursing to the colony of Connecticut, their expences in furnishing provisions and stores to the troops raised there in 1756; 20,000l. upon account, to the East India company, towards defraying the expence of a military force there; 4,000l. for repairing the church of St. Margaret, Westminster; 10,000l. for supporting the British forts on the coast of Africa. The said supplies to be applied as herein directed, and not otherwise. Regulations

to be obferved in the application of the half pay. Act 30 Geo. 2. Surplus of the half pay arifing from the laft year's grants, to be difpofed of
to fuch officers, widows, or children, as his Majefty fhall judge to be proper objects of charity.

CAP. XXXIV.

*An act for enlarging the times for the firft meetings of com-
miffioners or truftees, for putting in execution certain acts
of this feffion of parliament; and for other purpofes therein
mentioned.*

WHEREAS *by feveral acts of this prefent feffion of parliament,* Preamble.
*the firft meeting of the commiffioners or truftees for putting
fuch acts, or any part or parts thereof, in execution, hath been or may
be appointed or directed to be held before or upon the day of paffing of
fuch acts refpectively, whereby feveral doubts and difficulties may arife
with refpect to the due execution of the faid acts;* be it therefore
enacted by the King's moft excellent majefty, by and with the
advice and confent of the lords fpiritual and temporal, and
commons, in this prefent parliament affembled, and by the
authority of the fame, That in cafe any act of parliament hath Where the
paffed, or doth or fhall pafs, at any time whatfoever, during this firft meeting
prefent feffion of parliament, upon or after the day fpecified in of commiffion-
any fuch act, for the firft meeting of the commiffioners or truf- ers or truftees
tees appointed to put the fame, or any part thereof, in execution, fhall have been
in each and every fuch cafe, fuch commiffioners or truftees re- appointed, on
fpectively, or the fame number of fuch refpective commiffioners day the acts
or truftees, as is or fhall be authorized to hold fuch firft meeting, appointing the
or any greater number of them, fhall and may hold their firft fame fhall
meeting upon the fourteenth day after the paffing of this act, at have paffed,
fuch places as were refpectively appointed in fuch acts for holding is to be held
the firft meetings on the days therein fpecified; and all fuch on the 14th
commiffioners or truftees, or any number of them as aforefaid, day after the
being fo affembled refpectively on the faid fourteenth day after paffing of this
the paffing of this act, fhall and may proceed to the execution of act, &c.
fuch acts refpectively; and then, and from time to time afterwards, adjourn, and do and perform all fuch matters and things,
and execute all the powers and authorities granted to them in
the faid acts refpectively, in the fame manner, and as fully and
effectually to all intents and purpofes, as if fuch commiffioners
or truftees had been affembled in purfuance of, and on the refpective days fpecified or appointed in fuch acts, for holding the
firft meeting of faid commiffioners or truftees; any thing
therein contained to the contrary notwithftanding.

II. *And whereas feveral acts of parliament have been made for
amending and keeping in repair divers roads in Great Britain; and
whereas it may have happened that a fufficient number of the truftees
or commiffioners for putting fuch refpective acts in execution, have neglected to meet at fuch times and places, as were appointed or directed
in purfuance of the faid feveral acts, and that adjournments may not
have been made to meet at any future time: and whereas the clerks or*
                                                           other

other officers to the said trustees or commissioners, when proper adjournments have not been made, may have neglected, or omitted to give such proper notices, as the said respective acts have required to be made or given, of the next meeting of the said trustees or commissioners, notwithstanding which neglects or omissions, the said trustees or commissioners, have met and proceeded to put in execution the said several acts aforesaid: and whereas doubts have arisen, or may arise, with regard to the validity of the proceedings of the said trustees or commissioners, who have met and acted in the execution of the said several acts, notwithstanding such omissions or neglects had happened: for obviating whereof; be it further enacted by the authority aforesaid,

That where ever it has happened that any such trustees or commissioners as aforesaid, at any time before the passing of this act, have neglected to meet and adjourn, according to the direction of the said respective acts, or their clerks or officers shall have neglected to give such notice of any future meeting, as by the said respective acts is directed; such omission or neglect of the said trustees and commissioners, or of their clerks or other officers, shall not in any manner defeat, invalidate, or make void, any act, matter, or thing, already done by any of the said trustees or commissioners, in pursuance of the said acts of parliament, or any of them, but that every such act, matter, or thing, shall be good, valid, and effectual in the law, to all intents and purposes, and shall be so adjudged and taken, notwithstanding any such want of adjournment, or proper notice as aforesaid; any law or usage to the contrary thereof in any wise notwithstanding: and when it shall hereafter happen that a sufficient number of trustees or commissioners, do not meet to put the said several acts in execution, that then the clerk or other officer of the said trustees or commissioners, may and shall, at any time within the space of ten days after such omission or neglect of the said trustees to meet as aforesaid, appoint such trustees or commissioners, to meet at the house or place where the then last meeting was appointed to be held, on the day three weeks after the date of such notice; and in case such clerk or other officer, shall refuse or neglect to give such notice, for the space of ten days, that then it shall and may be lawful for any three or more of the said trustees or commissioners, appointed by the said respective acts, at any time within the space of ten days after such neglect or refusal of the clerk or other officer, to appoint such trustees or commissioners, to meet at the house or place where the then last meeting was appointed to be held, on the day three weeks after the date of such notice; which said respective notices in writing shall be affixed on such places as the said several acts respectively direct, and the same shall be deemed and taken to be sufficient notice; any law or usage to the contrary notwithstanding.

C A P.

CAP. XXXV.

An act to continue several laws therein mentioned, for grant-
ing a liberty to carry sugars of the growth, produce, or
manufacture, of any of his Majesty's sugar colonies in Ame-
rica, from the said colonies directly into foreign parts, in
ships built in Great Britain, and navigated according to
law; for the preventing the committing of frauds by
bankrupts; for giving further encouragement for the im-
portation of naval stores from the British colonies in
America and for preventing frauds and abuses in the ad-
measurement of coals in the city and liberty of Westminster;
and for preventing the stealing or destroying of madder
roots.

WHEREAS the laws herein after mentioned, which have *Preamble.*
by experience been found useful and beneficial, are near expiring; may it therefore please your most excellent Majesty, that it
may be enacted; and be it enacted by the King's most excellent
majesty, by and with the advice and consent of the lords spiritual
and temporal, and commons, in this present parliament assembled, and by the authority of the same, That an act made in the
twelfth year of the reign of his present Majesty, intituled, *An act*
for granting a liberty to carry sugars of the growth, produce, or ma- *Act 12 Geo. 2,*
nufacture of any of his Majesty's sugar colonies in America, from which was
the said colonies directly to foreign parts, in ships built in Great Bri- continued by
tain, and navigated according to law; which was to continue in quent acts,
force for five years, from the twenty ninth day of *September* one
thousand seven hundred and thirty nine, and from thence to
the end of the then next session of parliament; and which by several
acts made in the seventeenth and twenty fourth years of the
reign of his present Majesty, was further continued until the first
day of *September* one thousand seven hundred and fifty seven, and
from thence to the end of the then next session of parliament; *further conti-*
shall be, and the same is hereby further continued from the ex- *nued to 29*
piration thereof, until the twenty ninth day of *September* one *Sept. 1764.*
thousand seven hundred and sixty four, and from thence to the
end of the then next session of parliament.

II. And be it further enacted by the authority aforesaid, That *Act 5 Geo 2.*
an act made in the fifth year of the reign of his present Majesty, which was con-
intituled, *An act to prevent the committing of frauds by bankrupts;* tinued and a-
which was to continue in force for three years, from the twenty *mended by se-*
fourth day of *June* one thousand seven hundred and thirty two, quent acts,
and from thence to the end of the then next session of parliament; and which by several subsequent acts made in the ninth and
sixteenth years of the reign of his present Majesty, was further
continued until the twenty ninth day of *September* one thousand
seven hundred and fifty; and which by another act made in the
twenty fourth year of the reign of his present Majesty, was

amended and further continued to the first day of *September* one thousand seven hundred and fifty seven, and from thence to the end of the then next session of parliament; shall be, and the same is hereby further continued from the expiration thereof, until the twenty ninth day of *September* one thousand seven hundred and sixty four, and from thence to the end of the then next session of parliament.

further continued to 29 Sept. 1764.

III. And be it further enacted by the authority aforesaid, That so much of an act made in the eighth year of the reign of his late majesty King *George* the first, intituled, *An act for giving further encouragement of the importation of naval stores; and for other purposes therein mentioned;* as relates to the importation of wood and timber, and of the goods commonly called *lumber,* therein particularly enumerated, from any of his Majesty's *British* plantations or colonies in *America,* free from all customs and impositions whatsoever, which was to be in force for twenty one years, from the twenty fourth day of *June* one thousand seven hundred and twenty two; and which by several subsequent acts made in the sixteenth and twenty fourth years of the reign of his present Majesty, was further continued until the first day of *September* one thousand seven hundred and fifty seven, and from thence to the end of the then next session of parliament; shall be, and the same is hereby further continued from the expiration thereof, until the twenty ninth day of *September* one thousand seven hundred and sixty four, and from thence to the end of the then next session of parliament.

Part of the act of 8 Geo. 1. relating to the importation of wood, timber, and lumber, from America,

further continued to 29 Sept. 1764.

IV. And be it further enacted by the authority aforesaid, That an act made in the nineteenth year of the reign of his present Majesty, intituled, *An act more effectually to prevent the frauds and abuses committed in the admeasurement of coals within the city and liberty of* Westminster, *and several parishes near thereunto;* which was to continue in force from the twenty fourth day of *June* one thousand seven hundred and forty six, for the term of three years, and from thence to the end of the then next session of parliament; and which by two subsequent acts, one of the twenty third, and the other of the twenty fourth year of the reign of his present Majesty, was further continued until the first day of *September* one thousand seven hundred and fifty seven, and from thence to the end of the then next session of parliament; shall, and the same is hereby further continued from the expiration thereof, until the twenty fourth day of *June* one thousand seven hundred and fifty nine.

Act 19 Geo. 2. which was continued by several subsequent acts,

further continued to 24 June, 1759.

V. *And whereas the growth and cultivation of madder is of great consequence to the trade and manufactures of this kingdom: therefore, for preventing the stealing or destroying of madder roots;* be it enacted by the authority aforesaid, That if any person or persons shall steal and take away, or wilfully and maliciously pull up, or destroy, any madder roots growing or being in any lands or grounds belonging to any person or persons, and shall be thereof convicted before any justice or justices of the peace of the county, town, or place, where the offence shall be committed, either

Persons convicted of stealing or destroying madder roots,

either by confession of the party offending, or by the oath of any credible witness or witnesses (which oath such justice or justices is and are hereby authorized and impowered to administer) every person so offending, and being convicted of such offence in manner herein before mentioned, shall, for the first offence, give and pay to the owner or owners of the madder roots so stolen, pulled up, or destroyed, such satisfaction for his or their damage thereby sustained, and within such time, as the said justice or justices shall appoint; and shall over and above pay down upon such conviction unto the overseers of the poor of the parish where the offence or offences was or were committed, for the use of the said poor, such sum of money, not exceeding ten shillings, as to the said justice or justices shall seem meet; and if any such offender or offenders shall not make such recompence or satisfaction to the said owner or owners, and also pay such sum to the use of the poor, in manner and form aforesaid; then the said justice or justices shall and may commit such offender or offenders to the house of correction, for any space not exceeding one month; or shall and may order such offender or offenders to be whipped by the constable, or other officer, as to the said justice or justices shall seem meet; and if any such person or persons shall again commit the like offence, and be thereof convicted as aforesaid, then he, she, or they, so offending the second time, and being thereof convicted, as aforesaid, shall be committed to the house of correction for three months.

are, for the first offence, to make satisfaction for the damage;

and pay to the overseers of the poor of the parish a fine not exceeding 10s. or be committed to the house of correction for a month,

and on conviction of a like offence, the second time are to be committed for 3 months.

VI. Provided always, That no person or persons shall be prosecuted for any such offence of stealing, pulling up, or destroying of madder roots, unless such prosecution be begun within thirty days after the offence committed.

Prosecution to be within 30 days after the offence.

C A P. XXXVI.

An act for continuing certain laws therein mentioned relating to British sail cloth, and to the duties payable on foreign sail cloth; and to the allowance upon the exportation of British made gunpowder; and to the encouragement of the trade of the sugar colonies in America; and to the landing of rum or spirits of the British sugar plantations, before the duties of excise are paid thereon; and for regulating the payment of the duties on foreign exciseable liquors; and for the relief of Thomas Watson, with regard to the drawback on certain East India calicoes; and for rendering more commodious the new passage leading from Charing Cross.

WHEREAS *certain laws herein after mentioned, are found to be very useful and beneficial to the publick, and are near expiring, and it is fit they should be continued*; be it therefore enacted by the King's most excellent majesty, by and with the advice and consent of the lords spiritual and temporal, and commons, in this present parliament assembled, and by the authority

Preamble.

rity of the same, That an act made in the ninth year of the reign of his present Majesty, intituled, *An act for further encouraging and regulating the manufacture of* British *sail cloth; and for the more effectual securing the duties now payable on foreign sail cloth imported into this kingdom;* which was to continue in force from the twenty fourth day of *June,* one thousand seven hundred and thirty six, for the term of five years, and from thence to the end of the then next session of parliament; and which by several subsequent acts made in the thirteenth and twenty fourth years of the reign of his present Majesty, was further continued until the twenty fifth day of *December,* one thousand seven hundred and fifty seven, and from thence to the end of the then next session of parliament, shall be, and the same is hereby further continued from the expiration thereof, until the twenty ninth day of *September,* one thousand seven hundred and sixty four, and from thence to the end of the then next session of parliament.

II. And be it further enacted by the authority aforesaid, That an act made in the fourth year of the reign of his present Majesty, intituled, *An act for granting an allowance upon the exportation of* British *made gunpowder;* which was to continue in force for five years, from the twenty fourth day of *June,* one thousand seven hundred and thirty one, and from thence to the end of the then next session of parliament; and which by several subsequent acts made in the tenth, sixteenth, and twenty fourth years of the reign of his present Majesty, was further continued until the twenty fourth day of *June,* one thousand seven hundred and fifty seven, and from thence to the end of the then next session of parliament, shall be, and the same is hereby further continued from the expiration thereof until the twenty ninth day of *September,* one thousand seven hundred and sixty four, and from thence to the end of the then next session of parliament.

III. And be it further enacted by the authority aforesaid, That an act made in the sixth year of the reign of his present Majesty, intituled, *An act for the better securing and encouraging the trade of his Majesty's sugar colonies in* America; which was to continue in force for five years, to be computed from the twenty fourth day of *June,* one thousand seven hundred and thirty three, and to the end of the then next session of parliament; and which by several subsequent acts made in the eleventh, nineteenth, twenty sixth, and twenty ninth years of the reign of his present Majesty, was further continued until the twenty fourth day of *June,* one thousand seven hundred and fifty nine, shall be, and the same is hereby further continued from the expiration thereof, until the twenty ninth day of *September,* one thousand seven hundred and sixty one.

IV. And be it further enacted by the authority aforesaid, That so much of an act made in the fifteenth and sixteenth years of his present Majesty's reign, intituled, *An act to impower the importers or proprietors of rum, or spirits of the* British *sugar plantations,*

tations, to land the same before payment of the duties of excise charg- *landing of*
ed thereon, and to lodge the same in warehouses at their own expence; *rum, &c.*
and for the relief of Ralph Barrow, in respect to the duty on some *before duty*
rock salt lost by the overflowing of the rivers Weaver and Dane, as *paid, which*
relates to the landing of rum, or spirits of the *British* sugar *was continued*
plantations, before payment of the duties of excise, and to the *by several sub-*
lodging of the same in warehouses at the expence of the im- *sequent acts,*
porters or proprietors thereof; which was to continue in force
until the twenty ninth day of *September*, one thousand seven hundred and forty nine, and from thence to the end of the then
next session of parliament; and which, by an act made in the
twenty third year of the reign of his present Majesty, was further continued from the expiration thereof, until the twenty
ninth day of *September*, one thousand seven hundred and fifty
seven, and from thence to the end of the then next session of
parliament; shall be, and the same is hereby, further continued *further conti-*
from the expiration thereof, until the twenty ninth day of *Sep-* *nued to 29*
tember, one thousand seven hundred and sixty four, and from *Sep. 1764.*
thence to the end of the then next session of parliament.

V. *And whereas no certain time is appointed for the proprietor or
proprietors, importer or importers, of all or any kind of foreign liquors liable to the duties of excise on the importation thereof, to make
due entry thereof with the officer or collector appointed for the excise
in the port or place where the same shall be imported, and to pay the
duties for the same; and several persons have refused or neglected,
for a long time after the importation of such foreign excisable liquors,
to make due entry thereof, and have insisted to keep the same on board,
and even in some cases, when the ships have been put into the docks
to be repaired; by which means the payment of the duties due for the
same, have been unfairly postponed and kept back, and the revenue unnecessarily put to a very considerable expence by keeping tydesmen on
board; and great opportunities are also obtained for imbezzling or
running on shore all or part of the said foreign or exciseable liquors,
without payment of any duties for the same, notwithstanding the utmost care and vigilance of the officer to prevent the same:* for remedy whereof, be it enacted by the authority aforesaid, That from *Foreign li-*
and after the fifth day of *July*, one thousand seven hun- *quors liable to*
dred and fifty eight, the proprietor or proprietors, importer or *the duties of*
importers, of any kind of foreign liquors, liable to the duties *excise, are to*
of excise, within thirty days next after the master or purser for *be entered*
that voyage of the ship or vessel wherein the said foreign excise- *within 30 days*
able liquors, or any of them, shall be imported or brought in- *after the re-*
to the kingdom of *Great Britain*, shall have or ought to have *port is made of*
made a just and true entry or report upon oath, of the burthen, *the contents*
contents, and loading, of such ship or vessel, in pursuance of the *and loading of*
directions of the statute made in the thirteenth and fourteenth *the ship;*
years of the reign of King *Charles* the Second, intituled, *An act* *pursuant to the*
for preventing frauds, and regulating abuses in his Majesty's customs; *act of 13 & 14*
shall make due entry with the officer or collector appointed for *Car. 2.*
the excise, in the port or place where such foreign excisable liquors shall be imported, of all such foreign excisable liquors

on board of such ship or vessel belonging to such proprietor or
proprietors, importer or importers; and shall then, or before,
satisfy and pay the duties of excise due and payable for and in
respect of the said foreign exciseable liquors, and land the same,
on pain to forfeit for every neglect or refusal to make due entry
or payment, or to land the same, according to the directions of
this act, all such foreign exciseable liquors, with the casks and
package wherein the same shall be contained on board such ship
or vessel belonging to such proprietor or proprietors, importer or
importers, of the same, so neglecting or refusing, which shall
and may be seized by any officer or officers of the excise.

and the duties tobe paid then, or before, and the liquors landed, on forfeiture of the liquors, with the package.

VI. Provided always, and it is hereby declared and enacted
by the authority aforesaid, That so long as the said act of the fifteenth and sixteenth years of his Majesty's reign shall be continued and in force, nothing in the clause last before mentioned,
shall extend, or be construed to extend, in any wise to prevent
or hinder the proprietor or proprietors, importer or importers,
of any rum or spirits of the growth, produce, or manufacture,
of the *British* sugar plantations, as shall be imported into the
kingdom of *Great Britain* directly from the said sugar plantations, or any of them (an entry of such rum or spirits being first
made within the said thirty days, as directed by the said clause
last before mentioned) from forthwith landing such rum or spirits, and putting the same into such warehouse or warehouses,
and from giving such security for the due payment of the
duties of excise in pursuance of the directions of the said act of
the fifteenth and sixteenth years of his Majesty's reign, if he,
she, or they, shall chuse so to do, within the said term of thirty
days.

During the continuance of the recited act of 15 & 16 Geo. 2. the last mentioned clause is not to extend to rum or spirits of the British sugar plantations;

but the same maybe landed, and security given for the duties as the recited act directs.

VII. And it is hereby further enacted by the authority aforesaid, That in all entries or reports of any foreign liquors, liable to the duties of excise, to be made by the master or purser
of any ship or vessel, in pursuance of the said act of the thirteenth
and fourteenth years of the reign of King *Charles* the Second,
the number of casks or other package, with the particular numbers
and marks of each of them, and the particular kind of liquors
contained in each cask or other package, on board of each respective ship or vessel, shall be inserted in such entries or reports,
on pain for every neglect or refusal thereof, to forfeit such liquor,
with the cask or other package wherein the same shall be contained, which shall and may be seized by any officer of the excise; any law, custom, or usage, to the contrary thereof in any
wise notwithstanding: and that all seizures to be made in pursuance of any of the powers given by this act, shall (all necessa-
sary charges for the recovery thereof being first deducted) be employed, one moiety thereof to and for the use of his Majesty,
his heirs, and successors, and the other moiety to the seizer or
prosecutor.

In entries of foreign liquors, pursuant to act 13 & 14 Car. 2. the number of casks, or other package, with the numbers and marks thereon, and the contents, are to be inserted, on forfeiture of the liquor and package; One moiety to go to the King, the other to the seizer.

VIII. *And, in order to enable the gaugers or officers of the excise,
the better to ascertain the proof of all foreign imported liquors, liable to the duties of excise*; it is hereby further enacted by the authority

2

rity aforesaid, That it shall and may be lawful to and for the gaugers or officers of the excise, at any time or times, to take a sample or samples (not exceeding one quart in the whole) out of each of the casks or other package, containing such foreign spirituous liquors, paying for such sample or samples of liquors, after the rate of sixteen shillings *per* gallon.

Gauger may take a sample of the liquors, in order to ascertain the proof, paying for the same.

IX. *And whereas by a sudden fire which broke out in the work-shop of* Thomas Watson *of* Morris's Causeway *in the parish of* Lambeth *in the county of* Surry, *callicoe printer, on the eighth day of* September, *one thousand seven hundred and fifty five, two thousand two hundred and one pieces of printed* East India *callicoes, of the value of two thousand two hundred and forty nine pounds, fifteen shillings, and eleven pence, were burnt and destroyed: and whereas sundry duties were paid at the custom-house,* London, *upon the importation of the said callicoes; and the same were intended to have been exported to foreign parts, being by law prohibited to be worn in these kingdoms, and upon the exportation thereof, a drawback to the amount of seven hundred and thirty six pounds and four shillings, would have become payable to the exporter thereof:* for the relief therefore of the said *Thomas Watson*; be it enacted by the authority aforesaid, That the collector or other proper officer or officers of the customs at the port of *London*, shall, and he and they are hereby impowered and required, to make out and grant a proper debenture or debentures, for the said two thousand two hundred and one pieces of callicoes, whereby the said *Thomas Watson* may be intitled to draw back such part of the duties paid on the importation of the said callicoes, as would have been drawn back upon the exportation thereof, in the same manner as if the said callicoes had been exported to parts beyond the seas.

Debenture to be made out to Thomas Watson, for 2201 pieces of callicoes burnt, to intitle him to a drawback of the duties paid on the importation.

X. *And whereas the passage called* The New Passage *leading from* Charing Cross *into* Saint James's Park, *is very narrow, inconvenient, and dangerous, and it would be of publick convenience to widen and render the same commodious*; be it therefore enacted by the authority aforesaid, That the said passage shall from henceforth be deemed and taken to be one of the ways, streets, avenues, or passages, within the description of an act passed in the twenty ninth year of the reign of his present Majesty, intituled, *An act to enable the commissioners for building a bridge cross the river of* Thames, *from the city of* Westminster *to the opposite shore in the county of* Surry, *to purchase houses and grounds, and to widen the ways, and to make more safe and commodious the streets, avenues, and passages, leading from* Charing Cross, *to the two houses of parliament,* Westminster Hall, *and the courts of justice there, and* Westminster Bridge; *and to enable a less number of commissioners to execute the several acts relating to the said bridge, than at present are required by law; and for relief of* George *and* James King, *with regard to a lease taken by their late father from the said commissioners,* according to the true intent and meaning of the said act; and all and every the powers and authorities, clauses, rules, forms, directions, matters, and things, prescribed, mentioned, expressed, and contained in the said act, shall extend, and be

The New Passage from Charing Cross into S. James's Park, is to be deemed one of the ways intended to be widened, pursuant to the act of 29 Geo. 2.

B b 3 deemed

and the commiffioners are impowered to widen the fame accordingly ;

deemed and conftrued to extend, to impower the faid commiffioners, or any five or more of them, to widen and render fafe and commodious for carriages and paffengers on foot, the faid new paffage, as fully and effectually to all intents and purpofes whatfoever, and in fuch manner, and by fuch ways and means, as they the faid commiffioners, or any five or more of them, are authorized and impowered to open and widen any ways, ftreets, avenues, or paffages, leading from *Charing Crofs*, to the two houfes of parliament, *Weftminfter Hall*, and the courts of juftice there, and *Weftminfter Bridge*, by virtue of the faid recited act, or by any of the powers or authorities thereby to them given.

and to apply fuch of the furplus monies remaining in their hands after opening, &c. of the other ways and ftreets,

as fhall be fufficient to render the faid New Paffage fafe and commodious.

XI. And be it further enacted by the authority aforefaid, That when the faid commiffioners fhall have caufed to be opened and widened all fuch ways, ftreets, avenues, and paffages, from *Charing Crofs* aforefaid, to the two houfes of parliament, *Weftminfter Hall*, and the courts of juftice there, and *Weftminfter Bridge*, according to the directions of the faid recited act, if any monies granted by parliament, for the purpofes of the faid act, and the incidental expences thereof, fhall then remain in their hands, they the faid commiffioners, or any five or more of them, fhall and they are hereby authorized, directed, and required, to apply all fuch monies, or fo much thereof as fhall be fufficient for that purpofe, in opening, widening, and rendering fafe and commodious for carriages and paffengers on foot, the faid paffage now called *The New Paffage*, leading from *Charing Crofs* aforefaid, into Saint *James's Park*, and in defraying the incidental expences thereof, in fuch manner as they, or any five or more of them, fhall order, direct, and appoint, according to the true intent and meaning of this act.

CAP. XXXVII.

An act to permit the exportation of certain quantities of malt now lying in his Majefty's ftorehoufes ; and to allow the bounty upon fuch corn and malt as was fhipped and cleared for Ireland, *on or before a limited time ; and to authorize the tranfportation of flour, meal, bread, and bifcuit, to the iflands of* Guernfey *and* Jerfey, *for the ufe of the inhabitants there, in lieu of the wheat, malt, or barley, which may now, by law, be tranfported to thofe iflands.*

Preamble, reciting certain claufes and provifoes in act 30 Geo. 2.

WHEREAS *by an act of parliament made in the laft feffion of parliament, intituled,* An act to prohibit, for a time to be limited, the exportation of corn, malt, meal, flour, bread, bifcuit, and ftarch, *it was enacted, That no perfon or perfons whatfoever, at any time or times before the twenty fifth day of* December, *one thoufand feven hundred and fifty feven, fhould directly or indirectly export, tranfport, carry, or convey, or caufe or procure to be exported, tranfported, carried, or conveyed, out of or from* Great Britain *or* Ireland, *or load or lay on board, or caufe or procure to be laden or*
laid

laid on board, in any ship or other veffel or boat, in order to be exported or carried out of the faid kingdoms of Great Britain or Ireland, any fort of corn, meal, malt, flour, bread, bifcuit, or ftarch,
under the penalties therein mentioned; and wherein is contained a
provifo, That the faid act, or any thing therein contained, fhould not
extend to any of the faid commodities which fhould be exported, or
fhipped to be exported, out of or from Great Britain to Ireland, or
from Ireland to Great Britain, or from Great Britain or Ireland,
to Gibraltar, or unto any of his Majefty's iflands or colonies in A-
merica, that have ufually been fupplied with any of the faid commodities from Great Britain or Ireland, for the fuftentation of the inhabitants of the faid iflands, colonies, or dominions, or for the benefit
of the Britifh fifhery in thofe parts only, under fuch reftrictions, and
fubject to fuch forfeitures and penalties, as are therein mentioned;
and alfo another provifo, That the faid act, or any thing therein contained, fhould not extend to any wheat, malt, or barley, to be tranfported out of or from the port of Southampton only, unto the iflands
of Jerfey and Guernfey, or either of them, for the only ufe of the
inhabitants of thofe iflands, fo as the exporter complied with the requifites therein mentioned, and fo as the quantity of wheat, malt,
and barley, which at any time or times after the paffing of the faid
act, and before the twenty fifth day of December, one thoufand
feven hundred and fifty feven, fhould be fhipped at the faid port for
Jerfey and Guernfey, or either of them, as aforefaid, did not exceed in the whole, five thoufand quarters; and alfo another provifo,
That nothing in the faid act contained, fhould extend to any malt declared or made for exportation on or before the fourth day of December, one thoufand feven hundred and fifty fix, which fhould be exported, provided the requifites therein mentioned, were complied with
by the proprietor or proprietors thereof: and whereas the faid act
was by an act of parliament made in this prefent feffion of parliament,
further continued from the expiration thereof, until the twenty fourth
day of December, one thoufand feven hundred and fifty eight; and
in which faid laft-mentioned act is contained a provifo, That during
the continuance of fuch act, the bounty or bounties granted by any law
upon the exportation of any of the commodities therein before-mentioned, fhould not be allowed or paid to any perfon upon the exportation
thereof out of this kingdom, to any place whatfoever, or by whatfoever authority the fame may be exported: and whereas certain quantities of barley were making into malt and declared for exportation,
by or on the behalf of the merchants of Norwich and Yarmouth,
before, or about the time of, the paffing of the faid firft mentioned
act; and fuch malt was actually made before the end of January, one
thoufand feven hundred and fifty feven; and the fame malt is now
lying in his Majefty's ftorehoufes under the care of the proper officers
of excife: and whereas the faid malt is not fit for home confumption,
but was manufactured for the Holland market; and the faid merchants have not been able, by reafon of the act paffed in this feffion for
continuing the faid former act, to export the faid malt within the
time limited by an act for granting a duty upon malt; be it therefore
enacted by the King's moft excellent majefty, by and with the

B b 4

advice

advice and confent of the lords fpiritual and temporal, and commons, in this prefent parliament affembled, and by the authority of the fame, That it fhall be lawful for the merchants of
the city of *Norwich*, and borough of *Yarmouth*, in the county
of *Norfolk*, to export, and fhip to export, out of this kingdom,
on or before the twenty ninth day of *September*, one thoufand
feven hundred and fifty eight, to any of the ports in *Holland*,
two hundred lafts of malt, commonly called *Long Malt*, or any
part thereof, now lying in his Majefty's ftorehoufes, under the
care of the proper officers of excife, and which was entered and
declared for exportation, on or before the thirty firft day of *January*,
one thoufand feven hundred and fifty feven, in the fame manner, as if no act or acts had ever paffed to the contrary; fo as
the exporter, before the lading of fuch malt, or laying the fame
on board any fhip or veffel, do become bound with other fufficient fecurity, in the treble value thereof, to the commiffioners
or other chief officer or officers of his Majefty's cuftoms, belonging to the port or place where the fame fhall be fhipped or
put on board (who is hereby impowered to take fuch fecurity in
his Majefty's name, and to his Majefty's ufe, and for which fecurity no fee or reward fhall be given or taken) that fuch malt
fhall be landed in *Holland* (the danger of the feas and the enemy only excepted) and that fuch malt fhall not be landed or
fold in any other place whatfoever; any thing contained in any
former act or acts of parliament, to the contrary notwithftanding.

II. And be it further enacted by the authority aforefaid, That
each and every of the proprietors of the aforefaid two hundred
lafts of malt is and are hereby acquitted, freed, and difcharged,
of, and from all penalties whatfoever, by any former act of parliament laid or inflicted on him or them refpectively, or which
he or they refpectively may be fubject or liable to, for not removing or clearing the faid two hundred lafts of malt, or any
part thereof, out of the ftorehoufe or ftorehoufes, or other place
or places, within fifteen months after the fame was carried
therein refpectively; any thing contained in any former act or
acts of parliament to the contrary in any wife notwithftanding.

III. Provided always, That nothing herein contained fhall
intitle the proprietor or proprietors of the faid two hundred
lafts of malt, or of any part thereof, to any bounty or bounties
on fuch exportation; any thing herein contained to the contrary notwithftanding.

IV. *And whereas certain quantities of barley were making into
malt, and declared for exportation, by or on the behalf of feveral perfons inhabiting within the diftricts of* Lynn *and* Wells, *in the limits of the* Lynn *collection of excife in the county of* Norfolk, *on or
before the thirtieth day of* January, *one thoufand feven hundred and
fifty feven, and the faid malt is now lying in his Majefty's ftorehoufes,
and is not fit for home confumption;* be it therefore further enacted
by the authority aforefaid, That it fhall be lawful for the inhabitants of the faid diftricts of *Lynn* and *Wells*, to export, and
fhip

Side notes:

Merchants of Norwich and Yarmouth permitted to export to Holland, within a limited time, 200 lafts of Long Malt, lying in the King's ftore-houfes, which were enter'd for exportation on or before 31 Jan. 1757; they giving fecurity for the due landing, &c. thereof in Holland.

Proprietors difcharged from all penalties in refpect of not clearing the faid malt out of their ftore-houfes within the time limited by law.

Proprietors not intitled to any bounty on the exporta-tion.

Inhabitants of Lynn and Wells, per-

ship to export, out of this kingdom, on or before the said twenty ninth day of *September*, one thousand seven hundred and fifty eight, to any of the ports in *Holland*, three hundred and fifty lasts of malt, commonly called *Long Malt*, or any part thereof, now lying in his Majesty's storehouses, under the care of the proper officers of excise, and which was entered and declared for exportation, on or before the thirtieth day of *January*, one thousand seven hundred and fifty seven, in such and the same manner, and under the like regulations, as are herein before authorized and appointed with relation to the exportation of malt, by the merchants of *Norwich* and *Yarmouth*; and the inhabitants of the said districts, shall be, and are hereby also, in like manner, freed and discharged from all penalties incurred or to be incurred for not removing or clearing of the said three hundred and fifty lasts of malt, out of the storehouses or other place or places, within the time limited by any former law for that purpose; but nothing herein contained shall intitle any proprietor or proprietors of the said three hundred and fifty lasts of malt, to any bounty or bounties on such exportation; any thing contained in any former act or acts of parliament to the contrary notwithstanding.

mitted to export to Holland, under like regulations, 350 lasts of Long Malt, lying in the King's storehouses; which were enter'd for exportation on or before 30 Jan. 1757; and they are likewise discharged from all penalties in relation thereto.

V. *And whereas divers persons within this kingdom did actually ship, or cause to be shipped for exportation to* Ireland, *divers quantities of corn and malt, on or before the twenty fourth day of* December, *one thousand seven hundred and fifty seven, and the ships wherein the same were so shipped, were, on or before the said twenty fourth day of* December, *one thousand seven hundred and fifty seven, actually cleared;* be it therefore further enacted by the authority aforesaid, That the bounty or bounties granted on the exportation of corn and malt by each and every of the acts of parliament now in being, shall be allowed and paid to each and every of the exporter and exporters of corn or malt which was shipped and cleared for exportation to *Ireland*, on or before the twenty fourth day of *December*, one thousand seven hundred and fifty seven, in the same manner as if the said act made in this present session of parliament had never been made; any thing therein contained to the contrary notwithstanding.

Bounties granted by former acts, on exportation of corn and malt, to be allowed to exporters of such corn and malt as was shipped for Ireland, on or before 24 Dec. 1757.

VI. *And whereas it would be of great relief and advantage to the inhabitants of the islands of* Jersey *and* Guernsey, *if a sufficient quantity of meal, flour, bread, and biscuit, was allowed to be transported to the said islands, for the only use of the inhabitants there, instead of the like quantity of wheat, malt, or barley, now allowed by law to be transported to those islands;* be it therefore further enacted by the authority aforesaid, That it shall be lawful at any time or times before the twenty fourth day of *December*, one thousand seven hundred and fifty eight, to transport from the port of *Southampton* only, unto the said islands of *Jersey* and *Guernsey*, for the only use of the inhabitants there, any quantity or quantities of meal, flour, bread, or biscuit, in lieu of the like quantity or quantities of wheat, malt, or barley, now allowed by law to be transported to the said islands, so that the whole quantity

Liberty granted of exporting from the port of Southampton, within a limited time, and in limited quantities, meal, flour, bread, or biscuit, for the use of the

inhabitants of
Jersey and
Guernsey;

of wheat, malt, barley, meal, flour, bread, and biscuit, transported to the said islands before the said twenty fourth day of *December*, one thousand seven hundred and fifty eight, doth not exceed the quantity of wheat, malt, or barley, now limited by law to be transported to the said islands; and such transportation hereby authorized and allowed, shall be made under such

the same to
be transported
under certain
regulations.

and the like regulations, penalties, and forfeitures, as the transportation of wheat, malt, and barley, to the said islands is now subject; any thing in any former act or acts contained to the contrary notwithstanding.

70 lb. averdupoise wt.
deemed equal
to a bushel.

VII. And be it further enacted by the authority aforesaid, That in order to ascertain the amount of the said transportation, every seventy pounds averdupoise weight of bread or biscuit, shall be deemed respectively, for the purposes of this act, equal to one bushel of wheat, malt, or barley.

Account to be
laid before
parliament of
the quantities
so exported.

VIII. And be it further enacted by the authority aforesaid, That the commissioners of the customs for the time being, shall, and they are hereby required to give a full and true account in writing to both houses of parliament, at the beginning of the next session thereof, of all flour, meal, bread, and biscuit, that shall have been exported to each of the said islands of *Jersey* and *Guernsey*, by virtue or in pursuance of this act.

IX. And be it further enacted by the authority aforesaid, That if any action or suit shall be commenced against any person or persons for any thing done in pursuance of this act, the defendant or defendants in any such action or suit, may plead

General issue.

the general issue, and give this act, and the special matter, in evidence, at any trial to be had thereupon, and that the same was done in pursuance, and by the authority of this act; and if it shall appear so to have been done, the jury shall find for the defendant or defendants; and if the plaintiff shall be nonsuited, or discontinue his action, after the defendant or defendants shall have appeared; or if judgement shall be given upon any verdict or demurrer, against the plaintiff, the defendant or

Treble costs.

defendants shall and may recover treble costs, and have the like remedy for the same, as any defendant or defendants hath or have in other cases by law.

CAP. XXXVIII.

An act for applying a sum of money granted in this session of parliament towards carrying on the works for fortifying and securing the harbour of Milford in the county of Pembroke.

Preamble. 10,000 l. to be issued out of the monies granted for the service of the current year, towards carrying on the works for fortifying the harbour of Milford. Commissioners appointed for carrying the purposes of this act into execution. Commissioners may survey and set out the lands proper to be purchased for carrying on the said works; and determine, in a summary way, all claims and controversies, &c. relating thereto. Lands described within the boundaries of such survey, are vested in trustees, for the benefit of the parties interested, till the purchase-monies are paid; or certificates be made forth for the payment. Commissioners impowered to treat for the absolute purchase of such lands; conveyances thereof deemed valid. Where persons shall refuse to treat or agree, or shall be disabled from treating, &c. Warrant is to be issued to the sheriff for summoning
a jury

a jury to affefs the damage and recompence : fheriff to return and fummon a jury accordingly, and attend with his officers, to prove the fervice
of fuch fummons ; on penalty of forfeiting not exceeding 20 l. nor lefs
than 10 l. Juror neglecting his duty, without lawful excufe, liable to be
fined not exceeding 10 l. Fines to be eftreated into the exchequer. A fufficient jury not attending, the inqueft to be adjourned ; and a new warrant iffued for returning a fufficient number of jurors. Twelve to make a
jury ; and, upon their being fworn, commiffioners to fit till the inqueft be
taken, and judgement given thereon. Commiffioners may fummon and
examine witneffes upon oath, and caufe the evidences and writings of the
premiffes to be produced. 30 days notice to be given of the meetings of
commiffioners for determining claims ; and of the meetings of the juries.
Perfons fummoned, refufing to appear, or to produce the evidences of
their eftates ; liable to be fined not exceeding 5 l. Decrees of commiffioners relating to claims, agreements, conveyances, verdicts, and judgements
thereupon, to be final and conclufive. Where perfons interefted fhall ex-
prefs their defire to have their claims afcertained by a jury, the commiffioners are to caufe a jury to be impanelled and returned for that purpofe.
Verdict of the jury, and judgement of the commiffioners thereon, to be
final and conclufive. Entry to be made of all orders, judgements, decrees,
agreements, and verdicts ; fpecifying the houfes, number of acres, or parcels of land, their abuttals and boundaries, and parties interefted ; and
the fums to be paid for the fame. Duplicates thereof to be ingroffed on
parchment, and certified to the clerk of the crown, and remembrancer of
the exchequer. Certificates to be granted to the parties interefted ; furveyor general of the ordnance, to make out bills thereupon, with debentures for the fums certified, to be paid by the treafurer. Truftees thereupon, to ftand feifed of the premiffes. Certificates, on refufal to be accepted, may be depofited with the clerk of the peace. Where parties interefted fhall be incapable of taking and difpofing of the purchafe monies,
the commiffioners are to decree into whofe hands the fame fhall be paid
for their ufe ; and the money to be laid out in other purchafes, to be fettled to like trufts and ufes ; and till it fhall be fo employed, may be placed
out at intereft. Commiffioner not to act where he is interefted. Account
of the application of the monies for carrying on the works, to be laid every
year before parliament. Charges of this act to be firft paid. Limitation
of actions. General iffue. Treble cofts.

C A P. XXXIX.

An act for vefting certain meffuages, lands, tenements, and hereditaments, for the better fecuring his Majefty's docks, fhips, and ftores, at
Portfmouth, Chatham, and Plymouth, and for the better fortifying
the town of Portfmouth, and citadel of Plymouth, in truftees, for certain ufes ; and for other purpofes therein mentioned.

Preamble. Specification of land to be taken into the intended works and
fortifications at Plymouth, Portfmouth, and Chatham, and to veft in certain truftees, till the purchafe-money for the fame be afcertained and paid ;
Truftees names. 4 l. per cent. intereft allowed for 1 year, on the grofs
fum affeffed for the value of the premiffes. Purchafe money to be paid
out of the next aids granted in parliament. Commiffioners of claims to be
appointed by his Majefty ; who are to proceed in a fummary way in their
determinations, by examination of witneffes, and infpection of evidences,
or by a jury of inqueft ; with power to fend for perfons and papers ; and to
agree for, or determine the value of the premiffes, by any of thofe ways
and means ; their judgements and decrees to be entered in proper books,
fpecifying the particulars of the lands, the proprietors, and purchafe-
money ; and a duplicate thereof, ingroffed on parchment, to be certified
to the clerk of the crown in chancery, and to the remembrancer in the
exchequer ; the fame to be final and conclufive ; and copies thereof to be
laid before parliament, in order to the granting a compenfation to the
proprietors. Commiffioners may iffue warrants to the refpective fheriffs
for impanelling and fummoning juries ; fheriff to obey the faid warrants,
and fummon and return a jury accordingly ; and to attend on the return,
with

with his officers, to prove the service of such summons, if necessary. Sheriff neglecting his duty in any of the premisses, to be proceeded against
in a summary way, upon complaint to the court of chancery, &c. till he
shall have made satisfaction, and complied with such warrant. Juror neglecting his duty, without lawful excuse, may be fined in a sum not exceeding 20 l. Fines to be estreated into the exchequer. Inquest to be adjourned for want of a sufficient jury; and warrants to be issued for returning a proper number of jurors. Twelve to be a jury; and upon the jurors being sworn, commissioners to continue sitting, till the inquest be
taken, and judgement be given thereon. 30 days previous notice to be
given of commissioners meeting for the purposes aforesaid; and where the
persons refuse to appear, or produce the evidences of their claims, inquest,
&c. to be made upon the best information can be had, upon payment of
the sum awarded to the proprietors, the trustees are to stand seised of the
premisses, divested of all right and claim. No private buildings to be erected on the said lands; and the profits arising therefrom, to be applied in
reparation of the fortifications. Commissioners, upon complaint made to
them, are to enquire into, and make an estimate of, the damage done to
private grounds, by making the new works: and to report their opinions
as to what roads may properly be laid out for the conveniency of the adjacent lands. Lord of the manor of Stoke Damerell, allowed to dig lime
stones, and other stones, proper for building, or paving the streets of the
town, within a certain distance of the works, and to build lime kilns; and
to enjoy a foot-way and passage from the ferry to Dock Town, &c. and
also to enjoy a proper landing place on Mutton Cove, and ground to erect
keys and wharfs thereon, and a carriage-way to the same; with the several landing places, &c. now used over the creek and river. No ferry boat
to be made use of for passage over the creek, except in the King's service,
without licence of the lord of the manor. Commissioners exempted from
the penalties of the act of 25 Car. 2. 1 W. & M. 13 & 14 W. 3. and 2
Geo. 2. nor is their seat in parliament vacated thereby.

C A P. XL.

An act to ascertain the weight of trusses of straw, and to pu-
nish deceits in the sale of hay and straw in trusses in
London, *and within the weekly bills of mortality, and*
within the distance of thirty miles thereof, and pre-
vent common salesmen of hay and straw from buying the
same on their own account, to sell again; and also to restrain
salesmen, brokers, or factors in cattle, from buying on their
own account, to sell again, any live cattle in London, *or*
within the weekly bills of mortality, or which are driving
up thereto.

WHEREAS *great abuses are committed by persons selling straw*
in bundles or trusses in the city of London, *and within the*
limits of the weekly bills of mortality, and other places about London,
of less weight than the same ought to be, and are pretended to be, be-
tween buyer and seller; and also by putting into bundles or trusses of
straw and hay exposed for sale, straw and hay different in goodness or
quality from what the straw or hay, by the outside of such bundles or
trusses, appears to be, and also by putting other things into or amongst
such bundles or trusses of straw and hay, to make up or add thereto a
false weight: for remedy whereof, be it enacted by the King's
most excellent majesty, by and with the advice and consent of
the lords spiritual and temporal, and commons, in this present
parliament assembled, and by the authority of the same, That
from

from and after the twenty ninth of *September* one thousand seven hundred and fifty eight, all straw which shall be sold or delivered in, or brought to or exposed for sale in *London*, or any comprized within the limits of the weekly of mortality, shall be sold and delivered in bundles or trusses, each whereof shall be firmly bound or tied up; and that every such bundle or truss of straw shall be the full weight of thirty six pounds of good and sound straw, exclusive of any other thing which shall be put therein; and if any person or persons shall, after the said twenty ninth day of *September*, sell, or deliver, or bring into, or expose for sale, in *London*, or within the limits of the said weekly bills of mortality, or in any place within the distance of thirty miles from the extent of any part of the limits of the said weekly bills of mortality, where straw shall be sold in bundles or trusses, any bundle or truss of straw which shall be of less weight than thirty six pounds of good and sound straw, or which shall be in the inside of any such bundle or truss of different goodness of quality from what the same by the outside of any such bundle or truss, shall appear to be, he, she, or they, who shall so offend in the premisses, on being convicted thereof, in manner herein after mentioned, shall forfeit and pay every time any such straw shall be brought for sale, or sold or delivered in *London*, or within the limits of the weekly bills of mortality, not in bundles or trusses, the sum of twenty shillings; and the sum of one shilling for every bundle or truss of straw, which he, she, or they, shall sell, or bring into, or expose for sale in *London*, or within the limits of the said weekly bills of mortality, or in any place within the said distance of thirty miles from the extent of the limits of the said weekly bills of mortality, where straw shall be usually sold by the bundle or truss, which shall not be of the said full weight of thirty six pounds of good and sound straw, or which shall be proved to be, in the inside of any such bundle or truss, of different goodness or quality from what the same, by the outside of any such bundle or truss, shall appear to be.

Straw to be sold within the weekly bills, is to be made up into trusses firmly bound, and to weigh 36lb. of sound straw.

Where straw is usually sold in trusses, whether within the said weekly bills, or 30 miles distance, and shall be wanting of that weight, or shall be in the inside of a worse quality than the outside imports, the offender forfeits, for all straw not sold or delivered in trusses, 20s. and for every truss under weight, or of a mixt quality, 1s.

II. And be it further enacted by the authority aforesaid, That every truss of hay which, after the said twenty ninth day of *September*, shall be sold in, or brought into, or exposed for sale, in *London*, or any place comprized within the limits of the said weekly bills of mortality, or which shall be sold in any place within the said distance of thirty miles from the extent of the limits of the said weekly bills of mortality, where hay shall be sold in bundles or trusses, shall be made up with good and sound hay only, and such as the same shall appear to be by the outside of every such bundle or truss; and that such hay only as shall be good and sound shall be deemed and taken to be the hay which is to make up the weight every truss of hay by law ought to be.

Trusses of hay to be made up in like manner, of good and sound hay only, and of equal goodness throughout; and the sound hay to be allowed in weight only.

III. And be it further enacted by the authority aforesaid, That the pair of bands with which any truss of hay shall be bound, shall not exceed the weight of five pounds, upon pain that every person who shall sell any truss of hay with bands of a greater weight

Weight of the bands of a truss of hay not to exceed 5lb. on penalty of forfeiting 1s.

weight than five pounds, shall, for every such offence, forfeit and pay the sum of one shilling.

Persons employed to bind hay or straw, not conforming to the rules of this act, forfeit 3d. per truss, the owner objecting within 24 hours.

IV. And be it further enacted by the authority aforesaid, That if any person or persons employed to bind hay or straw, shall not bind up and make the same into bundles or trusses of such weight and quality as is directed by this act, every such person so offending shall forfeit and pay the sum of three pence for every bundle or truss of hay or straw, not being of such weight and quality; provided the same be objected to by the owner thereof within twenty four hours after the same shall be so bound or made up, and before the same shall be removed.

Salesman buying, after 29 September, hay or straw on his own account to sell again,

V. And be it further enacted by the authority aforesaid, That from and after the said twenty ninth day of September, no person who shall act as a common salesman in selling hay or straw for any other person, for gain or reward, or by commission, in London, or within the said limits of the said weekly bills of mortality, shall directly or indirectly buy any hay or straw on his own account, other than what he shall purchase to spend for his own use: and that if any such person who shall so act as a salesman of hay or straw shall, after the said twenty ninth day of September, buy any hay or straw on his own account to sell again; or shall sell in London, or within the said limits of the said weekly bills of mortality, any hay or straw which shall have been bought by him on his own account, he, she, or they, on being convicted thereof in manner herein after mentioned, shall, for every such offence, forfeit and pay the sum of one shilling for every truss of such hay or straw which shall be so sold by or for him.

or selling, after 29 September in London, or within the weekly bills, hay or straw bought by him on his own account, forfeits 1s. per truss.

VI. *And, in order to prevent any undue practices between the owners or salesmen of hay or straw, and the servants of the buyers thereof; and to the end it may be known at what price hay or straw sold within the limits aforesaid, shall be actually sold;* be it further enacted by the authority aforesaid, That from and after the said twenty ninth day of September, there shall be kept in the hay market in the city of London, and at every other hay market within the limits of the said weekly bills of mortality, where hay or straw is or shall be allowed to be sold, a book or register for entering and registering therein an account of all hay and straw which shall be sold in any such hay market respectively; and that such book or register shall be kept in London by the hay weigher, who shall be appointed by the mayor, commonalty, and citizens of the said city of London, to weigh the hay brought for sale into the said city, or his deputy or deputies; and out of the said city of London, within the limits of the said weekly bills of mortality, by the clerk or toll-gatherer of every hay market within the said limits, or his or their deputy or deputies; and that every person who shall sell any hay or straw in London, or within the limits of the said weekly bills of mortality, his servant or agent, shall, within six hours after any hay or straw shall, at any time, be sold in any publick hay market in London, or within the said limits of the weekly bills of mortality, and within seven days after every sale of hay or straw in London, or

A register to be kept in the hay markets within London, and the weekly bills;

in London, by the proper hay weigher,

and in other places by the clerk or toll gatherer.

Vender, within a limited time, to make an entry therein of the hay or straw sold by him,

within

within the said limits of the weekly bills of mortality, shall be made, out of any such hay market in *London*, or in any place within the limits of the said weekly bills of mortality, make an entry in the book or register of the hay market, in which any such hay or straw shall be sold; or where the same shall not be sold in any such hay market, then in the book or register of the hay market which shall be most contiguous to the place in *London*, or within the limits of the said weekly bills of mortality, in which any such hay or straw shall be sold; distinguishing therein the names and places of abode of the owners and sellers of any such hay or straw, and the names and places of abode of the respective buyer or buyers thereof, and also of the person or persons for whom or for whose use any such hay or straw shall be so bought, and also the day in which such hay or straw shall be so bought, and the true price at which the same shall be really sold; and every person who shall sell any such hay or straw, his servant or agent, shall sign his name, or set his mark, to every such entry which he shall so make or cause to be made, and shall pay for the same to the hay weigher, clerk, or toll-gatherer, of the market, who shall keep such book or register as aforesaid, the sum of one penny; and every such hay weigher, clerk, or toll-gatherer, of the market, or his deputy or deputies, shall, at all seasonable times in the day time, and during the market hours herein after mentioned, permit any person to have recourse to, and inspect any such book or register which shall be so kept for any such hay market, the person so desiring to inspect the same, paying for every such inspection the sum of one half-penny; and if the seller of any such hay or straw in *London*, or within the limits of the said weekly bills of mortality, his servant or agent, shall not make such entry as aforesaid in such book or register, within the said space of six hours after any sale shall be made of any such hay or straw in any publick hay market in *London*, or within the said limits of the weekly bills of mortality, and within the said space of seven days after every sale of any hay or straw in *London*, or within the said limits of the weekly bills of mortality, out of any such hay market, or shall not sign his name or put his mark thereto, or shall refuse to pay for making any such entry, or shall give in, or cause to be entered in any such book or register, any false or untrue account of the quantity of hay or straw sold, or of the price at which the same was really sold, or of the name or place of abode of any buyer of such hay or straw; every owner or seller of any such hay or straw, his servant or agent, who shall so offend, shall, on being convicted thereof in manner herein after mentioned, for every such offence forfeit and pay any sum not exceeding twenty shillings, nor less than ten shillings; and if any hay weigher in *London*, or clerk or toll-gatherer of any hay market within the limits aforesaid, or his or their deputy or deputies, shall omit or neglect to keep such book or register, or shall delay or refuse to let any entry hereby directed to be made therein, or shall demand any greater price than one penny for making any such entry, or one halfpenny for permitting such book

distinguishing the names and places of abode of the owners, sellers, and buyers, and for whose use the same was bought, with the date and price; and to sign the said entry, and pay 1d. fee to the clerk, &c.

Register to be inspected by any person on paying 1q.

Vender neglecting to make such entry, &c.

or giving in a false or untrue account, forfeits, not exceeding 20s. nor less than 10s.

and hay weigher or clerk, &c neglecting his duty in the premisses, forfeits in like manner.

book or register to be at any time perused or examined, or shall knowingly suffer or permit any untrue entry to be made in any such book or register, or shall refuse at any seasonable time in the day time, in market hours, to permit any person to inspect any entry which shall be made in any such book or register, every such person who shall so offend in the premisses, shall, for every such offence, on being convicted thereof in manner herein after mentioned, forfeit and pay any sum not exceeding twenty shillings, nor less than ten shillings.

VII. Provided always, and be it enacted by the authority aforesaid, That nothing in this act contained shall oblige any person to register any hay or straw which shall be sold within the limits aforesaid, in any less quantity than four trusses in any day, to any one person.

No Register to be made of hay or straw sold in a less quantity than 4 trusses, in a day, to one person; nor of any delivered on special contract; but such only to be registered as is brought to market for sale, and which shall be there sold.

VIII. Provided also, and be it further enacted by the authority aforesaid, That nothing in this act contained shall oblige any person to register any hay or straw which he shall deliver in London, or within the limits of the said weekly bills of mortality, on special contract or agreement; but such hay and straw only which shall be sent or brought into London, or some place within the limits of the said weekly bills of mortality, to be sold, and which shall be accordingly there sold, shall be registered as before is directed; any thing in this act before contained to the contrary thereof notwithstanding.

Proper scales and weights, or engines for weighing hay and straw, to be provided by the hay weighers and clerks of the markets.

IX. And be it further enacted by the authority aforesaid, That there shall be provided by the hay weigher of the said city of London, and by every clerk or toll-gatherer of every hay market, within the limits of the said weekly bills of mortality, and kept at every such hay market in London, and within the limits of the said weekly bills of mortality, proper scales and weights, or engines, for the weighing all hay and straw which shall be there brought for sale, or shall be required to be there weighed; and such hay weigher, clerk, or toll-gatherer, of the hay market, or his or their deputy, shall, on application to him or them for that purpose made, cause all hay or straw, which shall be there brought and required to be weighed, to be duly weighed, and with all convenient speed, after any request shall be made for weighing thereof; and such hay weigher, clerk, or toll-gatherer of the market, or his deputy, shall be paid by the party requiring any such hay or straw to be so weighed, the sum of one shilling and no more, for weighing every load of such hay or straw; and if less than a load of hay or straw shall be there weighed, then the sum of one halfpenny for every truss of such hay or straw which shall be there weighed; and if any doubt shall at any time arise, whether any hay or straw brought into London, or in any market or place within the limits of the said weekly bills of mortality, and which shall not have been weighed at any such hay market, is of the due weight the same ought to be, then and in such case it shall be lawful for the buyer thereof, on the delivery of such hay or straw at his or her abode, yard, loft, or other place, where the same shall be agreed by the seller to be delivered, to

Fees payable for the use thereof.

Where any doubt shall arise about the due weight of such hay or straw as shall not have been weighed in the markets, the buyer may.

cause

cauſe the ſame to be weighed in the preſence of the ſeller, or his ſervant or agent, who ſhall deliver the ſame; and if on the ſame being ſo weighed, the buyer or ſeller of any ſuch hay or ſtraw, his ſervant or agent, ſhall be diſſatisfied with any ſuch weighing thereof, it ſhall be lawful for any ſuch buyer or ſeller, his ſervant or agent, with all convenient ſpeed then afterwards to apply to the hay weigher, clerk, or toll-gatherer, of the hay market, his or their deputy or deputies, which ſhall be neareſt to the place where any ſuch hay or ſtraw ſhall be delivered, to ſee the ſame weighed over again, and on any ſuch application being made, the hay weigher, clerk, or toll-gatherer, of the market, who ſhall be ſo applied to, his deputy or deputies, ſhall, with all convenient ſpeed after any ſuch application ſhall be ſo made, come to the place where ſuch hay or ſtraw ſhall be, within the limits aforeſaid, and ſhall there ſee ſuch hay or ſtraw as ſhall be complained of as wanting in weight, again weighed, and the weight thereof which ſhall be aſcertained by any ſuch hay weigher, clerk, or toll-gatherer of the market, or his deputy or deputies, ſhall be concluſive to all parties; but the perſon who ſhall require any ſuch hay weigher, clerk, or toll-gatherer of the market, or his or their deputy or deputies, to attend and weigh any ſuch hay or ſtraw out of any ſuch hay market, ſhall pay to ſuch hay weigher, clerk, or toll-gatherer of the market as aforeſaid, or his or their deputy, to attend to ſee the ſame weighed, the ſum of two ſhillings, before any ſuch hay weigher, clerk, or toll-gatherer of the market, his deputy or deputies, ſhall be obliged to go to ſee any ſuch hay or ſtraw weighed out of any ſuch hay market; and if any hay or ſtraw which ſhall be weighed out of any ſuch hay market, ſhall be found by the hay weigher, clerk, or toll-gatherer of the market, or his or their deputy, to be of the due weight the ſame ought to be, then the two ſhillings which ſhall have been paid to or for ſuch hay weigher, clerk, or toll-gatherer of the market, to attend to ſee ſuch hay or ſtraw weighed, ſhall be forthwith repaid by the buyer of ſuch hay or ſtraw to the ſeller thereof, in caſe the ſeller paid ſuch two ſhillings; and if the hay or ſtraw which ſhall be ſo weighed, ſhall be found not to be of the due weight the ſame ought to be, then if the buyer thereof paid the ſaid two ſhillings, the ſame ſhall be forthwith repaid to him by the ſeller of ſuch hay or ſtraw; and if any hay weigher, clerk, or toll-gatherer of any ſuch hay market, or his or their deputy, ſhall omit to provide and keep proper ſcales and due weights or engines for the weighing hay or ſtraw at ſuch hay market, or ſhall neglect or refuſe to weigh any hay or ſtraw, which ſhall be required to be there weighed by him, or them, or to attend to ſee the ſame weighed out of ſuch hay market at any place within the limits aforeſaid, when thereunto required at any ſeaſonable time in the day time, and ſo as the ſaid ſum of two ſhillings ſhall have been paid or tendered to him ſo to attend, every ſuch hay weigher, clerk, or toll-gatherer of the market, his deputy or deputies, ſo offending in the premiſſes, ſhall, for every fuch offence, forfeit and pay any fum not exceeding twenty fhillings, nor lefs than ten fhillings.

Where there fhall be a doubt of want of weight, the hay or ftraw may be weighed at the place of delivery;

X. Provided always, and be it enacted by the authority aforefaid, That all hay or ftraw fold within the faid diftance of thirty miles from the extent of the limits of the weekly bills of mortality, and touching which there fhall be any doubt of want of weight, fhall and may, on the delivery thereof at the houfe, yard, loft, or any other place whereat the fame fhall be agreed to be delivered, or fhall be delivered by the feller thereof, be there weighed: and that no perfon fhall incur any penalty for felling, or expofing to fale, any hay or ftraw of lefs weight, or worfe quality than the fame ought to be, unlefs fuch hay or ftraw fhall be weighed either at or before the delivery, with the privity of the buyer, his fervant or agent, or complained of in refpect of the quality thereof, at the time and place at which the fame fhall be agreed to be delivered by the feller, in the prefence of fuch feller, his fervant, or agent; unlefs fuch feller, his fervant, or agent, on requeft made, or on notice given to him or them to attend to fee fuch hay or ftraw fo weighed, fhall refufe or neglect to attend to fee the fame fo weighed; any thing in this act, or any other act to the contrary thereof in any wife notwithftanding.

and the feller is not liable to a penalty either in refpect of weight or quality, unlefs the hay or ftraw be weighed either at or before the delivery, with the privity of the buyer, or complained of, as to its quality, at the time and place of delivery; and the feller refufe to attend, &c.

XI. *And whereas falefmen, brokers, or factors employed by feeders of cattle, or farmers, to fell their live cattle within the city of* London, *or within the faid limits of the weekly bills of mortality, may be guilty of many abufes greatly to the prejudice of their employers, by indirectly felling fuch cattle, and by that means, ftocking lands, which they may hire for that purpofe, near the markets within the faid city of* London, *or weekly bills of mortality, where fuch cattle may be brought to be fold again, whenever they fhall find a proper time or opportunity of felling the fame to advantage;* be it therefore further enacted by the authority aforefaid, That from and after the faid twenty ninth day of *September*, no falefman, or other broker, or factor, who fhall be employed to buy or fell any fort of cattle for others, by commiffion, or for reward, to be paid or taken, fhall by himfelf, or any fervant or agent, directly or indirectly, on or for his own account, buy any live ox, bull, cow, fteer, bullock, heifer, calf, fheep, lamb, or fwine, in *London*, or within the faid limits of the faid weekly bills of mortality, or at any place whilft any fuch cattle fhall be on the road, or be driving, bringing, or coming up, to be fold or offered to or for fale, in *London*, or at any other place within the faid limits of the faid weekly bills of mortality (other than fuch cattle which any fuch falefman, broker, or factor, fhall actually purchafe for the neceffary ufe or provifion of his family, and fhall actually ufe accordingly) and that no fuch falefman, broker, or factor, after the faid twenty ninth day of *September*, fhall fell or expofe to fale, or offer to or for fale, on his own account, in *London*, or at any place within the faid limits of the faid weekly bills of mortality, either by himfelf, or his fervant, or agent, any live ox, bull, cow,

Salefmen, &c. employed to buy or fell cattle for others, are not to buy or fell on their own account,

(Exception)

steer,

fteer, bullock, heifer, calf, fheep, lamb, or fwine, upon pain that every perfon who fhall fo offend in the premiffes, fhall every time he fhall be convicted of any fuch offence in manner herein after mentioned, forfeit and pay for every fuch offence, double the value of any live cattle, which he fhall fo buy or fell, on his own account, contrary to the tenor of this act.

on penalty of forfeiting double the value.

XII. And be it further enacted by the authority aforefaid, That from and after the faid twenty ninth day of *September*, no perfon or perfons fhall permit or fuffer his, her, or their waggon, cart, or carr, loaden with hay or ftraw for fale, to ftand or be in the hay market in *Smithfield* in *London*, or in any hay market within the weekly bills of mortality, from *Lady Day* to *Michaelmas*, after four of the clock in the afternoon, and from *Michaelmas* to *Lady Day*, after three of the clock in the afternoon, upon pain to forfeit and pay, for every fuch offence refpectively, five fhillings; but before any forfeiture for the faid laft mentioned offence fhall be incurred, the hay weigher, clerk, or tollgatherer, of the hay market, or his or their deputy, fhall, on every market day (to wit) *Tuefday*, *Thurfday*, and *Saturday*, in every week, ring a large hand bell round the hay market of which he fhall be hay weigher, clerk, or toll-gatherer, of the market, either in *London*, or within the limits of the weekly bills of mortality, one hour before the expiration of the time above appointed for perfons bringing hay or ftraw for fale into any fuch hay market, to leave the fame; and on any default of ringing fuch bell, as aforefaid, being made, no perfon ufing any fuch hay market, for the purpofe of felling hay or ftraw, fhall, the next immediate ufual market day or days after any fuch default in ringing fuch bell, as aforefaid, fhall be made, be liable to pay any toll for any waggon, cart, or carr, ftanding, or that fhall ftand, in any fuch hay market, to fell hay or ftraw; and every fuch hay market is hereby, in that cafe, and on the next market day in which any fuch default, as aforefaid, of ringing fuch bell fhall be made, declared to be toll-free.

Carts, &c. with hay or ftraw for fale, to quit the market by a certain hour on penalty of 5 l.

Hay weigher or clerk, &c. to give an hour's notice, by ringing of a bell;

and on default of fuch notice, no toll is to be paid for ftanding the next market day.

XIII. Provided always, and be it further enacted by the authority aforefaid, That no perfon fhall incur any penalty for fuffering his waggon, cart, or carr, loaden with hay or ftraw for fale, to be in any fuch hay market from *Lady Day* to *Michaelmas*, after three of the clock in the afternoon, and from *Michaelmas* to *Lady Day*, after two of the clock in the afternoon; any other law or ufage to the contrary thereof notwithftanding.

Carts ftanding in the market during certain hours only, not liable to forfeit.

XIV. Provided likewife, and it is hereby further enacted by the authority aforefaid, That no perfon fhall be convicted for any of the before-mentioned offences, unlefs profecution for any fuch offence fhall be committed within three days after the offence complained of fhall have been committed.

Profecution to be commenced within 3 days after the offence.

XV. And, for the more fpeedy recovery of all and every the money which fhall be forfeited by breach or non-obfervance of any part of this act, and for the difpofing thereof, be it further enacted by the authority aforefaid, That on complaint being made, on oath, to any juftice or juftices of the peace of any offence committed

Recovery and application of forfeitures, viz.

On complaint made, on oath, of the offence, the juftice is to

summon, &c.
the offender,
and witnesses,

mitted against this act, within his or their respective jurisdictions, such justice or justices is and are hereby required and authorized to issue his or their summons to convene the person or persons charged with being an offender or offenders against this act, and also any witness or witnesses for any of the parties, at a certain time and place in such summons to be specified; and if any one so summoned shall not appear on such summons, or offer some reasonable excuse for the default, then any such justice or justices shall issue his or their warrant or warrants for apprehending the party or parties so making default within the jurisdiction of any such justice or justices; and upon the party or parties complained against appearing, or being brought before any such justice or justices on his or their warrant or warrants;

and on the
parties appear-
ing or not ap-
pearing there-
upon, is to pro-
ceed to hear
and determine
the matter of
complaint in a
summary way;

or, in case the party or parties complained against shall not appear on such summons being served on him, or left for him or them at his or their usual place of abode, and proof shall be made thereof, by oath, before any such justice or justices; then every such justice and justices is and are hereby authorized and required to proceed to make enquiry touching the matters complained of, and to examine into the same by the oath or oaths of any credible person or persons as shall be requisite, and to hear and determine the matter of every such complaint; and, upon confession of the party, or proof of one credible witness, upon oath, to convict or acquit the party or parties against whom complaint shall be made; and if the money forfeited shall not

and on non-
payment of
the forfeiture,
on conviction,
is to issue his
warrant for
the levying
thereof by di-
stress and sale;

be paid down on every such conviction, every such justice or justices shall issue his or their warrant or warrants under his hand and seal, or their hands and seals, for levying thereof within his or their jurisdiction, by distress on the goods and chattels of every such offender, or offenders, and to cause sale to be made of such goods and chattels, in case the money forfeited, together with the charges of such distress and sale, shall not be paid within five days after the making any such distress and sale, rendering the overplus, if any, to the owner thereof, upon demand, after deducting the reasonable charges of every

and for want
of distress to
commit the
offender for
any time not
exceeding 1
month, nor
less than 10
days, unless
payment be
sooner made.

such distress and sale; and if any such offender shall not have any goods or chattels within the jurisdiction of such justice or justices, whereon the money forfeited can be presently levied, any justice or justices within whose jurisdiction any such offender or offenders shall be, shall and may issue a warrant or warrants under his hand and seal, or their hands and seals, on the application, or on the behalf, of any informer or informers, to apprehend every such offender and offenders, and to commit him or them to some publick prison or house of correction of the county, division, city, town, or place, in which any such offence shall have been committed, there to remain for any time not exceeding one calendar month, nor less than ten days, from the time of every such commitment, unless such offender or offenders shall sooner pay the money forfeited; and if any witness who shall appear or be brought by any warrant before any such justice or justices, shall refuse to be examined, any such person so

Witness refus-
ing to be exa-
mined, may
be committed

refusing

refusing to be examined, may be committed by any such justice *for any time* or justices to some prison of the county, city, or place, where *not exceeding* such witness shall so make default, for any time not exceeding *10 days.* ten days from the time of every such commitment, as any such justice or justices shall think fit.

XVI. Provided always, and be it further enacted, That if *Seller aggriev-* any person or persons convicted of any offence punishable by this *ed by the* act, or for selling any truss or trusses of hay, of less weight than *judgment of* the same ought to be, shall think him, her, or themselves ag- *a justice, may* grieved by the judgment or determination of any justice or ju- *appeal to the* stices as aforesaid, such person or persons may appeal against the *sions ;* same to the justices at the general or general quarter sessions of the peace of the county, city, or place, in which any such con- viction shall have been made, which shall be held next after any such conviction, unless such next general or general quarter ses- sions of the peace for any such county, city, or place, shall be held within six days next after any such conviction; and if any such general or general quarter sessions of the peace, shall hap- pen to be so held within the said space of six days next after any such conviction, then it shall be lawful for any such person or persons to appeal against any such judgment or determination, to the justices at the second general or general quarter sessions of the peace which shall be held for any such county, city, or place, next after any such conviction; but the party or parties who *entering into a* shall think fit so to appeal, shall, before any such appeal shall be *recognizance,* received, enter into a recognizance, with two sufficient sureties, *and giving se-* before such justice or justices as aforesaid, in double the sum *curity to pro-* which such person or persons shall have been adjudged to pay *secute the ap-* or forfeit, to prosecute every such appeal with effect, and to be *peal with ef-* forth coming to abide by and obey the judgment and determi- *fect ;* nation of the justices at any such general or general quarter ses- sions of the peace on every such appeal, and shall also give three *and giving due* days notice, in writing, of every such appeal, to, or leave the *notice thereof* same at the usual place of abode of the person or persons who *to the prosecu-* shall have prosecuted to conviction the party or parties so ap- *cutor.* pealing; and the justices of the peace at such general or general *Justices to* quarter sessions, are hereby authorized and required, on every *hear and de-* such appeal being made, finally to hear and determine the mat- *termine the* ter of every such appeal, and to make such order, and to award *matter of the* such costs therein, as they in their discretion shall deem meet; *appeal accord-* and the determination of such court of general or general quar- *ingly, and a-* ter sessions, on every such appeal, shall be final and conclusive *ward costs ;* to all parties thereto, and no *Certiorari* shall be allowed to re- *nation to be* move any such proceedings or determination. *final, &c.*

XVII. And be it further enacted by the authority aforesaid, *Forfeitures to* That one moiety of all money forfeited by this act, shall, when *be applied,* recovered, go and be paid to the person or persons who shall *one moiety to* prosecute to conviction any offender or offenders against this *the prosecut-* act, and that the other moiety thereof shall go and be paid to or *or, the other* for the use of the poor of the parish or place where the offence *to the poor* shall have been committed.

XVIII. Pro-

XVIII. Provided always, and it is hereby further enacted, That any inhabitant of the parish or place in which any offence shall be committed against this act, shall, notwithstanding such inhabitancy, be a good and competent witness.

Limitation of
actions.

XIX. And be it further enacted by the authority aforesaid, That if any plaint, action, or suit, shall be commenced or prosecuted against any person or persons, for what he or they shall do or have done in pursuance or in execution of this act, the same shall be commenced within six months after the offence committed, and shall be laid in the county or city where the offence shall have been committed; and such person or persons so

General issue. sued, in any court whatsoever, shall and may plead the general issue, not guilty, and may give this act, and the special matter in evidence, at any trial to be had thereupon; and if a verdict shall be found for the defendant or defendants, or if the plaintiff shall become nonsuit, or discontinue his action, after the defendant shall have appeared; or if judgment shall be given, upon a demurrer, against the plaintiff or plaintiffs, the defendant

Treble costs. or defendants, in every such action, shall recover treble costs, and have the like remedy for the same as any defendant or defendants hath or have in other cases for recovery of his or their costs.

CAP. XLI.

An act to amend and render more effectual an act passed in the twenty ninth year of his present Majesty's reign, intituled, An act for inclosing, by the mutual consent of the lords and tenants, part of any common, for the purpose of planting and preserving trees fit for timber or underwood; and for more effectually preventing the unlawful destruction of trees.

Preamble, re-
citing several
clauses in act
29 Geo. 2.

WHEREAS *by an act made in the twenty ninth year of the reign of his present Majesty, intituled,* An act for inclosing, by the mutual consent of the lord and tenants, part of any common, for the purpose of planting and preserving trees fit for timber or underwood; and for more effectually preventing the unlawful destruction of trees; *it is, among other things, enacted, That it shall and may be lawful to and for his Majesty, his heirs and successors, and all other owners of wastes, woods, and pastures, in that part of* Great Britain *called* England, *wherein any person or persons, or body or bodies politic or corporate, hath or have a right of common of pasture, by and with the assent of the major part in number and value of the owners and occupiers of tenements, to which the said right of common of pasture doth belong, and to and for the major part in number and value of the owners and occupiers of such tenements, by and with the assent of the owner or owners of the said wastes, woods, and pastures, and to and for any other person or persons, or body politic or corporate, by and with the assent and grant of the owner or owners of such wastes, woods, and pastures, and the major*

major part in number and value of the owners and occupiers of such
tenements, to inclose and keep in severalty, for the growth and pre-
servation of timber or underwood, any part of such wastes, woods,
and pastures, for such time, and in such manner, and upon such con-
ditions, as shall be agreed by them respectively: and whereas it is by
the said act provided, That in case any recompence shall be agreed to
be given for such inclosure, to or for the benefit of the owners and
occupiers of the tenements to which the right of common in such wastes,
woods, and pastures, doth belong, such recompence shall be made either
by a grant of a share of the profit which shall arise from the sale
of the timber or underwood growing on the ground or soil so inclosed,
or by a grant of other lands, tenements, or hereditaments, or by some
annuity or rent charge issuing out of the said ground or soil so in-
closed, or out of other lands, tenements, or hereditaments, or shall be
paid in money, to be placed out at interest on public securities, or laid
out in the purchase of lands, tenements, or hereditaments, or of some
annuity or rent charge issuing out of lands, tenements, or heredita-
ments; and the produce of such lands, tenements, or hereditaments
or such annuity or rent charge, or the interest of such money, until
the same shall be laid out in such purchase, as aforesaid, shall be
paid, from time to time, to the overseers or overseer of the poor of
the said parish or township, and shall be by them or him applied to-
wards the relief of the poor of the parish or township where such
wastes, woods, or pastures, shall lie, and accounted for in such man-
ner as the rates for relief of the poor are by law directed to be ac-
counted for: and whereas, in many cases, the right of common of
pasture in the ground or soil inclosed, or intended to be inclosed, may
not belong to all the owners and occupiers of tenements within the pa-
rishes or townships wherein such wastes, woods, or pastures, shall lie:
and whereas the owners and occupiers of such tenements, to which
such peculiar right of common doth belong, may refuse their assent to
an inclosure, the recompence for which is applicable to the general re-
lief of the poor of the parish, and not to them in proportion to their
particular interests; and yet they may be willing to accept a different
recompence from that which is provided by the said act; be it enacted by the King's most excellent majesty, by and with the
advice and consent of the lords spiritual and temporal, and commons, in this present parliament assembled, and by the authority of the same, That from and after the first day of *August,* The recom-
one thousand seven hundred and fifty eight, every recompence pence to be
to be made by virtue of the said act, shall be made to the per- made under
son or persons interested in the said right of common, in pro- the recited act
portion to their respective interest or interests therein; and not the rights of
to be paid to the overseer or overseers of the poor, as is directed common of
by the said act. pasture in
grounds to be
inclosed for planting trees, is to be paid to the persons respectively interested therein, and
not to the overseers of the poor.

II. *And whereas doubts may arise whether tenants for life, or for* Tenants for
terms of years, determinable upon one or more life or lives, be own- life, or for
ers, within the meaning of this act, and that of the twenty ninth of years deter-
terms of
his minable there-

C c 4

upon, may execute the powers given by the recited and this act, during their respective interests, But no act of theirs is to have effect, after the determination of such their estate.

his *present Majesty's reign*; be it enacted by the authority aforesaid, That the powers given to such owners by this act, and the said act of the twenty ninth of his present Majesty's reign, may be executed by such tenants for life, or years, during their respective interests.

III. Provided always, That nothing done by such tenants for life, or terms of years, by virtue of this act, or by the act of the twenty ninth of his present Majesty's reign, shall have effect or continuance after the determination of the estate of such tenants for life, or terms of years.

C A P. XLII.

An act for making perpetual several acts therein mentioned, for preventing theft and rapine on the northern borders of England; for the more effectual punishing wicked and evil disposed persons going armed in disguise, and doing injuries and violences to the persons and properties of his Majesty's subjects, and for the more speedy bringing the offenders to justice; and also two clauses to prevent the cutting or breaking down the bank of any river, or sea bank; and to prevent the malicious cutting of hop binds; for the more effectual punishment of persons maliciously setting on fire any mine, pit, or delph of coal, or canal coal; and of persons unlawfully hunting or taking any red or fallow deer in forests or chases; or beating or wounding the keepers or other officers in forests, chaces, or parks; and also so much of an act as relates to the power of appealing to the circuit courts in civil cases in Scotland.

Preamble.

WHEREAS *the laws herein after mentioned, which have by experience been found useful and beneficial, are near expiring*: may it therefore please your most excellent Majesty, that it may be enacted; and be it enacted by the King's most excellent majesty, by and with the advice and consent of the lords spiritual and temporal, and commons, in this present parliament assembled, and by the authority of the same, That an act made in the thirteenth and fourteenth years of the reign of King *Charles* the Second, intituled, *An act for preventing theft and rapine upon the northern borders of* England; which by several acts hath from time to time been continued; and by an act made in the sixth year of the reign of his present Majesty (for making perpetual several acts, and for other purposes therein mentioned) was further continued until the first day of *September* one thousand seven hundred and forty four, and from thence to the end of the then next session of parliament; and also several clauses, powers, and authorities, in the afore-mentioned act made in the sixth year of the reign of his present Majesty, for the more effectual preventing of theft and rapine upon the northern borders of *England*; and which by the said act were to continue in force until the first

Act 13 & 14 Car. 2.

and several clauses and powers in the act of 6 Geo. 2. relating thereto; and

day

day of *September* one thousand seven hundred and forty four, and
from thence to the end of the then next session of parliament;
and which said act, together with the said several clauses, powers, and authorities, were, by several subsequent acts made in the
seventeenth and twenty fourth years of the reign of his present
Majesty, further continued until the first day of *September* one
thousand seven hundred and fifty seven, and from thence to the
end of the then next session of parliament; are temporary, and
near expiring, shall be, and are hereby made perpetual. *(margin: which were continued by several subsequent acts, are made perpetual.)*

II. And be it further enacted by the authority aforesaid, That
an act made in the ninth year of the reign of his late majesty
King *George* the First, intituled, *An act for the more effectual
punishing wicked and evil disposed persons going armed in disguise,
and doing injuries and violences to the persons and properties of his
Majesty's subjects, and for the more speedy bringing the offenders to
justice*; which by several subsequent acts, one made in the
twelfth year of the reign of his late Majesty, and the others
made in the sixth, tenth, seventeenth, and twenty fourth years
of the reign of his present Majesty, was further continued until the first day of *September* one thousand seven hundred and
fifty seven, and from thence to the end of the then next session
of parliament; is temporary, and near expiring, shall be, and
is hereby made perpetual. *(margin: Act 9 Geo. 1. and which was continued by several subsequent acts, is made perpetual.)*

III. And be it further enacted by the authority aforesaid,
That a clause in an act made in the sixth year of the reign of
his present Majesty (for making perpetual several acts, and for
other purposes therein mentioned) to prevent the cutting or
breaking down the bank of any river, or sea bank, which was
to continue in force during the continuance of an act made in
the ninth year of the reign of his said late Majesty; and which
by another act made in the tenth year of the reign of his present Majesty, was further continued during the continuance
of the afore-mentioned act made in the ninth year of the reign
of his said late Majesty; and which by several subsequent acts
made in the seventeenth and twenty fourth years of his present
Majesty's reign, was further continued until the first day of
September one thousand seven hundred and fifty seven, and from
thence to the end of the then next session of parliament; is temporary, and near expiring, shall be, and is hereby made per-
petual. *(margin: Clause in act 6 Geo. 1. to prevent the cutting down the banks of rivers, and which was continued by several subsequent acts, is made perpetual.)*

IV. And be it further enacted by the authority aforesaid,
That a clause in an act made in the sixth year of the reign of his
present Majesty (for making perpetual several acts, and for
other purposes therein mentioned) to prevent the malicious cutting of hop binds growing on poles in any plantation of hops;
which was to continue in force during the continuance of an act
made in the ninth year of the reign of his said late Majesty, and
which by several subsequent acts made in the tenth, seventeenth,
and twenty fourth years of his present Majesty's reign, was further continued until the first day of *September*, one thousand seven hundred and fifty seven, and from thence to the end of the
then *(margin: Clause in act 6 Geo. 1. to prevent the malicious cutting of hop binds, and which was continued by several subsequent acts, is made perpetual.)*

then next seffion of parliament; is temporary, and near expiring, fhall be, and is hereby made perpetual.

Claufe in act 10 Geo. 2. for extending the powers in act 9 Geo. 1. to the feveral cafes of offences therein fet forth, and which was continued by feveral fubfequent acts, is made perpetual.

V. And be it further enacted by the authority aforefaid, That a claufe in an act made in the tenth year of the reign of his prefent Majefty (for continuing an act for the more effectual punifhing wicked and evil-difpofed perfons going armed in difguife, and doing injuries and violences to the perfons and properties of his Majefty's fubjects, and for the more fpeedy bringing the offenders to juftice; and for other purpofes therein mentioned) to extend, during the continuance of the faid act, all the provifions therein contained (for the more fpeedy and eafy bringing the offenders againft the faid act to juftice, and the perfons who fhall conceal, and abet or fuccour fuch offenders, and for making fatisfaction and amends to all and every the perfon and perfons, their executors and adminiftrators, for the damages they fhall have fuftained or fuffered by any offender or offenders againft the faid act; and for the encouragement of perfons to apprehend fuch offender and offenders; and for the better and more impartial trial of any indictment or information which fhall be found, commenced, or profecuted, for any of the offences committed againft the faid act; together with all reftrictions, limitations, and mitigations, by the faid act directed) to all cafes of offences committed by unlawfully and malicioufly cutting down the bank or banks of any river, or any fea bank, whereby any lands fhall be overflowed or damaged; or by unlawfully and malicioufly cutting any hop binds growing on poles in any plantation of hops; or by wilfully and malicioufly fetting on fire, or caufing to be fet on fire, any mine, pit, or delph of coal, or cannel coal, and which, by feveral fubfequent acts made in the feventeenth and twenty fourth years of his prefent Majefty's reign, was further continued until the firft day of September, one thoufand feven hundred and fifty feven, and from thence to the end of the then next feffion of parliament; is temporary, and near expiring, fhall be, and is hereby made perpetual.

Claufes in act 10 Geo. 2. for punifhing of perfons malicioufly fetting on fire any mine of coal; or unlawfully hunting and taking of deer; and beating and wounding the keepers of parks, &c. and which were continued by feveral fubfequent acts, are made perpetual. So much of the act of 20 Geo.

VI. And be it further enacted by the authority aforefaid, That the feveral claufes in an act made in the tenth year of the reign of his prefent Majefty (for the more effectual punifhment of perfons malicioufly fetting on fire any mine, pit, or delph of coal or cannel coal; or unlawfully hunting or taking any red or fallow deer in forefts or chaces; or beating and wounding the keepers or other officers in forefts, chaces, or parks) which were to continue in force during the continuance of an act made in the ninth year of the reign of his faid late Majefty, and which by feveral fubfequent acts, made in the feventeenth and twenty fourth years of his prefent Majefty's reign, were further continued until the firft day of September, one thoufand feven hundred and fifty feven, and from thence to the end of the then next feffion of parliament; are temporary, and near expiring, fhall be, and are hereby made perpetual.

VII. And be it further enacted by the authority aforefaid, That fo much of an act made in the twentieth year of his prefent
sent

fent Majesty's reign, intituled, *An act for taking away and abo-* *lishing the heritable jurisdictions in that part of* Great Britain *called* Scotland, *and for making satisfaction to the proprietors thereof, and for restoring such jurisdictions to the crown ; and for making more ef-* *fectual provision for the administration of justice, throughout that* *part of the united kingdom, by the King's courts and judges there ;* *and for obliging all persons acting as procurators, writers, or agents,* *in the law of* Scotland, *to take the oaths ; and for rendering the* *union of the two kingdoms more complete ;* as relates to the power of appealing to the circuit courts in civil cases, which was to continue in force for the space of ten years from the twenty fifth day of *March,* one thousand seven hundred and forty eight, and and from thence to the end of the then next session of parliament ; is temporary, and near expiring, shall be, and is hereby made perpetual.

2. as relates to the power of appealing to the circuit courts in civil cases, is made perpetual.

C A P. XLIII.

An act for repairing and widening several roads in the counties of Dorset and Devon, leading to and through the borough of Lyme Regis.

C A P. XLIV.

An act for repairing the road from the village of Magor, to the bridgefoot in the town of Chepstow, in the county of Monmouth ; and other roads in the counties of Monmouth and Gloucester.

C A P. XLV.

An act for ascertaining and collecting the poors rates, and for better regulating the poor in the parish of Saint Mary Magdalen Bermondsey in the county of Surry.

C A P. XLVI.

An act to amend an act passed in the last session of parliament, intituled, *An act for building a bridge or bridges cross the river of Thames, from a cer-* *tain place in Old Brentford, in the parish of Ealing, in the county of Middlesex,* *known by the name of Smith, or Smith's Hill, to the opposite shore in the county* *of Surrey.*

C A P. XLVII.

An act for the more easy and speedy repairing of publick bridges within the county of Devon.

C A P. XLVIII.

An act for enlarging the term and powers granted by an act of parliament passed in the twenty fourth year of his present Majesty's reign, for enlarging the term and powers granted by an act passed in the third year of the reign of his present Majesty, for repairing and amending the several roads leading from Woodstock, through Kiddington and Enstone, to Rollright Lane, and Enslow Bridge to Kiddington aforesaid ; and for making the said act more effectual.

C A P. XLIX.

An act for amending several roads leading from the town of Tiverton, in the county of Devon.

C A P. L.

An act for repairing and widening the roads from Donington High Bridge to Hale Drove, and to the Eighth Mile Stone, in the parish of Wigtoft, and to Langret Ferry, in the county of Lincoln.

C A P.

CAP. LI.

An act for repairing the high road leading from Brent Bridge in the county of Devon, to Gafking Gate, in or near the borough of Plymouth, in the faid county.

CAP. LII.

An act for enlarging the term granted by an act made in the twenty fixth year of his prefent Majefty's reign, intituled, *An act for laying a duty of two penny Scots, or a fixth part of a penny fterling, upon every Scots pint of ale and beer which fhall be brewed for fale, brought into, tapped, or fold, within the town and parifh of Prefton Pans, in the fhire of Eaft Lothian, otherwife Haddingtoun, for repairing the harbour of the faid town, and for other purpofes therein mentioned.*

CAP. LIII.

An act to explain, amend, and render more effectual an act paffed in the ninth and tenth years of the reign of his late majefty King William the Third, intituled, *An act for erecting hofpitals and workhoufes within the city and county of the city of Exon, for the better employing and maintaining the poor there.*

CAP. LIV.

An act for repealing fo much of the act of the fifteenth year of his prefent Majefty, for enlarging the term and powers granted by an act of the thirteenth year of his late Majefty King George the Firft, for repairing the roads from Cirencefter Town's End to Saint John's Bridge in the county of Gloucefter, as directs that the inhabitants of the feveral parifhes and hamlets therein named, fhall pafs toll free; and for repairing the ftreet from the High Crofs in Cirencefter to the Town's End there; and for other purpofes therein mentioned; and for enlarging the terms and powers granted by the faid two former acts.

CAP. LV.

An act for enlarging the term and powers granted by an act of the twenty fifth year of his prefent Majefty's reign, intituled, *An act for repairing the poft road from the city of Edinburgh, through the counties of Linlithgow and Stirling, from the Boat-houfe Ford, on Almond Water, and from thence to the town of Linlithgow, and from the faid town of Falkirk, and from thence to Stirling; and alfo from Falkirk to Kilfyth, and to Inch Bellie Bridge, on the poft road to the city of Glafgow*; and for building a bridge crofs Almond Water.

CAP. LVI.

An act for enlarging the powers granted by an act paffed in the eighteenth year of the reign of his prefent Majefty, intituled, *An act for rendering more effectual the feveral acts paffed for the erecting of hofpitals and workhoufes within the city of Briftol, for the better employing and maintaining of the poor thereof*; and for making the faid act more effectual.

CAP. LVII.

An act for making more effectual four feveral acts of parliament, made in the fixth year of the reign of her late majefty Queen Ann; the eleventh year of the reign of his late Majefty King George the Firft; and in the tenth and thirteenth years of the reign of his prefent Majefty refpectively, for repairing the highways from Old Stratford in the county of Northampton to Dunchurch, in the county of Warwick.

CAP. LVIII.

An act to continue and render more effectual two acts of parliament made in the twelfth year of the reign of his late Majefty, and in the eighteenth year of the reign of his prefent Majefty, for repairing the reads leading from Birmingham to Edghill, in the county of Warwick.

CAP,

CAP. LIX.

An act for building a bridge cross the river Trent, at or near a place called Wilden Ferry.

CAP. LX.

An act to enlarge, alter, and render more effectual, the term and powers of an act of the twelfth year of his present Majesty, for repairing the roads from Bakewell to Chesterfield in the county of Derby ; and from Chesterfield to Worksop in the county of Nottingham, and other roads therein mentioned.

CAP. LXI.

An act for repairing and widening the road from Cirencester in the county of Gloucester, to Cricklade in the county of Wilts.

CAP. LXII.

An act for repairing and widening the roads from Little Sheffield, in the county of York, through the towns of Hathersage, Hope, and Castleton, to Sparrowpit Gate, in the county of Derby: and from the Guide Post near Barber's Field Cupola, through Grindleford Bridge, Great Hucklow, Tidswell, Hardgate Wall, and Fairfield, to Buxton, in the county of Derby.

CAP. LXIII.

An act for repairing the road from Leeds to Sheffield, in the county of York.

CAP. LXIV.

An act for enlarging the terms and powers of two acts of parliament, one passed in the nineteenth year of the reign of his present Majesty, intituled, *An act for enlarging the term and powers granted by an act passed in the twelfth year of the reign of his late majesty King George the First, for repairing the road from the city of Gloucester to Stone, and other roads therein mentioned:* and for making the said act more effectual: and the other passed in the twenty second year of the reign of his present Majesty, intituled, *An act for continuing two acts of parliament, the one passed in the thirteenth year of the reign of his late majesty King George the First, for amending the several roads leading from the city of Bristol; and the other passed in the fourth year of the reign of his present Majesty, to explain and amend the same act, and for making the said acts more effectual: and also for repairing other roads therein mentioned:* and for making all the said acts more effectual: and for repairing, widening, and keeping in repair, several other roads.

CAP. LXV.

An act for repairing and widening the roads from Tetbury, to the gates on the west of Simond's Hall Down ; and from the turnpike gate at the top of Frocester Hill, to the turnpike road from Cirencester towards Bath ; and from the field called Bouldown Sleight, to the end of a lane adjoining to the road from Horsley to Tetbury, near Tiltup's Inn ; and from the Market-House in Tetbury, to the turnpike road on Minchin Hampton Common ; and from the said road in Minchin Hampton Field, unto the turnpike road from Cirencester to Stroud, near Burnt Ash ; and from the said turnpike road, to Tayloe's Millpond in Chalford Bottom, and through Hide, to the bottom of the Bourn Hill, in the county of Gloucester.

CAP. LXVI.

An act for amending, widening, and keeping in repair, the roads leading from Christian Malford Bridge, in the county of Wilts, to Shillingford Gate, in the county of Berks ; and also from Swindon to Lyddenton Wall, in the said county of Wilts.

CAP.

CAP. LXVII.

An act for widening and repairing several roads leading from the Welch Gate and Cotton Hill, in the town of Shrewsbury, in the county of Salop.

CAP. LXVIII.

An act for amending the road leading from Pengate in the parish of West-bury, in the county of Wilts, to Latchet's Bridge, near the east end of Market Lavington : and also the road leading from Market Lavington Down, to the turnpike road near Dewey's Water : and also the road leading from Bolesborough, to Studley Lane end ; and also the road leading from Yarnbrook, to the turnpike road at Melksham, in the said county of Wilts.

CAP. LXIX.

An act to continue and render more effectual an act made in the fifteenth year of his present Majesty's reign, intituled, *An act for laying a duty of two pennies Scots, or one sixth part of a penny sterling, upon every Scots pint of ale and beer which shall be brewed for sale, brought into, tapped, or sold, within the town of Kirkcaldy, and liberties thereof.*

CAP. LXX.

An act to enable the trustees appointed for putting in execution an' act passed in this session of parliament, intituled, *An act for repealing so much of the act of the fifteenth year of his present Majesty, for enlarging the term and powers granted by an act of the thirteenth year of his late majesty King George the First, for repairing the roads from Cirencester Town's end to Saint John's Bridge, in the county of Gloucester, as directs that the inhabitants of the several parishes and hamlets therein named, shall pass toll-free : and for repairing the Street from the High Cross in Cirencester, to the town's end there, and for other purposes therein mentioned; and for enlarging the terms and powers granted by the said two former acts ;* to reduce all or any of the tolls granted by the said act ; and for appointing additional trustees for putting the said acts in execution.

CAP. LXXI.

An act for regulating, governing, preserving, and improving, the oyster fishery in the river Colne, and waters thereto belonging.

CAP. LXXII.

An act for extending the navigation of the river Calder, to or near to Sowerby Bridge in the parish of Halifax ; and for making navigable the river Heble, Halig or Halifax Brook, from Brooksmouth to Saker Hebble Bridge, in the county of York.

CAP. LXXIII.

An act for repairing and widening the roads from Chawton Pond, in the parish of Chawton, in the county of Southampton, through Rumsdean Bottom, Westmeon, Warnford, Exton, Bishop's Waltham, and over Sherril Heath, and through Wickham and Fareham, to the town of Gosport ; and from Exon aforesaid, through Droxford, to the east end of Sherrill Heath, in the said county.

CAP. LXXIV.

An act for repairing and widening the roads from the town of Bishop's Waltham, in the county of Southampton, over the top of the down called Stephen's Castle Down, and through Salt Lane and Tichborne, to the town of New Alresford ; and from the Market House in the said town of New Alresford, through Old Alresford, Bradley Lane, and over Herriard Common, to the town of Odiham in the said county.

CAP. LXXV.

An act for repairing and widening the roads from the town of Stockbridge, in the county of Southampton, to the city of Winchester; and from the said city, through Be'lmour Lane, to the top of Steven's Castle Down, near the town of Bishop's Waltham, in the said county ; and from the said city of Winchester, through Otterborne, to Bargate, in the town and county of the town of Southampton.

CAP.

CAP. LXXVI.

An act for relief of the coalheavers working upon the river Thames; and for enabling them to make a provision for such of themselves as shall be sick, lame, or past their labour, and for their widows and orphans.

CAP. LXXVII.

An act for repairing and widening the road from the Swan Inn at Leatherhead, to the Maypole at the upper end of Spital or Somerset Street, in the parish of Stoake, near the town of Guldeford, in the county of Surrey.

CAP. LXXVIII.

An act for repairing and widening the road from the town of Guldeford, to the Directing Post near the town of Farnham, in the county of Surrey.

Anno Regni GEORGII II. Regis Magnæ Britanniæ, Franciæ, & Hiberniæ, tricesimo secundo.

AT the parliament begun and holden at Westminster, the thirty first day of May, Anno Dom. one thousand seven hundred and fifty four, in the twenty seventh year of the reign of our sovereign lord George the Second, by the grace of God, of Great Britain, France, and Ireland, King, defender of the faith, &c. And from thence continued by several prorogations to the twenty third day of November, one thousand seven hundred and fifty eight, being the sixth session of this present parliament.

CAP. I.

An act to continue, for a limited time, an act made in the last session of parliament, intituled, An act to permit the importation of salted beef, pork, and butter, from Ireland, for a limited time, and to amend the said act.

WHEREAS the permitting the importation of salted beef, pork, and butter, from Ireland into this kingdom, hath been found useful and beneficial; and that the time allowed for that purpose is near expiring, and it is expedient that the same should be prolonged: may it therefore please your most excellent Majesty, that it may be enacted; and be it enacted by the King's most excellent majesty, by and with the advice and consent of the lords spiritual and temporal, and commons, in this present parliament assembled, and by the authority of the same, That an act made in the last session of parliament, intituled, An act to permit the importation of salted beef, pork, and butter, from Ireland, for a limited time, which was to continue in force for the term of six months, from and after the twenty fourth day of June, one thousand seven hundred and fifty eight, shall be, and the same is hereby further continued from the expiration thereof, until the twen-

Preamble.

Act 31 Geo. 2.

further continued to 24 Dec. 1759.

twenty fourth day of *December*, one thoufand feven hundred and
fifty nine; except only with refpect to fuch parts thereof relating to the payment of the duty, and to the recovering of penalties, as are amended, or otherwife provided for by this act.

All kinds of salted pork, and hog meat, may be imported.

II. *And whereas doubts have arifen whether all kinds of falted
pork and hog meat may be imported from* Ireland, *by virtue of the
above recited act*; be it therefore declared and enacted by the
authority aforefaid, That the faid act does and fhall extend,
and fhall be deemed, conftrued, and taken to extend, to all kinds
of falted pork and hog meat imported, or to be imported, into
Great Britain from *Ireland*, during the continuance of the faid
act.

III. *And whereas the duty or impofition of one fhilling and three
pence charged and directed by the faid act to be laid on every hundred
weight of falted beef or pork fo to be imported from* Ireland *as a-
forefaid, is not adequate to, but falls fhort of, the duty laid upon,
and payable for, fuch quantity of falt as is requifite and neceffary to
be ufed in curing and falting the fame: and whereas the falted beef
and pork imported into this kingdom from* Ireland, *is generally packed up and contained in cafks, with the pickle or brine proper for preferving the fame; and the opening the faid cafks, in order to afcertain the net weight of the beef and pork liable to the faid duties on
importation, would not only be very expenfive to the revenue, but alfo
a great detriment and lofs to the faid provifions, and the owner and
importer of the fame; and that it would be more for the benefit and
advantage of the revenue, and alfo of fuch owner and importer, that
the rates and duties to be paid upon the importation of fuch beef and
pork, fhould be afcertained by, and laid upon, every barrel of the faid
commodities fo to be imported, according to the rate and proportion
herein after mentioned*; therefore be it enacted by the authority
aforefaid, That from and after the faid twenty fourth day of

Beef or pork, if in pickle, to pay 3s. 5d. per barrel, duty;

December, one thoufand feven hundred and fifty eight, and during the continuance of this act, there fhall be paid for every
barrel or cafk of falted beef or pork fo imported as aforefaid,
containing thirty two gallons, to the proper officer appointed
by the faid former act, the fum of three fhillings and four pence,
as and for cuftom or duty for, on, or in refpect thereof; and

if dried, 1s. 3d. per hundred weight;

fo in proportion for any greater or leffer quantity thereof: and
for every hundred weight of falted beef, called dried beef, or dried
neats tongues, or dried hog meat, fo imported, the fum of one
fhilling and three pence, and fo in proportion for every greater
or leffer quantity thereof, as and for cuftom or duty for, on, or
in refpect thereof.

IV. And it is hereby further enacted by the authority aforefaid, That if any perfon fhall after the faid twenty fourth day
of *December*, one thoufand feven hundred and fifty eight, during the continuance of this act, land any fuch falted beef, pork,
or butter, or any falted beef called dried beef, or dried neats

if landed without duty paid, to be forfeited, with

tongues, or dried hog meat, imported from *Ireland*, as aforefaid, before payment of the duty laid or directed by this act,
the fame, together with the cafks, veffels, and package, containing

taining the same, shall be forfeited and lost; and the importer *the package;* or proprietor of the said commodities shall also forfeit and pay *and importer* the sum of twenty shillings for every barrel of such salted beef, *also to pay 20s.* pork, or butter, and for every hundred weight of such salted *per barrel,* beef, called dried beef, or dried neats tongues, or dried hogs *weight.* meat, so imported and landed as aforesaid, and so in proportion for every greater or lesser quantity thereof; and that it shall and *Officer of* may be lawful to and for any person or persons (being an of- *customs, or* ficer of the customs, or of his Majesty's duties upon salt) to *salt duties,* take and seize all such commodities as shall be imported and *may seize the* landed, contrary to the true intent and meaning of this and the *same.* former act; and that all penalties and forfeitures inflicted and *Forfeitures to* directed to be levied by this act, shall be distributed in manner *and recovered,* as by the said former act, and may be recovered either by the *as by the for-* ways and means directed and appointed by the said former act, *mer act.* or may be sued for, recovered, and mitigated, by any of the laws of and relating to the excise.

CAP. II.

An act to continue, for a farther time, the prohibition of the exportation of corn, malt, meal, flour, bread, biscuit, and starch; and also to continue, for a further time, the prohibition of the making of low wines and spirits from wheat, barley, malt, or any other sort of grain, or from meal or flour; and to prohibit, for a limited time, the making of low wines and spirits from bran.

WHEREAS *an act made in the last session of parliament, in-* *Preamble, re-* *tituled,* An act for continuing certain laws made in the *citing several* last session of parliament, for prohibiting the exportation of *clauses in act* corn, malt, meal, flour, bread, biscuit, and starch; and for pro- *31 Geo. 2.* hibiting the making of low wines and spirits from wheat, bar- ley, malt, or any other sort of grain, or from meal or flour; and to allow the transportation of wheat, barley, oats, meal, and flour, to the *Isle of Man,* for the use of the inhabitants there; and for reviving and continuing an act made in the same session, for discontinuing the duties upon corn and flour imported, and upon corn, grain, meal, bread, biscuit, and flour, taken from the enemy; and to permit the importation of corn and flour into *Great Britain* and *Ireland,* in neutral ships; and to autho- rize his Majesty, with the advice of his privy council, to order and permit the exportation of such quantities of the commodi- ties aforesaid, as may be necessary for the sustentation of any forces in the pay of *Great Britain,* or of those of his Majesty's allies acting in support of the common cause; and to pro- hibit the payment of any bounty upon the exportation of any of the said commodities to be made during the continuance of this act, *is near expiring: and whereas it is expedient that so much of the said act as relates to the exportation of corn, malt, meal, flour, bread, biscuit, and starch; and also that the act made in the thir-*

and 30 Geo. 2.

tieth year of his prefent Majefty's reign, intituled, An act to prohibit, for a limited time, the making of low wines and fpirits
from wheat, barley, malt, or any other fort of grain, or from
any meal or flour, *which was continued by the faid firft mentioned
act, fhould be further continued;* be it therefore enacted by the
King's moft excellent majefty, by and with the advice and confent
of the lords fpiritual and temporal, and commons, in this prefent
parliament affembled, and by the authority of the fame, That

The recited
claufes in the
act of the laft
feffion,

fo much of the faid act made in the laft feffion of parliament,
intituled, *An act for continuing certain laws made in the laft feffion
of parliament, for prohibiting the exportation of corn, malt, meal,
flour, bread, bifcuit, and ftarch; and for prohibiting the making of
low wines and fpirits, from wheat, barley, malt, or any other fort
of grain, or from meal or flour; and to allow the tranfportation of
wheat, barley, oats, meal, and flour, to the* Ifle of Man, *for the
ufe of the inhabitants there; and for reviving and continuing an act
made in the fame feffion, for difcontinuing the duties upon corn and
flour imported, and upon corn, grain, meal, bread, bifcuit, and flour,
taken from the enemy; and to permit the importation of corn and
flour into* Great Britain *and* Ireland, *in neutral fhips; and to authorize his Majefty, with the advice of his privy council, to grant
and permit the exportation of fuch quantities of the commodities aforefaid, as may be neceffary for the fuftentation of any forces in the pay
of* Great Britain, *or of thofe of his Majefty's allies acting in fupport of the common caufe; and to prohibit the payment of any bounty
upon the exportation of any of the faid commodities, to be made during the continuance of this act,* as relates to the continuation of
the act made in the preceding feffion of parliament, for prohibiting the exportation of corn, malt, meal, flour, bread, bif-

and in act 30
Geo. 2.

cuit, and ftarch; and alfo the feveral claufes in the faid firft
mentioned act contained, for allowing the tranfportation of
wheat, barley, oats, meal, and flour, to the *Ifle of Man,* for the
ufe of the inhabitants there; to authorize his Majefty, by the
advice of his privy council, to order and permit the exportation
of fuch quantities of the commodities aforefaid, as may be neceffary for the fuftentation of any forces in the pay of *Great Britain,* or of thofe of his Majefty's allies, acting in fupport of the
common caufe; and to prohibit the payment of any bounty upon the exportation of any of the faid commodities; fhall be,

further con-
tinued to 24
Dec. 1759;
unlefs the
term fhall be
abridged by
parliament, or
by proclama-
tion, or order
of council.

and the fame are hereby further continued, from the expiration
thereof, until the twenty fourth day of *December,* one thoufand
feven hundred and fifty nine; unlefs fuch continuation fhall be
abridged or fhortened by any other act to be made in this prefent feffion of parliament, or unlefs fuch continuation fhall, during the recefs of parliament, be abridged or fhortened by his
Majefty's royal proclamation or proclamations, to be iffued with
the advice of his privy council, or his Majefty's order or orders
in council, to be publifhed in the *London Gazette;* which proclamation or proclamations, order or orders, his Majefty, during the recefs of parliament, and not otherwife, is hereby impowered, with the advice of his privy council, to iffue and make.

2   II. And

II. And be it further enacted by the authority aforesaid, That the said act made in the thirtieth year of his Majesty's reign, intituled, *An act to prohibit, for a limited time, the making of low wines and spirits from wheat, barley, malt, or any other sort of grain, or from any meal or flour,* shall be, and the same is hereby further continued, from the expiration thereof, until the said twenty fourth day of *December,* one thousand seven hundred and fifty nine.

Act 30 Geo. 2. continued to 24 Dec. 1759.

III. And be it further enacted by the authority aforesaid, That from and after the twenty fourth day of *December,* one thousand seven hundred and fifty eight, until the twenty fourth day of *December,* one thousand seven hundred and fifty nine, the several provisions made by the said act for prohibiting the making of low wines and spirits from wheat, barley, malt, or any other sort of grain, or from any meal or flour, shall, in like manner, extend to the prohibiting of the making of low wines and spirits from bran.

and the several provisions thereof extended to prohibiting the making of low wines and spirits from bran.

IV. *And whereas it would be of great relief and advantage to the inhabitants of the islands of* Jersey *and* Guernsey, *if a sufficient quantity of meal, flour, bread, and biscuit, was allowed to be transported to the said islands, for the only use of the inhabitants there, instead of the like quantity of wheat, malt, or barley, allowed by the said act made in the last session of parliament to be transported to those islands;* be it therefore further enacted by the authority aforesaid, That it shall be lawful, at any time or times before the expiration of this act, to transport, from the port of *Southampton* only, unto the said islands of *Jersey* and *Guernsey,* for the only use of the inhabitants there, any quantity or quantities of meal, flour, bread, or biscuit, in lieu of the like quantity or quantities of wheat, malt, or barley, allowed by the said act to be transported to the said islands, so that the whole quantity of wheat, malt, barley, meal, flour, bread, and biscuit, transported to the said islands, before the expiration of this act, doth not exceed the quantity of wheat, malt, or barley, limited by the said act to be transported to the said islands; and such transportation hereby authorized and allowed, shall be made under such and the like regulations, penalties, and forfeitures, as the transportation of wheat, malt, and barley, to the said islands is by the said act made subject; any thing in any former act or acts contained to the contrary notwithstanding.

Certain quantities of meal, flour, bread, or biscuit, may be transported from Southampton, for the use of the inhabitants of Jersey and Guernsey,

under certain regulations.

V. And be it further enacted by the authority aforesaid, That, in order to ascertain the amount of the said transportation, every seventy pounds avoirdupois weight of bread or biscuit, shall be deemed respectively, for the purposes of this act, equal to one bushel of wheat, malt, or barley.

70 lb. avoirdupois deemed equal to 1 bushel of wheat, &c.

VI. And be it further enacted by the authority aforesaid, That the commissioners of the customs for the time being shall, and they are hereby required, to give a full and true account in writing to both houses of parliament, at the beginning of the next session thereof, of all flour, meal, bread, and biscuit, that shall have been exported to each of the said islands of *Jersey* and *Guernsey,* by virtue or in pursuance of this act.

Return to be made to the parliament of the quantity of the said exports.

D d 2

CAP.

CAP. III.

An act for granting an aid to his Majesty by a land tax to be raifed in Great Britain, for the fervice of the year one thoufand feven hundred and fifty nine. 4s. in the pound.

CAP. IV.

An act for continuing and granting to his Majefty certain duties upon malt, mum, cyder, and perry, for the fervice of the year one thoufand feven hundred and fifty nine.

CAP. V.

An act for punifhing mutiny and defertion; and for the better payment of the army and their quarters.

CAP. VI.

An act to explain and amend an act paffed in the twenty fecond year of his prefent Majefty's reign, intituled, *An act for the more eafy and fpeedy recovery of fmall debts within the town and borough of Southwark, and the feveral parifhes of Saint Saviour, Saint Mary at Newington, Saint Mary Magdalen Bermondfey, Chrift Church, Saint Mary Lambeth, and Saint Mary at Rotherhith, in the county of Surry, and the feveral precincts and liberties of the fame*; and for extending the powers and provifions of the faid act to fuch part of the eaftern half of the hundred of Brixton, in the faid county; as is not included in the faid act.

CAP. VII.

An act to indemnify perfons who have omitted to qualify themfelves for offices and employments within the time limited by law; and for allowing further time for that purpofe.

Preamble, reciting the feveral qualifying acts of 1 Geo. 1, 13 Car. 2, 25 Car. 2, 13 Car. 2, 18 Geo. 2, 30 Geo. 2, and 31 Geo. 2. Further time to 28 Nov. 1759, allowed to perfons who have omitted to qualify themfelves, as the faid laws direct. Perfons qualifying themfelves in manner, and within the time, appointed, recapacitated and indemnified. Officers, &c. already avoided by judgment of a court, and filled up, confirmed. None indemnified where final judgment hath been given for the penalty incurred.

CAP. VIII.

An act for taking off the prohibition of the exportation of corn, malt, meal, flour, bread, bifcuit, and ftarch.

Act of this feffion.

WHEREAS *by an act made in this feffion of parliament, intituled,* An act to continue, for a farther time, the prohibition of the exportation of corn, malt, meal, flour, bread, bifcuit, and ftarch; and alfo to continue, for a farther time, the prohibition of the making of low wines and fpirits from wheat, barley, malt, or any other fort of grain, or from meal or flour; and to prohibit, for a limited time, the making of low wines and fpirits from bran; *it was enacted, That the prohibition of the exportation of corn, malt, meal, flour, bread, bifcuit, and ftarch, and likewife the prohibition of the payment of any bounty upon the exportation of any of the faid commodities, fhould be further continued until the twenty fourth day of* December, *one thoufand feven hundred and fifty nine, unlefs fuch continuation fhould be abridged or fhortened by any other act to be made in this prefent feffion of parliament, or in*

fuch

such other manner as by the said act is provided : and whereas it is expedient for the publick service, that the continuance of so much of the said act as relates to the prohibition of the exportation of corn, malt, meal, flour, bread, biscuit, and starch, and of the payment of any bounty on the exportation of any of the said commodities, should be abridged and shortened; be it enacted by the King's most excellent majesty, by and with the advice and consent of the lords spiritual and temporal, and commons, in this present parliament assembled, and by the authority of the same, That such continuance shall, from and after the twenty fifth day of *March*, one thousand seven hundred and fifty nine, cease and determine.

The exporta-
tion of corn,
malt, &c. pro-
visionally al-
lowed,

II. Provided always, and be it enacted by the authority aforesaid, That if, at any time before the twenty fifth day of *December*, one thousand seven hundred and fifty nine, his Majesty shall judge it to be most for the benefit and advantage of this kingdom to stop the exportation of the said commodities, it shall be lawful for his Majesty, by his royal proclamation, to be issued by the advice of his privy council, or by his Majesty's order in council, to be published in the *London Gazette*, to prohibit and stop the exportation of the said commodities, until the twenty fifth day of *December*, one thousand seven hundred and fifty nine ; except only in such cases in which the said commodities were allowed to be exported during such continuance of the said act of this session of parliament.

unless his Ma-
jesty by, pro-
clamation, or
order in coun-
cil, shall stop
the exporta-
tion thereof,
until 25 Dec.
1759.

Exception.

C A P. IX.
An act for the regulation of his Majesty's marine forces while on shore.

C A P. X.
An act for granting to his Majesty a subsidy of poundage upon certain goods and merchandizes to be imported into this kingdom; and an additional inland duty on coffee and chocolate; and for raising the sum of six millions six hundred thousand pounds, by way of annuities and a lottery, to be charged on the said subsidy and additional inland duty.

Most gracious Sovereign,

WE, your Majesty's most dutiful and loyal subjects, the commons of *Great Britain* in parliament assembled, towards raising, by the most easy means, the necessary supplies to defray your Majesty's publick expences, have freely and voluntarily resolved to give and grant unto your Majesty the several subsidies, rates, and duties, herein after mentioned; and do most humbly beseech your Majesty, that it may be enacted; and be it enacted by the King's most excellent majesty, by and with the advice and consent of the lords spiritual, and temporal and commons, in this present parliament assembled, and by the authority of the same, That from and after the fifth day of *April* one thousand seven hundred and fifty nine, there shall be raised, levied,

Preamble.

An additional
subsidy of 12d.
in the pound
granted upon

D d 3

certain goods
and merchan-
dizes import-
ed,

levied, collected, and paid unto and for the ufe of his Majefty, his heirs, and fucceffors, for and upon all tobacco, foreign linnens, fugar, and other grocery, as the fame is underftood in the books of rates, except currants; *Eaft India* goods, except coffee and raw filks; foreign brandy and fpirits, except rum of the produce of the *British* fugar plantations; and paper, which fhall be imported or brought into the kingdom of *Great Britain,* a

as the fame are
valued in the
books of
rates;

further fubfidy of poundage of twelve pence in the pound, according to the value or rate refpectively fet upon each of the faid commodities by the feveral books of rates, or any act or acts of parliament relating thereunto; which fubfidy fhall be paid by the importer of fuch goods and merchandizes, before the landing thereof, over and above all other duties charged or chargeable thereupon.

and to be le-
vied and paid
into the exche-
quer,

II. And be it further enacted and declared by the authority aforefaid, That the faid fubfidy of poundage by this act impofed, fhall be raifed, levied, collected, and paid into his Majefty's exchequer, for the purpofes in this act expreffed, in fuch and like form and manner, and with fuch allowances, difcounts, drawbacks, and exemptions, and under fuch penalties and forfeitures, and according to fuch rules, methods, and directions, as are

as the fubfidy
of 5l. per cent.
granted by 21
Geo. 2. &c.

prefcribed or appointed for raifing, levying, collecting, and paying, the fubfidy of five pounds *per centum,* granted by an act made in the twenty firft year of the reign of his prefent Majefty, intituled, *An act for granting to his Majefty a fubfidy of poundage upon all goods and merchandizes to be imported into this kingdom ; and for raifing a certain fum of money by annuities and a lottery, to be charged on the faid fubfidy ; and for repealing fo much of an act made in the twentieth year of his prefent Majefty's reign, as enacts,* That prize goods and merchandize may be exported without paying any duty of cuftom or excife for the fame; or as are contained in or by any other act or acts of parliament by the faid act of the twenty firft year of the reign of his prefent Majefty, referred unto, or any of them; and all and every the powers, authorities, rules, directions, penalties, forfeitures, claufes, matters, and things, now in force, contained in the faid act made in the twenty firft year of his prefent Majefty's reign, or in any other act or acts of parliament in the faid act referred unto, or any of them, for the raifing, levying, collecting, and paying, the fubfidies thereby granted, fhall be in full force, and be duly obferved, practifed, and put in execution, throughout this kingdom, for raifing, levying, collecting, and paying, the fubfidy of poundage of twelve pence in the pound by this act granted, as fully and effectually to all intents and purpofes, as if the fame or the like powers, authorities, rules, directions, penalties, forfeitures, claufes, matters, and things, were particularly repeated and re-enacted in the body of this prefent act.

Prize goods
are to be
charged only
with the du-
ties payable by
Act 30 Geo. 2.

III. Provided neverthelefs, That if any of the goods and merchandizes, charged with the fubfidy by this act impofed, have been, or, during the continuance of this prefent war with *France,* fhall be, taken and brought into any port of this kingdom

dom by any of his Majesty's ships or vessels of war, or by any private ships or vessels of war, and shall be condemned as lawful prize, the same shall not be liable to any other or further duty than what they are respectively charged with, by an act made in the thirtieth year of his present Majesty, intituled, *An act for the relief and encouragement of the captors of prizes, with respect to the bringing and landing prize goods in this kingdom*; unless the said goods and merchandizes so taken and condemned as prize, shall, for home consumption, be taken out of any warehouse wherein they are secured under the provisions of the said act; in which case, the person or persons so taking out the said goods and merchandizes shall first pay up the subsidy by this act granted, as well as all other duties payable to his Majesty thereon.

unless taken out of the warehouses for home consumption.

IV. Provided also, and it is the true intent and meaning of this act, that the importers of tobacco shall, upon paying down the subsidy hereby granted, have the same allowance with respect to this subsidy, as they are intitled to by any law now in force upon tobacco imported; but in case the said subsidy hereby granted, shall not be paid down as aforesaid, and the said importers shall become bound to his Majesty, his heirs, or successors, with one or more sufficient sureties, to be approved of by the collector of the port where the tobacco shall be imported, with the consent of the comptroller of such port, in one or more bond or bonds, at the election of the importer, for payment of the said subsidy within eighteen months, to commence at the end of thirty days after the master's report of the ship, or to commence from the merchant's entry of the goods within those thirty days, which shall first happen; that then the importers shall, in such case, have, and be intitled to, the same allowances and discounts, with respect to the subsidy hereby granted, or for paying the same before the bonds become due, as they are at this time intitled to by any law now in force upon bonds given for tobacco imported; any thing herein contained to the contrary thereof in any wise notwithstanding.

Allowance to be made to the importer of tobacco, on paying down the duty. Bond to be given on non-payment of the duty;

and the importers to have the usual allowances and discounts.

V. Provided always, and it is hereby enacted and declared by the authority aforesaid, That in all cases where any goods or merchandizes, that have paid the subsidy hereby granted, shall at any time or times be again exported by any merchant or merchants, within three years from the importation thereof, the subsidy by this act granted, and which shall have been actually paid for such goods, wares, or merchandizes, shall, without any delay or reward, be paid unto such merchant or merchants who shall export the same, or the security vacated; except for such goods or merchandizes, as by any former act or acts of parliament it is declared no drawback shall be paid or allowed upon exportation of.

Drawback of the duty allowed upon the exportation of goods within 3 years.

Exception.

VI. Provided always, and be it enacted by the authority aforesaid, That so much money as shall, from time to time, be paid for the duties granted by this or any former act or acts of parliament whatsoever, for any quantities of paper which

Drawback of the duty allowed on paper used in printing books

D d 4

shall

in the learned languages in both univerfities;

fhall be ufed in printing any books in the latin, greek, oriental, or northern languages, within the two univerfities of *Oxford* or *Cambridge*, or either of them, by permiffion of the vice chancellors of the fame refpectively, fhall and may be drawn back and repaid in fuch manner as is prefcribed by an act made in the tenth year of the reign of Queen *Anne*, intituled, *An act for laying feveral duties upon all foap and paper made in* Great Britain, *or imported*

as is prefcribed by act 10.° Anne.

into the fame; and upon chequered and ftriped linens imported; and upon certain filks, callicoes, linens, and ftuffs, printed, painted, or ftained; and upon feveral kinds of ftampt vellum, parchment, and paper; and upon certain printed papers, pamphlets, and advertifements, for raifing the fum of eighteen hundred thoufand pounds, by way of lottery, towards her Majefty's fupply; and for licenfing an additional number of hackney chairs; and for charging certain flocks of cards and dice; and for better fecuring her Majefty's duties to arife in the office for the ftamp duties by licences for marriages and otherwife; and for relief of perfons who have not claimed their lottery tickets in due time, or have loft exchequer bills, or lottery tickets; and for borrowing money upon flock. part of the capital of the South Sea *company, for the ufe of the publick.*

Like drawback allowed on paper ufed in printing books in the learned languages in the univerfities of Scotland.

VII. Provided always, and be it enacted by the authority aforefaid, That fo much money as fhall, from time to time, be paid for the duties granted by this or any former act or acts of parliament whatfoever, for any quantities of paper which fhall be ufed in printing any books in the latin, greek, oriental, or northern languages, within the univerfities of *Scotland*, or any of them, by permiffion of the principal of the fame refpectively, fhall and may be drawn back and repaid in fuch manner as is prefcribed by an act made in the tenth year of the reign of Queen *Anne*, intituled, *An act for laying feveral duties upon all foap and paper made in* Great Britain, *or imported into the fame; and upon chequered and ftriped linens imported; and upon certain filks, callicoes, linens, and ftuffs, printed, painted, or ftained; and upon feveral kinds of ftampt vellum, parchment, and paper; and upon certain printed papers, pamphlets, and advertifements, for raifing the fum of eighteen hundred thoufand pounds, by way of a lottery, towards her Majefty's fupply; and for licenfing an additional number of hackney chairs; and for charging certain flocks of cards and dice; and for better fecuring her Majefty's duties to arife in the office for the ftamp duties by licences for marriages and otherwife; and for relief of perfons who have not claimed their lottery tickets in due time, or have loft exchequer bills, or lottery tickets; and for borrowing money upon flock, part of the capital of the* South Sea *company, for the ufe of the publick.*

A Drawback of 3s. per hundred weight allowed on fugar refined in Great Britain, and exported, &c.

VIII. And be it further enacted by the authority aforefaid, That for every hundred weight of fugar imported into *Great Britain*, after the faid fifth day of *April* one thoufand feven hundred and fifty nine, and refined there (and fo in proportion for a greater or leffer quantity) that fhall be exported out of this kingdom, after the faid fifth day of *April* one thoufand feven hundred and fifty nine, during the continuance of this act, there fhall be repaid at the cuftom-houfe to the exporter, within thirty

days

days after the demand thereof, the fum of three fhillings, over and above the prefent bounties; oath being firft made by the refiner that the fugar fo exported was produced from brown and mufcovado fugar charged by this act, and that, as he verily believes, the fame was imported from his Majefty's plantations in *America*, and the duty duly paid at the time of the importation thereof, the exporter making oath that the fame was duly exported, and his Majefty's fearchers alfo certifying the fhipping thereof, and all other requifites being performed according to the refpective books of rates.

Refiner to make oath.

Exporter to make oath. Searcher to certify.

IX. And be it further enacted and declared by the authority aforefaid, That in the office of the auditor of the receipt of the exchequer, a book or books fhall be provided and kept, in which all the money arifing from the faid additional fubfidy of poundage of twelve pence in the pound, and paid into the faid receipt, fhall be entered feparate and apart from all other monies paid or payable to his Majefty, his heirs, or fucceffors, upon any account whatfoever; and the faid money fo arifing from the faid additional fubfidy of poundage of twelve pence in the pound, and paid into the faid receipt of the exchequer, fhall be part of the fund eftablifhed for the feveral purpofes herein after mentioned.

Books to be kept for entering the monies coming in by this act.

X. And be it further enacted and declared by the authority aforefaid, That from and after the fifth day of *April* one thoufand feven hundred and fifty nine, there fhall be charged, levied, collected, and paid, unto and for the ufe of his Majefty, his heirs, and fucceffors, for and upon all coffee to be fold in *Great Britain*, by wholefale or retail, and upon all chocolate to be made or fold in *Great Britain*, an additional inland duty, to be paid by the refpective fellers of fuch coffee, and by the refpective makers or fellers of fuch chocolate; that is to fay, For and upon all coffee to be fold in *Great Britain*, an additional duty of one fhilling *per* pound weight averdupoife; and in that proportion for a greater or leffer quantity, over and above the prefent inland duty, and over and above all cuftoms and duties payable upon the importation thereof; and for and upon all chocolate to be made or fold in *Great Britain*, an additional duty of nine pence *per* pound weight averdupoife; and in that proportion for a greater or leffer quantity, over and above the prefent inland duty payable thereupon.

An additional inland duty to be paid of 1s. per lb. on coffee.

and 9d. per lb. on chocolate.

XI. And be it further enacted and declared by the authority aforefaid, That the faid additional inland duties hereby granted to his Majefty, fhall be raifed, levied, collected, and paid, in the fame manner, and under fuch management, and under fuch penalties and forfeitures, and with fuch powers for recovering the fame, and by fuch rules, ways, and methods, as the former inland duties payable to his Majefty upon coffee and chocolate are raifed, levied, collected, and paid, as fully, and to all intents and purpofes, as if the feveral claufes, powers, directions, penalties, and forfeitures, relating thereto, were particularly repeated, and again enacted, in the body of this prefent act.

The faid duties on coffee and chocolate to be levied and paid, as the former inland duties payable thereon.

XII. And be it further enacted and declared by the authority afore-

Coffee lodged in warehouses on 6 April, 1759, to be charged with the new additional duty;

aforesaid, That all the coffee which, on the sixth day of April one thousand seven hundred and fifty nine, shall be lodged or secured in any warehouse or warehouses in pursuance of the directions of any former act or acts of parliament in that behalf made, shall be, and is hereby charged with the said additional duty of one shilling per pound, to be paid in like manner as the former inland duty on coffee is directed to be paid.

as also the stock in hand of coffee and chocolate (except for private use)

XIII. And be it further enacted and declared, That all the coffee and chocolate which any dealer in, or seller of, coffee, or any dealer in, or maker or seller of, chocolate, in Great Britain (other than, and except such persons who make chocolate for their family use, and not for sale, with respect only to their stock in hand) or any person or persons in trust for him, her, or them, or for his, her, or their use, shall be possessed of, or interested in, upon the said sixth day of April one thousand seven hundred and fifty nine, shall be, and is hereby, charged with the said additional inland duty of one shilling per pound for the said coffee, and nine pence per pound for the said chocolate; and that every

90 lb. of roasted coffee to be charged after the rate of 112 lb. of raw coffee. Duty to be paid into the office of excise.

ninety pounds weight of roasted coffee, by reason of the common decrease by shrinking in the roasting thereof, shall be charged after the rate of one hundred and twelve pounds of raw coffee; and so in proportion for a greater or less quantity; which said additional inland duty for the stock in hand shall be paid by the respective sellers of coffee, and such makers or sellers of chocolate as aforesaid, to the proper officer of excise for the said inland duties, at the office of excise within the limits of which they shall respectively inhabit; that is to say, All such duties as shall arise within the limits of the chief office of excise in London, shall be paid within fourteen days next after the said fifth day of April one thousand seven hundred and fifty nine; and all such duties as shall arise in any other part of Great Britain, shall be paid within six weeks next after the said fifth day of April one thousand seven hundred and fifty nine.

Stock in hand of chocolate (except for private use) to be brought to the proper offices in order to be stampt.

XIV. And it is hereby further enacted by the authority aforesaid, That all such chocolate as shall, on the sixth day of April one thousand seven hundred and fifty nine, be in the custody or possession of any maker or seller of chocolate, other than such makers as aforesaid, or of any person or persons in trust, or for the use, of him, her, or them, within the limits of the chief offices of excise in London, shall, within fourteen days next after the the said fifth day of April one thousand seven hundred and fifty nine, and all such chocolate as shall, on the sixth day of April one thousand seven hundred and fifty nine, be in the possession of any maker or seller of chocolate (other than such makers as aforesaid) or of any person or persons in trust, or for the use, of him, her, or them, in any other part of Great Britain, shall, within six weeks next after the said fifth day of April one thousand seven hundred and fifty nine, be brought to the respective offices where the entries for the same shall be, or ought to have been, made, and shall then have some new and additional stamp, mark, impression, or device, affixed thereon, to denote that it has been charg-

charged with the said additional inland duty; which stamp, mark, impression, or device, and all other stamps, marks, impressions, or devices, which shall be made use of to denote the charging the said additional duties, either on the stock in hand, or any future stock, the said respective commissioners of excise, and for the said inland duties, for the time being, are hereby directed to provide, in such manner as to them shall seem meet; which stamps, marks, impressions, or devices, or any of them, may, from time to time, be varied or altered in such manner as the said commissioners shall judge most proper; and if any person or persons whatsoever shall, at any time, counterfeit or forge, or cause to be counterfeited or forged, any such mark, stamp, impression, or device, which shall be made use of in pursuance of this act, or shall utter, vend, or sell, any chocolate with such counterfeit mark, stamp, impression or device thereon, knowing the same to be counterfeited; or shall, upon any chocolate which has not been duly entered with the proper officer, and for which the inland duties has not been duly charged or paid, fix or place any paper or papers having on it or them the impression of such mark or marks, stamp or stamps; or shall, in such paper or papers, inclose such chocolate as shall not have been duly entered with the proper officer, and for which the inland duties have not been duly charged or paid, with intent to defraud his Majesty of his inland duties for and respect of such chocolate; that then every such person or persons so offending therein shall, for every such offence, forfeit and lose the sum of five hundred pounds, and also shall be committed to the next county gaol, there to remain for twelve months without bail or mainprize.

New stamps to be provided on this occasion;

which may be altered from time to time. The penalty of counterfeiting or forging the same,

or being guilty of any fraud therein;

500l. and one year's imprisonment.

XV. And it is hereby further enacted by the authority aforesaid, That if any person or persons having, on the said sixth day of *April*, one thousand seven hundred and fifty nine, in his or their custody or possession, any stock or quantity of coffee or chocolate chargeable by this act with the said additional inland duties, shall clandestinely remove or carry away, or cause or suffer to be removed or carried away, the same, or any part thereof, before his Majesty's duties thereupon shall be paid as aforesaid; or shall fraudulently conceal or hide any part of his, her, or their said stock of coffee or chocolate; or shall neglect or refuse to bring or send, within the respective times appointed, his, her, or their said stock of chocolate to the respective offices where the entries for the same shall have been, or ought to have been, made, in order to have such chocolate stamped as aforesaid; or shall, after the said fifth day of *April*, one thousand seven hundred and fifty nine, sell or vend, or offer or expose to sale, any of their stock of chocolate, without being first marked or stamped to denote the payment of the said additional inland duty; that then, and in each and every of the said cases, he, she, or they, so offending, for every such offence, shall forfeit the sum of twenty shillings for every pound weight of such chocolate, and also the chocolate so found after the end of the said fourteen days, or six weeks respectively, without such mark,

The penalty of secreting or concealing the stock in hand of coffee or chocolate;

or not sending the chocolate to be new stampt;

or vending any without being duly stampt;

20s. per lb. and forfeiture of the chocolate.

stamp,

ftamp, impreffion, or device thereon, fhall be forfeited, and may be feifed.

XVI. *And whereas the provifion by the former law for packing up chocolate in pounds, has not been found fufficient to prevent frauds, and the permitting the fale of chocolate in fmall quantities not packed up and fecured in the manner herein after directed, has tended to encourage the clandestine and fraudulent making and felling thereof;* be it further enacted by the authority aforefaid, That all chocolate which, from and after the fifth day of *April,* one thoufand feven hundred and fifty nine, fhall be made in *Great Britain,* fhall be packed up, and a ftamp or mark put upon the fame, in manner herein after mentioned; that is to fay, all fuch makers or proprietors of chocolate, which fhall be made in *Great Britain,* fhall, from time to time, and at the refpective times and places, when and where they are required to make entries of the chocolate, by or for them refpectively made as aforefaid, produce all the chocolate contained in fuch entry, at the refpective offices where fuch entries are or ought to be made, to the refpective officers who are, or fhall be appointed for the receiving fuch entries, on pain of forfeiting the fum of twenty fhillings for every pound weight of fuch chocolate which fhall not then be produced; which chocolate fhall be brought, inclofed, packed, and tied up with thread, in papers, which faid papers fhall each of them contain either one pound, or half a pound, or a quarter of a pound weight of chocolate, and not more or lefs (at the election of the makers or proprietors) each of which papers fo tied up, fhall, by an officer appointed, or to be appointed, by the refpective commiffioners of excife and inland duties for that purpofe, or the major part of them refpectively, have fuch a mark, ftamp, impreffion, or device, affixed thereon, as fhall be by the faid refpective commiffioners for the time being, from time to time, devifed or appointed for that purpofe.

XVII. And it is hereby further enacted by the authority aforefaid, That if any perfon or perfons fhall fell chocolate in any lefs quantity than a quarter of a pound, or fhall fell and deliver any chocolate to any perfon not being at the time of the fale and delivery thereof duly marked or ftamped, or not being at that time inclofed, packed, and tied up with the identical piece of thread which is directed to be ufed in tying up the chocolate in a paper, before the fame is to have the mark, ftamp, impreffion, or device, affixed thereon, or fhall fell and deliver any chocolate, whereof the thread or ftamped label inclofing the fame at the time of the fale and delivery thereof, fhall have been broke or opened in any manner whatfoever, every perfon or perfons fo offending, fhall, for every fuch offence refpectively, forfeit twenty pounds.

XVIII. And be it further enacted and declared by the authority aforefaid, That in the office of the auditor of the receipt of the exchequer, a book or books fhall be provided and kept, in which all the monies arifing by the faid additional inland duties upon coffee and chocolate, and paid into the faid receipt, fhall be
entered

Rule to be obferved in packing up, and ftamping chocolate.

All chocolate entered, is to be duly brought to the proper offices, on forfeiture of 20 s. per lb. and to be tied up with thread in papers either of one pound, one half pound, or a quarter of a pound, which are to be feverally ftampt by the proper officers;

and none to be fold in lefs quantities than a quarter of a pound, nor without being ftampt, and tied up; and having the original thread and ftamp unbroken and un-opened; on forfeiture of 20 l.

Books to be kept for entering the duties apart from all others.

entered feparate and apart from all other monies paid or payable to his Majefty, his heirs, and fucceffors, upon any account whatfoever; and the faid money fo arifing from the faid additional duties, and paid into the faid receipt of exchequer, fhall be part of the fund eftablifhed for the feveral purpofes herein after mentioned.

XIX. And be it further enacted and declared by the authority aforefaid, That the feveral annuities which by this act are herein after directed to attend, as well the principal fum of fix millions fix hundred thoufand pounds, and the additional capital of five pounds to be added to every one hundred pounds thereof, as the additional capital which will arife by ten pounds, to be given in and by a lottery ticket to each fubfcriber, for and upon every one hundred pounds, advanced and paid towards the faid fum of fix millions fix hundred thoufand pounds, fhall be charged and chargeable upon, and payable out of the fubfidies, rates, and duties, compofing the fund hereby eftablifhed for the payment thereof, and the faid fubfidies, rates, and duties, are hereby appropriated for that purpofe accordingly. *These duties appropriated for the payment of the annuities chargeable on the monies borrowed on the credit of this act.*

XX. *And whereas the commons of* Great Britain *in parliament affembled, have refolved, That towards raifing the fupply granted to his Majefty in this prefent feffion of parliament, the fum of fix millions fix hundred thoufand pounds, be raifed by transferrable annuities, after the rate of three pounds* per centum per annum; *and that an additional capital of fifteen pounds be added to every one hundred pounds advanced; which additional capital fhall confift of ten pounds in a lottery ticket given to each fubfcriber on every one hundred pounds advanced, and of five pounds in like transferrable annuities, after the rate of three pounds* per centum per annum: *and whereas purfuant to, and upon the feveral terms and conditions expreffed in the faid refolution, feveral perfons have, in books opened at the bank of* England *for that purpofe, fubfcribed together the whole of the faid fum of fix millions fix hundred thoufand pounds, and made depofits of fifteen pounds* per centum, *on the refpective fums by them fo fubfcribed, with the cafhiers of the bank of* England: *and whereas feveral of the faid fubfcribers may have already paid, or may hereafter pay unto the faid cafhiers, the whole or fome further parts of the fums by them refpectively fubfcribed, previous to the days limited and appointed for the faid refpective payments*; be it therefore enacted by the authority aforefaid, That it fhall and may be lawful to and for all fuch fubfcribers who have made depofits with, or payments of further parts to the faid cafhiers, as aforefaid, to advance and pay, and they are hereby required to advance and pay, unto the faid cafhier or cafhiers of the faid governor and company of the bank of *England*, the feveral remainders of the fums by them refpectively fubfcribed, towards the faid fum of fix millions fix hundred thoufand pounds, at or before the refpective times or days, and in the proportions herein after limited and appointed on that behalf; that is to fay, the further fum of ten pounds *per centum*, being part of the fum fo remaining, on or before the thirtieth day of *March*, in the year *Times of payments in refpect of the fum of 6,600,000l. fubfcribed towards annuities.*

'one

one thoufand feven hundred and fifty nine; the further fum of ten pounds *per centum*, other part thereof, on or before the twenty feventh day of *April*, then next following; the further fum of ten pounds *per centum*, other part thereof, on or before thirty firft day of *May*, then next following; the further fum of ten pounds *per centum*, other part thereof, on or before the twenty eighth day of *June*, then next following; the further fum of fifteen pounds *per centum*, other part thereof, on or before the twenty feventh day of *July*, then next following; the further fum of ten pounds *per centum*, other part thereof, on or before the thirty firft day of *Auguft*, then next following; the further fum of ten pounds *per centum*, other part thereof, on or before the twenty eighth day of *September*, then next following; and the remaining fum of ten pounds *per centum*, on or before the twenty fixth day of *October*, then next following.

Contributors making their payments previous to the times limited,

to be allowed intereft for the fame, &c.

XXI. And be it further enacted by the authority aforefaid, That all fuch fubfcribers or contributors, their executors, adminiftrators, fucceffors, and affigns, paying in the whole, or any part of the fums by them refpectively fubfcribed, previous to the days appointed for the refpective payments herein before directed, in refpect to their proportionable fhare of the faid fum of fix millions fix hundred thoufand pounds, fhall be intitled to an allowance of fo much money as the intereft of the feveral fums fo previoufly paid, after the rate of three pounds *per centum per annum*, fhall amount to, from the days on which fuch previous payments fhall have been actually made, to the refpective times on which fuch payments are directed to be made; fuch allowance to be paid by the faid cafhier or cafhiers, out of the monies contributed towards the faid fum of fix millions fix hundred thoufand pounds, as foon as fuch refpective contributors, their executors, adminiftrators, fucceffors, and affigns, fhall have completed their payments herein before directed to be made.

Annuities to bear 3 l. per cent.

to commence from 5 Jan. 1759.

XXII. And be it further enacted by the authority aforefaid, That each and every fuch fubfcriber or fubfcribers, contributor or contributors, fhall be intitled to an annuity after the rate of three pounds *per centum per annum*, for and upon every one hundred pounds by him or them refpectively fubfcribed, advanced, and paid; and alfo to a like annuity of three pounds *per centum per annum*, for and upon an additional capital of five pounds, to be added to every one hundred pounds, by fuch fubfcriber or fubfcribers, contributor or contributors refpectively, advanced and paid; which faid annuities fhall commence and be computed from the fifth day of *January*, one thoufand feven hundred and fifty nine, and fhall be paid by half-yearly payments, by even and equal portions, on the fifth day of *July*, and the fifth day of *January*, in every year.

Subfcribers, for every 100 l. fubfcribed, intitled to a lottery ticket,

XXIII. And be it further enacted by the authority aforefaid, That each and every fuch fubfcriber or fubfcribers, contributor or contributors, fhall, for and upon every one hundred pounds by him or them refpectively fubfcribed, advanced, and paid, be likewife intitled to one ticket in the lottery, herein after mentioned;

tioned; which said ticket will be equal in value to, and is to be
taken and accepted as an addition of ten pounds capital, on every
one hundred pounds subscribed, advanced, and paid, as aforesaid, which sum shall carry an annuity at the rate of three pounds
per centum per annum; and the said annuity shall commence and to carry 3 l.
be computed from the fifth day of *January*, one thousand seven per cent.
hundred and sixty, and shall be paid by half-yearly payments
on the fifth day of *July*, and the fifth day of *January*, in every
year.

XXIV. And be it further enacted, That all the annuities a- Annuities
foresaid, shall be transferrable at the bank of *England*; subject transferrable.
nevertheless to such redemption as is hereafter mentioned.

XXV. And be it further enacted by the authority aforesaid, Cashier to give
That the cashier or cashiers of the governor and company of the receipts for
bank of *England*, who shall have received, or shall receive any money paid
part of the said contributions, towards the said sum of six mil- in,
lions six hundred thousand pounds, shall give a receipt or receipts in writing to every such contributor, for all such sums,
and that the receipts to be given shall be assignable by indorse- the same made
ment thereupon made at any time before the fifth day of *January*, assignable.
one thousand seven hundred and sixty, and no longer.

XXVI. Provided always, That such cashier or cashiers shall Cashier to give
give security to the good liking of any three or more of the com- security;
missioners of the treasury for the time being, or the high treasurer for the time being, for duly answering and paying into the
receipt of his Majesty's exchequer, for the public use, all the
monies which they have already received, and shall hereafter receive, from time to time, of and for the said sum of six millions
six hundred thousand pounds, and for accounting duly for the
same, and for performance of the trust hereby in them reposed; and to pay in
and shall, from time to time, pay all such monies so received, the monies
and account for the same, in the exchequer, according to the into the ex-
due course thereof. chequer.

XXVII. And be it further enacted by the authority aforesaid, Cashiers, on
That the said cashier or cashiers shall, and they are hereby au- receipt of 25 l.
thorized and required, upon the payment of twenty five pounds per cent. to
for every one hundred pounds so subscribed as aforesaid, and not give a note
before, to give a note or writing signed by him or them to such for the deli-
contributor or contributors, obliging himself or themselves to very of 1 lot-
deliver to such contributor or contributors, or their assigns, a tery ticket for
ticket in the lottery herein after-mentioned, of the value of ten every 100 l.
pounds, by way of additional capital, for every one hundred subscribed.
pounds by them respectively subscribed towards raising the sum
of six millions six hundred thousand pounds, for the purposes a-
foresaid, as soon as the managers and directors to be appointed
for preparing and delivering out the said tickets in the said lottery, shall deliver to the said cashier or cashiers the books comprehending the said tickets.

XXVIII. And be it further enacted by the authority afore- Treasury to
said, That it shall and may be lawful for three or more of the apply the mo-
commissioners of the treasury, or the high treasurer for the time nies to the services voted by
being, the commons.

being, to issue and apply, from time to time, all such sums of money as shall be so paid into the receipt of his Majesty's ex-chequer by the said cashier or cashiers, to such services as shall then have been voted by the commons of *Great Britain*, in this present session of parliament.

Contributors names, &c. to be entered in the office of the accomptant general of the bank.

XXIX. And be it further enacted by the authority aforesaid, That in the office of the accomptant general of the governor and company of the bank of *England* for the time being, a book or books shall be provided and kept, in which the names of the contributors shall be fairly entered; which book or books the said respective contributors, their respective executors, admini-strators, and assigns, shall and may, from time to time, and at all seasonable times, resort to and inspect, without any fee or charge; and that the said accomptant general shall, on or before the fifth day of *July*, one thousand seven hundred and sixty one, transmit an attested duplicate fairly written on paper of the said book or books, into the office of the auditor of the receipt of his Majesty's exchequer, there to remain for ever.

Duplicate thereof to be transmitted into the au-ditor's office.

The monies arising by the duties of this act appropri-ated to pay-ment of the annuities.

XXX. And be it further enacted by the authority aforesaid, That such contributors duly paying the whole sum subscribed, at or before the respective times in this act limited in that behalf, and their respective executors, administrators, and assigns, shall have, receive, and enjoy, and be entitled, by virtue of this act, to have, receive, and enjoy, the said several annuities by this act granted, in respect of the sum so subscribed out of the mo-nies appropriated by this act for payment thereof, and shall have good and sure interests and estates therein, according to the several provisions in this act contained; and that the said annuities shall be free from all taxes, charges and impositions whatsoever.

Contributors not making good their payments within the times limited, to forfeit their deposits.

XXXI. Provided always, That in case any such contributors who have already deposited with, or shall hereafter pay to, the the said cashiers, any sum or sums of money at the times, and in the manner before-mentioned, in part of the sum so by them respectively subscribed, or their respective executors, administra-tors, and assigns, shall not advance and pay to the said cashier or cashiers, the residue of the sums so subscribed, at the times, and in the manner before-mentioned; then, and in every such case, so much of the respective sums so subscribed as shall have been actually paid in part thereof, to the said cashier or cashiers, shall be forfeited for the benefit of the publick; any thing in this act contained to the contrary thereof in any wise notwith-standing.

Accomptant general to give credit for the sums nam-ed in the cer-tificates;

XXXII. And be it further enacted by the authority aforesaid, That the said accomptant general for the bank of *England*, for the time being, shall, in a book or books to be provided and kept for that purpose, give credit on or before the first day of *July* next, to the said respective contributors, and their respec-tive executors, administrators, and assigns, for the principal sums by them respectively subscribed and paid, and the said ad-ditional capital of five pounds *per centum* by this act allowed there-

thereon; and the perfons to whofe credit fuch principal fums with the faid additional capital fhall be fo placed, their refpective executors, adminiftrators, and affigns, fhall and may have power to affign and transfer the fame, or any part, fhare, or proportion thereof, to any other perfon or perfons, or body or bodies politick or corporate whatfoever, in other books to be provided and kept by the faid accomptant general for that purpofe; and every principal fum fo affigned and transferred, fhall carry an annuity after the rate of three pounds *per centum per annum*, and fhall be taken and deemed to be ftock transferrable according to the true intent and meaning of this act, until redemption thereof by parliament, according to a provifo herein after contained for that purpofe.

which may be transferred,

and carry 3 l. per cent. intereft.

XXXIII. *And whereas it is intended that every contributor of the fum of one hundred pounds, towards raifing the faid fum of fix millions fix hundred thoufand pounds, fhall have, and be intitled unto, an additional capital of ten pounds in a lottery ticket; which tickets are to be prepared, and a lottery to be drawn, in manner herein after mentioned*; be it therefore further enacted by the authority aforefaid, That fuch perfons as the commiffioners of his Majefty's treafury, or any three or more of them now being, or the high treafurer, or any three or more of the commiffioners of the treafury for the time being, fhall nominate or appoint, fhall be managers and directors for preparing and delivering out tickets, and to overfee the drawing of lots, and to order, do, and perform, fuch other matters and things as are hereafter in and by this act directed and appointed by fuch managers and directors to be done and performed; and that fuch managers or directors fhall meet together from time to time, at fome publick office or place for the execution of the powers and trufts in them repofed by this act; and that the faid managers or directors, or fo many of them as fhall be prefent at any fuch meeting, or the major part of them, fhall caufe books to be prepared, in which every leaf fhall be divided or diftinguifhed into three columns, and upon the innermoft of the faid three columns there fhall be printed fixty fix thoufand tickets, to be numbered one, two, three, and fo onwards, in an arithmetical progreffion, where the common excefs is to be one, until they rife to and for the number of fixty fix thoufand; and upon the middle column in every of the faid books fhall be printed fixty fix thoufand tickets of the fame breadth and form, and numbered in like manner; and in the extreme column of the faid books there fhall be printed a third rank or feries of tickets, of the fame number with thofe of the other two columns; which tickets fhall feverally be of an oblong figure, and in the faid books fhall be joined with oblique lines, flourifhes, or devices, in fuch manner as the faid managers and directors, or the major part of them, fhall think moft fafe and convenient; and that every ticket in the third or extreme column of the faid books fhall have written or printed thereupon (befides the number of fuch ticket, and the prefent year of our Lord Chrift) words to this effect:

Managers and directors of the lottery to be appointed by the treafury.

Method of the lottery books.

THIS *ticket will intitle the bearer thereof to fix pounds, or to a better chance, in a joint flock of annuities, after the rate of three pounds* per centum per annum, *transferrable at the bank of* England.

Managers to examine the books of tickets, and deliver them to the receivers;

XXXIV. And it is hereby enacted, That the faid managers and directors, or fo many of them as fhall be prefent at fuch meeting, or the major part of them then prefent, fhall carefully examine all the faid books, with the tickets therein ; and take care that the fame be contrived, numbered, and made according to the true intent and meaning of this act ; and fhall deliver or caufe to be delivered the fame books, and every or any of them, as they fhall be examined, to the faid cafhier or cafhiers, taking from fuch cafhier or cafhiers an acknowledgement in

taking receipts for them.

writing, under his or their hands, importing his or their receipt of fuch book or books, and fo many tickets therein, as fhall be delivered to him or them refpectively ; and all and every fuch

Receivers fhall cut out, and deliver tickets to the contributors.

cafhier or cafhiers refpectively ; is and are hereby directed and required, upon his or their receiving the full confideration-money to be contributed on this act, from any perfon or perfons contributing as aforefaid, to cut out of the faid book or books, fo to be put into his or their cuftody, through the faid oblique lines, flourifhes, or devices, indentwife, one of the tickets in the faid extreme columns ; which the faid cafhier or cafhiers fhall fign with his or their own name or names, and he or they fhall permit the contributor, if it be defired, to write his or her name or mark on the correfponding ticket in the fame book ; and at the fame time the faid cafhier or cafhiers fhall deliver to the faid contributor the ticket fo cut off, which he, fhe, or they, are to keep and ufe for the better afcertaining and fecuring of the intereft which he, fhe, or they, his, her, or their executors, adminiftrators, or affigns, fhall or may have in the faid fund.

Receivers to return the books with the remainder of the tickets.

XXXV. And be it further enacted by the authority aforefaid, That the faid cafhier or cafhiers, on or before the firft day of *November*, one thoufand feven hundred and fifty nine, fhall redeliver to the faid managers and directors, at their faid office or place of meeting, all the faid books, and therein all the tickets which the faid cafhier or cafhiers fhall not have cut out and delivered to the contributors as aforefaid ; and that the faid managers and directors, or the major part of them, which fhall be prefent at a meeting, as aforefaid, fhall forthwith caufe all the tickets of the faid outermoft columns, which fhall not have been delivered to the contributors as aforefaid, if any fuch be, to be delivered into the receipt of his Majefty's exchequer, there to be retained and kept, and to be difpofed of, as the commiffioners of his Majefty's treafury, or the high treafurer for the time being, fhall judge reafonable and fitting.

Tickets of the middle columns to be rolled up, and

XXXVI. And be it further enacted, That the faid managers and directors, or the major part of them, which fhall be prefent at a meeting as aforefaid, fhall caufe all the tickets of the middle

columns

columns in the books, made out with three columns, as afore-said, which shall be delivered back to them, by or from the said cashier or cashiers as aforesaid, to be carefully rolled up and made fast with thread or silk; and the said managers or directors, or the major part of them as aforesaid, shall, in their presence, and in the presence of such contributors or adventurers as will be there, cause all the said tickets, which are to be so rolled up, and made fast as aforesaid, to be cut off indentwise through the said oblique lines, flourishes, or devices, into a box, to be prepared for that purpose, and to be marked with the letter (A) which is presently to be put up into another strong box, and to be locked with seven different locks and keys, to be kept by as many of the said managers, and sealed with their seals, or the seals of some of them, until the said tickets are to be drawn, as is herein after mentioned; and that the tickets in the first or innermost columns of the said books, shall remain still in the books for discovering any mistake or fraud (if any such should happen to be committed) contrary to the true meaning of this act. *fastened with silk; and cut off indentwise into a box marked with the letter (A) Box to be locked up and sealed.*

XXXVII. And be it further enacted by the authority aforesaid, That the said managers and directors, or the major part of them, which shall be present at any meeting as aforesaid, shall also prepare, or cause to be prepared, other books, in which every leaf shall be divided or distinguished into two columns; and upon the innermost of those two columns there shall be printed sixty six thousand tickets, and upon the outermost of the said two columns there shall be printed sixty six thousand tickets, all which shall be of equal length and breadth, as near as may be; which two columns in the said books shall be joined with some flourish or device, through which the outermost tickets may be cut off indentwise; and that nine thousand three hundred and forty tickets, part of those to be contained in the outermost columns of the books last mentioned, shall be, and be called the fortunate tickets, to which extraordinary benefits shall belong, as is herein after mentioned; and the said managers and directors, or the major part of them, or such of them as shall be present at a meeting as aforesaid, shall cause the said fortunate tickets to be written upon, or otherwise expressed, as well in figures as in words at length, in manner following; that is to say, Upon two of them severally, twenty thousand pounds principal money; upon two of them severally, five thousand pounds principal money; upon two of them severally, three thousand pounds principal money; upon two of them severally, two thousand pounds principal money; upon every one of twenty five of them severally, one thousand pounds principal money; upon every one of thirty of them severally, five hundred pounds principal money; upon every one of one hundred and fifty of them severally, one hundred pounds principal money; upon every one of seven hundred of them severally, fifty pounds principal money; upon every one of eight thousand four hundred and twenty seven of them severally, twenty pounds principal money: *Books to be prepared with two columns, on each of which 60,000 tickets to be printed. The number and value of the fortunate tickets.*

money: which principal fums, fo to be written, or otherwife expreffed upon the faid fortunate tickets, together with five hundred pounds principal money, to be allowed to the owner of the firft drawn ticket, and one thoufand pounds principal money, to the owner of the laft drawn ticket, over and above the benefits which may happen to belong to the two laft mentioned tickets; and together with the fum of fix pounds to be paid or allowed for and upon each blank or unfortunate ticket of the faid lottery, will amount in the whole to the principal fum of fix hundred and fixty thoufand pounds; to be converted into annuities by virtue of this act, in refpect of the faid lottery; and the faid managers and directors, or the major part of them, who fhall be prefent at a meeting as aforefaid, fhall caufe all the faid tickets, contained in the outermoft columns of the faid laft mentioned books, to be, in the prefence of the faid managers and directors, or the major part of them, which fhall be prefent at a meeting as aforefaid, and in the prefence of fuch contributors or adventurers as will then be there, to be carefully rolled up and faftened with thread or filk, and carefully cut out indentwife through the faid flourifh or device, into another box, to be prepared for this purpofe, and to be marked with the letter (B) which box fhall be put into another ftrong box, and locked up with feven different locks and keys, to be kept by as many of the faid managers, and fealed up with their feals, or the feals of fome of them, until thefe tickets fhall alfo be drawn in the manner and form herein after mentioned; and that the whole bufinefs of rolling up, and cutting off, and putting into the faid boxes the faid tickets, and locking up and fealing the faid boxes, fhall be performed by the faid managers and directors, or fuch of them as aforefaid, before the laft fix days immediately preceding the day by this act appointed for the drawing the faid lottery: and to the end every perfon concerned may be well affured that the counterpart of the fame number with his or her ticket is put into the box, marked with the letter (A) from whence the fame may be drawn, and that other matters are done as hereby directed, fome publick notification in print fhall be given of the precife time or times of putting the faid tickets into the faid boxes, to the end that fuch adventurers, as fhall be minded to fee the fame done, may be prefent at the doing thereof.

XXXVIII. And be it further enacted by the authority aforefaid, That on or before the thirteenth day of *November*, one thoufand feven hundred and fifty nine, the faid managers and directors fhall caufe the faid feveral boxes, with all the tickets therein, to be brought into the guildhall of the city of *London*, fo that the fame may be there, and placed on a table provided for that purpofe, by nine of the clock in the forenoon of the fame day, and fhall then and there feverally attend this fervice, and caufe the two boxes containing the faid tickets, to be feverally taken out of the other two boxes, in which they fhall have been locked up; and the tickets or lots in the refpective innermoft

Marginal notes:

500 l. to the firft drawn ticket, and 1000 l. to the laft drawn.

Tickets of the outermoft columns to be rolled up and tied,

and cut out indentwife, into a box marked with the letter (B)

Box to be locked up and fealed.

Publick notice to be given of times of putting the tickets into the boxes.

Lottery to begin drawing on 13 Nov. 1759.

Method to be obferved in drawing, &c.

moft boxes being, in the prefence of the faid managers and directors, or fuch of them as fhall be then prefent, and of fuch
adventurers as will be there for the fatisfaction of themfelves,
well fhaken and mingled in each box diftinctly; fome one indifferent and fit perfon, to be appointed and directed by the faid
managers, or the major part of them, or fuch of them as fhall
be then prefent, fhall take out and draw one ticket from the box
where the faid numbered tickets fhall be as aforefaid put; and
one other indifferent and fit perfon, to be appointed and directed in like manner, fhall take out a ticket or lot from the box
where the faid nine thoufand three hundred and forty fortunate,
and fifty fix thoufand fix hundred and fixty blank tickets fhall
be promifcuoufly put as aforefaid; and immediately both the
tickets fo drawn fhall be opened, and the number, as well of
the fortunate as the blank ticket, fhall be named aloud; and if
the ticket taken or drawn from the box containing the fortunate
and blank lots fhall appear to be a blank, then the numbered
ticket fo drawn with the faid blank at the fame time drawn, fhall
both be put upon one file; and if the ticket fo drawn or taken
from the box containing the fortunate and blank lots, fhall appear to be one of the fortunate tickets, then the principal fum
written upon fuch fortunate ticket, whatfoever it be, fhall be
entered by a clerk, which the faid managers, or the major part
of them as aforefaid, fhall employ and overfee for this purpofe,
into a book to be kept for entering the numbers coming up with
the faid fortunate tickets, and the principal fums whereunto
they fhall be intitled refpectively, and two of the faid managers
fhall fet their names as witneffes to fuch entries; and the faid
fortunate and numbered tickets fo drawn together, fhall be put
upon another file; and fo the faid drawing of the tickets fhall
continue, by taking one ticket at a time out of each box, and
with opening, naming aloud, and filing the fame, and by entering the fortunate lots in fuch method as is before mentioned,
until the whole number of nine thoufand three hundred and
forty fortunate tickets, and one more for the laft drawn as aforefaid, fhall be compleatly drawn; and as the fame cannot be
performed in one day's time, the faid managers or directors fhall
caufe the boxes to be locked up and fealed in manner as aforefaid, and adjourn till the next day, and fo from day to day, and
every day (except *Sundays, Chriftmas* day, and faft days) and then
open the fame, and proceed as above, till the faid whole number of nine thoufand three hundred and forty fortunate tickets,
and one more, fhall be compleatly drawn as aforefaid; and afterwards the faid numbered tickets fo drawn, with the fortunate
tickets drawn againft the fame, fhall be and remain in a ftrong
box locked up as aforefaid, and under the cuftody of the faid
managers, until they fhall take them out to examine, adjuft, and
fettle the property thereof.

After each day's drawing, the boxes to be locked up and fealed.

XXXIX. And, to the end the fortunate may know, whether
abfent or prefent, to what degree they have been fo; be it enacted, That as foon as the drawing is over, the faid managers
Numbers of the fortunate

tickets, and
the sums, to
be printed.

Disputes relat-
ing thereto, to
be adjusted by
the managers.

Penalty of
forging tick-
ets or certifi-
cates.

are hereby required, as soon as conveniently may be, to cause to
be printed and published the number of the tickets drawn against
each fortunate ticket, and the principal sum written on the
same ; and if any contention or dispute shall arise in the adjusting the property of the said fortunate tickets, the major part of
the said managers, agreeing therein, shall determine to whom it
doth or ought to belong: and if any person or persons shall forge
or counterfeit any ticket or tickets, certificate or certificates, to
be made forth by this act, or made forth, or to be made forth,
upon any former lottery act, or alter any the numbers thereof,
or utter, vend, barter, or dispose of, or offer to dispose of, any
false, altered, forged, or counterfeit ticket or tickets, certificate
or certificates, or shall bring any forged or counterfeit ticket or
certificate, or any ticket or certificate the number whereof is
altered (knowing the same to be such) to the said managers, or
any of them, or to the cashier or accomptant general of the bank
of *England* for the time being, or to any other person or persons
whatsoever, to the intent to defraud his Majesty, or any contributor or adventurer, or the executors, administrators, and
assigns, of any contributor or adventurer upon this act ; that

Felony.

then every such person or persons, being thereof convicted in due
form of law, shall be adjudged a felon, and shall suffer death as
in cases of felony, without benefit of clergy: and the said managers or directors, or any two or more of them, are hereby
authorized, required, and impowered, to cause any person or
persons bringing or uttering such forged or counterfeit ticket or
tickets, certificate or certificates as aforesaid, to be apprehended, and to commit him, her, or them, to his Majesty's gaol of
Newgate, or to the common gaol of the county or place where
such person or persons shall be so apprehended, to be proceeded
against for the said felony according to law.

Managers to
be sworn.

XL. Provided always, and it is hereby enacted by the authority aforesaid, That every person that shall be appointed as aforesaid to be a manager and director for putting this act in execution, before his acting in such commission, shall take the oath
following; that is to say,

The oath.

I A. B. *do swear, That I will faithfully execute the trust reposed
in me ; and that I will not use any indirect art or means, or permit or direct any person to use any indirect art or means, to obtain a
prize or fortunate lot, for myself, or any other person whatsoever ;
and that I will do the utmost of my endeavour to prevent any undue
or sinister practice to be done by any person whatsoever ; and that I
will, to the best of my judgment, declare to whom any prize, lot, or
ticket, of right does belong, according to the true intent and meaning
of the act of parliament made in the thirty second year of his Majesty's
reign in that behalf.*

Which said oath shall and may be administered by any two or
more of the other managers and directors.

XLI. Pro-

XLI. Provided also, and it is hereby enacted by the authority aforesaid, That out of the monies to arise by and out of any of the supplies granted in this session of parliament, it shall and may be lawful to and for any three or more of the commissioners of the treasury, or the high treasurer for the time being, to reward the said managers and directors, and the clerks and officers to be employed by and under them, and any other officers and persons that shall and may be any ways employed in this affair, for their labour and pains, and to discharge such incident expences as shall necessarily attend the execution of this act, in such manner as any three or more of the commissioners of the treasury, or the high treasurer for the time being, shall, from time to time, think fit and reasonable in that behalf; any thing in this act contained to the contrary notwithstanding.

Managers, &c. to be paid by the commissioners of the treasury out of the lottery money.

XLII. And be it further enacted by the authority aforesaid, That no person or persons shall sell the chance or chances of any ticket or tickets in the said lottery, or any share or shares of any ticket or tickets in the said lottery, for a day, or part of a day, or for a longer time less than the whole time of drawing the lottery then to come; or shall receive any money whatsoever in consideration of the repayment of any sum or sums of money, in case any ticket or tickets in the said lottery shall prove fortunate; or shall lay any wager relating to the drawing of any ticket or tickets in the said lottery, either as to the time of such ticket or tickets being drawn, or whether such ticket or tickets be drawn fortunate or unfortunate; and all and every person and persons who shall offend in any of the aforesaid matters, shall forfeit and pay treble the sum and sums of money which shall have been received by such person and persons, contrary to the true intent and meaning of this act; to be recovered by action of debt, bill, plaint, or information, in any of his Majesty's courts of record at *Westminster*; in which no essoin, protection, privilege, or wager of law, or more than one imparlance shall be allowed; one moiety whereof to be for the use of his Majesty, his heirs, or successors, and the other moiety to be paid to the person or persons who shall sue for the same; and every such sale, wager, or contract, and every agreement relating thereto, shall be, and is hereby declared null and void.

Limitation of sale of chances, &c.

Penalty.

XLIII. And be it further enacted by the authority aforesaid, That if any person or persons shall keep any office or offices, or shall print or publish any scheme or proposal, for receiving any sum or sums of money in consideration of any interest to be granted for the same, in any ticket or tickets in the said lottery, whereof such person or persons shall not then be actually possessed, or in consideration of any sum or sums of money to be repaid in case any ticket, or number of tickets, in the said lottery, which shall not be in the actual possession of such person or persons, shall prove fortunate or unfortunate; all and every such person and persons shall forfeit and pay the sum of five hundred pounds; to be recovered by action of debt, bill, plaint, or information, in any of his Majesty's courts of record at *Westminster*;

Persons selling shares in tickets of which they are not possessed,

to forfeit 500l.

minster; in which no essoin, protection, or wager of law, or more than one imparlance, shall be allowed; one moiety whereof to be for the use of his Majesty, his heirs, or successors, and the other moiety to be paid to the person or persons who shall sue for the same; and also shall suffer three months imprisonment without bail or mainprize.

Offences committed in Ireland against acts for preventing unlawful lotteries, declared to be punishable, and may be sued for in Dublin.

XLIV. And be it further enacted by the authority aforesaid, That if any offence against any of the acts of parliament made in this kingdom, for preventing private and unlawful lotteries, shall be committed in *Ireland*, the offender shall incur the like penalty and punishment, to be inflicted in like manner as if the offence was committed in this kingdom; and that such penalties as, by any of the said acts, are directed to be recovered in any of his Majesty's courts of record at *Westminster*, shall, in case of offences committed against any of the said acts in *Ireland*, be recovered in any of his Majesty's courts of record in *Dublin*.

After the drawing of the lottery, the tickets to be exchanged for certificates.

XLV. And to the end that all and every the payments, as well upon the fortunate as upon the unfortunate tickets, may be more easily ascertained, settled, and adjusted, for the persons who shall be and become intitled thereunto; be it further enacted by the authority aforesaid, That as soon as conveniently may be after the drawing of the said lottery shall be completed and ended, all and every the said tickets, to be given out as aforesaid, shall be exchanged for certificates to be signed by such of the said managers as shall be appointed for that purpose.

Managers to give notice of the time for taking in the tickets, and delivering out the certificates, &c.

XLVI. And be it further enacted, That such of the said managers, as any three or more of the commissioners of the treasury, or the high treasurer for the time being, shall appoint to take in the said tickets, and deliver out the said certificates for and in lieu thereof, shall give timely notice, by advertisement to be printed and published in manner as they shall think fit, of the days and times for taking in the said tickets, and delivering out the said certificates, for and in lieu of the same; and every person's certificate shall be numbered in course, according to their bringing their tickets to the managers so to be appointed for exchanging the same; to which purpose, such managers shall

Books to be kept for entering persons names,

and the number of their tickets, &c.

enter, or cause to be entered, into a book or books to be by them kept for that purpose, the name of every person who shall bring any ticket or tickets to be exchanged for such certificate or certificates, and the number or numbers of the ticket or tickets which shall be so brought by such person or persons, the value in principal money payable thereupon, and the day of the month, and the year of our Lord, when the same was so brought, which book and books shall lie open in the office to be appointed for taking in the said tickets to be exchanged for such certificates, for all persons concerned to peruse; all which certificates shall be signed by the managers so to be appointed, or the major part of them, and be directed to the accomptant general of the bank of *England* for the time being.

Certificates to be signed, &c.

XLVII. And be it further enacted by the authority aforesaid,
That

That the faid accomptant general of the bank of *England* for the time being, to whom the faid certificates are to be directed as aforefaid, fhall, upon receiving and taking in the faid certificates, or any of them, give credit to the perfons named therein, in a book or books to be by him provided and kept for that purpofe, for the principal fums contained in every fuch certificate; and the perfons to whofe credit fuch principal fums fhall be entered in the faid book or books, his, her, or their executors, and ad-miniftrators, fhall and may have power to affign or tranfer the fame, or any part, fhare, or proportion thereof, to any other perfon or perfons, bodies politick or corporate whatfoever, in other books to be prepared and kept by the faid accomptant ge-neral for that purpofe; and the principal fums fo affigned or transferred, fhall carry the faid annuity of three pounds *per centum per annum*, and fhall be taken and deemed to be ftock trans-ferrable by this act, according to the powers and authorities herein after mentioned, until the redemption thereof as afore-faid; and the faid accomptant general of the bank of *England* for the time being, is hereby authorized and directed to cancel and file the certificates, as they fhall from time to time be re-ceived and taken in by him, and to give the perfons bringing in the fame a note under his hand, teftifying the principal money for which they fhall have credit in the faid book or books, by reafon or means of the certificates fo received, taken in, and cancelled as aforefaid, and of the annuities attending the fame.

Accountant general to give credit for the principal fums in the certificates.

Affignments may be made of the faid fums, &c.

Certificates to be filed and cancelled, and notes to be given in lieu thereof.

XLVIII. *And for the more eafy and fure payment of the faid transferrable annuities after the rate of three pounds* per centum per annum; be it further enacted by the authority aforefaid, That the faid governor and company of the bank of *England*, and their fucceffors, fhall, from time to time, until the faid an-nuities, after the rate of three pounds *per centum per annum*, fhall be redeemed as aforefaid, appoint and employ one or more fuf-ficient perfon or perfons within their office in the city of *Lon-don*, to be their chief or firft cafhier or cafhiers, and one other fufficient perfon within the fame office, to be their accomptant general; and that fo much of the monies from time to time arif-ing into the faid receipt of exchequer, from the faid fubfidies, rates, and duties, by this act granted and appropriated, as fhall be fufficient from time to time for payment of the faid annuities, after the rate of three pounds *per centum per annum*, fhall, by or-der of the commiffioners of the treafury, or any three or more of them, or the lord high treafurer for the time being, without any further or other warrant, to be fued for, had, and obtained, in that behalf, from time to time, at the refpective half-yearly days of payment in this act appointed for payment thereof, be iffued and paid at the faid receipt of exchequer, to the faid firft or chief cafhier or cafhiers of the faid governor and company of the bank of *England*, and their fucceffors, for the time being, by way of impreft, and upon account, for the payment of the faid annuities after the rate of three pounds *per centum per an-num*, at fuch times, and in fuch manner and form, as are by this

A chief ca-fhier, and ac-comptant ge-neral, to be appointed by the bank for paying the annuities.

Treafury to iffue money for that pur-pofe to the faid cafhier,

a act

who is to ac-
count for the
fame.

act prescribed in that behalf; and that such cashier or cashiers to whom the said money shall, from time to time, be issued, shall, from time to time, without delay, apply and pay the same accordingly, and render his or their account thereof, according to the due course of the exchequer.

Accomptant
general to ex-
amine the re-
ceipts and pay-
ments of the
cashier.
Annuities
deemed a per-
fonal estate,
&c.

XLIX. And be it further enacted by the authority aforesaid, That the said accomptant general for the time being shall, from time to time, inspect and examine all receipts and payments of the said cashier or cashiers, and the vouchers relating thereto, in order to prevent any fraud, negligence, or delay; and that all persons who shall be intitled to any of the said annuities, after the rate of three pounds *per centum per annum*, and all persons lawfully claiming under them, shall be possessed thereof as of a personal estate, which shall not be descendible to heirs, nor liable to any foreign attachment by the custom of *London*, or otherwise; any law, statute, or custom, to the contrary notwithstanding.

Annuities
deemed a joint
stock;

L. And be it further enacted by the authority aforesaid, That all the monies to be advanced or contributed by virtue of this act towards the said sum of six millions six hundred thousand pounds, on which the said annuities, after the rate of three pounds *per centum per annum*, shall be attending, shall be deemed one capital and joint stock; and that all persons and corporations whatsoever, in proportion to the monies by them severally advanced for the purchase of the said annuities, after the rate of three pounds *per centum per annum*, or to which they shall become intitled by virtue of this act, shall have, and be deemed to have, a proportional interest and share in the said stock, and in the said annuities attending the same, at the rate aforesaid; and that the said whole capital or joint stock, or any share or interest therein, shall be assignable and transferrable as this act directs, and not otherwise.

and made
transferrable.

Clause of re-
demption.

LI. Provided also, and it is hereby enacted by the authority aforesaid, That at any time upon six months notice to be printed in the *London Gazette*, and fixed upon the *Royal Exchange* in *London*, and upon repayment by parliament of the said sum of six millions six hundred thousand pounds, or any part thereof, by payments not less than five hundred thousand pounds at one time, in such manner as shall be directed by any future act or acts of parliament in that behalf, and also upon full payment of all arrearages of the said annuities, after the rate of three pounds *per centum per annum*; then, and not till then, such and so much of the said annuities as shall be attending on the principal sums so paid off, shall cease and determine, and be understood to be redeemed; and that any vote or resolution of the house of commons, signified by the speaker in writing, to be inserted in the *London Gazette*, and affixed on the *Royal Exchange* in *London* as aforesaid, shall be deemed and adjudged to be sufficient notice within the words and meaning of this act.

LII. And be it further enacted by the authority aforesaid,
That

That books fhall be conftantly kept by the faid accomptant ge- Transfer
neral for the time being, wherein all affignments or tranfers of books to be
the faid annuities, after the rate of three pounds *per centum per* kept by the
annum, fhall at all feafonable times, be entered and regiftered; accomptant
which entry fhall be conceived in proper words for that purpofe, general.
and fhall be figned by the parties making fuch affignments or Method of
transfers; or if fuch parties be abfent, by their refpective attor- transferring
nies thereunto lawfully authorized in writing under their hands ftock.
and feals, to be attefted by two or more credible witneffes; and
that the feveral perfons to whom fuch transfers fhall be made,
fhall refpectively underwrite their acceptance thereof; and that
no other method of affigning and transferring the faid annuities,
or any part thereof, or any intereft therein, fhall be good or
available in law.

LIII. Provided always, That all perfons poffeffed of any fhare Annuities de-
in the faid joint ftock of annuities, or eftate and intereft therein, vifeable by
may devife the fame by will in writing, attefted by two or more will.
credible witneffes; but that no payment fhall be made upon any Entry to be
fuch devife, till fo much of the faid will as relates to any fhare, made of fuch
eftate, or intereft, in the faid joint ftock of annuities, be entered claufe in the
in the faid office; and that in default of fuch transfer or devife, will.
fuch fhare, eftate, or intereft, in the faid joint ftock of annuities,
fhall go to the executors or adminiftrators; and that no ftamp Transfer not
duties whatfoever fhall be charged on any of the faid transfers; liable to ftamp
any law or ftatute to the contrary notwithftanding. duties.

LIV. Provided always, and be it enacted by the authority Treafury to
aforefaid, That out of the monies arifing from the contributions pay all inci-
towards raifing the faid fum of fix millions fix hundred thoufand dent charges
pounds, any three or more of the commiffioners of the treafury, attending the
or the high treafurer for the time being, fhall have power to execution of
difcharge all fuch incident charges as fhall neceffarily attend the this act;
execution of this act, in fuch manner as to them fhall feem juft
and reafonable; and alfo to fettle and appoint fuch allowances
as fhall be thought proper, for the fervice, pains, and labour, of
the faid cafhier or cafhiers, for receiving, paying, and accounting
for the faid contributions; and alfo fhall have power to make and to make
out of the fund hereby eftablifhed, or out of the finking fund, an allowance
fuch further allowances as fhall be judged reafonable, for the to the cafhier,
fervice, pains, and labour of the faid cafhier or cafhiers, for re- and accompt-
ceiving, paying, and accounting for the faid annuities, after the ant general;
rate of three pounds *per centum per annum*, payable by virtue of
this act; and alfo for the fervice, pains, and labour of the faid
accomptant general, for performing the truft repofed in him
by this act; all which allowances to be made as aforefaid in re- to be at the
fpect to the fervice, pains, and labour of any officer or officers of difpofal of the
the faid governor and company, fhall be for the ufe and bene- governor and
fit of the faid governor and company, and at their difpofal company of
only. the bank.

LV. Provided always, and be it further enacted by the au- Bank to con-
thority aforefaid, That the faid governor and company of the tinue a corpo-
bank of *England*, and their fucceffors, notwithftanding the re- ration till thefe
demp- annuities be
redeemed, &c.

demption of all or any of their own funds, in purfuance of the
acts for eftablifhing the fame, or any of them, fhall continue
a corporation till all the faid annuities, after the rate of three
pounds *per centum per annum*, by this act granted, fhall be redeemed by parliament, according to the provifo herein before
contained in that behalf; and that the faid governor and company of the bank of *England*, or any member thereof, fhall not
incur any difability for or by reafon of their doing any matter
or thing in purfuance of this act.

No fee for payment of contribution money.

LVI. And be it further enacted, That no fee, reward, or
gratuity whatfoever, fhall be demanded or taken of any of his
Majefty's fubjects, for receiving or paying the faid contribution
monies, or any of them, or for paying the faid feveral annuities,
or any of them, or for any transfer of any fum great or fmall, to
be made in purfuance of this act, upon pain that any offender
or perfon offending, by taking or demanding any fuch fee, reward, or gratuity, fhall forfeit the fum of twenty pounds to the
party aggrieved, with full cofts of fuit; and that all receipts and
iffues, and all other things directed by this act to be performed
in the exchequer, fhall be done or performed by the officer
there, without demanding or receiving, directly or indirectly,
any fee, reward, or gratuity for the fame; and in cafe the offi-

Penalty.

cers of the exchequer fhall take or demand any fuch fee or reward, or fhall mifapply or divert any of the monies to be paid
into the exchequer upon this act, or fhall pay or iffue out of the
fame, otherwife than according to the true intent of this act, or
fhall not keep fuch books, regifters, or make entries, and do
and perform all things which by this act they are directed and
required to do and perform, every fuch offender fhall forfeit his
place, and be for ever after incapable of any office or place of
truft whatfoever, and fhall anfwer and pay treble cofts of fuit
to any contributor or perfon claiming under him that will fue for
the fame, to be recovered by action of debt, bill, plaint, or information, in any of his Majefty's courts of record at *Weftminfter*, wherein no effoin, protection, privilege, or wager of law,
injunction, or order of reftraint, or any more than one impart-
lance fhall be granted or allowed; and in the faid action the
plaintiff, upon recovery, fhall have full cofts of fuit; one third
of which fum fhall be paid into the faid receipt of exchequer, for
the benefit of his Majefty, his heirs, and fucceffors, and the o-
ther two thirds fhall be to and for the ufe of the profecutor.

Deficiencies of the exche- quer, &c. how to be made good.

LVII. And it is hereby enacted by the authority aforefaid,
That if at any time or times it fhall happen that the produce of
the faid feveral fubfidies, rates, and duties, hereby granted, for
payment of the faid feveral annuities, fhall not be fufficient to
pay and difcharge the feveral and refpective annuities and other
charges directed to be paid thereout, at the end if any or either
of the refpective half-yearly days of payment, at which the fame
are hereby directed to be paid, then, and fo often, and in every
fuch cafe, fuch deficiency or deficiencies fhall and may be fupplied out of any of the monies which at any time or times fhall
be

be or remain in the receipt of the exchequer, of the furpluffes, exceffes, overplus monies, and other revenues, compofing the fund commonly called *The finking fund* (except fuch monies of the faid finking fund as are appropriated to any particular ufe or ufes, by any former act or acts of parliament in that behalf) and fuch monies of the faid finking fund, fhall and may be, from time to time, iffued and applied accordingly; and if at any time or times, before any monies of the feveral fubfidies, rates, and duties hereby granted fhall be brought into the exchequer as aforefaid, there fhall happen to be a want of money for paying the feveral annuities as aforefaid, which fhall be actually incurred and grown due at any of the half-yearly days of payments before-mentioned, that then, and in every fuch cafe, the money fo wanted fhall and may be fupplied out of the monies of the finking fund (except as before excepted) and be iffued accordingly.

LVIII. Provided always, and be it enacted by the authority aforefaid, That whatever monies fhall be iffued out of the finking fund, fhall, from time to time be replaced, by and out of the firft fupplies to be then after granted in parliament.
Sinking fund to be replaced.

LIX. Provided always, and be it enacted by the authority aforefaid, That in cafe there fhall be any furplus or remainder of the monies arifing by the faid feveral fubfidies, rates, and duties, after the faid feveral and refpective annuities, and all arrears thereof, are fatisfied, or money fufficient fhall be referved for that purpofe, fuch overplus or remainder fhall, from time to time, be referved for the difpofition of parliament, and fhall not be iffued but by the authority of parliament, and as fhall be directed by future act or acts of parliament, any thing in any former or other act or acts of parliament to the contrary notwithftanding.
Surplus monies how to be applied.

LX. And it is hereby enacted by the authority aforefaid, That if any perfon or perfons fhall, at any time or times, be fued or profecuted for any thing by him or them done or executed in purfuance of this act, or of any matter or thing in this act contained, fuch perfon or perfons fhall and may plead the general iffue, and give the fpecial matter in evidence for his or their defence: and if, upon trial, a verdict fhall pafs for the defendant or defendants, or the plaintiff or plaintiffs fhall become nonfuited, then fuch defendant or defendants fhall have treble cofts to him or them awarded againft fuch plaintiff or plaintiffs.
General iffue.
Treble cofts.

CAP. XI.

An act to permit the free importation of cattle from Ireland for a limited time.

WHEREAS *the permitting the free importation of cattle into Great Britain from Ireland for a limited time, may be of great advantage to both kingdoms;* be it therefore enacted by the King's moft excellent Majefty, by and with the advice and confent of the lords fpiritual and temporal, and commons, in this prefent parliament affembled, and by the authority of the fame,
Preamble.

That

That from and after the first day of *May*, one thousand seven hundred and fifty nine, the free importation of all sorts of cattle into this kingdom from *Ireland*, shall be, and is hereby permitted, allowed, and authorized, for and during the space of five years from the said first day of *May*, or at any time thereafter before the end of the then next session of parliament; and that all persons shall be, and are hereby exempted, freed, and discharged, from the payment of all subsidies, customs, rates, duties, or other impositions, and also from all penalties, forfeitures, payments, and punishments, for or upon account of importing or bringing cattle into this kingdom from *Ireland*, during the term aforesaid; any act or acts of parliament to the contrary notwithstanding.

II. And be it further enacted by the authority aforesaid, That if any action or suit shall be commenced against any person or persons for any thing done in pursuance of this act, the defendant or defendants in any such action or suit, may plead the general issue, and give this act, and the special matter in evidence, at any trial to be had thereupon; and that the same was done in pursuance and by the authority of this act; and if it shall appear so to have been done, the jury shall find for the defendant or defendants, and if the plaintiff shall be nonsuited or discontinue his action after the defendant or defendants shall have appeared; or if judgment shall be given upon any verdict or demurrer against the plaintiff, the defendant or defendants shall and may recover treble costs, and have the like remedy for the same, as any defendant or defendants hath or have in other cases by law.

(marginal notes:) Free importation of all sorts of cattle from Ireland, allowed for 5 years, from 1 May, 1759; the same to be duty free.

Limitation of actions.

General issue.

Treble costs.

CAP. XII.

An act to discontinue, for a limited time, the duties payable upon tallow imported from Ireland.

(marginal note:) Preamble.

WHEREAS the allowing, for a limited time, the free importation of tallow from Ireland, may tend to the ease of the publick, and advantage of the revenue, by reducing the price, and encouraging the consumption of candles in this kingdom; be it therefore enacted by the King's most excellent majesty, by and with the advice and consent of the lords spiritual and temporal, and commons, in this present parliament assembled, and by the authority of the same, That from and after the first day of *May*, one thousand seven hundred and fifty nine, no subsidy, custom, rate, duty, or other imposition whatsoever, shall be demanded, collected, received, or taken, upon any tallow un-manufactured into candles or soap, which shall be imported into this kingdom from *Ireland*; but that all such tallow shall and may be imported duty free for the space of five years, from the said first day of *May*, one thousand seven hundred and fifty nine, or at any time thereafter before the end of the then next session of parliament; any former law, statute, or act or acts of parliament, to the contrary notwithstanding.

(marginal note:) Free importation of tallow allowed for 5 years, from 1 May, 1759.

II. Provided always, and be it further enacted by the authority aforesaid, That a due entry shall be made of all such tallow at the custom-house belonging to the port into which the same

(marginal note:) Entry to be made thereof;

shall

shall be imported, in such manner and form, and expressing the quantities of such tallow, as were used and practised before the making of this act; and such tallow shall be landed in the presence of the proper officer or officers of the customs appointed for that purpose; and if any person or persons upon the importation of any tallow from *Ireland*, shall not observe and perform the said conditions and directions herein before mentioned, every such person shall be liable to, and pay such and the same duties, as such tallow would have been liable to if this act had not been made; any thing in this act contained to the contrary notwithstanding.

and the same to be landed in the presence of an officer.

Penalty.

III. And be it further enacted by the authority aforesaid, That if any action or suit shall be commenced against any person or persons for any thing done in pursuance of this act, the defendant or defendants in any such action or suit, may plead the general issue, and give this act, and the special matter in evidence, at any trial to be had thereupon; and that the same was done in pursuance and by the authority of this act; and if it shall appear so to have been done, the jury shall find for the defendant or defendants; and if the plaintiff shall be nonsuited, or discontinue his action, after the defendant or defendants shall have appeared; or if judgment shall be given upon any verdict or demurrer against the plaintiff, the defendant or defendants shall and may recover treble costs, and have the like remedy for the same, as any defendant or defendants hath or have in other cases by law.

Limitation of actions.

General issue.

Treble costs.

C A P. XIII.

An act for draining and preserving certain fen lands and low grounds in the parishes of Somersham, and Pidley with Fenton, and the parish of Colne, in the county of Huntingdon.

C A P. XIV.

An act for the more regular and easy collecting, accounting for, and paying, of post fines, which shall be due to the crown, or to grantees thereof under the crown; and for the ease of sheriffs in respect to the same.

WHEREAS *great trouble and expence arise in the execution of the office of sheriff, by the present method of collecting, accounting for, and paying, of post fines, which become due to the crown, or to grantees or proprietors thereof under the crown, by reason that the persons from whom such post fines are due, are frequently unknown to the sheriff, and reside out of his county; and the parishes, towns, precincts, or places, in which the lands lie, whereof the fine was levied, are frequently misnamed, whereby the sheriff is unable to find out the same: and forasmuch as the sheriff of every county, on the passing his accounts, is obliged to pay to the crown, before he can obtain his quietus, the several and respective post fines charged upon him, many of which he is never able to collect in and receive, to his manifest loss and detriment; for remedy whereof, and for the ease of sheriffs in the execution of their office, may it please your Majesty that it may* be

Preamble.

be enacted; and be it enacted by the King's moſt excellent majeſty, by and with the advice and conſent of the lords ſpiritu
and temporal, and commons, in this preſent parliament aſſem
bled, and by the authority of the ſame, That on all and ever
writ or writs of covenant which, from and after the firſt day o
Trinity term, one thouſand ſeven hundred and fifty nine, ſhall b
ſued out for the paſſing of fines in his Majeſty's court of *Common*
Pleas at *Weſtminſter*, the officer or officers, whoſe duty it is to k
and indorſe the preſine payable thereon, ſhall alſo at the ſam
time, ſet the uſual poſt fine, and indorſe the ſame on the back o
the ſaid writ or writs, together with his or their name or names
or mark of office thereto, in the like manner as the ſame are no
indorſed or ſtampt at the office called *The King's ſilver offic*
which ſaid poſt fine or poſt fines ſhall be forthwith paid to the
receiver of preſines at the alienation office, for the time being,
together with the ſum of four pence, as his fee for receiving the
ſame, inſtead, and in lieu, of the fee of four pence charged on
lands, tenements, and hereditaments, and payable to ſheriffs,
bailiffs, and others, on diſcharging the ſame, by virtue of the ad
of the third year of his late majeſty King *George* the Firſt, intituled, *An act for the better regulating the office of ſheriffs; and for aſ-*
certaining their fees, and the fees for ſuing out their patents and paſ-
ſing their accounts; which ſaid fee of four pence, by the ſaid act
granted, from and after the ſaid firſt day of *Trinity* term, one
thouſand ſeven hundred and fifty nine, ſhall ceaſe and determine;
and ſuch receiver ſhall indorſe upon the back of every ſuch writ
or writs of covenant, one particular or certain mark of office, in
like manner as is now uſed by him on the receipt of preſines at
the alienation office, together with the name of ſuch receiver,
and the ſum of money which ſhall be by him received as the poſt
fine due thereon; which mark and indorſement of ſuch receiver,
ſhall diſcharge the manors, lands, tenements, rents, commons,
and hereditaments, compriſed in the ſaid writ or writs of covenant, and the cognizee or cognizees named therein.

II. And be it further enacted by the authority aforeſaid, That
the officer or clerk of the King's ſilver office, or his deputy, from
and after the ſaid firſt day of *Trinity* term, one thouſand ſeven
hundred and fifty nine, ſhall continue to enter every ſuch fine or
fines upon record, in the way hitherto uſed in the paſſing of fines,
and make thereof the ſame entries, and ſhall put thereon the
ſame indorſements, with the ſame ſtamp or mark, and in the
like manner, as has hitherto been the conſtant uſage and practice
of the ſaid office in paſſing of fines; and that no fine, until the
ſame ſhall be ſtamped and marked with the ſum to which the
poſt fine amounts as aforeſaid in the ſaid King's ſilver office,
ſhall be deemed a fine valid and effectual in law.

III. *And whereas no preſine is payable on any writ of covenant*
where the lands and tenements contained therein are under the yearly
value of five marks; but a certain ſum of ſix ſhillings and eight pence
hath been antiently ſet and payable to the crown on every ſuch writ of
covenant, as and for the King's licence being granted to the parties in
ſuch

Marginal notes

The poſt fine to be indorſed on the back of the writ, by the officer who is to ſet the preſine, together with his name, or mark of office;

both fines to be paid toge-ther to the re-ceiver of the preſines at the alienation of-fice, with 4d. for his fee, in-ſtead of the fine granted by act 3 Geo. 1.

Receiver to in-dorſe on the back of the writ, his mark of office, name, and ſum re-ceived.

Clerk of the ſilver office to enter and mark the fines.

Fines not va-lid until ſtampt and mark'd with the poſt fine.

such writ of covenant named to accord; be it therefore further enacted by the authority aforesaid, That from and after the said first day of *Trinity* term, in all cases where no prefine shall be payable on any writ of covenant, the officer or officers at the said alienation office, whose duty it is to set and indorse the prefine on every writ of covenant on which a prefine is payable, shall set on every writ of covenant brought to the said alienation office, on which no prefine shall be payable, a post fine of six shillings and eight pence, as hath been antiently usually put, at the said King's silver office, on every writ of covenant on which no prefine was payable; and shall indorse such post fine of six shillings and eight pence on every such writ of covenant, together with his or their name or names, and mark of office, in the like manner as it hath been usual to indorse such writs of covenant at the said alienation office; and every such post fine of six shillings and eight pence, shall be paid to the said receiver of the said alienation office, before the writ of covenant on which no prefine is payable shall be passed at the said alienation office; and the said receiver, on payment of the said six shillings and eight pence, shall indorse on and mark every such writ of covenant, in like manner as other writs of covenant are by this act before directed to be indorsed and marked by such said receiver. *[margin: Where no prefine is payable on the writ, the officer at the alienation office is to put a post fine of 6s. 8d. thereon, and indorse the same, with his name and mark of office. The said sum of 6s. 8d. to be paid before the writ pass the alienation office. Receiver to indorse his name and mark the writ.]*

IV. And be it further enacted by the authority aforesaid, That the officer of clerk of the King's silver office, or his deputy, from and after the said first day of *Trinity* term, one thousand seven hundred and fifty nine, shall not receive any writ or writs of covenant, unless it shall appear by the mark and indorsement of such receiver as aforesaid, that the post fine has been paid thereon. *[margin: Clerk of the silver office to receive no writ where the post fine has not been paid.]*

V. Provided nevertheless, That if after the payment of such post fine or post fines as aforesaid, the said writ or writs of covenant shall, by the death of any of the parties named therein, or for any other cause whatsoever, be prevented or hindered from passing through the several other offices, so as the said fine or fines is or are not, or cannot be, compleated; that then, and in every such case, the said receiver shall repay to the cognizee or cognizees, in every such writ or writs of covenant, his, her, or their attorney or agent, on their producing and filing with him the said writ or writs of covenant, all and every such sum and sums of money as shall have been before by him received thereon as and for the post fine or post fines; and such writ or writs of covenant so remaining filed with such receiver, shall be, and is hereby declared to be a sufficient discharge to such receiver, for such sum or sums of money as he shall so repay as aforesaid. *[margin: If the writ shall be prevented from passing the several offices, the receiver to repay the post fine to the cognizee.]*

VI. And be it further enacted by the authority aforesaid, That every such receiver as aforesaid, before he takes upon him the execution of his said office, shall enter into a recognizance before one of the barons of his Majesty's court of *exchequer*, to his Majesty, his heirs, and successors, with one or more surety or sureties, as shall be thought proper by such baron, in *[margin: Receiver to enter into recognizance, with sureties, for the faithful discharge of his office, and making due payments of the monies received by him.]*

the penal fum of five thoufand pounds, conditioned for the due
and faithful execution of the faid office, and to pay unto every
refpective fheriff of every county, city, and town in *England*,
having a fheriff or fheriffs, or his under fheriff or lawful attorney,
on his or their producing to fuch receiver, his clerk or agent,
at his publick office, the *quietus* of the fheriff for whom payment
is required, the fum total of the poft fines which fhall be contained in fuch refpective *quietus*, and wherewith fuch fheriff fhall
have been charged in his account in the exchequer; and alfo
to pay unto all and every the lords of liberties, proprietors, or
grantees, of poft fines under the crown, or to their lawful bailiffs
or attorney, upon their producing refpectively unto the faid receiver, his clerk or agent, at his publick office, the refpective
fchedules of the foreign appofer, or clerk of the eftreats of the
faid court of *exchequer*, the feveral and refpective fums of money
in fuch fchedules contained, and fet over as poft fines to fuch

Sureties to
juftify them-
felves.

lords, proprietors, or grantees refpectively; which faid furety or
fureties, fhall refpectively juftify him or herfelf, before the baron
taking fuch recognizance, to be worth the fum of two thoufand
five hundred pounds, over and befides all juft debts and incumbrances; and every fuch recognizance fhall, with all convenient

Recognizance
to be tranf-
mitted to, and
filed in, the
court of exche-
quer.
Receiver and
fureties liable,
in the penalty
of the recog-
zance, to the
fheriff, lords
of liberties,
proprietors, or
grantees, for
the poft fines
received.
On the death,
&c. of a fure-
ty, a new one
to be provided
within one
month.

fpeed, after the taking thereof, be tranfmitted by the baron who
fhall take the fame to the King's remembrancer of the court of
exchequer, there to be filed and remain on record; and fuch receiver, and his faid fureties, fhall in all cafes be refpectively liable
to the amount of fuch penal fum, to make fatisfaction to each
refpective fheriff, and alfo to the refpective lords of liberties,
proprietors, or grantees, for all and every poft fine and poft fines
which fhall be received by fuch receiver, his deputy or agent,
on any fine levied of any lands, tenements, rents, or hereditaments, within their refpective fheriffwicks or liberties; and in
cafe of the death or infolvency of any of the faid fureties, at any
time after the entering into fuch recognizance as aforefaid, then
one or more furety or fureties in the room or place of him, her,
or them, fo dying or becoming infolvent as aforefaid, fhall,
within the fpace of one month then next, enter into fuch recognizance as the faid furety or fureties fo dying or becoming infolvent had entered into, and juftify himfelf, herfelf, or themfelves, in like manner as is before directed in this act; indefault of
which the faid office fhall immediately ceafe, determine, and be
utterly void.

Time of re-
ceiver's atten-
dance at office,
and delivery
of the writs.

VII. And be it further enacted by the authority aforefaid,
That from and after the faid firft day of *Trinity* term, every fuch
receiver, his clerk or agent, fhall daily (*Sundays* and holidays excepted) attend at the faid alienation office, from nine of the
clock in the morning, till one of the clock in the afternoon, and
fhall deliver back every fuch writ of covenant as aforefaid, when
the fame fhall be called for at the faid alienation office, during
the office hours herein before appointed for fuch receiver's attendance at the faid office, within two days after every fuch poft
fine fhall be paid thereon refpectively, unlefs the laft of the faid

two

two days shall happen to be a *Sunday* or holiday, and then on
the next succeeding day.

VIII. And be it enacted by the authority aforesaid, That
every such receiver as aforesaid shall pay unto every sheriff of any
of the counties, cities, or towns of *England*, his under sheriff or
lawful attorney, on his producing his *quietus*, the several and respective sums of money in the said *quietus* mentioned to have
been by him accounted for in the receipt of his Majesty's exchequer, on the passing of his accounts as and for post fines of his
Majesty's court of *Common Pleas* at *Westminster*; and also in like
manner pay unto all and every lords of liberties, proprietors, or
grantees, under the crown, of such post fines, or his or their bailiff or lawful attorney, upon their producing the schedules of the
foreign apposer, or clerk of the estreats of the said court of *exchequer*, the several and respective sums of money in the said schedules set and allowed to them as post fines; the said receiver deducting and retaining to himself, out of every twenty shillings
which he shall so pay, the sum of six pence only, for his trouble
and attendance on the due execution of this act, and so in proportion for any greater or less sum, and which he is hereby authorized and impowered to deduct and retain to his own use;
but neither the said receiver, nor any other person or persons
whatsoever, for his or their attendance on such receiver, shall
charge or be allowed any fee or reward for or on the account of
doing any thing by this act directed, except the said fees to such
receiver in this act particularly mentioned and expressed.

Receiver to pay the post fines to the sheriff, on producing his quietus,

and to the lords of liberties, proprietors, or grantees, on producing the schedules of the foreign apposer.

Receiver to deduct 6d. in the pound, and no more, of the sums paid by him.

IX. And be it further enacted by the authority aforesaid,
That if any person or persons from and after the said first day of
Trinity term, one thousand seven hundred and fifty nine, shall
make, forge, or counterfeit, or cause or procure to be made,
forged, or counterfeited, the mark or hand of such receiver as
aforesaid, whereby such receiver, or any other person or persons,
shall or may be defrauded, or suffer any loss thereby; every
person or persons convicted of such offence, shall be deemed
guilty of felony, and shall suffer death as a felon without benefit
of clergy.

Penalty of forging the receiver's hand or mark.

X. And be it also enacted by the authority aforesaid, That
every such receiver refusing or neglecting to pay such post fines
to the said respective sheriffs, lords of liberties, proprietors, or
grantees under the crown, or their lawful attornies or bailiffs,
shall be subject to such order as the barons of the said court of
exchequer of the degree of the coif shall make for the payment of
the same; and the said receiver, and every person or persons
who shall be guilty of any wilful default, extortion, or misdemeanor, contrary to the true intent and meaning of this act, shall
forfeit and pay to the party aggrieved treble damages with full
costs, which shall and may be ordered and awarded by the barons
of the court of *Exchequer*, upon application made to, and on due
proof thereof made before them, in such summary way and method as to them shall seem meet; provided every such application
or prosecution be made within the space of two years next after

Receiver made subject to the order of the court, for not paying the post fines;

and being guilty of any misdemeanor, to forfeit tre-ble damages.

Limitation of prosecutions,

any fuch offence fhall have been committed, and not otherwife; and fuch orders of the faid court of *exchequer*, fo to be made as aforefaid, fhall have the fame force, virtue, and effect, and the obfervance thereof fhall be inforced by fuch ways and means, as any other orders of the fame court.

XI. Provided always, and be it enacted by the authority aforefaid, That this act fhall not any way alter the operation of any fine which after the faid firft day of *Trinity* term, one thoufand feven hundred and fifty nine, fhall be levied in the court of *Common Pleas* at *Weftminfter*, or the courfe of paffing fines in that court, otherwife than in and by this act directed.

XII. And be it further enacted by the authority aforefaid, That this act fhall be deem'd and taken to be a publick act; and fhall be judicially taken notice of as fuch, by all judges, juftices, and other perfons whatfoever, without fpecially pleading the fame.

CAP. XV.

An act for the better prefervation of the turnpike roads in that part of Great Britain *called* Scotland.

WHEREAS *great fums of money have been expended in amending and repairing the turnpike roads in that part of* Great Britain *called* Scotland, *yet the faid roads cannot be kept in fufficient repair, and are in many places become ruinous by the great and exceffive weights which the number of horfes now allowed by law to draw waggons and other carriages, enable carriers, and other perfons ufing the faid roads, to carry upon the fame*; for remedy whereof, be it enacted by the King's moft excellent majefty, by and with the advice and confent of the lords fpiritual and temporal, and commons in this prefent parliament affembled, and by the authority of the fame, That from and after the firft day

of *September*, one thoufand feven hundred and fifty nine, where any waggon, wain, cart, or other carriage, is drawn by four or more horfes, or other beafts of draught, it fhall and may be lawful for all truftees or commiffioners appointed, or hereafter to be appointed, by any act or acts of parliament, for the repair of any highway or highways, in that part of *Great Britain* called *Scotland*, in their refpective diftricts, or any five or more of them, or any perfon or perfons impowered by them, or any five or more of them, to demand, receive, and take, and they are hereby required to demand, receive, and take, at all the gates and bars that are or fhall be erected for receiving and collecting any toll or duty, before fuch waggon, wain, cart, or other carriage, fhall be permitted to pafs through any fuch toll-gate or toll-bar, over and above the tolls or duties already granted, or hereafter to be granted, the fum of five fhillings fterling for each horfe, or other beaft of draught, drawing any fuch waggon, wain, cart, or other carriage; which faid additional toll or duty hereby granted and made payable, fhall and may be levied upon any perfon who fhall, after demand made thereof, refufe or neglect lest to pay the same, in such manner as any other toll or duty, payable at the same turnpike-gate or bar, is by law to be levied; and the money arising from such additional duty, shall be applied to the repair of the highway where the same shall be collected.

II. And be it further enacted by the authority aforesaid, That if any person or persons shall take off, or cause to be taken off, any horse or horses, or other beast of draught, from any carriage, at or before the same shall come to any of the said gates or turnpikes, with an intent to avoid paying the said additional toll or duty, each and every person so offending, and being convicted thereof before the said trustees, or any five or more of them, upon the oath of one or more credible witness or witnesses (which oath the said trustees, or any five or more of them, are hereby impowered to administer) shall forfeit and pay twenty shillings sterling; one half to the informer, and the other half to be applied to repairing such part or parts of the said road, as the said trustees, or any five or more of them, shall appoint. *10 s. penalty on taking off horse, &c. to avoid the additional toll.*

III. And be it further enacted and declared by the authority aforesaid, That every person who shall drive any waggon or other carriage upon any part of any turnpike road, with more horses than such waggon, or other carriage, shall, on the same day, pass through any turnpike-bar or gate with, shall be deemed and adjudged to have taken off the said horses, with intent to avoid paying the said additional toll or duty. *Travelling with fewer horses on one part of the road than on another, liable to forfeit.*

IV. And be it further enacted by the authority aforesaid, That from and after the first day of *September*, one thousand seven hundred and fifty nine, no waggon, wain, cart, or other carriage, shall be drawn by more than eight horses, or other beasts of draught, upon any turnpike road, in that part of *Great Britain* called *Scotland*, on pain of forfeiting the sum of five pounds sterling for every such offence; one half to the informer, and the other half to be applied to repairing the road where the offence shall be committed, as the trustees, or any five or more of them, shall appoint.

V. Provided always, and be it enacted by the authority aforesaid, That nothing in this act contained shall extend, or be construed to extend, to restrain the owner or owners of any carriage, or his or their servants, using or drawing with as many horses, or beasts of draught, as shall be necessary for drawing such carriages up any steep hill, as the said trustees, or any five or more of them, within their respective districts, where such steep hills do lie, shall, from time to time, order and direct; a copy of which order and direction, under the hand of the clerk of the said trustees, shall be kept by the person or persons impowered to levy the said tolls or duties, at the toll gate next adjacent to such hills; and shall, without fee or reward, be made patent to the owners of such carriages passing the road, or their servants, requiring to see the same. *Such number of horses may be used for drawing carriages up hill, as the trustees by an order for that purpose, shall allow. Copy of the order to be lodged with the collector of the tolls, &c.*

VI. Pro-

Waggons, &c. with broad wheels,

VI. Provided always, and be it enacted by the authority aforefaid, That nothing in this act contained fhall impofe or be conftrued to impofe the faid additional duty on any waggon, wain, cart, or other carriage, the fellies of the wheels whereof are of the breadth or gage of nine inches, from fide to fide, at the leaft; nor on any waggon, wain, cart, or other carriage,

or carrying only one block of marble, &c. not liable to additional duty.

employed in carrying one tree or piece of timber, one ftone or block of marble, or any machine or engine in one piece, which cannot be drawn by fewer than four horfes; nor on any waggon, wain, cart, or other carriage, drawn by oxen or neat cattle only, or along with two horfes, and no more.

Carriages with fellies of the wheels fix inches broad, drawn by 3 horfes, to pay the toll only of two.

VII. And, for the further encouraging the ufing of broad wheels, be it further enacted by the authority aforefaid, That from and after the firft day of September, one thoufand feven hundred and fifty nine, all waggons, wains, and carts, whereof the fellies of the wheels are of the breadth or gage of fix inches from fide to fide, at the leaft, drawn by three horfes, mares, or geldings, fhall only be liable and fubject to payment of fuch toll or duty as is at prefent impofed, by the acts of parliament already made, upon waggons, wains, and carts, drawn by two horfes.

Chaifes, coaches, &c. exempted.

VIII. Provided always, and be it further enacted by the authority aforefaid, That nothing in this act contained fhall be deemed or conftrued to extend to any chaife marine, coach, chariot, landau, berlin, chaife, chair, or calafh.

Truftees may order wheels to be meafured.

IX. And, for the better difcovering and detecting the offenders againft this act, it is hereby further enacted, That it fhall and may be lawful to and for the truftees appointed, or to be appointed, by any act or acts of parliament made, or to be made, for the repairing or amending any highway or highways within that part of Great Britain called Scotland, or any five or more of them, and they are hereby authorized and required, by writing under their hands, to order the fellies of the wheels of all waggons, wains, carts, and other carriages, which are, or ought to be, of the breadth or gage herein before directed and prefcribed, to be meafured and gaged at any turnpike or toll-gate erected, or to be erected, upon any part of the highway or road, in or upon which fuch waggon, wain, cart, or carriage refpectively, fhall travel, pafs, or be drawn.

Carriages with wheels reduced, by wearing, not more than one inch, allowed to pafs,

X. Provided always, That in cafe it fhall appear to the fatisfaction of the perfon or perfons appointed to meafure and gage the faid wheels, that the fellies of the wheels of any waggon or wheel carriage, travelling or paffing upon any fuch turnpike road, were originally, and when firft made, of the breadth of nine or fix inches refpectively, and, by long ufage and wearing, fhall have been reduced to, and become of, lefs breadth or gage then, and in fuch cafe, it fhall and may be lawful for fuch waggon or wheel carriage to travel, pafs, or be drawn upon any fuch turnpike road, fo as the fellies of all the wheels thereof refpectively be not diminifhed more than one inch of the full breadth required by this act.

XI. And

XI. And it is hereby further enacted and declared, That if any person or persons shall hinder, or attempt to prevent or obstruct, the measuring or gaging the fellies of such wheels, or shall use any violence to any person or persons employed or concerned in such measuring or gaging, each and every person so offending, and being convicted thereof before the said trustees, or any five or more of them, upon the oath of one or more credible witness or witnesses, which oath the said trustees, or any five or more of them, are hereby impowered to administer, shall forfeit and pay five pounds sterling; one half to the informer, and the other half to be applied to repairing such part or parts of the said road, as the said trustees, or any five or more of them, shall appoint. *(Persons hindering the measuring of wheels, forfeit 5 l. sterling.)*

XII. And be it further enacted by the authority aforesaid, That all tolls, duties, penalties, and forfeitures, by this act imposed, if not otherwise directed to be levied by this act, shall be levied by distress of the offender's goods and chattels, by warrant under the hands and seals of any two or more justices of the peace for the county, city, or place, where the offence shall be committed; and the persons distraining for such penalties are hereby authorised and impowered to sell the goods or chattels so distrained, and return the overplus money, if any there be, upon demand, to the owners of such goods and chattels, after such tolls, duties, penalties, or forfeitures, with the reasonable charges of such distress, shall be deducted and paid. *(Penalties, not otherwise directed, to be levied by distress. Distress may be sold.)*

XIII. And be it further enacted by the authority aforesaid, That if any person or persons shall think him or themselves aggrieved by any order or other proceedings of the said trustees or justices, it shall and may be lawful for him or them to appeal to the justices of the peace for the county or place where the cause of appeal shall arise, in their general quarter sessions assembled, who are hereby authorized and impowered to hear and determine the matter in dispute, and whose order therein shall be final and conclusive. *(Persons aggrieved may appeal to the quarter sessions.)*

XIV. And be it further enacted by the authority aforesaid, That if any action shall be brought, or suit commenced, against any person or persons for any thing done in pursuance of this act, or in relation to the premisses, or any of them, every such action or suit shall be laid or brought within one month after the fact done. *(Limitation of actions.)*

CAP. XVI.

An act to continue, amend, explain, and render more effectual, an act made in the sixth year of the reign of his present Majesty, for the better regulation of lastage and ballastage in the river Thames, and to prevent putting of rubbish, ashes, dirt, or soil, into the said river, and in the streets, passages, and kennels, in London, and in the suburbs thereof in Middlesex, and in Westminster, and such part of the dutchy of Lancaster as is in Middlesex;

F f 4

and

and for allowing a certain quantity of dung, compost,
earth, or soil, to be yearly shipped as ballast from the lay-
stalls in London *on board any collier or coasting vessel.*

Act 6 Geo. 2.

WHEREAS *an act made in the sixth year of the reign of his*
present Majesty, intituled, An act for the better regulation
of lastage and ballastage in the river Thames, *which was to con-*
tinue in force from the first day of June, *one thousand seven hundred*
and thirty three, for five years, and from thence to the end of the
then next session of parliament ; and which, by an act made in the
eleventh year of the reign of his said present Majesty, was further
continued for seven years, and from thence to the end of the then next
session of parliament ; and by an act made in the eighteenth year of
the reign of his said present Majesty, was further continued for
eleven years, and from thence to the end of the then next session of par-
liament ; is near expiring : and whereas the said act hath greatly
tended to the preventing the frauds and abuses theretofore committed
by the ballast-men employed under the master, wardens, and assistants
of the Trinity House *at* Deptford Strond *in the county of* Kent,
and also to the preservation of the navigation of the said river
Thames, *and the promoting and encouraging the trade of this king-*
dom, and for the maintenance and relief of decayed seamen, their
wives, widows, and orphans ; be it therefore enacted by the
King's most excellent majesty, by and with the advice and consent of the lords spiritual and temporal, and commons, in this
present parliament assembled, and by the authority of the same,
That the said act, and all every the powers, authorities, clauses,
and provisions therein contained, other than such as are herein-
after altered or amended, shall be and continue, and the same
is and are hereby continued, in force, from the expiration
thereof, until the twenty fourth day of *June,* one thousand
seven hundred and seventy, and from thence to the end of the
then next session of parliament.

The recited act further continued, except where altered by this act, to 24 June, 1770.

II. And, for the explaining and rendering more effectual the
said first recited act, and ascertaining the quantities of dung,
compost, earth, or soil, which may be shipped or transported as
ballast, be it therefore further enacted by the authority aforesaid,
That from and after the twenty fourth day of *June,* one thousand
seven hundred and fifty nine, any master, owner or owners, of
any ship or vessel, may ship, transport, and carry, in his or their
ship or ships, vessel or vessels, as ballast, from *London,* or any
part of the river *Thames,* any dung, compost, earth, or soil, or
any chalk rubbish, sope ashes, sope waste, flints, tobacco pipe
clay, or other clay, or any other goods or commodities, claimed to be furnished as ballast by the said corporation of *Trinity*
House (subject nevertheless to the payment of the rates and duties, and under the provisoes and restrictions herein-after mentioned and contained concerning the same) so that the whole
quantity together of all dung, compost, earth, or soil, which
shall be allowed to be shipped and transported for ballast as aforesaid, under the authority of this act, for the use of coasters and
colliers,

3000 tons of dung, compost, earth, or soil, allowed to be yearly shipped as ballast, from any part of the river Thames ;

colliers, or on any other account or pretence whatfoever, doth not exceed in any one year, to commence and be computed from the firft day of *June* inclufive in every year, the quantity of three thoufand tons, over and befides the quantity of two thoufand tons of dung, compoft, earth, or foil, herein after fpecified and allowed to be fhipped or put on board any coafting fhips or veffels in the faid river *Thames*, by the leffee or leffees, occupier or occupiers of the layftalls of the city of *London* for the time being, on the condition herein-after mentioned ; and fo alfo that the whole quantity of chalk and chalk rubbifh which fhall be fhipped and tranfported as ballaft, for the ufe of coafters and colliers in the faid river *Thames*, doth not exceed the quantity of three thoufand tons in any one year, to commence and be computed as aforefaid ; and fo likewife that the whole quantity of fope afhes, and of all other forts of commodities as aforefaid, claimed to be furnifhed as ballaft as aforefaid by the faid corporation, and licenfed by the authority of this act to be fhipped and tranfported as ballaft as aforefaid, for the ufe of coafters and colliers in the faid river, doth not exceed the quantity of two thoufand tons in any one year, to commence and be computed as aforefaid.

over and befides 2000 tons from the layftalls in London ;

and of chalk, and chalk rubbifh 3000 tons ;

and of fope afhes, &c. 2000 tons.

III. Provided neverthelefs, and be it enacted by the authority aforefaid, That before the mafter, owner or owners, of any fhip or veffel, fhall permit any of the faid commodities or things, claimed to be furnifhed as ballaft by the faid corporation, to be fhipped or put on board any fuch fhip or veffel, every fuch mafter, owner or owners, fhall make a due entry at the ballaft office of the *Trinity Houfe* in *London*, or with the officer of the faid *Trinity Houfe* at *Gravefend* (unlefs any of the faid commodities or things fhall be fhipped or put on board any fhip or veffel as aforefaid in the laft feven days of the month of *May* in any year, and then every entry thereof fhall be made at the office of the *Trinity Houfe* in *London*, and not in any other place) of all commodities and things as aforefaid which fhall be fhipped or put on board any fuch fhip or veffel as ballaft, and of the name of every fuch fhip or veffel, and of the mafter or commander thereof ; and alfo, at the time of the making of every fuch refpective entry, fhall pay to the faid corporation for fuch licence or authority, one penny for every ton of the faid commodities and things fo to be entered as aforefaid.

Entry to be made of all commodities fhipped for ballaft ;

and 1 d. per ton paid for a licence to the Trinity Houfe ; on penalty of 5 l.

IV. And be it further enacted by the authority aforefaid, That if any mafter, owner or owners, or officer of any fhip or veffel, fhall fhip or put on board, or fuffer to be fhipped or put on board, any fuch fhip or veffel, any of the commodities or things herein before-mentioned, fpecified, and enumerated, before every fuch entry and payment as aforefaid in refpect thereof fhall be made ; or fhall fhip or take on board any fuch fhip or veffel, any greater quantity thereof than what fhall be fo entered and paid for as aforefaid ; then, and in every fuch cafe, every perfon who fhall fo offend in the premiffes, and be thereof convicted

with like penalty for making a fraudulent entry.

victed in manner herein-after provided or directed, shall, for
every such offence, forfeit and pay the sum of five pounds.

V. Provided always, and it is hereby likewise enacted, That
from and after the said twenty fourth day of *June*, one thousand
seven hundred and fifty nine, it shall be lawful for any master
or owner of any ship or vessel, from time to time, to ship, transport, and carry, in any such ship or vessel, as ballast, from *London*, or any part of the river *Thames*, any quantity of bricks,
tyles, or lime, or any other merchandizeable commodities and
things (other than and except such of the said commodities and
things as are herein before enumerated and specified, and allowed to be taken or carried as ballast) without paying any thing
to the said corporation for the same.

Bricks, tyles, or lime, &c. may be shipped as ballast, duty-free.

VI. *And whereas it is necessary that the lighters, barges, or veffels, in which any dung, compost, earth, or foil, shall be loaded, in
order to be put on board any ships or vessels, for the use of coasters or
colliers in the said river* Thames, *should be weighed, marked, and
numbered*; be it further enacted by the authority aforesaid, That
from and after the said twenty fourth day of *June*, one thousand
seven hundred and fifty nine, no lighter, barge, or vessel whatsoever, shall be used or employed by any person or persons, for
carrying any dung, compost, earth, or foil, on board any ship
or vessel whatsoever in the said river *Thames*, for the use of coasters or colliers there, until every such lighter, barge, or vessel,
shall have been first weighed, marked, and numbered, by the
said corporation of the *Trinity House*, and at their costs, or by
some agent or officer who shall be appointed for that purpose by
them; and the said corporation, their agent or officer, is and
are hereby authorized and required, from time to time, at seasonable times in the day-time, as they shall fee occasion, to weigh
every such lighter, barge, or vessel, which shall be employed in
the said river *Thames*, for the carrying any dung, compost, earth,
or foil, on board any coaster or collier in the said river; and
also to affix a gauge mark, by painting the same, or otherwise,
in some conspicuous place or places, at the stem and stern of
every such lighter, barge, or vessel, as aforesaid, higher than the
same shall sink into the water when loaded, denoting the exact
tonage; and also the number of every such lighter, barge, or
vessel, in a legible manner, and in large white capital letters and
figures: and if any one shall offend in the premisses, or shall
remove, alter, deface, or counterfeit, any gauge mark of any
such lighter, barge, or vessel, as aforesaid, or the number thereof, which shall be set, painted, or affixed, by the said corporation, their agent or officer, on any such lighter, barge, or vessel;
every person so offending, and being thereof convicted in the
manner herein after directed, shall, for every such offence, forfeit and pay the sum of five pounds.

Lighters and vessels employed in the ballastage to be weighed, marked, and numbered, by the officers of the Trinity House;

Penalty of re-moving, de-facing, or counterfeit-ing, &c. the marks, 5 l.

VII. And be it further enacted by the authority aforesaid,
That in case the said corporation shall have reason at any time
to suspect that the gauge mark of any such lighter, barge, or
vessel, hath been removed, altered, or changed, then, and in
such

On suspicion of fraud, the lighters may be reweighed;

such case, it shall be lawful for the said corporation, their agent or officer, at all times hereafter, at seasonable times in the day-time, and at the costs of the said corporation, to reweigh any such lighter, barge, or vessel (so as that no more than one such lighter, barge, or vessel, shall be reweighed in any week) and in case upon the reweighing of any such lighter, barge, or vessel, the same shall be found to be of greater tonage than by the mark thereof, such lighter, barge, or vessel, shall be signified or de-noted, and ought to be, then the person or persons to whom *and the owner* such lighter, barge, or vessel, which shall be so found to be of *to forfeit 5l.* greater tonage than aforesaid shall belong, shall, for every such *on conviction* offence, on being convicted in manner by this act prescribed, *of the offence.* forfeit and pay the sum of five pounds.

VIII. *And whereas it frequently happens that ships and vessels which come within the port of* London, *bring in them large quantities of ballast, which, for convenience of the masters or owners of such ships or vessels, and to save expence, are frequently unloaded and thrown into the said river* Thames, *to the great prejudice and obstruction of the navigation thereof:* now, for preventing such annoyances for the future; be it further enacted by the authority aforesaid, That if any ship or vessel, after the said twenty fourth *Vessels to un-* day of *June,* one thousand seven hundred and fifty nine, shall *load their bal-* come into the said river with any ballast therein, no part of any *last on some* such ballast shall be unloaded, put, or thrown, from or out of *wharf or* any such ship or vessel, into the said river, but all such ballast *ground, above* shall be laid or put, at the expence of the owner or owners, or *high water* master, of every such respective ship or vessel, on some com-*mark;* mon wharf or quay near to the said river, or on some ground or place above high water mark; or otherwise, shall be unload-*or into light-* ed from every such respective ship or vessel, at the costs of the *ers of the Tri-* owner or owners, master or commander, of every such said ship *nity House.* or vessel, into one or more lighter or lighters belonging, or which shall belong, to the said corporation, which the said corporation are hereby required to furnish and send, on any demand for the same being made, or left in writing at the said ballast office, by or on the behalf of every such owner or owners, or master of any such ship or vessel; and in case the said corporation, on any *Trinity House* such application or demand as aforesaid, shall refuse, or shall ne-*to furnish* glect to furnish and send, sufficient lighter or lighters to take any *lighters ac-* ballast from any such ship or vessel, according to the true meaning *cordingly, on* of this act, within the space of three days after any such appli-*penalty of 50l.* cation or demand shall be made to them for that purpose, then, and in every such case, the said corporation shall forfeit and pay, for every such refusal or neglect, the sum of fifty pounds; unless such refusal or neglect shall be occasioned by frosty or tempestuous weather, preventing such lighter or lighters from being navigated to take away the same; to be recovered by action of *Application of* debt, bill, plaint, or information, in any of his Majesty's courts *the penalty.* of record at *Westminster,* wherein no essoin, protection, or wager of law, and no more than one imparlance shall be allowed; one moiety of which penalty shall be applied to the use of the

poor

poor of the parifh or place where the offence fhall be committed, and the other moiety to the perfon who fhall fue for the
fame.

IX. And be it further enacted by the authority aforefaid,
That the owner or owners, mafter or commander, of every fhip
or veffel, out of which any ballaft fhall be taken by any lighter
or veffel belonging to the faid corporation, fhall pay to the faid
corporation the fum of fix pence *per* ton, for every ton of ballaft which fhall be received by the faid corporation out of any
fuch fhip or veffel, within the fpace of twenty four hours after
any fuch ballaft fhall be carried away from, or out of, any fuch
fhip or veffel, by the ballaft-men, fervants, or agents, of the faid
corporation; which money, when received, fhall be applied and
difpofed of for the ufe of the poor of the faid corporation; and
in cafe of nonpayment thereof, the fame may be recovered for
the ufe aforefaid, by action of debt to be brought in any of his
Majefty's courts of record at *Weftminfter*, in the name of the
faid corporation, againft any fuch owner or owners, mafter or
commander, of any fuch fhip or veffel.

X. And be it further enacted by the authority aforefaid, That
if after the faid twenty fourth day of *June*, one thoufand feven
hundred and fifty nine, any ballaft, of any kind or denomination
whatfoever, fhall be unloaded, put, or thrown, out of any fhip
or veffel, into the river *Thames*, or be unloaded, laid, or put on
any fhore, ground, or place, below the high water mark in the
faid river, then, and in any fuch cafe, the mafter or commander
of every fuch refpective fhip or veffel from or out of which any
fuch ballaft fhall be fo unloaded, or put on any fuch fhore,
ground, or place, as aforefaid, on being thereof convicted in
the manner by this act prefcribed, fhall forfeit and pay for every
fuch offence the fum of five pounds.

XI. And be it further enacted by the authority aforefaid, That
if any perfon or perfons fhall, at any time or times after the faid
twenty fourth day of *June*, one thoufand feven hundred and
fifty nine, unload, put, or throw, into the faid river *Thames*,
any rubbifh, earth, afhes, dirt, or foil, from any wharf, quay,
or bank, adjoining or near to the faid river *Thames*, or from or
out of any barge or lighter; any perfon fo offending, and who
fhall be thereof convicted in manner by this act prefcribed, fhall
forfeit and pay for every fuch offence the fum of forty fhillings.

XII. *And, to the intent that no greater quantity of dung, compoft, earth, or foil, may be delivered or put on board any coafter or
collier, as or for ballaft, than is allowed of by this act, and that if
any greater quantity thereof than what is fo allowed of fhall be put on
board any coafter or coafters, difcovery may be made thereof;* be it
further enacted by the authority aforefaid, That from and after
the faid twenty fourth day of *June*, one thoufand feven hundred
and fifty nine, no dung, compoft, earth, or foil, fhall be delivered into or put on board any fuch coafter or collier immediately from any layftall, wharf, quay, or other place on fhore,
adjoining or near to the faid river *Thames*; and that all dung,
compoft,

compoft, earth, or foil, which, after the said twenty fourth day *ed lighter, and from* of *June*, shall, in pursuance of this act, be delivered or put on *thence de-* board any such coaster or collier as or for ballast, shall be taken *livered on* from the layftall, wharf, quay, or other place on shore, where-*board the* on the same shall lie, and therefrom shall be carried to every *coafter or* such coaster or collier, in and by some lighter, barge, or vessel, *collier.* which shall be weighed, marked, and numbered, as by this act is directed, and shall be delivered or put on board such coaster or collier from such numbered and marked lighter, barge, or vessel only, and not in any other manner : and if any person or *on penalty of* persons shall offend in the premisses, he or they, on being there-*5 l.* of convicted as by this act is directed, shall, for every such offence, forfeit and pay the sum of five pounds; one moiety *Application* thereof to the informer, and the other moiety thereof to the *thereof.* treasurer or treasurers of the said corporation of the *Trinity House*, for the use of the poor of the said corporation.

XIII. *And whereas great quantities of rubbish, earth, sand, ashes, dirt, filth, and soil, are frequently put or thrown into the streets, lanes, and common passages, of the city of* London, *and the liberties thereof, and of the suburbs of the said city in the county of* Middlesex *; and also in the streets, lanes, and common passages, of the city of* Westminster, *and the liberties thereof; and in such part of the liberty of the dutchy of* Lancaster, *as lies in the said county of* Middlesex *; and scavengers or rakers whose duty it is to cleanse such streets, lanes, and common passages, their servants or labourers, and also other persons, do frequently sweep or put rubbish, earth, sand, ashes, dirt, filth, and soil, into the kennels or channels in the said streets, lanes, and common passages, and by means thereof, such rubbish, earth, sand, ashes, dirt, filth, or soil, or part thereof, are frequently carried or forced down into the said river of* Thames, *to the manifest prejudice of the said river, and the navigation thereof, as well as to the annoyance of the docks and wharfs contiguous to the said river :* for remedy whereof, be it further enacted by the authority aforesaid, That from and after the said twenty fourth *Penalty of lay-* day of *June*, one thousand seven hundred and fifty nine, no *ing rubbish,* person or persons shall lay, throw, or put, any rubbish, earth, *ashes, or soil,* sand, ashes, dirt, filth, or soil, in any street, lane, court, com-*&c. in any of* mon way, or passage, within the said city of *London*, or the li-*the streets* berties thereof, or in the suburbs thereof in the said county of *or common* *Middlesex* ; or in any street, lane, court, common way, or pas-*ways in Lon-* sage, in the said city of *Westminster*, or the liberties thereof; or *don, Westmin-* in such part of the liberty of the dutchy of *Lancaster*, as lies in *iter, or the* the county of *Middlesex* ; other than such as is or are allowed *suburbs there-* by law to be laid or heaped up to drain, ready for the respective *of.* scavengers or rakers, within their several precincts, to carry away ; or sweep, throw, carry, or otherwise put, any rubbish, *or of sweeping* earth, sand, ashes, dirt, filth, or soil, into any kennel or chan-*or throwing* nel, in the said city of *London*, or the liberties thereof, or in the *any rubbish,* suburbs of the said city of *London*, or the liberties thereof; or *&c.* in the said city of *Westminster*, or the liberties thereof; or in such *into any of the* part of the liberty of the dutchy of *Lancaster*, as lies in the said *kennels.*

county

county of *Middlefex*; other than fuch as fhall be fwept away by the refpective inhabitants before their refpective habitations: and if any one fhall offend in the premiffes, and fhall be thereof convicted in the manner by this act directed, he, fhe, or they, fo offending, fhall, for every fuch offence, forfeit and pay the fum of ten fhillings.

But none are liable to forfeit for fweeping before their houfes immediately after fnow, thaw, or rain.

XIV. Provided always, and be it enacted by the authority aforefaid, That nothing before in this act contained fhall extend to prevent any inhabitant within the limits herein before mentioned, or his or her fervant, from fweeping immediately after fnow, thaw, or rain, into any kennel or channel within the limits aforefaid, any ice, fnow, dirt, or foil, which by means of any fuch fnow, thaw, or rain, fhall be before his or her houfe or tenement (other than and except rubbifh which fhall be caft out, thrown, or put, in any fuch ftreet, lane, or paffage, within the limits aforefaid, from repaired or decayed buildings, or otherwife) or to inflict any penalty on any fuch inhabitant, or his or her fervant, in refpect to his or her fo doing.

Leffees and occupiers of layftalls to infpect the ftreets and common paffages, and give information of offenders in the premiffes;

XV. And be it further enacted by the authority aforefaid, That it fhall be lawful for the leffee or leffees, occupier or occupiers, for the time being, of the layftalls of the faid city of *London*, and he and they is and are hereby required, either in perfon, or by fome proper fervant to be deputed by him or them, and at his or their charges, to go about and infpect the feveral ftreets, courts, lanes, and common paffages, in the faid city of *London*, and the liberties thereof, every day in the year (*Sundays* excepted) and to give information from time to time to the mayor of the faid city for the time being, or fome alderman of the faid city, of every perfon or perfons he or they fhall at any time difcover or detect offending in the premiffes, in the faid city of *London*, or the liberties thereof, contrary to the intent of this act, fo that every perfon and perfons fo offending in *London*, or the liberties thereof, may be proceeded againft, as by this act is directed, for every fuch offence.

XVI. And in cafe fuch leffee or leffees, occupier or occupiers, or his or their fervant, fhall duly, from time to time, make and perform the infpection hereby directed to be made, in London, *and the liberties thereof, according to the intent of this act, and give information againft the perfons found offending in the faid city of* London, *and the liberties thereof, to the mayor of the faid city for the time being, or fome alderman of the faid city;* be it further enacted by the authority aforefaid, That fuch leffee or leffees, occupier or occupiers, of the faid layftalls for the time being, fhall and may, between the firft day of *June*, one thoufand feven hundred and fifty nine, and the firft day of *June*, one thoufand feven hundred and fixty, fhip, or caufe to be fhipped, from any layftall of the faid city of *London*, as and for ballaft, but on no other account or pretence whatfoever, on board of any collier, or coafting fhip or fhips, veffel or veffels, in the faid river, any quantity of dung, compoft, earth, or foil, not exceeding two thoufand tons in the whole; and alfo, fhall and may, after the faid firft day

and on performing their duty therein, they are allowed to fhip annually, as ballaft, from any layftalls in London, 2000 tons of dung, &c.

day of *June*, one thousand seven hundred and sixty, yearly in every year then following, ship, or cause to be shipped, from any layftall or layftalls of the faid city of *London*, as and for ballaft, but on no other account or pretence whatfoever, on board any collier or coafting ship, veffel or veffels, any quantity of dung, compoft, earth, or foil, not exceeding two thoufand tons.

XVII. Provided neverthelefs, That fuch faid leffee or leffees, occupier or occupiers, of the faid layftalls, or the infpector or infpectors who fhall be employed by or under him or them, fhall do his or their duty in the premiffes, directed and intended by this act, and fhall yearly, after the faid firft day of *June*, one thoufand feven hundred and fixty, before the fhipping of any part of the faid additional two thoufand tons of dung, compoft, earth, or foil, obtain a teftimonial or certificate thereof, under the hand of the mayor of the faid city of *London* for the time being, and fhall deliver fuch certificate or teftimonial at the ballaft office of the faid mafter, wardens, and affiftants, of the faid *Trinity Houfe*, before the faid firft day of *June* in every fuch year, after the faid firft day of *June*, one thoufand feven hundred and fixty; and which faid additional two thoufand tons of dung, compoft, earth, or foil, fhall be befides and exclufive of the faid three thoufand tons allowed by the faid herein before recited act made in the faid fixth year of his prefent Majefty's reign, to be yearly fhipped and tranfported as ballaft; but fuch faid two thoufand additional tons of dung, compoft, earth, or foil, by this act allowed to be yearly fhipped and tranfported, as aforefaid, are to be, and fhall be, fubject and liable to the like penalties, payments, orders, reftrictions, and regulations, as in and by the faid firft herein before recited act are enacted and declared, concerning dung or compoft thereby allowed to be fhipped or tranfported as or for ballaft, other than fuch thereof as are altered or varied by this prefent act.

but before fhipping thereof, they are to obtain a certificate from the mayor, and deliver the fame at the ballaft office;

the faid quantity to be exclufive of the 3000 tons allowed by act 6 Geo. 1.

but fubject to like regulations, &c.

XVIII. And be it further enacted by the authority aforefaid, That any juftice or juftices of the peace, of the county, city, divifion, or place, in which any offence as aforefaid for unloading, putting, or throwing any ballaft from or out of any ship or veffel into the faid river *Thames*, or for putting, unloading, or throwing into the faid river *Thames*, any rubbifh, earth, fand, afhes, filth, dirt, or foil, from any wharf, quay, or bank, adjoining to or near the faid river, or from or out of any barge or lighter, or for putting or throwing any rubbifh, earth, fand, afhes, filth, dirt, or foil, in any ftreet, lane, or paffage, in the faid city of *London*, or the liberties thereof, or in the faid fuburbs of the faid city in the faid county of *Middlefex*, or in the faid city of *Weftminfter*, or the liberties thereof, or in fuch part of the liberty of the dutchy of *Lancafter* as lies in the faid county of *Middlefex*, except as herein before is excepted, or fweeping, putting, or throwing the fame into any kennel or channel in the faid city of *London*, or the liberties thereof, or in the fuburbs of the faid city in the faid county of *Middlefex*, or in the city of *Weftminfter*, or the liberties thereof, or in fuch part of the dutchy of *Lancafter*

Juftices, not being members of the Trinity houfe, may convict offenders on their own view and knowledge;

caſter

after as lies in the faid county of *Middlesex*, except as herein before is excepted, by means whereof the fame fhall or may be carried or forced down any fuch kennel or channel into the faid river *Thames*, fhall be committed, or wherein any fuch offender or offenders fhall be found, fuch juftice or juftices (not being a member of the faid corporation of the faid *Trinity House*) is and are hereby authorized and required to convict any fuch offender or offenders on the proper knowledge or view of any fuch

and hear all offences punifhable by pecuniary penalties (except where fuch are directed to be recovered in courts of record) and upon complaint or information, iffue warrants for apprehending offenders;

juftice or juftices; and every fuch juftice and juftices is and are hereby alfo authorized and required to hear all the offences punifhable by this act by any pecuniary penalties, other than fuch are herein before directed to be recovered by action of debt, bill, plaint, or information, in any of his Majefty's courts of record at *Weftminfter*; and upon an information exhibited, or complaint made, in that behalf, fo that every fuch information or complaint be exhibited upon oath before fuch juftice or juftices, within feven days after any fuch offence fhall be committed (which oath fuch juftice or juftices is or are hereby impowered and required to adminifter) every fuch juftice or juftices is and are hereby required, within their refpective jurifdictions, to iffue a warrant or warrants for the immediate apprehending of the party or parties accufed, and bringing him, her, or them, before any juftice or juftices, within his or their refpective jurifdiction, to anfwer the matters of complaint to be contained in fuch war-

which may be executed as well upon the river as on fhore;

rant or warrants; and which warrant or warrants the perfon and perfons to whom the fame fhall be directed is and are hereby authorized and impowered to execute upon the faid river *Thames*, or on any fhore adjoining thereto; and for that purpofe they, and every of them, is and are hereby authorized, impowered, and required, at all times in the day time, to go on board any fhip, veffel, boat, or craft, in the faid river, for apprehending any fuch offender or offenders who fhall be named in any fuch warrant or warrants: and on any fuch offender or offenders

offender, when taken, to be immediately carried before fome juftice, who is to fummon witneffes on either fide, and examine them on oath, &c.

being apprehended, he, fhe, or they fhall, with all convenient fpeed be carried before fome juftice or juftices of the peace, having jurifdiction in the premiffes; and every fuch juftice and juftices, within his and their refpective jurifdiction, is and are hereby authorized and required to fummon witneffes within jurifdiction of fuch juftice or juftices, as fhall be defired, on either fide, and, on their appearance, to examine them on oath (and which oath any fuch juftice and juftices is and are hereby authorized and required to adminifter) touching the premiffes, and thereupon to hear and determine the fame, and to give fuch judgment in the premiffes as fhall be juft, and according to the meaning of this act: and in cafe the party or parties accufed fhall be

Penalty, on conviction, may be levied by diftrefs and fale,

convicted, upon the proper knowledge or view of the juftice or juftices, of any offence cognizable by this act, or upon or by the oath of any credible witnefs, or by his, her, or their own confeffion, and the penalty thereby incurred or forfeited fhall not immediately be paid on fuch conviction, the fame fhall be recovered and levied by diftrefs and fale, in the like manner as any

of

of the penalties incurred and forfeited by the first-recited act are
thereby directed to be recovered and levied by distress and sale;
and in case sufficient distress cannot be found whereon the same **and for want**
may be recovered and levied, then such justice or justices shall, by **of sufficient**
warrant under his hand and seal, or their hands and seals, com- **distress, the**
mit the person or persons who shall be so convicted to the house **party be com-**
of correction of the county, city, or place, where such any offender **mitted.**
shall be apprehended, there to remain, without bail or mainprize, and be kept to hard labour, for any time not exceeding
one month, or until payment shall, before that time, be made,
of the pecuniary penalties or forfeitures, or composition shall be
made and accepted for the same.

XIX. Provided always, and it is hereby enacted and de- **Inhabitants**
clared, That any inhabitant of the parish or place in which **deemed com-**
any offence against this act shall be committed, shall, notwith- **petent wit-**
standing such inhabitancy, be a good and competent witness. **nesses.**

XX. And be it further enacted by the authority aforesaid, **Where wit-**
That if any person who shall be so summoned as a witness or **nesses refuse to**
witnesses, as aforesaid, before any justice or justices, shall refuse **appear upon**
or neglect to appear at the time by such summons appointed, **being sum-**
and no just cause shall be offered for such neglect or refusal; then **moned,**
(after proof on oath of such summons having been duly served
upon the party or parties so summoned) every such justice **warrants are**
and justices is and are hereby authorised and required to issue **to be issued out**
his or their warrant under his hand and seal, or their hands and **against them;**
seals, to bring every such witness or witnesses before any justice
or justice : and if any such witness or witnesses, on his or her **and where they**
appearance, or being brought before any such justice or justices, **refuse to give**
shall refuse to be examined on oath concerning the premisses, **evidence, they**
without offering some just excuse for such refusal, any such justice **are to be**
or justices, within the limits of his or their respective jurisdic- **committed.**
tion, may, by warrant under his hand and seal, or their hands
and seals, commit any person or persons so refusing to be examined to the house of correction of the county, city, or place,
where any such person shall be apprehended, there to remain for
any time not exceeding one month, nor less than one week, as
any such justice or justices shall direct.

XXI. Provided always, and be it further enacted, That every **Penalty of**
person who shall be summoned to appear and give evidence be- **witness not**
fore a justice or justices of the peace, concerning any offence cog- **appearing to**
nizable before him or them by this act, and shall refuse or ne- **the summons,**
glect to appear according to such summons, or appearing, shall **or refusing to**
refuse to give evidence, without offering some just cause, to be allow- **give evidence,**
ed of by such justice or justices, in excuse for such neglect or re- **40 s.**
fusal, shall, on being convicted thereof by such justice or justices,
forfeit and pay for every such neglect or refusal the sum of forty
shillings; to be recovered and levied by distress and sale of the **to be recover-**
goods and chattels of the party convicted of any such neglect or **ed by distress**
refusal, in like manner as any other pecuniary penalty incurred **and sale,**
under this act is hereby directed to be recovered and levied; and **and paid over**
that all money so forfeited, shall, when recovered, be paid and **for the use of**

applied **the poor of**
the parish;

applied for the ufe of the poor the parifh or place in which any fuch neglect or refufal fhall be made; but that no warrant fhall be figned by a juftice or juftices of the peace for committing to any houfe of correction any perfon who fhall be convicted of fuch neglect or refufal as aforefaid, until it fhall have been proved, by oath, to the fatisfaction of fuch juftice or juftices, that the money forfeited by fuch neglect or refufal had not been paid; and likewife that no fufficient diftrefs can be found, within the jurifdiction of fuch juftice or juftices, whereon the money fo forfeited may be recovered and levied.

but oath is to be made of nonpayment of the penalty, and want of diftrefs, before warrant of commitment be iffued.

XXII. And it is hereby further enacted, That in cafe any perfon againft whom a warrant fhall be iffued by any juftice or juftices before or after conviction as aforefaid, for any offence againft this act, fhall efcape, go into, refide, or be in any other county, riding, divifion, city, liberty, town, or place, out of the jurifdiction of fuch perfon granting fuch warrant or warrants as aforefaid; or if the goods and chattels of any offender convicted of any offence in purfuance of this act, fhall be in a different county, riding, divifion, city, liberty, town, or place, than where the faid party was convicted, or warrant of diftrefs granted; it fhall and may be lawful for any juftice of the peace of the county, riding, divifion, city, liberty, town, or place, into which fuch perfon fhall efcape, either before or after conviction, or where his goods and chattels fhall be after fuch conviction; and they and every of them are hereby required, upon proof made upon oath of the hand writing of any juftice or juftices granting fuch warrant or warrants, to indorfe his or their name or names on fuch warrant; and the fame, when fo indorfed, fhall be a fufficient authority to all peace officers to execute fuch warrant in fuch other county, riding, divifion, city, town, or place, out of the jurifdiction of the perfon or perfons granting the faid warrant: and any juftice or juftices refpectively, on the offender or offenders being apprehended and brought before him or them within their refpective jurifdictions, may proceed to hear and determine the complaint in the fame manner as if it had originally arofe within his or their refpective jurifdictions, or may direct the offender or offenders to be carried to the juftice or juftices who granted the original warrant, to be dealt with according to law.

Juftices may back warrants of apprehenfion or diftrefs, where the offender or goods fhall be out of the jurifdiction of the perfon firft granting the fame;

and may hear and determine the complaint, or remit the offender to the juftice who granted the original warrant.

XXIII. And be it further enacted by the authority aforefaid, That the juftice or juftices before whom any perfon fhall be convicted in manner prefcribed by this act, fhall caufe every fuch conviction to be drawn up in the form or to the effect following:

Form of conviction.

To wit, } BE it remembered, That on the   day of
                    in the   year of his
prefent Majefty's reign, A. B. *is convicted before
of his Majefty's juftices of the peace for the county of
or for the city of
(as the cafe fhall happen to be) for
and   do adjudge him, her, or
                                                         them*

them (as the case shall be) to pay and forfeit for the same the sum of

Given under   the day and
year aforesaid.

XXIV. And be it further enacted by the authority aforesaid, That no *Certiorari*, or other writ or process, for removal of any such conviction, or any proceedings thereon, into any of his Majesty's courts of record at *Westminster*, shall be allowed or granted; and that no person who shall be prosecuted under this act for any offence committed against the same, and who shall be thereupon convicted, shall be prosecuted or convicted for any such offence by or under any other law whatsoever.

No Certiorari issuable to remove the conviction or proceedings thereon. None to be prosecuted a second time for the same offence.

XXV. And be it further enacted by the authority aforesaid, That all pecuniary penalties and forfeitures which shall incur and become payable under or by virtue of this act (the application whereof is not herein before directed) shall, when recovered, go and be applied in manner following; that is to say, Where any person or persons shall be convicted under the authority of this act, on the view of any justice or justices, then the whole money forfeited shall go to the poor of the parish or place where such offence shall be committed; and where any person or persons shall be convicted by the oath of one or more credible witness or witnesses, or his, her, or their own confession, for any offence against this act not done on the river *Thames*, one moiety of the penalty so forfeited shall go to the poor of the parish or place where any such offence shall be committed, and the other moiety thereof to or for the use of the person or persons on whose information any such offender or offenders shall be convicted; and where the party or parties shall be convicted for any offence committed against this act on the said river *Thames*, then one moiety of the penalty forfeited shall go to, and be applied for, the benefit of the poor of the said corporation of *Trinity House*, and the other moiety thereof to the person or persons on whose information any person shall be convicted for any offence committed against this act on the said river *Thames*.

Application of the penalties, not otherwise directed how to be applied.

XXVI. Provided nevertheless, and it is hereby also enacted, That it shall be lawful to and for any justice or justices of the peace who shall convict any offender or offenders against this act, from time to time, as he or they shall see cause, to mitigate or lessen any of the forfeitures or penalties incurred by any such conviction, as any such justice or justices in his or their discretion shall think fit, so as such mitigation doth not extend to remit above one moiety of the penalty forfeited by any such conviction; and on the payment by the person or persons who shall have been so convicted of the sum to which any such penalty or forfeiture shall be so lessened or mitigated, the person or persons who shall have been so convicted, shall be acquitted and discharged of, from, and against, the penalty or forfeiture incurred by any such conviction.

Justices may mitigate the penalties, so as not to remit above one moiety thereof.

G g 2   XXVII. Pro-

XXVII. Provided also, and it is hereby further enacted, That if any person or persons shall find himself or themselves aggrieved, or remain unsatisfied, in the judgment or determination of any justice or justices as aforesaid, then such person or persons shall or may, by virtue of this act, complain or appeal to the justices of the peace at the next general or general quarter sessions of the peace which shall be held for the county, city, or place, wherein such offence shall be committed, who are hereby impowered to summon and examine witnesses upon oath,

and to hear and determine the matter of every such appeal; and which determination shall be final, and shall not be removeable by *Certiorari*, or otherwise, into any other court; and in case of conviction, to issue a warrant for levying or compelling, by the means by this act prescribed, the payment of the penalties and forfeitures hereby incurred, and the reasonable charges on any such appeal, if such charges at any such sessions shall be a-warded; and in case of nonpayment, to commit the offender

or offenders, on whose goods no sufficient distress can be made, to the house of correction of the county, city, or place, where any such offender shall be apprehended, there to remain without bail or mainprize, and be kept to hard labour, for any time not exceeding one month, or until payment shall, before that time, be made, of the pecuniary penalty or forfeiture incurred, and the reasonable charges of every such appeal, if the same at any such general or general quarter session of the peace, shall be ordered to be paid, or composition shall be made and accepted for such penalty or forfeiture and charges.

XXVIII. And be it further enacted by the authority aforesaid, That the several clauses, powers, penalties, forfeitures, provisions, and matters, herein before contained, shall continue in force and be executed from and after the respective commencements thereof, until the twenty fourth day of *June*, one thousand seven hundred and seventy, and from thence to the end of the then next session of parliament.

XXIX. And it is hereby further enacted and declared, That if any suit or action shall be brought or prosecuted against any person or persons for any thing done or to be done in pursuance of this act; in every such case, the action or suit shall be commenced within six months after the fact committed, and not afterwards; and shall be laid or brought in the county, city, or place, where the cause of action arises, and not elsewhere; and the defendant or defendants in such action or suit may plead the

general issue, not guilty, and give this act and the special matter in evidence at any trial to be had thereupon, and that the same was done in pursuance and by the authority of this act; and if it shall appear so to be done, or if any such action or suit shall be brought after the time limited for bringing the same, then the jury shall find for the defendant or defendants; or if the plaintiff or plaintiffs shall become nonsuited, or suffer a discontinuance of his, her, or their action or actions, or if a verdict shall pass against the plaintiff or plaintiffs; or if, upon demurrer-

murrer, judgment fhall be given againft the plaintiff or plaint- *Treble cofts.*
iffs, the defendant or defendants fhall have treble cofts, and have
fuch remedy for the fame, as any defendant or defendants hath
or have for cofts of fuit in other cafes by law.

XXX. And be it further enacted by the authority aforefaid, *Publick act.*
That this act fhall be deemed and taken to be a publick act;
and all judges, juftices, and other perfons, are to take notice
hereof.

CAP. XVII.

An act for obviating a doubt with refpect to the fummoning
of perfons for offences committed againft, or forfeitures
incurred by, the laws of excife.

WHEREAS *it has been doubted, where the commiffioners of* *Preamble.*
excife and juftices of the peace have refpectively iffued out any
fummons for the appearance of perfons offending againft, or for for-
feitures incurred by, the laws of excife, or other laws made for col-
lecting and fecuring the feveral other duties under the management of
the commiffioners of excife, which hath been left at the houfe or ufual
place of refidence, or with the wife, child, or menial fervant of fuch
perfons, whether the fame fhould be deemed and adjudged a good and
fufficient fummons, and as legal and effectual a notice, as if the fame
had been actually delivered to the proper hands of fuch perfon or per-
fons, to whom the fame was or were directed: now, in order to put
an end to fuch doubt; be it hereby enacted by the King's moft
excellent majefty, by and with the advice and confent of the
lords fpiritual and temporal, and commons, in this prefent par- *Summons left*
liament affembled, and by the authority of the fame, That every *at the houfe,*
fuch fummons, fo left as aforefaid, fhall be deemed to be a good *or ufual place*
and fufficient fummons, and as legal and effectual a notice, as *of the party,*
if the fame had been actually delivered to the proper hands of *deemed legal*
fuch perfons to whom the fame was by name directed. *notice.*

II. And for the future, it is hereby enacted, That in all cafes *In all cafes re-*
relating to the excife, or to any of the other duties, which now *lating to the*
or hereafter may be under the management of the commiffion- *excife, fum-*
ers of excife (except where particular provifions and directions *mons directed*
are or fhall be enacted for fummoning offenders, or for con- *to the party by*
demning of feizures made from perfons unknown) the leaving *his right or*
fuch fummons at the houfe, workhoufe, warehoufe, fhop, cel- *affumed name,*
lar, vault, or ufual place of refidence of fuch perfon or perfons, *or left at his*
directed to fuch perfon or perfons, by his, her, or their right or *ufual place of*
affumed name or names, fhall be deemed to be, and is hereby *refidence,*
declared to be, as legal and effectual a notice and fummons, to *deemed legal*
all intents and purpofes, as if the fame was perfonally given or *notice.*
delivered to or into the hands of the party or parties for whom *Exception.*
the fame fhall be defigned, and as if the fame was directed to
the party or parties to and for whom the fame fhall be defigned,
by his, her, or their, proper name or names.

CAP. XVIII.

An act to continue so much of an act made in the nineteenth year of the reign of his present Majesty, as relates to the further punishment of persons going armed or disguised, in defiance of the laws of customs or excise; and to the relief of the officers of the customs in informations upon seizures; and to appropriate certain penalties mentioned in an act made in the last session of parliament, for the due making of bread; and to regulate the price and assize thereof; and to punish persons who shall adulterate meal, flour, or bread.

Preamble.

WHEREAS the law here after mentioned, hath, by experience, been found useful, and beneficial, and is near expiring: may it therefore please your Majesty, that it may be enacted; and be it enacted by the King's most excellent majesty, by and with the advice and consent of the lords spiritual and temporal, and commons, in this present parliament assembled, and by the authority of the same, That so much of an act made in the **Act 19 Geo. 2.** nineteenth year of the reign of his present Majesty, intituled, *An act for the further punishment of persons going armed or disguised, in defiance of the laws of customs or excise; and for indemnifying offenders against those laws, upon the terms therein mentioned; and for relief of officers of the customs in informations upon seizures,* which act was to continue in force for the space of seven years, and from thence to the end of the then next session of parliament; as relates to the further punishment of persons going armed or disguised, in defiance of the laws of customs or excise, and to the relief of officers of the customs in informations upon seizures; which, by an act made in the twenty sixth year of the reign of his said Majesty, was further continued from the expiration thereof until the twenty fourth day of *June* one thousand seven hundred and fifty eight, and from thence to the end of the then **further conti-** next session of parliament, shall be further continued from the **nued to 29** expiration thereof, until the twenty ninth day of *September* one **Sept. 1764.** thousand seven hundred and sixty four, and from thence to the end of the then next session of parliament.

II. *And whereas several of the penalties or forfeitures made payable by an act passed in the thirty first year of his present Majesty's* **Act 31 Geo. 2.** *reign, intituled,* An act for the due making of bread; and to regulate the price and assize thereof; and to punish persons who shall adulterate meal, flour or bread; *were not by such said last mentioned act appropriated how or to whom the same should, when paid or recovered, go or be distributed;* be it therefore further enacted **Distribution of** by the authority aforesaid, That such of the penalties or for- **the unappro-** feitures which, from and after the twenty fourth day of *June* one **priated penal-** thousand seven hundred and fifty nine, shall incur or become **ties and for-** payable by or under the said last mentioned act, or by reason of **feitures under** any thing therein contained (as by the said act are not particu- **the said act;** larly

lan

larly difpofed of, or appropriated, how or to whom the fame
fhould go or be applied) fhall, when the fame fhall be recovered
or paid, go, and be diftributed, in manner following; that is to
fay, One moiety thereof, where any offender or offenders fhall
be convicted, either by his, her, or their own confeffion, or by
the oath of one or more credible witnefs or witneffes, fhall go
and be paid to the perfon or perfons who fhall inform againft,
and profecute to conviction, any fuch offender or offenders; and
the other moiety thereof, and alfo all penalties and forfeitures,
which, from the faid twenty fourth day of *June* one thoufand
feven hundred and fifty nine, fhall incur, be due, or payable,
under the faid laft mentioned act, on the weighing, trying, or
feizure of any bread, by any magiftrate or magiftrates, juftice or
juftices, fhall go and be applied for the better carrying into execution the purpofes of the faid laft mentioned act, as any fuch
magiftrate or magiftrates, juftice or juftices, within his or their
refpective jurifdiction, fhall, from time to time, think fit, and
order.

*viz. One moi-
ety to the pro-
fecutor, where
the offender
fhall be con-
victed by oath,
or felf confef-
fion; and the other
moiety, with
the penalties
on weighing,
trying, or
feizure of
bread, by a
magiftrate, to
fuch purpofes
as the magi-
ftrate fhall
think fit.*

C A P. XIX.

*An act to explain and amend an act paffed in the thirtieth year
of his prefent Majefty's reign, for granting to his Majefty
feveral rates and duties upon indentures, leafes, bonds, and
other deeds; and upon news papers, advertifements, and almanacks; and upon licences for retailing wine; and other
purpofes in the faid act mentioned; fo far as the fame relates to fome provifions with regard to licences for retailing
wine; and to preferve the privileges of the two univerfities
in that part of* Great Britain *called* England, *with refpect
to licences for retailing wine.*

WHEREAS *by an act paffed in the thirtieth year of his
prefent Majefty's reign, intituled,* An act *for granting to
his Majefty feveral rates and duties upon indentures, leafes,
bonds, and other deeds; and upon news papers, advertifements,
and almanacks; and upon licences for retailing wine; and upon
coals exported to foreign parts; and for applying from a certain
time the fums of money arifing from the furplus of the duties on
licences for retailing fpirituous liquors; and for raifing the fum
of three millions by annuities, to be charged on the faid rates,
duties, and fums of money; and for making perpetual an act
made in the fecond year of the reign of his prefent Majefty, intituled,* An act for the better regulation of attornies and folicitors; *
and for enlarging the time for filing aff-lavits of the execution of
contracts of clerks to attornies and folicitors; and alfo the time
for payment of the duties omitted to be paid for the indentures
and contracts of clerks and apprentices;* it was amongft other
things enacted, That from and after the fifth day of *July one thoufand
feven hundred and fifty feven, no perfon whatfoever, un'efs authorized
and enabled, by taking out fuch licence as is therein prefcribed, fubject*

*Preamble.
Act 30 Geo. 2.*

*Recital of a
claufe in the
faid act.*

to the payment of such duties as are therein respectively charged there-upon, should sell or utter by retail (that is) by the pint, quart, pottle, or gallon, or by any other greater or lesser retail measure, or in bottles, in any less quantity than should be equal to the measure of the cask or vessel in which the same should have been or might lawfully be imported, any kind of wine or wines, or any liquor called or reputed wine; upon pain to forfeit for every such offence, the sum of one hundred pounds: And whereas the said penalty of one hundred pounds inflicted by the said recited act of the thirtieth year of his present Majesty's reign, on all persons selling wine, or other liquor called or reputed wine, by re-tail, without a licence, in many instances is found to be attended with great inconvenience, and the greatest circumstances of hardship, and scarce ever to be recovered, on account of the largeness thereof; and which said penalty the commissioners for management of the said du-ties are not invested with any power to mitigate: now therefore, be

The commis-sioners are im-powered to mitigate, at their discre-tion, the 100l. penalty in the recited clause;

it enacted by the King's most excellent majesty, by and with the advice and consent of the lords spiritual and temporal, and commons, in this present parliament assembled, and by the au-thority of the same, That it shall and may be lawful to and for the commissioners for management of the said duties, or any two of them, where they shall see cause, to mitigate or lessen the said penalty of one hundred pounds already incurred, or hereafter to be incurred by all or any person or persons whatsoever, by vir-tue or in consequence of the said recited act of the thirtieth year of his present Majesty's reign, as they in their discretion, shall

but the costs and charges of the informa-tion and prose-cution, &c. are to be allow-ed over and a-bove such mi-tigation.

think fit; the reasonable costs and charges of the officers and in-formers, as well in making the discovery, as in the prosecution of the same, being always allowed over and above such mitiga-tion; any thing contained in any former act of parliament to the contrary notwithstanding.

II. *And whereas doubts and difficulties have arisen on the said recited act of the thirtieth year of his present Majesty's reign, whether wine merchants and other persons applying for a number of wine licences at one time, for enabling divers persons to sell wine by retail, were or are intitled to the benefit of the several discounts, drawbacks, and allow-ances, usually made and allowed to persons paying for a number of stamps at the same time, amounting to ten pounds, and upwards:*

No discount or drawback of the duty on wine licen-ces, to be al-lowed on tak-ing out any number thereof.

Now therefore, for obviating such doubts and difficulties for the future, be it enacted by the authority aforesaid, That no person or persons whatsoever paying for any number of wine licences at one and the same time, or at different times, shall be intitled to any discount, drawback, or allowance whatsoever, for or on ac-count of such payment for any number of wine licences whatso-ever; but that the said duty imposed by the said in part recited act of the thirtieth year of his present Majesty's reign on wine licences, shall be paid by all persons applying for the same, clear of all discounts, drawbacks, and allowances whatsoever; any thing contained in any former act of parliament to the con-trary notwithstanding.

III. And be it further enacted by the authority aforesaid, That no person or persons whatsoever licensed, or to be licensed, by

vir-

virtue of the said in part recited act of the thirtieth year of his present Majesty's reign, to retail wine, shall, by virtue of one licence, keep more than one place, house, shop, vault, cellar, warehouse, or other place, for selling or uttering wine by retail ; and that every retailer of wine shall cause the word WINE to be written or expressed in legible characters, either on a sign hung out, or in some visible place in or near the door in the front of his or her house, shop, vault, cellar, warehouse, or other place, made use of for the retailing of wine, to denote that such retailer is a dealer in wine, and subject and liable to take out a licence for the retailing thereof; and if any person or persons shall presume to sell or utter wine by retail, without fixing or hanging out such token as aforesaid, every person so offending shall, for every such offence, forfeit the sum of ten pounds, to be recovered in the same manner as the penalty inflicted on persons for selling wine by retail without licence is directed to be recovered; subject nevertheless to the like power of mitigation to be exercised by the commissioners of stamp duties, as in this act is before reserved and prescribed with regard to the penalty for selling wine by retail without licence.

One licence to serve but one house or place. Retailers to have the word WINE, expressed on their signs or houses, &c.

on penalty of 10l.

subject however to mitigation by the commissioners.

IV. Provided always, and be it further enacted by the authority aforesaid, That nothing in this or any former act of parliament, relating to wine licences, shall in any wise be prejudicial to the privileges of the two universities in that part of *Great Britain* called *England*, or either of them, or to the chancellors or scholars of the same, or their successors, but that they may use and enjoy such privileges as they have heretofore lawfully used and enjoyed; any thing to the contrary thereof in any wise notwithstanding.

Privileges of the two universities reserved to them.

CAP. XX.

An act for enforcing the execution of the laws relating to the militia; and for removing certain difficulties, and preventing inconveniencies, attending, or which may attend, the same.

WHEREAS *certain counties, ridings, and places, within that part of* Great Britain *called* England, *have made some progress in establishing the militia, according to the regulations and directions of an act passed in the thirtieth year of his Majesty's reign, intituled,* An act for the better ordering of the militia forces in the several counties of that part of *Great Britain* called *England, and of an act passed in the thirty first year of his Majesty's reign, intituled,* An act to explain, amend, and enforce the said act; *but have not yet completed the same: And whereas, in certain other counties, ridings, and places, little progress has been made therein; his Majesty's lieutenants, and the deputy lieutenants, and all others within such counties, ridings, and places, are hereby strictly required speedily and diligently to put the said acts, and this act, in execution: And, for removing certain difficulties, and preventing inconveniencies, attending, or which may attend, the execution of the said acts; be it enacted by* the King's most excellent majesty, by and with the advice and

Preamble.

Act 30 Geo. 2.

and 31 Geo. 2.

The recited acts, and this act, required to be put into speedy execution in such counties, &c. where little progress has been made therein.

con-

consent of the lords spiritual and temporal, and commons, in this present parliament assembled, and by the authority of the same, That in every county, riding, and place, within the part of *Great Britain* aforesaid, it shall be lawful for his Majesty's lieutenant together with any two or more deputy lieutenants, and on the death or removal, or in the absence, of his Majesty's lieutenant, or the deputy lieutenants, or any three or more of them, at a general meeting to be held after reasonable notice thereof given by his Majesty lieutenant, or by any two deputy lieutenants, to appoint subdivisions of the deputy lieutenants within their respective counties, ridings, and places, and the times and places for their first meetings within the said subdivisions; and also to change or alter such subdivisions, or any subdivision or subdivisions now appointed therein, whenever they shall find it convenient so to do; any thing in the said acts, or either of them, contained to the contrary notwithstanding.

II. And be it enacted, That if it shall happen that there shall not appear at any subdivision meeting, a sufficient number of deputy lieutenants, and justices of the peace, to act, the clerk of such meeting shall, by notice given in writing to all the deputy lieutenants within such subdivision, appoint another meeting to be held within fourteen days, at the same place where such meeting had been before appointed to be held, giving at least five days notice thereof.

III. And be it enacted, That the deputy lieutenants, or any three or more of them, or any two deputy lieutenants, together with any one justice of the peace, or any one deputy lieutenant, together with any two justices of the peace, in their several subdivisions, shall annually cause the lists of such persons in the several parishes, tythings, and places, within the same, as are in the said act passed in the thirty first year of his Majesty's reign described, to be made, and to be returned to them at their meetings within the respective subdivisions, on such days, and at such places, respectively, as his Majesty's lieutenant, together with any two or more deputy lieutenants, or on the death or removal, or in the absence, of his Majesty's lieutenant, any three or more deputy lieutenants, shall, at a general meeting, appoint; and that in the ordering, making out, and disposing of, such lists, and copies thereof, and also in all particulars subsequent to such first return so made, so much of the said last-mentioned act as relates to the method to be observed in returning, amending, and disposing of, the said lists, and copies thereof, and to the appointing, choosing, summoning, and inrolling, the militia men, and their substitutes, and administering the oath therein directed to be taken, and to the punishing persons refusing or neglecting to take the said oath, or to provide substitutes, and to the exemption of certain persons from serving in the militia, and to the appointing general meetings, and all subdivision meetings after the said first subdivision meetings, and is by the said act required to be observed in the
year

A general meeting to be held for appointing and regulating the subdivision meetings of the deputy lieutenants.

Subdivision meetings may be changed, as shall be found convenient.

When a sufficient number to act shall not appear at any subdivision meeting, the clerk is to give notice of another meeting to be held within 14 days after.

Deputy lieutenants and justices are annually to cause the lists described by Act 31 Geo. 2. to be returned to them in their subdivision meetings, at the times and places appointed at the general meeting; and all other the regulations, provisions and directions of the said act, subsequent thereto, and required to be observed in the year 1758, are to be duly complied with, and executed as the case shall require;

year one thousand seven hundred and fifty eight; shall be observed and executed, either in the whole, or in part, as the case shall require, until all the regulations, provisions, and directions, therein and herein contained, and which relate to the purposes aforesaid, be fully completed and performed: and that thereafter the method in the said act, and this act, prescribed for the performance of all the particulars here mentioned, shall be annually observed for and during the continuance thereof.

and thereafter, the method in this and the said act prescribed, is to be annually observed.

IV. And be it enacted, That each person liable to serve in the militia having more than one place of residence, shall be deemed to be, and shall serve as, a militia man within the county, riding, or place, where he shall have been first chosen by lot.

Militia men having more than one place of residence, to serve where he was first chosen.

V. And be it enacted, That it shall be lawful for the mayors, bailiffs, constables, tythingmen, headboroughs, and other chief magistrates and officers, of cities, towns, parishes, tythings, villages, and other places, within the part of *Great Britain* aforesaid, and, in their default or absence, for any one justice of the peace inhabiting in or near to any such city, town, parish, tything, village, or place, and for no others, and they are hereby required to quarter and billet the serjeants and drummers serving in the militia, in inns, livery stables, ale-houses, victualling-houses, and all houses of persons selling brandy, strong waters, cyder, or metheglin, by retail; the occupiers whereof are hereby required to provide for such serjeants and drummers, at such times for which no provision has by law been made for that purpose, convenient lodgings only.

Magistrates to quarter and billet serjeants and drummers in inns, livery stables, and ale-houses, &c.

Convenient lodgings to be found them.

VI. Provided always, and be it enacted, That the estates requisite for the qualification of the deputy lieutenants and officers of the militia, in the isle of *Ely* in the county of *Cambridge*, shall be as follows; a deputy lieutenant shall be seised or possessed, either in law or equity, for his own use and benefit, in possession of a freehold, copyhold, or customary estate for life, or for some greater estate, or of an estate for some long term of years, determinable on one or more life or lives, or of an estate for a certain term, originally granted for twenty years, or more, and renewable, over and above all rents and charges payable out of, or in respect of, the same, in manors, messuages, lands, tenements, or hereditaments, in *England, Wales*, or the town of *Berwick upon Tweed*, of the yearly value of two hundred pounds; a captain shall be, in like manner, seised or possessed of a like estate as aforesaid, of the yearly value of one hundred pounds; or be heir apparent of a person who shall be, in like manner, seised or possessed of a like estate as aforesaid, of the yearly value of two hundred pounds; a lieutenant or ensign shall be, in like manner, seised or possessed of a like estate as aforesaid, of the yearly value of fifty pounds; or be heir apparent of a person who shall be, in like manner, seised or possessed of a like estate as aforesaid, of the yearly value of one hundred pounds: one half of all which estates respectively shall be situate or arising within the said isle; and in case any person shall act as a deputy lieutenant,

Qualifications of officers in the isle of Ely;

for a deputy lieutenant 200l. per ann.

for a captain 100l. per ann.

for a lieutenant or ensign 50l. per ann.

A moiety of all estates to be situate or arising within or the said isle.

Penalty of acting where not qualified.

or officer of the militia, in the said isle, who shall not be respectively qualified as aforesaid, every such person shall be subject and liable to the same penalties and forfeitures as any person is subject and liable to for acting as a deputy lieutenant or officer of the militia, within any other part of the said county of *Cambridge*, not being qualified according to the directions of the said recited acts; any thing therein contained to the contrary notwithstanding.

Continuance of the act.

VII. Provided always, and be it enacted, That this act shall be and remain in force, for and during the continuance of the said recited acts, and no longer.

CAP. XXI.

An act for applying the money granted in this session of parliament, towards defraying the charge of pay and cloathing for the militia, from the thirty first day of December one thousand seven hundred and fifty eight, to the twenty fifth day of March one thousand seven hundred and sixty.

Preamble. Treasury to repay the 1,332l. 10s. advanced by his Majesty, in pursuance of the address from the commons. The money received to be accounted for to the receivers general of the land tax. Treasury, upon certificate that the number of officers and private men required in a regiment or battalion, are inrolled, &c. are to issue warrants to the receivers general for pay of the militia, four months in advance. The rates of pay to the adjutant; to non-commission officers, and private men; to the clerk of the battalion or regiment; and to the clerks of the general or subdivision meetings: rates for cloathing. Warrant to be delivered to the lieutenant of every county, &c. where the militia has been already cloathed, for payment of the rates for the additional cloathing. Warrants also to be issued for making the regular payments and issues, without new certificates from the lieutenants or deputy lieutenants for that purpose. The money to be paid to the clerks of the battalions, and four months pay in advance, to be paid within 14 days after the expiration of every three months. Clerks receipts to be a discharge to the receivers general. Clerk to pay one month's pay in advance to the adjutant, 14 days to the serjeant major and drum major, and two months in advance to each captain for his company. Captain to account yearly to the clerk for the pay of his company, and pay over the balance; money allowed for contingent expences, excepted; which is also to be accounted for annually, but the balance to be applied to the general use of the battalion. Clerk to retain money to make good his own salary; and discharge the cloathing account. Allowance of 5l. 5s. to be paid to the clerks of the general meetings, and of 1l. 1s. to the clerks of the subdivision meetings, for each meeting. Clerk of the battalion to give security. The bond to be lodged with the receiver general, and on nonperformance of the conditions to be put in suit by him, who is to receive full costs of suit, and 5l. per cent. of the money recovered thereon; residue to be accounted for to the auditor of the exchequer. Clerk of the battalion to render an account to the receiver general of the monies received and disbursed, with vouchers for the same, and pay over the balance; the said account to be transmitted to the auditor. Lieutenant neglecting to take proper security, or lodge the same with the receiver general, is made answerable for any loss of the publick money. Recovery of penalties, &c. No fee to be paid for issuing warrants for payment of money.

CAP. XXII.

An act for adding certain annuities granted in the year one thousand seven hundred and fifty seven, to the joint stack of three per centum annuities, consolidated by the acts of the twenty fifth, twenty eighth, and twenth ninth, years of his present Majesty's reign; and for carrying the several duties therein mentioned to the sinking fund; and for charging the annuities on single lives, granted in the year one thousand seven hundred and fifty seven, on the produce of the said fund.

WHEREAS, *in pursuance of an act of parliament made in the thirtieth year of his present Majesty's reign, intituled,* An act for granting to his Majesty several rates and duties upon indentures, leases, bonds, and other deeds; and upon news papers, advertisements, and almanacks; and upon licences for retailing wine; and upon coals exported to foreign parts; and for applying, for a certain time, the sums of money arising from the surplus of the duties on licences for retailing spirituous liquors; and for raising the sum of three millions, by annuities, to be charged on the said rates, duties, and sums of money; and for making perpetual an act made in the second year of the reign of his present Majesty, intituled, *An act for the better regulation of attornies and solicitors; and for enlarging the time for filing affidavits of the execution of contracts of clerks to attornies and solicitors; and also the time for payment of the duties omitted to be paid for the indentures and contracts of clerks and apprentices; several persons, bodies politick or corporate, have advanced and lent the sum of three millions upon the credit of the several rates, duties, and sums of money, by the said act granted, for the purchase of annuities after the rate of three pounds per centum per annum, transferrable at the bank of England, and redeemable by parliament; and also of annuities on single lives, payable at the receipt of the exchequer in respect of the same: and whereas it is thought necessary that the said principal sum of three millions should be (with the consent of the proprietors thereof, to be signified within the time herein after mentioned) added to, and made a part of, the joint stock of three pounds per centum transferrable annuities at the bank of England; and that the charges and expences in respect thereof should be charged upon, and paid out of, the fund commonly called* The Sinking Fund, *until redemption thereof by parliament, in the same and like manner as the annuities aforesaid are paid and payable; and that the several annuities on single lives, payable at the exchequer in respect of the aforesaid three millions, should likewise be charged upon, and made payable out of, the produce of the said sinking fund; and that the several rates, duties, and sums of money, which by the said act were made a fund for payment of the said three pounds per centum annuities, as also of the several annuities on single lives, should be carried to, and made a part of, the said fund commonly called* The Sinking Fund: *may it there-*

2

therefore please your most excellent Majesty, that it may be enacted; and be it enacted by the King's most excellent majesty, by and with the advice and consent of the lords spiritual and temporal, and commons, in this present parliament assembled, and by the authority of the same, That from and after the fifth day of *January* one thousand seven hundred and fifty nine, the principal sum of three millions borrowed by virtue of the said before recited act, carrying an interest after the rate of three pounds *per centum per annum*, payable at the bank of *England*, shall, with the consent of the proprietors as aforesaid, be added to, and made a part of, the joint stock of three pounds *per centum* transferrable annuities at the bank of *England*, consolidated by the acts made in the twenty fifth, twenty eighth, and twenty ninth, years of his present Majesty's reign, and shall be transferrable at the bank of *England*; and the charges and expences in respect thereof shall be charged upon, and paid out of, the fund commonly called *The Sinking fund*, until redemption thereof by parliament, in the same and like manner as the annuities consolidated as aforesaid are paid and payable; any thing in the said act made in the thirtieth year of his present Majesty's reign to the contrary thereof in any wise notwithstanding.

The sum of 3,000,000l. borrowed by virtue of the recited act, to be added, by consent of the proprietors, to the joint stock of 3l. per cent. consolidated annuities transferrable at the bank; and to be paid out of the sinking fund:

II. And be it further enacted by the authority aforesaid, That such proprietors who shall not, on or before the twentieth day of *June* one thousand seven hundred and fifty nine, signify their dissent to such consolidation as aforesaid, in books to be opened at the bank of *England* for that purpose, shall be deemed and taken to assent thereto; any thing to the contrary thereof in any wise notwithstanding.

And such as shall not enter their dissent before 20 June 1759, to be deemed assenting thereto.

III. And be it further enacted by the authority aforesaid, That from and after the said fifth day of *January* one thousand seven hundred and fifty nine, the several annuities on single lives by the said act granted, payable at the exchequer in respect of the aforesaid three millions, shall be charged upon, and made payable out of, the produce of the said fund commonly called *The Sinking Fund*; any thing to the contrary thereof in any wise notwithstanding.

The life annuities thereupon to be also paid out of the sinking fund.

IV. And be it further enacted by the authority aforesaid, That all the monies which have arisen since the fifth day of *January* one thousand seven hundred and fifty nine, or that shall or may hereafter arise, of the produce of the several additional stamp duties on pamphlets and printed papers, the additional duty on coals exported, the surplus on the new duty on licences for retailing wine, and the surplus on the duties on licences for retailing spirituous liquors, which were made a fund for payment of three pounds *per centum per annum* at the bank of *England*, on three millions borrowed by virtue of the said act made in the thirtieth year of the reign of his present Majesty, towards the supply of the year one thousand seven hundred and fifty seven, as also of the annuities on single lives, payable at the receipt of the exchequer in respect of the same, shall be carried to, and made

Produce of the additional stamp duties,

the duty on coals exported, and surplus of the new duty on wine licences, and retailing spirituous liquors granted by act 30 Geo. 2.

made a part of, the fund commonly called *The Sinking Fund*; Life annuities and the same shall be deemed and taken to be part of the said thereupon, to sinking fund, and shall be issued and applied to such uses and he made part purposes as the several excesses, surplusses, or overplus monies, fund and ap- composing the said sinking fund, are or may be issued and ap- plied accord- plied; any thing in the said before recited act to the contrary ingly. thereof in any wise notwithstanding.

C A P. XXIII.

An act to continue several laws therein mentioned, relating to the allowing a drawback of the duties upon the exporta- tion of copper bars imported; to the encouragement of the silk manufactures, and for taking off several duties on mer- chandize exported, and reducing other duties; to the pre- mium upon masts, yards, and bowsprits, tar, pitch, and turpentine; to the encouraging the growth of coffee in his Majesty's plantations in America; *to the securing the du- ties upon foreign made sail cloth, and charging foreign made sails with a duty; and for enlarging the time for payment of the duties omitted to be paid on the indentures and contracts of clerks, apprentices, or servants; and also for making affidavits of the execution of articles or con- tracts of clerks to attornies or sollicitors, and filing there- of.*

WHEREAS the laws herein after mentioned, which have by Preamble. experience been found useful and beneficial, are near expiring: may it therefore please your most excellent Majesty, that it may be enacted; and be it enacted by the King's most excellent ma- jesty, by and with the advice and consent of the lords spiritual and temporal, and commons, in this present parliament assem- bled, and by the authority of the same, That a clause in an act Clause in an made in the ninth and tenth years of the reign of his late maje- act 9 & 10 sty King *William* the Third, intituled, *An act to settle the trade to* Will. 3. relat- *Africa*; for allowing, during a limited time, a drawback of the back of the duties upon the exportation of copper bars imported; and duties upon which clause was to continue in force for the term of thirteen copper bars, years, and from thence to the end of the then next session of &c. parliament; and which clause, after the expiration thereof, was, by an act made in the twelfth year of the reign of her late majesty Queen *Anne*, revived and continued; and also a proviso in the last mentioned act contained, That no drawback should be allowed on the exportation of any copper, but such as had been or should be imported from the *East Indies* and the coast of *Barbary* only; and which said clause and proviso, by several and the provi- subsequent acts of the thirteenth year of the reign of his late so in act 12 majesty King *George* the First, and of the fifteenth and twenty *Annæ*, relat- sixth years of the reign of his present Majesty, were continued ing thereto, until the twenty fourth day of *June*, one thousand seven hun- dred

further conti-nued to 24 June, 1766.

dred and fifty eight, and from thence to the end of the then next session of parliament; shall be, and the same are hereby further continued, from the expiration thereof, until the twenty fourth day of *June*, one thousand seven hundred and sixty six, and from thence to the end of the then next session of parliament.

Part of act 8 Geo. 1. relating to the encouragement of the silk manufactures, further continued to 24 June, 1766.

II. And be it further enacted by the authority aforesaid, That so much of an act made in the eighth year of the reign of his late majesty King *George* the First, for the encouragement of the silk manufactures of this kingdom; and for taking off several duties on merchandizes exported; and for reducing the duties upon beaver skins, pepper, mace, cloves, and nutmegs, imported; and for importation of all furs of the product of the *British* plantations, into this kingdom only; and that the two corporations of assurance, on any suits brought on their policies, shall be liable only to single damages and costs of suit; as relates to the encouragement of the silk manufactures of this kingdom, and to the taking off several duties on merchandizes exported; which was to continue in force for three years, from the twenty fifth day of *March*, one thousand seven hundred and twenty two, and from thence to the end of the then next session of parliament; and which, by several subsequent acts made in the eleventh year of the reign of his late majesty King *George* the First, and in the second, eighth, fifteenth, twentieth, and twenty sixth years of the reign of his present Majesty, hath been continued until the twenty fourth day of *March*, one thousand seven hundred and fifty eight, and from thence to the end of the then next session of parliament; shall be, and the same is hereby further continued from the expiration thereof, until the said twenty fourth day of *June*, one thousand seven hundred and sixty six, and from thence to the end of the then next session of parliament.

So much of the act 2 Geo. 2. &c. as relates to premiums on masts, tar, and pitch, &c. continued to 24 June, 1766.

III. And be it further enacted by the authority aforesaid, That so much of an act made in the second year of the reign of his present Majesty, for the better preservation of his Majesty's woods in *America*, and for the encouragement of the importation of naval stores from thence; and to encourage the importation of masts, yards, and bowsprits, from that part of *Great Britain* called *Scotland*; as relates to the premiums upon masts, yards, and bowsprits, tar, pitch, and turpentine, which was to continue in force from the twenty ninth day of *September*, one thousand seven hundred and twenty nine, for the term of thirteen years, and from thence to the end of the then next session of parliament; and which, by several subsequent acts made in the thirteenth and twenty fourth years of his said Majesty's reign, was further continued until the twenty fifth day of *December*, one thousand seven hundred and fifty one, and from thence to the end of the then next session of parliament; and which, by another act made in the twenty fifth year of the reign of his said Majesty, was amended, and further continued until the twenty fifth day of *March*, one thousand seven hundred and fifty

fifty eight, and from thence to the end of the then next feffion of parliament; fhall be, and the fame is hereby further continued from the expiration thereof, until the faid twenty fourth day of *June*, one thoufand feven hundred and fixty fix, and from thence to the end of the then next feffion of parliament.

IV. Provided, That no bounty fhall be paid upon any tar, unlefs each barrel fhall contain thirty one gallons and one half; and that the officers who furvey fuch barrel, fhall not furvey the fame, till the water fhall be all drawn off, and every barrel filled up with tar. *Quantity of tar in each barrel intitled to bounty, not to be lefs than 32 gallons.*

V. And be it further enacted by the authority aforefaid, That an act made in the fifth year of the reign of his prefent Majefty, for encouraging the growth of coffee in his Majefty's plantations in *America*, which was to continue in force from the twenty fifth day of *March*, one thoufand feven hundred and thirty five, until the twenty fifth day of *March*, one thoufand feven hundred and thirty nine, and from thence to the end of the then next feffion of parliament; and which, by feveral fubfequent acts made in the eleventh, nineteenth, and twenty fifth years of his faid Majefty's reign, was further continued until the twenty fifth day of *March*, one thoufand feven hundred and fifty eight, and from thence to the end of the then next feffion of parliament; fhall be, and the fame is hereby further continued from the expiration thereof, until the faid twenty fourth day of *June*, one thoufand feven hundred and fixty fix, and from thence to the end of the then next feffion of parliament. *Act 5 Geo. 2. for encouraging the growth of coffee, continued to 24 June, 1766.*

VI. And be it further enacted by the authority aforefaid, That an act made in the nineteenth year of the reign of his prefent Majefty, for the more effectual fecuring the duties now payable on foreign-made fail cloth imported into this kingdom; and for charging all foreign-made fails with a duty; and for explaining a doubt concerning fhips being obliged, at their firft fetting out to fea, to be furnifhed with one complete fet of fails made of *Britifh* fail cloth; which was to continue in force from the twenty fourth day of *June*, one thoufand feven hundred and forty fix, for the term of feven years, and from thence to the end of the then next feffion of parliament; and which, by another act made in the twenty fixth year of the reign of his prefent Majefty, was further continued until the twenty fourth day of *June*, one thoufand feven hundred and fifty eight, and from thence to the end of the then next feffion of parliament; fhall be, and the fame is hereby further continued from the expiration thereof, until the faid twenty fourth day of *June*, one thoufand feven hundred and fixty fix, and from thence to the end of the then next feffion of parliament. *Act 19 Geo. 2. for fecuring the duties on foreign-made fail cloth imported, &c. continued to 24 June, 1766.*

VII. *And, for the relief of perfons who through neglect or inadvertency have omitted to pay the feveral rates and duties upon money given, paid, contracted, or agreed for, with or in relation to any clerk, apprentice, or fervant, who hath been put or placed to or with any mafter or miftrefs, to learn any profeffion, trade, or employment, and to have the indenture, or other writing which contains the cove-*

nants, articles, contracts, or agreements, relating to the service of any such clerk, apprentice, or servant, stamped within the time by the several acts of parliament for those purposes respectively limited, or who have neglected or omitted to insert and write in words at length, in any such indenture, or other writing, as aforesaid respectively, the full sum or sums of money received, or in any wise directly or indirectly given, paid, agreed, or contracted for, with or in relation to any such clerk, apprentice, or servant, as aforesaid;

be it further enacted, That upon payment on or before the first day of September, one thousand seven hundred and fifty nine, of the rates and duties neglected or omitted to be paid upon any money given, paid, contracted, or agreed for, with or in relation to any clerk, apprentice, or servant, as aforesaid, to such person or persons to whom the same ought to be paid, the indenture or other writing by which any such clerk, apprentice, or servant, was respectively put out as aforesaid, shall, on the same being tendered at the proper place in the stamp office (where the same ought to have been stamped) during the time of office hours, be stamped with the proper stamp forthwith after every such payment and tender of every such respective indenture or writing shall be there made; and every such inden-

ture, or other writing, as aforesaid, being so stamped, shall be good and available in law and equity, and may be given in evidence in any court whatsoever; and the several clerks, apprentices, or servants, therein respectively named, shall be capable of following and exercising their respective intended profession, trade, employment, or business, as fully as if the rates or duties so neglected or omitted to have been paid, had been duly paid, and as if the full sum or sums of money received or agreed to be paid as aforesaid, had been inserted and wrote in words at length in every such indenture, or other writing, as aforesaid respectively; and that all and every person and persons who hath

or have incurred any penalty by any such neglect or omission, as aforesaid, shall be acquitted and discharged of, from, and against the same; any thing in any former act to the contrary hereof notwithstanding: and the commissioners of his Majesty's stamp

duty are hereby required, with all convenient speed, after the passing this act, to cause notice of this clause to be published in the London Gazette, in such manner as they shall think fit.

VIII. And whereas some persons have omitted to cause affidavits to be made, and afterwards to be filed in the proper offices, of the actual execution of several contracts in writing entered into by them, to serve as clerks to attornies or solicitors, within the time in which the same ought to have been done, and many infants, and others, may thereby incur certain disabilities: for preventing whereof, and for relieving such persons; be it likewise enacted by the authority

aforesaid, That every person who hath neglected or omitted to cause any such affidavit or affidavits as aforesaid to be made and filed, and who on or before the first day of September, one thousand seven hundred and fifty nine, shall cause one or more affidavit or affidavits to be made, and afterwards to be filed, in such manner as the

the fame ought to have been made and filed, in due time, shall be, and is hereby indemnified, freed, and difcharged, from and against all penalties, forfeitures, incapacities, and difabilities, in or by any act or acts of parliament mentioned and incurred, or to be incurred, for or by reafon of any fuch neglect or omiffion, in not caufing fuch affidavit or affidavits to be made and filed, in fuch manner as the fame ought to have been; and every fuch affidavit and affidavits fo to be made, and which fhall be duly filed, on or before the faid firft day of *September*, one thoufand feven hundred and fifty nine, as aforefaid, fhall be as effectual to all intents and purpofes, as if made and filed within the refpective times the fame ought, by the laws now in being for that purpofe, to have been fo made and filed.

CAP. XXIV.

An act to amend an act made in the laft feffion of parliament, for repealing the duty granted by an act made in the fixth year of the reign of his late Majefty on filver plate, and for granting a duty on licences to be taken out by all perfons dealing in gold or filver plate, by permitting the fale of gold or filver plate in fmall quantities without licence; and by granting a duty inftead of the duty now payable upon licences to be taken out by certain dealers in gold or filver plate: and alfo a duty upon licences to be taken out by pawnbrokers dealing in gold or filver plate, and refiners of gold or filver.

WHEREAS *by an act made in the laft feffion of parliament,* *intituled,* An act for repealing the duty granted by an act made in the fixth year of the reign of his late Majefty, on filver plate, made, wrought, touched, affayed, or marked in *Great Britain*; and for granting a duty on licences to be taken out by all perfons dealing in gold or filver plate; and for difcontinuing all drawbacks upon filver plate exported; and for more effectually preventing frauds and abufes in the marking or ftamping of gold or filver plate; *it was enacted, That in lieu of the duty thereby repealed, there fhould, from and after the fifth day of* July, *one thoufand feven hundred and fifty eight, be paid unto his Majefty, his heirs, and fucceffors, a duty of forty fhillings for every licence to be taken out in manner therein after-mentioned, by each perfon trading in, felling, or vending gold or filver plate, and by the faid act fuch licences were directed to be taken out annually; and it was alfo thereby further enacted, That all perfons ufing the trade of felling or vending gold or filver plate, or any goods or wares compofed of gold or filver, or any goods or wares in which any gold or filver was or fhould be manufactured, and alfo all perfons employed to fell any gold or filver plate, or any fuch goods or wares aforefaid, at any auction, or publick fale, or by commiffion, fhould refpectively be deemed traders in, fellers or venders of, gold or filver plate, within the intent and meaning of the faid act, and fhould take out a licence for the fame: and whereas fo*

much

much of the faid laft recited claufe, as directs that every perfon trading in, felling, or vending gold or filver plate, or any goods or wares compofed of gold or filver, or any goods or wares in which any gold or filver was or fhould be manufactured, fhould take out a licence for that purpofe, has been found detrimental to the toy and cutlery trades of this kingdom : and your Majefty's moft dutiful and loyal fubjects, the commons of Great Britain in parliament affembled, are therefore defirous that all perfons may be permitted to trade in, fell, or vend any goods or wares in which the gold or filver fhall not exceed the refpective quantities herein after mentioned, without being obliged to take out a licence for that purpofe, and in lieu thereof, to grant unto your Majefty a duty upon fuch licences as are herein after mentioned ; and therefore do moft humbly befeech your Majefty that it may be enacted, and be it enacted by the King's moft excellent majefty, by and with the advice and confent of the lords fpiritual and temporal, and commons, in this prefent parliament affembled, and by the authority of the fame, That from and after the fifth day of *July*, one thoufand feven hundred and fifty nine, no perfon or perfons whatfoever fhall be fubject or liable to take out any licence for or in refpect of his, her, or their trading in, vending, or felling, any quantity of gold not exceeding two penny weights in any one feparate and diftinct ware or piece of goods, or any quantity of filver not exceeding five penny weights in any one feparate and diftinct ware or piece of goods ; but that all perfons may, from time to time, after the faid fifth day of *July*, one thoufand feven hundred and fifty nine, trade in, vend, or fell, any ware or piece of goods, in which the gold or filver fhall not exceed the refpective quantities aforefaid, without being fubject in refpect thereof to any penalty for not having taken out a licence, or paid the duty granted by the faid act made in the laft feffion of parliament ; any thing in the faid act contained to the contrary notwithftanding.

Traders in, or venders of, fmall gold and filver wares, exempted from taking out a licence for the fame ;

II. *And, in order to make good any deficiency which may happen in the produce of the faid duty, by reafon of the exemption aforefaid;* be it further enacted by the authority aforefaid, That there fhall, from and after the faid fifth day of *July*, one thoufand feven hundred and fifty nine, be paid unto his Majefty, his heirs, and fucceffors, a duty of five pounds for every licence to be taken out by each trader in, vender or feller of, gold or filver plate, or of any goods or wares in which any gold or filver is or fhall be manufactured, who fhall trade in, vend, or fell, any piece of plate, or goods, or any ware in which the gold or filver fhall be of the refpective weights herein after mentioned, or of any greater weight, and by all pawnbrokers trading in, vending, or felling, gold or filver plate, or any goods or wares in which any gold or filver is or fhall be manufactured, and all refiners of gold or filver.

but fuch as fhall trade in, or vend larger quantities, as alfo pawnbrokers, and refiners, to take out a licence, for which they are to pay 5 l.

III. And be it further enacted by the authority aforefaid, That from and after the faid fifth day of *July*, one thoufand feven hundred and fifty nine, no perfon or perfons whatfoever, who now, or at any time or times hereafter, doth, do, or fhall trade in, vend

What quantity of gold or filver wares fhall fubject the traders

or sell, any gold or silver plate, or any goods or wares in which *in, or venders* any gold or silver is or shall be manufactured, shall presume by *thereof, to* him, her, or themselves, or by any other person or persons *take out a* whatsoever employed by him, her, or them, for his, her, or *licence.* their benefit, either publickly or privately, to trade in, vend or sell, any piece of plate or goods, or any ware in which the quantity of gold shall be of the weight of two ounces or upwards, or in which the quantity of silver shall be of the weight of thirty ounces or upwards, unless he, she, or they, shall have first paid a duty of five pounds for a licence, which shall have been taken out in the manner required by the said act made in the last session of parliament; and every person who shall so trade in, vend or sell, any such piece of plate or goods, or ware as aforesaid, shall pay the like duty of five pounds for every licence which shall be taken out in each year, in pursuance of the said act, instead and in lieu of the duty of forty shillings thereby granted; any thing in the said act contained to the contrary notwithstanding: and if any person or persons trading in, vend- *20l. penalty* ing, or selling gold or silver plate, or any goods or wares in *for not taking* which any gold or silver is or shall be manufactured, shall, after *out such li-* the said fifth day of *July*, one thousand seven hundred and fifty *cence,* nine, presume or offer to trade in, vend or sell, any such piece of plate or goods, or any such ware as aforesaid, without first taking out a licence, for which the said duty of five pounds shall have been paid, and renewing the same licence, and making the like *and renewing* payment yearly as aforesaid, he, she, or they, shall respectively *the same year-* forfeit and lose, for every such offence, the sum of twenty *ly.* pounds.

IV. And be it further enacted by the authority aforesaid, *Pawnbrokers,* That from and after the said fifth day of *July*, one thousand *and refiners,* seven hundred and fifty nine, no pawnbroker or pawnbrokers *deemed trad-* shall presume, by him, her, or themselves, or by any other *ers in, and* person or persons whatsoever employed by him, her, or them, *venders of,* for his, her, or their benefit, either publickly or privately, to *gold and silver* trade in, vend or sell, any gold or silver plate, or any goods or *wares,* wares in which any gold or silver is or shall be manufactured; nor shall any person or persons presume, either by him, her, or *and liable to* themselves, or by any other person or persons whatsoever em- *take a licence,* ployed by him, her, or them, for his, her, or their benefit, to use or practice the trade or business of a refiner of gold or silver, without first taking out a licence, in such manner as persons using the trade of selling or vending gold or silver plate are, by the said act made in the last session of parliament, required to take out licences; and every such pawnbroker, and also every such refiner of gold or silver, shall take out a fresh licence in every year, *and renew the* in such manner as persons using the trade of selling or vending *same yearly;* gold or silver plate, are by the said act required to do: and for the more effectual enforcing the taking out of the said licences, and recovery of the duty herein after directed to be from time to time paid upon the taking out thereof, every such pawnbroker and refiner of gold or silver respectively shall be deemed, for the purpofes of this act, to ufe the trade of felling or vending gold or filver plate; any thing in the faid former act contained to the contrary notwithstanding: and every fuch pawnbroker as aforefaid, and alfo every fuch refiner of gold or filver, fhall refpec- **for which 5l. is to be paid;** ively pay a duty of five pounds for every licence which fhall be taken out by each fuch pawnbroker or refiner; and which faid duty of five pounds fhall be paid in each year at the times when fuch licences are taken out, and to fuch perfon or perfons, and in fuch manner, as the duty of forty fhillings granted by the faid act is thereby directed to be paid: and if, after the faid fifth day of July, one thoufand feven hundred and fifty nine, any pawnbroker fhall prefume or offer to trade in, vend or fell, any gold or filver plate, or any goods or wares in which any gold or filver is or fhall be manufactured; or if any perfon fhall prefume or offer to ufe or practice the trade or bufinefs of a refiner of gold or filver, and fuch pawnbroker or perfon refpectively fhall not have firft taken out a licence, for which the faid duty of five pounds fhall have been paid, or fhall not have renewed the fame licence, and made fuch payment yearly as aforefaid; **on penalty of forfeiting 20l.** every fuch pawnbroker and perfon fhall refpectively, for every fuch offence, forfeit and lofe the fum of twenty pounds.

Licences taken out under the former act, upon payment of the additional fum of 3l. to be good for the fubfifting term thereof. V. Provided always, and be it further enacted by the authority aforefaid, That if, at any time or times, any perfon or perfons who fhall have taken out a licence in the manner prefcribed by the faid former act, and have paid, in refpect thereof, the faid duty of forty fhillings, fhall, before the expiration of fuch licence, produce the fame, and pay the further fum of three pounds to any perfon or perfons authorized by virtue of the faid former act to grant licences (all which perfons are hereby required to accept fuch payment, and to indorfe a memorandum thereof, without fee or reward, upon the licence fo produced) every perfon paying fuch additional fum of three pounds may, and is hereby impowered, from the time of the payment thereof, and during the continuance of the remainder of the term of the faid licence, to trade in, vend, or fell, any gold or filver plate, or any goods or wares in which any gold or filver is or fhall be manufactured; or to ufe or practice the trade or bufinefs of a refiner of gold or filver, in fuch manner as any other perfon who fhall have paid the duty of five pounds upon the original granting of any licence is by this act impowered to do; any thing herein before contained to the contrary notwithstanding.

Perfons in partnerfhip, carrying on trade or bufinefs in one houfe only, &c. not liable to take out more than one licence. Licence to ferve but for one fhop or houfe, VI. Provided always, That perfons in partnerfhip, and carrying on their trade or bufinefs in one houfe, fhop, or tenement only, fhall not be obliged to take out more than one licence in any one year for the carrying on fuch trade or bufinefs: and that no licence which fhall be granted by virtue of this act, fhall authorize or impower any perfon or perfons to whom the fame may be granted, and who fhall fell gold or filver plate in fhops, to trade in, fell, or vend, fuch gold or filver plate in any other fhop or place, except in fuch houfes or places thereunto belonging, wherein he, fhe, or they fhall inhabit and dwell at

the

the time of granting such licence, or in booths or stalls at fairs booths and stalls at fairs or markets excepted.
or markets.

VII. And be it further enacted by the authority aforesaid, That all prosecutions for recovery of penalties and forfeitures incurred for offences committed against this act, shall and may be heard and determined, and such penalties and forfeitures recovered, levied, and applied, and in case of want of sufficient distress whereon to levy the same, the offender shall be imprisoned, in such and the same manner, and with the same powers and authorities, as are prescribed, given, and appointed, in the said act made in the last session of parliament with respect to prosecutions for, and the recovering, levying, and applying of, the penalties and forfeitures incurred for offences committed against the said act, and to the imprisonment of the party or parties offending until satisfaction shall be made. Penalties and forfeitures to be recovered and applied, as by the act of 31 Geo. 2. is prescribed.

VIII. Provided always, and it is hereby enacted, That the several penalties and forfeitures of twenty pounds, created and inflicted by the said recited act, and this present act, may be mitigated by such ways, means, and methods, as any fine, penalty, or forfeiture, may be mitigated by any law or laws of excise; any thing in the said recited act, or this present act, to the contrary in any wise notwithstanding. Mitigation of penalties.

IX. And be it further enacted by the authority aforesaid, That all the monies which shall arise by the duty hereby directed to be paid upon licences (the necessary charges of raising and accounting for the same excepted) shall, from time to time, be paid into the receipt of his Majesty's exchequer at *Westminster*, together with the monies arising by the duty on licences granted by the said act made in the last session of parliament; and shall be applied to such uses and purposes, and in such manner, as the monies arising by the duty granted by the said act are thereby made applicable, and to and for no other use or purpose whatsoever. Duties to be paid into the exchequer; and to be applied as the duties under the former act are directed.

X. And be it further enacted by the authority aforesaid, That the said act made in the last session of parliament (except such parts thereof as are varied or altered by this act) shall continue in full force and effect, and the provisions and powers therein contained (except as aforesaid) shall extend, and are hereby extended to, and shall operate and be executed, with respect to this act, and to all matters and things to be done in pursuance thereof, in as full and ample manner, to all intents and purposes, as if the said provisions and powers were, with such variations and alterations, herein especially repeated and re-enacted; any thing in this act contained to the contrary notwithstanding. The recited act, except where altered by this act, continued and enforced.

CAP. XXV.

*An act to explain and amend an act made in the twenty ninth
year of his present Majesty's reign, intituled,* An act for
the encouragement of seamen, and the more speedy
and effectual manning his Majesty's navy ; *and for the
better prevention of piracies and robberies by crews of
private ships of war.*

Preamble.

WHEREAS *repeated complaints have of late been made of
divers outragious acts of piracy and robbery, committed on
board great numbers of ships, more particularly by the crews of small
ships, vessels, or boats, being, or pretending to be,* English *privateers : and whereas it is of the utmost importance to the honour of this
nation, to detect and bring to justice persons who (in violation of the
laws of nations in general, and of this kingdom in particular) have
been, or shall be, guilty of such piracies and robberies : and whereas
by a clause in an act of parliament passed in the twenty ninth year of
the reign of his present Majesty, intituled,* An act for the encouragement of seamen, and the more speedy and effectual manning his Majesty's navy, *it is, amongst other things, enacted,
That the lord high admiral of* Great Britain, *or the commissioners for
executing the office of lord high admiral of* Great Britain *for the time
being, or any three or more of them, or any person or persons by him
or them impowered and appointed, shall, at the request of any owner
or owners of any ship or vessel, giving such bail and security as have
been usually taken upon granting commissions or letters of marque (except only for the payment of the tenths of the value of prizes which
shall be taken, to the lord high admiral, or commissioners for executing the office of lord high admiral for the time being) cause to be issued forth, in the usual manner, one or more commission or commissions
to any person or persons whom such owner or owners shall nominate to
be commander, or, in case of death, successively commanders of such
ship or vessel, for the attacking, surprizing, seizing, and taking, by
and with such ship or vessel, or with the crew thereof, any place or
fortress upon the land, or on any ship or vessel, goods, ammunition,
arms, stores of war, or merchandize, belonging to, or possessed by,
any of his Majesty's enemies, in any sea, creek, haven, or river : and
whereas it is apprehended that most of the acts of piracy and robbery
complained of as aforesaid, have arisen from the obligation on the said
lord high admiral, or the said commissioners for executing the office of
lord high admiral, at such request as aforesaid, to grant such commissions to the commanders of all ships or vessels, of what burthen soever, without distinction :* to remedy which inconveniency ; be it
enacted by the King's most excellent majesty, by and with the
advice and consent of the lords spiritual and temporal, and
commons, in this present parliament assembled, and by the
authority of the same, That from and after the first day of *June*
in the year of our Lord one thousand seven hundred and fifty
nine, so much of the said recited clause in the above-mentioned

Clause in act
29 Geo. 2.

So much of
the recited
clause, as di-
rects the ad-
miralty, upon
application,
and security
given, to grant
commissions

act

act of parliament, passed in the twenty ninth year of the reign of his present Majesty, as directs the lord high admiral of *Great Britain*, or the commissioners for executing the office of lord high admiral of *Great Britain* for the time being, or any three or more of them, or any person or persons by him or them impowered and appointed, at the request of any owner or owners of any ship or vessel giving such bail and security as therein is mentioned, to cause to be issued forth, in the usual manner, one or more commission or commissions to any person or persons whom such owner or owners shall nominate to be commander, or, in case of death, successively commanders of such ship or vessel, for the purposes in the said recited clause mentioned, shall be, and the same is hereby declared and enacted to be absolutely repealed and made void. *to privateers, repealed.*

II. And be it further enacted by the authority aforesaid, That the lord high admiral of *Great Britain*, or the commissioners for executing the office of lord high admiral of *Great Britain* for the time being, or any three or more of them, or any person or persons by him or them impowered and appointed, shall, from and after the said first day of *June*, one thousand seven hundred and fifty nine, at the request of any owner or owners of any ship or vessel, giving such bail and security as is herein after-mentioned and expressed, cause to be issued forth one or more commission or commissions to any person or persons whom such owner or owners shall nominate to be commander, or, in case of death, successively commanders of such ship or vessel, for the attacking, surprizing, seizing, and taking, by and with such ship or vessel, or with the crew thereof, any place or fortress upon the land, or any ship or vessel, goods, ammunition, arms, stores of war, or merchandize, belonging to, or possessed by, any of his Majesty's enemies, upon the land, or in any sea, creek, haven, or river; and that such ship or ships, vessel or vessels, or any goods, ammunition, arms, stores of war, and merchandizes whatsoever, with all their furniture, tackle, and apparel, so to be taken, by or with such private owner or owners ship or vessel, according to such last-mentioned commission or commissions (being first adjudged lawful prize in any of his Majesty's courts of admiralty) shall wholly and entirely belong to, and be divided between and among, the owner and owners of such ship or vessel, and the several persons which shall be on board the same, and be aiding and assisting to the taking thereof, in such shares and proportions as shall be agreed on with the owner or owners of such ship or vessel as shall be the captor thereof, their agents or factors, as the proper goods and chattels of such owner or owners, and the persons that shall be intitled thereto by virtue of such agreements among themselves; and that neither his Majesty, his heirs, or successors, or any admiral, vice admiral, governor, or other person, commissioned by, or claiming, under his Majesty, his heirs, or successors, or any person or persons whatsoever, other than the owner or owners of such ship or vessel, being the captor of such prize ship or vessel, goods, ammunition, arms, stores of war, and merchandizes, and the per- *Admiralty to grant commissions, upon owners, &c. giving such bail and security as is herein after-mentioned.*

Prizes to belong solely to, and be divided among, the owners and captors, as shall be agreed between them;

reserving only the customs and duties payable by act 29 Geo. 2.

No commission to be granted to vessels, in Europe, under 100 tons burthen, 10 guns, and 40 men; unless the admiralty shall think fit; the owners giving bail and security as herein after mentioned.

Admiralty may revoke any former or future commissions;

of which notice is to be forthwith sent to the ship's owners, agents, or sureties.

Times limited for order of revocation to take place, viz.

If the vessel be in the channel; or northern seas; if to the south of Cape Finisterre, or in the Mediterranean; in North America, the West Indies, or East Indies.

Complaint may be made to the King in

persons claiming under him or them, shall be intitled to any part or share thereof (except as to the customs and duties mentioned in the said act of the twenty ninth year of his Majesty's reign) any custom, statute, or other law to the contrary notwithstanding.

III. Provided nevertheless, and it is hereby further enacted, That no such commission as aforesaid shall be issued forth or granted to any person or persons by virtue of this act, unless the ship or vessel for which the same shall be granted, in *Europe*, shall be of the burthen of one hundred tons, and carry ten carriage guns, being three pounders, and forty men at the least; or unless the lord high admiral, or commissioners for executing the office of lord high admiral, or any three or more of them, or any person or persons by him or them impowered and appointed, shall, in their discretion, think fit to grant the same to any ship or vessel of inferior force or burthen, the owner or owners of such ship or vessel giving such bail and security as is herein after mentioned and expressed.

IV. And be it further enacted by the authority aforesaid, That it shall and may be lawful to and for the lord high admiral of *Great Britain*, or the commissioners for executing the office of lord high admiral of *Great Britain* for the time being, or any three or more of them, at any time or times hereafter, to revoke and make void, by any order or orders in writing under his or their hand or hands, any commission or commissions which hath, have been, or shall be, issued forth to any person or persons who hath, have been, or shall be, nominated commander or commanders of any ship or vessel, either by virtue of the said act of the twenty ninth year of the reign of his present Majesty, or this present act.

V. Provided nevertheless, That the secretary of the admiralty for the time being shall, with all convenient speed, after any and every such commission shall be so revoked, cause notice thereof in writing to be forthwith sent to the owner or owners, or agent or agents, or surety or sureties, or some one of them, of the ship or vessel named or described in such order of revocation: and in case such ship or vessel shall be in the chanel, the said order of revocation shall be effectual to supersede and annul the said commission, at the expiration of twenty days from and after such notice given as aforesaid, or sooner, if notice shall be actually given in writing by the secretary of the admiralty to the captain or commander thereof; and in case such ship or vessel shall be in the northern seas, at the expiration of thirty days; and in case such ship or vessel shall be to the southward of *Cape Finisterre*, or in the *Mediterranean*, at the expiration of six weeks; and in case such ship or vessel shall be in *North America*, or the *West Indies*, at the expiration of three months; and in case such ship or vessel shall be in the *East Indies*, at the expiration of six months: and any commander or commanders, owner or owners, agent or agents, surety or sureties, of any such ship or vessel, whereof such commission or commissions issued or to be issued forth as aforesaid shall be so revoked, may complain thereof

to his Majesty in council, within thirty days next after the fe- *council of*
cretary of the admiralty for the time being shall cause notice *fuch revoca-*
thereof to be given as aforesaid; and the determination of his *tion.*
Majesty in council, touching every such complaint, shall be *The council's*
final. *determination*
to be final;

VI. Provided always, That in case any such order of revoca- *and if the or-*
tion shall be superseded, such commission shall be deemed and *der shall be*
taken to have continued in force: and all prizes taken by virtue *superseded,*
thereof shall belong to, and be the property of, such owners and *the commif-*
captors, in such manner as the same would have been in case *fion to stand*
such order of revocation had not been made. *good.*

VII. Provided also, That no person shall be liable to be pu- *None liable to*
nished for doing, before he shall have received personal notice *punishment*
of such order of revocation, any matter or thing which he might *before perfon-*
have lawfully done under the authority of such commission, in *al notice re-*
case such order of revocation had not been made. *ceived of fuch*
order of re-
vocation.

VIII. And be it further enacted by the authority aforesaid, *Usual bail and*
That before the granting or issuing of any commission in pur- *fecurity to be*
suance of this act, such bail and security shall be taken as have *taken;*
been usual upon the granting or issuing of commissions for private ships of war; and that, previous to the taking of such bail *the parties*
and security, the persons who propose to be bound, and give *making oath*
such security, shall severally make oath before the judge of the *of their qua-*
high court of admiralty of *England*, or his surrogate, or other *lification;*
person or persons by such judge, or surrogate, lawfully commissioned, that, at the time of their being sworn, they are respectively worth more money than the sum for which they are
then to be bound, over and above all their just debts: and
moreover, the marshal of the said high court of admiralty for the *and the mar-*
time being, or his deputy, or the person or persons so commissi- *shal fatisfying*
oned as aforesaid, is or are hereby required and directed to make *himself as to*
diligent enquiry into, and satisfy himself or themselves of, the *the fufficiency*
sufficiency of such bail and security, and make a report thereof *thereof.*
to the said judge, or his surrogate, before any such commission
shall be granted or issued.

IX. And be it further enacted by the authority aforesaid, That *Perfons apply-*
from and after the first day of *June*, one thousand seven hundred *ing for com-*
and fifty nine, all and every person and persons who shall apply *miffions, to*
to the said lord high admiral, or the commissioners for execut- *make applica-*
ing the office of lord high admiral for the time being, in order *tion in writ-*
to obtain any commission to be granted or issued forth in pur- *ing,*
suance of this act, shall make every such application in writing,
and therein set forth a particular, true, and exact description of *and fet forth a*
the ship or vessel for which such commission is requested, speci- *defcription of*
fying the burthen of such ship or vessel, and the number and *the veffel, &c.*
nature of the guns on board the same, to what place belonging,
and the name or names of the principal owner or owners of such
ship or vessel, and the number of men intended to be put on *the particu-*
board the same (all which particulars shall be inserted in every *lars thereof to*
commission to be granted or issued in pursuance of this act) and *be inferted in*
that every commander of a private ship or vessel of war, for which *the commif-*
fion;

a

a commiſſion ſhall be granted or iſſued in purſuance of this act,

which commiſſion is to be produced to the collector or other officer of the port, who is to examine the ſhip, and ſee how far ſhe agrees in all reſpects with the ſaid deſcription ; and if ſhe agrees thereto, or be of a greater force or burthen,

ſhall produce ſuch commiſſion to the collector, cuſtomer, or ſearcher, for the time being, of his Majeſty's cuſtoms, reſiding at, or belonging to, the port from whence ſuch ſhip or veſſel ſhall be firſt fitted out, or to the lawful deputy or deputies of ſuch collector, cuſtomer, or ſearcher ; and the ſaid collector, cuſtomer, or ſearcher, or his or their lawful deputy or deputies, ſhall, as ſoon thereafter as conveniently may be, without fee or reward, inſpect and examine ſuch ſhip or veſſel, ſo as to aſcertain the burthen thereof, and the number of men, and number and nature of the guns on board the ſame : and if ſuch ſhip or veſſel ſhall thereupon be found to be of ſuch burthen, and be manned and armed according to the tenor of the deſcription inſerted in ſuch commiſſion as aforeſaid, or be of a greater burthen or force than ſhall be mentioned in ſuch commiſſion, then

is to grant a certificate, which ſhall be a clearance to ſuch veſſel.

ſuch collector, cuſtomer, or ſearcher, or his or their lawful deputy or deputies, ſhall, and he or they is and are hereby required immediately upon the requeſt of the commander of ſuch ſhip or veſſel, to give a certificate thereof in writing under his or their hand or hands *gratis*, to ſuch commander ; which certificate ſhall be deemed a neceſſary clearance, before ſuch private ſhip or veſſel ſhall be permitted to ſail from that port ; and if the com-

Penalty of departing without ſuch clearance.

mander of any ſhip or veſſel for which any commiſſion ſhall have been granted or iſſued in purſuance of this act, ſhall depart with ſuch ſhip or veſſel from ſuch port or clearance, before he hath received ſuch certificate, or ſhall depart from any ſuch

or with a force inferior to that ſpecified in the commiſſion.

port, or proceed upon a cruize, with a force inferior to the force ſpecified in ſuch commiſſion, or required by this act ; in every ſuch caſe, the commiſſion for ſuch ſhip or veſſel ſhall from thenceforth be abſolutely null and void ; and the commander ſo offending, being convicted thereof before any court of admiralty, ſhall be impriſoned without bail or mainprize, for ſuch ſpace as the ſaid court ſhall direct, not exceeding one year for any one offence.

Collector, &c. granting a falſe certificate,

X. And be it further enacted by the authority aforeſaid, That if any collector, cuſtomer, or ſearcher of his Majeſty's cuſtoms, or his or their lawful deputy or deputies, ſhall grant a certificate for any ſhip or veſſel which ſhall not be of the burthen and force ſpecified in the commiſſion granted to the commander or commanders thereof, or of greater burthen and force than ſhall be mentioned in ſuch commiſſion, he ſhall, for ſuch of-

to forfeit his office, and 100 l. Recovery and application thereof.

fence, forfeit his ſaid office, and be for ever after incapable of holding any office in the cuſtoms, and ſhall alſo forfeit the ſum of one hundred pounds, to be recovered by any perſon or perſons who will ſue for the ſame, by action of debt, bill, plaint, or information, in any of his Majeſty's courts of record at *Weſtminſter*, in which no eſſoin, protection, wager of law, or more than one imparlance, ſhall be allowed ; and one moiety of the ſaid penalty of one hundred pounds, when recovered, ſhall be paid to the informer or informers, and the other moiety to the treaſurer for the time being to the corporation for the relief and support of sick, maimed, and disabled seamen, and of the widows and children of such as shall be killed, slain, or drowned, in the merchants service, for the use of such corporation; or where such forfeitures shall be incurred in any of the out-ports in which a corporation is established, or shall hereafter be established, for the purposes aforesaid, then the moiety of such penalty shall be paid to the trustees for the use of the corporation so established.

XI. Provided always, That the number of tons so to be certified, be ascertained according to the rules laid down by an act passed in the eighth year of the reign of her late majesty Queen *Anne*, intituled, *An act for making a convenient dock or bason at Liverpool, for the security of all ships trading to or from the said port of Liverpool.*

Tonage to be ascertained according to the rules prescribed by act 8 Annæ.

XII. And be it further enacted by the authority aforesaid, That in case at any time or times after the first day of *June*, one thousand seven hundred and fifty nine, any commander or commanders of any private ship or ships, or vessel or vessels, of war, duly commissioned by virtue of the said act of the twenty ninth year of his Majesty's reign, or this act, shall agree with the commander or commanders, or other person or persons, of or belonging to any neutral or other ship or ships, vessel or vessels (except those of his Majesty's declared enemies) for the ransom of any such neutral or other ship or ships, vessel or vessels, or the respective cargo or cargoes thereof, or any part thereof, after the same shall have been taken as prize, and shall, in pursuance of any such agreement or agreements, actually quit, set at liberty, or discharge, any such prize or prizes, instead of bringing the same into some port or ports belonging to his Majesty's dominions; that then all and every of the commander and commanders of such private ship or ships, or vessel or vessels of war, who shall so agree for any such ransom (except as aforesaid) and shall quit, set at liberty, or discharge, any such prize or prizes in manner aforesaid, shall be deemed, adjudged, and taken to be guilty of piracy, felony, and robbery; and he, they, and every of them, being duly convicted thereof in the manner herein before-mentioned, shall have and suffer such pains of death, loss of lands, goods, and chattels, as pirates, felons, and robbers upon the seas, ought to have and suffer according to the laws now in being.

Privateers agreeing for the ransom of neutral ships made prizes, and discharging them without bringing them into port, deemed guilty of piracy; and to suffer death and confiscation of goods, &c.

XIII. Provided always, and be it further enacted, That it shall be lawful for the commander of any private ship of war, upon the capture of any neutral ship or vessel which by any law or treaty shall be liable only to the forfeiture of such contraband goods as shall be on board thereof, to receive such goods from such ship or vessel, in case the commander thereof is willing to deliver the same; and the commander of such private ship of war may thereupon quit, set at liberty, or discharge, such neutral ship or vessel; any thing herein before contained to the contrary notwithstanding: and if any person or persons shall purloin

Privateers may take contraband goods from on board neutral ships, with consent of the commanders and set the vessels at liberty.

loin

2

Penalty of em-
bezzling the
fame.

loin or embezzle any fuch contraband goods before condemnation thereof, every fuch perfon fhall be fubject to fuch pains
and forfeitures as are inflicted by law upon perfons purloining
or embezzling goods out of any captured fhip.

All papers,
&c. found on
board prize
veffels, to be
brought into
the regiftry of
the admiralty;

but fuch only
as fhall be
thought ne-
ceffary by the
proctors to be
tranflated and
made ufe of,
&c.

XIV. And be it further enacted by the authority aforefaid,
That from and after the firft day of June, one thoufand feven
hundred and fifty nine, all books, papers, and writings, found
in any fhip or veffel taken as prize, fhall, without delay, be
brought into the regiftry of the court or admiralty wherein fuch
fhip or veffel may be proceeded againft, in order to condemnation ; but that fuch only of the faid books, papers, and writings,
fhall be made ufe of and tranflated, as fhall be agreed or infift-
ed upon by the proctors of the feveral parties, captors, or claimants, or in cafe of no claim, by the captor or regifter, to be
neceffary for afcertaining the property of fuch fhip or veffel, and
the cargo thereof.

No officer of
the court of
admiralty,

or advocate,
&c. of the
court to be
any ways in-
terefted in pri-
vateers;

XV. And be it further enacted by the authority aforefaid, That
from and after the faid firft day of June, one thoufand feven
hundred and fifty nine, no judge, regifter, or deputy regifter,
marfhal, or deputy marfhal, or any other officer whatfoever, of
or belonging to any court of admiralty or vice admiralty in
Great Britain or Ireland, or in any of his Majefty's colonies or
plantations in America, or elfewhere, nor any perfon or perfons
practifing either as advocate, proctor, or otherwife, in any fuch
court or courts, fhall be concerned or interefted, directly or indirectly, as owner, part owner, fharer, or adventurer, in any
private fhip or fhips, or veffel or veffels, of war whatfoever,
having any commiffion or commiffions as aforefaid : and in cafe
any fuch judge, regifter, deputy regifter, marfhal, deputy marfhal, or other officer, advocate, or proctor whatfoever, fhall,
notwithftanding this act, be directly or indirectly concerned or
interefted as aforefaid ; fuch judge, regifter, deputy regifter, or
marfhal, deputy marfhal, or other officer refpectively, fhall, for
fuch offence (being thereof lawfully convicted, either upon an

on forfeiture
of his employ-
ment, and
100 l.

information or an indictment) abfolutely forfeit his office and
employment in and belonging to any fuch court of admiralty or
vice admiralty, of what kind or nature foever fuch office or employment may happen to be, and fhall alfo forfeit and pay to
the ufe of his Majefty, his heirs, and fucceffors, the fum of one

and advocate,
&c. to be dif-
qualified from
practifing in
the faid courts.

hundred pounds ; and every fuch advocate or proctor refpectively fhall, for fuch laft-mentioned offence (being thereof lawfully
convicted in manner aforefaid) be from thenceforth abfolutely
difqualified, and rendered for ever incapable of practifing either
as an advocate or proctor in any of his Majefty's courts of admiralty or vice admiralty wherefoever.

Regifters and
marfhals of
the court dif-
qualified from
acting as ad-
vocates or
proctors.

XVI. And be it further enacted by the authority aforefaid,
That from and after the firft day of June, one thoufand feven
hundred and fifty nine, no regifter or deputy regifter, nor any
marfhal or deputy marfhal, of or belonging to any of his Majefty's faid courts of admiralty or vice admiralty whatfoever,
fhall, either directly or indirectly, by himfelf or themfelves, or

by

by any agent or agents, or other perfon or perfons whatfoever, act or be concerned in any manner, either as an advocate or proctor, in any caufe, matter, or bufinefs whatfoever, that fhall be depending in any fuch court or courts of admiralty or vice admiralty, to which fuch regifter, deputy regifter, marfhal, or deputy marfhal, fhall then belong; and that every regifter, deputy regifter, marfhal, or deputy marfhal, who fhall be guilty of fuch offence (being thereof lawfully convicted, either upon an information or indictment) fhall from thenceforth abfolutely forfeit his refpective office and employment of regifter, deputy regifter, marfhal, or deputy marfhal, in and belonging to the fame court. *on forfeiture of their refpective offices.*

XVII. And be it further enacted by the authority aforefaid, That all and every commiffion and commiffions which have been iffued forth or granted in purfuance of the aforefaid act of parliament made and paffed in the twenty ninth year of his prefent Majefty's reign, to the commander or commanders of any private fhip or fhips, or veffel or veffels, of war, in *Europe*, fuch fhip or fhips, veffel or veffels, not being refpectively of the burthen of one hundred tons, and carrying each ten carriage guns, being three pounders, and forty men at the leaft (except fuch fhips or veffels of an inferior burthen or force whofe commiffions fhall be refpectively confirmed by any order in writing under the hand or hands of the lord high admiral of *Great Britain*, or the commiffioners for executing the office of lord high admiral of *Great Britain*, or any three or more of them, or any perfon or perfons by him or them impowered and appointed) fhall, from and after the firft day of *July*, one thoufand feven hundred and fifty nine, be null and void; and the fame, and every of them, is and are hereby accordingly enacted and declared to be abfolutely revoked and made null and void, to all intents and purpofes whatfoever. *Commiffions heretofore granted to veffels of inferior force and burthen, than this act allows, except fuch as fhall be confirmed by the admiralty; are revoked, and declared void.*

XVIII. Provided always, That every fuch confirmation of any commiffion as aforefaid, fhall be made and granted without fee or reward. *Confirmation of commiffions to be granted without fee.*

XIX. *And, to the end that the owners of fuch fhips or veffels, not being under fifty, or above one hundred, tons, whofe commiffions are by this act made void, which, fince the twenty feventh day of May, one thoufand feven hundred and fifty fix, have conftantly ferved as private fhips of war to the time of fuch revocation, may not be injured thereby*; it is hereby further enacted, That it fhall and may be lawful for his Majefty, under his royal fign manual, to appoint fuch perfon or perfons as his Majefty fhall think fit to receive and adjuft the claims of fuch owners, for any lofs or damage they may refpectively fuftain by reafon of the revocation of any of the faid commiffions hereby made void; and the fums which fhall by fuch perfon or perfons, fo appointed by his Majefty, be certified to be due on fuch claims, fhall be paid out of the next aids to be granted in parliament. *Where the commiffions of inferior veffels are vacated by revocation, His Majefty to appoint perfons to adjuft the claims of the owners for damages; and the fums certified by them, to be paid out of the next fupplies.*

XX. *And, for the more fpeedy bringing of offenders to juftice, and to prevent the inconveniencies occafioned by want of frequently holding*

a

a *feffion of admiralty for the trial of offences committed on the high*
feas ; be it further enacted by the authority aforefaid, That from

A feffion of
the court of
admiralty to
be held in
March and
October yearly.

and after the firft day of *June*, one thoufand feven hundred and
fifty nine, a feffion of *Oyer* and *Terminer* and gaol delivery, for
the trial of offences committed upon the high feas within th:
jurifdiction of the admiralty of *England*, fhall be held twice at
the leaft in every year; that is to fay, In the feveral months of
March and *October* in each year, at *Juftice Hall* in the *Old Bai-
ley, London*; except at fuch times as the feffions of *Oyer* and
Terminer and gaol delivery for the city of *London* and county of
Middlefex fhall be appointed to be there held; or in fuch other
place, within that part of *Great Britain* called *England*, as the
lord high admiral of *Great Britain*, or the commiffioners for
executing the office of lord high admiral of *Great Britain* for the
time being, or any three or more of them, fhall, by any letter,
or order in writing, under their hands, directed to the judge of
the high court of admiralty in *England* for the time being, appoint.

Commiffioners
of the court,
and juftices of
the peace, im-
powered to
take informa-
tions of pi-
racy, &c.

XXI. And be it further enacted by the authority aforefaid,
That from and after the firft day of *June*, one thoufand feven
hundred and fifty nine, it fhall and may be lawful, not only to
and for any one or more of the commiffioners for the time being, named in the commiffion of *Oyer* and *Terminer* for the trying of offences committed within the jurifdiction of the admiralty of *England*, but alfo to and for any one or more of the juftices of the peace for the time being of any county, riding,
divifion, or place, within that part of *Great Britain* called *England*, and they are hereby refpectively authorized and impowered,
from time to time, to take any information or informations of
any witnefs or witneffes in writing upon oath, touching any piracy, felony, or robbery, done or committed, or charged to have
been done or committed, in or upon the fea, or in any haven,
river, creek, or place, where the admiral or admirals hath or
have power, authority, or jurifdiction; and thereupon (if fuch
commiffioner or commiffioners, or juftice or juftices of the peace

and, if they
fee caufe, to
apprehend
and commit
the offenders;

refpectively, fhall fee caufe) by any warrant or warrants under
his or their hand and feal, or hands and feals, to caufe the perfon
or perfons accufed in fuch information or informations to be apprehended and committed to the gaol of the county or place
wherein the fame information or informations fhall be taken,
there to remain until difcharged by due courfe of law.

and to oblige
the profecu-
tors and evi-
dences to en-
ter into recog-
nizances, to
appear and
profecute;

XXII. And it is hereby further enacted, That fuch of the
faid commiffioners, or juftices of the peace, who fhall caufe any
fuch perfon or perfons to be committed as is laft mentioned,
fhall, and he or they is or are hereby refpectively required, at
the fame time, to oblige all and every fuch other perfon or perfons whom fuch commiffioner or commiffioners, or juftice or juftices of the peace, fhall judge neceffary to profecute and give
evidence againft the perfon or perfons who fhall be fo committed
as aforefaid, to enter into one or more recognizance or recognizances to his Majefty, in a fufficient penalty, for his, her, or
their

their appearing at the then next session of *Oyer* and *Terminer*, and gaol delivery, to be held for the jurisdiction of the admiralty of *England*, there to prosecute and give evidence against the person or persons who shall be committed as aforesaid : and if any person shall refuse to enter into such recognizance to prosecute or give evidence, as shall be required, he, she, or they, so refusing, shall be committed by any such commissioner or commissioners, justice or justices, to the gaol of the county or place in which the person so refusing shall be, until the next sessions of admiralty shall be held, or such person shall enter into such recognizance as shall be required as aforesaid ; which recognizance or recognizances, together with the information or informations taken, touching the offence or offences wherewith the person or persons to be committed as aforesaid shall be charged, the said commissioner or commissioners, or justice or justices of the peace, before whom the same shall be taken, shall, and they are hereby respectively required, to transmit, with all convenient speed, to the register for the time being of the high court of admiralty of *England*, to be by him forthwith laid before the judge for the time being of the same court, and afterwards to be kept among the records of that court.

and on refusal, to commit them.

Recognizances and informations to be transmitted to the register of the court, to be laid before the judge, and kept among the records.

XXIII. And be it further enacted by the authority aforesaid, That the marshal of the admiralty for the time being, and his deputy or deputies, and all sheriffs, bailiffs, stewards, constables, headboroughs, tythingmen, keepers of gaols and prisons, and all other officers whatsoever, for keeping of the peace (as well within liberties as without) shall, and they, and every of them, are hereby respectively authorized and required, from time to time, diligently to execute, perform, and obey all such precept and precepts, warrant and warrants, and other order and orders, as shall at any time or times hereafter be made, directed, issued, or given to them, or any of them respectively, by any one or more of the said commissioners named in the commission of *Oyer* and *Terminer*, or justices of the peace, by virtue or in pursuance of this act, touching any of the matters or things herein contained.

The marshal, sheriffs, and other peace officers, are to obey and execute all precepts and orders of the commissioners and justices.

XXIV. And be it further enacted by the authority aforesaid, That in case any appeal shall be interposed from a sentence given in any admiralty court, concerning any goods and effects which may hereafter be seised or taken as prize, in pursuance of the aforesaid act of parliament of the twenty ninth year of his Majesty's reign, or of this act ; that then, and in such case, the judge of such court of admiralty shall and may, at the request, costs, and charges, either of the captor or claimant, or of the claimant only, in cases where the privilege is reserved in favour of the claimant by any treaty or treaties subsisting between his Majesty and foreign powers, make an order to have such capture appraised, unless the parties shall otherwise agree upon the value thereof, and an inventory taken, and then take security for the full value thereof, and thereupon cause such capture to be delivered to the party giving such security, in like manner as, by the

Where an appeal shall be interposed from the sentence of the court, concerning goods taken as prize,

the capture may be appraised, and upon security given, be delivered to the said party ;

said former act, such judge ought or could have done, before sentence given, notwithstanding such appeal: and if there shall be any difficulty or objection to the giving or taking of security, the said judge shall, at the request of either of the parties, order such goods and effects to be entered, landed, and sold by publick auction, as prize goods now are, under the care and custody of the proper officers of the customs, and under the direction and inspection of such persons as shall be appointed by the claimants and captors; and the monies arising by such sale shall be deposited in the bank of *England*, or in some publick securities, and in the names of such trustees as the captors and claimants shall jointly appoint, and the court shall approve, for the use and benefit of the parties who shall be adjudged to be intitled thereto: and if such security shall be given by the claimants, then it is hereby also enacted, That such judge shall give such capture a pass, to prevent it's being taken again by his Majefty's fubjects in it's destined voyage.

XXV. Provided always, and be it further enacted by the authority aforesaid, That this act shall continue in force during the present war with *France*, and no longer.

Side note: and if there shall be any difficulty or objection to the giving or taking security, the judge may order the goods to be landed, and fold by auction, and the money to be deposited in the bank, &c. If security be given by the claimants, judge to give the capture a pass. Act to be in force during the present war with France.

CAP. XXVI.

An act for applying a sum of money granted in this session of parliament towards carrying on the works for fortifying and securing the harbour of Milford in the county of Pembroke; and to amend and render more effectual an act of last session of parliament, for applying a sum of money towards fortifying the said harbour.

Preamble, reciting a clause in act 31 Geo. 2. 10,000l. to be issued out of the supplies granted for the year 1759, towards fortifying the harbour of Milford. Commissioners for putting this act in execution. Fortifications to be erected on the places here mentioned, under direction of the master general and other officers of the ordnance. Commissioners impowered to appoint and pay secretaries, and other proper officers under them. Account of the application of the monies to be laid before parliament. Charges of obtaining this act to be first paid out of the monies granted.

CAP. XXVII.

An act for continuing, amending, explaining, and making more effectual, an act made in the nineteenth year of his present Majefty's reign, intituled, An act more effectually to prevent the frauds and abuses committed in the admeasurement of coals within the city and liberty of Weftminfter, and that part of the duchy of Lancaster adjoining thereto, and the several parishes of Saint Giles in the Fields, Saint Mary le Bon, and such part of the parish of Saint Andrew, Holborn, as lies in the county of Middlesex.

WHEREAS *by an act made and passed in the nineteenth year of the reign of his present Majefty, intituled,* An act more effectually to prevent the frauds and abuses committed in the admeasurement of coals within the city and liberty of *Weftminfter,*

Side note: Preamble, reciting act 19 Geo. 2.

fter, and that part of the duchy of *Lancaster* adjoining thereto, and the several parishes of Saint *Giles in the Fields,* Saint *Mary le Bon,* and such part of the parish of Saint *Andrew, Holborn,* as lies in the county of *Middlesex; it was enacted, That from and after the twenty fourth day of* September *one thousand seven hundred and forty six, there should be erected and continued within the city and liberty of* Westminster, *one publick office, to be called by the name of* The land coal meters office for the city and liberty of *Westminster; and which should, from time to time, be managed by two persons to be nominated and appointed by his Majesty, his heirs, and successors, and to be called and known by the name of* The principal land coal meters for the city and liberty of *Westminster; and divers fees, rules, orders, powers, authorities, penalties, punishments, forfeitures, and provisions, were thereby given, granted, made, established, prescribed, and directed, to be levied and inflicted respectively, for the better enforcing and carrying the said act into execution for the purposes therein mentioned; and which were to continue and be in force for three years, from the twenty fourth day of* September *one thousand seven hundred and forty six, and to the end of the then next session of parliament: and it was thereby, amongst other things, enacted and provided, That if the driver of any cart loaded with coals, or any person belonging thereto, or employed therewith, should deliver, or suffer to be delivered or taken from such cart, any coals under his care, otherwise than to or for the use of the owner or owners thereof, and should be convicted of such offence, he should, for every such offence, forfeit and pay the sum of five pounds; and it was thereby further enacted and provided, That if any person or persons should be dissatisfied with, or think himself or herself aggrieved by or in the measure of any coals, under or by virtue of the said act, the same coals should, either upon acquainting the seller of such coals, or the carman driving or leading the same, at any time during the delivery thereof, and before the carman should be discharged thereof by the consumer, or his, her, or their, agent or agents, be remeasured either in the presence of a sea coal meter, from the sea coal meters office in the city of* London, *or one of the meters, or their agents, appointed in pursuance of the said act, for which there should be paid four pence for every chaldron, and no more; and in case the coals so to be re-measured, should not amount to the measure for which they were originally sold and measured, the sellers of such coals are thereby respectively made liable to the penalties and punishments thereby inflicted, to be recovered and applied in manner therein mentioned; and that, from and after notice should have been given in writing of any such dissatisfaction or grievance as aforesaid, to the seller of such coals, or to the carman leading or driving the same, and whilst such coals should so remain in their or either of their possession or power, such seller or carman, in whose possession or power such coals should be at the time of such notice, should not leave or depart from the cart in which such coals should have been laden, but that he and they should remain with the same, and take all possible care both of the coals and cart, till a meter or meters, appointed in pursuance of the said act, could be procured to re-measure such coals; and they are thereby respectively required, from time to time, with all con-*

venient fpeed, on notice for that purpofe to be delivered or left at the faid office in writing in any of the office hours, to attend for that purpofe: And whereas the faid act of parliament (having by experience been found ufeful and beneficial within the city and liberty of Weftminfter, and the other places and limits therein mentioned) was, by three fubfequent acts, one of the twenty third, another of the twenty fourth, and another of the thirty firft year of the reign of his prefent Majefty, further continued until the twenty fourth day of June one thoufand feven hundred and fifty nine: And whereas it would be of great fervice to the inhabitants of the city and liberty of Weftminfter, and the faid feveral parts and places of the county of Middlefex, that the faid act fhould, under certain reftrictions, be further continued; and in cafe proper provifions were made for obviating mifchiefs and abufes which were not forefeen, and not fufficiently provided for by the faid former act, the fame would be ftill of greater benefit and advantage to the faid inhabitants, and more effectually anfwer the purpofes thereby intended: May it therefore pleafe your Majefty, that it may be enacted; and be it enacted by the King's moft excellent majefty, by and with the advice and confent of the lords fpiritual and temporal, and commons, in this prefent parliament affembled, and by the authority of the fame, That if the driver of any cart loaded with coals, or any perfon belonging thereto, or employed therewith, fhall deliver, or fuffer to be delivered or taken from fuch cart, any coals under his care, otherwife than to or for the ufe of the owner or owners thereof, and fhall be lawfully convicted in fuch manner as in the faid act is mentioned; he fhall, for every fuch offence, be publickly whipt, or committed to the houfe of correction, there to remain without bail or mainprize for the fpace of three months.

Carter, &c. fraudulently delivering, or fuffering coal to be taken from his cart, to be publickly whipt, and committed for 3 months.

II. And it is hereby further enacted, That in cafe any perfon or perfons fhall be diffatisfied with, or think himfelf or herfelf aggrieved by or in the meafure of any coals, under or by virtue of the faid former act, and fuch coals fhall be remeafured in purfuance or under the authority of the faid acts, and fhall, upon fuch remeafuring, fall fhort of, and be deficient of, the true quantity or meafure, at or for which the fame were originally contracted for, fold, and meafured; then, and in fuch cafe, the principal coal meter or coal meters fhall, for every bufhel which the faid coals fo to be remeafured fhall fall fhort of or be deficient in the true quantity or meafure fo originally contracted for, fold, and meafured, forfeit and pay the fum of forty fhillings; to be recovered and applied in fuch and the fame manner as the pecuniary penalties inflicted and directed to be levied by the firft mentioned act, are thereby ordered, directed, and appointed, to be levied, recovered, and applied refpectively.

And if coals upon remeafurement, fhall fall fhort of the quantity they were originally fold and meafured for, the principal coal meters to pay 40s. for every bufhel wanting of the meafure.

III. And it is hereby further enacted, That if any labouring coal meter fhall deliver a ticket to any perfon or perfons for any quantity of coals, without having been prefent at, and feen the meafuring of, the whole quantity thereof fpecified and expreffed in fuch ticket, in every fuch cafe the principal coal meters fhall forfeit and pay the fum of five pounds; to be recovered and applied

Labouring coal meter delivering tickets for coals, which he was not prefent at the meafuring of,

6   plied

plied in such manner as the pecuniary penalties, inflicted and directed to be levied by the first-mentioned act, are thereby ordered, directed, and appointed, to be levied, recovered, and applied, respectively: and every labouring coal meter so offending, upon complaint thereof made unto any one or more justice or justices of the peace for the city and liberty of *Westminster*, or for the said county of *Middlesex*, and, upon due proof made to his or their satisfaction, shall be committed to the house of correction, there to remain, and be kept to hard labour, for any time not exceeding thirty days; and shall be for ever rendered incapable of acting as a labouring coal meter under this act. *(margin: to be committed to hard labour for 30 days, and incapacited; and the principals to forfeit 5l.)*

IV. *And whereas by an act passed in the third year of his present Majesty's reign, it was therein enacted, That all coals should be carried to the respective buyers, within the limits therein mentioned, in linen sacks, sealed and marked with white paint in oil at* Guildhall, London, *or at the exchequer office at* Westminster, *by the proper officer there; which sacks shall be full four feet and two inches in length, and six and twenty inches in breadth, after they shall be made: And whereas it has been found by experience that these dimensions have not been quite sufficient, by reason of the great shrinking of the sacks from wet, and other causes*; be it therefore enacted, That from and after the twenty fourth day of *December* one thousand seven hundred and fifty nine, all sacks made use of for the carriage of coals within the limits mentioned in the aforesaid act, shall be full four feet four inches in length, and full twenty six inches in breadth, after they are made; nor shall any of less dimensions be sealed and marked at the above mentioned offices: And if any person or persons dealing in or selling coals within the limits aforesaid, shall use, or cause to be used, sacks of any less dimensions than the dimensions herein before directed, every such person shall, for every such offence, forfeit the sum of forty shillings, to be recovered, levied, and applied, in such manner as the pecuniary penalties, inflicted and directed to be levied by the said act of the nineteenth year of his present Majesty's reign, are thereby directed and appointed to be levied, recovered, and applied, respectively. *(margin: Clause in act 3 Geo. 2. Sacks to be 4 feet 4 inches long, and 26 inches broad. 40s. penalty on using sacks of less dimensions.)*

V. *And, for the more effectually preventing any frauds by false admeasurement of coals*; it is hereby further enacted, That if any person employed as a labouring coal meter shall suffer any coal sacks to be made use of for the carriage of coals, being less than full four feet in length, and full two feet in breadth, within side the sack, or shall neglect to attend and perform his duty at the wharfs, as in the said act of the nineteenth year of his present Majesty's reign is directed, he shall, for every such offence, forfeit the sum of forty shillings; to be recovered, levied, and applied, in such and the like manner as the pecuniary penalties inflicted and directed to be levied by the said act of the nineteenth year of his present Majesty's reign, are thereby directed and appointed to be levied, recovered, and applied, respectively. *(margin: Labouring coal meter using sacks of less dimensions than here allowed, or neglecting his duty, forfeits 40s. Application thereof.)*

VI. And it is hereby further enacted, That such justice or justices as aforesaid, upon every such complaint so to him or them made *(margin: Justices, upon application and complaint.)*

in any of the cafes aforefaid, to fummon and examine the parties;

made in the cafes before-mentioned, is and are hereby authorized and required to call and fummon the parties before him or them, and to hear and examine every fuch complaint upon oath, or upon affirmation of fuch witnefs or witnefles as fhall be of the people called *Quakers* (and which oath or affirmation fuch juftice or juftices is and are hereby refpectively impowered and required to adminifter and take) and upon due proof of fuch offence as

and upon proof of the offence, to commit the offender.

aforefaid to his or their fatisfaction to grant a warrant or warrants under his or their hand and feal, or hands and feals, for the commitment of fuch offender or offenders to the houfe of correction, there to remain and be dealt with as aforefaid.

Provifions relating to the fee for the admeafurement of coals, or punifhment of dealers or carters, to take place in fuch cafes only, where a meter fhall have attended the admeafurement at the buyer's defire.

VII. Provided always, and it is hereby further enacted by the authority aforefaid, That from and after the commencement of this act, none of the provifions made by the faid former act of the nineteenth year of the reign of his prefent Majefty, or by this prefent act, relating to the payment of any fum or fums of money for or on account of the admeafurement or infpection of the admeafurement of coals, or to the punifhment of any dealer in coals, or carter, on account of fending, carrying, or leading, coals from any wharf or place within the limits aforefaid, fhall take place and be in force, except in fuch cafes only where the buyer of fuch coals fhall have fignified, by notice in writing to one of the principal coal meters, or one of the labouring coal meters, his or her defire to have the attendance of a coal meter to infpect the admeafurement of his or her coals, and where a coal meter fhall, purfuant to fuch notice, attend and actually infpect the admeafurement of the whole quantity of fuch coals; any thing contained in the faid recited act, or this act, to the contrary thereof in any wife notwithftanding.

The powers, &c. of 19 Geo. a.

except where altered by this act,

to be in force during the continuance of this act.

Commencement and continuance of this act.

VIII. And it is hereby further enacted and declared, That the faid act made in the nineteenth year of the reign of his prefent Majefty, and continued by the fubfequent acts herein before-mentioned and referred to, and all the powers, penalties, forfeitures, remedies, provifions, rules, orders, directions, claufes, matters, and things, given, granted, ordered, appointed, prefcribed, inferted, and contained, in and by the faid acts refpectively, or any of them, which are now in force (other than fo far forth as the fame, or any of them refpectively, are varied, altered, explained, rendered unneceffary, or otherwife provided for by the force of this prefent act) fhall be exercifed, practifed, ufed, enforced, and put in execution, during the continuance, and for the purpofes, of this prefent act, in as full, extenfive, and beneficial manner, to all intents and purpofes, as if the faid powers, penalties, forfeitures, remedies, provifions, rules, orders, directions, claufes, matters, and things, were particularly expreffed, and again enacted in the body of this prefent act: and alfo that this act fhall take effect, continue, and be in force, from the faid twenty fourth day of *June*, one thoufand feven hundred and fifty nine, for and during the further term of feven years then next enfuing, and from thence to the end of the then next feffion of parliament; and fhall be deemed, adjudged, and

taken

taken to be a publick act, and be judicially taken notice of as
fuch by all judges, juftices, and other perfons whatfoever.

CAP. XXVIII.

An act for relief of debtors with refpect to the imprifon-
ment of their perfons ; and to oblige debtors, who fhall
continue in execution in prifon beyond a certain time, and
for fums not exceeding what are mentioned in the act, to
make difcovery of, and deliver upon oath, their eftates for
their creditors benefit.

WHEREAS *many perfons fuffer by the oppreffion of inferior* Preamble.
officers in the execution of procefs for debt, and the exaction
of jaylors to whom fuch debtors are committed: for remedy whereof, it may be reafonable not only to enforce the execution of the
laws now in being againft fuch oppreffions and exactions, more
efpecially feveral claufes in a ftatute made at a parliament held
in the twenty fecond and twenty third years of the reign of King Act 22 & 23
Charles the Second (intituled, *An act for the relief and releafe of* Car. 2.
poor diftreffed prifoners for debt) but likewife to make fome further provifions for the eafe and relief of debtors who fhall be
willing to fatisfy their creditors to the utmoft of their power;
be it therefore enacted by the King's moft excellent majefty, by
and with the advice and confent of the lords fpiritual and temporal, and commons, in this prefent parliament affembled, and
by the authority of the fame, That no fheriff, under fheriff, Officer may
bailiff, ferjeant at mace, or other officer or minifter whatfoever, not carry his
fhall at any time or times hereafter convey or carry, or caufe to any tavern
be conveyed or carried, any perfon or perfons by him or them or other pub-
arrefted, or being in his or their cuftody by virtue or colour of lick houfe,
any action, writ, procefs, or attachment, to any tavern, ale- without his
houfe, or other publick victualling or drinking houfe, or to the consent;
private houfe of any fuch officer or minifter, of any tenant or
relation of his, without the free and voluntary confent of the
perfon or perfons fo arrefted or in cuftody; nor charge any fuch nor charge
perfon or perfons with any fum of money for any wine, beer, him for liquor
ale, victuals, tobacco, or any other liquor or things whatfoever, or other
fave what he, fhe, or they, fhall call for of his, her, or their own things, other
free accord; nor fhall caufe or procure him, her, or them, to he fhall freely
call or pay for any fuch liquor or things, except what he, fhe, or and particu-
they, fhall particularly and freely afk for; nor fhall demand, larly call for;
take, or receive, or caufe to be demanded, taken, or received, nor demand
directly or indirectly, any other or greater fum or fums of mo- for caption or
ney than is or fhall be by law allowed to be taken or demanded any other than
for any arreft or taking, or for detaining, or waiting till the per- his legal fee;
fon or perfons fo arrefted or in cuftody fhall have given an appearance or bail, as the cafe fhall require, or agreed with the perfon or perfons at whofe fuit or profecution he, fhe, or they fhall
be taken or arrefted, or until he, fhe, or they, fhall be fent to the
proper gaol belonging to the county, riding, divifion, city, town,

nor exact any gratuity money; nor carry his prisoner to gaol within 24 hours after his arrest, unless he shall refuse to be carried to some safe house of his own appointment within some city or town, if arrested there, or within 3 miles thereof.

or place, where such arrest or taking shall be; nor shall exact or take any reward, gratuity, or money, for keeping the person or persons so arrested or in custody out of gaol or prison; nor shall carry any such person to any gaol or prison within four and twenty hours from the time of such arrest, unless such person or persons, so arrested, shall refuse to be carried to some safe and convenient dwelling house of his, her, or their own nomination or appointment, within a city, borough, corporation, or market town, in case such person or persons shall be there arrested; or within three miles from the place where such arrest shall be made, if the same shall be made out of any city, borough, corporation, or market town, so as such dwelling house be not the house of the person arrested, and be within the county, riding, division, or liberty, in which the person under arrest was arrested; and then, and in any such case, it shall be lawful to and for any such sheriff, or other officer or minister, to convey or carry the person or persons so arrested, and refusing to be carried to such safe and convenient dwelling house as aforesaid, to such gaol or prison as he, she, or they, may be sent to, by virtue of the action, writ, or process, against him, her, or them.

Nor may officer take for the lodging, diet, and other expences of such prisoner, more than shall be allowed, in such cases, by an order of the justices in their general or quarter sessions, which order they are required to make with all expedition;

II. And be it further enacted by the authority aforesaid, That no sheriff, under sheriff, bailiff, serjeant at mace, or other officer or person, shall, at any time or times hereafter, take or receive any other or greater sum or sums for one or more nights lodging, or for a day's diet, or other expences of any person or persons under arrest, on any writ, action, attachment, or process, other than what shall be allowed as reasonable in such cases by some order or orders already made, or which shall hereafter be made, by the justices of the peace at some general or quarter sessions which shall be held for the county, riding, division, city, town, or place, where such arrest or taking shall be, who are hereby authorized and required, with all convenient expedition, to make some standing order or orders for ascertaining such charges and expences, within their respective counties, ridings, divisions, cities, towns, and jurisdictions, if the same hath or have not already been there made; and if any such order or orders hath or have been there already made, such justices for the time being, at their respective general or quarter sessions, are hereby authorized and required to vary or alter the same, from time to time, as they shall see occasion; and also are hereby required to cause a copy of every such order, and of every variation or alteration thereof, signed by the clerk of the peace of every such county, riding, division, city, town, or place, respectively, to be put and kept up in some conspicuous place in the sessions house, or some other proper place, of every such respective county, riding, division, city, town, or place, as such justices shall order, so as the same may be there seen and examined as occasion may require.

a copy whereof is to be hung up in some conspicuous part of the sessions house, or other proper place.

Sheriffs, and the seconda-

III. And, to the intent that no person may suffer by reason of his ignorance of the provisions made by this act, be it further enacted by the authority aforesaid, That all and every sheriff, under sheriff,

sheriff, and bailiff of any liberty, and also the respective secondaries and clerks sitters in the respective compters in *London*, and all other persons intrusted with the execution of process, or who shall enter any actions, or make any warrant or warrants, or any writ or process, in order to have the same executed, shall deliver a printed copy of the several clauses contained in this act relating to bailiffs, serjeants, and other officers and persons who shall be employed under them respectively to execute any writ, process, or attachment, or who shall arrest any person on any action which shall be entered, or otherwise, within their respective sheriffwicks or jurisdictions, to every such bailiff, serjeant, officer, and other person, and shall make it part of the condition of every security or bond which shall be given or made to any such sheriff or under sheriff, or bailiff of any liberty, by any bailiff, serjeant at mace, or other officer or person, who shall be employed or intrusted to execute any such writ or process as aforesaid under him, them, or any of them, that every such bailiff, serjeant at mace, or officer, and other person respectively, shall and will shew and deliver a copy of the said clauses to every person he shall arrest by virtue of any process, action, writ, or attachment, or under any warrant made out thereon, and carry or go with to any publick or other house where any liquor shall be sold; and also shall and will permit every such person who shall be so arrested, or any friend of him or her, to read over the same clauses, before any liquor, meat, or victuals, shall be, at any such publick or other house, called for, or brought to, any such person who shall be so under arrest there; and in case any bailiff, serjeant at mace, or other officer or person, shall, in any respect, offend in the premisses, every such offence, besides the breach of the condition of every such security bond, shall be accounted and deemed a misdemeanor in the execution of the process or action on which any such person was arrested, and shall be punishable as such by virtue of this act.

ries of the compters, to deliver printed copies of these clauses to bailiffs and other officers employed in the execution of writs, &c. and make it a part of the condition of the bond to be given by them, that they shall shew and deliver a copy of the said clauses to the prisoner, if carried to a publick house, and permit him or his friend to read over the same, before any liquor or victuals be brought or called for. Officer offending in the premisses, besides the breach of covenant, liable to be punished for a misdemeanor.

IV. And be it further enacted by the authority aforesaid, That every sheriff, under sheriff, bailiff of any liberty, gaoler and keeper of any prison or gaol, and other person and persons, to whose custody or keeping any one hath been, or hereafter shall be, arrested, taken, committed, or charged in execution, by virtue of any writ, process, or action, or attachment, shall, at all times hereafter, permit and suffer every such person and persons, during his, her, and their respective continuance under arrest or in custody, or in execution for any debt, damages, costs, or contempt, at his, her, and their free will and pleasure, to send for, or have brought to him, her, or them, at seasonable times in the day time, any beer, ale, victuals, or other necessary food, from what place he, she, or they shall think fit, or can have the same; and also to have and use such bedding, linen, and other necessary things, as he, she, or they shall have occasion for and think fit, or shall be supplied with, during his, her, or their continuance under any such arrest or commitment, without purloining or detaining the same, or any part thereof, or inforcing or re-

Sheriffs and gaolers to allow debtors in custody, to send for, or have brought to them, victuals and beer from what place they shall think fit; and to have and use such bedding and linen, &c. as they shall think fit, or shall be supplied with,

quiring

without pur-
loining or de-
taining there-
of, or obliging
them to pay
for the same.

quiring him, her, or them, to pay for the having or using thereof, or putting any manner of restraint or difficulty upon him,
her, or them, in the using thereof, or relating thereto; and no
such prisoner or prisoners shall pay any thing in respect thereof to any such sheriff, under sheriff, bailiff of any liberty, gaoler,
keeper, or other person as aforesaid.

The L. C. Ju-
stices of the
King's Bench,
Common
Pleas, and Ex-
chequer, with
the mayor
and two al-
dermen of
London, for
the prisons
within the
said city;
and the L. C.
Justices, and
L. C. Baron,
with three
justices of the
peace for Mid-
dlesex and Sur-
ry, for the
prisons in the
said counties,
to meet and
settle a table
of the fees to
be taken by
the respective
gaolers there-
of;
and to vary
the same as
they shall see
occasion;
and justices at
their general
or quarter
sessions of the
peace, to
make like ta-
bles of fees to
be taken by
the gaolers
within their
respective ju-
risdictions.
Tables of the
fees for Lon-
don, Middle-
sex, and Surry
gaols, to be
signed by the
persons mak-
ing or altering
the same:
those for other
places to be

V. And be it further enacted by the authority aforesaid, That
the lord chief justice of the court of *King's Bench*, the lord chief
justice of the court of *Common Pleas*, and the lord chief baron of
the court of *exchequer*, for the time being, or any two of them,
together with the mayor and two of the aldermen, or with three
of the aldermen of the city of *London* without the mayor for the
time being, for and in respect of the gaols and prisons within the
said city of *London*; and the said lords chief justices, and lord
chief baron, or any two of them, with three justices of the peace
of the counties of *Middlesex* and *Surry* respectively, for and in respect of the gaols and prisons in the said counties of *Middlesex*
and *Surry* respectively; are hereby respectively required, with
all convenient speed, to meet, from time to time, at such place
as they shall think fit and appoint, and there to settle and establish a
table of the rates and fees which shall be allowed to be taken by
any gaoler or keeper in *London*, or in the several counties of *Middlesex* and *Surry*, where the same hath not been already established; and where the same hath been already established, they are
hereby respectively authorized to meet together as aforesaid, and
vary the same from time to time as they shall see occasion; and
the justices of the peace of every other county, riding, division,
city, and place, for and in respect of the gaols and prisons in
each other respective county, riding, division, city, town, and
place, are hereby respectively authorized and required, at any general or quarter session of the peace to be held for such county,
riding, division, city, town, or place respectively, with all convenient speed, to settle and establish a table of the respective rates
and fees, which shall be allowed to be taken by any gaoler or
keeper, within their respective jurisdictions, where the same hath
not been already settled and established, and where the same hath
been already settled and established, then to vary and alter the
same, from time to time, as there shall be occasion; and that
the respective tables of such fees which shall be so made, varied,
or altered, for or in respect of the several gaols and prisons within the city of *London*, and counties of *Middlesex* and *Surry* aforesaid, shall be signed, from time to time, by the said lords chief
justices, and lord chief baron, or two of them, and the mayor
and two aldermen of the said city of *London*, or by three aldermen of the said city of *London* without the mayor, and by three
justices of the peace of the counties of *Middlesex* and *Surry* respectively, within their respective jurisdictions, by whom the
same shall be respectively made, varied, or altered; and that the
tables of such fees, which shall be made, or altered, or varied,
for or in respect of the rest of the said gaols and prisons, shall,
from time to time, be signed by three or more of the justices of
the

the peace who shall so make or vary, or alter, the same, at any *signed by 3* such general or quarter session of the peace as aforesaid, and shall *justices at the* be afterwards reviewed and confirmed, or moderated, within that *quarter ses-* part of *Great Britain* called *England*, by the judges of assize, and *and to be re-* if within the principality of *Wales*, or county palatine of *Chester*, *viewed, con-* by the justices of great sessions respectively, at the next assizes, *firmed, or* or great sessions, which shall be held in the respective counties, *the judges of* within their several circuits next after the making, or varying, or *assize, or ju-* altering of any such table of fees; and the same shall be after- *stices of great* wards signed by the respective judges of assize, or justices of great *sessions, with-* sessions, who shall respectively review, confirm, or moderate the *in their re-* same, and three or more justices of the peace of such respective *spective cir-* county, riding, division, city, town, or place, under their respec- *and be after-* tive hands, for and in respect of the respective gaols and prisons *wards signed* within their respective circuits, counties, ridings, divisions, ci- *by them.* ties, towns, or jurisdictions.

VI. And be it also enacted by the authority aforesaid, That *Rules and or-* proper rules and orders for the better government of the respect- *ders for the* ive gaols and prisons in that part of *Great Britain* called *Eng-* *vernment of* land, and of the prisoners who are or shall be therein, where *the gaols, and* such rules and orders have not already been made, shall, with *prisoners* all convenient speed, be made by the several courts in *Westmin-* *therein, to be* *ster Hall*, for and in respect of the several gaols or prisons be- *respective* longing to such courts respectively; and by the said lords chief *courts in* justices, and lord chief baron, or any two or more of them, to- *Westminster* gether with the mayor and two aldermen of the said city of *Lon-* *gaols belong-* don, or three or more aldermen of the said city of *London* with- *ing to such* out the said mayor, for and in respect of the gaols and prisons *courts;* within the said city of *London*; and by the said lords chief justices, *and by the L.* and lord chief baron, or any two of them, for the time being, *and L. C. Ba-* together with three or more justices of the peace, for and in re- *ron, with the* spect of the gaols and prisons within the said counties of *Middle-* *mayor and* sex and *Surry*; and by three or more justices of the peace of each *two aldermen,* county, riding, or division, city, borough, town corporate, or *in London;* place, for and in respect of the gaols and prisons within their re- *and by the* spective counties, ridings, divisions, cities, boroughs, towns *L. C. Justices* corporate, or places, at some general or quarter sessions, as afore- *and L. C. Ba-* said; and the same shall afterwards be reviewed, and may be *justices of the* altered, if thought necessary, by the judge or judges of assize, or *peace, for* justice or justices of great sessions respectively, at the next assizes *those in Mid-* or great sessions which shall be held by them respectively, with- *dlesex and* in their several circuits, after the making or altering of any such *Surry;* rules or orders; and where any rules or orders for regulating or *stices of the* governing any such gaols or prisons have already been made, or *peace, for* hereafter shall be made, the same may, at all times hereafter, be *those in any* enlarged, altered, or amended, as there shall be occasion, by the *other county,* respective courts in *Westminster Hall*, and other the persons for *These to be* the time being respectively authorized by this act to make and *afterwards re-* alter the same: and after every making, enlarging, altering, or *viewed, and* amending thereof, all such rules or orders so enlarged, altered, *may be alter-* or amended, shall be signed by the judges of each respective court *judges of as-* *in size, and ju-*

stices of great
sessions re-
spectively.
Rules to be
enlarged, al-
tered, or a-
mended as
there shall be
occasion;
and to be du-
ly signed.
Duplicates of
such orders,
and tables of
fees, to be
enrolled, and
entered upon
record in the
proper courts;

in *Westminster Hall*, where any such rules or orders shall be made, enlarged, altered, or amended, for and in respect of the prisons and prisoners belonging to the said courts respectively; and in respect to the other gaols or prisons, or the prisoners therein, by the respective persons, for the time being, hereby before authorized to make, and review, or alter, such rules or orders, within their respective jurisdictions, as aforesaid: and duplicates of every such table of fees which shall be made, enlarged, altered, or varied, and of all rules or orders which shall be hereafter made for regulating any gaol or prison in pursuance of this act, belonging to the said respective courts in *Westminster Hall*, shall be entered and inrolled on record in every such respective court, by the proper officer thereof, without any fee to be paid for the same; and a like duplicate of every such table of fees, rules, or orders, which shall be so made, varied, altered, or amended, and which shall concern or relate to any other gaol or prison, or the prisoners therein, in that part of *Great Britain* called *England*, shall, from time to time, with all convenient speed after the making or altering, enlarging or varying thereof, be transmited to the respective clerks of the peace of the several counties, ridings, divisions, cities, or places, in or for which the same shall be made, altered, enlarged, or varied, and shall be by every such respective clerk of the peace, entered or registered on the rolls

and copies
thereof to be
hung up in all
courts of as-
size, great
sessions, and
quarter ses-
sions;
and transmit-
ted to the re-
spective gaol-
ers,
and kept hung
up in some
publick room
of each pri-
son.

of the respective sessions without fee; and every such clerk of the peace shall cause another copy thereof to be hung up in the court where every assize, great sessions, or quarter sessions of the peace, for every such county, riding, division, city, or place respectively, within his jurisdiction, shall be held, there to remain and be inspected as occasion shall require; and shall also cause another copy thereof to be transmitted to every gaoler or keeper of any prison, within the jurisdiction of any such respective clerk of the peace; and every such gaoler or keeper shall forthwith, after the receipt of any such table of fees, rules, or orders, cause the same to be hung up in some open or publick room or place, and in a conspicuous manner, in his gaol or prison; and it shall be incumbent on every such gaoler or keeper, to take care that the same shall, from time to time, be kept up there, and preserved, so as that the prisoners in his gaol or prison may have free and easy resort thereto, at seasonable times in the day time, as occasion shall require, without paying any thing for the same.

Courts in
Westminster
Hall to enquire
annually, whe-
ther such ta-
bles of fees
and orders
are duly hung
up and com-
plied with,
and to give
notice to the
prisoners of
the time ap-

VII. And be it further enacted by the authority aforesaid, That the several courts of record in *Westminster Hall* aforesaid shall hereafter, in every *Michaelmas* term, appoint some day in such term, to inquire whether such table of fees, and such rules or orders, as aforesaid, are hung up, and remain publick, and easy to be resorted to, in the several prisons to the said courts respectively belonging, and whether the same be duly complied with, and observed; and shall cause eight days notice to be given in every such *Michaelmas* term, to the prisoners in every of the respective prisons belonging to the said respective courts in *Westminster Hall*, of the time appointed for such inquiry, and shall

in-

inform themselves touching the same in the best manner they pointed for can, and supply and redress whatever they shall find neglected or such inquiry. transgressed.

VIII. And be it also enacted by the authority aforesaid, That the judges and justices of assize, gaol delivery, and great sessions as aforesaid respectively, within their respective jurisdictions, shall, at all assizes and sessions of gaol delivery and great sessions, as aforesaid, which shall hereafter be held by them, make enquiry whether such table of fees, and rules or orders, as aforesaid, are hung up, and remain publick, to be resorted to in the several gaols or prisons within their respective jurisdictions, and whether the same be duly complied with, and observed : and shall inform themselves touching the same in the best manner they can, and supply and redress whatever they shall find neglected or transgressed relating thereto, and shall expressly give in charge to every grand jury impanelled and sworn before them respectively, to make enquiries concerning the same.

Judges and justices of assize, &c. to make a like inquiry; and supply and redress what shall be necessary; and charge the grand jury to make inquiries therein.

IX. And be it further enacted by the authority aforesaid, That the several courts of *King's Bench, Common Pleas*, and *Exchequer*, judges of assize, and justices of great sessions, and justices of the peace within their respective jurisdictions, and all commissioners for charitable uses, do, from time to time, use their best endeavours and diligence to examine after and discover the several gifts, legacies, and bequests, bestowed or given for the benefit or advantage of the poor prisoners in the several gaols or prisons within their respective jurisdictions; and they are hereby severally authorized, within their respective jurisdictions, to send for, and cause to be brought before them respectively, any deeds, wills, writings, books of account, and papers, as they shall receive information of to be in the custody of any person within their respective jurisdictions, and to concern the premisses ; and also may summon, and cause to come before them respectively, any person or persons whom they shall have any just reason to apprehend may be able to make any discovery concerning the same ; and they are hereby authorized, within their respective jurisdictions, to examine any such person or persons on oath, in order to get at a true discovery thereof, and to order and settle the payment, recovery, and receipt of any such gifts, legacies, or bequests, when so discovered and ascertained, in such easy and expeditious manner and way as shall be thought proper by them respectively, that the prisoners for the future may not be defrauded, but may, without delay, receive the full benefit of all such gifts, legacies, and bequests, according to the true intent of the respective donors thereof.

Courts at Westminster, judges of assize, justices of peace, and commissioners for charitable uses, impowered to enquire concerning bequests to poor prisoners, to send for any papers and persons that may give insight therein,

and to settle the payment, recovery, and receipt of such bequests.

X. And be it further enacted by the authority aforesaid, That a list or table of such gifts, legacies, and bequests, for the benefit of the prisoners in every gaol or prison respectively, as aforesaid, shall, after every settling thereof, be transmitted by the persons hereby authorized to settle the same, unto the clerks of the peace of the respective counties or places, and shall be registered by them respectively, in the manner tables of fees and orders are

Table of benefactions to be transmitted to, and registered by, the clerks of the peace,

herein

and alfo to the gaolers of the prifons to which the fame relate, and be hung up in fome publick place of fuch prifons.

herein before directed to be regiftered by them refpectively, without any fee to be paid for the fame; and that a lift or table of fuch gifts, legacies, and bequefts, fhall be fairly written and tranfmitted, by order of fuch perfons as aforefaid, to the gaoler or keeper of every gaol or prifon to which the gifts, charities, or bequefts, therein contained relate, and forthwith after the receipt thereof, fhall be hung up by the gaoler or keeper, who fhall receive the fame, in a confpicuous manner in fome publick place in his gaol or prifon, and where the prifoners in fuch gaol or prifon may have free and eafy refort thereto, as occafion may require, without fee; and it fhall be the duty of every fuch gaoler or keeper, to take care that every fuch lift or table of gifts which fhall be tranfmitted to any fuch gaol or prifon, or a true copy thereof, fhall, from time to time thereafter, be kept hung up as aforefaid in his refpective gaol or prifon.

Where gaolers, bailiffs, or others, fhall be guilty of extortion, or other abufes, the court, &c. upon petition of the prifoner, is to examine into the fame in a fummary way;

XI. And, for the more fpeedy punifhing gaolers, bailiffs, and others, employed in the execution of procefs, for extortion, or other abufes in their refpective offices and places, be it further enacted by the authority aforefaid, That upon the petition, in term time, of any prifoner or perfon being, or having been, under arreft or in cuftody, complaining of any exaction or extortion by any gaoler, bailiff, or other officer or perfon, in or employed in the keeping or taking care of any gaol or prifon, or other place, where any fuch prifoner or perfon under, or having been under, arreft or in cuftody, by any procefs or action, is or fhall have been carried or in refpect of the arrefting or apprehending any perfon or perfons, by virtue of any procefs, action, or warrant, or of any other abufe whatfoever committed or done in their refpective offices or places, unto any of his Majefty's courts of record at Weftminfter, from whence the procefs iffued, by which any perfon who fhall fo petition was arrefted, or under whofe power or jurifdiction any fuch gaol, prifon, or place, is; or in vacation time, to any judge of any fuch courts at Weftminfter, from whence any fuch procefs fo iffued; or to the judges of affize, or juftices of great feffions, in their refpective circuits; or to the judge or judges of any other court of record, where any prifoner or perfon being, or having been, under arreft or in cuftody, was arrefted or in cuftody by procefs iffued out of, or action entered in, any fuch other court of record within that part of Great Britain called England; and if within the principality of Wales, or county palatine of Chefter, then to the juftices at fome great feffions to be holden for the county in the principality of Wales, or for the county palatine of Chefter, where any fuch prifoner or perfon being, or having been, under arreft or in cuftody, was arrefted or in cuftody, in the faid principality of Wales, or county palatine of Chefter; every fuch court, judges of affize, and juftices of great feffions, and judge and judges of all inferior courts of record, are hereby authorized and required refpectively, within their feveral jurifdictions, to hear and determine the fame in a fummary way, and to make fuch order thereupon for redreffing the abufes which fhall, by any fuch petition, be complained of, and for punifh-

and make fuch order thereupon, for

nishing such officer or person complained against, and for making **redressing the** reparation to the party or parties i injured, as they shall think **abuse, and** just, together with the full costs of every such complaint; and **punishing the** all orders and determinations which shall be thereupon made, **they shall** by any of the said courts, or any of the said judges, justices of **think just;** assize, justices of great sessions, judge or judges of any such in- **and may in-** ferior court as aforesaid respectively, in such summary way as is **ence to such** herein prescribed, shall have the same effect, force, and virtue, **orders.** and obedience thereunto may be inforced by the respective courts, judges, justices of assize, justices of great sessions, judge or judges of any such inferior court, by attachment, or in any other manner, as other orders of the said respective courts, judges, justices of assize and great sessions, judge or judges of inferior courts of record, may be inforced.

XII. And be it further enacted by the authority aforesaid, **Gaoler to take** That no gaoler or keeper of any goal, or prison, or other per- **no other fees** son thereto belonging, shall demand, take, or receive, directly **than what** or indirectly, of any prisoner or prisoners, for debt, damages, **shall be allow-** costs, or contempt, any other or greater fee or fees whatsoever **in the authen-** for his, her, or their commitment, or coming into gaol, cham- **of fees.** ber rent there, release or discharge, than what shall be men- tioned or allowed in the list or table of fees which is or shall be settled, inrolled, and registered as aforesaid; and that every **and sheriffs** sheriff, under sheriff, bailiff of any liberty, bailiff, serjeant at **and other of-** mace, gaoler, and other officer and person as aforesaid, who **ficers offend-** shall in any wise offend against this act, shall, for every such **ing against** offence against this present act (over and above such penalties or **forfeit 50l.** punishments as he or they shall be liable unto by the laws now **(exclusive of** in force) forfeit and pay to the party thereby aggrieved the sum **other penal-** of fifty pounds, to be recovered with treble costs of suit, by **party aggriev-** action of debt, bill, plaint, or information, in any of his Ma- **ed.** jesty's courts of record at *Westminster*; wherein no essoin, pro- tection, or wager of law, or more than one imparlance, shall be allowed.

XIII. *And, for the ease and relief of prisoners who shall be charg- ed in execution for any sum or sums of money, not exceeding in the whole the sum of one hundred pounds, and who shall be willing to sa- tisfy their respective creditors as far as they are able*, be it further enacted by the authority aforesaid, That from and after the **Debtor charg-** fifteenth day of *June*, one thousand seven hundred and fifty nine, **ed in execu-** if any person or persons shall be charged in execution for any **tion for any** sum or sums of money, not exceeding in the whole the sum of **not exceeding** one hundred pounds, or on which execution or executions there **100l. &c.** shall at any time remain due, as shall be made appear by oath, a sum or sums of money, not amounting to above the said sum of one hundred pounds, and shall be minded to deliver up to his, her, or their creditor or creditors who shall so charge him, her, or them, in execution, all his, her, or their estate and ef- fects, for or towards the satisfaction of the debt or debts where- with he, she, or they, shall so stand charged; it shall and may **may exhibit a** be lawful to and for any such prisoner, before the end of the first **petition to the** term **court,** term which shall be next after any such prisoner shall be charged in execution by his creditor or creditors, to exhibit a petition to any court of law, from whence the process issued upon which any such prisoner was or were taken and charged in execution as aforesaid, or to the court into which any such prisoner shall be removed by *Habeas Corpus*, or shall be charged in custody, and shall remain in the prison thereof,

certifying therein the causes of his imprisonment, with a schedule of his real and personal estate at the time,

certifying the cause or causes of his, her, or their imprisonment; and not only setting forth, in every such petition, a just and true account of all the real and personal estate which he, she, or they so petitioning, or any person or persons in trust for him, her, or them, is, was, or were intitled to at the time of his, her, or their so petitioning,

and charges affecting the same,

and of all incumbrances and charges (if any there be) affecting any such real or personal estate of the person or persons so petitioning, but also a just and true account of all the real and personal estate which any such prisoner or prisoners, or any person or persons in trust for him, her, or them, or for his, her, or their use, was or were interested in, or intitled to, at the

and also the state of his effects at the time of his first imprisonment,

time of his, her, or their first imprisonment, in the action in which such person is charged in execution, either in possession, reversion, remainder, or expectancy, to the best of the belief of every such prisoner or prisoners, and so far as his, her, or their respective knowledge extends concerning the same; and like-

and the securities, bonds, notes, and books, relating thereto, with the names and places of abode of the witnesses.

wise a just and true account of all securities wherein any part of the estates of any such prisoner or prisoners consists, and of all the deeds, evidences, writings, books, bonds, notes, and papers, concerning the same, or relating thereto; and the names and places of abode of the witnesses to all securities, bonds, or notes, and where they are to be respectively met with, so far as his, her, or their knowledge extends concerning the same: and before any such petition from any such prisoner or prisoners shall be received by any such court, every such prisoner or prisoners shall give or leave, or cause to be given or left, unto or for all and every the creditor or creditors at whose suit any such prisoner

14 days previous notice of such intended petition to be given to the creditor, or his attorney, at whose suit he is charged in execution;

or prisoners shall stand charged in execution as aforesaid, or his, her or their executors or administrators, and at his, her, or their usual place of abode, or to or for his, her, or their attorney or agent last employed in any such action, suit, cause or causes, in case any such creditor or creditors, his, her, or their executors or administrators, cannot be met with, but not otherwise, fourteen days at least before any such petition shall be presented and received, a notice in writing, signed with the proper name or mark of every such prisoner or prisoners, importing therein, That such prisoner or prisoners as aforesaid, doth or do intend to petition the court from whence the process issued, upon which he, she, or they stand charged in execution, or into the prison to which any such prisoner shall have been removed by *Habeas Corpus*, or shall stand charged in execution on any judgement, recovered on any bill or declaration filed or

with a copy of the schedule he intends to

delivered in any such court; and also setting forth in every such notice or writing, a true copy of the account or schedule, in-

cluding

cluding the whole real and personal estate of the person or per- deliver into court.
sons so designing to petition, which he, she, or they doth or do
intend to deliver into any such court (other than and except the
necessary wearing apparel and bedding of the prisoner or prisoners, and his, her, or their family, and the tools or instruments
of his, her, or their trade or calling, not exceeding ten pounds Affidavit of
in value in the whole) and an affidavit of the due service of every the due ser-
such notice shall be delivered with every such petition, at the vice of such
time of presenting thereof, and openly read in the court to notice to be
which any such petition shall be addressed : and if such court delivered at
shall thereupon be satisfied of the regularity of every such notice, the same time
such petition shall be received, and such court shall thereupon, with the peti-
by order or rule of the same court, cause the prisoner or pri- tion into
soners so petitioning to be brought up to such court, on some court, and
certain day in such order or rule to be specified, and the credi- read openly ;
tor, or several creditors, at whose suit any such prisoner or pri- and a rule to
soners shall stand charged in execution, as aforesaid, his, her, be made, upon
or their executors or administrators, to be summoned to appear receiving the
personally, or by his, her, or their attorney, in such court, at petition, for
some certain day to be specified in such rule or order for that bringing the
purpose : and if any creditor or creditors of any such prisoner or prisoner into
prisoners, who shall be so summoned, his or her executors or court, and
administrators, shall appear in person, or by his, her, or their at- summoning
torney ; or if any such creditor or creditors, his or her executors the creditor,
or administrators, shall refuse or neglect to appear in person, or &c.
by his, her, or their attorney ; then upon affidavit of the due and the cre-
service of such rule or order on him, her, or them, or his, ditor appear-
her, or their attorney, if any such creditor or creditors, his, ing or not ap-
her, or their executors or administrators, cannot be met with, pearing there-
such court shall, in a summary way examine into the matter of to.
every such petition, and hear what can or shall be alledged on Oath being
either side, for or against the discharge of any such prisoner or made of the
prisoners who shall so petition ; and upon such examination, due service of
every such court is hereby required to administer or tender to the rule,
the prisoner or prisoners respectively who shall so petition, and the court to
give such previous notice thereof as herein before is directed, examine into
an oath to the effect following : that is to say, the matter of the petition in a summary way ; and admini- ster the oath following to the prisoner.

I A. B. do swear, in the presence of Almighty God, That the ac- The oath.
count by me set forth in my petition presented to this honourable
court, doth contain a full and true account of the real and personal
estate, debts, credits, and effects whatsoever, which I, or any in
trust for me, at the time of my first imprisonment in this action, or
at any time since, had, or was in any respect intitled to, in possession,
reversion, or remainder (except the wearing apparel and bedding of or
for me and my family, and the tools or instruments of my trade or
calling, not exceeding ten pounds in value in the whole) and also an
account how much of my real and personal estate, debts, credits, or
effects, hath since been disposed of, released, or discharged, and how,
to whom, and on what consideration, and for what purpose, and how
much thereof I, or any person or persons in trust for me, have, or, at

*the time of my presenting my said petition to this honourable court,
had, or which I am or was, or any person in trust for me, or for
my use, is any ways interested in, or intitled to, in possession, reversion, remainder, or expectancy, and also a true account of all deeds,
writings, books, papers, securities, bonds, and notes, relating thereto, and where the same respectively now are, to the best of my knowledge and belief, and what charges are now affecting the real estate I
am now seised of, or intitled to (if any such prisoner or prisoners
shall be then seised of any real estate) and that I have not, at any
time before or since my imprisonment, directly or indirectly, sold,
leased, assigned, mortgaged, pawned, or otherwise disposed of, or
made over in trust for myself, or otherwise than is mentioned in such
account, any part of my messuages, lands, tenements, estates, goods,
stock, money, debts, or other real or personal estate, whereby to have
or accept any benefit, advantage, or profit, to myself or my family, or
with any view, design, or intent, to deceive, injure, or defraud, any
of my creditors to whom I am indebted.*

So help me God.

Court may thereupon order an assignment to be made, on the back of the petition, of the prisoner's estate and effects, and conveyed to the creditor, &c.

And in case any prisoner or prisoners as aforesaid shall, in open court, take the said oath, such court in which any such oath as aforesaid shall be taken, may then immediately order the messuages, lands, tenements, goods, and effects, contained in such account, or so much of them as may be sufficient to satisfy the debt or debts wherewith any such prisoner or prisoners shall stand charged in execution, and the fees due to the warden, marshal, or keeper of the gaol or prison from which any such prisoner was brought, to be, by a short indorsement on the back of such petition, and to be signed by the prisoner, assigned and conveyed to the creditor or creditors who shall have charged any such prisoner in execution (if more than one) his, her, or their heirs, executors, administrators, and assigns, for the benefit of him, her, or them, who shall have so charged any such

the same to be subject to prior incumbrances.

prisoner in execution (subject nevertheless to all prior incumbrances affecting the same) and the estate, interest, or property, of all messuages, lands, goods, debts, estates, and effects, which shall belong to any such prisoner, shall, by such assignment and conveyance as aforesaid, be vested in the person or persons to whom such assignment and conveyance shall be made, according to the estate and interest such prisoner or prisoners had therein respectively; and the creditor or creditors to whom

Creditor may thereupon take possession, and sue in like manner as assignees of commissioners of bankrupts; and no release of the prisoner, subsequent to such assignment, may be pleaded in

any such assignment and conveyance shall be made, shall and may take possession of, and sue in his, her, or their name or names for the recovery thereof, in like manner as assignees of commissioners of bankrupts can or may sue for the recovery of the estates and effects of bankrupts which shall be assigned and conveyed to them; and no release of any such prisoner or prisoners, his or her executors or administrators, or any trustee for him, her, or them, subsequent to such assignment and conveyance, shall be pleadable, or be allowed of in bar of any action or suit which shall be commenced by any such assignee or

assignees

assignees of any such prisoner or prisoners, for the recovery of *bar of any* any of his, her, or their estate or effects; and upon every such *such action.* assignment and conveyance being executed by any such prisoner *Court there-* or prisoners, he, she, or they, shall be discharged out of custody *upon to make* by rule or order of such court, which shall be petitioned by any *charge of the* such prisoner; and such rule or order being produced to, and a *prisoner;* copy thereof being left with, any such sheriff, gaoler, or keeper, of any prison as aforesaid, shall be a sufficient warrant to him to discharge every such prisoner or prisoners, if charged in execution, or detained for the causes mentioned in his, her, or their respective petition, and no other: and every such she- *and the she-* riff, gaoler, or keeper, is hereby required, on having such or- *riff or gaoler,* der produced to him, and a copy thereof left with him, to dis- *being served* charge and set at liberty forthwith, every such prisoner and pri- *with a copy* soners who shall be ordered as aforesaid to be so discharged, *thereof, to set* without taking any fee, or detaining him, her, or them, in re- *the prisoner at* spect of any demand of any such sheriff, warden, marshal, gaol- *liberty.* er, or keeper, for or in respect of chamber rent or lodging, or otherwise; or for or in respect of any fees theretofore claimed, or due to any such sheriff, goaler, or keeper, or any employed by or under him or them: and no such sheriff, gaoler, or keep- *Sheriff not li-* er, shall afterwards be liable to any action of escape, or other *able to action* suit or information on that account, or for what he shall do in *of escape* pursuance of this act; and the person or persons to whom the *thereupon.* estate and effects of any such prisoner or prisoners shall be as- *Assignee to* signed and conveyed, shall, with all convenient speed, sell and *make sale of* dispose of the estates and effects of every such prisoner which *the estate and* shall be so assigned and conveyed, and shall divide the net pro- *effects of the* duce of all such estates and effects amongst the creditors of every *prisoner,* such prisoner and prisoners, if more than one, who shall have *and make a* charged any such prisoner in execution, before the time of such *dividend ac-* prisoner's petition to be discharged shall have been presented, *cordingly a-* rateably and in proportion to their respective debts; but in case *mongst the* the person or persons at whose suit any such prisoner or prison- *other credi-* ers stood charged in execution as aforesaid, shall not be satisfied *But if the* with the truth of any such prisoner's oath, and shall either per- *creditor shew* sonally, or by his, her, or their attorney, if he, she, or they *cause of disbe-* cannot personally attend, and proof shall be made thereof to *lieving the* the satisfaction of any such court as aforesaid, desire further time *prisoner's* to inform him, her, or themselves of the matters contained *oath,* therein, any such court may remand any such prisoner or pri- *and desire fur-* soners, and direct him, her, or them, and the person or persons *ther time for* dissatisfied as aforesaid with such oath, to appear either in per- *information,* son, or by his, her, or their attorney, on some other day to be *the court is to* appointed by such said court, some time at furthest within the *remand the* first week of the term next following the time of such examina- *prisoner back* tion, but sooner, if any such court shall so think fit; and all ob- *to a further* jections which shall be made as to the insufficiency in point of *day.* form against any prisoner's schedule of his estates and effects, *Objections to* shall be only made the first time any such prisoner shall be *the form of* brought up; and if at such second day which shall be appoint- *the schedule,* ed, *to be made* *the first time* *the prisoner is* *brought up.*

Creditor not appearing the second day, or not making a further discovery; Court to make a rule for discharge of the prisoner;

unless the creditor infist upon his detention,

and covenant to allow him 2 s. 4 d. per week;

but upon failure, at any time in the payment thereof, the prisoner, upon application to the court, to be discharged,

upon executing such affignment and conveyance as aforefaid. Prisoner refusing to take the oath, or being detected of falfity therein, or refusing to execute an affignment, &c. of his eftate, to be continued in execution.

ed, the creditor or creditors diffatisfied with such oath fhall make default in appearing, either in person, or by his, her, or their attorney, or in cafe he, fhe, or they fhall appear, if he, fhe, or they fhall be unable to difcover any eftate or effects of the prifoner omitted in the account fet forth in fuch his or her petition; then, and in any fuch cafe, fuch court fhall, by rule or order thereof, immediately caufe the faid prifoner or prifoners to be difcharged, upon fuch prifoner or prifoners executing fuch affignment and conveyance of his or her eftates and effects, in manner as affignments and conveyances of prifoners eftates and effects are herein before directed to be made, unlefs fuch creditor or creditors who fhall have charged any fuch prifoner or prifoners in execution as aforefaid, his, her, or their executors or adminiftrators, doth or do infift upon fuch prifoner or prifoners being detained in prifon, and fhall agree, by writing figned with his, her, or their name or names, mark or marks, or under the hand of his, her, or their attorney, in cafe any fuch creditor or creditors, his, her, or their executors or adminiftrators fhall be out of *England*, to pay and allow weekly a fum not exceeding two fhillings and four pence, as any fuch court fhall think fit, unto the faid prifoner, to be paid every *Monday* in every week, fo long as any fuch prifoner fhall continue in prifon in execution at the fuit of any fuch creditor or creditors; and in every fuch cafe, every fuch prifoner and prifoners fhall be remanded back to the prifon or gaol from whence he, fhe, or they was or were fo brought up, there to continue in execution; but if any failure fhall, at any time, be made in the payment of the weekly fum which fhall be ordered by any fuch court to be paid to any fuch prifoner, fuch prifoner, upon application in term time to the court where the fuit in which any fuch prifoner fhall be charged in execution was commenced, or fhall have been carried on, or in the prifon of which court any fuch prifoner fhall ftand committed on any *Habeas Corpus*, or in vacation time, to any judge of any fuch court, may, by the order of any fuch court, or judge, be difcharged out of cuftody on every fuch execution, proof being made before fuch court, or judge, on oath, of the nonpayment, for any week, of the fum of money ordered and agreed to be weekly paid; but every fuch prifoner and prifoners, before he, fhe, or they fhall be fo difcharged out of cuftody by any fuch rule or order, fhall execute an affignment and conveyance of his, her, or their eftates and effects, in manner herein before directed: and if any prifoner who fhall petition or apply for his or her difcharge under this act, fhall refufe to take the faid oath herein before directed to be taken, or taking the fame, fhall afterwards be detected before any fuch court, or judge, of falfity therein, or fhall refufe to execute fuch affignment and conveyance of his, her, or their eftates and effects as aforefaid, as herein before is required to be made by him, her, or them refpectively, he, fhe, or they fhall be prefently remanded and continue in execution.

6

XIV. Pro-

XIV. Provided always, and be it further enacted, That where more creditors than one shall charge any prisoner or prisoners in execution, and shall desire to have such prisoner or prisoners detained in prison, each and every such creditor and creditors shall only respectively pay such weekly sum of money, not exceeding one shilling and six pence a week, on every *Monday* in every week, to or for such respective prisoner, as the court before whom any such prisoner or prisoners shall be brought up to be discharged shall, at the time of his, her, or their being remanded, on such note for payment of the weekly sum ordered to be paid being given, direct or appoint.

Where more creditors than one insist on the prisoner's detention, they are to pay him each not exceeding 1 s. 6 d. per week.

XV. And be it further enacted by the authority aforesaid, That from and after the said fifteenth day of *June*, one thousand seven hundred and fifty nine, where any prisoner or prisoners shall be charged in execution in any county gaol, or in any other gaol or prison above the space of twenty miles distant from *Westminster Hall*, or the court or courts out of which the execution or executions shall be issued out against any such prisoner or prisoners, then upon petition being made by any such prisoner or prisoners to the court from whence any such execution against any such prisoner or prisoners issued, or in the prison of which court any such prisoner shall be and stand charged in execution, in the like form and manner as the petitions herein before-mentioned of prisoners are directed to be made, and on an affidavit to the purport as affidavits are herein before directed to be made in the case of prisoners in gaol not above twenty miles distant from the court out of which the execution against such prisoner issued, being made and left with such petition, such court (on being satisfied with the truth of such affidavit) is hereby authorized and required to make a rule or order to cause the prisoner or prisoners, so petitioning, to be brought to the next assizes which shall be holden for the county or place where he, she, or they, shall be imprisoned, if the same shall be within that part of *Great Britain* called *England*; and if within the principality of *Wales*, or county palatine of *Chester*, then to cause such prisoner or prisoners to be brought to the next great sessions to be holden for the county in *Wales*, or county palatine of *Chester*, in which any such prisoner or prisoners shall be imprisoned; and the expence of bringing every such prisoner to any such assizes, not exceeding one shilling a mile, shall be paid to the gaoler, keeper, or officer, who shall bring any such prisoner to any such assizes or great sessions, in obedience to any such rule or order as aforesaid served on him, out of every such prisoner's estate or effects, if the same shall be sufficient to pay such expence; and if not, then such expence shall be paid by the treasurer of the county, riding, division, or place, in which any such prisoner shall be imprisoned, out of the stock of the county, riding, division, or place, as the same shall be allowed, directed, or ordered, by any such court from which any such execution shall have been issued against any such prisoner or prisoners, or in the prison of which any such prisoner shall be, by

Prisoner charged in execution in county and other gaols, distant from Westminster, to proceed in like manner by petition, and affidavit; and the court to make a rule thereupon, for his being brought up to the next assizes, &c.

1 s. per mile to be paid to the gaoler for his expences, out of the prisoner's estate; or by the treasurer of the county.

one or more of the judge or judges of affize, juftice or juftice
of great feffions: and the creditor, or feveral creditors, his,
Creditors to her, or their executors or adminiftrators, at whofe fuit any fuch
be fummoned, prifoner or prifoners fhall ftand charged in execution as aforefaid, fhall, by rule or order of the court from whence the procefs iffued, be fummoned to appear at the faid next affizes or
great feffions, if fuch creditor or creditors, his, her, or their ex-
and a copy of ecutors or adminiftrators, can be met with; and if not, the
the rule ferv- the attorney laft employed for fuch creditor or creditors fhall be
ed on them; fummoned to appear there; and a copy of every fuch rule or
order fhall be ferved on every of fuch creditor or creditors, his,
her, or their executors or adminiftrators, or be left at his, her,
or their dwelling houfe or ufual place of abode, or with his, her,
or their attorney laft employed as aforefaid, fourteen days at
leaft before the holding of any fuch affizes or great feffions;
and upon af- and on an affidavit of fuch fervice thereof being laid before the
fidavit made judge or judges of affize, juftice or juftices of great feffions as
of fuch fervice, aforefaid, fuch judge or judges of affize, juftice or juftices of great
the court to feffions refpectively, on being fatisfied with the truth of fuch affi-
appoint a time davit, is and are hereby required to appoint a time for hearing the
for hearing matter upon every fuch petition as aforefaid, on fome certain day
the matter of and time, on the crown fide of every fuch court or great feffions,
the petition; during fuch affizes or great feffions; and upon the appearance there
and the credi- of the creditor or creditors who fhall be fummoned in purfuance of
tors appearing this act, his, her, or their executors or adminiftrators, or in
thereto, or default of the appearance, either in perfon or by attorney, of
not, the party or parties who fhall have been fummoned fo to ap-
Proof being pear, then on proof of his, her, or their being duly ferved with
made of their the notice hereby required to be given, and a copy of the ac-
being duly count of the real and perfonal eftate of the prifoner or prifoners
ferved with defiring to be difcharged being comprifed in fuch notice, and
the notice, alfo of the rule of fuch court for his, her, or their appearance at
and copy of fuch affizes or great feffions, having been duly ferved as herein be-
the fchedule fore is directed, the judge or judges of fuch affizes or great feffions
of the prifo- refpectively, as the cafe fhall happen to be, fhall there, in a
ner's eftate, fummary way, examine into the matter of every fuch petition,
the court to and hear what can or fhall be alledged, on either fide, for or
proceed there- againft the difcharge of the prifoner or prifoners fo petitioning;
in in a fum and upon every fuch examination, fuch judge and judges of af-
mary way; fize and great feffions refpectively, or any one of them, is and
are hereby impowered and required refpectively, within their
and adminifter refpective jurifdictions, to adminifter or tender to every fuch
the oath to prifoner, the fame oath as herein before is directed and appoint-
the prifoner; ed to be taken by any prifoner, before the judges of the court
and make fuch out of which the procefs, upon which any fuch prifoner was
order in the taken in execution, iffued; and fuch faid judge or judges of
premiffes as affize, juftice or juftices of great feffions refpectively, or any one
fhall feem of them, is and are hereby refpectively authorized and required
meet, and pro- to make fuch order in the premiffes as to him or them fhall feem
ceed as afore- meet, and to proceed in the fame manner concerning the dif-
faid concern- charge of any prifoner or prifoners in any prifon within their
ing the prifon-
er's difcharge.

respective jurisdictions, and to give the same judgement, relief, and directions relating thereto, as any court out of which any process shall issue against any such prisoner as aforesaid, is herein before impowered and directed to do : and every order which shall be made in the premisses by any such judge or judges of assize or great sessions, shall be as valid and effectual as if the same had been made in the court out of which the process issued on which any such prisoner was charged in execution ; and the same shall be made a record of the proceedings at such assizes or great sessions, as the case shall happen to be, and a copy thereof shall, from thence, be transmitted to the court from whence the execution against the prisoner or prisoners discharged, issued, or was awarded, signed by the judge or judges of assize or great sessions, to be a record of the said court, and to be kept as such amongst the other records thereof.

Order to stand good, and be enter'd upon record.

XVI. *And whereas it sometimes happens that persons who are prisoners in execution in gaol for debt or damages, will rather spend their substance in prison, than discover and deliver up the same towards satisfying their creditors their just debts, or so much thereof as such substance will extend to pay*; be it therefore further enacted, That if any prisoner now committed to any prison or gaol, and charged in execution for any debt or damages not exceeding the sum of one hundred pounds, besides costs of suit, shall not, on or before the twenty ninth day of *September*, one thousand seven hundred and fifty nine, make satisfaction to the creditor or creditors, his, her, or their, executors or administrators, at whose suit any such prisoner shall be so charged in execution for such debt or damages, and the costs of such suit ; or if any prisoner, who after the said fifteenth day of *June*, one thousand seven hundred and fifty nine, shall be committed or charged in execution in any prison or gaol, for any debt or damages not exceeding the sum of one hundred pounds, besides costs of suit, shall not, within three months next after every such prisoner, after the said fifteenth day of *June*, one thousand seven hundred and fifty nine, shall be committed or charged in execution as aforesaid, make satisfaction to his, her, or their, creditor or creditors, who shall charge any such prisoner in execution as aforesaid, his, her, or their, executors or administrators, for such debt, damages, and costs ; then, and in any of the said cases, any such creditor or creditors, his, her, or their, executors or administrators, is and are hereby authorized and impowered to require every such respective prisoner or prisoners, on giving twenty days notice in writing to him or her respectively, that such creditor or creditors, his, her, or their, executors or administrators, design to compel any such prisoner to give in to the court at law, from which the writ or process issued on which any such prisoner is or shall be charged in execution as aforesaid, or into the court in the prison of which any such prisoner hath been or shall be removed by *Habeas Corpus*, or shall remain, or be charged in execution, within the first seven days of the term which shall next ensue the expiration of the said twenty days, in respect to any

Prisoner refusing to deliver up his estate and effects to satisfy his creditors,

Creditors may compel such prisoner to be brought up and deliver in to court a schedule of his estate and effects, and the incumbrances affecting the same, upon oath ; giving the prisoner 20 days notice of such intention ;

prisoner charged in any of the prisons belonging to any of the courts in *Westminster Hall*; and at the second court which shall be held by any such other court of record after the expiration of the said twenty days, in respect to any prisoner charged in any prison belonging to any such other court; and where any such prisoner is or shall be charged in execution, in any county gaol, or other gaol or prison, above the space of twenty miles distant from *Westminster Hall*, or the court or courts out of which the writ or process on which any such prisoner is or shall be so charged in execution issued, or shall issue; then to give in, upon oath, at the assizes or great sessions as aforesaid, and on the crown side thereof, which shall be held for the county or place in the prison of which any such prisoner shall be, next after the expiration of such twenty days from the time of giving any such notice as aforesaid to any such prisoner, a true account in writing, and to be signed with the proper name or mark of every such prisoner, of all the real and personal estate of such prisoner, and of all incumbrances affecting the same, to the best of the

in order that his estate and effects may be divested out of him, and assigned and conveyed as herein after directed.

knowledge and belief of such prisoner, in order that the estate and effects of such prisoner may be divested out of him or her, and may, by the court, judge or judges, justice or justices, as aforesaid, be ordered to be assigned and conveyed, in manner and for the purposes herein after declared: and every such creditor or creditors, as aforesaid, who shall require any such prisoner to be brought up as aforesaid, for the purpose aforesaid,

Like notice to be given of such intention to the other creditors;

shall also give twenty days like notice in writing, of such his, her, or their intention, to require any such prisoner to be brought up as aforesaid, to discover and deliver up his or her estate as aforesaid, to all and every other creditor and creditors of every such prisoner, at whose suit any such prisoner shall be detained or charged in custody in any such gaol or prison, if such prisoner shall be there detained in custody, or charged in execution, at the suit of any other creditor or creditors besides the creditor or creditors giving such notice as aforesaid, if such other creditor or creditors can be found out or met with, and if not, then to the several attornies last employed in the respective actions or suits, in which any such prisoner or prisoners shall be so detained or charged in custody by any such other creditor or creditors of such prisoner; and shall likewise give a like no-

and also to the sheriff and gaoler,

tice in writing to the sheriff or sheriffs, gaoler or keeper of the gaol or prison in which any such prisoner or prisoners shall be detained in custody, or committed or charged in execution as aforesaid, of such his or her intention to have any such prison-

requiring them to bring up such prisoner;

er so brought up, and to require such sheriff or sheriffs, gaoler or gaolers, respectively, to bring up every such prisoner accordingly: and every such notice which shall be so given to any such sheriff or sheriff, gaoler or gaolers, shall be so given to him or them respectively, twenty days at least before the time ap-

who is to be brought accordingly at the costs of the creditors,

pointed for any such prisoner to be so brought up; and thereupon every such sheriff or sheriffs, gaoler or keeper, respectively, to whom any such notice as aforesaid shall be so given, shall, at the costs of such creditor or creditors, his, her, or their, exe-

cuecutors or administrators, cause every such prisoner to be brought, as by such notice in writing shall be required, to such court, assizes, or great sessions as aforesaid, together with a copy or causes of his or her respective detainer or detainers there; and if any such sheriff or sheriffs, gaoler or keeper, on any such notice in writing being given to him or them as aforesaid, and tender being made to him or them, by or on the behalf of any such creditor or creditors aforesaid, of reasonable charges, not exceeding one shilling a mile, to bring up the prisoner or prisoners required as aforesaid to be so brought up to any such court, assizes, or great sessions as aforesaid, shall neglect to refuse to bring there the prisoner or prisoners so required to be brought there as aforesaid, and at the time he or she shall be so required to be brought there, together with a copy of his, her, or their detainer or detainers in any such gaol or prison; every such sheriff and sheriffs, gaoler and keeper, who shall so offend in the premisses, shall, for every such offence, forfeit and pay the sum of twenty pounds, to be recovered by the party aggrieved by action of debt, bill, or information, in any of his Majesty's courts of record at *Westminster*, if any such offence shall be committed out of the said principality of *Wales*, or county palatine of *Chester*; and if any such offence shall be committed in the principality of *Wales*, or county palatine of *Chester*, then in some court of record in the said principality of *Wales*, or county palatine of *Chester*, within the jurisdiction of which any such offence shall be so committed, together with treble costs of suit.

XVII. And be it further enacted by the authority aforesaid, That every prisoner charged, or who shall be charged, in execution as aforesaid, and who, in pursuance of this act, shall, at the desire of any of his, her, or their creditor or creditors, his her, or their executors or administrators, be brought up to any such court, assizes, or great sessions, as aforesaid, shall, on proof being there first made of such notices as are herein before directed to be given having been given, deliver in there in open court, upon oath, within the time herein before for that purpose prescribed, a full, true, and just account, disclosure, and discovery, in writing, of the whole of his or her real and personal estate, and of all books, papers, writings, and securities, relating thereto, and also of all incumbrances then affecting the same, and the respective times when made, to the best of his or her knowledge and belief (other than and except the necessary wearing apparel, and bedding of such prisoner, and his or her family, and the necessary tools or instruments of his or her respective trade or calling, not exceeding the value of ten pounds in the whole) which account shall be subscribed with the proper name or mark of the prisoner respectively who shall so deliver in the same; and on the delivering in of any such account, the estate and effects of every such prisoner shall be assigned and conveyed by such prisoner respectively, by a short endorsement on the back of every such account as shall be so delivered in, to such person or persons as the court, judge or judges, justice or justices, in which, or to whom, any such account shall be so given in, shall order or direct,

Marginal notes:

with a copy of his detainer.

Sheriff or gaoler making default in the premisses, after due notice given, and tender of reasonable charges,

forfeit 20l. to the party aggrieved,

with treble costs of suit.

Prisoner, upon proof of due notice as aforesaid having been given him, is to deliver in, upon oath, to the court a schedule of his estate and effects, and signed by him;

and is to assign and convey the same in trust, for the benefit of his creditors,

rect, in trust, and for the benefit of the creditor or creditors who shall have required any such prisoner to be brought up as aforesaid, and of such other creditor or creditors (if any) of every such respective prisoner at whose suit or suits any such prisoner shall be charged in custody, or in execution, in any such prison or gaol, and who shall, by any memorandum or writing to be signed by such creditor or creditors respectively, before any such conveyance or assignment shall be made, consent to any such prisoner's being discharged out of gaol or prison, at his, her, or their suit or suits, and also agree to take or accept a proportionable dividend of such prisoner's estate and effects, with the creditor or creditors who shall have required any such prisoner to be brought up as aforesaid; and if there shall be no other creditor or creditors as aforesaid of such prisoner, or there being any such, if such other creditor or creditors as aforesaid shall not agree in writing to discharge such prisoner, and accept such proportionable dividend as aforesaid of the estate and effects of any such prisoner; then in trust for the creditor or creditors only who shall require any such prisoner to be brought up for the purpose aforesaid: and by such assignment and conveyance as aforesaid, all the prisoner's estate and effects shall be vested in the creditor or creditors to whom the same shall be assigned and conveyed, in trust as aforesaid; and if any overplus shall remain of any such prisoner's estate, after payment of the debt, or damages, and costs, which shall be due to any creditor or creditors respectively at whose suit or suits any such prisoner as aforesaid shall, in pursuance of this act, be discharged out of gaol or prison, on delivering up his or her estate and effects as aforesaid, and all reasonable charges expended in or by means of getting in of such estate or effects, the same shall be paid to such prisoner, his or her executors, administrators, or assigns: and upon every such discovery, assignment, and conveyance, being made and executed by any such prisoner, to the satisfaction of the court, judge or judges of assize, justice or justices of great sessions, before whom the same shall be respectively made, every such prisoner, and prisoners shall, by such court, judge or judges, justice or justices, be discharged, and set at liberty, in the actions and charges, at the suit of the creditor or creditors, his, her, or their executors or administrators, who shall require any such prisoner to be so brought up, and also in the actions and charges of every other creditor of any such prisoner, his, her, or their executors or administrators, who shall sign any such consent as aforesaid, for any such prisoner's discharge, with the same benefit of making use of such his or her discharge, as is herein before provided for prisoners seeking, and who shall obtain, their discharge, under the provisions contained in the former part of this act; and no greater fee than two shillings and six pence in the whole, shall be paid or taken for any such discharge, by all or any officer or officers of any such courts, assizes, or great sessions; and no stamp shall be necessary on any such assignment and conveyance as aforesaid, or any rule or order, which shall
be

(marginal notes:) they agreeing to his discharge, and to accept a proportionable dividend of his effects; but if any shall refuse to agree thereto, then the same to be in trust, for the creditors only requiring the prisoner to be brought up for the purpose aforesaid. Overplus remaining after all charges, to be paid to the prisoner.

Prisoner complying, to the satisfaction of the court, to be set at liberty;

paying for his discharge fees 2s. 6d.

be made for any such discharge; but all the future effects of every such prisoner (other than except the necessary wearing apparel, and bedding, of such prisoner, and his or her family, and the necessary tools or instruments of his or her respective trade or calling) shall be and remain liable to satisfy his or her debts, if the same shall not be fully paid from his or her estate which shall be assigned and conveyed as aforesaid; and no advantage shall be had or taken in any action or suit which shall be hereafter commenced against any such prisoner, his or her heirs, executors, or administrators, for that the cause of action did not accrue within six years next before the commencing of any such action or suit, unless such prisoner was intitled to take such advantage before he or she stood charged in custody by virtue of the original suit or action; and in any such case the same may be pleaded by any such prisoner, his or her heirs, executors, or administrators: and if any prisoner charged, or who shall be charged, in execution, in any prison or gaol, and who shall be required as aforesaid to be brought up to any such court, assizes, or great sessions as aforesaid, shall neglect or refuse to deliver in and subscribe such just and true account of his or her whole estate and effects in any such court, or at any such assizes, or great sessions as aforesaid, as the case may happen to be, within the time herein before limited or appointed for the doing thereof, or within sixty days then next following, without offering and making appear some just excuse for every such neglect or refusal, to be allowed of by the court, judge or judges of assize, justice or justices of great sessions as aforesaid, or who shall refuse to assign or convey his or her estate and effects, according to the order of any such court, judge or judges, justice or justices as aforesaid; he or she so offending in any of the said cases, and who shall be convicted of any such offence upon any indictment found against him or her, shall thereupon have judgment for transportation pronounced against him or her, and shall be transported, according to the laws made and now in force for transportation of felons, to some of his Majesty's colonies or plantations in America, for the term of seven years: and if any such prisoner shall deliver in any false or untrue account of his or her estate or effects, or shall designedly conceal, and not insert in the account he or she shall deliver in and subscribe as aforesaid, any books, papers, securities, or writings, relating to his or her estate and effects, with intent to defraud his or her creditor or creditors, and shall be thereof convicted on any indictment found against him or her in respect thereof; he or she so offending, and being convicted as aforesaid thereof, shall suffer the pains and penalties which by law are to be inflicted on any person convicted of wilful perjury.

XVIII. Provided also, and be it further enacted by the authority aforesaid, That if any person who shall take any oath as by this act is required to be taken, shall, upon any indictment for perjury, be convicted by his, her, or their own confession, or by verdict of twelve lawful men; the person so convicted shall

Marginal notes:

Future effects of the prisoner liable to debts unsatisfied;

and no advantage to be taken of the statute of limitation, unless he was intitled thereto before he stood charged in custody on the original suit.

Prisoner neglecting or refusing to deliver in a schedule of his estate and effects,

or to make an assignment and conveyance thereof,

to be transported for 7 years; and delivering in a false account,

to suffer the pains and penalties of wilful perjury.

Persons convicted of perjury to suffer in like manner;

suffer

and be liable to be taken on a procefs de novo, and charged in execution for the debt; and never have the benefit of this act. If the prifoner's effects fhall not fatisfy his debt, and warden's fees, &c. Warden to receive only a proportional dividend with the other creditors.

fuffer the pains and forfeitures which by law are to be inflicted on any perfon convicted of wilful perjury; and fhall likewife be liable to be taken on any procefs *de novo*, and charged in execution for the faid debt, in the fame manner as if he or fhe had not been difcharged, or not taken or charged in execution before, and fhall never after have the benefit of this act; any thing herein before contained to the contrary notwithftanding.

XIX. Provided likewife, and it is hereby further enacted, That if the effects of any prifoner or prifoners, which fhall be affigned and conveyed in purfuance of this act, fhall not extend to fatisfy the whole debt due to the creditors as aforefaid of the prifoner who fhall be fo difcharged, and the fees due to the warden, marfhal, or gaoler, from any fuch prifoner; then fuch warden, marfhal, or gaoler, fhall only receive a proportional dividend from fuch prifoner's eftate, in refpect of fuch fees, *pro rata* with the other creditors as aforefaid of fuch prifoner or prifoners.

Prifoner difcharged not liable to arreft, or action, for the fame debt, unlefs convicted of perjury; but the judgement to remain in force, and execution may be had thereon againft his eftate and effects.

XX. Provided further, and be it hereby alfo enacted, That the prifoner or prifoners who fhall be fo difcharged by virtue of this act, fhall never after be arrefted for the fame debt or debts; nor fhall any action of debt be brought againft him, her, or them, on any fuch judgment, unlefs he, fhe, or they fhall, under this act, be convicted of wilful perjury; but notwithftanding any difcharge obtained by virtue of this act for the perfon of any fuch prifoner or prifoners, the judgment obtained againft every fuch prifoner and prifoners fhall continue and remain in force, and execution may at any time be taken out thereon againft the lands, tenements, rents, or hereditaments, goods or chattels, of any fuch prifoner or prifoners, other than and except the neceffary wearing apparel, and bedding for him, her, or themfelves and family, and the neceffary tools for the ufe of his, her, or their trade or occupation, not exceeding ten pounds in value in the whole, as if he, fhe, or they had never been before arrefted, taken in execution, and releafed out of prifon, by virtue of, or under, this act.

Affignees may compound with the creditors in full difcharge of their debts;

and fubmit difputes relating to the prifoner's eftate and debts, &c. to arbitration, &c.

XXI. And be it further enacted by the authority aforefaid, That any affignee or affignees to whom, by virtue of this act, the eftate or effects of any prifoner or prifoners difcharged by this act fhall be affigned, is and are hereby impowered to make compofition with any debtors or accountants to fuch prifoner or prifoners, where the fame fhall appear neceffary or reafonable, and to take fuch reafonable part of any debt due, as can, upon any fuch compofition, be gotten, in full difcharge of fuch debt or account; and alfo to fubmit any difference or difpute concerning any part of any fuch prifoner's eftate or effects, or by reafon or means of any matter, caufe, or thing relating thereto, or to fuch prifoner or prifoners, or in refpect of any debt claimed to be due to fuch prifoner or prifoners, to the final end and determination of arbitrators to be chofen by the faid affignee or affignees, and the party or parties with whom any fuch difference fhall be; and if fuch arbitrators cannot agree in the fame, then to fubmit the fame to the determination of any umpire to be chofen by them,

of

or otherwife to fettle and agree the matter in difference or difpute between them, in fuch manner as fuch affignee or affignees fhall think fit, and can agree; and the fame fhall be binding. as well to all other of the faid prifoner or prifoners creditors as aforefaid, who fhall have charged him, her, or them, in cuftody or exe- cution, as alfo to every fuch prifoner and prifoners; and every fuch affignee and affignees is and are indemnified for what he or they fhall fairly, and without any fraudulent defign, do in the premiffes, according to the direction of this act. *the fame to be binding to creditors and prifoners. Affignees in- demnified therein.*

XXII. *And, to the intent the eftate and effects of fuch prifoner or prifoners who fhall be difcharged by virtue of this act may be truly and fairly applied;* be it further enacted by the authority aforefaid, That it fhall be lawful for the refpective courts at *Weftminfter,* from whence any procefs iffued upon which any fuch prifoner or prifoners was or were charged in execution, and whofe eftate and effects in purfuance of this act fhall have been affigned as by this act is directed, or where any fuch prifoner fhall have been charged in execution by procefs iffued out of any other court, it fhall be lawful for the judges of the courts of *King's Bench, Common Pleas,* and *Exchequer,* or any one of them, from time to time, on the petition of any creditor of fuch prifoner or prifoners who had charged any fuch prifoner in execution, or of fuch prifoner or prifoners, to any fuch court, or any judge thereof, complaining of any infufficiency, fraud, mifmanagement, or other mifbeha- viour of any fuch affignee or affignees, to order the refpective parties concerned to attend fuch court or judge on the matter of every fuch petition, at fome certain time in fuch order to be mentioned; and every fuch court at *Weftminfter,* and alfo every judge thereof, on hearing the parties concerned therein, is hereby authorized to make fuch order, and give fuch directions in the premiffes, either for the removal or difplacing fuch affig- nee or affignees, and appointing any new or other affignee or affignees in the place or ftead of fuch affignee or affignees fo to be removed or difplaced, or for the prudent, juft, or equitable management or diftribution of the faid eftate and effects, for the benefit of the refpective creditors as aforefaid of fuch prifoner or prifoners, as any of the faid courts at *Weftminfter,* or judges there, refpectively fhall think fit; and in cafe of the removal or difplacing of any affignee or affignees, and the appointing of any new affignee or affignees, the eftate or effects of fuch prifoner or prifoners fhall from thenceforth be divefted out of the affignee or affignees fo removed or difplaced, and be vefted in, and de- livered over to, the new affignee or affignees, in the fame manner, and for the like intents and purpofes, as the fame were before vefted in the former affignee or affignees. *On complaint to court of any infufficiency, fraud, mifma- nagement, or other mifbeha- viour of the affignees, the parties to be ordered to attend the court thereon; and the court make fuch order therein as they fhall think juft. On removal of any affig- nees, the prifoner's eftate and effects to be vefted in and delivered over to the new affignees.*

XXIII. And be it further enacted, That in all and every cafe and cafes where mutual credit fhall have been given between any prifoner or prifoners who fhall be difcharged under this act, and any other perfon or perfons, bodies politick or corporate, before the delivery of any fchedule or inventory of the eftate and effects of any fuch prifoner or prifoners, upon oath, as by this *Where mutual credit hath been given,*

act

the assignees may only state the account, and demand the balance.

act is herein before directed; then, and in every such case, the respective assignee or assignees of such prisoner or prisoners shall have power, and is and are hereby required, on his or their part or parts, to state and allow an account between them; and nothing more shall be deemed to be vested by any assignment which shall be made in pursuance of this act, as the estate or effects of such prisoner or prisoners, than what shall appear to have been due to him, her, or them respectively, and to be justly coming to him, her, or them, on or for the balance of such account when truly stated.

None intitled to the benefit of this act, who have taken, or shall take, the benefit of any act of insolvency; unless compelled by a creditor to deliver up his estate and effects.
This act not to extend to Scotland.

XXIV. Provided always, and be it further enacted by the authority aforesaid, That no person or persons who hath or have already taken, or shall hereafter take, the benefit of any act for the relief of insolvent debtors, shall have or receive any benefit or advantage of or under this act, or be deemed to be within the meaning hereof, so as to gain any discharge, unless compelled by any creditor to discover and deliver up his or her estate and effects; any thing herein contained to the contrary notwithstanding.

XXV. And be it also enacted by the authority aforesaid, That this act, or any thing herein contained, shall not extend, or be construed to extend, to that part of *Great Britain* called *Scotland.*

C A P. XXIX.

An act for further regulating the power of taking samples of foreign spirituous liquors by the officers of excise; and also for impowering the traders to take such samples before the duties are charged.

Preamble, reciting clause in act 31 Geo. 2.

WHEREAS by a clause in an act of parliament passed in the last session of parliament, intituled, An act for continuing certain laws therein mentioned relating to *British* sail cloth, and to the duties payable on foreign sail cloth; and to the allowance upon the exportation of *British* made gunpowder; and to the encouragement of the trade of the sugar colonies in *America*; and to the landing of rum or spirits of the *British* sugar plantations, before the duties of excise are paid thereon; and for regulating the payment of the duties on foreign exciseable liquors; and for the relief of *Thomas Watson*, with regard to the drawback on certain *East India* callicoes; and for rendering more commodious the new passage leading from *Charing Cross*, *in order to enable the gaugers or officers of excise the better to ascertain the proof of all foreign imported liquors liable to the duties of excise, it was enacted, That it should be lawful to and for the gaugers or officers of the excise at any time or times to take a sample or samples (not exceeding one quart in the whole) out of each of the casks, or other package, containing such foreign spirituous liquors, paying for such sample or samples of liquors after the rate of sixteen shillings per gallon: and whereas the taking so great a quantity as a quart out of each of the said casks, or other package, is unnecessary, and the paying for the same at the before mentioned rate will be detrimental to the*

re-

revenue; and whereas till of late the importers or proprietors of such foreign spirituous liquors, or their factors or agents, were permitted to take a sample out of each cask, or other package, and to land such sample without paying any duty for the same, by means whereof they were enabled to, and did for the most part, fell such foreign spirituous liquors whilst on shipboard: And whereas for some time last past, such permission hath, in many instances, been refused, which hath proved a great inconvenience to the said trade: For remedy whereof it is hereby enacted by the King's most excellent majesty, by and with the advice and consent of the lords spiritual and temporal, and commons, in this present parliament assembled, and by the authority of the same, That it shall and may be lawful for the gaugers or other officers of excise, at any time before the gauging, to take a sample or samples, not exceeding half a pint in the whole, out of each of the casks, or other package, containing such spirituous liquors, without paying for the same; and that it shall and may be lawful for the importers or proprietors of such foreign spirituous liquors, their factors or agents, to take, in the presence of one or more of the gaugers or other officers of excise, a sample or samples, not exceeding half pint in the whole, out of every cask, or other package, containing such spirituous liquors, whilst the same shall be on shipboard, and before the landing thereof, and to land such sample or samples, without paying any duty for the same.

Gaugers, &c. impowered to take samples gratis of spirituous liquors, not exceeding half a pint, out of each cask; and importers, &c. allowed to take a like quantity as samples also, before the landing thereof;

II. Provided nevertheless, That still it shall and may be lawful for the said officers of excise to take the like sample or samples, not exceeding half a pint in the whole, out of each cask, or other package, containing such spirituous liquors, in any shop, warehouse, or other place, belonging to any dealer in the same, paying for such sample or samples (if demanded) according to the market price liquor of the like quality shall be sold for at the time such sample or samples shall be taken.

Officers may also take like samples, after the landing and being lodged in warehouses, &c. paying for the same.

CAP. XXX.

An act for making compensation to the proprietors of such lands and hereditaments as have been purchased for the better securing his Majesty's docks, ships, and stores, at Chatham, Portsmouth, and Plymouth, and for better fortifying the town of Portsmouth, and citadel of Plymouth, in pursuance of an act of the last session of parliament; and for other purposes therein mentioned.

Preamble, reciting act 31 Geo. 2. A sum not exceeding 34,521l. 15s. 9d. to be issued and applied out of the aids granted for the service of the year 1759, towards making compensation to the parties interested. Bills to be made out for the respective sums and interest by the surveyor general of the ordnance, and debentures to be issued thereupon; which are to be paid by the treasurer of the ordnance. Where the debentures shall be refused to be accepted, they are to be deposited with the clerk of the peace of the county, and acquitances taken for the same; and the lands thereupon to vest to his Majesty's use. Where the parties interested shall be disabled by law from taking and disposing of the money, it is then to be paid to the remembrancer of the exchequer, and to be laid out in the purchase of other lands, to be conveyed and settled to the same uses; and till such purchases can be made, is to be placed out at interest. The lands, &c. taken in for fortifying the docks at Portsmouth and Chatham, chargeable

able to the land tax and parifh taxes, &c. which are to be paid by the ftorekeeper, and allowed in his accounts; and in cafe of nonpayment may be levied on him.

CAP. XXXI.

An act for granting to his Majefty certain fums of money out of the finking fund; and for applying certain monies remaining in the exchequer for the fervice of the year one thoufand feven hundred and fifty nine; and for relief of Samuel Taylor, with refpect to a bond entered into by him for fecuring the duties on tobacco imported.

Preamble. 180,076l. 17s. 3q. furplus remaining in the exchequer of the produce of the finking fund, for the quarter ending 5 April 1759, to be iffued and applied towards the fupplies granted for the year 1759. A further fum not exceeding 2,250,000l. to be iffued and applied out of the growing produce of the faid fund, towards the faid fupply. Surplus remaining of the fum of 100,000l. granted in the laft feffion towards defraying the charge of pay and cloathing of the militia; as alfo the fum of 73,308l. 3s. 10d. 3q. overplus of the grants for the year 1758; with the fum of 100,000l. repaid into the exchequer, being the fum voted to the Emprefs of Ruffia in the year 1755, to be iffued and applied towards the faid fupply. In cafe of want of money for carrying on the current fervice, the treafury may borrow a fum to make good fuch deficiency, upon the credit of the growing produce of the faid fund; to be repaid quarterly with intereft. Bank may advance thereon any fum not exceeding 2,250,000l. notwithftanding the act of 5 & 6 W. & M. Treafury impowered to difcharge Samuel Taylor from the penalty and payment of the bond entered into by him for fecuring the duties on tobacco imported.

CAP. XXXII.

An act for the more effectual preventing the fraudulent importation of cambricks and French lawns.

WHEREAS *the acts made in the eighteenth and twenty firft years of the reign of his prefent Majefty, for prohibiting the wearing and importation of cambricks and* French *lawns, have not been effectual to prevent the fraudulent importation thereof*; therefore, for the amending and enforcing the faid acts, be it enacted by the King's moft excellent majefty, by and with the advice and confent of the lords fpiritual and temporal, and commons; in this prefent parliament affembled, and by the authority of the fame, That from and after the firft day of *Auguft* one thoufand feven hundred and fifty nine, no cambricks, *French* lawns, or other linnens whatfoever, of the kind ufually entered under the denomination of cambricks, fhall be imported, or brought into any port or place whatfoever within *Great Britain*, unlefs the fame be packed in bales, cafes, or boxes, covered with fackcloth or canvas, each of which bales, cafes, or boxes, fhall contain one hundred whole pieces, or two hundred demi or half pieces, of fuch cambricks or *French* lawns.

No cambricks or French lawns to be imported but in bales, &c. covered with cloth, containing each 100 whole pieces, or 200 half pieces;

on penalty of forfeiture thereof.

II. And be it further enacted, That in cafe any cambricks or *French* lawns fhall be imported in any other form or manner, or in any lefs quantity, than is herein before mentioned and allowed, in each and every of the faid cafes, the cambricks or *French* lawns fo imported, or found on board any fhip or veffel in this kingdom, fhall be forfeited, and fhall and may be feifed by any officer or officers of the cuftoms.

III. And

III. And be it further enacted by the authority aforesaid, That from and after the said first day of *August* one thousand seven hundred and fifty nine, cambricks and *French* lawns shall be imported for exportation only, and shall be lodged in such warehouse belonging to his Majesty, his heirs, and successors, as the commissioners of the customs, or any three or more of them, for the time being, shall appoint; and shall not be delivered out of such warehouse, but under the like security and restrictions as *East India* goods, prohibited to be consumed in *Great Britain*, are now liable to.

The same to be imported for exportation only, and to be lodged in the King's warehouses, and delivered out under like security and restrictions as prohibited East India goods.

IV. And be it further enacted by the authority aforesaid, That from and after the said first day of *August*, there shall be no customs or duties whatsoever paid, or secured to be paid, for any cambricks or *French* lawns imported, or which shall be imported, and deposited in such warehouse as aforesaid, other than one half of the old subsidy, which is to remain by law, after the goods are exported again.

One half of the old subsidy payable only upon the importation.

V. And be it further enacted by the authority aforesaid, That all and every person and persons having in their custody any cambricks or *French* lawns imported before the said first day of *August*, for the exportation whereof, within the time limited by law, bond has been given, shall, on or before the first day of *August* next, bring and deposite, or cause to be brought or deposited, all such cambricks and *French* laws, in such warehouse as shall be approved of by the commissioners aforesaid for that purpose; and upon the depositing of such goods in such warehouse as aforesaid, the bonds for the exportation thereof shall be delivered up to the person or persons who gave the same, or his or their heirs, executors, administrators, or assigns, who shall likewise receive at the same time from the collector, or other proper officer of the customs at the port where such bond was given, all the duties which such goods would be intitled to draw back upon exportation: and such goods shall not be again delivered out of the said warehouse but for the exportation thereof, in like manner as if the same had been deposited therein at the importation: and in case any person or persons shall sell, offer, or expose to sale, or, after the said first day of *August*, have in his, her, or their custody or possession, for that purpose, any cambricks or *French* lawns (other than in such warehouse as shall be approved of by the said commissioners as aforesaid) the same shall be forfeited, and shall be liable to be searched for and seised in like manner as other prohibited and uncustomed goods are, and every such person shall also forfeit two hundred pounds, over and above all other penalties and forfeitures inflicted upon such person or persons by any former act.

What goods shall be in private custody, are to be deposited by 1 august next in the King's warehouses, and the bonds thereupon to be delivered up, and the drawback upon exportation to be paid, and the goods not to be delivered out again but for exportation. Goods exposed to sale, or found in private possession, after the said day, may be seised, and the offender to forfeit 200l. extra.

VI. And be it further enacted by the authority aforesaid, That if any doubt or question shall arise with respect to the species or quality of the said goods seised by virtue of this act, or where the same were manufactured, the proof shall lie on the owner or owners thereof, and not upon the prosecutor; any law, custom, or usage, to the contrary notwithstanding.

In doubts concerning the species or quality, &c. of the goods, onus probandi to lie on the owner.

Goods seised
to be carried
to the next
custom-house,
VII. And be it further enacted by the authority aforesaid, That all the goods seised by virtue of this act, or any other cause of forfeiture, shall upon seizure thereof, be carried to the next custom-house, and after condemnation in due course of law, shall not be consumed or used in this kingdom, but shall
be exported; and shall not be sold or delivered out of such ware-house, otherwise than on condition to be exported, nor until the buyer or buyers shall have given security for the exportation thereof, and observing all the regulations and restrictions pre-scribed for the exportation of *East India* goods prohibited to be consumed or used in *Great Britain*.

VIII. And be it further enacted by the authority aforesaid, That all the penalties and forfeitures by this act imposed, shall and may be sued for and recovered in any of his Majesty's courts of record at *Westminster*, or in the court of *exchequer* at *Edinburgh*, respectively, by action, bill, plaint, or information, in the name of his Majesty's attorney general, or in the name of his Majesty's advocate in *Scotland*, or in the name or names of some officer or officers of the customs; and that one moiety of every such penalty and forfeiture shall be to his Majesty, his heirs, and successors, and the other moiety thereof to such officer or officers of the customs who shall seize, inform, or prosecute for the same.

Upon actions
entered for
pecuniary pe-
nalties, a ca-
pias in the first
process to be
issued;
and the de-
fendant may
give bail
thereto, &c.
IX. And be it further enacted by the authority aforesaid, That upon every action, bill, plaint, or information, entered and filed as aforesaid, for any pecuniary penalty imposed by this act, a *capias* in the first process shall and may issue, specifying the sum of the penalty sued for; and the defendant or defendants shall be obliged to give sufficient bail or security by natural born subjects or denisons, to the person or persons to whom such *capias* shall be directed, to appear in the court out of which such *capias* shall issue, at the day of the return of such writ, to answer such suit or prosecution; and shall likewise, at the time of such appearance, give sufficient bail or security, by such persons as aforesaid, in the said court, to answer and pay all the forfeitures and penalties incurred for such offence or offences, in case he, she, or they shall be convicted thereof, or to yield his, her, or their body or bodies to prison.

X. And be it further enacted by the authority aforesaid, That if any action or suit shall be commenced against any person or persons for any thing done in pursuance of this act, the defend-ant or defendants in any such action or suit, may plead the gene-
ral issue, and give this act, and the special matter in evidence, at any trial to be had thereupon; and that the same was done in pursuance and by the authority of this act; and if it shall appear so to have been done, then the jury shall find for the defendant or defendants, and if the plaintiff shall be nonsuited or discontinue his action after the defendant or defendants shall have appeared; or if judgment shall be given upon any verdict or demurrer a-gainst the plaintiff, the defendant or defendants shall recover
treble costs, and have the like remedy for the same, as defend-ants have in other cases by law.

CAP.

CAP. XXXIII.

An act to explain and amend an act made in the last session of parliament, intituled, An act for granting to his Majesty several rates and duties upon offices and pensions; and upon houses; and upon windows or lights; and for raising the sum of five millions by annuities and a lottery, to be charged on the said rates and duties; so far as the same relates to the rates and duties on offices and pensions.

WHEREAS *by an act made in the last session of parliament, intituled,* An act for granting to his Majesty several rates and duties upon offices and pensions; and upon houses; and upon windows or lights; and for raising the sum of five millions by annuities and a lottery, to be charged on the said rates and duties, *it is (among other things)* declared and enacted, *That a deduction shall be made of the sum of one shilling out of every twenty shillings payable for or in respect of the salary, wages, or fees, of any offices and employments payable by the crown in* Great Britain, *which exceed one hundred pounds per annum; and for or in respect of any pension or gratuity, which is or shall be payable out of any revenue belonging to his Majesty in* Great Britain, *exceeding the value of one hundred pounds per annum; and that the money so deducted by the officers of his Majesty's exchequer in* England, *shall remain there for the purposes in the said act declared; and that such part of the money as shall be so deducted by any officer or officers of the dutchies of* Lancaster *and* Cornwall, *or by any other commissioners, officers, and persons, by whom the said salaries, wages, fees, pensions, and gratuities, are or shall be respectively payable in* England, *shall be by them paid into the receipt of his Majesty's exchequer at* Westminster: *and whereas the said recited directions may be expensive in the execution thereof, by subjecting each of the officers, commissioners, and persons, by the said act required to make the deduction aforesaid, to a separate account before the auditors of the imprests, for the several sums by them respectively deducted: and whereas the said recited directions have appeared to be in other respects inconvenient;* be it enacted by the King's most excellent majesty, by and with the advice and consent of the lords spiritual and temporal, and commons, in this present parliament assembled, and by the authority of the same, That all sums of money which on the fifth day of *July,* one thousand seven hundred and fifty nine, and afterwards from time to time, shall become due, and be deducted by virtue of the said act, for or in respect of the salaries, fees, or wages, of any offices and employments payable by the crown in that part of *Great Britain* called *England, Wales,* or *Berwick* upon *Tweed,* and for or in respect of any pension or gratuity payable out of any revenue belonging to his Majesty, in *England, Wales,* or *Berwick* upon *Tweed,* shall, by the commissioners, officers, and persons deducting the same, be respectively paid into the hands of a receiver or receivers to be for that purpose appointed by his Ma-

3 d. in the
pound allowed
him for his
trouble.

Security to be
given by him.

Deductions of
the duties to
be paid over
quarterly to
the receiver,
and by him,
within the
quarter fol-
lowing, into
the exche-
quer.
An account
of the falaries,
fees, and pen-
fions, &c. to be
delivered to
the receivers;
and entered
by them in
proper books.

The monies
which have
been, or ought
to have been
deducted un-
der the faid
act, to be ac-
counted for, to
the faid re-
ceivers, and
paffed by
them.

Difputes con-
cerning the
charging any
particular of-
fice or penfion,
or fums to be
deducted
thereout,
to be heard
and deter-
mined by the
barons of the
Exchequer in

jefty, his heirs, and fucceffors; and it fhall and may be lawful
to and for fuch receiver or receivers to retain, out of the monies
fo paid into his or their hands as aforefaid, fuch fum, as a reward or compenfation for his or their trouble, as his Majefty, his
heirs, and fucceffors fhall appoint, not exceeding three pence in
the pound; and the faid receiver or receivers fhall give fecurity
for their good behaviour in difcharging the truft in them repofed, by giving bond in fuch penalty, and with fuch furety or
fureties, as the commiffioners of his Majefty's treafury for the
time being, or any three or more of them, or the lord high
treafurer for the time being, fhall think fit; and the payment
of the feveral fums deducted as aforefaid, fhall be made into the
the hands of fuch receiver or receivers, in the courfe of the quarter
wherein the faid fums fhall have been deducted; and fuch receiver or receivers fhall, within the compafs of the next enfuing
quarter, pay the fame fums refpectively into the receipt of his
Majefty's exchequer at *Weftminfter*: and the feveral commiffioners, officers, and perfons, making the deductions aforefaid,
are hereby directed and required, at the requeft of fuch receiver
or receivers, to deliver to him or them a juft and true account
of all and every the falaries, fees, and wages, and likewife of
the annual penfions and gratuities by the faid commiffioners,
officers, and perfons refpectively payable, and of the names of
the perfons intitled to receive the fame; of which accounts the
faid receiver or receivers are to enter exact copies in books to
be by them kept for that purpofe.

II. And be it further enacted by the authority aforefaid, That
all fums of money which have been, or ought to have been,
deducted or retained under the faid act, by the officers of the
exchequer, or of any other officer, or by any commiffioner or
commiffioners, or other perfons in *England*, *Wales*, or *Berwick*
upon *Tweed*, for the duties payable under the faid act of the
thirty firft year of his prefent Majefty's reign, for or in refpect
of the falaries, fees, or wages of any office or employment, or
for or in refpect of any penfion or gratuity out of any revenue
belonging to his Majefty, fhall be accounted for to fuch receiver
or receivers as fhall be, in purfuance of this prefent act, appointed by his Majefty, his heirs, and fucceffors; and the accounts thereof fhall be examined, audited, and paffed, by fuch
receiver or receivers, or one of them, and not by the auditors
of the imprefts, or the auditors of the court of *Exchequer*.

III. And be it further enacted by the authority aforefaid,
That if any difpute fhall arife whether the fees, falary, or wages
of any office or employment, or whether any penfion or gratuity, be chargeable under the faid act of the thirty firft year of
his prefent Majefty's reign, or under this act, or touching the
fum of money which ought to be ftopped and deducted out of
fuch falary, fees, wages, penfions, or gratuities, fuch difputes
fhall be heard by the barons of the *Exchequer* in *England*, if the
office or employment in queftion is exercifed, or the penfion or
gratuity is payable, in *England*, *Wales*, or *Berwick* upon *Tweed*;

or

or by the barons of the *Exchequer* in *Scotland*, if the office or employment in question is exercised, or the pension or gratuity is payable, in that part of *Great Britain*; and such hearing is to be given on the complaint or representation laid in writing before the barons of the *Exchequer* in *England* or *Scotland* respectively, either by the party who shall think himself aggrieved, or by such receiver or receivers who shall be appointed in pursuance of this act, in respect of *England*, *Wales*, or *Berwick* upon *Tweed*, and by the receiver general or receivers in *Scotland*, in respect of that part of the united kingdom.

IV. Provided always, That the complainant shall give a copy of his complaint or representation to the person or persons against whom the same is made, within ten days after the same shall have been lodged with the said barons; and the said barons in *England* and *Scotland* respectively shall hear and determine such disputes in a summary way, and their determination shall be binding without further appeal.

V. *And whereas the profits of several offices and employments in Great Britain arise in the whole, or in part, from perquisites which are due and payable in the course of office; and it is therefore, by the said act of the thirty first year of his present Majesty's reign, enacted, That such part of the sums of money thereby granted as are payable for or in respect of the profits of any office or employment in any* part of England, Wales, or Berwick upon Tweed, *which arise from such perquisites, shall be computed, raised, levied, and paid, according to the annual value at which such profits stood valued and rated to the last assessment to the land tax; with a proviso, That such profits arising from such perquisites as aforesaid, should be deemed and taken to have been valued and rated in such last assessment to the land tax, at so much only as the entire sum at which any such office was valued and rated in the said assessment should exceed the amount of the salaries, wages, and fees, payable as aforesaid in respect of the same office: and whereas, for the better rating, ordering, levying, and collecting of the duty by the said act charged upon such perquisites of such of the said offices and employments as are in that part of* Great Britain *called* England, Wales, *and* Berwick upon Tweed, *the commissioners of the land tax for the time being are thereby authorized and required to ascertain, and set down in writing, the amount of the duty of one shilling in the pound, to be paid in pursuance of the said act by all commissioners and other officers, their clerks, agents, secondaries, substitutes, and other inferior ministers and persons whatsoever, having, using, or exercising, any of the said offices or employments, the salaries, wages, fees, and perquisites whereof, exceed the value of one hundred pounds per annum, within their respective hundreds, laths, wapentakes, rapes, wards, or other divisions, in proportion to the annual value at which the profits of such offices or employments respectively stood valued and rated in the last assessment to the land tax for the said respective hundreds and divisions respectively: and whereas it hath been found that, in consequence of the said beforerecited limitations put by the said act upon the rating, valuing, and assessing, of the profits of offices and employments arising from per-* quisites

quisites due and payable in the course of office, the said offices and employments have not contributed in equal proportion with those whereof the profits arise from salaries, fees, and wages, payable by the crown; be it therefore enacted by the authority aforesaid, That the commissioners of the land tax for the time being shall fix and ascertain, according to their best judgement and discretion, the sum total or amount of the perquisites arising from each and every office within their respective districts, distinct from the salary, fees, and wages, thereunto belonging, which are to be deducted under the said act, and independently of any former valuation or assessment of the same to the land tax; and shall rate and assess all such of the said offices and employments, whereof the perquisites shall be found to exceed one hundred pounds a year, at one shilling for every twenty shillings arising by the said offices and employments.

VI. And, to the end that the duty of one shilling in the pound may be paid upon all offices and employments whereof the salary, fees, and wages, together with the perquisites, shall exceed one hundred pounds a year; it is hereby further enacted by the authority aforesaid, That the receiver or receivers to be appointed by virtue of this act, shall transmit to the commissioners of the land tax in every district where any office or employment is to be assessed, an account of all such offices and employments, whereof the fees, wages, and salaries, do not exceed one hundred pounds a year; and if the said commissioners of the land tax shall find the perquisites arising from the said office, with the salary, fees, and wages, of the same, as certified by such receiver or receivers, to exceed together the amount of one hundred pounds a year, then the said commissioners are to rate and assess such office and employment, and to cause the duty of one shilling in the pound to be levied and collected thereon.

VII. Provided nevertheless, That in all future assessments to the land tax, the said offices and employments shall not be valued or assessed at any higher rates than those whereat the same offices and employments were respectively assessed and rated towards the land tax imposed by an act made in the thirty first year of his present Majesty's reign; any thing to the contrary thereof in any wise notwithstanding.

VIII. And, to prevent any doubts which might arise concerning the meaning of the word Perquisites, in the said act, and in this present act mentioned; be it declared and enacted by the authority aforesaid, That the same shall for the purposes of the said act, and likewise of this present act, be construed, deemed, and taken, as and for such profits of offices and employments in Great Britain, as arise from fees established by custom or authority, and payable either by the crown, or the subjects, in consideration of business done, from time to time, in the course of executing such offices and employments.

IX. And whereas in and by the said act it is provided, That no commissioner of the land tax in England, Wales, or Berwick upon Tweed,

Tweed, or commissioner of supply in Scotland, who shall be possessed of any office or employment subject and liable to the duty thereby imposed, shall sit, or act, or any ways interfere, in rating his own office or employment, but shall withdraw until the rating thereof be settled and determined by the rest of the commissioners then present: and whereas a doubt hath arisen whether any commissioner possessed of any such office or employment, can sit, or act, or any ways interfere, in the execution of the said act, in regard that the commissioners of the land tax are thereby constituted the assessors, and that the making and signing any assessment to be made in pursuance of the said act by any commissioner possessed of any office or employment, might be deemed and taken to be sitting, acting, or interfering, in the rating of his own office or employment, although such commissioner had withdrawn, until the rating of his office was settled and determined; be it therefore enacted by the authority aforesaid, That nothing in this or in the said in part recited act contained, shall be deemed or construed to extend to any such commissioner, for or in respect of his making or signing any assessment made, or to be made, in pursuance of the said in part recited act, or of this act; provided such commissioner shall have withdrawn, or shall withdraw, until the rating of his own office or employment shall have been, or shall be, settled or determined.

Commissioners of the land tax not liable to penalties for acting in the cases here mentioned, provided they withdraw during the rating of their respective employments.

X. Provided also, That the duty of one shilling in the pound charged by the said act made in the thirty first year of his present Majesty's reign upon pensions and gratuities, shall not, for the future, be charged on, or payable out of, such pensions or gratuities which his Majesty, his heirs, and successors, shall be pleased to declare in the warrant, order, or other instrument, directing payment thereof, to be intended as charitable donations; any thing to the contrary thereof in any wise notwithstanding.

Charitable donations exempted from duties;

XI. Provided also, That nothing in the said act contained shall extend, or be construed to extend, to the charging of the said duty upon any military officers serving on the staff, or belonging to any of his Majesty's garrisons, regiments, troops, companies, the royal hospital of *Chelsea*, or the hospitals of the army; any thing to the contrary thereof in any wise notwithstanding.

as also officers of the army, and the hospitals;

XII. Provided always, and be it further enacted by the authority aforesaid, That the said recited act passed in the thirty first year of his Majesty's reign, or this act, or any thing therein or herein contained, shall not charge, or be construed, deemed, or taken to charge, any pension, annuity, yearly payment, rent, or sum, issuing out of, or charged upon, any revenues belonging to his Majesty in *Great Britain*, that have been by his Majesty's royal predecessors, Kings or Queens of *England*, or by act of parliament, granted unto any person or persons in fee or fee-tail, or till redeemed by payment of any sum or sums of money mentioned in any grant or act of parliament, with the said duty or payment in the said recited act of one shilling out of every twenty shillings thereof by the year, but that such pensions,

and the pensions, annuities, and rents, &c. granted in fee, or fee-tail, &c. by former Kings and Queens of England;

annuities, yearly payments, rents, or fums, fhall be acquitted and difcharged of, from, and againft, the faid duty, as if the faid recited act had never been made; any thing therein or here in contained to the contrary notwithftanding.

and offices in both univerfities.

XIII. Provided always, and be it farther enacted by the authority aforefaid, That nothing in this act contained fhall extend, or be conftrued to extend, to charge any offices or employments in either of the two univerfities in that part of *Great Britain* called *England*, with the duty by this act impofed.

CAP. XXXIV.

An act for the better preventing the importation of the woollen manufactures of France *into any of the ports in the* Levant *fea, by or on the behalf of any of his Majefty's fubjects; and for the more effectual preventing the illegal importation of raw filk and mohair yarn into the kingdom.*

Preamble.

WHEREAS the importation of woollen broad cloth of the manufacture of France into any ports or places within the Levant feas, by or on the behalf of British fubjects, is not only a manifeft difcouragement and prejudice to the woollen manufactures of Great Britain, but is alfo a means of affording relief to the enemy, and thereby enabling them to carry on the war againft thefe kingdoms now: for the more effectually preventing fuch deftructive commerce for the future, may it pleafe your Majefty that it may be enacted; and be it enacted by the King's moft excellent majefty, by and with the advice and confent of the lords fpiritual and temporal, and commons, in this prefent parliament affembled, and by the authority of the fame, That from and after the paffing of this act, no woollen broad cloth, or woollen goods of the manufacture of *France*, fhall directly or indirectly be imported or carried into any port or place in the *Levant* feas, within the limits of any letters patent or charter granted to the governor and company of merchants of *England* trading into the *Levant* feas, commonly called *The Turkey Company*, by or on the account of any member of the faid company, or any fubject of this realm.

No woollen manufactures of France, may be imported by or on behalf of any English fubject, into any of the ports in the Levant feas;

nor may English goods be fo imported, except directly from Great Britain, unlefs certificate attefted by the conful be produced from the laft place of exportation, that the faid goods are originally British, &c.

II. And be it further enacted by the authority aforefaid, That no woollen broad cloth, or other woollen goods, of the produce or manufacture of this kingdom, fhall be imported into any port or place in the *Levant* feas, within the limits of the faid company's charter, except directly from this kingdom, by, for, or on account of, any *British* fubject; unlefs the importer fhall produce to his Majefty's ambaffador, or to the conful or vice conful, or other proper officer appointed by the *Levant* company, at the port or place where fuch goods fhall be imported, a certificate upon oath, from the exporter or fhipper of fuch goods, at the port or place where the fame goods were laft exported from, that the fame were brought or received from *Great Britain*; and in fuch certificate fhall be defcribed the name of

the

the ship or vessel, and also of the master thereof, and the particular day or time when the same goods were imported into such last loading port or place from *Great Britain*; which certificate shall be attested by the *British* consul, or person acting as consul in his absence, residing at such last loading port or place; and the said shipper shall also produce to the said *British* consul, or person acting as consul in his absence, the bill or bills of lading of the said goods, which shall have been given or made out upon the shipping thereof from *Great Britain*; and the said consul, or person acting as consul in his absence, shall take notice in the attestation of such certificate, that such bill or bills of lading were produced to him. *and the bills of lading upon the exportation from Great Britain, be also produced, and notified in the attestation.*

III. And be it further enacted by the authority aforesaid, That upon granting every certificate for the exportation of *British* cloths or other woollen manufactures of this kingdom, for any port or place within the limits of the charter of the *Levant* company, the consul, vice consul, or person acting as such, is hereby required to enter a duplicate of the said certificate in a book to be by him kept for that purpose; in which book the said duplicate being entered at the time of granting the certificate shall be signed by the exporter or shipper of the goods, taking the oath before required to be taken upon making out such certificate; which book and entry of the duplicates of all such certificates shall be referred to, and received as final evidence, in all disputes which may arise with respect to the truth or authenticity of such certificates; and such entries shall and may be examined by all parties without fee or reward. *Consul to enter a duplicate of such certificate in a book to be kept for that purpose; which is to be signed by the exporter; and the same may be admitted as evidence, and examined gratis.*

IV. And be it further enacted by the authority aforesaid, That in all cases where the consul, or person acting as such, shall receive information, upon oath, setting forth good reason to suspect the truth or authenticity of any certificate, the said consul, or person acting as such, shall, and is hereby required, to signify such information to the importer, and to take security in double the value of the goods: which security shall be forfeited, in case, upon a reference to the entries and books of the consul, or person acting as such, at the port from whence such goods shall be pretended to be imported, it shall appear that no such certificate was granted; such security to be assigned to the informer for his sole use and benefit. *Where the certificate shall be suspected, the consul is to signify the same to the importer, and take double security; and if fraud be discovered, the security to be forfeited, and assigned to the informer.*

V. Provided always, and it is hereby enacted, That as often as any such objections shall be made to any certificate produced by any importer of woollen cloths, or manufactures, into any port or place within the limits of the charter of the *Levant* company, and security shall be taken of the said importer as by this act is directed to be taken; that in every such case, the ambassador, consul, or person acting as such, shall, by the first opportunity, transmit to the consul, or person acting as such, at the port or place at which such disputed certificate shall be alledged to have been granted, notice of such dispute, requiring from such consul or person, at the same time, an attestation under his hand and seal, determining whether the certificate in dispute *Notice of such disputed certificate to be transmitted to the consul at the port where the same shall be alledged to have been granted;*

was

was granted by him; and such attestation shall be transmitted by the said consul, or person acting as such, by the first opportunity, to the ambassador, consul, or person acting as such, at the port or place where the dispute shall arise, who is hereby required, upon the receipt thereof, to lay such attestation before the said importer; and in case the certificate be by such attestation verified, the security shall be immediately cancelled; but if the certificate shall by such attestation be found not to have been granted, the ambassador, consul, or person acting as such, is hereby required to levy the penalty by distress and sale of the goods and chattels of the person or persons giving the former security, by warrant under the hand and seal of such ambassador, consul, or person acting as such; which warrant he is hereby authorized to issue; and the said penalty, when recovered, shall be applied in manner as is before by this act directed.

who is to return an attestation concerning the same, which is to be laid before the importer, and the security to be vacated or forfeited accordingly.

VI. And be it further enacted by the authority aforesaid, That all such woollen goods as shall be imported into any port or place within the limits of the said *Levant* company's charter, by, for, or on the account or behalf of any *British* subject, without such certificate as aforesaid, other than such as shall be imported directly from *England*, shall be deemed, and construed, and taken, to be woollen goods of the manufacture of *France*, within the true intent and meaning of this act; and his Majesty's ambassador, and the consul, or vice consul, or other proper officer appointed by the said *Levant* company are hereby impowered and required respectively to cause the same to be seized and confiscated.

Woollen goods imported without such certificate, otherwise than directly from England, deemed to be French,

and may be seized.

VII. And be it further enacted by the authority aforesaid, That every merchant or factor who shall be a subject of *Great Britain*, or residing under the protection of the *British* ambassador, or any consul, or vice consul, or the person acting as such in his absence, within the limits of the said company's charter, shall, before the exportation of any goods or merchandize whatsoever from any port or place within the limits aforesaid, make oath before the said ambassador, or such consul, or vice consul, or the person acting as such in his absence as aforesaid, that such goods or merchandize so intended to be exported, were not purchased by such merchant or his factor, with his knowledge, with the produce of, or taken in barter or exchange for, *French* woollen broad cloth, or any other woollen manufactures of *France*, since the passing of this act.

Factor to make oath, before exportation, that the goods were not purchased with, or taken in barter for, French goods.

VIII. And be it further enacted by the authority aforesaid, That from and after the passing of this act, every person who shall import into *Great Britain* or *Ireland* any goods, wares, or merchandize whatsoever, of the growth, produce, or manufacture, of the *Turkish* dominions, within the limits of the said company's charter, shall, before such goods, wares, or merchandize, shall be permitted to be landed, make oath before his Majesty's commissioners of the customs, or the collector or comptroller, or other principal officer of the customs of such port or place where such goods, wares, or merchandize, shall be

Importer of Turkish goods into Great Britain, to make oath, before the landing, that the same were not purchased with, or taken in barter for, French woollen goods,

be imported, that the same, or any part thereof, were, or was not, by himself, or his correspondent, with his knowledge, directly, or indirectly purchased by or with the produce of, or taken in barter or exchange, for any kind of woollen broad cloth, or any other woollen manufactures of *France*, since the passing of this act, except such as shall have been condemned as lawful prize.

except the same shall be prize goods.

IX. And be it further enacted by the authority aforesaid, That in case any certificate to be granted pursuant to this act shall happen to be lost or mislaid, the master or other person having charge of the ship or vessel, on board whereof the goods to which such certificate did relate shall be loaden, shall, before the landing of such goods, make oath before his Majesty's ambassador, or the consul or vice consul of the port of discharge of the said ship, thereby setting forth, according to the best of his remembrance and belief, the purport of such certificate, and that the same is so lost or mislaid, and that he doth not know what is become thereof, and that the same hath not been with his privity, consent, or knowledge, delivered or disposed of to any person or persons whatsoever; and the said master or other person navigating the said ship or vessel, or the consignee or consignees of the goods to which such certificate did relate, shall also give sufficient security, in the penalty of double the value of the said goods, to his Majesty's ambassador, or to the consul or vice consul, or the person acting as such in his absence, of the port or place where the said goods shall be imported, for procuring and delivering to his Majesty's ambassador, or to the said consul or vice consul, or the person acting as such in his absence, within a reasonable time to be by him appointed, a duplicate of such certificate so lost or mislaid: and, upon making such oath, and giving such security, as aforesaid, his Majesty's ambassador, or the said consul or vice consul, shall grant the said master, or the consignee of the said cargo, leave or licence to import the goods mentioned in the said oath; and the same shall and may thereupon be lawfully landed and imported.

If a certificate shall be lost or mislaid, the master to make oath concerning the same, and the purport thereof,

and give security for producing a duplicate thereof;

Licence thereupon to be granted to import the goods.

X. Provided nevertheless, That nothing in this act contained shall extend, or be deemed, construed, or taken to extend, to hinder or prevent the shipping, transporting, importing, selling, or disposing of, any woollen goods or woollen manufacture of any country whatsoever, which shall have been taken from the enemies of the crown of *Great Britain*, and condemned as lawful prize, by any ship or ships of war, or privateer, belonging to, or bearing commission from, his Majesty, his heirs, or successors.

Prize woollen goods may be imported, &c.

XI. Provided, That at the time of the importation of such prize cloths, a copy of the sentence of condemnation, signed by the person condemning the same, shall be delivered to the consul, or person acting as such, at the port or place of importation.

upon producing a copy of the sentence of condemnation to the consul.

XII. *And whereas by an act of parliament passed in the twelfth year of the reign of his late majesty King* Charles *the Second, intituled,*

Recital of clauses in act 12 Car. 2.

tuled, An act for the encouragement and increasing of shipping
and navigation, it was, amongst other things, enacted, That no
goods or commodities of foreign growth, production, or manufacture,
and which should be brought into England, Ireland, Wales, the
islands of Guernsey or Jersey, or town of Berwick upon Tweed,
in English built shipping, or other shipping, as therein before mentioned, should be shipped or brought from any other place or places,
country or countries, but only from those of the said growth, production, or manufacture, or from those ports where the said goods or
commodities could only or usually had been first shipped for transportation, and from none other places or countries, under the penalty of the
forfeiture of all such goods as should be imported from any other place
or country, contrary to the true intent and meaning of the said act, as
also of the ship in which the same were imported, with all her guns,
furniture, ammunition, tackle, and apparel, one moiety to his Majesty, his heirs, and successors, and the other moiety to him or them
that should seize, inform, or sue for the same, in any court of record, to be recovered as in the said act is expressed: and it was by
the same act provided, That the said act, or any thing therein contained, should not extend or be meant to restrain and prohibit the importation of any of the commodities of the Streights or Levant seas
loaded in English built shipping, and whereof the master, and three
fourths of the mariners at least, were English, from the usual ports
or places for loading of such commodities theretofore, within the said
Streights or Levant seas, though the same were not of the very
growth of the said places: and whereas by another act of parliament

6 Geo. 1.

made in the sixth year of the reign of his late majesty King George
the First, intituled, An act for prohibiting the importation of
raw silk and mohair yarn of the product or manufacture of Asia,
from any ports or places in the Streights or Levant seas, except
such ports and places as are within the dominions of the Grand
Seignior; after reciting the aforesaid clause, and also the aforesaid
proviso in the said act of the twelfth year of the reign of his said
late majesty King Charles the Second, herein before recited, and also
reciting that the woollen manufacture in France had since that time
been greatly increased, and very large quantities of such goods were
then annually imported from thence to Turkey, in return whereof,
were brought from thence raw silk, and other commodities, to Mar-
seilles, and other ports in France, great quantities whereof were carried into Italy, and from thence imported into Great Britain, in
English shipping, greatly to the discouragement of the woollen
manufactures of Great Britain, and the advancement thereof in
France, and that without some speedy care therein, the British trade
to Turkey would be daily lessened, and was in danger of being lost;
it was by the said act enacted, That from and after the twenty ninth
day of September one thousand seven hundred and twenty, the said
recited clause or proviso, as to the importation of raw silk and mohair
yarn of the product or manufacture of Asia, should be, and was thereby repealed, excepting only as to the ports and places in the said Streights
or Levant seas, which were within the dominions of the Grand
Seignior: and whereas by another act of parliament passed in the

thir-

thirteenth and fourteenth years of the reign of his said late majesty &13&14Car.2.
King Charles *the Second,* intituled, *An act* for preventing frauds,
and regulating abuses, in his Majesty's customs; *reciting, that
there were great practices and combinations between the importers and
owners of goods and merchandizes, and the seizers and informers,
with design and intent to defraud the force of the law; and his Majesty, of his duties and customs, it was enacted, That no ship or ships,
goods, wares, or merchandizes, should be seised as forfeited, for or
by reason of unlawful importation, or exportation, into, or out of, this
kingdom of* England, *dominion of* Wales, *or port and town of* Berwick, *but by the person or persons who were or should be appointed by
his Majesty to manage his customs, or officers of his Majesty's customs
for the time being, or such other person or persons as should be deputed and authorized thereunto, by warrant from the lord treasurer, or
under treasurer, or by special commission from his Majesty under the
great or privy seal; and if any seizure should thereafter be made by
any other person or persons whatsoever, for any the causes therein
before-mentioned, such seizure should be void and of none effect: and
whereas great quantities of raw silk of the product or manufacture
of* Asia *have imported into this kingdom, under various denominations
and pretences, from* Leghorn, *and other ports and places from whence
the same may not be lawfully imported into* England, *contrary to the
said acts prohibiting the same, and to the great prejudice of the trade
of this kingdom:* now, for the more effectually preventing such Where raw
illegal practices for the future, be it further enacted by the autho- filk, or mo-
rity aforesaid, That in case any raw silk or mohair yarn, or any hair yarn, or
ship or vessel bringing the same into *England,* Ireland, *Wales,* the the vessel im-
islands of *Guernsey* or *Jersey,* or town of *Berwick upon Tweed,* porting the
at any time from and after the passing of this act, shall be seiz- seized, as for-
ed, as forfeited by virtue of all or any of the said herein before feited by vir-
in part recited acts of parliament, then, and in any such case, the recited
it shall not be lawful for any officer or officers, or other person acts,
or persons who shall make such seizure, to releafe or abandon the seizure
the fame, or delay or omit to proceed to judgment for the con- may not be
demnation thereof, as the law in that behalf directs, without abandoned,
first acquainting the governor, deputy governor, treasurer, or quainting the
husband, of the said company, or their successors, or their known company of
secretary for the time being, by writing, of his or their inten- such intention to relinquish or abandon such seizure; and such officer or and delivering
officers, or other person or persons, shall, at the same time, de- in a schedule
liver to the said governor, deputy governor, treasurer, husband, of the seizure;
or secretary of the said company, or of their successors, a copy of
the schedule of such seizure: and in case the said governor and and where the
company, or any committee thereof, shall, within seven days company shall
after such notice, give bond, or offer to give bond, under the give bond to
common seal of their corporation, in the penal sum of one thou- indemnify the
sand pounds, with condition thereunder written for indemnifying officer;
and saving harmless such officer or officers, or other person or
persons, of, from, and against, all costs of suit, charges, damages,
and expences, which such officer or officers, or other person or
persons, shall be necessarily put to, or may pay or sustain, in
case

cafe such ship, vessel, or goods, so seized, shall not be adjudged, upon the trial or hearing concerning the condemnation thereof, to have been forfeited; that then such officer, or other person or persons, shall not voluntarily abandon or relinquish such seizure, or omit to commence or bring, nor discontinue any proceedings commenced for the condemnation of such ship, vessel, or goods, without the consent of the said company, or some committee thereof; but shall, with all convenient speed, proceed to judgment concerning the legality of such seizure; any law, or construction of law, to the contrary notwithstanding.

the suit may not be discontinued without their consent,

but be prosecuted to judgment.

XIII. Provided nevertheless, That any person, being a member of the said company, shall be admitted to give evidence, either for the plaintiff or plaintiffs, relator or relators, or defendant or defendants, upon any trial, hearing, or examination, concerning the condemnation or legality of the feizure of the goods, ship, or vessel, to which any such bond, so to be given as aforesaid, shall relate; any such bond, or any law, or construction of law, to the contrary notwithstanding.

Member of the company admitted to give evidence upon the trial.

XIV. And be it further enacted, That this act shall be deemed, adjudged, and taken to be, a publick act, and be judicially taken notice of as such, by all judges and other persons whatsoever, without the same being specially pleaded.

Publick act.

XV. And be it further enacted by the authority aforesaid, That if any person or persons shall, at any time or times, be sued or prosecuted for any thing by him or them done or executed in pursuance of this act, or of any matter or thing in this act contained, such person or persons shall and may plead the general issue, and give the special matter in evidence for his or their defence; and if, upon the trial a verdict shall pass for the defendant or defendants, or the plaintiff or plaintiffs shall become nonsuited, or discontinue his or their action, then such defendant or defendants shall have treble costs to him or them awarded, against such plaintiff or plaintiffs.

General issue.

Treble costs.

XVI. Provided always, That this act, and every thing contained therein, shall continue and be in force during the present war with *France*, and no longer.

Continuance of the act.

CAP. XXXV.

An act for augmenting the salaries of the puisne judges in the court of King's Bench, *the judges in the court of* Common Pleas, *the barons of the coif in the court of* Exchequer *at* Westminster, *the judges in the courts of* Session *and* Exchequer *in* Scotland, *and justices of* Chester, *and the great sessions for the counties in* Wales.

WHEREAS *the salaries of the puisne judges in the court of* King's Bench, *the judges in the court of* Common Pleas, *the barons of the coif in the court of* Exchequer *at* Westminster, *the judges in the courts of* Session *and* Exchequer *in* Scotland, *and the justices of* Chester, *and of the great sessions for the counties in* Wales, *are inadequate to the dignity and importance of their offices:*
and

Preamble.

and your Majesty's most dutiful and loyal subjects, the commons of *Great Britain* in parliament assembled, being desirous to augment the said salaries, do give and grant unto your Majesty, in order to establish in the first place a proper fund for the augmentation of the salaries of the said judges in the courts at *Westminster*, and justices of *Chester*, and the great sessions for the counties in *Wales*, the duties herein after mentioned, and do therefore most humbly beseech your Majesty that it may be enacted; and be it enacted by the King's most excellent majesty, by and with the advice and consent of the lords spiritual and temporal, and commons, in this present parliament assembled, and by the authority of the same, That from and after the fifth day of *July*, one thousand seven hundred and fifty nine, there shall be throughout *England*, the dominion of *Wales*, and town of *Berwick upon Tweed*, raised, collected, levied, and paid, unto and for the use of his Majesty, his heirs, and successors, for every piece of vellum, parchment, or paper, on which the several and respective matters and things herein after mentioned, shall be ingrossed or written at any time or times after the said fifth day of *July* (over and above the rates, duties, charges, and sums of money, now due and payable to his Majesty for or in respect of the same) the further several and respective rates, duties, charges, and sums of money following; that is to say,

Additional stamp duties charged on every piece of vellum, parchment, or paper, used in such matters, to take place 5 July, 1759.

For every piece of vellum or parchment, or sheet or piece of paper, upon which any affidavit to be made use of in any court of law or equity at *Westminster*, or in any court of the great sessions for the counties in *Wales*, or in the court of the county palatine of *Chester*, shall be ingrossed or written (except affidavits taken pursuant to several acts made in the thirtieth and two and thirtieth years of the reign of King *Charles* the Second, for burying in woollen; and except such affidavits as shall be taken before the officers of the customs, or any justice or justices of the peace, or before any commissioners appointed, or to be appointed, by any act of parliament, for the assessing and levying any aids or duties granted or to be granted to his Majesty, his heirs and successors, and which affidavits shall be taken by the said officers of the customs, justices, or commissioners, by virtue of their authority as justices of the peace, or commissioners respectively, and not otherwise) the sum of six pence.

viz. upon affidavits filed or read in courts, 6d. (Affidavits for burying in woollen, and those taken before officers of the customs, justices, or commissioners of the publick taxes, excepted.)

For every piece of vellum or parchment, or sheet or piece of paper, upon which any copy of such affidavit as is herein before charged, that shall be filed or read in any of the said courts, shall be ingrossed or written, the sum of six pence.

Upon copies of the said affidavits, 6d.

For every piece of vellum or parchment, or sheet or piece of paper, upon which any common bail to be filed in any court of law at *Westminster*, or in any of the aforesaid courts, and upon which any appearance that shall be made upon such bail, shall be ingrossed or written, the sum of six pence.

Upon filing a common bail or appearance, 6d.

For every piece of vellum or parchment, or sheet or piece of paper, upon which any rule or order made or given in any the courts

Upon a rule or order of court, 6d.

courts at *Westminster*, either courts of law or equity, shall be ingroffed or written, the sum of six pence.

Upon a copy of such rule or order, 6d.

For every piece of vellum or parchment, or sheet or piece of paper, upon which any copy of such rules or orders entered, shall be ingroffed or written, the sum of six pence.

Upon original writs, &c. (except where a Capias issues) or other process of court, where the debt or damage amounts to 40s. or more, 6d.

For every piece of vellum or parchment, or sheet or piece of paper, upon which any original writ (except such original on which a writ of *Capias* issues) *Sub Pœna*, bill of *Middlesex*, *Latitat*, writ of *Capias Quo Minus*, writ of *Dedimus Potestatem*, to take answers, examine witnesses, or appoint guardians, or any other writ whatsoever, or any other process or mandate, that shall issue out or pass the seals of any the courts at *Westminster*, courts of the great sessions in *Wales*, courts in the counties palatine, or any other court whatsoever holding plea, where the debt or damage doth amount to forty shillings, or above, or the thing in demand is of that value, shall be ingroffed or written (writs of covenant for levying fines, writs of entry for suffering common recoveries, and writs of *Habeas Corpus*, alway excepted) the sum of six pence.

(particular writs excepted)

Upon depositions taken in Chancery, or other court of equity (paper draughts thereof excepted)

For every piece of vellum or parchment, or sheet or piece of paper, upon which any deposition taken in the court of *Chancery*, or other court of equity at *Westminster* (except the paper draughts of depositions, taken by virtue of any commission, before they are ingroffed) or upon which any copy of any bill, answer, plea, demurrer, replication, rejoynder, interrogatories, depositions, or other proceedings whatsoever, in such courts of equity, shall be ingroffed or written, the sum of one penny.

Copies of bills, answers, pleas, or other proceedings in such courts, 1d.
Upon declarations, and other pleadings in courts of law, 1d.

For every piece of vellum or parchment, or sheet or piece of paper, upon which any declaration, plea, replication, rejoynder, demurrer, or other pleading whatsoever, in any court of law at *Westminster*, or in any of the courts of the principality of *Wales*, or in any of the courts in the counties palatine of *Chester*, *Lancaster*, or *Durham*, shall be ingroffed or written, the sum of one penny; and,

Upon any copy thereof, 1d.

For every piece of vellum or parchment, or sheet or piece of paper, upon which any copy thereof shall be written or ingroffed, the sum of one penny.

These duties to be under the management of the commissioners for the other stamp duties;

II. And be it further enacted by the authority aforesaid, That for the better and more effectual raising, levying, collecting, and paying, all the said additional and new rates and duties herein before granted, the same shall be under the government, care, and management, of the commissioners for the time being appointed to manage the duties payable to his Majesty, his heirs, and successors, and charged on stamped vellum, parchment, and paper, by former acts of parliament in that behalf made; who,

who are to employ proper officers under them, and provide fit stamps for the purpose, and do all other matters

or the major part of them, are hereby required and impowered to employ such officers under them for that purpose as they shall think proper; and to use such dyes and stamps to denote the stamp duties hereby charged as they shall think fit, and to repair, renew, or alter the same, from time to time, as there shall be occasion; and to do all other acts, matters, and things, necessary to be done for putting this act in

in execution, with relation to the said several rates and duties
hereby granted, in the like and in as full and ample manner as
they, or the major part of them, are authorized to put in execution any former law concerning stamped vellum, parchment, or
paper.

necessary for carrying this act into exe-cution.

III. Provided always, and be it further enacted by the authority aforesaid, That to prevent the multiplication of stamps upon such pieces of vellum or parchment, or sheets or pieces of
paper, on which several duties are by several acts of parliament
imposed, it shall and may be lawful for the said commissioners,
instead of the distinct stamps directed to be provided to denote
the several duties on the vellum, parchment, or paper, charged
therewith, to cause one new stamp to be provided, to denote the
said several duties on every piece of vellum or parchment, or
sheet or piece of paper, charged with the said several duties,
from time to time, as shall be by them thought needful.

One new stamp to be provided to denote the several duties.

IV. And it is hereby further enacted, That all vellum, parchment, and paper, charged by this act with any of the stamp duties hereby granted, which hath been, or shall, before the said
fifth day of *July*, be stamped or marked in pursuance of the former acts of parliament relating to his Majesty's stamp duties, or
any of them, shall, before any of the matters and things in respect whereof any rate or duty is hereby made payable shall be
ingrossed or written thereupon, such ingrossing or writing being
at any time after the said fifth day of *July*, be brought to the
head office for stamping or marking of vellum, parchment, and
paper, to be stamped or marked with another mark or stamp,
over and besides the marks or stamps put or to be put thereupon
in pursuance of the said former acts, or any of them; and that
all vellum, parchment, and paper, which hath not been, or shall
not, before the said fifth day of *July*, be stamped or marked in
pursuance of the said former acts, or any of them, shall, before
any of the matters or things in respect whereof any stamp duty
is payable hereby, and by the said former acts, or any of them,
shall be thereupon ingrossed or written, such ingrossing or writing being after the said fifth day of *July*, be brought to the said
head office, and there marked and stamped with the proper
marks or stamps, or mark or stamp, provided, used, or appointed, or to be provided or appointed in pursuance of the said former acts, or of this act, to denote the respective duties thereby
and hereby respectively charged thereupon: and if any of the said
matters and things so to be ingrossed or written as aforesaid, shall
be ingrossed or written, contrary to the true intent and meaning
hereof, upon vellum, parchment, or paper, not appearing to
have been duly marked or stamped, according to this act; that
then, and in every such case, there shall be due, answered, and
paid (over and above the stamp duties payable hereby, and by
the said former acts, or any of them) for or in respect of every
such matter and thing the sum of five pounds; and that no such
matter or thing shall be available in law or equity, or be given
in evidence, or admitted in any court, unless as well the said duty

Former stamps not made use of before 5 July, to be brought to the office, and have an addi-tional stamp put on them.

All papers, &c. made use of after the said day, to be duly stampt according to this act;

on penalty of forfeiting 5 l. besides the duties.

The penalty and duties to be paid,

hereby charged in respect thereof, as the said sum of five pounds, shall be first paid to the receiver general for the time being of the stamp duties, or his deputy or clerk ; and until the vellum, parchment, or paper, upon which such matter or thing is so ingrossed or written, shall be marked or stamped according to the tenor and true meaning hereof : and the said receiver general, and his deputy or clerk, are hereby enjoined and required, upon payment or tender of the said duties, and of the said sum of five pounds, and such other sums as by the said former acts are payable in that behalf, to give a receipt for such monies ; and the other proper officers are thereupon required to mark or stamp such matters or things with the proper marks or stamps, or mark or stamp, required in that behalf; which said sum of five pounds, is to be applied to the same uses and purposes as the duties hereby granted are to be applied.

V. And be it further enacted by the authority aforesaid, That the several rates and duties herein before granted, shall be paid, from time to time, into the hands of the receiver general for the time being of the duties on stamped vellum, parchment, and paper; who shall keep a separate and distinct account of the several rates and duties arising by virtue of this act, and pay the same (the necessary charges of raising, paying, and accounting for, such rates and duties being deducted) into the receipt of the exchequer, for the purposes herein after expressed, at such time and in such manner as any former duties on stamped vellum, parchment, or paper, are directed to be paid : and that in the office of the auditor of the said receipt, shall be provided and kept a book or books, in which all the monies arising from the several rates and duties hereby granted and paid into the said receipt, as aforesaid, shall be entered separate and apart from all other monies paid and payable to his Majesty, his heirs, and successors, upon any account whatsoever, and shall be applied in such manner as is herein after mentioned.

VI. And be it further enacted by the authority aforesaid, That the said commissioners, and all other officers who shall be employed in the collection or management of the said several rates and duties herein before granted, shall, in the execution of their offices, observe and perform such rules and orders as they respectively shall, from time to time, receive from the high treasurer, or the commissioners of the treasury, or any three or more of them, for the time being ; and that no fee or reward shall be taken or demanded by any such commissioners or officers from any of his Majesty's subjects, for any matter or thing to be done in pursuance of this act : and in case any officer employed in the execution of this act in relation to the said rates and duties, shall refuse or neglect to do or perform any matter or thing by this act required or directed to be done or performed by him, whereby any of his Majesty's subjects, shall or may sustain any damage whatsoever; such officer, so offending, shall be liable by any action to be founded on this statute, to answer to the party grieved all such damages, with treble costs of suit.

VII. And

Marginal notes:

and the papers, &c. duly stampt, before the same shall be available in law or equity. Uponpayment of the penalty and duties, papers admitted to be stampt.

Duties to be paid to the receiver general ;

and a separate account kept thereof, and to be paid over by him into the exchequer.

Books to be kept in the auditor's office for entering these duties apart from all others.

Commissioners, and officers under them, to observe the orders of the treasury in the execution of their offices.

No fees to be taken.

Officer making default in his duty, to pay damages, and treble costs, to the party grieved.

VII. And be it further enacted by the authority aforesaid, That the said commissioners and their officers shall be subject to such penalties and forfeitures for any breach of the trusts in them reposed, or for diverting or misapplying the money received in pursuance of this act, as by any former law relating to stamped vellum, parchment, or paper, are inflicted; and that all powers, provisions, articles, clauses, penalties, forfeitures, distribution of penalties and forfeitures, and all other matters and things prescribed, inflicted, or appointed, by any former act or acts of parliament relating to the duties on vellum, parchment, and paper, on which any affidavit, or any other matter or thing herein before mentioned, in respect whereof any rate or duty is by this act granted, shall be ingrossed or written, and not hereby altered, shall be in full force and effect with relation to the additional rates and duties hereby imposed, and shall be applied and put in execution for the raising, levying, collecting, and securing, the said additional rates and duties, according to the true intent and meaning of this act, as fully, to all intents and purposes, as if the same had severally and respectively been herein enacted with relation to the additional rates and duties hereby imposed.

Penalties and forfeitures for breach of trust.

Powers and provisions,&c. of former acts relating to the stamp duties, extended to these duties.

VIII. And be it further enacted by the authority aforesaid, That if any person, from and after the said fifth day of *July*, shall counterfeit or forge, or procure to be counterfeited or forged, any seal, stamp, or mark, to resemble any seal, stamp, or mark, directed or allowed to be used by this act for the purpose of denoting the duties hereby granted, or shall counterfeit or resemble the impression of the same, with an intent to defraud his Majesty, his heirs, and successors, of any of the said duties, or shall utter, vend, or sell any vellum, parchment, or paper, liable to any such stamp duty, with such counterfeit stamp or mark, knowing the same to be counterfeit; or shall privately or fraudulently use any seal, stamp, or mark, directed or allowed to be used by this act, with intent to defraud his Majesty, his heirs, and successors, of any of the said duties; every person so offending, and being thereof lawfully convicted, shall be adjudged a felon, and shall suffer death as in cases of felony, without benefit of clergy.

Penalty of forging or counterfeiting the stamps,

or privately or fraudulently making use of the true ones.

death.

IX. And be it further enacted by the authority aforesaid, That, from and after the fifth day of *July*, there shall be issued, paid, and applied, in every year, out of the monies which shall arise by the duties herein before granted, and be paid into the receipt of the exchequer as aforesaid, the sums of money following to the several judges herein after mentioned, as an addition to, and in augmentation of, their respective salaries; that is to say, The sum of five hundred pounds to each of the puisne judges for the time being in the court of *King's Bench*; the sum of five hundred pounds to each of the judges for the time being in the court of *Common Pleas* at *Westminster*; the sum of one thousand pounds to the chief baron for the time being in the court of *Exchequer* at *Westminster*; and the sum of five hundred pounds to

The following sums to be paid out of the duties, in augmentation of the judges salaries;

viz 500l. to each of the puisne judges of the court of King's Bench; 500l. to each of the judges in the court of Common Pleas;

each of the other barons of the coif for the time being in the faid court of *Exchequer*; the fum of two hundred pounds to the chief juftice of *Chefter* for the time being; the fum of one hundred and fifty pounds to the fecond juftice of *Chefter* for the time being; and the fum of one hundred and fifty pounds to each of the juftices for the time being of the great feffions for the counties in *Wales*: which faid feveral and refpective fums of money fhall be and are hereby charged upon the rates and duties herein before granted, and fhall be paid thereout, in every year, at fuch time or times, and in fuch manner, as the falaries to the faid judges now are or have accuftomarily been paid.

X. And be it further enacted by the authority aforefaid, That if the faid rates and duties fhall prove deficient in any year to make good and anfwer the fums herein before appointed to be paid, and applied yearly in augmentation of the falaries of the faid judges, it fhall, from time to time, as often as fuch defi- ciency fhall happen, be lawful for the high treafurer, or com- miffioners of the treafury, or any three or more of them for the time being, out of any money that is then, or fhall thereafter be, in the exchequer, and that hath arifen, or fhall arife, by the faid rates and duties, and not otherwife applied by parliament, to direct any fum or fums of money to be iffued and paid for or towards making good fuch parts of the faid annual fums as fhall be, from time to time, deficient or in arrear.

XI. Provided always, That when and as often as any fuch deficiency fhall happen, the payments to be made to the faid feveral and refpective judges fhall be in proportion to the refpec- tive fums which are herein before directed and appointed to be paid to fuch judges refpectively.

XII. And be it further enacted by the authority aforefaid, That all the refidue and furplus of the monies arifing by the faid rates and duties which fhall, from time to time, remain in the exchequer, and fhall not have been iffued and applied for the augmentation of the falaries to the faid judges, and for the making good any fuch deficiencies as aforefaid, fhall be, from time to time, referved for the difpofition of parliament, and fhall not be iffued but by authority of parliament, and as fhall be directed by future act or acts of parliament; any thing in any former act or acts contained to the contrary notwith- ftanding.

XIII. *And for the augmenting of the falaries of the judges in the courts of feffion and exchequer in that part of* Great Britain *called* Scotland, be it further enacted by the authority aforefaid, That from and after the faid fifth day of *July*, there fhall be iffued, paid, and applied, in every year, out of the monies which fhall arife, from time to time, of or for any the duties and revenues in that part of *Great Britain* called *Scotland*, which by an act made in the tenth year of the reign of Queen *Anne*, were charged or made chargeable with the payment of the fees, falaries, and other charges allowed or to be allowed by her Majefty, her heirs, or fucceffors, for keeping up the courts of feffion and jufticiary and

exche-

exchequer court in *Scotland*, the feveral fums of money following, to the judges herein after mentioned, as an addition to, and in augmentation of, their refpective falaries; that is to fay, The fum of three hundred pounds to the prefident for the time being of the faid court of feffion; the fum of three hundred pounds to the chief baron for the time being of the faid court of exchequer; and the fum of two hundred pounds to each of the other judges for the time being in the faid courts of feffion and exchequer refpectively: which faid feveral and refpective fums of money fhall be, and are hereby, charged upon the faid duties and revenues, and fhall be paid thereout in every year, at fuch time or times, and in fuch manner, as the fees, falaries, and other charges of keeping up the faid courts, now are or have accuftomarily been paid fince the union of the two kingdoms, in purfuance of any act or acts of parliament.

viz. 300l. to the prefident of the court of feffion; 300l. to the chief baron of the court of exchequer; 200l. to each of the other judges in the faid courts; to be paid yearly, as the falaries have accuftomarily been paid.

XIV. And it is hereby enacted by the authority aforefaid, That if any perfon or perfons fhall, at any time or times, be fued or profecuted for any thing by him or them done or to be done or executed in purfuance of this act, or of any matter or thing in this act contained, fuch perfon or perfons fhall and may plead the general iffue, and give the fpecial matter in evidence, for his or their defence; and if upon the trial a verdict fhall pafs for the defendant or defendants, or the plantiff or plaintiffs fhall become nonfuited, then fuch defendant or defendants fhall have treble cofts to him or them awarded againft fuch plaintiff or plaintiffs.

General iffue.

Treble cofts.

CAP. XXXVI.

An act for enabling his Majefty to raife the fum of one million for the ufes and purpofes therein mentioned; and for further appropriating the fupplies granted in this feffion of parliament.

Preamble. Credit of loan granted to his Majefty for 1,000,000l. Treafury may raife the fame by loans or exchequer bills, in like manner as is prefcribed by the land tax act of this feffion, concerning loans or exchequer bills thereby to be made out. The claufes, &c. in the faid act relating to the loans or exchequer bills, extended to the loans and exchequer bills to be made forth in purfuance of this act; principal and intereft, with the charges attending, to be paid out of the next fupplies, and if none fufficient be granted before 5 July 1760, then they are to be paid out of the finking fund; and the monies fo iffued to be replaced out of the firft fupplies. The bank impowered to advance on the faid credit of loan, any fum or fums not exceeding 1,000,000l. the act of 5 & 6 W. & M. notwithftanding. Appropriation of the fupplies in general. The monies arifing by the land tax, malt act, fubfidy and lottery act, and other fums remaining in the exchequer, and finking fund. Savings upon the fum granted for pay and cloathing of the militia for the year 1758, overplus of the grants for the year 1758 remaining in the exchequer, and the fum of 100,000l. granted to the emprefs of Ruffia in 1755, repaid into the exchequer, with the fum of 1,000,000l. granted by this act; viz. out of the aids in general, 3,558,491l. 9s. 8d. towards naval fervices herein fpecified. 1,000,000l. towards paying off the navy debt. 10,000l. towards the fupport of Greenwich Hofpital. 544,777l. 5s. for charge of the office of ordnance for land fervice. 4,592,444l. 1s. 9d. 3q. towards the land forces in general; of which 1,256,130l. 15s. 2d. for troops in Germany and the Weft Indies, and for guards and garrifons, &c in Great Britain, Guernfey, and Jerfey. 52,484l. 1s. 8d. for the ftaff officers, and officers of the hofpitals. 742,531l. 5s. 7d. for guards and garrifons, &c. in the plantations, and Gibraltar, Nova Scotia, Newfoundland, Providence,

dence, Cape Breton, and Senegal. 40,879l. 13s. 9d. for troops on the Irifh eftablifhment ferving in North America and Africa. 34,367l. 15s. 10d. to the reduced officers of the land forces and marines. 2,958l. 19s. 7d. to the officers and gentlemen of horfe guards, &c. reduced. 2,122l. for penfions of officers widows. 16,000l. for out-penfioners of Chelfea Hofpital. 466,785l. 10s. 5d. 3q. for extraordinary expences of land forces, and other fervices, incurred in the year 1758. 398,697l. 17s. 2d. 3q. for the troops of Hanover, Wolfenbuttel, Saxe Gotha, and count Buckeburg, employed againft the common enemy, in concert with the King of Pruffia. 59,646l. 1s. 8d. 3q. for the troops of Heffe Caffel, in the pay of Great Britain, with the fubfidy, purfuant to treaty, from 25 Dec. 1758, to 24 March, 1759. 182,251l. 2s. 11d. 1q. refidue for charge of the faid troops, from 25 Dec. 1758, to 25 Dec. 1759. 97,582l. 17s. 10d. &c. for charge of additional troops of Heffe Caffel, in the pay of Great Britain, from 1 Jan. 1759, to 31 Dec. 1759. 500,000l. upon account, for forage and other contingent expences of the combined army under prince Ferdinand. 670,000l. to the King of Pruffia, purfuant to treaty. 60,000 l. to the landgrave of Heffe Caffel, purfuant to treaty. 800,000l. to difcharge the like fum borrowed on a vote of credit of the laft feffion. 1,000,000l. upon account, to defray the extraordinary expences of the war. 9,902l. 5s. upon account, for fupporting the colony of Nova Scotia. 11,278l. 18s. 5d. upon account, for charges incurred in 1757, for fupporting the faid colony, and not provided for. 4,057l. 10s. upon account, for defraying the civil eftablifhment of Georgia. 667,771l. 19s. 7d. for charges of tranfport fervice, &c. incurred in the year 1758. 2,500l. to make good the like fum iffued by his Majefty to John Mill efquire, and to be paid over by him to the victuallers, &c. of Southampton, in confideration of their expences in quartering the Heffian troops. 11,450l to make good the like fum iffued by his Majefty in augmentation of the judges falaries. 778l. 16s. 6d. to make good the like fum iffued by his Majefty to Jane Hardinge, balance of her husband's account for printing the journals of the houfe of commons. 69,910l. 15s. 1q. upon account, for difcharging incumbrances on the Perth eftate, purfuant to act 25 Geo. 2. 24,371l. 6s. 11d. 3q. to replace to the finking fund the like fum paid thereout, to make good the deficiency of the additional ftamp duties, &c. on 5 July, 1758. 8,881l. 11. 10d. 2q. to replace to the finking fund the like fum paid thereout, to make good the deficiency of the duties on glafs, &c. on 5 July, 1758. 15,000l. without account, towards repairing London Bridge, Act 29 Geo. 2. 20,000l. to the Foundling Hofpital, to be paid without fee. 30,000l. to the Foundling Hofpital, for receiving, &c. fuch children as fhall be brought thither before 1 Jan. 1760, to be paid without fee. 10,000l. towards maintaining the forts and fettlements in Africa. 1,280l. to R. Long, D. D. to enable him to difcharge a mortgage upon the eftate devifed by T. Lowndes Efq; for the endowment of an aftronomical and geometrical profefforfhip in Cambridge. 90,000l. upon account, for pay and cloathing of the militia, and repayment to his Majefty of 1,332l. 10s. advanced by him for the fervice of the militia. 10,000l. to the Eaft India company, in lieu of the King's troops withdrawn from thence. 200,000l. upon account, to make compenfation to the provinces of North America, for expences incurred by them in levying, cloathing, and pay of troops raifed there. 2,443l. 3s. 1d. for purchafing lands for fecuring Portfmouth, Chatham, and Plymouth docks. Thefe aids to be applied to no other ufes. Rules to be obferved in the application of the half-pay. Claufe in act 31 Geo. 2. Application of the favings of the faid fum of 35,602l. granted the laft feffion towards half-pay. Treafury may iffue to the banks of Scotland, the fum of 69,910l. 15s. 9d. 1q. for difcharging the incumbrances of the Perth eftate. The decrees fuftaining the claims thereupon, to be produced to the court on or before 5 July 1759; and debentures to be then made out for the fame, with the intereft due; which are to be paid at fight by the bank. Decrees not then produced, the claims not to bear intereft after the faid day. Barons of the Exchequer, with confent of the treafury, to fettle the rewards due to the officers of the court, and iffue debentures for the fame, &c. No fee to be taken by the officers of the Exchequer from the creditors of the faid

faid eftate, on penalty of 100l. and repayment of the fee, with cofts. Surplus monies, after difcharging the incumbrances on the Perth eftate, to be referved for the future difpofition of parliament.

CAP. XXXVII.

An act for repairing and widening the high road leading from the town of Mansfield in the county of Nottingham, through the towns of Plea-fley, Glapwell, Heath, and Normenton, and the liberty of Hafland, to the turnpike road leading from the town of Derby, to the town of Che-fterfield in the county of Derby.

CAP. XXXVIII.

An act for repairing and widening the roads from Chappel Bar, near the weft end of the town of Nottingham, to Newhaven ; and from The Four-Lane-Ends near Oakerthorpe, to Afhborne ; and from the crofs poft on Wirkfworth Moor, to join the road leading from Chefterfield, to Chappel-en-le-Frith, at or near Longfton in the county of Derby ; and from Selfton, to Annefley Woodhoufe in the county of Notting-ham.

CAP. XXXIX.

An act for repairing and widening the roads from the eaft end of the town of Chard, to the fouth end of Weft Moor ; and from the weft end of the Yeovil turnpike road, through Ilmifter, to Kenny Gate; and from the weft end of Peafe Marfh Lane, to Horton Elm ; and from Saint Raine Hill, to Ilmifter ; and from White Crofs, to Chillington Down ; and from a place called Three Oaks, over Ilford Bridges, to Bridge Crofs in the county of Somerfet.

CAP. XL.

An act for repairing feveral roads leading to the town of Bridgewater, in the county of Somerfet; and for amending and rendering more effec-tual feveral acts for amending feveral roads from the cities of Gloucefter and Briftol, and feveral other roads in the faid acts mentioned, in the counties of Somerfet and Gloucefter.

CAP. XLI.

An act for repairing and widening the road from the crofs at Broken Crofs in Macclesfield, in the county of Chefter, through Macclesfield Foreft, to the prefent turnpike road at the fouth end of the townfhip of Bux-ton, in the county of Derby.

CAP. XLII.

An act for making the river Stort navigable, in the counties of Hertford and Effex, from the New Bridge in the town of Bifhop Stortford, into the river Lee, near a place called The Rye, in the county of Hertford.

CAP. XLIII.

An act for repairing and widening the road from Chefterfield to the turn-pike road at Hernftone-Lane-Head ; and alfo the road branching from the faid road upon the Eaft Moor, through Baflow and Wardlow, to the joining of the faid roads again near Wardlow Mires; and alfo the road leading between the faid road and branch from Calver-Bridge, to Ba-flow-Bridge ; and alfo the road from the turnpike road near Newhaven Houfe, to the turnpike road near Grindleford Bridge, in the county of Derby.

CAP. XLIV.

An act to continue, amend, and make effectual an act paffed in the twelfth year of the reign of his prefent Majefty, intituled, *An act for repairing the roads from the north-weft parts of the county of Lincoln, through Nettlam Fields, Wragby Lane, and Baumber Fields, to the Wolds, or North-eaft part of the faid county ;* and alfo for repairing and widening the

M m 4

roads

roads from the Well, in Eaſt-gate in the city of Lincoln, and from the
north-weſt end of Horncaſtle, and from the Guide Poſt at the eaſt end
of Hainton, through Barkwith, to the roads directed to be repaired by
the ſaid act.

CAP. XLV.

An act for repairing, widening, and rendering ſafe and commodious,
ſeveral roads leading from the town of Southmolton in the county of
Devon.

CAP. XLVI.

An act for repairing and widening the road from a place called The Old
Gallows, in the pariſh of Sunning, in the county of Berks, through
Wokingham, New Bracknowl, and Sunning Hill, to Virginia Water, in
the pariſh of Egham, in the county of Surry.

CAP. XLVII.

An act to amend and explain an act made in the third year of his pre-
ſent Majeſty's reign, intituled, *An act for making navigable the river
Stroudwater, in the county of Gloceſter, from the river Severn, at or near
Framiload, to Wallbridge, near the town of Stroud, in the ſame county.*

CAP. XLVIII.

An act for repairing the road from Wakefield to Auſterlands, in the weſt
riding of the county of York.

CAP. XLIX.

An act for the better enlightening and cleanſing the open places, ſtreets,
ſquares, lanes, courts, and other paſſages, within the part of the manor and liberty of Norton Folgate, otherwiſe Norton Folley, in the
county of Middleſex, which is extraparochial: and regulating the
nightly watch and beadles therein.

CAP. L.

An act for repairing and widening the roads from Oxdown Gate, in
Popham Lane, to the city of Wincheſter: and from the ſaid city,
through Hurſley, to Chandler's Ford: and from Hurſley aforeſaid, to
the turnpike road at Romſey: and from the ſaid turnpike road, through
Ringwood, in the county of Southampton, to Longham Bridge and
Winborne Minſter, in the county of Dorſet.

CAP. LI.

An act to explain, amend, and render more effectual, the powers granted
by ſeveral acts of parliament for repairing ſeveral roads leading to the
city of Bath; and for amending ſeveral other roads near the ſaid
city.

CAP. LII.

An act for amending, widening, and keeping in repair the road from
the Hollow Way on the weſt ſide of lord Clifford's park gate, where the
Exeter turnpike road ends, to a place called Biddaford, in the county
of Devon.

CAP. LIII.

An act for repairing and widening the roads from Grantham, in the
county of Lincoln, through Botteſford and Bingham, to Nottingham
Trent Bridge; and from Chappel Bar, near the weſt end of the town
of Nottingham, to Saint Mary's Bridge in the town of Derby; and
from the guide poſt in the pariſh of Lenton, to Sawley Ferry.

CAP. LIV.

An act for repairing and widening the road from Dewsbury to Ealand, in
the weſt riding of the county of York.

CAP.

CAP. LV.

An act for repairing and widening the roads from the town of Mold to the town of Denbigh, and from thence to Tal-y-Cafn and Conway; and from the town of Wrexham to the towns of Ruthin, Denbigh, and the town and port of Ruthland, in the counties of Denbigh, Flint, and Carnarvon.

CAP. LVI.

An act for laying a duty of two pennies fcots, or one fixth part of a penny fterling, upon every fcots pint of ale, porter, and beer, which fhall be brewed for fale, brought into, tapped, or fold, within the town of Kelfo, in the fhire of Roxburgh, for finifhing a bridge crofs the river Tweed, and for other purpofes therein mentioned.

CAP. LVII.

An act for repairing and widening the roads from a place called Little-gate, at the top of Leadenham Hill, in the county of Lincoln, to the weft end of Barnby Gate, in Newark upon Trent; and from the guide poft at the divifion of Kelham and Muskham Lanes, to Mansfield; and from Southwell to Oxton; in the county of Nottingham.

CAP. LVIII.

An act for eftablifhing, regulating, and maintaining a nightly watch, and for enlightening the open places and ftreets, within the town of Guild-ford in the county of Surrey.

CAP. LIX.

An act to explain, amend, and render more effectual, an act paffed in the fixth year of the reign of her late majefty Queen Anne, intituled, *An act for erecting a workhoufe in the town and borough of Plymouth in the county of Devon; and for fetting the poor on work, and maintaining them there;* and for obliging the mayor and commonalty of Plymouth to contribute towards the county rates of Devon: and for applying, for the relief of the poor in the faid workhoufe, certain furplus monies which have for-merly arifen by the affeffments for raifing the land tax in the faid town.

CAP. LX.

An act for repairing and widening the road from the town of Derby to the town of Newcaftle under Lyne, in the county of Stafford.

CAP. LXI.

An act for difcharging the inhabitants of the town of Manchefter, in the county palatine of Lancafter, from the cuftom of grinding their corn and grain, except malt, at certain water corn mills in the faid town, called The School Mills; and for making a proper recompence to the febffees of fuch mills.

CAP. LXII.

An act for improving the navigation of the river Clyde to the city of Glafgow; and for building a bridge crofs the faid river, from the faid city to the village of Gorbells.

CAP. LXIII.

An act to continue and amend two acts, one made in the thirteenth year of the reign of his late majefty King George the Firft, and the other in the feventeenth year of his prefent Majefty, for repairing certain roads leading from Chippenham, and for repairing feveral roads lead-ing from Chippenham Bridge; and to repeal fo much of an act made in the twenty ninth year of his prefent Majefty, as relates to the road be-tween the faid bridge and Lower Stanton in the county of Wilts.

CAP. LXIV.

An act for making and completing the navigation of the river Wear, from and including South Biddick, or Biddick Ford, in the county of Durham,

ham, to the city of Durham ; and for repealing fo much of an act made in the twentieth year of his prefent Majefty's reign, intituled, *An act for the better prefervation and improvement of the river Wear, and port and haven of Sunderland, in the county of Durham* ; as relates to making the faid river, navigable between the faid two places called South Biddick, or Biddick Ford, and New Bridge, in the county of Durham.

CAP. LXV.

An act for continuing, amending, and rendering more effectual, fo much of an act made in the twentieth year of his prefent Majefty's reign, intituled, *An act for the better prefervation and improvement of the river Wear, and port and haven of Sunderland, in the county of Durham* ; as relates to the port and haven of Sunderland, and the river Wear, between South Biddick, or Biddick Ford, and the faid port and haven.

CAP. LXVI.

An act for amending and widening the roads leading from Stretford's Bridge in the county of Hereford, to the new inn in the parifh of Winftanftow in the county of Salop ; and alfo the road from Blue Mantle Hall, near Mortimer's Crofs, to Aymftrey in the faid county of Hereford ; and for repealing fo much of an act made in the twenty fecond year of the reign of his prefent Majefty, as relates to the road from Mortimer's Crofs to Aymftrey Bridge.

CAP. LXVII.

An act for repairing the road from the fouth end of the fouth ftreet, in the parifh of South Malling, near the town of Lewes, to Glyndbridge ; and from thence through Firle Street under the Hill, to Longbridge in the parifh of Alfrifton, in the county of Suffex.

CAP. LXVIII.

An act for repairing and widening the road from Modbury, through the town of Plympton, to the north end of Lincotta Lane, in the county of Devon.

CAP. LXIX.

An act for repairing, amending, and widening the roads from the fouth weft end of NetherBridge, in the county of Weftmorland, by Sizerghfellfide, to Levens Bridge, and from thence through the town of Millthrop, to Dixes ; and from the town of Millthrop aforefaid, to Hangbridge, and from thence to join the Heron Syke turnpike road, at the guide poft near Clawthrop Hall, in the county aforefaid.

CAP. LXX.

An act for repairing and widening the road leading from the eaft fide of Barnfley Common, in the county of York, to the middle of Grange Moor, and from thence to White Crofs ; and alfo the road from the guide poft, in Barugh, to a rivulet called Barugh Brook, and from thence for two hundred yards over and beyond the fame rivulet or brook into the townfhip of Cawthorne, in the faid county.

CAP. LXXI.

An act for repairing and widening the high road from Wetherby to Graffington, in the county of York.

The END *of the Twenty-Second Volume.*

Flood   1979

4

157